Lecture Notes in Computer Science 4961

Commenced Publication in 1973
Founding and Former Series Editors:
Gerhard Goos, Juris Hartmanis, and Jan van Leeuwen

Editorial Board

David Hutchison
  Lancaster University, UK
Takeo Kanade
  Carnegie Mellon University, Pittsburgh, PA, USA
Josef Kittler
  University of Surrey, Guildford, UK
Jon M. Kleinberg
  Cornell University, Ithaca, NY, USA
Alfred Kobsa
  University of California, Irvine, CA, USA
Friedemann Mattern
  ETH Zurich, Switzerland
John C. Mitchell
  Stanford University, CA, USA
Moni Naor
  Weizmann Institute of Science, Rehovot, Israel
Oscar Nierstrasz
  University of Bern, Switzerland
C. Pandu Rangan
  Indian Institute of Technology, Madras, India
Bernhard Steffen
  University of Dortmund, Germany
Madhu Sudan
  Massachusetts Institute of Technology, MA, USA
Demetri Terzopoulos
  University of California, Los Angeles, CA, USA
Doug Tygar
  University of California, Berkeley, CA, USA
Gerhard Weikum
  Max-Planck Institute of Computer Science, Saarbruecken, Germany

José Luiz Fiadeiro   Paola Inverardi (Eds.)

Fundamental Approaches to Software Engineering

11th International Conference, FASE 2008
Held as Part of the Joint European Conferences
on Theory and Practice of Software, ETAPS 2008
Budapest, Hungary, March 29-April 6, 2008
Proceedings

 Springer

Volume Editors

José Luiz Fiadeiro
University of Leicester
Department of Computer Science
University Road, Leicester LE1 7RH, UK
E-mail: jose@mcs.le.ac.uk

Paola Inverardi
Università degli Studi l'Aquila
Dipartimento di Informatica
Via Vetoio, 67100 L'Aquila (AQ), Italy
E-mail: inverard@di.univaq.it

Library of Congress Control Number: 2008923360

CR Subject Classification (1998): D.2, F.3, D.3

LNCS Sublibrary: SL 1 – Theoretical Computer Science and General Issues

ISSN   0302-9743
ISBN-10 3-540-78742-9 Springer Berlin Heidelberg New York
ISBN-13 978-3-540-78742-6 Springer Berlin Heidelberg New York

This work is subject to copyright. All rights are reserved, whether the whole or part of the material is
concerned, specifically the rights of translation, reprinting, re-use of illustrations, recitation, broadcasting,
reproduction on microfilms or in any other way, and storage in data banks. Duplication of this publication
or parts thereof is permitted only under the provisions of the German Copyright Law of September 9, 1965,
in its current version, and permission for use must always be obtained from Springer. Violations are liable
to prosecution under the German Copyright Law.

Springer is a part of Springer Science+Business Media

springer.com

© Springer-Verlag Berlin Heidelberg 2008
Printed in Germany

Typesetting: Camera-ready by author, data conversion by Scientific Publishing Services, Chennai, India
Printed on acid-free paper   SPIN: 12244720   06/3180   5 4 3 2 1 0

Foreword

ETAPS 2008 was the 11th instance of the European Joint Conferences on Theory and Practice of Software. ETAPS is an annual federated conference that was established in 1998 by combining a number of existing and new conferences. This year it comprised five conferences (CC, ESOP, FASE, FOSSACS, TACAS), 22 satellite workshops (ACCAT, AVIS, Bytecode, CMCS, COCV, DCC, FESCA, FIT, FORMED, GaLoP, GT-VMT, LDTA, MBT, MOMPES, PDMC, QAPL, RV, SafeCert, SC, SLA++P, WGT, and WRLA), nine tutorials, and seven invited lectures (excluding those that were specific to the satellite events). The five main conferences received 571 submissions, 147 of which were accepted, giving an overall acceptance rate of less than 26%, with each conference below 27%. Congratulations therefore to all the authors who made it to the final programme! I hope that most of the other authors will still have found a way of participating in this exciting event, and that you will all continue submitting to ETAPS and contributing to make of it the best conference in the area.

The events that comprise ETAPS address various aspects of the system development process, including specification, design, implementation, analysis and improvement. The languages, methodologies and tools which support these activities are all well within its scope. Different blends of theory and practice are represented, with an inclination towards theory with a practical motivation on the one hand and soundly based practice on the other. Many of the issues involved in software design apply to systems in general, including hardware systems, and the emphasis on software is not intended to be exclusive.

ETAPS is a confederation in which each event retains its own identity, with a separate Programme Committee and proceedings. Its format is open-ended, allowing it to grow and evolve as time goes by. Contributed talks and system demonstrations are in synchronized parallel sessions, with invited lectures in plenary sessions. Two of the invited lectures are reserved for 'unifying' talks on topics of interest to the whole range of ETAPS attendees. The aim of cramming all this activity into a single one-week meeting is to create a strong magnet for academic and industrial researchers working on topics within its scope, giving them the opportunity to learn about research in related areas, and thereby to foster new and existing links between work in areas that were formerly addressed in separate meetings.

ETAPS 2008 was organized by the John von Neumann Computer Society jointly with the Budapest University of Technology and the Eötvös University, in cooperation with:

 ▷ European Association for Theoretical Computer Science (EATCS)
 ▷ European Association for Programming Languages and Systems (EAPLS)
 ▷ European Association of Software Science and Technology (EASST)

and with support from Microsoft Research and Danubius Hotels.

The organizing team comprised:

Chair	Dániel Varró
Director of Organization	István Alföldi
Main Organizers	Andrea Tósoky, Gabriella Aranyos
Publicity	Joost-Pieter Katoen
Advisors	András Pataricza, Joaõ Saraiva
Satellite Events	Zoltán Horváth, Tihamér Levendovszky, Viktória Zsók
Tutorials	László Lengyel
Web Site	Ákos Horváth
Registration System	Victor Francisco Fonte, Zsolt Berényi, Róbert Kereskényi, Zoltán Fodor
Computer Support	Áron Sisak
Local Arrangements	László Gönczy, Gábor Huszerl, Melinda Magyar, several student volunteers.

Overall planning for ETAPS conferences is the responsibility of its Steering Committee, whose current membership is:

Vladimiro Sassone (Southampton, Chair), Luca de Alfaro (Santa Cruz), Roberto Amadio (Paris), Giuseppe Castagna (Paris), Marsha Chechik (Toronto), Sophia Drossopoulou (London), Matt Dwyer (Nebraska), Hartmut Ehrig (Berlin), Chris Hankin (London), Laurie Hendren (McGill), Mike Hinchey (NASA Goddard), Paola Inverardi (L'Aquila), Joost-Pieter Katoen (Aachen), Paul Klint (Amsterdam), Kim Larsen (Aalborg), Gerald Luettgen (York) Tiziana Margaria (Göttingen), Ugo Montanari (Pisa), Martin Odersky (Lausanne), Catuscia Palamidessi (Paris), Anna Philippou (Cyprus), CR Ramakrishnan (Stony Brook), Don Sannella (Edinburgh), João Saraiva (Minho), Michael Schwartzbach (Aarhus), Helmut Seidl (Munich), Perdita Stevens (Edinburgh), and Dániel Varró (Budapest).

I would like to express my sincere gratitude to all of these people and organizations, the Programme Committee Chairs and members of the ETAPS conferences, the organizers of the satellite events, the speakers themselves, the many reviewers, and Springer for agreeing to publish the ETAPS proceedings. Finally, I would like to thank the Organizing Chair of ETAPS 2008, Dániel Varró, for arranging for us to have ETAPS in the most beautiful city of Budapest

January 2008   Vladimiro Sassone

Preface

Software products are increasingly dominating our lives. Their pervasiveness makes it crucial for both economical and social progress that producing software of high quality and at low cost becomes routine. In order to achieve this goal, software engineers need to have at their disposal theories, languages, methods, and tools that derive from both the systematic research of the academic community and the distilled experience of practitioners. The International Conference on Fundamental Approaches to Software Engineering (FASE)—one of the European Joint Conferences on Theory and Practice of Software (ETAPS)—is concerned with the foundations on which Software Engineering is built. Its focus is on the principles on which methods, tools or techniques are based and on the way in which these contribute to making Software Engineering a more mature and responsible professional activity.

This year, FASE received 119 submissions. Each submission was reviewed by at least three technical experts from the program committee or the external research community. Each paper was discussed during a two-week "electronic" meeting. We wish to express our sincere thanks to all of the referees for the time, effort and care taken in reviewing and discussing the submissions.

The program committee selected a total of 31 papers, 5 of which were tool demonstrations. Accepted papers address a fair range of topics including requirements and architectures, models and models transformation, service oriented systems, adaptable systems, verification and testing, objects and components, and design. The technical program was complemented by the invited lectures of Connie Heitmeyer, *On the Utility of Formal Methods in Building Software: A Panacea or Academic Poppycock?* and Tom Reps, *WYSINWYX: What You See Is Not What You eXecute* .

FASE 2008 was held in Budapest (Hungary) as part of the 11th edition of ETAPS. Arrangements were the responsibility of the local organization committee and overall coordination of ETAPS was carried out by its steering committee. We would like to thank the chairs of these committees, Daniel Varr and Vladimiro Sassonne, as well as Perdita Stevens as chair of the steering committee until September 2007, for the professional and friendly support with which we were provided throughout this process.

The planning and coordination of the FASE series of conferences is the responsibility of EASST (European Association of Software Science and Technology). We would like to thank Maura Cerioli, as chair of the steering committee of FASE in 2006, for having invited us to be co-chairs of this 2008 edition. We wish all the best to the co-chairs of the 2009 edition, Marsha Chechik and Martin Wirsing.

As always, the stars of the show are the authors of the papers, especially the presenters. We would like to thank them all for having put so much effort into the papers and presentations (and meeting all the deadlines!). As to the attendees of FASE 2008, we are sure that they will have been inspired by the quality of the program (both technical and social) and will have started planning their submissions to FASE 2009.

January 2008

José Fiadeiro
Paola Inverardi

Organization

Committees

Program Chair José Fiadeiro and Paola Inverardi

Program Committee

Don Batory, University of Texas at Austin (USA)

Ruth Breu, University of Innsbruck (Austria)

Carlos Canal, University of Málaga (Spain)

Maura Cerioli, University of Genova (Italy)

Shing-chi Cheung, Hong Kong University of Science and Technology (China)

Vittorio Cortellessa, University of l'Aquila (Italy)

Laurie Dillon, Michigan State University (USA)

Marlon Dumas, Queensland University of Technology (Australia)

Schahram Dustdar, Technical University of Vienna (Austria)

Harald Gall, University of Zürich (Switzerland)

Dimitra Giannakopoulou, NASA Ames Research Center (USA)

Holger Giese, University of Paderborn (Germany)

Martin Glinz, University of Zürich (Switzerland)

Reiko Heckel, University of Leicester (UK)

Valerie Issarny, Inria Rocquencourt (France)

Daniel Le Metayer, Inria Alpes (France)

Gary T. Leavens, Iowa State University (USA)

Antonia Lopes, University of Lisbon (Portugal)

Angelika Mader, University of Twente (The Netherlands)

Tom Maibaum, McMaster University (Canada)

Dominique Mery, University of Nancy (France)

Oscar Nierstrasz, University of Berne (Switzerland)

David Rosenblum, University College London (UK)

Tetsuo Tamai, University of Tokyo (Japan)

Gabriele Taentzer, Philipps-Universität Marburg (Germany)

Sebastian Uchitel, Imperial College London (UK)

Martin Wirsing, University of Munich (Germany)

Pamela Zave, AT&T Labs (USA)

Reviewers

Adrian Lienhard
Amancio Bouza
Andreas Seibel
Antonio Vallecillo
Apostolos Zarras
Arend Rensink
Basel Katt
Basil Becker
Beat Fluri
Berthold Agreiter
Carlos Matos
Christian Soltenborn
Claudia Ermel
David Workman
Denes Bisztray
Dirk Muller
E. Cuesta
Emanuel Giger
Emilio Tuosto
Emmanuel Letier
Ernesto Pimentel
Filippo Ricca
Frank Innerhofer-Oberperfler
Ghaith Haddad
Giacomo Ghezzi
Gianna Reggio
Guillaume Brat
Gwen Sala
Hermann Haussler
Jacques Carette
James Worrell
Jan Mendling
Javier Camra
Javier Cubo
Joanna Chimiak-Opoka
Jochen Kuester

Katharina Mehner
Kevin Lano
Leen Lambers
Luciano Baresi
Manuel Fernandez-Bertoa
Marc Lohmann
Marcus Denker
Massimiliano De Leoni
Mats Heimdahl
Matthias Tichy
Mauro Caporuscio
Michael Butler
Michael Jackson
Michael Wuersch
Mihaela Gheorghiu
Mukhtiar Memon
Nazareno Aguirre
Nikolaos Georgantas
Norman Fenton
Pascal Poizat
Patrick Knab
Peter Mehlitz
Peter Schmitt
Robert Wagner
Roberto Speicys-Cardoso
Samuel Fricker
Sarah Thompson
Stefan Henkler
Stefan Jurack
Stefan Neumann
Thomas Hettel
Tony Modica
Ulrike Prange
Yi Huang
Yu Zhou

Table of Contents

Verification and Testing I

Verification and Testing II

Objects and Components

Models, Model Transformations II

Deriving Non-zeno Behavior Models from Goal Models Using ILP*

Dalal Alrajeh[1], Alessandra Russo[1], and Sebastian Uchitel[1,2]

[1] Imperial College London
{da04,ar3,su2}@doc.ic.ac.uk
[2] University of Buenos Aires
s.uchitel@dc.uba.ar

Abstract. This paper addresses the problem of automated derivation of non-zeno behaviour models from goal models. The approach uses a novel combination of model checking and machine learning. We first translate a goal model formalised in linear temporal logic into a (potentially zeno) labelled transition system. We then iteratively identify zeno traces in the model and learn operational requirements in the form of *preconditions* that prevent the traces from occurring. Identification of zeno traces is acheived by model checking the behaviour model against a time progress property expressed in linear temporal logic, while learning operational requirements is achieved using Inductive Logic Programming. As a result of the iterative process, not only a non-zeno behaviour model is produced but also a set of preconditions that, in conjunction with the known goals, ensure the non-zeno behaviour of the system.

1 Introduction

Goal oriented requirements engineering (GORE) is an increasingly popular approach to elaborating software requirements. Goals are prescriptive statements of intent whose satisfaction requires the cooperation of components in the software and its environment. One of the limitations of approaches to GORE [5,6,14] is that the declarative nature of goals hinders the application of a number of successful validation techniques based on executable models such as graphical animations, simulations, and rapid-prototyping. They do not naturally support narrative style elicitation techniques, such as those in scenario-based requirements engineering and are not suitable for down-stream analyses that focus on design and implementation issues which are of an operational nature.

To address these limitations, techniques have been developed for constructing behaviour models automatically from declarative descriptions in general [22] and goal models specifically [12]. The core of these techniques is based on temporal logic to automata transformations developed in the model checking community. For instance, in [12] Labelled Transition Systems (LTS) are built automatically from KAOS goals expressed in Fluent Linear Temporal Logic (FLTL) [8].

---

* We acknowledge EPSRC EP/CS541133/1, ANPCyT PICT 11738, and the Leverhulme Trust for partially funding this work.

J. Fiadeiro and P. Inverardi (Eds.): FASE 2008, LNCS 4961, pp. 1–15, 2008.
© Springer-Verlag Berlin Heidelberg 2008

The key technical difficulty in constructing behaviour model from goal models is that the latter are typically expressed in a synchronous, non-interleaving semantic framework while the former have an asynchronous interleaving semantics. This mismatch relates to the fact that it is convenient to make different assumptions for modelling requirements and system goals than for modelling communicating sequential processes. One of the practical consequences of this mismatch is that the construction of behaviour models from a goal model may introduce deadlocks and progress violations. More specifically, the resulting behaviour model may be *zeno*, i.e exhibit traces in which time never progresses. Clearly these models do not adequately describe the intended system behaviour and thus are not suitable basis for analysis.

A solution proposed in [12] to the problem of zeno traces is to construct behavior models from a fully *operationalised* goal model rather than from a set of high-level goals. This involves identifying system operations and extracting operational requirements in the form of *pre-* and *trigger-conditions* from the high-level goals [13]. One disadvantage of this approach is that operationalisation is a manual process for which only partial support is provided. Support comes in the form of derivation patterns restricted to some common goal patterns [6].

This paper addresses the problem of non-zeno behaviour model construction using a novel combination of model checking and machine learning. The approach starts with a goal model and produces a non-zeno behaviour model that satisfies all goals. Briefly, the proposed method first involves translating automatically the goal model, formalised in Linear Temporal Logic (LTL), into a (potentially zeno) labelled transition system. Then, in an iterative process, zeno traces in the behaviour model are identified mechanically, elaborated into positive and negative scenarios, and used to automatically learn preconditions that prevent the traces from occurring. Identification of zeno traces is achieved by model checking the behaviour model against a time progress property expressed in LTL, while preconditions are learned using Inductive Logic Programming (ILP).

As a result of the proposed approach, not only a non-zeno behaviour model is constructed, but also a set of precondition is produced. These preconditions, in conjunction with the known goals, ensure the non-zeno behaviour of the system. Consequently, the approach also supports the operationalisation process of goal models described in [13].

The rest of the paper is organizes as follows: Section 2 provides background on goal-models, LTSs and FLTL. Section 3 describes the problem of derivation of non-zeno behaviour models and presents a formalisation of the problem resolved in this paper. Section 4 presents the details of the proposed approach. Section 5 discusses the results and observations obtained from applying the approach. Finally, Sections 6 and 7 conclude the paper by a comparison with related work and discussion on future work.

2   Background

In this section we discuss goal and behaviour modelling. The examples we use refer to a simplified version of the mine pump control system [10]. In this system, a pump controller is used to prevent the water in a mine sump from passing some threshold and flooding the mine. To avoid the risk of explosion, the pump may only be on when the level of methane gas in the mine is not critical. The pump controller monitors the water and methane levels by communicating with two sensors, and controls the pump in order to guarantee the safety properties of the system.

2.1 Goal Models

Goals focus on the objectives of the system. They are state-based assertions intended to be satisfied over time by the system. By structuring goals into refinement structures, GORE approaches aim to provide systematic methods that support requirements engineering activities. Goals are expected to be refined into sub-goals that can be assigned either to the software-to-be, to other components or to the environment as domain assumptions. Goals assigned to the software-to-be are used to derive operational requirements in the form of pre-, post- and trigger-conditions for operations provided by the software.

In this paper, we define a goal model to be a collection of system goals and operation descriptions. We specify goals informally using natural language and formally using LTL [16]. We follow the KAOS [5] approach assuming a discrete-model of time in which consecutive states in a trace are always separated by a single time unit. The time unit corresponds to some arbitrarily chosen smallest possible time unit for the application domain. Hence, the goal *PumpOffWhenLowWater* can be informally described as *"when the water is below the low level, the pump must be off within the next time unit"* and formally specified as $\Box(\neg HighWater \rightarrow \bigcirc \neg PumpOn)$, where $\Box$ is the temporal operator meaning *always*, $\bigcirc$ is the *next* time point operator, and *HighWater* and *PumpOn* are propositions meaning that "the water in the sump is above the low level threshold" and "the pump is on", respectively.

LTL assertions are constructed using a set P of propositions that refer to state-based properties, the classical connectives, $\neg, \wedge$ and $\rightarrow$, and the temporal operators $\bigcirc$ (next), $\Box$ (always), $\Diamond$ (eventually) and U (strong until). Other classical and temporal operators can be defined as combinations of the above operators (e.g. $\phi \vee \psi \equiv \neg(\neg\phi \wedge \neg\psi)$, and $\phi \mathsf{W}\psi \equiv (\Box\phi) \vee (\phi\mathsf{U}\psi)$). The semantics of LTL assertions is given in terms of traces (i.e. infinite sequences of states s_1, s_2, ...). Each state defines the set of propositions true at that state. In addition, each state is classified as an *observable* or a *non-observable* state.

LTL assertions are evaluated only on observable states. In the case of goal models, an observable state corresponds to a time point where a time unit ends and another one starts. A proposition p is said to be satisfied in a trace σ at position i, written $\sigma, i \models p$, if it is true at the ith observable state in that trace. Note this state is not necessarily the ith state of the trace, as non-observable states may appear between observable ones. The semantics of Boolean operators is defined in a standard way over each observable state in a sequence. The semantics of the temporal operators is defined as follows:

- $\sigma, i \models \bigcirc\phi$ iff $\sigma, i+1 \models \phi$
- $\sigma, i \models \Box\phi$ iff $\forall j \geq i.\ \sigma, j \models \phi$

- $\sigma, i \models \Diamond\phi$ iff $\exists j \geq i.\ \sigma, j \models \phi$
- $\sigma, i \models \phi \cup \psi$ iff $\exists j \geq i.\ \sigma, j \models \psi$ and $\forall i \leq k < j.\ \sigma, k \models \phi$

Given the above semantics, a formula $\bigcirc p$ is satisfied at the ith observable state in σ if p is true at the $(i+1)^{th}$ observable state in σ. An LTL assertion ϕ is said to be *satisfied in a trace* σ if and only if it is satisfied at the first observable state in the trace. Similarly, a set Γ of formulae is said to be satisfied in a trace σ if each formula $\psi \in \Gamma$ is satisfied in the trace σ; Γ is said to be consistent if there is a trace that satisfies it.

Goal models also include domain and required conditions of operations. An *operation* causes the system to transit from one state to another. Conditions over operations can be domain *pre-* and *post-conditions* and required *pre-* and *trigger-conditions*. Domain pre- and post-conditions describe elementary state transitions defined by operation applications in the domain. For instance, the operation *switchPumpOn* has as domain pre- and post-condition the assertions $\neg PumpOn$ and $PumpOn$. Required pre- and trigger-conditions are prescriptive conditions defining respectively the weakest necessary conditions and the sufficient conditions for performing an operation. Conditions on operations are evaluated at the beginning/end of time units. For instance, if a required precondition holds at the beginning of a time unit (i.e. at an observable state in a trace), then the operation *may* occur within the time unit (i.e. before the next observable state in that trace). It is expected that the required pre- and trigger-conditions guarantee the satisfaction of system goals.

2.2   Behaviour Models

Behaviour models are event-based representations of system behaviors. Different formalisms have been proposed for modelling and analyzing system behaviors (e.g. [9]), among which LTS is a well known formalism for modelling systems as a set of concurrent components. Each component is defined as a set of states and possible transitions between these states [15]. Transitions are labelled with events denoting the interaction that the component has with its environment. The global system behavior is captured by the parallel composition of the LTS model of each component, by interleaving their behavior but forcing synchronization on shared events.

LTSA [15] is a tool that supports various types of automated analyses over LTSs such as model checking and animation. The logic used by LTSA is the asynchronous linear temporal logic of fluents (FLTL) [8]. This logic is an LTL in which propositions in P are defined as fluents. Fluents represent time varying properties of the world that are made true and false through the occurrence of events. A fluent can be either state-based or event-based. We denote the set of state fluents as P_f whereas event fluents as P_e. A *fluent definition* is a pair of disjoint sets of events, referred to as the *initiating* and *terminating* sets, and an initial truth value. Events of the initiating (resp. terminating) set are those events that, when executed, cause the fluent to become true (resp. false). For instance, the fluent definition for the state fluent $PumpOn$ would be

$PumpOn= \langle\{switchPumpOn\},\{switchPumpOff\}\rangle$, meaning that the event *switchPumpOn* (resp. *switchPumpOff*) causes the fluent *PumpOn* to be true (resp. false). Given an event e, the event fluent also denoted as e is always defined as $\langle\{e\}, L - \{e\}\rangle$ where L is the universe of events.

Asynchronous FLTL assertions are evaluated over traces of states and events (i.e. $s_0 \xrightarrow{e_1} s_1 \xrightarrow{e_2} s_2...$). A position i in a trace σ, for $i \geq 0$, denotes the ith state in σ. The satisfiability of fluents over an LTS is defined with respect to positions in a given traces. A fluent f is said to be true at position i in a trace σ if and only if either of the following conditions hold: (i) f is initially true and no terminating event has occurred since; and (ii) some initiating event has occurred before position i and no terminating event has occurred since. As the satisfiability depends on the fluent definition, we use $\sigma, i \models_D f$ to denote that f is satisfied in σ at i with respect to a given set of fluent definitions D.

LTS models are *untimed*. To support the derivation of behavior models from goal models, which are timed models, time must be represented explicitly in the LTSs. We adopt the standard approach to discrete timed behaviour models by introducing an event *tick* to model the global clock with which each timed-process synchronizes [15]. In the context of this paper, a *tick* signals the end of a time unit (as assumed by the goal model) and the beginning of the next.

When modelling discrete-timed systems using LTS with *tick* events, it is important to check the system does not exhibit traces in which a finite number of ticks occur. These traces, called *zeno traces*, represent executions in which time does not progress. We refer to an LTS with zeno traces as a *zeno model*.

3 Problem Formulation

In this section we discuss and exemplify why the construction of behaviour models from goal models can result in models with zeno executions. We then describe formally the problem that this paper addresses in Section 4.

3.1 From Goal Models to Behaviour Models

Let G_s be a consistent goal model as described in Section 2.1. It is possible to construct an LTS satisfying G_s by transforming G_s into a semantically equivalent set of asynchronous FLTL assertions G_a and then computing an LTS model using an adaptation [12] of the temporal logic to automata algorithms in [8].

The transformation of a goal model G_s into asynchronous FLTL assertions G_a requires (i) translating the LTL goals in G_s to FLTL assertions using the technique described in [12] and (ii) coding the operations descriptions in G_s into asynchronous FLTL.

Goal assertions in G_s are translated into semantically equivalent asynchronous FLTL using an event fluent *tick* to model observable states where LTL formulae are evaluated. The translation $Tr : LTL \rightarrow FLTL_{Async}$ is defined as follows (where ϕ and ψ are LTL assertions):

$$Tr(\Box\phi) = \Box(tick \rightarrow Tr(\phi)) \qquad Tr(\phi\mathsf{U}\psi) = tick \rightarrow Tr(\phi)\mathsf{U}(tick \wedge Tr(\psi))$$
$$Tr(\Diamond\phi) = \Diamond(tick \wedge Tr(\phi)) \qquad Tr(\bigcirc\phi) = \bigcirc(\neg tick\mathsf{W}(tick \wedge Tr(\phi)))$$

The translation of the synchronous (LTL) next operator (see $Tr(\bigcirc\phi)$) exemplifies well the difference between synchronous and asynchronous semantics. The synchronous formula $\bigcirc\phi$ asserts that at the next time point ϕ is true. The translation assumes that the formula $Tr(\bigcirc\phi)$ will be evaluated at the start of a time unit, in other words at the occurrence of a *tick*, and requires that no *ticks* shall occur from that point onwards until the asynchronous translation of ϕ holds and *tick* occurs. Consider the synchronous goal *PumpOffWhenLowWater* formalised in Section 2.1. Its translation gives the asynchronous assertion $\Box(tick \rightarrow (\neg HighWater \rightarrow \bigcirc (\neg \; tick\mathbf{W}(tick \wedge \neg PumpOn))))$.

The operations defined in G_s correspond to events in the behaviour model constructed, and the operation descriptions are expressed as FLTL assertions using the associated event fluents. For instance, if *DomPre* is the domain precondition for an operation e, then its asynchronous FLTL assertion is $\Box((tick \rightarrow (\neg DomPre) \rightarrow \bigcirc \neg e \; \mathbf{W} \; tick))$ (intuitively, if *DomPre* is false at the start of a time unit, then e may not occur until the next tick). The coding of required preconditions *ReqPre* in G_a is analogous to domain preconditions. The FLTL assertion coding of required trigger-condition *ReqTrig* for an operation e is $\Box(tick \rightarrow ((ReqTrig \wedge DomPre) \rightarrow \bigcirc \neg tick\mathbf{W}e))$. Finally, the domain postcondition *DomPost* for an operation e in G_s is coded within the fluent definition associated with it. If f is the fluent appearing positively (resp. negatively) in the domain postcondition for e, then it is added to the fluent f's initiating (resp. terminating) set of events.

Computing an LTS model from the asynchronous FLTL representation of a goal model requires using an adaptation [12] of a temporal logic to automata algorithm used in model checking of FLTL [8]. This adaptation consists of applying the technique, described in [8], to each FLTL assertion and then composing in parallel the individual LTS models, which amounts to logical conjunction. We shall see in the next subsection that this is not sufficient and that the resulting LTS may exhibit problematic behaviour in the form of zeno executions.

3.2   The Problem with Zeno Models

The LTS models constructed from asynchronous FLTL goal assertions are not good models of a system behavior, as they constrain the event *tick* which cannot be controlled by the system and do not impose any constraints on the controllable events. The latter are only introduced by conditions on operations (i.e. domain and required conditions). If the goal model has insufficient conditions on operations then spurious executions may be exhibited by the goal model. For instance, the LTS model for the goal *PumpOffWhenLowWater* includes the infinite trace ⟨tick, switchPumpOn, switchPumpOff, switchPumpOn, switchPumpOff,...⟩ which does not exhibit a second tick events, so violating the expectation that time progresses (also referred as *time progress property*). Such trace occurs because there is no restriction as to when the pump may be switched on or off (i.e. preconditions for *switchPumpOn* or *switchPumpOff* is missing). In conclusion, although the LTS model constructed automatically from an asynchronous FLTL encoding of a goal model may satisfy all goals, it may contain zeno executions due to missing conditions over operations.

3.3 Problem Formulation

The problem the remainder of this paper addresses is providing automated support to extending a goal model with conditions over its operations in order to guarantee the construction of a non-zeno behaviour model. In other words, given the asynchronous transformation G_a of a synchronous goal model G_s, the aim is to find a set of required preconditions Pre, referred to as the *correct operational extension of G_a*, such that the LTS model constructed from $G_a \cup Pre$ satisfies the *time progress* (TP) property .

4 The Approach

This section presents a novel approach for extending a goal model with the necessary set of required preconditions for deriving a non-zeno behavior model that satisfies a given goal model. The approach uses model checking to provide automated support for generating zeno traces and ILP to produce the preconditions.

4.1 Overview of the Approach

Figure 4.1 depicts an overview of the approach. A goal model G_s is initially transformed into an asynchronous model G_a and a set of fluent definitions D. The actual computation of the correct operational extension of G_a is then iteratively done in three phases: (i) the *analysis phase* in which the LTSA model checking tool is used to construct an LTS model satisfying G_a with respect to D and then checks the LTS against the time progress property. If the property does not hold, a counter example trace is generated, (ii) the *scenario elaboration phase* in which the violation trace is elaborated into a set of positive and negative scenarios and (iii) the *learning phase* which first transforms asynchronous goal model, fluent definitions and scenarios into a logic program and then uses an ILP system to find a set of required preconditions that cover the positive but none of the negative scenarios. Once computed, these preconditions are added to the initial goal model and the steps above repeated. The final output is an extended goal model from which a non-zeno behavior model can be constructed.

4.2 Analysis Phase

This phase considers an asynchronous FLTL encoding of a goal model as input and produces a zeno trace if the goal model does not guarantee time progress.

The LTSA model checker is used to build automatically the least constrained LTS model from the asynchronous FLTL assertions [8]. LTSA is then used to verify that time progresses by checking the property $\Box\Diamond tick$ against the model. The output of LTSA, in the case of a zeno model, is an infinite trace in which from one position onwards, no *tick* event occurs.

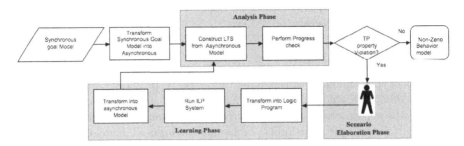

Fig. 1. Approach overview

The check is performed by assuming maximal progress of the system with respect to the environment (a standard assumptions for reactive systems), and weak fairness [15]. Fairness ensures that the environment will eventually perform *tick* instead of other environment controlled events (assuming the environment itself is consistent with time progress).

In our running example, the full set G_s of initial goals includes, in addition to the *PumpOffWhenLowWater*, the following LTL goal assertions: *PumpOffWhen-Methane*=$\Box$(*CriticalMethane* → $\bigcirc\neg$*PumpOn*), and *PumpOnWhenHighWater-AndNoMethane*=$\Box$(¬*CriticalMethane* ∧ *HighWater* → $\bigcirc$*PumpOn*).

The application of the analysis phase to the asynchronous FLTL translation of G_s and asynchronous preconditions $\Box$(*tick*∧¬*HighWater*→ $\bigcirc\neg$*switchPumpOn*) and $\Box$(*tick*∧*HighWater*∧¬*CriticalMethane*→ $\bigcirc\neg$*switchPumpOff*), gives the following output:

```
Violation of LTL property: AlwaysEventuallyTick
Trace to terminal set of states:
tick
signalCriticalMethane        CRITICALMETHANE
signalHighWater              HIGHWATER && CRITICALMETHANE
tick                         HIGHWATER && CRITICALMETHANE
switchPumpOn                 HIGHWATER && CRITICALMETHANE && PUMPON
switchPumpOff                HIGHWATER && CRITICALMETHANE
Cycle in terminal set:
switchPumpOn
switchPumpOff
LTL Property Check in: 8ms
```

The output represents an infinite trace compactly displayed as a (finite) trace with the prefix ⟨tick,signalCriticalMethane,signalHighWater,tick, switchPumpOn, switchPumpOff⟩ followed by a cycle in which *tick* does not occur ⟨switchPumpOn, switchPumpOff, switchPumpOn,...⟩. The capitalized text on the right column indicates the fluents that are true after the occurrence of each event of the trace prefix on the left. The trace indicates that a precondition for at least one of the system controlled events *switchPumpOn* and *switchPumpOff* is missing or requires strengthening. Indeed, consider the second *tick* of the trace, where *HighWater* and *CriticalMethane* are true. At this point the goals proscribe *tick* from occurring while *PumpOn* is still true. Hence, the occurrence of *switchPumpOff* is desirable. However, as soon as *switchPumpOff* happens, there are no preconditions preventing the pump being switched on again. Note that switching the pump back on does not violate any goals as the requirement is that the pump be off at the next *tick* and nothing is stated about the number of times the pump may be switched on during the time unit. A reasonable outcome of this analysis is to conclude that the precondition for *switchPumpOn* needs strengthening to prevent the pump being switched on unnecessarily.

4.3   Scenario Elaboration Phase

This phase assumes the engineer will elaborate the violation trace generated by the LTSA and produce a set of positive and negative scenarios. The engineer is assumed to identify an event in the trace returned by the LTSA that should not have occurred at a particular position in the trace. The prefix starting from the initial state of that trace up to and including the undesirable event is identified as a negative scenario. Hence, given a trace of the form $\langle w_1, e, w_2 \rangle$, a negative scenario is $\langle w_1, e \rangle$. The intended meaning of $\langle w_1, e \rangle$ is that if the system exhibits w_1 then e should not happen. The task of producing a negative scenario from the trace returned by the LTSA is believed to be an intuitive task that can be performed manually, in particular because the negative scenarios will always be sub-traces of the trace produced by the LTSA.

The engineer is also assumed to provide a scenario which shows a positive occurrence of e. This is a scenario that starts from the same initial state, is consistent with the goal model and terminates with a tick (i,e, $\langle x_1, e, x_2 \rangle$ where *tick* is the last event in x_2). Note that because scenarios are finite traces, positive scenarios are not meant to exemplify non-zeno traces. They merely capture desirable system behavior which is consistent with the given model. Note that the same model generated by LTSA can be walked through or animated by the engineer to generate positive scenarios that are consistent with existing goals and operation conditions.

Returning to the zeno trace described above, the engineer may identify the first occurrence of `switchPumpOn` as incorrect. A negative scenario becomes ⟨`tick`, `signalCriticalMethane`, `signalHighWater`, `tick`, `switchPumpOn`⟩ stating that the pump should not have been switched on after high water and methane have been signalled. In addition, a positive scenario exemplifying a correct occurrence of *switchPumpOn* must be provided. A positive scenario could be ⟨ `tick`, `signalHighWater`, `tick`, `switchPumpOn`, `tick`⟩. The completion of this phase is noted by the identification of at least one positive and one negative scenario.

4.4   Learning Phase

This phase is concerned with the inductive learning computation of missing event preconditions with respect to a given set of positive and negative scenarios. It makes use of an ILP framework, called XHAIL [19].

In general an inductive learning task is defined as the computation of an hypothesis H that explains a given set E of examples with respect to a given background knowledge B [20,18]. Intuitively, within the context of learning preconditions, the background knowledge is the fluent definitions D and the goal model G_a, currently considered by the analysis phase. The set of positive and negative scenarios generated during the scenario elaboration phase form the examples. The learned (set of) asynchronous preconditions, Pre, is the hypothesis that added to G_a generates an LTS model that accepts the positive scenarios but none of the negative ones. We refer to Pre as the *correct extension of a goal model with respect to scenarios*.

To apply XHAIL to the task of learning preconditions, the asynchronous FLTL goal model G_a, with preconditions computed in previous iterations, fluent definitions D, and the elaborated positive and negative scenarios $\Sigma_P \cup \Sigma_N$ are encoded into a, semantically equivalent, Event Calculus (EC)[17] logic program Π.

Event Calculus Programs. Our EC programs include a sort A of events ($e_1, e_2, \ldots$), a sort F of fluents ($f_1, f_2, \ldots$), a sort S of scenarios ($s_1, s_2, \ldots$), and two sorts $P = (p_1, p_2, \ldots)$ and $T = (t_1, t_2, \ldots)$ both isomorphic to the set of non-negative integers. The two sorts P and T denote, respectively, positions (of (non-)observable states) and time units along a trace.

EC programs make use of the basic predicates `happens`, `initiates`, `terminates`, `holdsAt`, `impossible` and `attempt`. The atom `happens(e,p,t,s)` indicates that event e occurs at position p, within time unit t in scenario s, the atom `initiates( e,f,p,s)` (resp. `terminates(e,f,p,s)`) means that if, in a scenario s, event e were to occur at position p, it would cause fluent f to be true (resp. false) immediately afterwards. The predicate `holdsAt(f,p,s)` denotes, instead, that in a scenario s, fluent f is true at position p. The atoms `impossible(e,p,t,s)` and `attempt(e,p,t,s)` are used, respectively, to state that in a scenario s, at position p within a time unit t, the event e is impossible, and that an attempt has been made to perform e. The first four predicates are standard, whereas the last two are adapted from the EC extension presented in [17].

To relate positions and time units within a given scenario, our EC programs use the predicate `posInTime(p,t,s)`. For example, the scenario ⟨tick, signalHighWater, tick, switchPumpOn, tick⟩ is encoded using the ground atoms `happens(tick,0,0,s)`, `happens(signalHighWater,1,0,s)`, `happens(tick,2,1,s)`,... for the event transitions, `posInTime(0,0,s)`, `posInTime(1,0,s)`, `posInTime(2,1,s)`, `posInTime(3,1,s)`, `posInTime(4,2,s)`, ... for the relation between position and time units. Finally, to capture the notion of synchronous satisfiability in terms of asynchronous semantics our programs make use of the predicates `holdsAtTick` and `notHoldsAtTick`, which are defined as follows:

$$holdsAtTick(f,t,s):\text{-} attempt(tick,p,t,s),holdsAt(f,p,s), \\ posInTime(p,t,s) \tag{1}$$

$$notHoldsAtTick(f,t,s) :\text{-} attempt(tick,p,t,s), not\ holdsAt(f,p,s) \\ posInTime(p,t,s) \tag{2}$$

where p, t and s are respectively position, time unit and scenarios[1]. Axioms (1) and (2) state that a fluent f holds (resp. does not hold) at the beginning of a time unit t in a scenario s if it holds (resp. does not hold) at the position p where its starting `tick` is attempted.

EC programs are equipped with a set of domain-independent core axioms suitable for reasoning about effects of events over fluents. A full definition of these axioms is given in [21]. These include, in particular, an axiom for differentiating the possibility of an event occurring from it actually occurring. This is defined as follows: `happens(e,p,t,s):-attempt(e,p,t,s), not impossible(e,p,t,s)`. It is one of the key axioms in our learning process, as it relates the occurrence of an event (`happens(e,p,t,s)`) with the notion of its preconditions, captured by rules defining the predicate `impossible`.

From Goal Models to EC Programs. Given a goal model G_a, written in asynchronous FLTL, and a set of fluent definitions D, a mapping τ has been defined that automatically generates from G_a and D an EC program of the type described above. In brief, the mapping assigns to each FLTL fluent definition $f \equiv \langle\{a_i\}, \{b_i\}\rangle$ *initially* I the set of atomic literals comprising of `initially(f,S)`, for those fluents f where I is set to true, `initiates(a`$_j$`,f,P,S)`, for each a_i in the initiating set of f and `terminates(b`$_i$`,f,P,S)`, for each b_i in the terminating set of f. For example, the mapping function τ would generate from the fluent definition $pumpOn \equiv \langle\{switchPumpOn\}, \{switchPumpOff\}\rangle$, the facts `initiates(switchPumpOn, pumpOn,P,S)` and `terminates(switchPumpOff, pumpOn,P,S)`.

Asynchronous FLTL goal assertions are, instead, encoded into integrity constraints[2], using only `holdsAtTick` and `notHoldsAtTick` predicates. For instance, applying the function τ to the asynchronous formalisation of the goal *PumpOffWhenLowWater* gives the EC integrity constraint

`:- notHoldsAtTick(highWater,T,S),next(T2,T),holdsAtTick(pumpOn,T2,S)`

where `next(T2,T)` means $T2$ is the next time point. Asynchronous FLTL preconditions are encoded into rules for the predicate `impossible`. So a precondition $\Box(\bigwedge_{1\leq i\leq n}(\neg)f_i) \rightarrow \bigcirc\neg e$ *W tick)* would be expressed by the EC rule:

$$
\texttt{impossible(e,P,T,S):-(not)HoldsAtTick(f}_1\texttt{,T,S),}\dots, \\
\texttt{(not)HoldsAtTick(f}_n\texttt{,T,S)} \tag{3}
$$

In [1] the authors have shown that the above translation function is sound with respect to the stable model semantics [7].

Learning Preconditions. To learn event preconditions, positive and negative scenarios generated during the scenario elaboration phase have to be translated into our EC program. The translation depends on the event for which the precondition axiom is to be learnt. Without loss of generality, we assume that

---

[1] The operators : − and , denote implication and conjunction operators respectively in logic programming.

[2] An integrity constraint (IC) is a disjunction of literals with no positive literal.

preconditions are to be learnt always for the last event of each negative scenario. The encoding of negative and positive scenarios contribute to both the background knowledge and the examples of our learning task. For a positive scenario $\sigma_P = \langle e_1, e_2, ..., e_k \rangle$, the facts `attempt(e`$_\texttt{i}$`,i-1,t,`$\sigma$`p)` and `posInTime(i-1,t,`$\sigma$`p)` are added to the background knowledge, and the facts `happens(e`$_\texttt{i}$`,i-1,t,`σ`p)` are added to the example. For each negative scenario of the form $\sigma_N = \langle e_1, e_2, ..., e_l \rangle$ in Σ_N, the facts `attempt(e`$_\texttt{j}$`,j-1,t,`σ`N)` and `posInTime(j-1,t,`σ`N)` are added to the background knowledge, and the facts `happens(e`$_\texttt{j}$` ,j-1,t,`σ`N)` together with the atom `not happens(e`$_\texttt{l}$`,l-1,t,`σ`N)` are added to the examples.

The search space of all possible preconditions is defined by a language bias, which specifies the predicates that can appear in the hypothesis. In our learning task, the language bias defines the predicate `impossible` to appear in the head of the H rule, and the predicates `holdsAtTick` and `notHoldsAtTick` to appear in the body. For a detailed description of the XHAIL learning algorithm the reader is refer to [20]. To describe an example of learned precondition, consider again our example of the Mine Pump system, where the set of goals are as states in Subsection 4.2, with associated fluent definitions, and the positive and negative scenarios in Subsection 4.3. The XHAIL is applied to the EC programs B and E generated from these inputs. The system computes the ground rule:

```
impossible(switchPumpOn,4,2,σN) :- holdsAtTick(highWater,2, σN),
                                   notHoldsAtTick(pumpOn,2,σN),
                                   holdsAtTick(criticalMethane,2,σN),
                                   posInTime(4,2,σN).
```

And then generalizes it into the hypothesis: `impossible(switchPumpOn,X,Y,Z) :- holdsAtTick(criticalMethane,Y,Z)`. This output is then translated back into the FLTL assertion $\Box($ $tick \wedge criticalMethane \rightarrow \bigcirc \neg switchPumpOn$ W $tick)$.

4.5   The Cycle

At the end of each iteration, the learned preconditions are translated back into asynchronous FLTL and added to the goal model. The LTS resulting from the extended goal model is guaranteed not to exhibit the zeno trace detected by the LTSA in that iteration and captured by the elaborated negative scenario. In addition, the LTS is guaranteed to accept the positive scenarios identified by the engineer and, of course, all previously elicited goals and operational requirements. The property is formally captured by the following theorem and constitutes the main invariant of the approach.

Theorem 1. *Let G_a be an asynchronous goal model, D a set of fluent definitions, and $\Sigma_P \cup \Sigma_N$ a set of positive and negative scenarios. Let $(B, E) = \tau(G_a, D, \Sigma_P, \Sigma_N)$ be the EC programs generated by the translation function τ. Let H be the set of preconditions computed by the XHAIL system as inductive solution for the programs (B, E) such that $B \cup H \models E$. Then the corresponding set Pre of asynchronous FLTL preconditions, such that $\tau(Pre) = H$, is a correct extension of G_a with respect to $\Sigma_P \cup \Sigma_N$.*

This process is expected to be repeated until all the preconditions necessary to guarantee, together with the initial goal model, the construction of a non-zeno

LTS model. Although the convergence of this process has not yet been studied fully, experiments have shown so far that to avoid the derivation of a zeno-model, one only needs to learn a sufficient set of preconditions, i.e. triggering conditions are not necessary to avoid non-zeno traces.

5   Validation of the Approach

We validated our approach with two case studies, the Mine Pump Controller [10], parts of which have been used as a running example in this paper, and the Injection System [2]. The methodology used was to start with goal models formalised in the KAOS goal oriented approach (the mine pump [13] and the safety injection [12] systems), to apply the approach iteratively using informal existing documentation on the case studies to inform the elaboration of zeno traces into positive and negative scenarios and to compare the preconditions learned against the manually operationalised models of the provided goal models.

In the mine pump case study, it was necessary to learn three preconditions where as the safety injection system required only two. Moreover, in the safety injection system the set of preconditions needed for the process to converge, and reach a goal model from which a non-zeno behaviour model can be derived, was a subset of the preconditions of the fully operationalised goal model[12]. This indicates that the operationalisation process presented in [13] and required in [12] to build non-zeno models introduces unnecessary (and labour intensive) work. This also indicates that the process of resolving time progress violation in behavior models synthesized from goal models is a first step towards an automated procedure to produce a complete operationalisation of goal models.

6   Related Work

Automated reasoning techniques are increasingly being used in requirements engineering [11,3,4]. Among these, the work most related to our approach is [11], where an *ad-hoc* inductive inference process is used to derive high-level goals, expressed as temporal formulae, from manually attuned scenarios provided by stake-holders. Each scenario is used to infer a set of goal assertions that explains it. Then each goal is added to the initial goal model, which is then analyzed using state-based analysis techniques (i.e. goal decomposition, conflict management and obstacle detection). The inductive inference procedure used in [11] is mainly based on pure generalization of the given scenarios and does not take into account the given (partial) goal model. It is therefore a potentially unsound inference process by the fact that the generated goals may well be inconsistent with the given (partial) goal model. In our approach learned requirements are guaranteed to be consistent with the given goals.

The work in [3] also proposes the use of inductive inference to generate behavior models. It provides an automated technique for constructing LTSs from a set of user-defined scenarios. The synthesis procedure uses a grammar induction to derive an LTS that covers all positive scenarios but none of the negative ones.

The generated LTS can then be used for formal event-based analysis techniques (e.g. check against the goals expressed as safety properties). Our approach, on the other hand, uses the LTSA to generate the LTS models directly from goal models, so our LTS models are always guaranteed to satisfy the given goals.

The technique in [12] describes the steps for transforming a given KAOS goal and operational model into an FLTL theory that is used later by the LTSA to construct an LTS. Deadlock analysis reveals inconsistency problems in the KAOS model. However, the technique assumes these are resolved by manually reconstructing the operational model. Our approach builds on the goal to LTS transformation of [12] but does not require a fully operationalised model. Rather it provides automated support for completing an operational model with respect to the given goals.

7   Conclusion and Future Work

The paper presents an approach for deriving non-zeno behavior model from goal models. It deploys established model checking and learning techniques for the computation of precondition from scenarios. These preconditions can incrementally be added to the initial goal model so to generate at the end of the cycle a non-zeno behavior model. The precondition learned at each iteration has the effect of removing zeno traces identified by the LTS model at the beginning of that iteration. The cycle terminates when no more zeno traces are generated from the LTSA on the current (extended) goal model. A formal characterization of termination of the cycle is currently under investigation. But our experiments and case study results have so far confirmed the convergence of our process. Furthermore, the approach assumes, in the second phase, that the engineer will manually elaborate the violation trace into a set of scenarios. The possibility of automating the elaboration process by using other forms of learning techniques (e.g. abduction) is being considered. Future work includes learning other forms of requirements such as trigger conditions, learning preconditions with bounded temporal operators that refer to the past such as B and S in [13], and to integrate the approach within a framework for generating a set of required pre- and trigger-conditions that is complete [13] with respect to a given goal model.

References

1. Alrajeh, D., Ray, O., Russo, A., Uchitel, S.: Extracting requirements from scenarios with ILP. In: Muggleton, S., Otero, R., Tamaddoni-Nezhad, A. (eds.) ILP 2006. LNCS (LNAI), vol. 4455, pp. 64–78. Springer, Heidelberg (2007)
2. Courtois, P.J., Parnas, D.L.: Documentation for safety critical software. In: Proc. 15th Int. Conf. on software engineering (1993)
3. Damas, C., Dupont, P., Lambeau, B., van Lamsweerde, A.: Generating annotated behavior models from end-user scenarios. IEEE Transactions on Software Engineering 31(12), 1056–1073 (2005)

4. Damas, C., Lambeau, B., van Lamsweerde, A.: Scenarios, goals, and state machines: a win-win partnership for model synthesis. In: Proc. of the Intl. ACM Symp. on the Foundations of Software Engineering (2006)
5. Dardenne, A., van Lamsweerde, A., Fickas, S.: Goal-directed requirements acquisition. Science of Computer Programming 20 (1), 3–50 (1993)
6. Darimont, R., van Lamsweerde, A.: Formal refinement patterns for goal-driven requirements elaboration. In: Proc. of the 4th ACM Symp. on the Foundations of Software Engineering (1996)
7. Gelfond, M., Lifschitz, V.: The stable model semantics for logic programming. In: Kowalski, R.A., Bowen, K. (eds.) Proc. of the 5th Intl. Conf. on Logic Programming, MIT Press, Cambridge (1988)
8. Giannakopoulou, D., Magee, J.: Fluent model checking for event-based systems. In: Proc. 11th ACM SIGSOFT Symp. on Foundations Software Engineering (2003)
9. Heitmeyer, C., Bull, A., Gasarch, C., Labaw, B.: Scr*: A toolset for specifying and analyzing requirements. In: Proc. of the 10th Annual Conf. on Computer Assurance (1995)
10. Kramer, J., Magee, J., Sloman, M.: Conic: An integrated approach to distributed computer control systems. In: IEE Proc., Part E, vol. 130 (January 1983)
11. Van Lamsweerde, A., Willemet, L.: Inferring declarative requirements specifications from operational scenarios. IEEE Transactions on Software Engineering 24(12), 1089–1114 (1998)
12. Letier, E., Kramer, J., Magee, J., Uchitel, S.: Deriving event-based transitions systems from goal-oriented requirements models. Technical Report 02/2006, Imperial College London (2006)
13. Letier, E., Van Lamsweerde, A.: Deriving operational software specifications from system goals. In: Proc. 10th ACM SIGSOFT Symp. on Foundations of Software Engineering (2002)
14. Letier, E., van Lamsweerde, A.: Agent-based tactics for goal-oriented requirements elaboration. In: Proc. of the 24th Intl. Conf. on Software Engineering (2002)
15. Magee, J., Kramer, J.: Concurrency: State Models and Java Programs. John Wiley and Sons, Chichester (1999)
16. Manna, Z., Pnueli, A.: The Temporal Logic of Reactive and Concurrent Systems. Springer, Heidelberg (1992)
17. Miller, R., Shanahan, M.: Some alternative formulation of event calculus. In: Computer Science; Computational Logic; Logic programming and Beyond, vol. 2408 (2002)
18. Muggleton, S.H.: Inverse Entailment and Progol. New Generation Computing, Special issue on Inductive Logic Programming 13(3-4), 245–286 (1995)
19. Ray, O.: Using abduction for induction of normal logic programs. In: Proc. ECAI 2006 Workshop on Abduction and Induction in AI and Scientific Modelling (2006)
20. Ray, O., Broda, K., Russo, A.: A hybrid abductive inductive proof procedure. Logic Journal of the IGPL 12(5), 371–397 (2004)
21. Shanahan, M.P.: Solving the Frame Problem. MIT Press, Cambridge (1997)
22. Uchitel, S., Brunet, G., Chechik, M.: Behaviour model synthesis from properties and scenarios. In: Proc. of the 29th IEEE/ACM Intl. Conf. on Software Engineering (2007)

What's in a *Feature*:
A Requirements Engineering Perspective

Andreas Classen*, Patrick Heymans, and Pierre-Yves Schobbens

PReCISE Research Centre, Faculty of Computer Science, University of Namur
5000 Namur, Belgium
{acs,phe,pys}@info.fundp.ac.be

Abstract. The notion of feature is heavily used in Software Engineering, especially for software product lines. However, this notion appears to be confusing, mixing various aspects of problem and solution. In this paper, we attempt to clarify the notion of *feature* in the light of Zave and Jackson's framework for Requirements Engineering. By redefining a problem-level feature as a set of related requirements, specifications and domain assumptions—the three types of statements central to Zave and Jackson's framework—we also revisit the notion of feature interaction. This clarification work opens new perspectives on formal description and verification of software product lines. An important benefit of the approach is to enable an early identification of feature interactions taking place in the systems' environment, a notoriously challenging problem. The approach is illustrated through a proof-of-concept prototype tool and applied to a Smart Home example.

1 Introduction

Software product lines engineering (SPLE) is an emergent software engineering paradigm institutionalising reuse throughout the software lifecycle. Pohl *et al.* [1] define a software product line (SPL) as *"a set of software-intensive systems that share a common, managed set of features satisfying the specific needs of a particular market segment or mission and that are developed from a common set of core assets in a prescribed way"*. In SPLE, features appear to be first class abstractions that shape the reasoning of the engineers and other stakeholders [2,1]. This shows up, for instance, in feature modelling languages [3,4,5], which are popular notations used for representing and managing the variability between the members of a product line in terms of features (see Fig. 1 and Section 2.2).

In their seminal paper, Kang *et al.* introduce FODA (Feature-oriented domain analysis), a SPL approach based on feature diagrams [3]. In this context, they define a feature as *"a prominent or distinctive user-visible aspect, quality or characteristic of a software system or systems"*. We term this definition *problem-oriented* as it considers features as being an expression of the user's requirements. Eisenecker and Czarnecki, on the other hand, define a feature in

---

* FNRS Research Fellow. Work originated in a research stay at the Open University.

J. Fiadeiro and P. Inverardi (Eds.): FASE 2008, LNCS 4961, pp. 16–30, 2008.
© Springer-Verlag Berlin Heidelberg 2008

Table 1. Definitions for the term "feature" found in the literature and their overlaps with the descriptions of the Zave and Jackson framework (excerpt of [14])

Reference	Definition	R	W	S	D	other
Kang *et al.* [3]	"a prominent or distinctive user-visible aspect, quality or characteristic of a software system or systems"	✓		✓		
Kang *et al.* [8]	"distinctively identifiable functional abstractions that must be implemented, tested, delivered, and maintained"	✓		✓	✓	
Eisenecker and Czarnecki [6]	"anything users or client programs might want to control about a concept"	✓	✓	✓	✓	✓
Bosch *et al.* [9]	"A logical unit of behaviour specified by a set of functional and non-functional requirements."	✓		✓	✓	
Chen *et al.* [10]	"a product characteristic from user or customer views, which essentially consists of a cohesive set of individual requirements"	✓				
Batory [11]	"an elaboration or augmentation of an entity(s) that introduces a new service, capability or relationship"			✓	✓	✓
Batory *et al.* [12]	"an increment in product functionality"	✓		✓		
Apel *et al.* [13]	"a structure that extends and modifies the structure of a given program in order to satisfy a stakeholder's requirement, to implement and encapsulate a design decision, and to offer a configuration option."		✓	✓	✓	

a more general way as "*anything users or client programs might want to control about a concept*" [6]. This broader definition also subsumes elements of the solution space such as communication protocols, for instance.

As shown in the first two columns of Table 1, many other definitions exist that mix to a varying degree elements of solution and problem. This leads to confusion as to what a feature generally represents, and hence to a need for clarification. Most definitions, however, make sense in their respective context. Judging them by comparing them to one another irrespective of this context would not be very sensible. In this paper, we limit our scope to requirements engineering, and complement our previous work on disambiguating feature models. In [4,5], we devised a generic formal semantics for feature diagrams. There, we clarified and compared constructs used to combine features, but did not question the notion of feature itself. In [7], we further disambiguated feature models by distinguishing features and variability that represent product management decisions from those that denote extension capabilities of the SPL's reusable software assets.

In this paper, we propose a complementary perspective that looks at features as expressions of problems to be solved by the products of the SPL. We rely on the extensive work carried out by Jackson, Zave and others during the past decade in a similar attempt to clarify the notion of requirement [15,16]. Their work has resulted in more precise definitions of the terms "requirement", "specification" and "domain assumption". Their clarifications have allowed to improve the methodological guidance given to requirements engineers in eliciting, documenting, validating and verifying software related needs. One of the most notable outcomes of their work is the identification of a fundamental *requirements concern*, i.e. a logical entailment that must hold between the various components of a requirements document. Roughly, this concern can be stated as: given a set of assumptions W on the application domain, and given a system that behaves according to its specification S, we should be able to guarantee that the requirements R are met. More formally: $S, W \vdash R$.

In their ICSE'07 roadmap paper, Cheng and Atlee [17] acknowledge that *"reasoning about requirements involves reasoning about the combined behaviour of the proposed system and assumptions made about the environment. Taking into consideration environmental conditions significantly increases the complexity of the problem at hand"*. In this paper, we propose concepts, methods and tools to address the combined complexity of highly environment-dependent systems and systems that have to be developed in multiple (possibly many) exemplars. In such systems, a particularly difficult problem is to detect feature interactions that involve the environment [18].

In the present paper, building on Jackson *et al.*'s clarification work, we redefine the notion of feature as a subset of correlated elements from W, S and R. Doing so, we ambition to demonstrate that:

(i) a clearer definition of the notion of feature is useful to guide modellers in their abstraction process;
(ii) the relationships between feature models and other kinds of descriptions needed during SPL requirements engineering become clearer;
(iii) the requirements concern can be redefined in the context of SPLE, giving the engineers a clear target in terms of a "proof obligation";
(iv) the notion of "feature interaction" can be revisited in the light of this adapted proof obligation, further clarifying concepts and guidelines for SPL engineers.

The remainder of this paper is structured as follows. In Section 2 we recall Feature Diagrams as well as Zave and Jackson's framework for requirements engineering. We illustrate them on a Smart Home System example. The redefinition of "feature" follows in Section 3, accompanied by a discussion of its implications on the concept of "feature interaction" and a proposal for a general approach to feature interaction detection in SPLs. As a proof of concept for the definitions and the general approach, we present a particular verification approach and prototype tool in Section 4. This is followed in Section 5 by a discussion on possible improvements and future work. Related works are described in Section 6 before Section 7 concludes the paper.

2   Background

2.1   Zave and Jackson's Reference Model

The starting point of Zave, Jackson *et al.*'s work is the observation that specifying indicative and optative properties of the environment is as important as specifying the system's functionality [15,16,19].

They identify three types of descriptions: *Requirements R* describe what the purpose of the system is. They are optative descriptions, i.e. they express how the world should be once the system is deployed. For an alarm system, this could be: 'Notify the police of the presence of burglars'. *Domain assumptions W* describe the behaviour of the environment in which the system will be deployed. They are indicative, i.e. they indicate facts, as for instance 'Burglars cause movement when they break in' and 'There is a movement sensor monitoring the house, connected to the system'. The *specification* then describes how the system has to behave in order to bring about the changes in the environment as described in R, assuming the environment to be as described in W. In our example, this would be 'Alert the police if the sensor captures movement'. The central element of the reference model is the following relationship between these three descriptions:

$$S, W \vdash R, \tag{1}$$

i.e. the machine satisfies the requirements if S combined with W *entails R*. For the remainder of the paper, we will use the symbol $\vdash\!\sim$ to make explicit the fact that the entailment relationship is not necessarily monotonic [20].

2.2   Modelling Variability

To reason on the variability of a SPL, Feature Diagrams (FDs) are perhaps the most popular family of notations. An example (using the FODA [3] syntax) is shown in Fig. 1 and further discussed in Section 2.3. Generally, a FD is a tree or a directed acyclic graph that serves as a compact representation of all valid combinations of features (depicted as boxes). A formal semantics of FDs can be devised by considering non-leaf boxes as Boolean formulae over their descendants [21,4]. For example, Fig. 1 uses three *or*-decompositions (depicted as dark 'pie slices'), but other operators (*and*, *xor*, cardinalities...) as well as cross-cutting constraints (*excludes*, *requires*) are also commonly used.

In our previous work [4,5], we devised a generic formalisation of the syntax and semantics of FDs, on top of which most popular FD dialects were (re)defined and compared. In this paper, we reuse this formalisation and its associated tool. More specifically, we will make use of the tool's product derivation capabilities, that is, its ability to generate valid feature combinations.

2.3   Illustrative Example

As an illustration, let us consider the case of a Smart Home System (SHS) [22]. Such a system has a high degree of integration with its environment as it mainly observes and controls properties of a house that are part of the physical world. In order to be able to build a SHS right, it is important to understand how these properties influence each other [22].

A SHS is also a typical product line [1] since the company developing and selling such systems has to be able to adapt them to each customer's home. In addition, such companies need to be able to leave configuration choices to the customer, such as the features to be included, and specificities of theses features, which allows to address different market segments. A house located in a very warm region, for instance, will probably not need a heating system. A house under surveillance by an external security company will need an adapted security system as part of the smart home package, and so on.

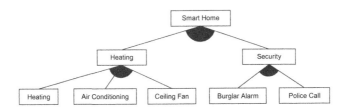

Fig. 1. Feature diagram for the SHS

The simplified system we use as an illustration consists of two features. Each feature has several sub-features as depicted on the FD in Fig. 1. All features are decomposed with an *or*-operator. This means that a product might only consist of the security feature, for instance. A short description of the two main features is given below.

Heating. Its objective is to assure that the temperature of the room lies within a range of user-defined values. In order to achieve this, the system can use the heating, the air conditioning and a ceiling fan.

Security. The security feature has to make sure that the police and the neighbourhood are alerted of any burglars and intruders. The system is equipped with a movement sensor, a telephone connection to alert the police, and an alarm to alert the neighbours.

A problem diagram [19] for a particular product consisting of the ceiling fan and the police call features is depicted in Fig. 2. It shows two requirements (dashed ovals) on the right-hand side, one for each feature, and the SHS on the left-hand side (rectangle with two stripes). In between there are real world domains. When a domain can directly control or observe properties of another domain, those domains are said to share phenomena. This is depicted by a line between the domain boxes. Dashed lines denote the phenomena in terms of which the requirements are defined. The arrow heads point to the domains of which the phenomena are constrained by the requirement. The problem diagram basically shows the problem's topology, it is schematic and is to be completed by precise descriptions of R, S and W.

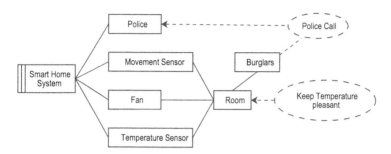

Fig. 2. Composite problem diagram for the simplified SHS

As shown in Section 2.1 and in Fig. 2, the description of the security feature indeed covers all of the above constituents. We also showed that, intuitively, its $S, W \mathrel{|\!\sim} R$ relation holds. Yet, it is still easy to imagine that other features can differ, overlap or conflict with this feature in terms of their S, W and R constituents. Conflicts are typically called feature interactions. As we will see in the next section, a new and precise definition of "feature interaction" will follow from our redefinition of "feature".

3   Towards a General Definition of "Feature" in Requirements Engineering

Table 1 shows how, in the context of requirements engineering, current definitions of "feature" mix or ignore the various elements (R, W, S) and sometime also subsume design (D) or other concerns. The irregular distribution of checkmarks, although subjective and debatable, still suggests that there is room for clarification.

3.1   "Feature" Revisited

Based on the previous observations, and following to some extent an idea suggested by Chen *et al.* [10], we redefine a feature as a set of related requirements, domain properties and specifications:

Definition 1 (Feature). *A feature is a triplet, $f = (R, W, S)$, where R represents the requirements the feature satisfies, W the assumptions the feature takes about its environment and S its specification.*

By adopting this definition, we emphasise three essential constituents of features. We can then relate them using the central proof obligation of the reference model, which acts as a consistency criterion for a feature. A feature $f_1 = (R_1, W_1, S_1)$ is said to be consistent if we have $S_1, W_1 \mathrel{|\!\sim} R_1$.

Just as in the Zave-Jackson framework, we are not prescriptive about the formalisms to use for the descriptions of S_1, W_1 and R_1. Hence, they can be chosen freely. This also means that the form this proof should take is not fixed either. In this, we follow Hall *et al.* in [23]: if judged sufficiently dependable, the proof can be provided by any mean, including non-exhaustive tests, or even arguments such as *"Dijkstra programmed it"*, as long as the choice is justified with respect to the level of confidence expected by the developers. Being general, the definition thus allows all kinds of formal or informal proofs. If we want to be able to automate the approach, however, we have to restrict ourselves to automatable modes of proof. This path will be further explored in Section 4, where we present a prototype tool that automates this proof.

Checking each feature on its own, however, is not sufficient. A SPL can contain hundreds of features, the combination of which define the products. Most of the complexity of variability management resides in the interoperation of features: some can depend on each other, and some, conversely, can disrupt each other. This means that a system cannot be proven correct by proving each feature separately. We now address this issue.

3.2 "Feature Interaction" Revisited

Feature interactions have long been a research topic in the telecommunications domain. The particularity of an interaction is that it is a property that two or more features only exhibit when put together, and not when run individually [24].

Based on the previous definition of feature, and based on the Zave-Jackson framework, we propose the following definition.

Definition 2 (Feature interaction). *Given a set of features $p = f_1..f_n$, expressed as R_i, W_i, S_i for $i = 1..n$ and $n \geq 2$, features $f_1..f_n$ are said to interact if*

(i) they satisfy their individual requirements in isolation,
(ii) they do not satisfy the conjunction of these requirements when put together,
(iii) and removing any feature from p results in a set of features that do not interact.

i.e. if:

$$\forall f_i \in p \, . \, S_i, W_i \mathrel{\vdash\mkern-10mu\sim} R_i$$
$$\wedge \bigwedge_{i=1}^{n} S_i, \bigwedge_{i=1}^{n} W_i \mathrel{\not\vdash\mkern-10mu\sim} \bigwedge_{i=1}^{n} R_i$$
$$\wedge \forall f_k \in p \, . \, \bigwedge_{i \in \{1..k-1,k+1..n\}} S_i, \bigwedge_{i \in \{1..k-1,k+1..n\}} W_i \mathrel{\vdash\mkern-10mu\sim} \bigwedge_{i \in \{1..k-1,k+1..n\}} R_i$$

A feature interaction in a system $s = \{f_1..f_q\}$ is then any set $p \subseteq s$ such that its features interact.

Points (i) and (ii) of Definition 2 express the fact that an interaction only occurs when features are put together. The objective of point (iii) is to make sure that a feature interaction is always minimal, i.e. all features that are part of an interaction have to be present for the interaction to occur. If a feature could be taken out of a set of interacting features without affecting the interaction, it would not be part of the interaction anyway. Ignoring (iii) would also mean that for each interaction between i features ($i < |allfeatures|$), a new interaction of $i + 1$ features could be found simply by adding any of the remaining features.

3.3   Two Kinds of Interactions

Since a feature can add elements on both sides of the $\vdash\!\sim$ relation, non-satisfaction of the proof obligation is not necessarily a monotonic relation. This is, however, assumed in the previous paragraph, i.e. we assumed that:

$$\bigwedge_{i=1}^{k} S_i, \bigwedge_{i=1}^{k} W_i \not\vdash\!\sim \bigwedge_{i=1}^{k} R_i \wedge S_{k+1}, W_{k+1} \vdash\!\sim R_{k+1} \quad \Rightarrow \quad \bigwedge_{i=1}^{k+1} S_i, \bigwedge_{i=1}^{k+1} W_i \not\vdash\!\sim \bigwedge_{i=1}^{k+1} R_i$$

As a counterexample consider a situation in which two features need a third one to work properly: features f_1 and f_2, for instance, both do print logging, which means that both require access to some dot-matrix printer connected to the system in order to print their logs. These features interact because each works fine in isolation, but once both are put together the first one that gains access to the printer would exclude the other from doing so, thereby preventing it from printing its logs, hence violating the global requirement. If we consider now a third feature f_3 that is a wrapper for the printer API and allows simultaneous access from multiple processes, then it is easy to imagine that f_3 would prevent f_1 and f_2 from interacting. Assuming that $f_i = (S_i, W_i, R_i)$ we would have the following relations:

$$S_1, W_1 \vdash\!\sim R_1 \qquad S_2, W_2 \vdash\!\sim R_2 \qquad S_3, W_3 \vdash\!\sim R_3$$
$$S_1, S_2, W_1, W_2 \not\vdash\!\sim R_1, R_2 \qquad S_1, S_2, S_3, W_1, W_2, W_3 \vdash\!\sim R_1, R_2, R_3$$

The above example shows that adding a feature to a set of interacting features could as well solve the interaction. This observation does not invalidate the preceding definition of a feature interaction. It merely points out a second type of interaction, which we do not consider. What we define as an interaction is basically the fact that *simultaneous* presence of several features causes malfunctions, and that these features *cannot be present* in the system at the same time. A second type of interaction would be just the opposite, i.e. the fact that a number of features *have to be* present in the system at the same time, because *individual* presence would lead to malfunctions. While interactions of the first type are harmful and have to be prevented, interactions of the second one are desired and have to be assured. For the FD, this generally results in adding *excludes*-constraints between features concerned by the first case and *requires*-constraints between features concerned by the second case.

3.4   Systematic Consistency Verification

Building on the preceding definitions and assuming that descriptions S, W and R are provided for each feature of a SPL, we now propose a set of consistency rules that need to be satisfied by these descriptions. We then present four algorithms as a general approach to feature interaction detection based on these consistency rules. A proof-of-concept instance of this approach is presented in Section 4.

The starting point is again the $S, W \hspace{0.2em}\vdash\hspace{-0.6em}\sim R$ relation which has to be proven correct for all products of the SPL. Unfortunately, proving this relation alone is not sufficient, as it would be trivially satisfied if we had $S, W \hspace{0.2em}\vdash\hspace{-0.6em}\sim false$. Similarly, if $R \hspace{0.2em}\vdash\hspace{-0.6em}\sim false$, or $R, W \hspace{0.2em}\vdash\hspace{-0.6em}\sim false$, the requirement would be too restrictive. As these cases need to be excluded, we have to perform several preliminary proofs. In consequence, we identify a total of six proofs:

$$S \hspace{0.2em}\not\vdash\hspace{-0.6em}\sim false \qquad W \hspace{0.2em}\not\vdash\hspace{-0.6em}\sim false \qquad R \hspace{0.2em}\not\vdash\hspace{-0.6em}\sim false$$
$$S, W \hspace{0.2em}\not\vdash\hspace{-0.6em}\sim false \qquad W, R \hspace{0.2em}\not\vdash\hspace{-0.6em}\sim false \qquad (2)$$
$$S, W \hspace{0.2em}\vdash\hspace{-0.6em}\sim R$$

These proofs have to be verified for each single feature, as well as for each product of the SPL. The whole process can be described by the following four algorithms.[1]

A1 *Feature consistency check:* verify the proofs (2) on all features of the SPL. This algorithm has to be run first, because we have to make sure that all features are consistent before the SPL is verified. Its algorithmic complexity is $O(n\gamma)$ where γ is the complexity of verifying one relation of the form $S_i, W_i \hspace{0.2em}\vdash\hspace{-0.6em}\sim R_i$ an n the number of features in the SPL.

A2 *Product consistency check:* verify the proofs (2) for a given product that is part of the SPL. If the complexity of verifying a relation of the form $\bigwedge_{i=1}^{n} S_i, \bigwedge_{i=1}^{n} W_i \hspace{0.2em}\vdash\hspace{-0.6em}\sim \bigwedge_{i=1}^{n} R_i$ is assumed to be $\Gamma(n)$, then this algorithm is of complexity $O(\Gamma(n))$. It is invoked by algorithm A3.

A3 *Product line consistency check:* verify the consistency of the whole SPL. Given the feature diagram d, generate all products that are part of the SPL and invoke the preceding algorithm (A2) for each one. The complexity in this case is $O(2^n + |[[d]]|\Gamma(n))$.

A4 *Find interactions:* identify the actual feature interaction in the case an inconsistency has been detected by algorithm A3. This algorithm will be invoked by A3 as needed. The complexity here is $O(2^n \Gamma(n))$.

We believe that this approach is sufficiently general to act as an umbrella for a large number of feature interaction detection techniques, depending on the form the $S, W \hspace{0.2em}\vdash\hspace{-0.6em}\sim R$ proof takes. The next section provides one proof-of-concept instance.

4   A Proof-of-Concept Instance

In order to experiment with the general approach introduced in the preceding section we created an instance of this approach by choosing an automatable formalism (viz. the Event Calculus), based on which we developed a proof-of-concept prototype that automates all composition and validation tasks.

---

[1] Due to space constraints, the descriptions of these algorithms as well as their complexity results are shortened and simplified. For a detailed account please refer to [14].

4.1   Prototype Tool

If all descriptions are expressed in a formalism that allows for automated reasoning, the algorithms presented in Section 3.4 can be largely automated. We chose the Event Calculus (EC) [25], because it is intuitive and well suited for "commonsense" descriptions such as those found in many domain properties. Among the available EC implementations, we chose the *discrete event calculus reasoner (Decreasoner)*, an EC implementation by Mueller [25]. Decreasoner does model-checks on a set of EC formulae by transforming them into a SAT problem to be solved by a third-party SAT solver. After running the SAT-solver, Decreasoner analyses the model it found and presents it as a narrative of time points, events and fluents.

Using the EC and the Decreasoner implementation, we developed a prototype reasoning tool, called *FIFramework*,[2] as a plugin for the Eclipse platform. The tool offers a dedicated EC editor, which simplifies the editing of formulae through syntax highlighting and code assistance and enforces feature descriptions to be conform to Definition 1. It also adds a number of new buttons to the toolbar, which allow the user to launch the verifications introduced in Section 3.4 and thus provides the capability of proving the absence of interactions as defined in Definition 2 behind a push-button interface. Each time a specific verification is launched, the tool automatically gathers all formulae needed for the particular verification. These formulae are then written to a Decreasoner compatible input file, and Decreasoner is invoked to process the file. Once this is done, the result is analysed, a report generated and the final result presented to the user.

As depicted on the workflow shown in Fig. 3, the tool builds on and implements the ideas and definitions of Section 3. The starting point is a SPL which has its variability documented in a FD. The features of this diagram are modelled using problem diagrams, and formalised using the EC. Processing the feature diagrams delivers a list of products (sets of features) [4], and the associated problem diagrams are represented by a set of EC files. Given this input, our tool automates all EC formulae composition and verification tasks. Through interactive usage, the algorithms of Section 3.4 (except algorithm A4) can then be effectively automated.

4.2   Results

An in-depth illustration of the approach as well as of FIFramework can be found in [14], where the author models and analyses a SHS product line consisting of 16 different features (actually an extended version of the example used in Section 2.3). The illustration starts with a feature analysis and a problem analysis which identifies the different domains and requirements. Based on this analysis, a product consisting of 11 features is specified formally with the EC. This results in a total of 30 EC formulae expressing domain assumptions, requirements and specifications which are then introduced into FIFramework.

---

[2] Available online at www.classen.be/work/mscthesis

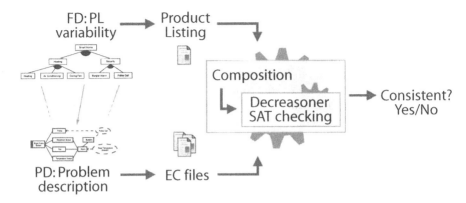

Fig. 3. FIFramework workflow

Using the feature interaction detection algorithms of Section 3.4, we were able to identify two interactions, one between the away-from-home and the energy control feature (two features not included in this paper) and one between the police call and the heating feature (those of the Section 2.3). The two features work just fine in isolation. Once deployed in the same room, however, they interact. This is due to the fact that the movement sensor of the police call feature will not only capture burglars, but also the movement of the ceiling fan, leading to false alarms.

We reiterate that our example and tool are not realistic, but only intend to demonstrate the feasability of the general approach. Before trying a real-world case study, we need to improve the scalability of our tool.

5   Discussion

During SPL requirements engineering, if one looks at variability only from the lens of FDs, one will be limited by the fuzzy notion of feature. The only formal notion of product validity that one will be able to use is that of a product (set of features) satisfying the constraints in the FD. Since features are very coarse-grained abstractions, and in the absence of more detailed verification, the safety of such approaches can seem questionable. On the contrary, further distinction and formalisation of the features' constituents (S, W and R), as proposed in this paper, allows to uncover hidden interactions while still remaining at the problem definition level. The approach relies on a stronger notion of product satisfiability relying on the satisfaction of its first proof obligation, i.e. absence of feature interactions and a guarantee of the overall requirement being met. The results of this formal analysis, however, should be in turn reflected in the FD, updating it with *excludes* and *xor* constraints so that their satisfaction implies satisfaction of the first proof obligation. Furthermore, it is conceivable to use the approach to identify unnecessary constraints in the FD that should be relaxed because they prevent useful combinations that have no harmful interaction. This bi-directional model co-evolution process, further discussed in [14], is a topic of on-going work.

As we have seen, the first instance of our general feature interaction detection framework is a running prototype that relies on the EC and its Decreasoner implementation. Although the EC and Decreasoner are powerful tools to express and reason on many "common sense" descriptions, branching time properties and behaviour are out of its scope. Furthermore, the Decreasoner implementation only uses finite-time discrete EC, putting the burden of defining valid time intervals on the analyst. We are already considering moving to temporal logic, because of the abundance of literature and powerful model checkers.

On a more conceptual note, we found in various experiments that several descriptions, mainly among the domain assumptions, are shared by all features. We thus intend to extend Definition 2 (and consequently our consistency checking procedure) so that it accounts for shared descriptions explicitly. It is, for instance, conceivable to assume that there exists a *base configuration*, i.e. some R_b, W_b and S_b that hold for all features, and to include it in each proof.

Another crucial point for the scalability of our approach is the modularity of the manipulated models. Although there exist guidelines for structuring FDs [8,26], such models can become very large, and feature decomposition criteria can be quite subjective, making it hard to navigate through models. On the other hand, over the years, the Zave-Jackson framework has evolved into the Problem Frames (PF) approach [19]. PFs facilitate the description of complex problems by decomposing them into "basic problems" that match patterns (frames) from a repertoire of recurrent simple situations. This decomposition approach provides much clearer criteria and better modularity than feature-based decomposition. However, it sometimes appears that very large problems are hard to decompose, and a prior feature decomposition allows for a high-level exploration of the problem space. Also, PFs lack a way to represent variability explicitly. The complementarity of the two approaches and the co-evolution of their respective diagrams (FDs and problem diagrams) was already investigated by the authors in [27], but still has to be linked to our feature interaction detection approach.

6   Related work

The Feature-Oriented Reuse Method (FORM) [8] has its own typology of features. It extends the basic FD notation with four classes of features organised in four respective layers: capability features, operating environment features, domain technology features and implementation technique features. This classification is similar to the S, W, R classification of the reference framework, but is less formal. In particular, no proof obligation is proposed. The main purpose is to structure the FD.

Several authors suggest other classifications for variability in general. Pohl *et al.* [1] distinguish *internal* and *external* variability. External variability is what is relevant to customers, while internal variability is technical. No formal relation between them is defined though. Similar, yet different, is the distinction of *product line variability* and *software variability* by Metzger *et al.* [7], who separated business-related variability *decisions* from platform variability *data*. However, all these distinctions consider features as black boxes. They do not distinguish or restrict the content of the features for each variability class.

Silva [28] introduces a method for detecting and solving discrepancies between different viewpoints. The suggested approach is similar to what we presented here, in that Silva also uses the same RE framework and compares different descriptions against each other. It differs from our case, in that Silva considers descriptions of the same feature, that stem from different analysts, while we consider descriptions of different features.

Laney *et al.* [29] also work with problem diagrams and EC to detect and solve run-time behavioural inconsistencies. In case of a conflict, the feature with the highest priority (expressed using composition operators) prevails. Their approach is focused on run-time resolution using composition operators whereas ours focuses on design-time resolution in the SPLE context.

We also note that there are efforts underway in the feature interaction community to detect and solve inconsistencies in SHS [22]. Although they allow to discover interactions in the physical world, their approach remains domain-specific whereas our framework is domain-independent.

7   Conclusion

In this paper, we laid down the foundations for a general approach to automated feature interaction detection supporting the early stages of software product line engineering. Central to this approach are novel definitions of two fundamental concepts: "feature" and "feature interaction". These definitions are themselves grounded in the Zave-Jackson framework for requirements engineering and allow to link it to the popular notation of feature diagrams. The most important benefit of the approach is to allow for a formal, fine-grained analysis of feature interactions, which is one of the most challenging problems in software product lines. More and more widespread, but particularly difficult to detect, are interactions that involve the environment. Our framework provides a general means to tackle them as early as possible in the development lifecycle, when the corrective actions are orders-of-magnitude cheaper than in subsequent stages.

We also reported on the instance of the general approach into a proof-of-concept prototype that uses the Event Calculus as a concrete specification language, and an off-the-shelf SAT solver. The tool could be tried out on a SHS, exemplifying our concepts and allowing to uncover non-trivial feature interactions occurring in the system's environment.

Our future work will target scalability mainly by (i) adopting temporal logic and its associated industrial-strength model-checkers, (ii) improving the modularity of the models by integrating our approach with problem frames, (iii) investigating possibilities to do compositional verification, and (iv) integrating the tool into a toolchain that we are currently developing for formal specification and analysis of software product lines. Cooperation is also underway with industry to apply our techniques to a real SHS.

Acknowledgements

This work was partially funded by the Interuniversity Attraction Poles Programme, Belgian State, Belgian Science Policy, by the Belgian National Bank and the FNRS.

References

1. Pohl, K., Bockle, G., van der Linden, F.: Software Product Line Engineering: Foundations, Principles and Techniques. Springer, Heidelberg (2005)
2. Batory, D.S.: Feature-oriented programming and the ahead tool suite. In: 26th International Conference on Software Engineering (ICSE 2004), Edinburgh, United Kingdom, May 23-28, 2004, pp. 702–703 (2004)
3. Kang, K., Cohen, S., Hess, J., Novak, W., Peterson, S.: Feature-Oriented Domain Analysis (FODA) Feasibility Study. Technical Report CMU/SEI-90-TR-21, Software Engineering Institute, Carnegie Mellon University (November 1990)
4. Schobbens, P.Y., Heymans, P., Trigaux, J.C., Bontemps, Y.: Feature Diagrams: A Survey and A Formal Semantics. In: Proceedings of the 14th IEEE International Requirements Engineering Conference (RE 2006), Minneapolis, Minnesota, USA, September 2006, pp. 139–148 (2006)
5. Schobbens, P.Y., Heymans, P., Trigaux, J.C., Bontemps, Y.: Generic semantics of feature diagrams. In: Computer Networks (2006). special issue on feature interactions in emerging application domains, vol. 38 (2006), (doi:10.1016/j.comnet.2006.08.008)
6. Eisenecker, U.W., Czarnecki, K.: Generative Programming: Methods, Tools, and Applications. Addison-Wesley, Reading (2000)
7. Metzger, A., Heymans, P., Pohl, K., Schobbens, P.Y., Saval, G.: Disambiguating the documentation of variability in software product lines: A separation of concerns, formalization and automated analysis. In: Proceedings of the 15th IEEE International Requirements Engineering Conference (RE 2007), New Delhi, India, October 2007, pp. 243–253 (2007)
8. Kang, K.C., Kim, S., Lee, J., Kim, K., Shin, E., Huh, M.: Form: A feature-oriented reuse method with domain-specific reference architectures. Annales of Software Engineering 5, 143–168 (1998)
9. Bosch, J.: Design and use of software architectures: adopting and evolving a product-line approach. ACM Press/Addison-Wesley, New York (2000)
10. Chen, K., Zhang, W., Zhao, H., Mei, H.: An approach to constructing feature models based on requirements clustering. In: Proceedings of the 13th IEEE International Conference on Requirements Engineering (RE 2005), pp. 31–40 (2005)
11. Batory, D.: Feature modularity for product-lines. In: OOPSLA 2006 Generative Programming and Component Engineering (GPCE) (tutorial) (October 2006)
12. Batory, D., Benavides, D., Ruiz-Cortes, A.: Automated analysis of feature models: Challenges ahead. Communications of the ACM (December 2006)
13. Apel, S., Lengauer, C., Batory, D., Möller, B.: Kästner, C.: An algebra for feature-oriented software development. Technical report, Fakultät für Informatik und Mathematik, Universität Passau (2007)

14. Classen, A.: Problem-oriented modelling and verification of software product lines. Master's thesis, Computer Science Department, University of Namur, Belgium (June 2007)
15. Zave, P., Jackson, M.A.: Four dark corners of requirements engineering. ACM Transactions on Software Engineering and Methodology 6(1), 1–30 (1997)
16. Gunter, C.A., Gunter, E.L., Jackson, M., Zave, P.: A reference model for requirements and specifications. IEEE Software 17(3), 37–43 (2000)
17. Cheng, B.H., Atlee, J.M.: Research directions in requirements engineering. In: Proceedings of the 29th International Conference on Software Engineering (ICSE 2007), May 20-26 (2007)
18. Metzger, A., Bühne, S., Lauenroth, K., Pohl, K.: Considering Feature Interactions in Product Lines: Towards the Automatic Derivation of Dependencies between Product Variants. In: Feature Interactions in Telecommunications and Software Systems VIII (ICFI 2005), June 2005, pp. 198–216. IOS Press, Leicester (2005)
19. Jackson, M.A.: Problem frames: analyzing and structuring software development problems. Addison-Wesley, Boston (2001)
20. Makinson, D.: General Patterns in Nonmonotonic Reasoning. In: Handbook of Logic in Artificial Intelligence and Logic Programming, vol. 2, pp. 35–110. Oxford University Press, Oxford (1994)
21. Batory, D.S.: Feature Models, Grammars, and Propositional Formulas. In: Obbink, H., Pohl, K. (eds.) SPLC 2005. LNCS, vol. 3714, pp. 7–20. Springer, Heidelberg (2005)
22. Wilson, M., Kolberg, M., Magill, E.H.: Considering side effects in service interactions in home automation - an online approach. In: Proceedings of the 9th International Conference on Feature Interactions in Software and Communication Systems (ICFI 2007), Grenoble, France, September 2007, pp. 187–202 (2007)
23. Hall, J.G., Rapanotti, L., Jackson, M.: Problem frame semantics for software development. Software and System Modeling 4(2), 189–198 (2005)
24. Calder, M., Kolberg, M., Magill, E.H., Reiff-Marganiec, S.: Feature interaction: a critical review and considered forecast. Computer Networks 41(1), 115–141 (2003)
25. Mueller, E.T.: Commonsense Reasoning. Morgan Kaufmann, San Francisco (2006)
26. Lee, K., Kang, K.C., Lee, J.: Concepts and guidelines of feature modeling for product line software engineering. In: Gacek, C. (ed.) ICSR 2002. LNCS, vol. 2319, pp. 62–77. Springer, Heidelberg (2002)
27. Classen, A., Heymans, P., Laney, R., Nuseibeh, B., Tun, T.T.: On the structure of problem variability: From feature diagrams to problem frames. In: Proceedings of the First International Workshop on Variability Modelling of Software-intensive Systems, Limerick, Ireland, LERO, January 2007, pp. 109–117 (2007)
28. Silva, A.: Requirements, domain and specifications: a viewpoint-based approach to requirements engineering. In: ICSE 2002: Proceedings of the 24th Int. Conference on Software Engineering, pp. 94–104. ACM Press, New York (2002)
29. Laney, R., Tun, T.T., Jackson, M., Nuseibeh, B.: Composing features by managing inconsistent requirements. In: Proceedings of the 9th International Conference on Feature Interactions in Software and Communication Systems (ICFI 2007), Grenoble, France, September 2007, pp. 141–156 (2007)

Formal Approach to Integrating
Feature and Architecture Models

Mikoláš Janota[1] and Goetz Botterweck[2]

[1] School of Computer Science and Informatics,
Lero, University College Dublin, Dublin, Ireland
`mikolas.janota@ucd.ie`
[2] Lero, University of Limerick, Limerick, Ireland
`goetz.botterweck@lero.ie`

Abstract. If we model a family of software applications with a feature model and an architecture model, we are describing the same subject from different perspectives. Hence, we are running the risk of inconsistencies. For instance, the feature model might allow feature configurations that are not realizable by the architecture.

In this paper we tackle this problem by providing a formalization of dependencies between features and components. Further, we demonstrate that this formalization offers a better understanding of the modeled concepts. Moreover, we propose automated techniques that derive additional information and provide feedback to the user. Finally, we discuss how some of these techniques can be implemented.

1   Introduction

Many companies providing software-intensive systems have to deal with the challenge to fulfill the expectation of each individual customer and, at the same time, to perform the necessary engineering processes in an efficient manner.

One way to approach this challenge is by focusing on building a whole set of similar systems in a systematic way. This phenomenon shaped a field known as *software product lines (SPL)* [6]. A software product line is "a set of software-intensive systems that share a common, managed set of features satisfying the specific needs of a particular market segment [..] and that are developed from a common set of core assets in a prescribed way" [21]. SPL approaches use miscellaneous models to describe the various aspects of a product-line. This includes feature models [13,8] or architecture models containing the components that implement the features. We will now use very simple examples of such models to illustrate the motivation for our research presented in this paper.

Imagine a product-line of mobile phones that has only two features which distinguish the various products: the capability to play MP3 files, and a built-in camera. Fig. 1 shows the corresponding models. In SPL engineering such models are created by the *domain engineer* in order to describe the scope of the whole product-line. Further, these models are given to the *application engineer* to be used during the configuration and derivation of a concrete product.

J. Fiadeiro and P. Inverardi (Eds.): FASE 2008, LNCS 4961, pp. 31–45, 2008.
© Springer-Verlag Berlin Heidelberg 2008

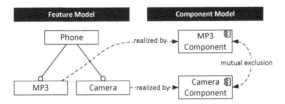

Fig. 1. Feature model and component model of a mobile phone product-line

The feature model in Fig. 1 does not capture any dependencies between the features MP3 and Camera. Nevertheless, the feature MP3 is realized by MP3Component, the feature Camera is realized by CameraComponent, and there is a mutual exclusion between the two components. This means that the feature model permits a combination of features that is not realizable with respect to the component model. In other words, there is an *implicit* dependency (exclusion) between the two features.

This poses a problem, as during the feature configuration the application engineer often deals solely with the feature model since it is simply too time-consuming to walk through subsequent implementation steps (to check each possible feature configuration for its realizability). In this small example the chain of dependencies is easy to spot. In real SPL projects with their complex models and large number of dependencies these implicit dependencies pose a big problem. Hence, it is desirable to enhance the feature model in Fig. 1 with the mutual exclusion between the features MP3 and Camera.

In this article we are focusing on how to find such implicit (missing) dependencies. The feature model enhanced with the missing dependencies will provide a better guidance to the application engineering during the configuration process as the additional dependencies disallow void configurations. We are offering a means of finding these implicit dependencies by providing a semantics for the involved models and analyses of this semantics.

The remainder of this text is structured as follows. First we provide a background on basic concepts (Sect. 2). We then give an overview of our approach (Sect. 3) and explain it for the general case (Sect. 4). We discuss how the relation "realized by" can be interpreted (Sect. 5) and specialize the general case for propositional logic (Sect. 6). This includes the automatic calculation of the defined properties, which has been implemented in a prototype (Sect. 6.1). We conclude with an overview of related work (Sect. 7), a short summary, and an outlook on potential topics for future work (Sect. 8).

2   Background

Kang et al. define a feature as "a prominent or distinctive user-visible aspect, quality, or characteristic of a software system or system" [13]. In the literature there are numerous suggestions for feature modeling languages, e.g., in [13,7].

Defining the semantics of a modeling language in a mathematical form is preferred, because it rules out ambiguity. For instance, for the feature model in Fig. 1 we demand that a feature cannot be selected without its parent, and, that the root is always selected. This is expressed by the following formulas.

root must be selected: *children require parent:*

Phone   MP3 $\Rightarrow$ Phone

Camera $\Rightarrow$ Phone

Other primitives of feature modeling languages are mapped to their formal representation in a similar fashion. For instance, the missing exclusion would be expressed as $\neg(\text{MP3} \wedge \text{Camera})$.

Such mappings from models to formal descriptions are used as a foundation for (automated) reasoning. This area has been addressed by a number of researchers [16,2,19], including our own work on formalizing feature models in higher-order logic [12].

Feature models are not the only way to describe the capabilities of a product line. For instance, a *domain architecture* takes a more solution-oriented perspective and describes potential implementation structures. This includes variable elements that can be configured and, hence, enables the derivation of different *product-specific architectures* from the domain architecture. In this paper we will focus on the components contained in such an architecture and abstract from other details. We will use a *component model* to capture constraints for the whole product line and *component configurations* to describe the components selected for one particular product.

Analogously to the feature model, the component model is interpreted by mapping it to a formal representation. For instance, the mutual exclusion in the example component model in Fig. 1 is interpreted as

$$\neg(\text{MP3Component} \wedge \text{CameraComponent})$$

All these mappings depend on the interpretation of the particular feature or component modeling language and the type of logic used as a formal representation. It should be mentioned that the approach presented in this paper is designed to be independent of particular meta-models and independent of a specific forms of logic (e.g., propositional logic or first order logic).

3   Overview of Our Approach

We will now start to conceptualize our approach by defining four interrelated models. We identified two major aspects that we want to concentrate on, features and components. These can be modeled on two levels, resembling the distinction between product line and products.

A *feature model* (see ❶ in Fig. 2) describes the capabilities of the product line and defines the constraints for potential products. A *feature configuration* ❷ describes the features selected for one particular product. It no longer contains

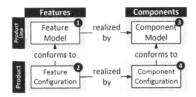

Fig. 2. Two aspects (features, components) on two levels (model, configuration)

variability since all configuration decisions have been made. It can be checked for conformity with the feature model.

Analogously a *component model* ❸ describes the elements used in the implementation of the products. A *component configuration* ❹ describes which components have been selected for a particular product.

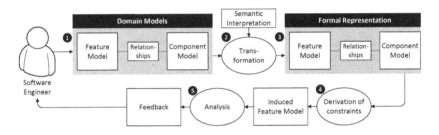

Fig. 3. Overview of our approach

We proceed by describing an overview of our approach (see Fig. 3): The domain engineer starts by creating models of features and the related components ❶. By applying a semantic interpretation ❷ these models are transformed into formal representations ❸.

This formal representation is then used to derive ❹ additional information which then is further analyzed ❺. The resulting information is used to provide feedback to the domain engineer.

In the end, this additional information should be used to enhance the feature model to provide guidance to the application engineer during the configuration process. More specifically, the contributions of our article are as follows: (1) We provide a formalization that integrates features, components, and the dependencies between them. This formalization is independent of particular feature or architecture modeling languages. (2) We specialize the formalization for models that are expressible in propositional logic. (3) This enables the implementation of automatic reasoning techniques to derive additional constraints from the models. (4) Consequently, we are able to cut down the configuration space and provide the desired guidance to the software engineer.

4   Feature-Component Models: General Case

Feature models appear in a variety of forms. They can have attributes, cardinalities and various types of constraints. For the following discussion, we will abstract from these different representations and instead directly operate on the actual semantics. Hence, we will treat a model as an oracle which, given a particular configuration, answers 'yes' or 'no' to indicate whether that configuration conforms to the model or not.

4.1   Definitions of the Basic Concepts

When modeling a particular product line, we assume that we are given a *set of feature configurations*, denoted as $\mathbb{F}$, and a *set of component configurations*, denoted as $\mathbb{C}$.

In this text, we will represent constraints on configurations as sets. A given configuration satisfies a given constraint if and only if this configuration is an element of the set representing that constraint. Taking this approach, the following definitions establish the building blocks for the rest of this article. We begin by defining entities that capture constraints on features and components.

Definition 1 (feature and component models)

1. *a feature model $\mathcal{M}_f$ is a set of feature configurations:* $\mathcal{M}_f \subseteq \mathbb{F}$
2. *a feature configuration $\mathbf{f} \in \mathbb{F}$ conforms to the feature model $\mathcal{M}_f$ if and only if $\mathbf{f} \in \mathcal{M}_f$*
3. *a component model $\mathcal{M}_c$ is a set of component configurations:* $\mathcal{M}_c \subseteq \mathbb{C}$
4. *a component configuration $\mathbf{c} \in \mathbb{C}$ conforms to the component model $\mathcal{M}_c$ if and only if $\mathbf{c} \in \mathcal{M}_c$*

Building on the preceding definition, we define concepts for capturing constraints on features and components together.

Definition 2 (feature-component model)

1. *a feature-component configuration $\langle \mathbf{f}, \mathbf{c} \rangle$ is a pair consisting of a feature configuration and a component configuration:* $\langle \mathbf{f}, \mathbf{c} \rangle \in \mathbb{F} \times \mathbb{C}$
2. *a feature-component model $\mathcal{M}_{fc}$ is a set of feature-component configurations:* $\mathcal{M}_{fc} \subseteq \mathbb{F} \times \mathbb{C}$
3. *a feature-component configuration $\langle \mathbf{f}, \mathbf{c} \rangle \in \mathbb{F} \times \mathbb{C}$ conforms to the feature-component model $\mathcal{M}_{fc}$ if and only if $\langle \mathbf{f}, \mathbf{c} \rangle \in \mathcal{M}_{fc}$*

The following two examples illustrate the concepts introduced by Defs. 1 and 2.

Example 1. Let us consider a case with two features, f_1 and f_2, and two components, c_1 and c_2. We will represent a configuration as a set of the features or components that are selected — a feature or component not in the set is unselected. Hence, feature configurations will correspond to the subsets of $\{f_1, f_2\}$; similarly, the component configurations will correspond to the subsets of $\{c_1, c_2\}$.

To express this in a mathematical notation, we utilize the concept of a powerset, denoted $\mathcal{P}(\cdot)$, as follows: $\mathbb{F} \equiv \mathcal{P}(\{f_1, f_2\})$ and $\mathbb{C} \equiv \mathcal{P}(\{c_1, c_2\})$. The feature model $\mathcal{M}_f$ requires that at least one feature is selected and component model $\mathcal{M}_c$ states that whenever c_1 is selected, c_2 must be selected, expressed as follows.

$$\mathcal{M}_f \equiv \mathbb{F} \setminus \{\emptyset\} = \{\{f_1\}, \{f_2\}, \{f_1, f_2\}\}$$
$$\mathcal{M}_c \equiv \{\mathbf{c} \in \mathbb{C} \mid c_1 \in \mathbf{c} \Rightarrow c_2 \in \mathbf{c}\} = \{\emptyset, \{c_2\}, \{c_1, c_2\}\}$$

We introduce an auxiliary relation $\mathcal{R}$ to impose additional constraints on the combinations of feature and component configurations:

$$\mathbf{f}\,\mathcal{R}\,\mathbf{c} \Leftrightarrow ((f_1 \in \mathbf{f} \Rightarrow c_1 \in \mathbf{c}) \wedge (f_2 \in \mathbf{f} \Rightarrow c_2 \in \mathbf{c}))$$

(Note that the relation $\mathcal{R}$ states that f_1 requires c_1 and f_2 requires c_2.)

To obtain the overall feature-component model $\mathcal{M}_{fc}$ we combine all these constraints together: $\mathcal{M}_{fc} \equiv (\mathcal{M}_f \times \mathcal{M}_c) \cap \mathcal{R}$.

In plain language, a feature-component configuration conforms to $\mathcal{M}_{fc}$ if and only if its feature part conforms to $\mathcal{M}_f$, its component part conforms to $\mathcal{M}_c$, and the whole pair belongs to the relation $\mathcal{R}$.

For this feature-component model, $\langle \emptyset, \{c_1\}\rangle$ and $\langle \{f_2\}, \{c_1\}\rangle$ are examples of non-conforming configurations, whereas $\langle \{f_1\}, \{c_1, c_2\}\rangle$ is a conforming configuration.

Example 2. Let the set of feature configurations $\mathbb{F}$ where each configuration is a pair consisting of the set of selected features and a natural number representing an attribute of the feature f_1: $\mathbb{F} \equiv \mathcal{P}(\{f_1, f_2\}) \times \mathbb{N}$. Let the feature model disallow selecting the feature f_2 when f_1 is selected with the value less than 100:

$$\mathcal{M}_f \equiv \{\langle \text{sel}, \text{attr}_1\rangle \in \mathbb{F} \mid (f_1 \in \text{sel} \wedge \text{attr}_1 < 100) \Rightarrow f_2 \notin \text{sel}\}$$

Let $\mathbb{C} \equiv \mathcal{P}(\{c_1, c_2\})$ and $\mathcal{M}_c \equiv \mathbb{C}$, i.e., $\mathcal{M}_c$ is imposing no restrictions on the component configurations. To express how features relate to components, we define the following three relations:

$$(\langle \text{sel}, \text{attr}_1\rangle\,\mathcal{R}_1\,\mathbf{c}) \Leftrightarrow (f_1 \in \text{sel} \wedge \text{attr}_1 < 500 \Rightarrow c_1 \in \mathbf{c})$$
$$(\langle \text{sel}, \text{attr}_1\rangle\,\mathcal{R}_2\,\mathbf{c}) \Leftrightarrow (f_1 \in \text{sel} \wedge \text{attr}_1 \not< 500 \Rightarrow c_1 \in \mathbf{c} \wedge c_2 \in \mathbf{c})$$
$$(\langle \text{sel}, \text{attr}_1\rangle\,\mathcal{R}_3\,\mathbf{c}) \Leftrightarrow (f_2 \in \text{sel} \Rightarrow c_2 \in \mathbf{c})$$

The relation $\mathcal{R}_1$ expresses that if the feature f_1 is selected and the value of its attribute is less than 500, then the component c_1 is required. The relation $\mathcal{R}_2$, however, requires the component c_2 must be selected on top of c_1 once the attribute's value is not less than 500. The relation $\mathcal{R}_3$ records that the feature f_2 requires the component c_2. Let relation $\mathcal{R}$ be the intersection of these relations $\mathcal{R} \equiv \mathcal{R}_1 \cap \mathcal{R}_2 \cap \mathcal{R}_3$, then all the constraints combined are $\mathcal{M}_{fc} \equiv (\mathcal{M}_f \times \mathcal{M}_c) \cap \mathcal{R}$.

4.2   From Overall Constraints to Feature Models

In the introduction we have promised that we will investigate how overall constraints, constraints on a composite feature-component model, are projected back onto the features. The following definition formalizes the meaning of this projection.

Definition 3 (induced feature model). *For a feature-component model $\mathcal{M}_{fc}$, the induced feature model $\mathcal{I}_{\mathcal{M}_{fc}} \subseteq \mathbb{F}$ is a set of feature configurations for which there exists a component configuration such that together they conform to the feature-component model:*

$$\mathcal{I}_{\mathcal{M}_{fc}} \equiv \{\mathbf{f} \in \mathbb{F} \mid (\exists \mathbf{c} \in \mathbb{C})\, \langle \mathbf{f}, \mathbf{c} \rangle \in \mathcal{M}_{fc}\}$$

Intuitively, for any feature configuration conforming to the induced feature model, we are *guaranteed* that there is an implementation of this feature configuration (with respect to the pertaining feature-component model). On the other hand, if the induced feature model is not equal to the feature model given by the user, it means that the feature model permits a feature configuration without implementation and thus should be improved. This is illustrated by the following example.

Example 3. Let $\mathbb{F} \equiv \mathcal{P}(\{f_1, f_2\})$, $\mathbb{C} \equiv \mathcal{P}(\{c_1, c_2\})$, and the feature-component model $\mathcal{M}_{fc}$ defined as follows.

$$\mathcal{M}_f \equiv \mathbb{F} \quad \mathcal{M}_c \equiv \mathbb{C} \smallsetminus \{c_1, c_2\}$$
$$\mathbf{f}\,\mathcal{R}\,\mathbf{c} \Leftrightarrow ((f_1 \in \mathbf{f} \Rightarrow c_1 \in \mathbf{c}) \wedge (f_2 \in \mathbf{f} \Rightarrow c_2 \in \mathbf{c}))$$
$$\mathcal{M}_{fc} \equiv (\mathcal{M}_f \times \mathcal{M}_c) \cap \mathcal{R}$$

We see that f_1 and f_2 require c_1 and c_2, respectively, and that c_1 and c_2 are mutually excluded. Therefore, there is no implementation for the feature configuration $\{f_1, f_2\}$, even though it is permitted by the feature model $\mathcal{M}_f$. In other words, the induced feature model for $\mathcal{M}_{fc}$ is $(\mathbb{F} \smallsetminus \{f_1, f_2\})$.

4.3   Configurations with Preference

In this section we consider that the software engineer *prefers* some configurations over other configurations. To motivate further discussion let us look at some of the configurations for Example 1. The configuration $\langle \{f_1\}, \{c_1, c_2\} \rangle$ conforms to $\mathcal{M}_{fc}$, but we are not getting the best out of the included components as the feature f_2 could be added with no further consequences (no additional component is required). However, it is not possible to remove any of the components while keeping the feature f_1. Dually, the configuration $\langle \{f_2\}, \{c_1, c_2\} \rangle$ uses more components than necessary, i.e., c_1 can be removed while keeping the same features. So we can say that we *prefer* configurations with more features and with less components.

To record this formally, we assume that we are given two partial orderings, one on feature configurations, denoted as $\sqsubseteq_f$, and one on component configurations, denoted as $\sqsubseteq_c$. Intuitively, $\sqsubseteq_f$ corresponds to the increase of capabilities expressed by the features; whereas $\sqsubseteq_c$ corresponds to the weight, or price, ordering on component configurations and we will prefer cheaper solutions to the expensive ones. To reflect the discussion above, for Example 1 we define the orderings as $\sqsubseteq_f \equiv \subseteq$ and $\sqsubseteq_c \equiv \subseteq$. For Example 2, we can, for instance, define the orderings in the same fashion by ignoring the feature attribute as follows.

$$(\langle \text{sel}, \text{attr}_1 \rangle \sqsubseteq_f \langle \text{sel}', \text{attr}_1' \rangle) \Leftrightarrow (\text{sel} \subseteq \text{sel}') \qquad (\mathbf{c} \sqsubseteq_c \mathbf{c}') \Leftrightarrow (\mathbf{c} \subseteq \mathbf{c}')$$

The following definition utilizes these orderings to characterize feature-component configurations.

Definition 4 (strong conformity). *For a feature-component model $\mathcal{M}_{\mathrm{fc}}$. A configuration $\langle \mathbf{f}, \mathbf{c} \rangle$ strongly conforms to $\mathcal{M}_{\mathrm{fc}}$ if and only if $\langle \mathbf{f}, \mathbf{c} \rangle \in \mathcal{M}_{\mathrm{fc}}$ and the following holds.*

$$(\forall \langle \mathbf{f}', \mathbf{c}' \rangle \in \mathcal{M}_{\mathrm{fc}})((\mathbf{f} \sqsubseteq_{\mathrm{f}} \mathbf{f}' \wedge \mathbf{c}' \sqsubseteq_{\mathrm{c}} \mathbf{c}) \Rightarrow (\mathbf{f} = \mathbf{f}' \wedge \mathbf{c} = \mathbf{c}'))$$

Intuitively, we cannot add features to a strong conforming configuration without adding components, or, remove components without reducing the features. In Example 1, the configuration $\langle \{f_2\}, \{c_2\} \rangle$ strongly conforms to $\mathcal{M}_{\mathrm{fc}}$. Whereas, the configuration $\langle \{f_1\}, \{c_1, c_2\} \rangle$ does not strongly conform to $\mathcal{M}_{\mathrm{fc}}$ because we can add the feature f_2 (the required component c_2 is already in place). Nevertheless, the cost of the configuration cannot be improved while keeping the feature f_1 as this feature requires both components.

5   Semantics of "Realized by"

As we have seen in the preceding examples, it is natural to express feature-component models in the form $(\mathcal{M}_{\mathrm{f}} \times \mathcal{M}_{\mathrm{c}}) \cap \mathcal{R}$. The user specifies the feature model $\mathcal{M}_{\mathrm{f}}$ in a feature modeling language and $\mathcal{M}_{\mathrm{c}}$ in an architecture modeling language that supports variability. Both types of languages have been widely studied from various angles and tool support exists. Little work, however, has been done to study the glue between the two representations, the relation $\mathcal{R}$ in our formalism.

We would like to enable the domain engineer to express herself at a higher level of abstraction — using concepts as "The feature f is realized by the component c." First, we need to define a language concept for expressing such facts and second, provide semantics for it in a mathematical form.

It might seem, at first glance, that it is sufficient to have a single mapping from each feature to the component that realizes that feature. In practice, however, we need to cope with more complex scenarios. For instance, when a feature can be implemented by different components, or, when a feature requires multiple components. Dually, a combination of features as a whole might impose different requirements in contrast to the combination of the requirements imposed by each of them. Hence, we introduce a language construct that maps sets of feature configurations to sets of component configurations.

Definition 5. *Let $\mathcal{S}_{\mathrm{f}} \subseteq \mathbb{F}$ and $\mathcal{S}_{\mathrm{c}} \subseteq \mathbb{C}$, then* realized-by$(\mathcal{S}_{\mathrm{f}}, \mathcal{S}_{\mathrm{c}})$ *is a realized-by expression. If a realized-by expression is in the form* realized-by$(\{\mathbf{f} \in \mathbb{F} \mid f_{\mathrm{r}} \in \mathbf{f}\}, \mathcal{S}_{\mathrm{c}})$ *then we say that the feature f_{r} is realized by $\mathcal{S}_{\mathrm{c}}$.*

Example 4. Let $\mathbb{F} \equiv \mathcal{P}(\{f_1, f_2\})$ and $\mathbb{C} \equiv \mathcal{P}(\{c_1, c_2, c_3\})$

realized-by$(\{\mathbf{f} \in \mathbb{F} \mid f_2 \in \mathbf{f}\}, \{\mathbf{c} \in \mathbb{C} \mid c_1 \in \mathbf{c} \vee c_2 \in \mathbf{c}\})$
realized-by$(\{\mathbf{f} \in \mathbb{F} \mid \{f_1, f_2\} \subseteq \mathbf{f}\}, \{\mathbf{c} \in \mathbb{C} \mid \{c_1, c_2\} \subseteq \mathbf{c}\})$

Intuitively, each realized-by expression imposes a restriction on the feature-component configurations. The first one in Example 4 specifies that either of c_1 or c_2 is an implementation of f_2; the second expression specifies that the combination c_1 and c_2 is an implementation of the combination f_1 and f_2.

Before we proceed with the semantics of the realized-by expressions, we will put them in the context of feature and component models.

Definition 6. *A product line model is a triple $\langle \mathcal{M}_f, \mathcal{M}_c, Q \rangle$, where $\mathcal{M}_f$ is a feature model, $\mathcal{M}_c$ is a component model, and Q is a set of realized-by expressions.*

To formally analyze this model, we have to define our interpretation of it (see ❷ in Fig. 2). For this, we present three alternatives:

1. Interpretation with $\Rightarrow$
2. Interpretation with $\Leftrightarrow$
3. Interpretation with $\Rightarrow$ and strong-conformity (see Def. 4)

Definition 7. *Semantics of product line models is a function that maps a software product line model to a feature-component model. We will use the notation $\llbracket \cdot \rrbracket$ for a function of the type $\langle \mathcal{M}_f, \mathcal{M}_c, Q \rangle \to \mathcal{P}(\mathbb{F} \times \mathbb{C})$.*

1. Interpretation with $\Rightarrow$. Let the relation $\mathcal{R} \subseteq \mathbb{F} \times \mathbb{C}$ be defined as follows

$$\mathbf{f} \, \mathcal{R} \, \mathbf{c} \Leftrightarrow \bigwedge_{\text{realized-by}(\mathcal{S}_f, \mathcal{S}_c) \in Q} \mathbf{f} \in \mathcal{S}_f \Rightarrow \mathbf{c} \in \mathcal{S}_c$$

Then $\llbracket \langle \mathcal{M}_f, \mathcal{M}_c, Q \rangle \rrbracket_1 \equiv (\mathcal{M}_f \times \mathcal{M}_c) \cap \mathcal{R}$. In other words, the inclusion of features implies the inclusion of related components — but not necessarily the other way around.

2. Interpretation with $\Leftrightarrow$. Let the relation $\mathcal{R} \subseteq \mathbb{F} \times \mathbb{C}$ be defined as follows

$$\mathbf{f} \, \mathcal{R} \, \mathbf{c} \Leftrightarrow \bigwedge_{\text{realized-by}(\mathcal{S}_f, \mathcal{S}_c) \in Q} \mathbf{f} \in \mathcal{S}_f \Leftrightarrow \mathbf{c} \in \mathcal{S}_c$$

Then $\llbracket \langle \mathcal{M}_f, \mathcal{M}_c, Q \rangle \rrbracket_2 \equiv (\mathcal{M}_f \times \mathcal{M}_c) \cap \mathcal{R}$. In other words, the inclusion of features implies the inclusion of related components — and vice versa.

3. Interpretation with $\Rightarrow$ and strong conformity. Given the orderings $\sqsubseteq_f$ and $\sqsubseteq_c$. Let $\mathcal{M}_{fc} = \llbracket \langle \mathcal{M}_f, \mathcal{M}_c, Q \rangle \rrbracket_1$ then

$$\llbracket \langle \mathcal{M}_f, \mathcal{M}_c, Q \rangle \rrbracket_3 \equiv$$
$$\{ \langle \mathbf{f}, \mathbf{c} \rangle \in \mathbb{F} \times \mathbb{C} \mid \langle \mathbf{f}, \mathbf{c} \rangle \text{ strongly conforms to } \mathcal{M}_{fc} \text{ w.r.t. } \sqsubseteq_f \text{ and } \sqsubseteq_c \}$$

In other words, we use the first interpretation and in addition require strong-conformity. Hence, we reduce the feature-component models to those configurations that cannot be improved in their capability or cost.

The following examples will illustrate the different semantics on two product line models, PLM_a and PLM_b, with $\mathbb{F} \equiv \mathcal{P}(\{f_1, f_2\})$, $\mathbb{C} \equiv \mathcal{P}(\{c_1, c_2\})$, and the orderings $\sqsubseteq_f \equiv \subseteq$ and $\sqsubseteq_c \equiv \subseteq$.

Example 5. Let $\mathrm{PLM_a} \equiv \langle \mathcal{M}_f, \mathcal{M}_c, Q \rangle$ be a product line model where:

$$\mathcal{M}_f \equiv \mathbb{F} \qquad \mathcal{M}_c \equiv \{\mathbf{c} \in \mathbb{C} \mid c_1 \in \mathbf{c} \Rightarrow c_2 \in \mathbf{c}\}$$
$$Q \equiv \{\text{ realized-by}(\{\mathbf{f} \in \mathbb{F} \mid f_1 \in \mathbf{f}\}, \{\mathbf{c} \in \mathbb{C} \mid c_1 \in \mathbf{c}\}),$$
$$\text{realized-by}(\{\mathbf{f} \in \mathbb{F} \mid f_2 \in \mathbf{f}\}, \{\mathbf{c} \in \mathbb{C} \mid c_2 \in \mathbf{c}\})\}$$

According to Def. 7, the semantics $[\![\cdot]\!]_1$ and $[\![\cdot]\!]_2$ of $\mathrm{PLM_a}$ correspond to the following feature-component models.

$$\langle \mathbf{f},\, \mathbf{c} \rangle \in [\![\mathrm{PLM_a}]\!]_1 \Leftrightarrow \qquad\qquad \langle \mathbf{f},\, \mathbf{c} \rangle \in [\![\mathrm{PLM_a}]\!]_2 \Leftrightarrow$$
$$f_1 \in \mathbf{f} \Rightarrow c_1 \in \mathbf{c} \wedge \qquad\qquad f_1 \in \mathbf{f} \Leftrightarrow c_1 \in \mathbf{c} \wedge$$
$$f_2 \in \mathbf{f} \Rightarrow c_2 \in \mathbf{c} \wedge \qquad\qquad f_2 \in \mathbf{f} \Leftrightarrow c_2 \in \mathbf{c} \wedge$$
$$c_1 \in \mathbf{c} \Rightarrow c_2 \in \mathbf{c} \qquad\qquad\quad c_1 \in \mathbf{c} \Rightarrow c_2 \in \mathbf{c}$$

To obtain the semantics $[\![\mathrm{PLM_a}]\!]_3$ we compute the strongly conforming configurations of $[\![\mathrm{PLM_a}]\!]_1$, which are the following.

$$[\![\mathrm{PLM_a}]\!]_3 \equiv \{\langle \emptyset, \emptyset \rangle, \langle \{f_2\}, \{c_2\} \rangle, \langle \{f_1, f_2\}, \{c_1, c_2\} \rangle\}$$

Interestingly, the feature component models $[\![\mathrm{PLM_a}]\!]_2$ and $[\![\mathrm{PLM_a}]\!]_3$ are equal. Intuitively, the reason for this is that once c_2 is included in a configuration, there is nothing that prevents f_2 from being included.

If we look at the resulting models from the perspective of induced feature models (see Def. 3), we see that the induced feature model for $[\![\mathrm{PLM_a}]\!]_1$ is imposing no restrictions on the features. Here the user might feel that there is some information lost, since originally there was a dependency between the realizing components but now there is no dependency between the features themselves.

For $[\![\mathrm{PLM_a}]\!]_2$ and $[\![\mathrm{PLM_a}]\!]_3$ the induced feature model is $\{\mathbf{f} \in \mathbb{F} \mid f_1 \in \mathbf{f} \Rightarrow f_2 \in \mathbf{f}\}$, due to the bi-implication between the inclusion of a feature and the inclusion of the implementing component.

Hence, for $\mathrm{PLM_a}$ the semantics $[\![\cdot]\!]_2$ and $[\![\cdot]\!]_3$ return the same result and they project dependencies between components to dependencies between features. Whereas the semantics $[\![\cdot]\!]_1$ does not project dependencies between the components onto the features.

The next example, $\mathrm{PLM_b}$, strengthens the constraints of $\mathrm{PLM_a}$ by adding an exclusions between the two features.

Example 6. Let $\mathrm{PLM_b} \equiv \langle \mathcal{M}_f, \mathcal{M}_c, Q \rangle$ be a product line model such that:

$$\mathcal{M}_f \equiv \{\mathbf{f} \in \mathcal{P}(\{f_1, f_2\}) \mid \neg(f_1 \in \mathbf{f} \wedge f_2 \in \mathbf{f})\}$$
$$\mathcal{M}_c \equiv \{\mathbf{c} \in \mathcal{P}(\{c_1, c_2\}) \mid c_1 \in \mathbf{c} \Rightarrow c_2 \in \mathbf{c}\}$$
$$Q \ \equiv \{\text{realized-by}(\{\mathbf{f} \in \mathbb{F} \mid f_1 \in \mathbf{f}\}, \{\mathbf{c} \in \mathbb{C} \mid c_1 \in \mathbf{c}\}),$$
$$\text{realized-by}(\{\mathbf{f} \in \mathbb{F} \mid f_2 \in \mathbf{f}\}, \{\mathbf{c} \in \mathbb{C} \mid c_2 \in \mathbf{c}\})\}$$

The three semantics yield the following feature-component models (enumerated as conforming feature-component configurations).

$$[\![\mathrm{PLM_b}]\!]_1 \equiv \{\langle \emptyset, \emptyset \rangle, \langle \{f_1\}, \{c_1, c_2\} \rangle, \langle \{f_2\}, \{c_2\} \rangle, \langle \{f_2\}, \{c_1, c_2\} \rangle\}$$
$$[\![\mathrm{PLM_b}]\!]_3 \equiv \{\langle \emptyset, \emptyset \rangle, \langle \{f_1\}, \{c_1, c_2\} \rangle, \langle \{f_2\}, \{c_2\} \rangle\}$$
$$[\![\mathrm{PLM_b}]\!]_2 \equiv \{\langle \emptyset, \emptyset \rangle, \langle \{f_2\}, \{c_2\} \rangle\}$$

Now, let us compare these sets. The feature-component model given by $[\![\cdot]\!]_1$ is formed by exactly the combinations where the implementation provides sufficient functionality for the selected features. The semantics $[\![\cdot]\!]_3$ additionally 'filters out' the configuration $\langle\{f_2\}, \{c_1, c_2\}\rangle$ as c_1 is not needed for f_2.

The semantics $[\![\cdot]\!]_2$, however, yields a somewhat surprising feature-component model. Due to the bi-implication between features and realizing components, f_1 is not selectable since if we are to select f_1, we need to select c_1 which requires c_2 but f_2 cannot be selected due to the restriction imposed by the feature model. A feature that does not appear in any product (is not selectable), is called a *dead feature* and it is most likely an undesired property of the feature-component model.

Hence, for PLM_b, each of the semantics yields a different feature-component model. Note, however, that $[\![PLM_b]\!]_1$ and $[\![PLM_b]\!]_3$ have the same induced feature model. The semantics $[\![\cdot]\!]_2$ appears to be inappropriate for PLM_b as the feature f_2 is dead under this semantics.

To conclude this section, a summary of the observations follows.

1. translate via implication, the relation between features and components is somewhat "loose": the features require their implementations but there is no dependency in the other direction,
2. translate via bi-implication, the resulting model requires for the features to be "on" whenever they are implemented; this dependency might bee too strong in some cases,
3. translate via implication and strong-conformity, in that case a feature is required to be "switched on" whenever it is *possible* to switch it on.

6   Feature-Component Models with Propositional Logic

In this section we specialize the concepts introduced so far for propositional logic. We focus on features and components that can just be selected or deselected (in contrast to having attributes) and hence, can be expressed as boolean variables.

Before we proceed, let us recall some basic concepts from propositional logic. Let F be a boolean formula on the set of variables V, $m \subseteq V$, and let F' be obtained from F by replacing every variable $v \in m$ by *true* and every variable $v' \notin m$ by *false*, then m is a *model* of F if and only if F' evaluates to *true*. For the evaluation we assume the standard semantics of boolean connectives, such as $true \wedge false$ evaluates to *false*.

For the following we assume $\mathcal{F}$ to be a finite set of features and $\mathcal{C}$ a finite set of components such that $\mathcal{F} \cap \mathcal{C} = \emptyset$. The domain of feature configurations then becomes $\mathbb{F} \equiv \mathcal{P}(\mathcal{F})$ and the domain of component configurations becomes $\mathbb{C} \equiv \mathcal{P}(\mathcal{C})$. We will say that a feature or component is *selected* by a configuration if and only if it is in that configuration. We will use the subset relation to define the orderings on configurations, i.e., $\sqsubseteq_f \equiv \subseteq$ and $\sqsubseteq_c \equiv \subseteq$.

Feature and component models will be represented as boolean formulas on the variables $\mathcal{F}$ and $\mathcal{C}$, respectively; the feature-component models will be represented as formulas on the variables $\mathcal{F} \cup \mathcal{C}$ (recall that $\mathcal{F}$ and $\mathcal{C}$ are disjoint). The conforming configurations will correspond to models of the formulas. The correspondence between the general form and the boolean representation is illustrated by the following example.

Example 7. For the model in Example 1 we have $\mathcal{F} \equiv \{f_1, f_2\}, \mathcal{C} = \{c_1, c_2\}$. The propositional formulas corresponding to $\mathcal{M}_f$, $\mathcal{M}_c$, $\mathcal{R}$, and $\mathcal{M}_{fc}$, respectively, are:

$$M_f \equiv f_1 \vee f_2 \qquad R \equiv (f_1 \Rightarrow c_1) \wedge (f_2 \Rightarrow c_2)$$
$$M_c \equiv c_1 \Rightarrow c_2 \qquad M_{fc} \equiv M_f \wedge M_c \wedge R$$

For which $\{f_2, c_2\}$ is an example of a model of the formula M_{fc}, corresponding to the feature-component configuration $\langle \{f_2\}, \{c_2\} \rangle$.

6.1   On Implementing Propositional Feature-Component Models

When using models whose semantics is expressible in propositional logic, we have the advantage, over first-order logic for example, that the problems we are dealing with are typically decidable. We should note, however, that the complexity of many interesting problems remains a significant obstacle, e.g., consistency of a feature model is NP-complete [19].

We have implemented the ideas presented in this paper for the propositional logic case where the underlying data structure of the computations are binary decision diagrams (BDDs) [18]. The implementation is in an experimental stage and techniques that would make the approaches applicable in practice are under investigation. For the lack of space we cannot give the full account of the details but the reader is most welcome to contact the authors to obtain the source code. Here we briefly describe the main concepts used in the implementation.

Propositional induced feature models. Once the feature-component model is represented as a boolean expression, it is straight-forward to compute the induced feature model (see Def. 3) by applying the *existential quantification* [18, Sect 10.2.3]. Schematically, an existential quantifier from the formula $((\exists v)\phi)$ is eliminated by computing the formula $\phi[v \mapsto true] \vee \phi[v \mapsto false]$.

Propositional logic and strong conformity. Strong conforming configurations in the propositional case map directly to maximal models of a formula [14] by inverting the variables corresponding to components.

Realized-by expressions and their semantics. The realized-by expressions translate directly. For instance, realized-by($\{\mathbf{f} \in \mathbb{F} \mid f_1 \in \mathbf{f}\}, \{\mathbf{c} \in \mathbb{C} \mid c_1 \in \mathbf{c}\})$) translates as realized-by(f_1, c_1), which in semantics $[\![\cdot]\!]_1$ is translated to $f_1 \Rightarrow c_1$.

6.2   Deriving Propositional Models

In practice, often, more complex constraints than propositional ones are needed. Here we wish to note that for certain types of constraints on attributes it is possible to generate an equivalent propositional constraint. We illustrate this idea on an example.

Example 8. Let size : $\mathcal{C} \to \mathbb{N}$ be a function assigning a size to each component. Let $l, h \in \mathbb{N}$ and the component model $\mathcal{M}_c \subseteq \mathcal{P}(\mathcal{C})$ be given in the form:

$$\mathbf{c} \in \mathcal{M}_c \Leftrightarrow \left(l \leq \sum_{c \in \mathbf{c}} \mathrm{size}(c) \leq h \right)$$

Such a constraint can be translated into a propositional formula that disables the combinations of components whose total size is outside the given boundaries. Once this formula is computed, it can be "anded" to the formula obtained from the propositional feature-component model. Mathematically speaking, if a feature-component model is expressed by the formula M_{fc} and an additional constraint is expressed by the formula C, then we put $M'_{\mathrm{fc}} \equiv M_{\mathrm{fc}} \wedge C$ to impose the restriction C on M_{fc}.

7   Related Work

Kumbang [1] provides tool support for integrated feature and component modeling. The semantics of the modeling languages is defined in terms of the *weight constraint language*, which is supported by the smodels reasoning engine [20]. The reasoning is used during the configuration process, i.e., when certain selections are made, the engine is executed to infer the consequences of these selections. The reasoning of smodels is based on *stable models* semantics which guarantees that selections are not enforced without justification, which is similar to the component-minimality requirement in the semantics $[\![\cdot]\!]_3$ (see Sect. 5).

Thaker et al. [22] in the context of AHEAD Tool Suite [3] utilize a SAT solver to ensure that a feature model does not permit compositions that yield invalid Java programs (programs that do not type-check).

Van der Storm [23] maps features to components, which are organized in a dependency tree. Further, he maps this model to propositional logic semantics enabling reasoning on it.

Czarnecki and Pietroszek [9] investigated UML models with variability, so-called *model templates*, and utilized OCL to specify and the consistency requirements. These are utilized to check consistency of the models.

The works [22,23,9], described above, rely on propositional logic; Kumbang framework [1] enables more expressive constraints than propositional. We believe that all these works can be mapped to our formalism.

Automated reasoning was applied on feature models by a number of researchers. For example, Mannion applied Prolog to detect inconsistencies [16], Batory applied *logic truth maintenance systems* to facilitate the configuration process [2]. Benavides et al. investigated the use of constraint solving to automated analysis of feature models [5]. See [4] for a more complete overview.

McCarthy's *circumscription* [17] is a form of non-monotonic reasoning in principal similar to the semantics $[\![\cdot]\!]_3$ defined in Sect. 5. When using circumscription we are reasoning only with respect to minimal interpretation of a formula, similarly as in our approach we reason only about configurations that are strong conforming.

In Sect. 6.2 we have suggested how the techniques that reason on models expressible in propositional logic can be used to reason about other models that are not expressed as such. In a similar fashion, Eén and Sörensen preprocess so-called *pseudo-boolean constraints* inputted to a SAT solver [11].

8   Summary and Future Work

We have provided a unified mathematical approach to formalizing models for features and their implementations. We have shown how this formalization can be utilized to improve our understanding of the modeling primitives and provide automated feedback to the software engineer who uses such models.

We see the following challenges for future work.

Feedback to the user. If the induced feature model contains new derived dependencies not present in the original model, how should this "delta" be presented to the user? For this, we are investigating research by Czarnecki and Wąsowski [10] on turning boolean formulas to feature models.

Relating to languages used in practice. We have provided a formal foundations for expressing dependencies for integrated feature and component modeling. How can modeling languages used in practice be described using our formalism?

Other models. This work focuses on feature and component models. Could this approach be extended for an arbitrary number of models?

Implementation and Evaluation. We will further improve our prototype implementation to evaluate the efficiency issues arising for larger numbers of features and to find out which of the semantics defined in Sect. 5 are useful in practice.

Acknowledgments. We thank Ondřej Čepek for his valuable insight that improved the definition of strong conformity. This work is partially supported by Science Foundation Ireland under grant no. 03/CE2/I303_1.

References

1. Asikainen, T., Männistö, T., Soininen, T.: Kumbang: A domain ontology for modelling variability in software product families. Advanced Engineering Informatics 21 (2007)
2. Batory, D.: Feature Models, Grammars, and Propositional Formulas. In: Obbink, H., Pohl, K. (eds.) SPLC 2005. LNCS, vol. 3714, Springer, Heidelberg (2005)
3. Batory, D., Sarvela, J.N., Rauschmayer, A.: Scaling step-wise refinement. IEEE Transactions on Software Engineering 30(6) (2004)
4. Benavides, D., Ruiz-Cortés, A., Trinidad, P., Segura, S.: A Survey on the Automated Analyses of Feture Models. In: Jornadas de Ingeniería del Software y Bases de Datos (JISBD) (2006)
5. Benavides, D., Trinidad, P., Ruiz-Cortés, A.: Automated Reasoning on Feature Models. In: Pastor, Ó., Falcão e Cunha, J. (eds.) CAiSE 2005. LNCS, vol. 3520, Springer, Heidelberg (2005)
6. Clements, P., Northrop, L.: Software Product Lines: Practices and Patterns. Addison–Wesley Publishing Company, London (2002)

7. Czarnecki, K., Eisenecker, U.W.: Generative Programming. Addison Wesley, Reading (2000)
8. Czarnecki, K., Helsen, S., Eisenecker, U.: Staged Configuration Using Feature Models. In: Nord, R.L. (ed.) SPLC 2004. LNCS, vol. 3154, Springer, Heidelberg (2004)
9. Czarnecki, K., Pietroszek, K.: Verifying Feature-Based Model Templates Against Well-Formedness OCL Constraints. In: Proceedings of the 5th International Conference on Generative Programming And Component Engineering (2006)
10. Czarnecki, K., Wąsowski, A.: Feature Diagrams and Logics: There and Back Again. In: Kellenberger (ed.) 15
11. Eén, N., Sörensen, N.: Translating Pseudo-Boolean Constraints into SAT. Journal on Satisfiability, Boolean Modeling and Computation (2006)
12. Janota, M., Kiniry, J.: Reasoning about Feature Models in Higher-Order Logic. In: Kellenberger (ed.) 15
13. Kyo, C., Kang, S.G., Cohen, J.A., Hess, W.E.: Novak, and A. Spencer Peterson. Feature-oriented domain analysis (FODA), feasibility study. Technical Report CMU/SEI-90-TR-021, Software Engineering Institute, Carnegie Mellon University (November 1990)
14. Kavvadias, D.J., Sideri, M., Stavropoulos, E.C.: Generating all maximal models of a Boolean expression. Information Processing Letters 74(3-4), 157–162 (2000)
15. Kellenberger, P. (ed.): Software Product Lines Conference (2007)
16. Mannion, M.: Using First-Order Logic for Product Line Model Validation. In: Chastek, G.J. (ed.) SPLC 2002. LNCS, vol. 2379, Springer, Heidelberg (2002)
17. McCarthy, J.: Circumscription—A Form of Non-Monotonic Reasoning. Artificial Intelligence 13, 27–39 (1980)
18. Meinel, C., Theobald, T.: Algorithms and Data Structures in VLSI Design: OBDD-foundations and applications. Springer, Heidelberg (1998)
19. Schobbens, P.-Y., Heymans, P., Trigaux, J.-C.: Feature Diagrams: A Survey and a Formal Semantics. In: Proceeding of 14th IEEE International Requirements Engineering Conference (RE) (2006)
20. Simons, P., Niemelä, I., Soininen, T.: Extending and implementing the stable model semantics. Artificial Intelligence 138(1-2) (2002)
21. Software Engineering Institute. What is a software product line?, http://www.sei.cmu.edu/productlines/
22. Thaker, S., Batory, D., Kitchin, D., Cook, W.: Safe Composition of Product Lines. In: Proceedings of the 6th International Conference on Generative Programming and Component Engineering (GPCE) (2007)
23. van der Storm, T.: Generic Feature-Based Software Composition. In: Proceedings of 6th International Symposium on Software Composition (2007)

Correctness-Preserving Configuration of Business Process Models

Wil M.P. van der Aalst[1,2], Marlon Dumas[2,3], Florian Gottschalk[1],
Arthur H.M. ter Hofstede[2], Marcello La Rosa[2], and Jan Mendling[2]

[1] Eindhoven University of Technology, The Netherlands
{w.m.p.v.d.aalst,f.gottschalk}@tue.nl
[2] Queensland University of Technology, Australia
{a.terhofstede,m.larosa,j.mendling}@qut.edu.au
[3] University of Tartu, Estonia
{marlon.dumas}@ut.ee

Abstract. Reference process models capture recurrent business operations in a given domain such as procurement or logistics. These models are intended to be configured to fit the requirements of specific organizations or projects, leading to individualized process models that are subsequently used for domain analysis or solution design. Although the advantages of reusing reference process models compared to designing process models from scratch are widely accepted, the methods employed to configure reference process models are manual and error-prone. In particular, analysts are left with the burden of ensuring the correctness of the individualized process models and to manually fix errors. This paper proposes a foundation for configuring reference process models incrementally and in a way that ensures the correctness of the individualized process models, both with respect to syntax and behavioral semantics. Specifically, assuming the reference process model is behaviorally sound, the individualized process models are guaranteed to be sound.

Keywords: Reference process model, model configuration, Petri net.

1 Introduction

The design of business process models is labor-intensive, especially when such models need to be detailed enough to support the development of software systems. To avoid having to repeatedly create process models from scratch, consortia and vendors have defined so-caled *reference process models*. These models capture recurrent business operations in a given domain. They are generic and are intended to be individualized to fit the requirements of specific organizations or IT projects. Commercial process modeling tools come with standardized libraries of reference process models such as the IT Infrastructure Library (ITIL) [21] or the Supply Chain Operations Reference (SCOR) model [20]. Also, the SAP Reference Model [6] incorporates a collection of process models corresponding to common business operations supported by SAP's platforms.

J. Fiadeiro and P. Inverardi (Eds.): FASE 2008, LNCS 4961, pp. 46–61, 2008.
© Springer-Verlag Berlin Heidelberg 2008

Reference process models in commercial use lack a representation of configuration alternatives and decisions. As a result, their individualization is manual [18]. Analysts take the reference models as a source of inspiration, but ultimately, they design their own model on the basis of the reference model, with little guidance as to which model elements need to be removed, added or modified to meet a requirement. To address this shortcoming, we introduced in previous work the concept of *configurable process models* [18]. A configurable process model represents multiple variants of a business process model in an integrated manner. In line with methods from software product lines [17], these alternatives are captured as *variation points*. For example, the fact that a task in a reference process model may or may not appear in an individualized model is captured by attaching a variation point to that task. Individualized models are obtained from configurable models by interpreting the values for each variation point.

While configurable process models provide guidance to analysts during individualization, they do not guarantee that the individualized models are correct, whether syntactically or semantically. For example, if a model element or an entire path in a reference process model is removed during configuration, the remaining model elements need to be re-connected to maintain syntactic correctness. Also, the configuration of variation points attached to parallel splits, decision points and synchronization points in a configurable process model may lead to the introduction of deadlocks. And if the individualized process model contains such semantic errors, it needs to be manually fixed.

The contribution of this paper is a framework for configuring reference process models in a correctness-preserving manner. The framework includes a technique to derive propositional logic constraints that, if satisfied by a configuration step, guarantee the syntactic correctness of the resulting model. We prove that for a large class of process models, these constraints also ensure that semantic correctness is preserved. The framework supports *staged configuration* [8]. In other words, it allows correctness to be checked at each intermediate step of the configuration procedure. Whenever a value is assigned to a variation point, the current set of constraints is evaluated. If the constraints are satisfied, the configuration step is applied. If on the other hand the constraints are violated, we compute a reduced propositional logic formula, from which we can identify additional variation points that need to be configured simultaneously in order to preserve correctness (e.g. if an edge in the process model is removed, all nodes in a path starting with that edge need to be removed). The set of constraints is incrementally updated after each step of the configuration procedure.

The proposal is intended as a foundation for reference process model configuration. Accordingly, we adopt a Petri net-based representation of process models, thus abstracting from the specificities of process modeling notations used in practice (e.g. UML Activity Diagrams, EPC, BPMN). We use a class of Petri nets, namely workflow nets, which are specifically designed to represent business processes [1]. Workflow nets come with a notion of behavioral correctness known as soundness, which ensures the absence of deadlocks and improper completion. In this paper, we enhance workflow nets with the notion of variation point, leading to the concept of a configurable workflow net. We then define a notion of configuration step over such nets and we show how to derive correctness-preserving constraints for such steps. A core result of the paper is that, for workflow nets that satisfy the "free-choice" property [9], if the outcome of a configuration step starting from a sound workflow net is a workflow net, then this latter workflow net is sound. This means that for this class of nets, configuration steps that preserve syntactic correctness also preserve behavioral correctness.

The paper is structured as follows. Section 2 introduces workflow nets and the notion of soundness while Section 3 introduces the notion of configurable workflow net and configuration step. Section 4 discusses the derivation of constraints that guarantee the preservation of syntactic correctness, and proves that these constraints also guarantee soundness for free-choice nets. The paper concludes with a section on related work, a summary, and an outlook on open issues.

2   Background

Petri nets are a formal model of concurrent systems [16]. Petri nets benefit from a rich body of theoretical results, analysis techniques and tools. They have been extensively applied to the formal verification of business process models [23]. These features make Petri nets suitable for establishing a formal foundation for business process model configuration. In addition, mappings exist between process modeling languages used in practice (e.g. UML Activity Diagrams, EPC, BPMN, BPEL) and Petri nets. These mappings provide a basis for extending the results outlined in this paper to concrete process modeling notations.

We use a class of Petri nets, namely workflow nets, specifically designed for business process modeling. Workflow nets have a single starting point and ending point, which captures the intuition that business processes are instantiated, and each process instance progresses independently through a series of activities until completion. A desirable property is that an instance of a workflow net always completes properly. This is captured by the notion of soundness. To make the paper self-contained, we provide an introduction to workflow nets and soundness.

2.1   Workflow Nets: Syntax

Petri nets are composed of two types of elements, namely transitions and places, connected by directed arcs. Transitions represent tasks while places represent the status of the system before or after the execution of a transition. Formally:

Definition 1 (Petri net, Preset, Postset). *A Petri net is a triple $PN = (P, T, F)$, such that:*

- P *is a finite set of places,*
- T *is a finite set of transitions $(P \cap T = \varnothing)$,*
- $F \subseteq (P \times T) \cup (T \times P)$ *is a set of arcs (flow relation).*

For each node $x \in P \cup T$, we use $\bullet x$ and $x \bullet$ to denote the set of inputs to x (preset) and the set of outputs of x (postset).   □

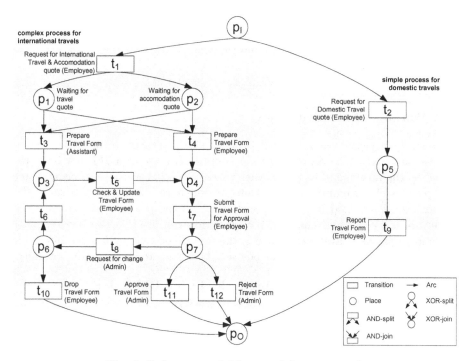

Fig. 1. Reference model for travel form approval

Fig. 1 shows a process model for travel requisition approval as a Petri net. It consists of two variants: the left one for international travel and the right one for domestic travel. After requesting a quote for international travel, either the employee or an assistant prepares the travel requisition form. In case of the latter, the employee needs to check the form before submitting it for approval. The administrator can then approve or reject the requisition, or make a request for change. At this point, the employee can update the form according to the administrator's suggestions and re-submit it, or drop the case. In contrast, the application for domestic travel only requires the employee to ask for a quote and to report the travel requisition to the administration.

A business process model may be executed a number of times to deal with different cases (e.g. different travel requests in the example). Each of these cases (called *process instances*) has a distinct start (input) and an end (output). Accordingly, we are only interested in Petri nets with a unique source place (representing the input) and a unique sink place (output), and such that all other nodes are on a directed path between the input and the output places. A Petri net satisfying these conditions represents a *structurally correct* process model and is known as a *workflow net* [1]. Formally:

Definition 2 (Workflow net). *Let $PN = (P, T, F)$ be a Petri net and F^* is the reflexive transitive closure of F. PN is a workflow net (WF-net) iff:*

- there exists exactly one $p_I \in P$ such that $\bullet p_I = \varnothing$, and
- there exists exactly one $p_O \in P$ such that $p_O \bullet = \varnothing$, and
- for all $n \in P \cup T$, $(p_I, n) \in F^*$ and $(n, p_O) \in F^*$.   □

The Petri net in Fig. 1 is a *WF*-net.

2.2   Workflow Nets: Semantics

Behavioral correctness of a *WF*-net is defined with respect to the states that a process instance can be in during its execution. A state of a *WF*-net is represented by the marking of its places with tokens. In other words, in a given state, each place is either empty, or it contains one or more tokens (i.e. it is marked). A transition is enabled in a given marking, if all the places in the transition's preset are marked. Once enabled, the transition can fire (i.e. can be executed) by removing a token from each place in the preset and putting a token into each subsequent place of the transition's postset. This leads to a new state. Formally:

Definition 3 (Marking, Enabling Rule, Firing Rule). *Let $N = (P, T, F)$ be a WF-net with source place p_I and sink place p_O:*

- *$M : P \to \mathbb{N}$ is a marking of N and $\mathbb{M}(N)$ is the set of markings of N,*
- *M_I is the initial marking of N with one token in place p_I, i.e. $M_I = [p_I]$,*
- *M_O is the final marking of N with one token in place p_O, i.e. $M_O = [p_O]$,*
- *$M(p)$ returns the number of tokens in place p if $p \in dom(M)$,*
- *For any two markings $M, M' \in \mathbb{M}(N)$, $M \geq M'$ iff $\forall_{p \in P} M(p) \geq M'(p)$,*
- *For any transition $t \in T$ and any marking $M \in \mathbb{M}(N)$, t is enabled at M, denoted as $M[t\rangle$, iff $\forall_{p \in \bullet t} M(p) \geq 1$. Marking M' is reached from M by firing t and $M' = M - \bullet t + t\bullet$,*
- *For any two markings $M, M' \in \mathbb{M}(N)$, M' is reachable from M in N, denoted as $M' \in N[M\rangle$, iff there exists a firing sequence $\sigma = \langle t_1, t_2, ..., t_n \rangle$ leading from M to M', and we write $M \xrightarrow{\sigma}_N M'$. If $\sigma = \langle t \rangle$, we use the notation $M \xrightarrow{t}_N M'$. N can be omitted if clear from the context.*   □

The execution of a process instance starts with the state in which the input place has one token and no other place is marked. The execution of this process instance should then progress through transition firings until a proper completion state. This intuition is captured by three requirements [1]. Firstly, every process instance should always have the option to complete. If a *WF*-net satisfies this requirement, it will never run into a deadlock or livelock. Secondly, every process instance should eventually reach the state in which there is one token in the output place p_O, and no tokens are left behind in any other place, since this would signal that there is still work to be done. Thirdly, for every transition, there should be at least one execution sequence from the initial marking (where only p_I is marked) to the final marking (where only p_O is marked) that includes at least one firing of this transition. In other words, no transition in the *WF*-net should be spurious. A *WF*-net fulfilling these requirements is *sound*. Formally:

Definition 4 (Sound WF-net). *Let $N = (P, T, F)$ be a WF-net and M_I, M_O be the initial and end markings. N is sound iff:*

- *option to complete: for every marking M reachable from M_I, there exists a firing sequence leading from M to M_O, i.e. $\forall_{M \in N[M_I\rangle} M_O \in N[M\rangle$, and*
- *proper completion: the marking M_O is the only marking reachable from M_I with at least one token in place p_o, i.e. $\forall_{M \in N[M_I\rangle} M \geq M_O \Rightarrow M = M_O$,*
- *no dead transitions: every transition can be reached by the initial marking, i.e. $\forall_{t \in T} \exists_{M \in N[M_I\rangle} M[t\rangle$.* □

3 Process Model Configuration

There are several ways to capture variation points for the purpose of representing a configurable process model [7,11,18]. In this paper we choose the approach presented in [11], which is based on the concept of inheritance of process behavior [2], since it abstracts from vendor-specific process modeling notations and can easily be applied to Petri nets. Accordingly, we define the notion of *configurable WF-net*, where each transition captures a variation point whose possible values (or *variants*) are: *allowed*, *hidden* and *blocked*.

Hiding a transition refers to skipping its execution while it is fired, without affecting the rest of the process flow. Consider for example the *WF*-net in Fig. 1. Some organizations may not require a quote for domestic travels. Thus, the task to request a quote can be skipped from the process model by hiding transition t_2. The process continues without forcing the employee to request a quote.

Blocking a transition implies to inhibit it in the process model. Blocked transitions cannot forward cases and all the subsequent transitions will never be executed if they cannot be enabled via other paths. For example, if t_2 in Fig. 1 is blocked, the process for domestic travels cannot be triggered and all travel approvals must be done via the complex variant.

If a transition is neither blocked nor hidden, we say it is allowed, meaning nothing changes in the model. To configure a *WF*-net each transition has to be assigned one value among hidden, blocked or allowed. Formally:

Definition 5 (Configuration). *Let $N = (P, T, F)$ be a WF-net, then $c_N \in T \rightarrow \{allow, hide, block\}$ is a configuration for N. We define:*

- *$A_N^c = \{t \in T \mid c(t) = allow\} \subseteq T$ as the set of all allowed transitions,*
- *$H_N^c = \{t \in T \mid c(t) = hide\} \subseteq T$ as the set of all hidden transitions,*
- *$B_N^c = \{t \in T \mid c(t) = block\} \subseteq T$ as the set of all blocked transitions.[1]*

If N is clear from the context, we drop the subscript. □

Based on these configuration values, a configured net is obtained representing the new behavior of the process model. This new Petri net is a restriction of the behavior of the starting model (the reference model), where all the hidden

---

[1] $A_N^c \cap H_N^c \cap B_N^c = \varnothing$ follows from the definition of N.

transitions are replaced by silent τ transitions and all the blocked transitions are removed. Also, all the places connected only to blocked transitions and all the flow relations from/to blocked transitions have to be removed too. Formally:

Definition 6 (Configured net). *Let* $N = (P, T, F)$ *be a WF-net and let* c *be a configuration of* N. *The resulting configured net* $N^c(P^c, T^c, F^c)$ *is defined as follows:*

- $T^c = (T \setminus (B^c \cup H^c)) \cup \{\tau_t \mid t \in H^c\}$,
- $F^c = (F \cap ((P \cup T^c) \times (P \cup T^c))) \cup \{(p, \tau_t) \mid (p, t) \in F \wedge t \in H^c\} \cup \{(\tau_t, p) \mid (t, p) \in F \wedge t \in H^c\}$,
- $P^c = (P \cap \bigcup_{(x,y) \in F^c} \{x, y\}) \cup \{p_I, p_O\}$. $\square$

As an example, Fig. 2a shows a configuration derived from the *WF*-net in Fig. 1, where the transitions t_2 and t_9 have been blocked to allow the complex approval process only. In this configuration employees have to prepare the approval form on their own, as t_3 has been blocked, and cannot drop a form application if a change is requested after approval (t_{10} also blocked). Place p_5 has been removed as it became disconnected after removing t_2 and t_9.

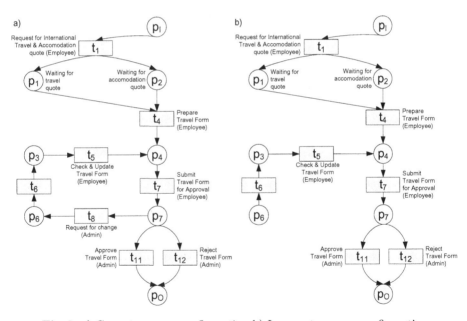

Fig. 2. a) Correct process configuration b) Incorrect process configuration

A process configuration has to comply with the requirements of the domain. This may prevent users from configuring the values of transitions freely. For example, in the travel management domain, if an employee submits a travel form for approval there must be at least an option to accept the request and an option to reject it. This is clearly a requirement of the domain, which forbids users to block both t_{11} and t_{12} in the process model. In [14] we showed how propositional logic expressions can be used to encode domain constraints. By evaluating each transition's value against these constraints with a SAT solver, it is possible to prevent all the configurations which would violate the constraints.

Nonetheless, the set of constraints derived from the domain are in most cases not sufficient to guarantee the syntactic and semantic correctness of the configured model. Indeed, as per Definition 6, a configured net can be any Petri net, which means that it can contain elements that are not on a path from p_I to p_O, or which are completely disconnected. For example, forbidding the request for a change by blocking t_9 in the WF-net of Fig. 2a would make p_6, t_6, p_3 and t_5 unreachable, yielding the net of Fig. 2b. Such a configuration is not syntactically correct and hence not semantically correct either, according to Definition 4. So, as soon as t_3 and t_8 are blocked, it would be desirable to suggest the user to block t_6 and t_5 too, so as to get rid of the unreachable branch. In the following section we present an approach to automatically derive a set of constraints from a WF-net that preserve the model correctness during its configuration.

4   Correctness-Preserving Configuration

Existing tools like Woflan [23] support the verification of Petri net-based process models. These tools could be used to check every single configured net that can be derived from a reference process model. If the net is incorrect, the configuration that has generated this net should be excluded from the set of possible configurations. However, this approach is costly, considering that reference process models can potentially yield thousands of individualized process models.

Our aim is therefore to define a framework which allows incorrect configuration steps to be discarded incrementally and without computing all possible configurations of the reference model. In addition, the framework needs to seamlessly integrate the domain constraints, so that a user can derive a correct process model which also satisfies any domain constraints.

To this end, we complement the domain constraints with a set of process constraints to guarantee the preservation of syntactic and semantic correctness in the configured net. Both sets of constraints are captured in propositional logic over the nodes of a WF-net and are reduced by a BDD solver. In this way we can provide interactive support to the user, by pinpointing the impact of each configuration step on the resulting net and by eliminating unfeasible options.

4.1   Preserving Syntactic Correctness

In a staged configuration, users make configuration decisions one after another in steps, and the set of configuration options is recalculated after each step. To remain syntactically correct, a WF-net must thus be checked on which configuration options are still viable among the transitions that have not been configured yet. For this, we have to consider the configuration decisions already taken.

To distinguish nodes which remain in the net from nodes which do not, we use a boolean variable for each node. If the variable is set to *true*, the node remains part of the net; if it is set to *false*, the node is dropped in the configured net. Accordingly, we assign a blocked transition the value *false*, while a transition that is allowed or hidden is assigned the value *true*. Since silent transitions have the same routing behavior as the original transitions, we do not need to distinguish hidden from allowed transitions. All transitions that are not explicitly configured remain as variables (i.e. unset).

According to Definition 6, any internal place remains in the net if there is a non-blocked transition in its present or postset. Translating this definition in boolean logic, if one such transition is *true*, the place has also to be set to *true*; if all the connected transitions are *false*, the place has to be set to *false*; if some transitions have no value assigned yet, the place remains unset. Since a configuration is defined over the transitions of a net, we have to derive the values of the places. We do that by imposing that each transition set to *true* implies *true* for all the places in its preset and in its postset. Formally: $\bigwedge_{t \in T^c} [\, t \Rightarrow \bigwedge_{p \in \bullet t} p \wedge \bigwedge_{p \in t \bullet} p].$[2]

Assuming the original net is a *WF*-net, to guarantee the configured net is still a *WF*-net, we have to ensure that each node that remains in the configured net be on a directed path from p_I to p_O. This is the only requirement of *WF*-net to be verified, as p_I and p_O are part of the configured net by definition. This means all the nodes composing the directed path should not be *false*. For each node, we can decompose this path into two sub-paths: one from p_I to the node in question and the other from the node to p_O, and verify the property over the nodes of each sub-path. However, as per Definition 6, we can restrict the verification to the places of each sub-path, by deriving the places' values from the ones of the transitions. Indeed, if a non-blocked transition has at least one place in its preset on a directed path from p_I and at least one place in its postset on a directed path to p_O, then the transition is on a directed path from p_I to p_O. When searching for such paths we can restrict our analysis to acyclic paths. In fact a cycle always leads back to the same node, but does not provide any valuable progress from p_I to p_O. Formally, we define an acyclic path as follows:

Definition 7 (Acyclic Path). *Let* $PN = (P, T, F)$ *be a Petri Net:*

- $\phi = \langle n_1, n_2, ..., n_k \rangle$ *is an* acyclic path *of* PN *such that* $(n_i, n_{i+1}) \in F$ *for* $1 \leq i \leq k - 1$ *and* $i \neq j \Rightarrow n_i \neq n_j$,
- $\alpha(\phi) = \{n_1, n_2, ..., n_k\}$ *is the alphabet of* ϕ,
- Φ_{PN} *is the set of all acyclic paths of* PN;
- *for all* $n \in P \cup T$, $AC_I(n) = \{\phi \in \Phi_{PN} \mid \phi = \langle p_I, ..., n \rangle\}$ *is the set of all acyclic paths from* p_I *to* n,
- *for all* $n \in P \cup T$, $AC_O(n) = \{\phi \in \Phi_{PN} \mid \phi = \langle n, ..., p_O \rangle\}$ *is the set of all acyclic paths from* n *to* p_O. $\qquad\square$

The set of process constraints is called PC and is defined as follows:

Definition 8 (Process Constraint). *Let* $N = (P, T, F)$ *be a WF-net. Treating each place and each transition of N with a propositional variable, the process*

---

[2] Where with t, p we indicate a transition, resp. a place, which is set to *true*.

constraint $PC(N)$ is a propositional logic formula over these variables, given by the conjunction of the following expressions:

- p_I and p_O are always true, i.e. $p_I \wedge p_O$;
- each place p implies the disjunction of all acyclic paths from p_I to p and the disjunction of all acyclic paths from p to p_O: $\bigwedge_{p \in P} [p \Rightarrow \bigvee_{\phi \in AC_I(p)} (\bigwedge_{n \in \alpha(\phi)} n) \wedge \bigvee_{\phi \in AC_O(p)} (\bigwedge_{n \in \alpha(\phi)} n)]$.   □

The following theorem shows that any configured net derived from a configuration that satisfies PC is a WF-net.

Theorem 1. Let $N = (P, T, F)$ be a WF-net and $PC(N)$ be its process constraint. Let c be a configuration of N and let $N^c = (P^c, T^c, F^c)$ be the resulting configured net. Let $v \in T \cup P \rightarrow \{true, false\}$ be such that $v(q) = true$ iff $q \in T^c \cup P^c$. Then N^c is a WF-net $\Leftrightarrow v \models PC(N)$.

Proof. By construction.   □

PC has to be satisfied over a system of variables represented by the nodes of the net, where the values of the transitions are configured by the user and the values of the places are derived automatically. Checking the satisfiability of PC is an NP-complete problem. To overcome this issue, we propose to use a SAT solver[3] based on Shared Binary Decision Diagrams (SBDDs). Existing SBDD solvers can efficiently deal with systems made up of around one million possibilities [15]. Hence they are reasonably adequate to capture all the configurations produced by a reference process model.

We propose to use the solver to obtain a reduced representation of PC in conjunctive normal form, where each variable is initially unset. Then we conjunct this formula with each new transition valuation as provided by the user during the configuration process, and further reduce the formula. In this way we do not recalculate PC for each configuration step. The solver can only reduce the formula if this is satisfiable, i.e. if the configuration can yield a syntactically correct process model. This may imply to automatically force to *true* or *false* the conjunction or disjunction of other transitions which are still unset, in order to keep the formula satisfiable. For example, after blocking t_8 in the model of Fig. 2a, the solver would force to *false* t_5 and t_6 as well.

This solver can be embedded in a tool to support staged configuration of process models, where invalid configurations are identified when a configuration step is applied and alternatives are suggested to keep the model correct.

4.2 Preserving Semantic Correctness

In addition to structural correctness, a configuration should be semantically correct. The example in Fig. 3 shows that a configuration conforming to the WF-net properties is not automatically sound, even if it is derived from a sound WF-net. The WF-net in (a) is a sound WF-net: if t_8 fires before t_4, the token

---

[3] Available at http://www-verimag.imag.fr/~raymond/tools/bddc-manual

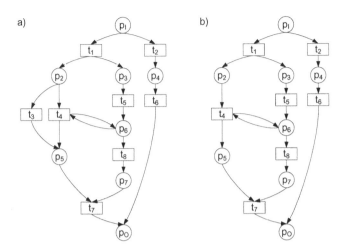

Fig. 3. Blocking t_3 in (a) leads to an unsound *WF*-net (b)

in p_2 can reach p_5 via t_3. However, if t_3 is blocked (b), t_4 needs to fire before t_8 as t_4 depends on the token in p_6 which is removed when t_8 fires. Since this behavior is not enforced in the net, the process might deadlock, and is therefore not sound, although (b) is still a valid *WF*-net.

Soundness is only defined for *WF*-nets (Definition 2), but it can be generalized to any Petri net with a designated source and sink place. However, it is easy to show that any non *WF*-net would still violate this generalized soundness notation. Therefore, the process constraint defined in Definition 8 is a necessary requirement for soundness, but as Fig. 3 shows, it is not sufficient.

Below, we prove that *PC* is a sufficient requirement to guarantee soundness of a configured net, if the original model is a sound extended free-choice *WF*-net. The restriction to this class of Petri nets provides a good compromise between expressiveness and verification complexity. Not only do extended free-choice *WF*-nets have several desirable properties [9], but the large majority of constructs of process modeling languages such as EPCs, BPMN or BPEL can be mapped to Petri nets in this class. An extended free-choice is defined as follows [16]:

Definition 9 (Extended Free-choice *WF*-Net). *Let $N = (P, T, F)$ be a Petri net. N is extended free-choice (eFC) if for every couple of places sharing transitions in their postset, these postsets coincide, i.e. $\forall_{p_1, p_2 \in P \setminus p_O} [p_1 \bullet \cap p_2 \bullet \neq \varnothing \Rightarrow p_1 \bullet = p_2 \bullet]$.* □

Assuming the reference process model is a sound, *eFC WF*-net, we are able to identify several configuration properties relevant for the preservation of soundness during the configuration process:

Proposition 1 (Properties of Configuration). *Let $N = (P, T, F)$ be a sound, eFC WF-net with source place p_I and sink place p_O, let c be a configuration* *of N, and let $N^c = (P^c, T^c, F^c)$ be the configured net resulting from c. If N^c is a WF-net (i.e. $PC(N)$ evaluates to* true*), then:*

a) $\forall_{t \in T^c} [(\bullet_N t = \bullet_{N^c} t) \wedge (t \bullet_N = t \bullet_{N^c})]$.
b) $p_I \in P^c$ *and* $p_O \in P^c$.
c) $\forall_{t \in B_N^c} [(\bullet_N t \cap P^c = \varnothing) \vee \exists_{t' \in T^c} (\bullet_N t = \bullet_N t')]$ *(a blocked transition is either not consuming any tokens from P^c or there is a transition in T^c with the same input set).*
d) $\forall_{\sigma \in T^{c*}} (M_I \xrightarrow{\sigma}_N) \Leftrightarrow (M_I \xrightarrow{\sigma}_{N^c})$ *(the input and output sets of transitions in T^c are the same in both nets, therefore, the respective behaviors are identical when considering only firing sequences $\sigma \in T^{c*}$).*
e) $\forall_{\sigma \in T^{c*}} \forall_M [(M_I \xrightarrow{\sigma}_N M) \Leftrightarrow (M_I \xrightarrow{\sigma}_{N^c} M)]$.
f) $N^c[M_I\rangle \subseteq N[M_I\rangle$ *(all firing sequences of N^c are also possible in N).*
g) N^c *is eFC.*
h) $\forall_{M \in N^c[M_I\rangle \setminus \{M_O\}} \exists_{t' \in T^c} [M[t'\rangle]$ *(N^c has no deadlock markings).*

Proof

a) *Follows directly from the construction of N^c.*
b) *Idem.*
c) *Suppose that some $t \in B_N^c$ consumes a token from a place $p \in P^c$ in N. Because N^c is a WF-net with source place p_I and sink place p_O, there has to be a path from p to p_O. Hence there is a transition $t' \in T^c$ consuming a token from p. Hence $\bullet_N t \cap \bullet_N t' \neq \varnothing$, thus $\bullet_N t = \bullet_N t'$ (N is eFC).*
d) *Follows directly from (a).*
e) *Follows directly from (d).*
f) *Follows directly from (e).*
g) *Let $t, t' \in T^c$ such that $\bullet_{N^c} t \cap \bullet_{N^c} t' \neq \varnothing$. Given that $\bullet_N t' = \bullet_{N^c} t'$ and $\bullet_N t = \bullet_{N^c} t$, we have $\bullet_{N^c} t \cap \bullet_{N^c} t' = \bullet_N t \cap \bullet_N t' \neq \varnothing$. Hence $\bullet_N t = \bullet_N t'$ and thus $\bullet_{N^c} t = \bullet_{N^c} t'$. Therefore N^c is eFC.*
h) *Let $M \in N^c[M_I\rangle \setminus \{M_O\}$. Then using (e) we can deduce $M_I \twoheadrightarrow_N M$, thus there exists a $t \in T$ such that $M[t\rangle$ (as N is sound). If $t \in T^c$ then we are done. If $t \in B_N^c$ then there exists a $t' \in T^c$ such that $\bullet_N t = \bullet_{N^c} t'$ (c). Therefore $M[t'\rangle$.* $\square$

While propositions a, b, d, e and f follow directly from the construction of configured nets and hold for non *eFC* WF-nets, propositions c, g, and h are particularly interesting for soundness. The problem in the example of Fig. 3 is that the configuration may yield an unsound model when a transition is blocked which shares part of its preset with another transition. By definition, in an *eFC* WF-net such a situation cannot exist and therefore a deadlock marking cannot occur (propositions c and h). Further on, the deadlock in the example prevents all tokens from reaching the final place. As the configured net derived from an *eFC* WF-net remains *eFC* (proposition g), the *eFC* property prevents also this problem as it permits any token to move towards the final place.

These properties allow us to prove that if a configured net, derived from a sound *eFC WF*-net, is a *WF*-net, it fulfills the soundness criteria. Formally:

Theorem 2. *Let $N = (P, T, F)$ be a sound, eFC WF-net with source place p_I and sink place p_O, let c be a configuration of N and let $N^c = (P^c, T^c, F^c)$ be the resulting configured net. If N^c is a WF-net, then N^c is sound.*

Proof. Note that changing a transition into a silent transition (hiding) has no implications for soundness analysis.

- proper completion: *since $N^c[M_I\rangle \subseteq N[M_I\rangle$ (Proposition 1f), M_O is the only state marking p_O.*
- option to complete: *because N^c is an eFC WF-net (Proposition 1g), any token can decide to move towards p_O. If p_O is marked, all other places are empty (N^c has proper completion). Hence, marking M_O can be reached (and the property holds) or the net is in a deadlock M. However, this is not possible as N^c has no deadlock markings (Proposition 1h).*
- no dead transitions: *we define a length function as follows: $L : T^c \to \mathbb{N}$. If $p_I \in \bullet t$ then $L(t) = 0$. Otherwise $L(t) = 1 + min_{p \in \bullet t, t' \in \bullet p} L(t')$. Given that every transition in N^c is on a path from p_I, the function is well-defined. Using induction we prove $\forall_{n \in \mathbb{N}} \forall_{t \in T^c} [L(t) = n \Rightarrow t$ is not dead in $N^c]$.*
  (Base case) If $n = 0$ then $\bullet t = \{p_I\}$ and as $p_I \in P^c$ (Proposition 1b), $M_I[t\rangle$, hence t is not dead.
  (Induction Hypothesis (IH)) If $t \in T'^c$ is such that $L(t) = n+1$, there exists a transition t' such that $L(t') = n$ and $t' \bullet \cap \bullet t \neq \varnothing$. t' is not dead (IH), hence there exists an $M \in N^c[M_I\rangle$ such that $M[t'\rangle$. Let M' be such that $M \xrightarrow{t'} M'$, then M' marks at least one input place (i.e., p) of t. As N^c has the option to complete, $M' \twoheadrightarrow M_O$. This implies that some transition t'' exists which removes the token from p in some marking M', hence $p \in \bullet t''$. Therefore $\bullet t \cap \bullet t'' \neq \varnothing$, and thus, given that N^c is eFC (Proposition 1g) $\bullet t = \bullet t''$. Therefore $M'[t\rangle$ and t is not dead. □

Theorems 1 and 2 can be combined to show that a configured net is sound if and only if the process constraint PC is satisfied for the corresponding configuration. If the configured net is not an *eFC WF*-net, the implication only holds in one direction and in the other direction soundness cannot be guaranteed. In these cases PC can be used to rule out all the syntactically incorrect process models and conventional analysis tools such as Woflan [23] have to be used in addition.

5   Related Work

Variability modeling has been widely studied in the field of Software Product Line Engineering (SPLE) [17]. Techniques developed in the field enable the configuration of software artifacts based on models that relate these artifacts to domain concepts (e.g. parameters, options or features). The techniques differ in the way domain models are captured and related to software artifacts, and also in the way they capture constraints. The Adele Configuration Manager [10] and the Cosmic Configurable Middleware [22] use first-order logic to capture constraints. In contrast, we use propositional logic, for which we can apply efficient techniques to discard incorrect configuration steps or to suggest ways of repairing them. Batory [5] presents a Feature-Oriented Domain Analysis (FODA) technique in which constraints are captured in propositional logic. The respective tool uses a SAT solver to determine if a configuration is valid. A similar approach is adopted in [4]. Our work is inspired by these approaches but it is targeted at business process model configuration. Thus, we deal with graph-oriented models (hence, structural correctness needs special attention) and we are concerned with ensuring absence of deadlocks or livelocks and other behavioral properties.

We outlined a technique to derive propositional logic constraints from process models. Similar techniques have been used for analyzing Petri nets [3] and process graphs [19]. However, the constraints we derive are specifically aimed at checking that a configuration step preserves the structural properties of workflow nets.

Our previous work includes the definition of variation mechanisms for existing process modeling languages: EPCs [18], YAWL [13] and SAP WebFlow [12]. In [14] we proposed a framework which ensures domain conformance (but not syntactic or behavioral correctness) by linking configurable process models to domain models expressed as questionnaires. Finally, the use of the hiding and blocking operators for variation points is sketched in [11].

6   Summary and Outlook

We have proposed a framework for staged correctness-preserving configuration of reference process models. Assuming the initial (reference) process model is correct, the framework guarantees that the individualized process models are also correct at each stage of the configuration procedure. This is achieved by capturing the syntactic correctness constraints as a propositional logic formula. This formula, in conjunction with another formula capturing the domain constraints, is used to check the correctness-preservation of each configuration step. If a configuration step violates the constraints, a formula is derived to suggest ways of making the configuration step correctness-preserving. A cornerstone of the framework is a proof that, for free-choice process models, the enforcement of these syntactic constraints also ensures the preservation of semantic correctness.

The proposal is framed in the context of Petri net-based process models. Existing mappings from other process modeling notations to Petri nets provide a basis to enhance the framework's applicability in practice. This will be a direction for future work. Another goal is to provide tool support based on the proposed framework. In previous work [14], we have developed a tool for questionnaire-driven configuration of C-EPC and C-YAWL process models. After adapting the framework to the syntax of these languages, we will be able to extend this tool with the ability to derive and to enforce correctness-preserving constraints.

References

1. van der Aalst, W.M.P.: Verification of Workflow Nets. In: Azéma, P., Balbo, G. (eds.) ICATPN 1997. LNCS, vol. 1248, pp. 407–426. Springer, Heidelberg (1997)
2. van der Aalst, W.M.P., Basten, T.: Inheritance of workflows: an approach to tackling problems related to change. Theoretical Computer Science 270(1-2), 125–203 (2002)
3. Abdulla, P.A., Iyer, S.P., Nyln, A.: SAT-solving the coverability problem for Petri nets. Formal Methods in System Design 24(1), 25–43 (2004)
4. Antkiewicz, M., Czarnecki, K.: FeaturePlugIn: Feature modeling plug-in for Eclipse. In: Proceedings of the 2004 OOPSLA workshop on eclipse technology eXchange, pp. 67–72 (2004)
5. Batory, D.S.: Feature Models, Grammars, and Propositional Formulas. In: Obbink, H., Pohl, K. (eds.) SPLC 2005. LNCS, vol. 3714, pp. 7–20. Springer, Heidelberg (2005)
6. Curran, T., Keller, G.: SAP R/3 Business Blueprint: Understanding the Business Process Reference Model, Upper Saddle River (1997)
7. Czarnecki, K., Antkiewicz, M.: Mapping Features to Models: A Template Approach Based on Superimposed Variants. In: Glück, R., Lowry, M. (eds.) GPCE 2005. LNCS, vol. 3676, pp. 422–437. Springer, Heidelberg (2005)
8. Czarnecki, K., Helsen, S., Eisenecker, U.: Staged configuration using feature models. In: Nord, R.L. (ed.) SPLC 2004. LNCS, vol. 3154, pp. 266–283. Springer, Heidelberg (2004)
9. Desel, J., Esparza, J.: Free Choice Petri Nets. In: Cambridge Tracts in Theoretical Computer Science, vol. 40, Cambridge University Press, Cambridge (1995)
10. Estublier, J., Casallas, R.: The Adele Software Configuration Manager. In: Configuration Management, pp. 99–139. John Wiley & Sons, Chichester (1994)
11. Gottschalk, F., van der Aalst, W.M.P., Jansen-Vullers, M.H.: Configurable Process Models – A Foundational Approach. In: Becker, J., Delfmann, P. (eds.) Reference Modeling, pp. 59–78. Springer, Heidelberg (2007)
12. Gottschalk, F., van der Aalst, W.M.P., Jansen-Vullers, M.H.: SAP WebFlow Made Configurable: Unifying Workflow Templates into a Configurable Model. In: Alonso, G., Dadam, P., Rosemann, M. (eds.) BPM 2007. LNCS, vol. 4714, pp. 262–270. Springer, Heidelberg (2007)
13. Gottschalk, F., van der Aalst, W.M.P., Jansen-Vullers, M.H., La Rosa, M.: Configurable Workflow Models. BETA Working Paper 222, Eindhoven University of Technology, The Netherlands (2007)
14. La Rosa, M., Lux, J., Seidel, S., Dumas, M., ter Hofstede, A.H.M.: Questionnaire-driven Configuration of Reference Process Models. In: Krogstie, J., Opdahl, A., Sindre, G. (eds.) CAiSE 2007 and WES 2007. LNCS, vol. 4495, pp. 424–438. Springer, Heidelberg (2007)
15. Minato, S., Ishiura, N., Yajima, S.: Shared Binary Decision Diagram with Attributed Edges for Efficient Boolean function Manipulation. In: Proceedings of the 27th ACM/IEEE Conference on Design Automation, pp. 52–57 (1990)
16. Murata, T.: Petri Nets: Properties, Analysis and Applications. Proceedings of the IEEE 77(4), 541–580 (1989)
17. Pohl, K., Böckle, G., van der Linden, F.: Software Product-line Engineering – Foundations, Principles and Techniques. Springer, Berlin (2005)
18. Rosemann, M., van der Aalst, W.M.P.: A Configurable Reference Modelling Language. Information Systems 32(1), 1–23 (2007)

19. Sadiq, S.W., Orlowska, M.E., Sadiq, W.: Specification and validation of process constraints for flexible workflows. Information Systems 30(5), 349–378 (2005)
20. Stephens, S.: The Supply Chain Council and the SCOR Reference Model. Supply Chain Management - An International Journal 1(1), 9–13 (2001)
21. Taylor, C., Probst, C.: Business Process Reference Model Languages: Experiences from BPI Projects. In: Proceedings of INFORMATIK 2003, Jahrestagung der Gesellschaft für Informatik e. V (GI), pp. 259–263 (2003)
22. Turkay, E., Gokhale, A.S., Natarajan, B.: Addressing the Middleware Configuration Challenges using Model-based Techniques. In: Proceedings of the 42nd ACM Southeast Regional Conference, Huntsville AL, pp. 166–170. ACM Press, New York (2004)
23. Verbeek, H.M.W., Basten, T., van der Aalst, W.M.P.: Diagnosing Workflow Processes using Woflan. The Computer Journal 44(4), 246–279 (2001)

Consistent Integration of Models Based on Views of Visual Languages

Hartmut Ehrig[1], Karsten Ehrig[2], Claudia Ermel[1], and Ulrike Prange[1]

[1] Technische Universität Berlin, Germany
ehrig,lieske,uprange@cs.tu-berlin.de
[2] University of Leicester, United Kingdom
karsten@mcs.le.ac.uk

Abstract. The complexity of large system models in software engineering nowadays is mastered by using different views. View-based modeling aims at creating small, partial models, each one of them describing some aspect of the system. Existing formal techniques supporting view-based visual modeling are based on typed attributed graphs, where views are related by typed attributed graph morphisms. Such morphisms up to now require a fixed type graph, as well as a fixed data signature and domain. This is in general not adequate for view-oriented modeling where only parts of the complete type graph and signature are known and necessary when modeling a partial view of the system.

The aim of this paper is to extend the framework of typed attributed graph morphisms to *generalized* typed attributed graph morphisms, short GAG-morphisms, which involve changes of the type graph, data signature, and domain. This allows the modeler to formulate type hierarchies and views of visual languages defined by GAG-morphisms between type graphs, short GATG-morphisms. In this paper we study the interaction and integration of views, and the restriction of views along type hierarchies. In the main result we present suitable conditions for the integration and decomposition of consistent view models. As a running example we use a visual domain-specific modeling language to model coarse-grained IT components and their connectors in decentralized IT infrastructures.

1 Introduction

In recent years, the complexity of large system models in software engineering is mastered by using different views or viewpoints. View-based modeling rather aims at creating small, partial models, each one of them describing some aspect of the system instead of building complex monolithic specifications. Visual techniques nowadays form an important part of the overall software development methodology. Usually, visual notations like the UML [1], Petri nets or other kinds of graphs are used in order to specify static or dynamic system aspects. Hence, the syntax definition of visual modeling languages is an important basis for the implementation of tools supporting visual modeling (e.g. visual editor generation) and for model-based system verification.

J. Fiadeiro and P. Inverardi (Eds.): FASE 2008, LNCS 4961, pp. 62–76, 2008.
© Springer-Verlag Berlin Heidelberg 2008

Two main approaches to visual language (VL) definition can be distinguished: grammar-based approaches or meta-modeling. Using graph grammars and graph transformation [2], multidimensional representations are described by graphs. Graph rules are used to manipulate the graph representation of a language element. Meta-modeling (see e.g. [3]) is also graph-based, but uses constraints instead of a grammar to define a visual language. The advantage of meta-modeling is that UML users, who probably have basic UML knowledge, do not need to learn a new external notation to be able to deal with syntax definitions. Graph grammars are more constructive, i.e. closer to the implementation, and provide a formal basis for visualizing, validating and verifying system properties.

For the application of graph transformation techniques to VL modeling, typed attributed graph transformation systems and grammars [2] have proven to be an adequate formalism. A VL is modeled by a type graph capturing the definition of the underlying visual alphabet, i.e. the symbols and relations which are available. Sentences or models of the VL are given by graphs typed over (i.e. conforming to) the type graph. Such a VL type graph corresponds closely to a meta model. In order to restrict the set of valid visual models, a syntax graph grammar may be defined, consisting of a set of language-generating graph transformation rules, typed over the abstract syntax part of the VL type graph.

In this paper we extend the graph transformation framework in order to allow an adequate specification of different views and their relations. In the literature, approaches already exist to model views as morphisms between typed attributed graphs [4]. Up to now such morphisms require a fixed type graph, as well as a fixed data signature and domain. This is in general not adequate for view-oriented modeling where only parts of the complete type graph and signature are known and necessary when modeling a partial view of the system. Hence, in this paper we develop the notion of *generalized attributed graph morphisms* (GAG-morphisms) which allows the modeler to change the type graph, data signature and domain. GAG-morphisms are the basis for more flexible, view-oriented modeling since views are independent of each other, now also with respect to the data type definition.

For view-oriented modeling, mechanisms are needed to integrate different views to a full system model. In order to integrate two or more views, their intended correspondences have to be specified. Here, typed graphs and the underlying categorical constructions support an integration concept which goes much further than an integration merely based on the use of common names. In this paper, we define type hierarchies and views based on GAG-morphisms, and study the interaction and integration of views, as well as the restriction of views along type hierarchies, the notion of view consistency, and the integration and decomposition of models based on consistent views.

As a running example we use a visual domain-specific modeling language to model coarse-grained IT components and their connectors in decentralized IT infrastructures. An infrastructure model has to provide the basis to handle structural security issues, like firewall placements, of such distributed IT components. In order to provide support to model, build, administrate, monitor and control such a local IT landscape, we present a formal, visual domain-specific language family based on attributed type graph hierarchies and views. A simplified visual language for this purpose using typed graphs *without* attributes was first introduced in [5], serving as a basis to transform domain-specific IT infrastructure models to a Reo coordination model [6] for further analysis.

The paper is structured as follows: Section 2 defines the category **GAGraphs** of typed attributed graphs and GAG-morphisms, and introduces the sample VL for IT infrastructures. On this basis, views are defined in Section 3, and the view relations *interaction* and *integration* are given by categorical constructions. Moreover, the interplay of type hierarchies of VLs and views is considered. Section 4 studies models of visual languages and models of views (view-models) and states as main result conditions for the consistency, integration and decomposition of view-models. In Section 5, related work is presented and compared to our approach. We conclude and discuss future work in Section 6.

2   Visual Language Definition by Typed Attributed Graphs

We use the meta-model approach in combination with typed attributed graphs to define visual languages. A meta-model is given by an attributed type graph ATG together with structural constraints, and the corresponding visual language VL is given by all attributed graphs typed over ATG which satisfy the constraints. In the following, we introduce the necessary definitions for typed attributed graphs.

The definition of attributed graphs is based on E-graphs, which give a structure for graphs with data elements. An E-graph $G = (V_G, V_D, E_G, E_{NA}, E_{EA}, (source_j, target_j)_{j \in \{G,NA,EA\}})$ has two different kinds of nodes, namely graph nodes V_G and data nodes V_D, and different kinds of edges, namely graph edges E_G and, for the attribution, node attribute edges E_{NA} and edge attribute edges E_{EA}, with corresponding source and target functions according to the signature on the right.

As presented in [2], attributed graphs are defined as E-graphs combined with a *DSIG*-algebra, i.e. an algebra over a data signature *DSIG*. In this signature, we distinguish a set of attribute value sorts. The corresponding carrier sets in the *DSIG*-algebra can be used for attribution. In addition to attributed graph morphisms in [2], generalized attributed graph morphisms are mappings of attributed graphs with possibly different data signatures.

Definition 1 (Attributed graph and generalized attributed graph morphism). *An* attributed graph $AG = (G, DSIG, D)$ *consists of*

- *an E-graph* $G = (V_G, V_D, E_G, E_{NA}, E_{EA}, (source_j, target_j)_{j \in \{G,NA,EA\}})$,
- *a data signature* $DSIG = (S, S_D, OP)$ *with attribute value sorts* $S_D \subseteq S$, *and*
- *a DSIG-algebra* D *such that* $\dot{\bigcup}_{s \in S_D} D_s = V_D$.

Given attributed graphs $AG^i = (G^i, DSIG^i, D^i)$ for $i = 1, 2$, a generalized *attributed graph morphism (GAG-morphism) $f = (f_G, f_S, f_D) : AG^1 \to AG^2$ is given by*

- *an E-graph morphism $f_G : G^1 \to G^2$,*
- *a signature morphism $f_S : DSIG^1 \to DSIG^2$, and*
- *a generalized homomorphism $f_D : D^1 \to D^2$, which is a $DSIG^1$-morphism $f_D : D^1 \to V_{f_S}(D^2)$ with $f_D = (f_{D,s_1} : D^1_{s_1} \to D^2_{f_S(s_1)})_{s_1 \in S^1}$*

with the following compatibility property: $f_S(S^1_D) \subseteq S^2_D$ and the diagram on the right commutes for all $s_1 \in S^1_D$, where the vertical (curling) arrows are inclusions. A GAG-morphism $f = (f_G, f_S, f_D)$ is called

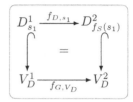

- injective, *if f_G, f_S, f_D are injective,*
- signature preserving, *if f_S is isomorphic,*
- persistent, *if f_D is isomorphic.*

Attributed graphs with generalized attributed graph morphisms form the category **GAGraphs**.

Note that AG-morphisms in [2] correspond to signature preserving GAG-morphisms.

For the typing, we use a distinguished attributed type graph ATG. According to [2], attributed type graphs and typed attributed graphs are now defined using GAG-morphisms presented above.

Definition 2 (Typed attributed graph and typed attributed graph morphism). *An attributed type graph $ATG = (TG, DSIG, Z_{DSIG})$ is an attributed graph where Z_{DSIG} is the final DSIG-algebra, i.e. $Z_{DSIG,s} = \{s\}$ for all $s \in S$, and $V_D = \dot{\bigcup}_{s \in S_D} Z_{DSIG,s} = S_D$.*

Given an attributed type graph ATG, a typed attributed graph $TAG = (AG, t)$ (over ATG) is given by an attributed graph AG and a GAG-morphism $t : AG \to ATG$.

Given an attributed type graph ATG and typed attributed graphs $TAG^i = (AG^i, t : AG^i \to ATG)$ over ATG for $i = 1, 2$, a typed attributed graph morphism $f : TAG^1 \to TAG^2$ is given by a GAG-morphism $f : AG^1 \to AG^2$ such that $t_2 \circ f = t^1$.

Given an attributed type graph ATG, typed attributed graphs over ATG and typed attributed graph morphisms form the category **GAGraphs$_{ATG}$**.

As a special case of GAG-morphisms we obtain generalized attributed type graph morphisms based on attributed type graphs.

Definition 3 (Generalized attributed type graph morphism). *Given attributed type graphs $ATG^i = (TG^i, DSIG^i, Z_{DSIG^i})$ for $i = 1, 2$, a* generalized *attributed type graph morphism (GATG-morphism) $f = (f_G, f_S, f_D) : ATG^1 \to ATG^2$ is given by*

- an E-graph morphism $f_G : TG^1 \to TG^2$,
- a signature morphism $f_S : DSIG^1 \to DSIG^2$, and
- a generalized homomorphism $f_D : Z_{DSIG^1} \to Z_{DSIG^2}$, which is uniquely determined by $f_{D,s_1}(s_1) = f_S(s_1)$ for all $s_1 \in S^1$.

A GATG-morphism f is also a GAG-morphism since the compatibility property is automatically satisfied because $f_{G,V_D}(s_1) = f_S(s_1)$ for all $s_1 \in S_D^1$ and f_D, f_{G,V_D} are uniquely determined by f_S. Moreover, if f is a GATG-morphism then f is persistent.

Now we are able to define visual languages. For simplicity, we consider only visual languages over attributed type graphs, without any constraints. For the case with constraints we refer to [7].

Definition 4 (Visual language). *Given an attributed type graph ATG, the visual language VL of ATG consists of all typed attributed graphs $(AG, t : AG \to ATG)$ typed over ATG, i.e. VL is the object class of the category* **GAGraphs$_{ATG}$**.

Example 1 (VL for network infrastructures). Fig. 1 shows at the top the attributed type graph ATG_{DSL} which represents a meta-meta model (or schema) for domain-specific languages for IT infrastructures. The *DSL* schema defines that all its instances (domain-specific languages) consist of node types for components, connections and interfaces. In the center of Fig. 1, the attributed type graph $ATG_{Network}$ defines a simple modeling language for network infrastructures which has component types for personal computers (PC), application servers (AS), and databases (DB). Interfaces are refined into HTTP-client and HTTP-server ports, as well as database client and server ports. Connections may be secure (i.e. with firewall) or insecure, which is modeled by the new boolean attribute secure.

There is a generalized attributed type graph morphism h from $ATG_{Network}$ to ATG_{DSL}, indicated by equal numbering of mapped nodes. Note that in order to be able to define the signature morphism f_S and the *DSIG*-morphism f_D for any GAG-morphisms $f : ATG_1 \to ATG_2$ between different type graphs, we assume that each node type in ATG_2 has at least one sort "*", and one attribute $attr : *$, where all sorts and attributes from ATG_1 can be mapped to which are not already defined in ATG_2. Thus we can have new attributes, sorts and methods at the more detailed type level ATG_1 which need not be defined already in ATG_2. For our sample GAG-morphism h in Fig. 1, this is the case for the new attribute $secure : Bool$ of the type Connection in $ATG_{Network}$. The new sort $Bool$ is mapped by the signature morphism to the sort "*", and the attribute $secure$ is mapped by the *DSIG*-morphism to the constant $attr$.

At the bottom of Fig. 1, a sample computer network is depicted as graph $G_{Network}$ which is an element of the visual $Network$ language since $G_{Network}$ is typed over $ATG_{Network}$: $(G_{Network}, t : G \to ATG_{Network}) \in VL_{Network}$. Obviously, all graphs G in $VL_{Network}$ are also in VL_{DSL}, since every $(G, t : G \to ATG_{Network})$ is also typed over ATG_{DSL} by the composition of typing morphisms: $(G, h \circ t : G \to ATG_{DSL}) \in VL_{DSL}$.

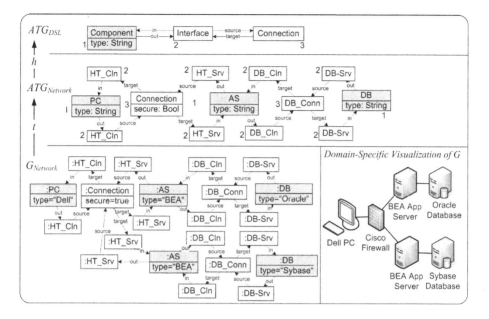

Fig. 1. *Example 1:* Domain-Specific Languages for IT Infrastructures

3   Type Hierarchies and Views of Visual Languages

In this section, we study type hierarchies and views of visual languages based on morphisms in **GAGraphs**, which allow to change not only the graph structure but also the data signature and data type. Note that in this section we only consider the attributed type graphs and their relations, but not yet models over them. This is done in the next section.

A restriction of a visual language to a specific subpart of the language is called a view.

Definition 5 (View). *A view of a visual language VL over an attributed type graph ATG is given by an injective $GATG$-morphism $v_1 : ATG_1 \to ATG$.*

For the interaction and integration of views we need the categorical constructions of pullbacks and pushouts in **GAGraphs**. Proofs for the pushout and pullback construction lemmas are given in [7]. Pullbacks are a kind of generalized intersection of objects over a common object.

Lemma 1 (Pullback construction in GAGraphs). *Given GAG-morphisms $f : AG^2 \to AG^3$ and $g : AG^1 \to AG^3$ then the pullback in **GAGraphs** is constructed componentwise in the G-, S- and D-components. Moreover, pullbacks preserve injective, signature preserving, and persistent morphisms.*

Pushouts generalize the gluing of objects, i.e. a pushout emerges from the gluing of two objects along a common subobject using the amalgamation of data types in the sense of [15].

Lemma 2 (Pushouts in GAGraphs over persistent morphisms). *Given persistent morphisms* $f' : AG^0 \rightarrow AG^1$ *and* $g' : AG^0 \rightarrow AG^2$ *in* **GAGraphs** *then the pushout* (1) *in* **GAGraphs** *is constructed componentwise in the G- and S-components, with attribute value sorts* $S_D^3 = g_s(S_D^1) \sqcup f_S(S_D^2)$, *and in the D-component by amalgamation as* $D_3 = D^1 +_{D^0} D^2$. *Moreover, pushouts preserve injective, signature preserving, and persistent morphisms.*

$$
\begin{array}{ccc}
AG^0 = (G^0, DSIG^0, D^0) & \xrightarrow{\ f'=(f_G',f_S',f_D')\ } & (G^1, DSIG^1, D^1) = AG^1 \\
{\scriptstyle g'=(g_G',g_S',g_D')}\Big\downarrow & (1) & \Big\downarrow{\scriptstyle g=(g_G,g_S,g_D)} \\
AG^2 = (G^2, DSIG^2, D^2) & \xrightarrow{\ f=(f_G,f_S,f_D)\ } & (G^3, DSIG^3, D^3) = AG^3
\end{array}
$$

Based on the concepts of pullbacks and pushouts, we are now able to define the interaction and integration of views. Roughly spoken, the interaction is the intersection, and the integration is the union of views.

Definition 6 (Interaction and integration of views). *Given views* (ATG_1, v_1) *and* (ATG_2, v_2) *over* ATG *the interaction* (ATG_0, i_1, i_2) *is given by the following pullback* (1) *in* **GAGraphs**, *where* (ATG_0, v_0) *with* $v_0 = v_1 \circ i_1 = v_2 \circ i_2$ *is a view over* ATG *and also called subview of* (ATG_1, v_1) *and* (ATG_2, v_2).

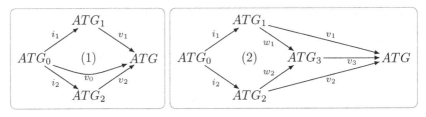

The integration of views (ATG_1, v_1) and (ATG_2, v_2) with interaction (ATG_0, i_1, i_2) is given by the above pushout (2) in **GAGraphs**. Due to the universal pushout property there is a unique injective GATG-morphism $v_3 : ATG_3 \rightarrow ATG$ such that (ATG_3, v_3) is a view over ATG.

ATG is covered by views (ATG_i, v_i) with $i = 1, 2$ if v_1 and v_2 are jointly surjective.

There is a close relationship between covering by views and view integration.

Fact 1 (Integration of views). *If* ATG *is covered by views* (ATG_i, v_i) *for* $i = 1, 2$ *then the integration* ATG_3 *is equal to* ATG *up to isomorphism.*

Proof. According to Def. 6, there is a unique morphism v_3 with $v_3 \circ w_1 = v_1$ and $v_3 \circ w_2 = v_2$. This morphism is injective in the G- and S-components due to general properties of graph and signature morphisms, and v_3 is injective in the D-component as a general property of GATG-morphisms. Surjectivity of v_3 follows from joint surjectivity of v_1 and v_2.

Example 2 (Interaction and integration of views on IT networks). Fig. 2 shows two views $(ATG_{Components}, v_1)$ and $(ATG_{Connections}, v_2)$ of the visual language over ATG_{DSL} (see Fig. 1). The type graph $ATG_{Components}$ consists of a node type for Computer linked to a node type for Port, whereas the type graph $ATG_{Connections}$ contains a node type Channel which is linked to a node type ChEnd. The view embedding v_1 maps Computer to Component and Port to Interface, and v_2 maps Channel to Connection and ChEnd to Interface. Edges are mapped accordingly. The interaction $(ATG_{interaction}, i_1, i_2)$ is constructed as pullback (1) in **GAGraphs** which is the intersection of v_1 and v_2 with suitable renaming. Given the interaction, the integration of the views $(ATG_{Components}, v_1)$ and $ATG_{Connections}, v_2$ over $(ATG_{Interaction}, i_1, i_2)$ can be constructed as pushout (2) in **GAGraphs**, resulting in the type graph $(ATG_{Integration})$. According to Fact 1, $(ATG_{Integration})$ is isomorphic to ATG_{DSL}, since ATG_{DSL} is covered by $(ATG_{Components}, v_1)$ and $(ATG_{Connections}, v_2)$.

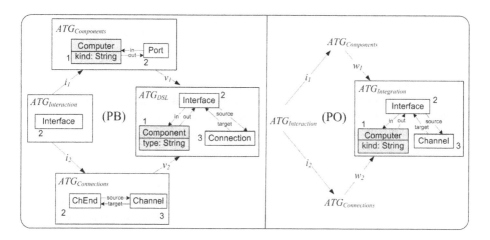

Fig. 2. *Example 2:* Interaction and Integration of two Views on ATG_{DSL}

In order to support stepwise language development, visual languages can be structured hierarchically: one attributed type graph ATG may specify the abstract concepts a set of visual languages VL_i have in common, and different type graphs ATG_i for these visual languages refine the types in ATG by specifying multiple concrete subtypes for them. The type hierarchy relation is formalized by GATG-morphisms h_i from ATG_i to ATG. The morphism $h : ATG_{Network} \rightarrow ATG_{DSL}$ depicted in Fig. 1 is such a type hierarchy morphism. The next step is to define the restriction of views along type hierarchies by pullbacks.

Definition 7 (Type hierarchy and restriction of views). *A* type hierarchy *of visual languages VL and VL' given by attributed type graphs ATG and ATG', respectively, is a GATG-morphism $h : ATG' \rightarrow ATG$.*

Given a type hierarchy morphism $h : ATG' \to$ ATG and a view (ATG_1, v_1) over ATG then the restriction (ATG'_1, v'_1) of this view along h is defined by the pullback (1) in **GAGraphs**.

The restriction (ATG'_1, v'_1) is a view over ATG' because pullbacks preserve injectivity.

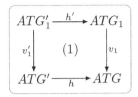

Fact 2 (Hierarchy and covering views). *Given a hierarchy morphism* $h : ATG' \to ATG$ *and views* (ATG_i, v_i) *for* $i = 1, 2$ *covering* ATG, *then the restrictions* (ATG'_i, v'_i) *along* h *are covering* ATG'.

Proof. In the diagram to the right, v_1 and v_2 being jointly surjective implies that also v'_1 and v'_2 are jointly surjective because (1) and (2) are componentwise pullbacks.

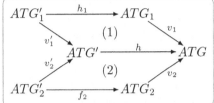

Example 3 (Hierarchy and covering views). The morphism $h : ATG_{Network} \to ATG_{DSL}$ in Fig. 1 is a type hierarchy morphism. Moreover, we have two views $(ATG_{Components}, v_1)$ and $(ATG_{Connections}, v_2)$ on ATG_{DSL}, shown in Fig. 2, which are covering ATG_{DSL}. Fig. 3 shows the restrictions v'_1 and v'_2 of the views along the hierarchy morphism h which are covering $ATG_{Network}$ due to Fact 2.

4 Models and View-Models of Visual Languages

In this section we study models of visual languages and of views of visual languages, called view-models, and we present our main result on the integration and decomposition of models.

Definition 8 (Model). *Given a meta-model of a visual language* VL *by an attributed type graph* ATG, *then a* model *of* VL *is a typed attributed graph* AG, *typed over* ATG *with a GAG-morphism* $t : AG \to ATG$.

The model (AG, t) *is called* signature-conform *if* t *is signature-preserving.*

Similar to the restriction of views at the type level we now define the restriction of models at the model level.

Definition 9 (Restriction). *Given a view* $f : ATG_1 \to ATG$, *i.e. an injective GATG-morphism, and an* ATG-*model* (AG, t) *then the* restriction (AG_1, t_1) *of* (AG, t) *to the view* (ATG_1, f) *is defined by the pullback (1), written* $f^<(AG, t) = (AG_1, t_1)$.

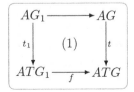

The construction $f^<(AG, t)$ is called backward typing and can be extended to a functor $f^<(AG, t) : \mathbf{GAGraphs_{ATG}} \to \mathbf{GAGraphs_{ATG_1}}$, as opposed to the extension of view models defined by forward typing $f^>(AG_1, t_1) = (AG_1, f \circ t_1)$.

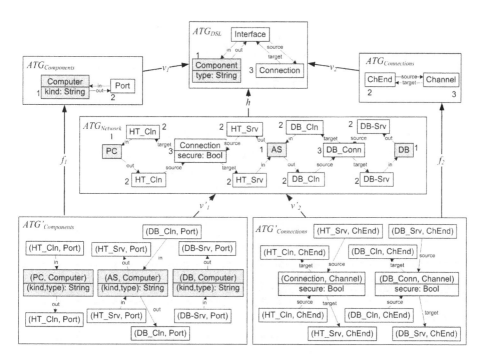

Fig. 3. *Example 3:* Restriction of two Views along Hierarchy Morphism h

In order to state the main result on integration and decomposition of models, we have to define the notions of consistency and integration for models. Roughly, models AG_1 and AG_2 of type ATG_1 and ATG_2, respectively, are consistent if they agree on the interaction type ATG_0. In this case, there is an integrated model AG such that the restrictions of AG to ATG_1 and to ATG_2 are equal to the given models AG_1 and AG_2, respectively.

Definition 10 (Consistency and integration). *Given views (ATG_i, v_i) for $i = 1, 2$ of ATG with interaction (ATG_0, i_1, i_2) defined by the pullback in the bottom face of the following cube, then the models (AG_i, t_i) of the views (ATG_i, v_i) are called* consistent *if there is a model (AG_0, t_0)*

of ATG_0 such that the back faces are pullbacks, i.e. $i_1^<(AG_1, t_1) = (AG_0, t_0) = i_2^<(AG_2, t_2)$.

A model (AG, t) of ATG is called integration *(or amalgamation) of consistent (AG_1, t_1) and (AG_2, t_2) via (AG_0, t_0) if the front faces of the above cube are pullbacks, i.e.*

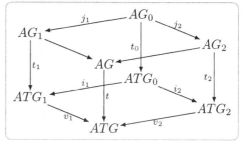

$v_1^<(AG, t) = (AG_1, t_1)$ *and* $v_2^<(AG, t) = (AG_2, t_2)$, *and the top face commutes.*

Example 4 (Inconsistent models). Consider the view models AG_1 and AG_2 in Fig. 4. These models are inconsistent since the squares (1) and (2) are pullbacks corresponding to the back squares of the cube in Def. 10, but the resulting pullback objects AG_0 and AG'_0 are different (and non-isomorphic), so we have $i_1^<(AG_1, t_1) = (AG_0, t_0) \neq i_2^<(AG_2, t_2) = (AG'_0, t'_0)$. In this case, there is no integration (AG, t) s.t. $v_1^<(AG, t) = (AG_1, t_1)$ and $v_2^<(AG, t) = (AG_2, t_2)$.

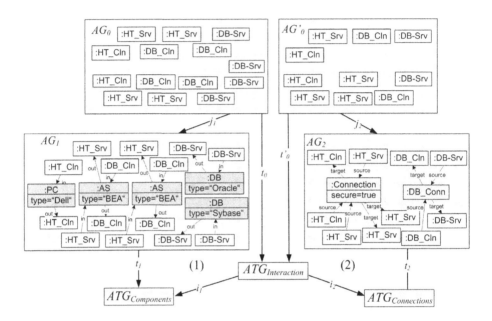

Fig. 4. *Example 4:* Inconsistent View Models

Theorem 1 (Integration and decomposition of models). *Let ATG be covered by the views (ATG_i, v_i) for $i = 1, 2$.*

Integration. *If (AG_i, t_i) are consistent models of (ATG_i, v_i) via (AG_0, t_0) then there is up to isomorphism a unique integration (AG, t) of (AG_i, t_i) via (AG_0, t_0).*

Decomposition. *Vice versa, each model (AG, t) of ATG can be decomposed uniquely up to isomorphism into view-models (AG_i, t_i) with $i = 1, 2$ such that (AG, t) is the integration of (AG_1, t_1) and (AG_2, t_2) via (AG_0, t_0).*

Bijective Correspondence. *Integration and decomposition are inverse to each other up to isomorphism.*

Proof
Integration. Since ATG is covered by (ATG_i, v_i) for $i = 1, 2$ it is also the integration of these views by Fact 1. This means that the bottom pullback is already a pushout in **GAGraphs** with injective and persistent morphisms. Now assume that (AG_i, t_i) with $i = 1, 2$ are consistent models. This means that the back

faces of the cube in Def. 10 are pullbacks with injective and persistent j_1 and j_2. This allows to construct AG in the top face as pushout in **GAGraphs** leading to a unique t such that the front faces commute. According to a suitable van Kampen property (see [7]), the front faces are pullbacks such that (AG, t) is the integration of (AG_i, t_i) for $i = 1, 2$ via (AG_0, t_0). In order to show the uniqueness let also $(AG', t' : AG' \rightarrow ATG)$ be an integration of (AG_i, t_i) for $i = 1, 2$ via (AG_0, t_0). Then the front faces are pullbacks with (AG', t') and the top face commutes. Now the van Kampen property in the opposite direction implies that the top face is a pushout in **GAGraphs**. This implies that (AG, t) and (AG', t') are equal up to isomorphism.

Decomposition. Vice versa, given a model (AG, t) of ATG we construct the front and one of the back faces as pullbacks such that the remaining back face also becomes a pullback and the top face commutes. This shows that (AG_1, t_1) and (AG_2, t_2) are consistent w.r.t (AG_0, t_0), and, similar to the previous step, (AG, t) is the integration of both via (AG_0, t_0). The decomposition is unique up to isomorphism because the pullbacks in the front faces are unique up to isomorphism.

Bijective Correspondence. Uniqueness of integration and decomposition as shown above implies that both constructions are inverse to each other up to isomorphism.

Example 5 (Integration and decomposition of models). The graph $G_{Network}$ from Fig. 1 is a model, typed over $ATG_{Network}$. From the two views $ATG'_{Components}$ and $ATG'_{Connections}$ given in Fig. 3 we can construct two consistent view models $G_{Components}$ and $G_{Connections}$ in Fig. 5 according to the *Decomposition* in Thm. 1 such that $G_{Network}$ is the integration of $G_{Components}$ and $G_{Connections}$ via $G_{interaction}$. Vice versa, starting with consistent models $G_{Components}$ and $G_{Connections}$, via $G_{interaction}$ we obtain $G_{Network}$ as the integration.

5   Related Work

Viewpoint-oriented software development is well-known in the literature [8, 9, 4], however identifying, expressing, and reasoning about meaningful relationships between view models is hard [10]. Up to now existing formal techniques for visual modeling of views and distributed systems by graph transformation support the definition of non-hierarchical views which require a common fixed data signature [2, 11]. This is in general not adequate for view-oriented modeling where only parts of the complete type graph and signature are known and necessary when modeling a view of the system. Moreover, hierarchical relations between views could not be defined on the typing and data type level resulting in a lack of composition and decomposition techniques for view integration, verification, and analysis.

In [12] domain specific languages are defined using graphical and textual views based on the meta-modeling approach used in the $AToM^3$ tool. In this approach the language designer starts with the common (integrated) meta-model and selects parts of the meta-model as different diagram views. So a common abstract meta-model is missing allowing to define hierarchical relations between the models.

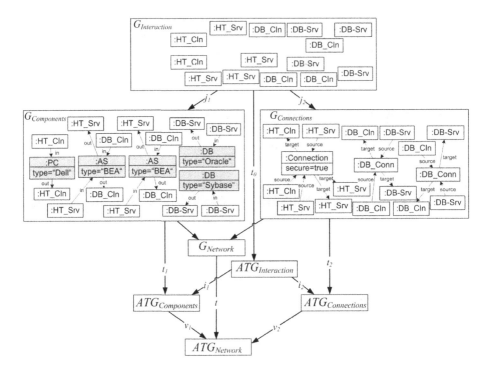

Fig. 5. *Example 5:* Integration and Decomposition of View Models

In [13] abstract graph views are defined, abstracting from specification details allowing a convenient usage of modules. To fulfill this purpose, reference relations have been introduced for the definition of mapping between view elements and abstract model elements (e.g. the database). Given this relations, there are different semantics for modifying view objects which are not studied yet in full detail. In comparison with the presented approach, generalized attributed graph morphisms have a unique formal semantics on the one hand and they provide the flexibility to define hierarchical relations on the other hand.

As a related approach *xlinkit* [14] provides rule-based link generation in web content management systems. In this approach semantics are defined using first order logic allowing automatic link generation to manage large document repositories. According to its purpose, this approach is limited to XML documents using XPath and XLink and thus requires an XML based storage format for models.

6   Conclusion

In this paper we have studied the interaction and integration of views and the restriction of views along type hierarchies. The main result shows under which condition models of these views can be composed to a unique integrated model.

The condition is called *consistency* of view models which means roughly that the models agree on the interaction type of the views. Vice versa, each model can be decomposed up to isomorphism into consistent models of given views. The paper is based on an extended version of typed attributed graph morphisms which allow changes of the type graph including those of data signatures and domains. In this paper we have considered visual languages based on meta-models given by attributed type graphs without constraints. But we claim that most of the results in this paper can be extended to visual languages including constraints and/or generating grammars. Together with full proofs of all technical lemmas used in this paper, some of the extended results are given in our technical report [7].

An important consequence of our work is that we provide the ability to rapidly compose "small" visual languages both at the view (type graph) level and at the view-model level, thus laying the formal basis for multi-view modeling environments. Hence, rather than a "one modeling language does all" approach, we favor a confederation of small, relatively orthogonal visual languages for different system aspects. Future work is planned to investigate the interplay of views and models with behaviour, which is related to the field of merging behavioural models [16, 17].

The concept of type hierarchies should allow a language designer to adapt language definitions by performing model transformations at an abstract hierarchy level and "inheriting" the transformation results at the more concrete levels of the hierarchy. Work is in progress to analyze model transformations for hierarchically structured visual languages.

References

[1] Object Management Group: Unified Modeling Language: Superstructure – Version 2.0, Revised Final Adopted Specification, ptc/04-10-02 (2004), http://www.omg.org/cgi-bin/doc?ptc/2004-10-02

[2] Ehrig, H., Ehrig, K., Prange, U., Taentzer, G.: Fundamentals of Algebraic Graph Transformation. In: EATCS Monographs in Theor. Comp. Science, Springer, Heidelberg (2006)

[3] Object Management Group: Meta-Object Facility (MOF), Version 1.4 (2005), http://www.omg.org/technology/documents/formal/mof.htm

[4] Engels, G., Ehrig, H., Heckel, R., Taentzer, G.: A combined reference model- and view-based approach to system specification. Int. Journal of Software and Knowledge Engineering 7(4), 457–477 (1997)

[5] Braatz, B., Brandt, C., Engel, T., Hermann, F., Ehrig, H.: An approach using formally well-founded domain languages for secure coarse-grained IT system modelling in a real-world banking scenario. In: Proc. 18th Australasian Conference on Information Systems (2007)

[6] Arbab, F.: Reo: A channel-based coordination model for component composition. Mathematical Structures in Computer Science 14(3), 329–366 (2004)

[7] Ehrig, H., Ehrig, K., Ermel, C., Prange, U.: Generalized typed attributed graph transformation systems based on morphisms changing type graphs and data signatures. Technical report, TU Berlin (2008), http://tfs.cs.tu-berlin.de/publikationen/Papers08/EEEP08a.pdf

[8] Goedicke, M., Enders, B., Meyer, T., Taentzer, G.: ViewPoint-Oriented Software Development: Tool Support for Integrating Multiple Perspectives by Distributed Graph Transformation. In: Schwartzbach, M.I., Graf, S. (eds.) TACAS 2000. LNCS, vol. 1785, pp. 43–47. Springer, Heidelberg (2000)

[9] Goedicke, M., Meyer, T., Taentzer, G.: ViewPoint-oriented Software Development by Distributed Graph Transformation: Towards a Basis for Living with Inconsistencies. In: Proc. 4th IEEE Int. Symposium on Requirements Engineering, IEEE Computer Society, Los Alamitos (1999)

[10] Nuseibeh, B., Finkelstein, A., Kramer, J.: ViewPoints: Meaningful Relationships are difficult. In: Proc. Int. Conf. on Software Engineering (ICSE 2003), IEEE Computer Society, Los Alamitos (2003)

[11] Guerra, E., Diaz, P., de Lara, J.: A Formal Approach to the Generation of Visual Language Environments Supporting Multiple Views. In: Proc. IEEE Symposium on Visual Languages and Human-Centric Computing (VL/HCC 205), IEEE Computer Society, Los Alamitos (2005)

[12] Andrés, F.P., de Lara, J., Guerra, E.: Domain Specific Languages with Graphical and Textual Views. In: Proc. Third Int. Symposium of Application of Graph Transformation with Industrial Relevance (AGTIVE 2007). LNCS, pp. 79–94. Springer, Heidelberg (to appear)

[13] Ranger, U., Gruber, K., M., H.: Defining Abstract Graph Views as Module Interfaces. In: Proc. Third Int. Symposium of Application of Graph Transformation with Industrial Relevance (AGTIVE 2007). LNCS, pp. 117–133. Springer, Heidelberg (to appear)

[14] Nentwich, C., Capra, L., Emmerich, W., Finkelstein, A.: xlinkit: A Consistency Checking and Smart Link Generation Service. In: of Computer Science, D., ed.: University College London (2007)

[15] Ehrig, H., Mahr, B.: Fundamentals of Algebraic Specification 1: Equations and Initial Semantics. In: EATCS Monographs on Theoretical Computer Science, vol. 6, Springer, Heidelberg (1985)

[16] Brunet, G., Chechik, M., Easterbrook, S., Nejati, S., Niu, N., Sabetzadeh, M.: A Manifesto for Model Merging. In: Proc. of the Int. Workshop on Global Integrated Model Management (GaMMa 2006), pp. 5–12. ACM Press, New York (2006)

[17] Uchitel, S., Chechik, M.: Merging Partial Behavioural Models. In: Proc. of the 12th Int.ACM SIGSOFT Symposium on Foundations of Software Engineering, pp. 43–52. ACM Press, New York (2004)

Translating Model Simulators
to Analysis Models

Juan de Lara[1] and Hans Vangheluwe[2]

[1] Polytechnic School, Universidad Autónoma (Madrid, Spain)
jdelara@uam.es
[2] School of Computer Science, McGill University (Montréal, Canada)
hv@cs.mcgill.ca

Abstract. We present a novel approach for the automatic generation of model-to-model transformations given a description of the operational semantics of the source language by means of graph transformation rules. The approach is geared to the generation of transformations from Domain-Specific Visual Languages (DSVLs) into semantic domains with an explicit notion of transition, like for example Petri nets. The generated transformation is expressed in the form of operational triple graph grammar rules that transform the static information (initial model) and the dynamics (source rules and their execution control structure). We illustrate these techniques with a DSVL in the domain of production systems, for which we generate a transformation into Petri nets.

1 Introduction

Domain-Specific Visual Languages (DSVLs) are becoming increasingly popular in order to facilitate modelling in specialized application areas. Their use in software engineering is promoted by recent development paradigms such as Model Driven Development (MDD). Using DSVLs, designers are provided with high-level intuitive notations which allow building models with concepts of the domain and not of the solution space or target platform (often a low-level programming language). This makes the construction process easier, having the potential to increase quality and productivity.

Usually, the DSVL is specified by means of a meta-model with the abstract syntax concepts. Additionally, the concrete syntax can be given by assigning visual representations to the different elements in the meta-model. For the semantics, several possibilities are available. For example, it is possible to specify semantics by using visual rules [4,8], which describe the pre-conditions for a certain action to be triggered, as well as the effects of such action. The pre- and post- conditions are given visually as models that use the concrete syntax of the DSVL. This technique has the advantage of being intuitive, as it uses concepts of the domain for describing the rules, thus facilitating the specification of simulators for the given DSVL.

Graph transformation [3] is one such rule-based technique. One of the most commonly used formalizations of graph transformation is based on category

J. Fiadeiro and P. Inverardi (Eds.): FASE 2008, LNCS 4961, pp. 77–92, 2008.
© Springer-Verlag Berlin Heidelberg 2008

theory [4] and supports a number of interesting analysis techniques, such as detecting rule dependencies [1,4,7]. However, graph transformation lacks advanced analysis capabilities that have been developed for other formalisms for expressing semantics, such as Place/Transition Petri nets (P/T nets) [14]. In this case, the high-power analysis is thanks to the fact that P/T nets are less expressive than graph transformation.

To address the lack of analysis capabilities, another common technique for expressing the semantics of a DSVL is to specify a mapping from the source DSVL into a semantic domain [7,8] and then back-annotate the analysis results to the source notation. This possibility allows one to use the techniques specific to the semantic domain for analysing the source models. However, this approach is sometimes complicated and requires from the DSVL designer deep knowledge of the target language in order to specify the transformation.

To reap the benefits of both approaches, we have developed a technique for deriving a transformation from the source DSVL into a semantic domain, starting from a rule-based specification of the DSVL semantics using graph transformation [3]. Such a specification uses domain-specific concepts only and is hence domain specific in its own right. In addition, such behavioural specification may include control structures for rule execution (such as layers [1] or priorities [8]). The main idea is to automatically generate triple graph grammar (TGG) rules [15] to first transform the static information (i.e., the initial model) and then the dynamics (i.e., the rules expressing the behaviour and the rule control structure). We exemplify this technique by using P/T nets as the target language, but other formalisms with an explicit representation of a "simulation step" or transition (such as Constraint Multiset Grammars [12] and process algebras) could also be used. This explicit representation of a transition allows encoding the rule dynamics in the target model by creating a transition for each possible execution (i.e., match) of the original rule.

Paper organization. Section 2 presents the rule-based approach for specification of behaviour by means of a DSVL for production systems. Section 3 shows how the initial model (i.e., the static information) is transformed. Section 4 presents the approach for translating the rules and the control structure. Section 5 gives an overview of the algorithms for the generation of the TGG rules. Section 6 presents related research and finally, Section 7 ends with the conclusions. Due to space limitation we keep the discussion at an informal level, omitting a theoretical presentation of the concepts when possible. A short, preliminary version of some parts of this work appeared as a technical report [16].

2   Rule-Based Specification of Operational Semantics

In this section we provide a description of a DSVL for production systems using meta-modelling, and its operational semantics using graph transformation. The top of Fig. 1 shows a meta-model for the example language. It contains different kinds of machines (all concrete subclasses of Machine), which can be connected through conveyors. Human operators are needed to operate the

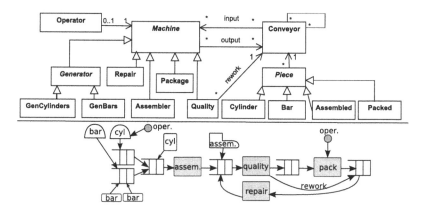

Fig. 1. Meta-Model for the Example Language (up). Example Model (down).

machines, which consume and produce different types of pieces from/to conveyors. These machines can be connected.

The bottom of Fig. 1 shows a production model example using a visual concrete syntax. It contains six machines (one of each type), two operators, six conveyors and four pieces. Machines are represented as boxes, except generators, which are depicted as semi-circles with the kind of piece they generate inside. Operators are shown as circles, conveyors as lattice boxes, and each kind of piece has its own shape. In the model, the two operators are currently operating a generator of cylindrical pieces and a packaging machine respectively.

Fig. 2 shows some of the graph transformation rules that describe the DSVL's operational semantics. Rule "assemble" specifies the behaviour of an assembler machine, which converts one cylinder and a bar into an assembled piece. The rule can be applied if every specified element (except those marked as "{new}") can be found in the model. When such an occurrence is found, then the elements marked as "{del}" are deleted, and the elements marked as "{new}" are created. Note that even if we depict rules using this compact notation, we use the Double Pushout (DPO) formalization [4] in our graph transformation rules. In practice, this means that a rule cannot be applied if it deletes a node but not all its adjacent edges. In addition, we consider only injective matches.

Rule "move" describes the movement of pieces through conveyors. The rule has a negative application condition (NAC) that forbids the movement of the piece if the source conveyor is also connected to any kind of machine having an operator. In this case we use *abstract objects* in rules (i.e., piece and machine are abstract classes). Of course, no object with an abstract typing can be found in the models, but the abstract object in the rule can get instantiated to objects of any concrete subclass [9]. In this way, rules become much more compact. The rule in the example is equivalent to 24 concrete rules, resulting from the substitution of *piece* and *machine* by their children concrete classes.

Finally, rule "change" models the fact that an operator may move from one machine (of any kind) to another one when the target machine is unattended and it has at least one incoming piece (of any kind). The NAC forbids its application if the target machine is already being controlled by an operator. This rule is also abstract and equivalent to 144 concrete rules. Additional rules, not shown in the paper, model the behaviour of the other machine types.

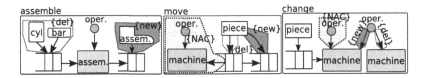

Fig. 2. Some Rules for the Production Systems DSVL

By default, graph grammars use a non-deterministic execution model. In this way, in order to perform a *direct derivation* (i.e., a simulation step), a rule is chosen at random, and is applied if its pre-condition holds in some area of the model. This is a second source of non-determinism, as a rule may be applicable in different parts of the model, and then one match is chosen at random. The grammar execution ends when no more rules are applicable. Different rule control structures can be imposed on grammars to reduce the first source of non-determinism, and to make them more usable for practical applications. We present two of them (layers and priorities) later in Section 4.1.

As the example has shown, graph transformation is an intuitive means to describe the operational semantics of a DSVL. Its analysis techniques are limited however, as is for example difficult to determine termination and confluence (which for the general case are non-decidable), state reachability, reversibility, conservation and invariants. For these purposes, the next sections show how to automatically obtain a transformation into P/T nets starting from the previous rule-based specification (with rules using the DSVL syntax).

3   Transforming the Static Information

In this and the next sections, we explain how, starting from the previous definition of the DSVL syntax and semantics, a transformation into P/T nets can be automatically derived. We illustrate the techniques by example, the details of the constructions are left to Section 5.

In a first step, the static information of the source model is transformed. For this purpose, the designer has to select the roles that the elements of the source DSVL will play in the target language. This is specified with a *meta-model triple* [6], a structure declaring the allowed relations between two meta-models. A meta-model triple for the example is shown in Fig. 3. The Petri nets metamodel is in the lower component, the meta-model of the source DSVL is placed in the upper component, while the correspondence meta-model in the middle is used to relate elements of both meta-models. The references (dotted arrows) depict the allowed relations for the elements in the other two meta-models. These

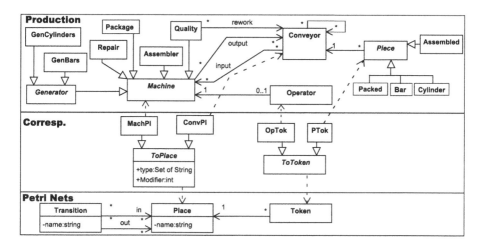

Fig. 3. Meta-Model Triple for the Transformation

references are inherited, thus, for example a "Repair" object can be related to a "Place" object through a mapping object of type "MachPl".

This process of identifying roles for source elements is a kind of *model marking* [13], i.e., annotating the model before the transformation actually takes place. In the example, we state that machines and conveyors play the roles of *places* in Petri nets (i.e., they are holder-like or place-like elements), whereas operators and pieces are *token*-like entities (i.e., they can "move around", being associated with machines and conveyors respectively). For this particular transformation into P/T nets, the meta-model triple provides two standard mappings: *ToPlace* and *ToToken*, which allow relating source elements to places and tokens respectively, by subclassing both classes. As we are translating the *static* information, no element can play the role of a Petri net transition. As the next section will show, the role of Petri net transition is reserved for the dynamic elements in the source specification: the rules modelling the operational semantics.

From this meta-model triple, a number of *operational* TGG rules [15] are generated. These rules manipulate structures (triple models) made of source and target models, and their interrelations. They specify how the target model (a Petri net in our case) should be modified taking into consideration the structure of the source model. Thus, TGG rules manipulate triple models conforming to a meta-model triple (such as the one in Fig. 3).

The TGG rules we automatically generate associate with each place-like entity (in the source language) as many places as different types of token-like entities are connected to it in the meta-model. In the example, class *Machine* (place-like) is connected to class *Operator*, a token-like entity. Thus, we have to create one place for each machine in the model. Conveyors are also place-like, and are connected to pieces (token-like). Thus, we have to create four different places for each conveyor (to store each different kind of piece). This is necessary as tokens are indistinguishable in P/T nets. Distinguishing them is done by placing them in distinct places. We give additional details of this construction in Section 5. Here we only give some insight through examples.

Fig. 4 shows some of the resulting TGG rules. Rule "add 1-Op-Machine" associates a place to each machine in the source model (because operators can be connected to machines). The place in the target model, together with the mapping to the source element is marked as *new* (so it is created), and also as *NAC*, so that it is created only once for each source machine. Attribute "type" of the mapping object stores the type (and all supertypes) of the token-like entity associated with the place. Rule "init 1-Op-Machine" creates the initial marking of the places associated to machines. It adds one token in the place associated to each machine for every operator connected to it. We represent tokens as black dots connected to places. Rule "add 1-Cyl-Conv" associates one place (of type "cylinder") to every conveyor in the source model. Similar rules associate additional places for each concrete type of piece in the source meta-model.

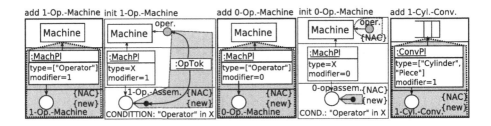

Fig. 4. Some TGG Rules for Transforming the Model

In addition, as the number of operators in each machine is bounded (there is a "0..1" cardinality in the source meta-model), an additional place (which we call *zero-testing* place) is associated to machines to denote the absence of operators in the given machine. This is performed by the automatically generated rule "add 0-Op-Machine". Distinguishing between normal places and zero-testing ones is done through the *modifier* attribute of the mapping object. The initialization of the zero-testing place for operators is done by rule "init 0-Op-Machine", which adds a token in the place if no operator is connected to the machine. We use this kind of places to test negative conditions on token-like entities (e.g., NACs as well as non-applicability of rules). We cannot generate such kinds of places for conveyors, as the number of pieces that can be stored in a conveyor is not bounded. This restricts the kind of negative tests that can be done for conveyors. The zero-testing places are not needed if the target language has built-in primitives for this kind of testing, like Petri nets with inhibitor arcs [14]. These kinds of nets, though more expressive, have fewer analysis capabilities. Reachability for example is not decidable in a net with at least two inhibitor arcs.

Applying the generated rules to the source model in Fig. 1, the Petri net in Fig. 5 is obtained (we do not show the mappings to the source model for simplicity, but tag each group of places with the type of the source holder-like element). The next section shows how the translation of the dynamics is performed.

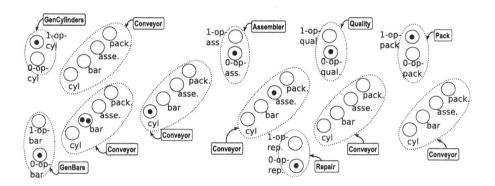

Fig. 5. First Step in the Transformation

4 Transforming the Dynamic Behaviour

In order to translate the rules implementing the operational semantics (shown in Fig. 2) into the target language, a number of additional TGG rules are needed. These rules "embed" each operational rule in the target language, in each possible way (i.e., for each possible match of the original rules in the initial model). Thus, in our case, we make explicit in the Petri net (by means of transitions) all allowed movement of token-like entities: pieces and operators. This reflects the fact that rules for the movement of pieces and operators in the source language can be applied non-deterministically at each possible occurrence.

Fig. 6 shows some of the generated rules. Rule "create assemble" is generated from rule "assemble" in Fig. 2. It creates a Petri net transition that takes two pieces (a cylinder and a bar), checks that an operator is present, and then generates an assembled piece. The triple rule uses the source model to identify all relevant place-like elements in the pre- and post- conditions of the operational rule. This TGG rule will be applied at each possible occurrence of two conveyors connected by an assembler machine, producing a corresponding Petri net transition in the target model. Thus, we are identifying a priori (by adding Petri net transitions) all possible instantiations of the rules implementing the operational semantics. This can be done because the TGG rules contain as pre-conditions the place-like entities present in the pre-conditions of the original rules.

Rule "create change" is generated from rule "change" in Fig. 2, and adds a Petri net transition to model the movement of operators between any two machines. The NAC in rule "change" has been translated by using the zero-testing place associated with the target machine (to ensure that it is currently unattended). Note, however, that the original rule "change" cannot have NACs involving pieces, as we may have an unbounded number of them in conveyors. Moreover, we allow an arbitrary number of NACs in the original rules, but each one of them is restricted to have at most one token-like element, as otherwise we cannot test such condition in the Petri net in one step.

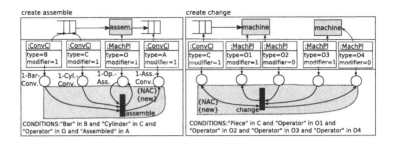

Fig. 6. Some TGG Rules for Translating the Operational Rules

Fig. 7 shows the rules generated from rule "move" in Fig. 2. Note that the original rule has a NAC involving both token-like and place-like entities. TGG rule "create move-1" assumes that the place-like entities exist, and therefore the token-like entities must not exist. The latter condition is tested by means of the zero-testing place. TGG rule "create move-2" assumes that the place-like entities do not exist. As can be seen in the rules, the handling of abstract objects in the original rule depends on their role. On the one hand, the abstract place-like entites are copied in the TGG rule (e.g., machine in the rule). On the other hand, abstract token-like elements (e.g., piece element in the rule) are handled by the attribute "type" of the mapping object (this also ocurred in rule *change*).

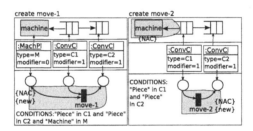

Fig. 7. Additional TGG Rules for Translating the Operational Rules

Fig. 8 shows the result of applying the generated triple rules to the model in Fig. 5. It is only partially shown for clarity, as many other transitions are generated. In particular, we show only two applications of rule "change" to move an operator to another machine: from the assembler machine to quality checking the availability of an assembled piece (transition labelled *a2q-ass*) and from quality to package seeking an assembled piece (transition labelled *q2p-ass*). The full transformation generates transitions to move the operators between all combinations of machines and types of pieces. Transitions "c2b" and "b2c" are generated by a specialized rule "change generator" (not shown) applicable to generator machines (which do not need an incoming conveyor). Again, the mappings from the Petri net places to the original model are omitted.

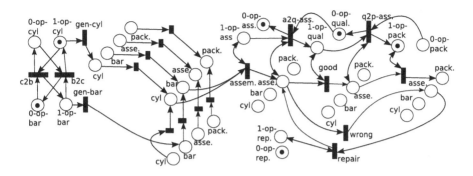

Fig. 8. Second Step in the Transformation (Some Transitions Omitted for Clarity)

4.1 Transforming the Rules Execution Control

Up to now, we have not assumed any control structure for rule execution. That is, rules are tried at random, and the execution finishes when no more rule are applicable. With this control scheme, no further transformations are needed, and in the example, the resulting Petri net is the one in Fig. 8. However, it is also possible to translate rule control structures. For example, one can assign priorities to rules [8], such that rules with higher priorities are executed first. If more than one rule has the same priority, one is executed at random. Each time a rule is executed, the control goes back to the highest priority. When no rule in a given priority can be executed, the control goes to the next lower priority. The execution ends when none of the rules with the lowest priority can be executed.

This execution policy can be embedded in the resulting Petri net as well, and we illustrate the translation with the scheme shown in Fig. 9. The figure assumes two rules ($r1$ and $r2$) with the highest priority (priority one). These transitions, in addition, would be connected to the pre- and post- condition places, resulting from the previous step in the transformation. The idea is that in priority 1, modelled by the $prio-1$ place, rules $r1$ and $r2$ are tried. Both cannot be executed, because place $p1+$ makes them mutually exclusive. Transitions $\neg r1$ and $\neg r2$ are constructed from the operational rule specifications in such a way that they can be fired whenever $r1$ and $r2$ cannot be fired, respectively (details are shown later). Thus, if both $\neg r1$ and $\neg r2$ are fired, the control goes to the next priority (as this means that $r1$ nor $r2$ can be executed). If either $r1$ or $r2$ can be fired, then the control remains in priority one. The transitions that move the priority take care of removing the intermediate tokens from $r1$, $r2$, $\neg r1ex$ and $\neg r2ex$. Of course, a rule for the original DSVL can be transformed into many Petri net transitions, one for each possible match. The resulting transitions are given the same priority as the original rule.

Thus, an important issue in this transformation is that we need to check when rules are not applicable (as transitions $\neg r1$ and $\neg r2$ did in the previous figure). This in general is possible only if the places associated with the rule are bounded. Thus, in the case of the example of previous sections, we cannot test whether

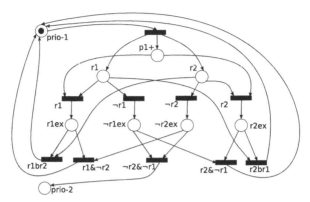

Fig. 9. Scheme for Transforming a Control Structure Based on Priorities

rules "assemble", "move" or "change" cannot be fired, since the number of pieces in conveyors is not bounded.

Fig. 10 shows examples of the construction of the transitions for testing non-executability of a rule. Rule "rest" deletes an operator, while rule "work" models the creation of a new operator in an unattended machine. Triple rule "create ¬rest" generates a Petri net transition that tests if the machine is not attended. If this is the case, transition "¬rest" can fire, which means that "rest" cannot (i.e., the rule cannot be applied at that match). Note that the "¬rest" transition makes use of the zero-testing place. TGG rule "create ¬work" creates a transition that can fire when the machine has an operator, and therefore rule "work" cannot be fired. The generated transitions can only by fired if the original rule cannot, and the firing does not produce any other effect.

Note that these kinds of TGG rules cannot be generated if the original rule has more than one NAC involving token-like elements, or a NAC and a pre-condition, both containing token-like elements, or a pre-condition with more than one token-like element. The reason is that in these cases we cannot test the non-executability of the rules in just one step, we need more than one transition. This is feasible using several transition firings, but a more sophisticated scheme than the one in Fig. 9 is needed, which we leave for future work.

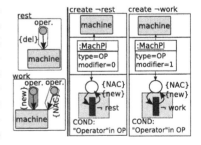

Fig. 10. Generation of Rules for Testing Non-Applicability

Typical control structures in graph transformation, such as layers, can be transformed in a similar way as priorities. For layers, the only difference is that when a rule in a layer is executed, the control remains in the current layer and does not go back to the first layer. Note that the transformation of the control structure can be kept independent of the two previous transformation steps. We are thus in effect *weaving* two transformations.

5   Algorithms for the Construction of the TGG Rules

This section gives the details for the construction of the TGG rules.

TGG Rules for the Static Information. In order to construct the TGG rules to transform the static information (like those in Fig. 4), we first explicitly copy the reference edges through the inheritance hierarchies in the meta-model triple. Thus, in the meta-model triple of Fig. 3, we add references from "MachPl" to each subclass of "Machine", from "PTok" to each subclass of "Piece", from "Place" to each subclass of "ToPlace" and from "Token" to each subclass of "To-Token". A similar closure is performed for the normal associations in the upper part of the meta-model triple (the meta-model corresponding to the DSVL).

Fig. ?? shows the approach for the generation of two of the TGG rules. We seek all possible instantiations (injective matches) of the pattern to the left in the meta-model triple (where node Z depicts a concrete class), and we generate the two rules to the right for each occurrence. The first rule adds one place for each instance of each place-like entity in the meta-model. Function *supers* returns all the superclasses of a given class. The second rule sets the initial marking of the place related to each place-like instance connected with a token-like instance. The condition checks that the name of the type of the token-like entity is included in attribute "type". For simplicity, we do not use the abstract syntax of class diagrams in the meta-model triple.

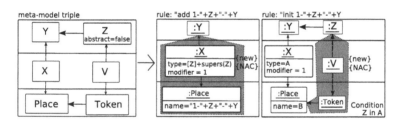

Fig. 11. Constructing the Rules for Translating the Static Information

Additional rules (similar to "add 0-op-machine" and "init 0-op-machine" in Fig. 4) are constructed for creating a zero-testing place for the bounded token-like entities. The pattern is similar to the one in the figure, but looks for a "0..1" multiplicity in the association connecting the token-like entity to the place-like entity (to the side of the latter).

TGG Rules for the Dynamic Behaviour. In addition, a TGG rule is constructed for each rule of the source DSVL. As stated before, we consider rules with an arbitrary number of NACs, but each with at most one token-like element. The construction algorithm proceeds as follows:

1. Initialize the upper part (i.e., corresponding to the source DSVL) of the TGG rule with all the place-like elements (and the connections between them) of the source DSVL rule that are tagged *NAC*, *del* or untagged. Fig. 12 shows this first step for rule "work" (shown in Fig. 10).

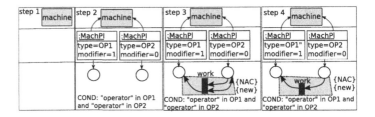

Fig. 12. Steps for Deriving the TGG rule from Rule "work"

2. For each element in the upper part of the TGG rule which was associated with a token-like element in the original rule (with tags *new*, *del* or untagged), add a mapping and a place in the middle and lower sections. Add an attribute condition stating that the type of the token-like entity is included in attribute "type" of the corresponding mapping object. If the token-like entity is bounded, or was marked as "NAC", then add an additional mapping identifying the associated zero-testing place. Do not add a mapping twice to the same place. In Fig. 12 we do not add place "1-op-machine" or the mapping twice, even when the operator appears twice in the original rule (tagged *new* and *NAC*).

3. Add a Petri net transition in the lower part of the TGG rule. Connect it to each place added due to a token-like entity marked as *new* in the original rule. Conversely, connect each place added due to a token-like element marked as *del* in the original rule to the transition. Connect the transition with a loop to each zero-testing place coming from a token-like element tagged *NAC* in the original rule. Moreover, for each connection starting or departing from the place associated with a bounded element, add the reverse connection to the associated zero-testing place. Add a loop to the transition for each place added due to an untagged token-like entity in the original rule.

   Tag the Petri net transition and the created connections in the TGG rule as *new* and *NAC*. In Fig. 12, we create a connection to place "1-op-machine" as the operator is tagged *new*. We create a loop to the zero-testing place, as the operator is marked *NAC*. Finally, we add the connection from the zero-testing place because the operator is bounded, and we added the reverse edge to the other place.

4. Simplify connections to/from the Petri net transition to zero-testing places. An incoming edge can be cancelled with an outgoing one. If a loop remains, it can be eliminated only if the place is related to a token-like element which was not marked *NAC* in the original rule (this is to allow rewriting of token-like entities by a single rule, but to retain the semantics of NACs). In the example we can cancel one outgoing and one incoming edge.

5. NACs of the original rule involving only place-like elements are copied into the TGG rule.

6. If the original rule has NACs involving both place-like and token-like elements, create an additional TGG rule following the previous steps, but

ignoring the token-like elements connected to the place-like elements in the NACs (see rule "create move-2" in Fig. 7).

TGG Rules for Testing Non-Executability. These rules generate transitions that can be fired if the original rule cannot be executed at a certain match. The procedure for their construction is similar to the previous one. The first two steps are the same. In step 3, we neglect each elements tagged *new*. Then, for each element tagged *del* or not marked, we create a self-loop from its associated zero-testing place to the Petri net transition. For each element marked *NAC*, we create a self-loop from its related place to the transition. See the rule in Fig. 10.

6 Discussion and Comparison with Related Work

Many contributions in the field of model-to-model transformation have concentrated on devising high-level means to express them. On the more formal side, we can find the seminal work on TGGs [15], which proposed an algorithm to generate operational rules (deriving for example source-to-target or target-to-source translations) from declarative ones. Recent work tries to provide even higher-level means to express the transformations, for example using *triple patterns* [10] from which operational TGG rules are generated. This is closely related to the notion of "model transformation by example" [17] (where transformation rules are derived starting from a mapping between two meta-models) and transformation models [2] (which express transformations as a MOF model relating source and target elements, and OCL constraints).

However, our work is very different from these, as we express the semantics of the graph grammar rules (which express the operational semantics of the source model) with Petri nets. Petri nets can be seen as a restricted kind of graph grammar, as the token game can be considered as a graph transformation step on discrete graphs. Some work has tried to encode graph transformation rules in Petri nets, and then use the analysis techniques of the latter to investigate the former. For example, in [18] a graph transformation system is abstracted into a Petri net to study termination. However, there are several fundamental differences with our work. First, they only consider rules, while we consider rules and an initial graph. Therefore we are able to consider all possible instantiations (occurrences) of the source rules. Second, they end up with an abstraction of the original semantics, as, when the transformation is done, the topology of the source model is lost (i.e., tokens represent instances of the original types, but their connections are lost). However, the fact that we consider an initial model and that we use TGGs that create mappings to the Petri net model allows us to retain the source model topology, thus the transformation does not lose information (the obtained Petri net perfectly reflects the semantics of the original language). This is thanks to the fact that a Petri net transition is constructed for each possible application of the original rule. Finally, we consider control structures for the rules and abstract rules.

In [5], graph grammars are defined for transforming DSVL models into Petri nets, without explicitly considering the original DSVL rules. Then, the transformations are applied to the DSVL rules themselves, resulting in grammar rules simulating the Petri net. Our approach is different as we translate the DSVL rules into transitions, accurately reflecting the source DSVL semantics.

Note that we cannot translate arbitrary behavioural specifications. The source DSVL and its semantics are constrained by the following:

– The DSVL has to include elements that can be mapped to places and tokens.
– For the case of P/T nets as the target language, rules cannot create or delete place-like entities, as this would change the topology of the target model. We would need reconfigurable Petri nets [11], for example.
– Moving token-like entities (i.e., deleting and creating the edge connecting the token-like entity to the place-like entity instead of deleting and creating the edge and the entity) is possible if the target notation is place/transtion Petri nets (as we have shown when moving the operator). However care should be taken if tokens have distinct identities such as in Coloured Petri nets.
– Token-like entities are usually required to be bounded. If rules have NACs, then all token-like elements in the NAC should be bounded. Boundedness is also necessary if we are translating control structures like layers or priorities.
– NACs may have at most one token-like element. Restrictions w.r.t. the number of NACs (involving token-like elements) a rule may have, and the number of token-like elements in the pre-conditions also apply for generating negative tests. However, rules may have arbitrary NACs involving place-like elements only, as they are translated into NACs for the TGG rules and do not involve checking for tokens at run-time.

7   Conclusions

We have presented a new technique for the automatic generation of transformations into a semantic domain given a rule-based specification of the operational semantics of the source DSVL. The presented technique has the advantage that the language designer has to work mainly with the concepts of the source DSVL, and does not have to provide directly the model-to-model transformation (which can become a complex task) or have deep knowledge of the target notation.

We have illustrated this technique by transforming a production system into a Petri net. The designer has to specify the simulation rules for the source language, and the roles of the source language elements. From this information, TGG rules are generated that perform the transformation. Once the transformation is executed, the Petri net can be simulated or analyzed, for example to check for deadlocks or state reachability. Thus, by using Petri net techniques, we can answer difficult questions about the original operational rules, such as termination or confluence (which for the case of general graph grammars are undecidable).

We are working on tool support for this transformation generation, as well as studying other source and target languages. Moreover, we believe that for P/T nets the roles played by the source DSVL elements can be inferred by analysing the source rules (checking the static and the dynamic elements). It will also be interesting to study how graph grammar analysis techniques are translated into P/T nets and viceversa (e.g., rule conflicts can be analysed by studying transition persistence).

Acknowledgements. Work sponsored by the Spanish Ministry of Science and Education, project MOSAIC (TSI2005-08225-C07-06). We thank the referees for their useful comments.

References

1. AGG, `http://tfs.cs.tu-berlin.de/agg/`
2. Bézivin, J., Büttner, F., Gogolla, M., Jouault, F., Kurtev, I., Lindow, A.: Model Transformations? Transformation Models! In: Nierstrasz, O., Whittle, J., Harel, D., Reggio, G. (eds.) MoDELS 2006. LNCS, vol. 4199, pp. 440–453. Springer, Heidelberg (2006)
3. Ehrig, H., Engels, G., Kreowski, H.-J., Rozenberg, G.: Handbook of Graph Grammars and Computing by Graph Transformation, vol. 1. World Scientific, Singapore (1999)
4. Ehrig, H., Ehrig, K., Prange, U., Taentzer, G.: Fundamentals of Algebraic Graph Transformation. Springer, Heidelberg (2006)
5. Ermel, C., Ehrig, K.: Simulation and Analysis of Reconfigurable Systems. In: Proc. AGTIVE 2007, pp. 261–276 (to appear)
6. Guerra, E., de Lara, J.: Event-Driven Grammars: Relating Abstract and Concrete Levels of Visual Languages. In: SoSyM, vol. 6(3), pp. 317–347. Springer, Heidelberg (2007)
7. Heckel, R., Küster, J.M., Taentzer, G.: Confluence of Typed Attributed Graph Transformation Systems. In: Corradini, A., Ehrig, H., Kreowski, H.-J., Rozenberg, G. (eds.) ICGT 2002. LNCS, vol. 2505, pp. 161–176. Springer, Heidelberg (2002)
8. de Lara, J., Vangheluwe, H.: Defining Visual Notations and Their Manipulation Through Meta-Modelling and Graph Transformation. JVLC 15(3-4), 309–330 (2004)
9. de Lara, J., Bardohl, R., Ehrig, H., Ehrig, K., Prange, U., Taentzer, G.: Attributed graph transformation with node type inheritance. Theor. Comput. Sci. 376(3), 139–163 (2007)
10. de Lara, J., Guerra, E., Bottoni, P.: Triple Patterns: Compact Specifications for the Generation of Operational Triple Graph Grammar Rules. In: Proc. GT-VMT 2007. Electronic Communications of the EASST, vol. 6 (2007)
11. Llorens, M., Oliver, J.: Structural and Dynamic Changes in Concurrent Systems: Reconfigurable Petri Nets. IEEE Trans. Computers 53(9), 1147–1158 (2004)
12. Marriott, K., Meyer, B., Wittenburg, K.: A survey of visual language specification and recognition. In: Theory of Visual Languages, pp. 5–85. Springer, Heidelberg (1998)
13. Mellor, S., Scott, K., Uhl, A., Weise, D.: MDA Distilled: Principles of Model-Driven Architecture. Addison Wesley, Reading (2004)
14. Peterson, J.L.: Petri Net Theory and the Modelling of Systems. Prentice-Hall, Englewood Cliffs (1981)
15. Schürr, A.: Specification of Graph Translators with Triple Graph Grammars. In: Mayr, E.W., Schmidt, G., Tinhofer, G. (eds.) WG 1994. LNCS, vol. 903, pp. 151–163. Springer, Heidelberg (1995)

16. Vangheluwe, H., de Lara, J.: Automatic Generation of Model-to-Model Transformations from Rule-Based Specifications of Operational Semantics. In: DSM 2007 workshop, Tech.Rep Univ. Jyväskilä (2007)
17. Varro, D.: Model Transformation by Example. In: Nierstrasz, O., Whittle, J., Harel, D., Reggio, G. (eds.) MoDELS 2006. LNCS, vol. 4199, pp. 410–424. Springer, Heidelberg (2006)
18. Varro, D., Varro-Gyapay, S., Ehrig, H., Prange, U., Taentzer, G.: Termination Analysis of Model Transformations by Petri Nets. In: Corradini, A., Ehrig, H., Montanari, U., Ribeiro, L., Rozenberg, G. (eds.) ICGT 2006. LNCS, vol. 4178, pp. 260–274. Springer, Heidelberg (2006)

Orthographic Modeling Environment

Colin Atkinson and Dietmar Stoll

Lehrstuhl für Softwaretechnik, University of Mannheim, Germany
{atkinson,stoll}@informatik.uni-mannheim.de

Abstract. The rise in importance of component-based and service-oriented software engineering approaches over the last few years, and the general uptake in model-driven development practices, has created a natural interest in using languages such as the UML to describe component-based systems. However, there is no standard way (de jure or de facto) of using the various viewpoints and diagram types identified in general model-driven development approaches to describe components or assemblies of components. To address this problem, we have developed a prototype IDE which provides a systematic and user-friendly conceptual model for defining and navigating around different views of components and/or component-based systems. This is supported by an infrastructure that allows the IDE to be extended with tools that create views and check consistency in an easy and systematic way, and a unifying metamodel which allows all views to be generated automatically from a single underlying representation of a component or component-based system.

1 Introduction

Over the last few years, two of the most significant trends in software engineering have been the move towards component and service-based ways of constructing software systems [1] and the use of model-based approaches to describe their properties and architecture [2]. This has naturally generated an interest in using the two approaches together. However, there is no standard (de jure or de facto) approach for using the various viewpoints and diagram types identified in general model-driven development approaches (e.g. UML class diagrams, UML state diagrams, UML activity diagrams, constraints etc.) to describe components and services or systems assembled from them.

In practice, therefore, developers today use an ad-hoc collection of views which are only loosely related to one another. This not only creates significant consistency problems, because there are no built-in mechanisms for making sure that the different views are consistent, it also creates significant management and navigation problems, because the mapping between logical components and concrete views has to be remembered by developers in their heads. Moreover, each difTcrent view generator or editor that is integrated into a development environment such as Eclipse has its own storage artifacts, data persistence formats and navigation trees which usually have to be managed and navigated separately.

There are two main challenges that need to be overcome to provide a clean and logically coherent environment for the model-based development of component and

J. Fiadeiro and P. Inverardi (Eds.): FASE 2008, LNCS 4961, pp. 93–96, 2008.
© Springer-Verlag Berlin Heidelberg 2008

service-based systems. The first is to devise a flexible and efficient mechanism by which individual views can be generated on the fly from a single, unified model of the component or system. The second is to provide a single coherent navigation mechanism which allows the appropriate view to be selected and managed as needed. In this paper we provide a brief introduction to the tool that we have been developing to meet these challenges. The underlying conceptual foundation for the approach is provided by the KobrA method for component modeling [3], although the ideas developed are more generally applicable. Moreover, the tool was originally customized to support the generation of workflows using pre-developed components [4], but the approach can be used in any domain.

2 "On the Fly" View Generation

During the development of a component, all kinds of artifacts like UML class diagrams, UML state charts and source code are produced. All represent different views of a component and are usually related to each other. As the number of views increases, navigation becomes more tedious and maintaining consistency between related views becomes increasingly difficult. An ideal solution to this problem would be for every tool of the IDE to work on a single underlying model (SUM) and for changes made to individual views to be synchronized directly with this model. In this way, the consistency between the editors and the model is automatically ensured, as long as each individual change to a view is checked for validity against this model. This "on the fly" generation of views is schematically depicted in Fig 1.

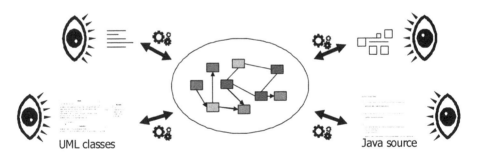

UML classes   Java source

Fig. 1. On the fly generation of views

Our long term goal is to create an implementation of the IDE in which all views are generated on the fly in this way, regardless of their form (graphical or textual) or their level of abstraction (executable code or platform independent model). However, it is obviously impossible to populate the IDE overnight with all the editors and view generators needed to usefully model components. Therefore, as a pragmatic intermediate solution the current version supports a mixture of different "tool-native" formats as well as the single, underlying model.

3   Dimension-Based Navigation

Having the ability to generate views on the fly when needed, and to add new kinds of views by simply adding a new view metamodel and associated generation transformations, provides a powerful foundation for the view-based modeling of components, but it doesn't help define what views are most useful and how they should be managed and navigated around. We address this problem by applying KobrA's notion of organizing views around different, fundamental dimensions of concern. Various dimensions can be considered, but in the current version of the IDE the following dimensions are supported –

Composition: This dimension covers the (de)composition of components into sub-components. Selecting a point along this dimension corresponds to the specification of the component or subcomponent which is currently being worked on, e.g. a Bank component or an AccountManager as a subcomponent.

Abstraction: This dimension addresses the platform independence of a view. In other words, selecting a point on the abstraction dimension identifies the level of detail at which the component is being viewed. There are currently three levels of abstraction: specification, realization and implementation. The most abstract level is the specification which provides a black box view of the component. It describes all externally visible properties of a component and thus serves as its requirements specification. The realization of a component describes the design of the component and provides a white box view of its internal algorithms and subcomponents. The implementation level describes the source code and tests.

Projection: This dimension deals with the types of information contained in a view. The three projections currently available are the structural, functional and behavioral projections. The structural projection includes classes and associations involving the component as well as taxonomical information. Operations of a component and their interaction with other artifacts are modeled in the functional projection by means of operation specifications and interaction diagrams. Finally, the behavioral projection focuses on the sequencing and algorithmic properties of the component as manifest by state charts and activity diagrams.

Other dimensions are possible and can easily be added. For example, to model a family of components according to a product line approach, a variant dimension could be added in which each point defines a particular variant. Alternatively, to support views of realizations of different cross-cutting concerns along the lines of aspect-oriented programming, an aspect dimension could be added in which each point defines a different aspect (and one of them defines the core functionality). Since this approach of defining views according to particular combinations of orthogonal perspectives resembles the way in which orthographic projections of physical objects such as houses or cars are defined and organized, we refer to the approach as orthographic software modeling.

Fig. 2 shows a screenshot of the IDE. This particular picture shows a UML diagram representing the structural projection of the specification of a Bank component. The particular points along each dimension occupied by this view can be seen on the left hand side. These can be selected independently.

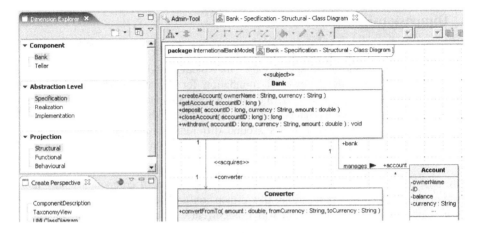

Fig. 2. IDE with the UML class diagram of a bank

4 Conclusion

In this paper we have outlined the key features of our tool for the orthographic modeling of component and service-based systems – an approach based on the metaphor of multiple orthogonal views. The current prototype version is a heterogeneous mix of native tool views and pure views dynamically generated from the single underlying model. We are currently implementing a view generation engine using a transformation language and aim to reduce the number of native tools to zero in the near future.

Acknowledgements. This work was largely performed as part of the AristaFlow project under the support of the State of Baden-Württemberg.

References

[1] Szyperski, C., Gruntz, D., Murer, S.: Component Software - Beyond Object-Oriented Programming? 2nd edn., 608 pages. Addison-Wesley / ACM Press (2002), ISBN 0-201-74572-0

[2] Mukerji, J., Miller, J.: Overview and guide to OMG's architecture (June 2003), http://www.omg.org/cgi-bin/doc?omg/03-06-01

[3] Atkinson, C., Bayer, J., Bunse, C., Kamsties, E., Laitenberger, O., Laqua, R., Muthig, D., Paech, B., Wüst, J., Zettel, J.: Component-Based Product Line Engineering with UML. Addison-Wesley Publishing Company, Reading (2002)

[4] Dadam, P., Reichert, M., Rinderle, S., Atkinson, C.: Auf dem Weg zu prozessorientierten Informationssystemen der nächsten Generation - Herausforderungen und Lösungskonzepte. In: Spath, D., Haasis, K., Klumpp, D. (eds): Aktuelle Trends in der Softwareforschung - Tagungsband zum doIT Software-Forschungstag 2005, June 2005, Schriftenreihe zum doIT Software-Forschungstag, Band 3, MFG Stiftung, pp. 47–67 (2005)

HOL-OCL:
A Formal Proof Environment for UML/OCL

Achim D. Brucker[1] and Burkhart Wolff[2]

[1] SAP Research, Vincenz-Priessnitz-Str. 1, 76131 Karlsruhe, Germany
achim.brucker@sap.com
[2] Information Security, ETH Zurich, 8092 Zurich, Switzerland
bwolff@inf.ethz.ch

Abstract. We present the theorem proving environment HOLOCL that is integrated in a Model-driven Engineering (MDE) framework. HOLOCL allows to reason over UML class models annotated with OCL specifications. Thus, HOLOCL strengthens a crucial part of the UML to an object-oriented formal method. HOLOCL provides several derived proof calculi that allow for formal derivations establishing the validity of UML/OCL formulae. These formulae arise naturally when checking the consistency of class models, when formally refining abstract models to more concrete ones or when discharging side-conditions from model-transformations.

Keywords: HOLOCL, UML, OCL, Formal Method, Theorem Proving.

1 Introduction

The HOLOCL system (http://www.brucker.ch/projects/hol-ocl/) is an interactive proof environment for UML [5] and OCL [4] specifications that we developed as a conservative, shallow embedding into Isabelle/HOL. This construction ensures the consistency of the underlying formal semantics as well as the correctness of the derived calculi. Together with several automated proof-procedures, we provide an effective logical framework supporting object-oriented modeling and reasoning with a particularly clean semantic foundation.

2 The Architecture and Its Components

2.1 Overview

HOLOCL [1, 2] is integrated into a framework [3] supporting a formal, model-driven software engineering process (see Figure 1). Technically, HOLOCL is based on a repository for UML/OCL models, called su4sml, and on Isabelle/HOL; both are written in SML. HOLOCL is based on the SML interface of Isabelle/HOL. Moreover, HOLOCL also reuses and extends the existing Isabelle front-end called Proof General well as the Isabelle documentation generator. Figure 2 gives an overview of the main system components of HOLOCL, namely:

J. Fiadeiro and P. Inverardi (Eds.): FASE 2008, LNCS 4961, pp. 97–100, 2008.
© Springer-Verlag Berlin Heidelberg 2008

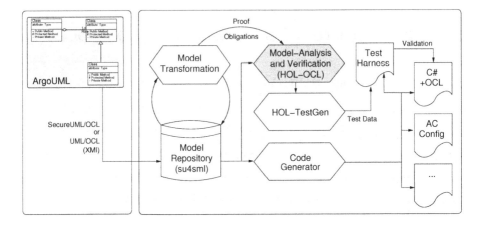

Fig. 1. A Toolchain Supporting a Formal Model-driven Engineering Process

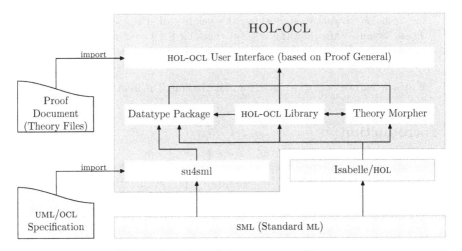

Fig. 2. Overview of the HOLOCL architecture

- the data repository, called su4sml, providing XMI import facilities,
- the datatype package, or *encoder*, which encodes UML/OCL models into HOL; from a user's perspective, it yields a semantic interface to the model,
- the HOLOCL library which provides the core theorems needed for verification and also a formal semantics for the OCL built-in operators, and
- a suite of automated proof procedures based on rewriting and tableaux techniques.

2.2 The Model Repository: su4sml

The model repository *su4sml* [3] provides a data base for syntactic elements of UML core, namely class models and statemachines as well as OCL expressions.

Moreover, su4sml provides an import mechanism based on the XMI, which is a standardized XML file format for UML models. Most CASE tools for UML can export models in XMI.

For class models, su4sml resembles the tree structure given by the containment hierarchy. For example, a class contains attributes, operations, or statemachines. OCL expressions naturally translate into an abstract SML datatype in SML. This abstract datatype is modeled closely following the standard OCL 2.0 metamodel. In addition to these datatype definitions, the repository structure defines a couple of normalization functions, for example for converting association ends into attributes with corresponding type, together with an invariant expressing the cardinality constraint.

2.3   The Encoder: An Object-Oriented Datatype Package

Encoding object-oriented data structures in HOL is a tedious and error-prone activity if done manually. We therefore provided a *datatype package* automating this task. In the theorem prover community, a datatype package is a module that allows one to introduce new datatypes and automatically derive certain properties over them.

Our datatype packages extends the given theory by a HOLOCL-representation of the given UML/OCL model. This is done in an extensible way, i. e., classes can be added to an existing theory while preserving all proven properties. The theory extension comprises the following activities:

1. declaration of HOL types for the classifiers of the model,
2. encoding of type-casts, attribute accessors, and dynamic type and kind tests implicitly declared in the imported data model, and
3. encode the OCL specification (including invariants and operation specifications) and combine it with the core data model.

Overall, the datatype package encodes conservatively the user supplied model and derives the usual algebraic properties on object-oriented structures (up casts followed by down casts are idempotent, casts do not change the dynamic type, etc.; [1, 2] describe the details). The package also provides automatically proofs that the generated HOL model is a faithful representation of object-orientation; for example, inheritance is expressed as inclusion of the sets of objects along the subclass hierarchy of the model. This strategy, i. e., deriving properties of the UML/OCL model from generated conservative definitions in HOL, ensures two very important properties:

1. our encoding fulfills the required properties, otherwise the proofs fail, and
2. doing all definitions conservatively ensures the consistency of our model.

The time spent for all these proof activities during the import is typically below a minute; the approach is therefore feasible in a proof environment.

2.4 The Library

An important part of HOLOCL is a collection of Isabelle theories describing the built-in operations of UML/OCL. This comprises over 10 000 definitions and theorems such as properties of basic types like `Integer`, `Real`, and `String` as well as collection types such as `Bag`, `Sequence` and `Set`, and also the common superclass `OclAny`. Besides the model-specific part covered by the datatype package described in Section 2.3, the library with its body of derived rules represents the generic part of data-structure related reasoning in OCL. Moreover, these theories also contain new proof tactics written in SML.

2.5 Automated Proof Procedures

The operations of OCL have a certain representational distance to the operations of HOL: for example, the logical connectives `and`, `or`, `forAll`, `exists` are based on a three-valued logic (i. e., a strong Kleene logic) with an additional element `OclUndefined` ($\bot$) and properties such as `OclUndefined and false = false`. Moreover, all operations are implicitly parametrized over the pre-sate and the post-state; OCL expressions are *assertions* and not only logical formulae.

The major Isabelle proof procedures, e. g., `simp` and `auto`, cannot handle this logic directly, except for a fairly trivial fragments. We therefore implemented our own versions of a context-rewriter and a tableaux-prover. These language specific variants offer a reasonably high degree of proof automation for OCL.

3 Conclusion

We provide a proof-environment for an object-oriented specification method based on UML class models annotated with OCL constraints. On this bases, we can formally reason over such UML/OCL models. For example, we can prove the satisfyability of class invariants, that postconditions do not contradict with class invariants, or proof-obligations arising from stating that one class-model is a refinements from another.this The system has been used in several smaller and medium-sized case studies [1, 2].

References

[1] Brucker, A.D.: An Interactive Proof Environment for Object-oriented Specifications. Ph.d. thesis, ETH Zurich (March 2007), ETH Dissertation No. 17097, http://www.brucker.ch/bibliography/abstract/brucker-interactive-2007

[2] Brucker, A.D., Wolff, B.: The HOL-OCL book. Technical Report 525, ETH Zurich (2006), http://www.brucker.ch/bibliography/abstract/brucker.ea-hol-ocl-book-2006

[3] Brucker, A.D., Doser, J., Wolff, B.: An MDA framework supporting OCL. Electronic Communications of the EASST, 5 (2006), ISSN 1863-2122, http://www.brucker.ch/bibliography/abstract/brucker.ea-mda-2006-b

[4] Object Management Group. UML 2.0 OCL specification (October 2003), OMGdocumentptc/03-10-14

[5] Object Management Group. Unified modeling language specification (version 1.5) (March 2003), OMGdocument,formal/03-03-01

Towards Faithful Model Extraction Based on Contexts

Lucio Mauro Duarte*, Jeff Kramer, and Sebastian Uchitel

Department of Computing, Imperial College London
180 Queen's Gate, London, SW7 2AZ, UK
{lmd,jk,su2}@doc.ic.ac.uk

Abstract. Behaviour models facilitate the analysis of software systems using model-checking tools to detect errors and generate counterexamples. Such models can be generated from existing implementations using a model extraction process. This process should guarantee that an extracted model is a faithful representation of the system, so that analysis results may be trusted. This paper discusses the formal foundations of our model extraction process based on contexts. Contexts are abstractions of concrete states of a system, providing valuable information about dependencies between actions. Models are generated by a tool called LTS Extractor and can be refined to improve correctness by augmenting context information. This refinement process eliminates some false negatives and is property-preserving. Completeness of the models depends on the coverage provided by a set of traces describing behaviours of the system. We discuss the faithfulness of our models and results of two case studies.

1 Introduction

Behaviour models are abstract representations of the intended behaviours of systems [22]. They can normally be handled in situations where the real systems could not [18], and have been successfully used to uncover errors that would go undetected otherwise, such as violations of program properties [4].

In this work, we focus on the construction of behaviour models of existing systems. The process of obtaining a model from an implementation is called *model extraction* [15]. An essential requirement of this process is that the generated model should be a *faithful representation* of the system behaviour. Any analysis based on an incorrect model may mislead the developer into an erroneous understanding of how the system behaves [16].

Research has been carried out on techniques for model extraction in recent years (e.g., [6], [15], [7], [1] and [2]) and the results have been encouraging. Nevertheless, the extensive use of model extraction, and, therefore, of model checking [5] for existing systems, has been slowed down by the *model construction problem* [7]. It corresponds to finding a way of bridging the gap between the semantics of current programming languages and that of the less expressive

---

* Supported by CAPES (Brazil) under the grant BEX 1680-02/1.

J. Fiadeiro and P. Inverardi (Eds.): FASE 2008, LNCS 4961, pp. 101–115, 2008.
© Springer-Verlag Berlin Heidelberg 2008

languages used as inputs in model-checking tools. This is necessary to meet the requirement of model faithfulness.

In [8], an approach for model extraction based on the use of contexts was presented. A *context* represents an abstraction of a state of the system, composed of the identification of a block of code and the values of a set of attributes. Contexts allow the detection of relations between actions of a system and the inference of additional feasible behaviours from samples of execution [8]. Models based on contexts can be built using the LTS Extractor (LTSE), which implements most of the extraction process. Their use for verifying temporal properties of concurrent systems in the LTSA tool [19] has proved that they are good approximations of the behaviours of the systems they describe.

The aim of this paper is to discuss the formal foundations of the approach for model extraction based on contexts, focusing on factors that determine the faithfulness of models. *Completeness* of the models is shown to depend on the coverage provided by a set of traces obtained during the model extraction process, whereas *correctness* is affected by the selection of attributes used in the identification of contexts. We discuss how completeness and correctness can be improved and how to interpret property-checking results according to these characteristics of a behaviour model. We also present a description of our refinement process, which can eventually lead to a correct abstraction of the system behaviour by the addition of more attributes to contexts. This refinement process is demonstrated to be property-preserving.

This paper is organised as follows. The next section discusses basic concepts involved in our work and Sec. 3 presents our approach for model extraction using context information. In Sec. 4 we discuss the faithfulness of the extracted models and Sec. 5 describes results of two case studies. Finally, Sec. 6 compares our work to similar approaches and Sec. 7 presents the conclusions and future work.

2   Background

We build models where behaviours are described in terms of sequences of actions a system can execute. An *action* is an atomic event of the system that causes an indivisible change on the program state [19]. In this work, an action usually represents the execution of a method, but user-defined actions are also accepted, according to the format described in [9]. More specifically, we model behaviours using Labelled Transition Systems.

Definition 1 Labelled Transition System (LTS). *A labelled transition system $M = (S, s_i, \Sigma, T)$ is a model where*

- *S is a finite set of abstract states,*
- *$s_i \in S$ represents the initial state,*
- *Σ is an alphabet (set of actions), and*
- *$T \subseteq S \times \Sigma \times S$ is a transition relation.*

In a LTS, transitions are labelled with the name of the actions that cause the system to progress from the current state to a new one. Therefore, given two states $s_0, s_1 \in S$ and an action $a \in \Sigma$, then a transition $s_0 \xrightarrow{a} s_1$ means that it is possible to go from state s_0 to state s_1 through the execution of an action with name a. Thus, a transition can only take place if the associated action occurs.

The following definitions apply to LTS models following Definition 1. A *behaviour* is a finite sequence of actions $\pi = \langle a_1...a_n \rangle$ such that $a_1, ..., a_n \in \Sigma$. The set $L(M) = \{\pi_1, \pi_2, ...\}$ of all behaviours of M is called its *language*.

For a state $s \in S$, $E(s) = \{a \in \Sigma | \exists s' \in S \cdot (s, a, s') \in T\}$ represents the non-empty finite set of actions *enabled* in s. A *path* $\lambda = \langle s_1, a_1, s_2, a_2, s_3, ... \rangle$ is a sequence of alternating states $s_1, s_2, s_3, ... \in S$ and actions $a_1, a_2, ... \in \Sigma$ labelling transitions connecting these states, such that, for $i \geq 1$, for every transition $t_i = (s_i, a, s_{i+1})$ composing λ, $t_i \in T$. A path always starts and ends with a state. We use $\Lambda(M)$ to denote the set of all paths of M.

An LTS model M is a *faithful* representation of the behaviour of a program *Prog* if the satisfaction/violation of a certain property by M implies that *Prog* also satisfies/violates the property. This means that, ideally, $L(M) = L(Prog)$, where $L(Prog)$ represents the language of *Prog*. However, the faithfulness of a model is affected by its completeness and correctness.

Definition 2 Completeness. *M is complete w.r.t. Prog iff* $L(Prog) \subseteq L(M)$.

Definition 3 Correctness. *M is correct w.r.t. Prog iff* $L(M) \subseteq L(Prog)$.

Completeness, therefore, is related to language containment, whereas correctness is related to the absence of invalid behaviours. If the model is not complete, then *false positives* may occur, i.e., properties might be checked to hold in the model even though they are violated by the system. If the model is not correct, then the model might violate a property not violated by the system, representing a *false negative*.

3   Contexts

As described in [9], we build models combining a *control component*, which indicates the execution point where the system is at, and a *data component*, representing the state of the system in terms of values of program variables. The control component is obtained based on the control flow graph of the implementation of the system.

Definition 4 Control Flow Graph (CFG). *Let Prog be a program. Then* $CFG_{Prog} = (Q, q_i, Act, \Delta)$ *is its* control flow graph, *where*

- *Q is a finite set of control components of Prog, where each control component $q \in Q$ is a pair (bc, cp), with bc representing a block of code and cp describing the logic test associated with bc (i.e., its control predicate),*
- *$q_i = (bc_i, \text{true}) \in Q$, where bc_i is the initial block of code,*
- *Act is the set of actions of Prog, and*
- *$\Delta \subseteq Q \times Act \times Q$ is a transition relation.*

As for the data component, we adopt the values of attributes (system state). Let P_{Prog} be the finite set of data components of $Prog$ and $val(p)$ be the value of an attribute $p \in P_{Prog}$. A finite tuple $v = \{val(p_1), ..., val(p_n)\}$ represents one possible combination of values of attributes $p_1, ..., p_n \in P_{Prog}$. The set $V(P_{Prog}) = \{v_1, ..., v_n\}$ is composed of all possible system states of $Prog$, such that $v_1 = \emptyset$, representing the beginning of the execution, when values of attributes are yet unknown. The finite set $V(P) \subseteq V(P_{Prog})$ represents all possible combinations of values of attributes $p_1, ..., p_n \in P$, where $P \subseteq P_{Prog}$.

We define a context as the conjunction of a control component with a data component, thus representing an abstract state of the actual system.

Definition 5 Context. *Given a program Prog, a context $C = (bc, val(cp), v)$ is the combination, at a certain point of the execution of Prog, of the current block of code bc being executed, the value val(cp) of its control predicate cp and the current set of values $v \in V(P)$ of attributes in $P \subseteq P_{Prog}$.*

The information collected to identify contexts is denominated *context information*. Using this information, our model extraction approach builds LTS models from Java source code. This is done in the steps discussed next, which, except for the first one, are all implemented by the LTSE[1].

3.1   Information Gathering

We obtain context information from the system through the instrumentation of the source code. Annotations are included for each block of code (selection and repetition statements, method calls and method bodies) and action (methods). The result of executing the instrumented code is the creation of a set of traces, which are recorded in log files.

For a given program $Prog$, a recorded trace t, produced by the execution of the instrumented $Prog$, is a finite sequence $\langle CA_1, AA_1, CA_2, ..., AA_n, CA_n \rangle$, where $CA_1, CA_2, ..., CA_n$ are *context annotations*, which contain context information, and $AA_1, ..., AA_n$ are *action annotations* describing the actions that happened between two consecutive contexts. We use $Tr(Prog)$ to denote the set of all traces that $Prog$ can produce when instrumented and executed. F_{Prog} is the set of log files containing traces of $Prog$. Therefore, $Tr(F_{Prog})$ represents the set of all traces of $Prog$ recorded in files in F_{Prog}, such that $Tr(F_{Prog}) \subseteq Tr(Prog)$.

As an example, we use the code of the buffer component presented in [13], which is part of a producer-consumer system and has a storage capacity of two elements. An action **halt** is used by the producer to signal that it has finished its operations on the buffer. An exception is generated whenever the consumer attempts to get a new element from the buffer but it is empty and the producer has stopped.

We created test cases considering the number of operations each of these components carries out on the buffer. Below, we show the traces obtained after instrumenting the code of the buffer as described in [8]. Due to lack of space, we

---

[1] Available at http://www.doc.ic.ac.uk/~lmd/ltse

only present the sequence of actions produced in each trace. For the format of complete recorded traces, refer to [9].

T1 = ⟨ put.1 get.0 put.1 get.0 put.1get.0 put.1 get.0 halt ⟩
T2 = ⟨ put.1 get.0 put.1 get.0 put.1 get.0 halt halt_exception ⟩
T3 = ⟨ put.1 get.0 put.1 get.0 put.1 get.0 put.1 halt ⟩

The number after the action name describes the number of elements in the buffer as a result of the execution of the operation.

3.2 Context Identification

The context information collected from traces is recorded in a *context table* $CT = \{c_1, ..., c_n\}$, where $c_1, ..., c_n$ are entries of the table. Each entry is assigned a *context ID* (CID), which is a unique sequential numeric identifier, and contains a set of values of attributes defining a context, including an identification of the executed block of code (BID), and the evaluation of the control predicate associated with this block. The CT is initialised with an *initial context*, which represents the beginning of the execution.

The LTSE tool constructs the CT by reading each annotation from the log files, identifying contexts and comparing each context found to every context already recorded. A context C is identified as in the CT if, when compared to a context C' (stored as an entry c' of the CT), C and C' have the same context information, i.e., the same set of values for the attributes, including the same BID and the same value of the control predicate. When the context is not in the CT yet, a new entry is created to store it, which is assigned a new CID. Table 1 shows part of the CT of the buffer example. Note that no attributes were selected to identify contexts in this example.

The result of the context identification phase is the generation of a set of context traces. A *context trace* $ctr = \langle s_1, a_1, s_2, ..., a_n, s_n \rangle$ is a finite sequence of abstract states $s_1, s_2, ..., s_n$ that correspond to CIDs, such that, for $1 \geq j \geq n$, for every CID_j there exists a state s_j which represents that context, and actions $a_1, ..., a_n \in Act$. It describes the contexts the system went through during the execution, according to context annotations, and the actions that happened in between them, defined by action annotations. As an example, this is part of the context trace generated based on the trace T1: ⟨0 1 2 3 4 put.1 5 6 7 get.0 2 ...⟩. Note that some states might not be connected by actions. In this case, we use an empty action ϵ to represent a transition that is always enabled.

3.3 LKS Creation

As previously stated, we use context information to generate LTS models. However, in order to use values of attributes during the construction of the models, we need an intermediate structure which can deal with both actions and states. We have adopted Labelled Kripke Structures as our intermediate structure.

Table 1. Part of the CT for the buffer component

CID	Predicate	Val	Attribs	BID
0		true		-1
1	put	true		9
2	(usedSlots == 0)	true		5
3	get	true		8
4	(halted)	false		6
5	(usedSlots == SIZE)	false		7
...	...	...	...	...

Definition 6 Labelled Kripke Structure (LKS). *A* Labelled Kripke Structure $K = (S, s_i, P, \Gamma, \Sigma, T)$ *is an abstract model where*

- *S is a finite set of abstract states,*
- *$s_i \in S$ represents the initial state,*
- *P is a finite set of attributes used to label states in S,*
- *$\Gamma : S \to N^P$ is a state-labelling function, where N is the sum of the ranges of values of attributes in P,*
- *Σ is a finite set of actions, i.e., an* alphabet, *and*
- *$T \subseteq S \times \Sigma \times S$ is a transition relation.*

Our definition slightly differs from the one presented in [2] in that, instead of propositions, which are always of boolean type, we use attributes to label states. Because of that, in our case, the state-labelling function Γ labels every state with the values of every attribute in P. Moreover, we use a singleton set of initial states to guarantee conformance to Definition 1 when creating the LTS model. This also reflects the fact that the initial state of our models represents the initial context, which is unique.

Our mapping from context traces collected from *Prog* to an LKS involves translating concrete states of *Prog* (information from context annotations) into abstract states of K. Let $CFG_{Prog} = (Q, q_i, Act, \Delta)$ be the CFG of *Prog* and $V(P_{Prog})$ be the set of possible system states. A concrete state $\theta = (q, v)$ of *Prog* comprises a control component $q = (bc_q, cp_q) \in Q$, where bc_q is a block of code and cp_q is its associated control predicate, and a data component $v \in V(P_{Prog})$. We use $\Theta(Prog) = \{\theta_1, \theta_2, ...\}$ to denote the set of all possible concrete states of *Prog* and $\Omega \subseteq \Theta(Prog) \times Act \times \Theta(Prog)$ to represent the transition relation between them. The mapping from concrete to abstract states is described bellow:

- Every concrete state $\theta = (q, v) \in \Theta(Prog)$, where $v = \{val(p_1), ..., val(p_n)\} \in V(P)$ for $P = \{p_1, ..., p_n\} \subseteq P_{Prog}$, is modelled by an abstract state $s \in S$, such that $\Gamma(s) = v$, where s is derived from a CID appearing in the context traces generated by *Prog*. This abstract state includes only the values of attributes in the selected set P. Hence, s may represent a set of concrete states $\Theta(Prog)_s = \{\theta_1, ...\theta_n\}$, where $\Theta(Prog)_s \subseteq \Theta(Prog)$. These concrete states are indistinguishable when the information used for comparison is restricted to system states containing only attributes in P;

- The initial state $s_i \in S$ models a concrete state $\theta_i = (q_i, v_i) \in \Theta(Prog)$, where $v_i = \emptyset$ and, thus, $\Gamma(s_i) = \emptyset$;
- $\Sigma \subseteq Act$ and, therefore, the alphabet of the model is also restricted to a subset of that of the program;
- The transition relation T is defined in this way: Given a set of attributes $P \subseteq P_{Prog}$, let s and s' be two abstract states of K. Abstract state s models a set of concrete states $\Theta(Prog)_s = \{\theta_1, ..., \theta_n\}$, such that $\Theta(Prog)_s \subseteq \Theta(Prog)$, where, for $1 \geq i \geq n$, $\theta_i = (q_i, \{v_i\} \cap V(P))$. Abstract state s' models a set of concrete states $\Theta(Prog)_{s'} = \{\theta'_1, ..., \theta'_m\}$, such that $\Theta(Prog)_{s'} \subseteq \Theta(Prog)$, where, for $1 \geq j \geq m$, $\theta'_j = (q'_j, \{v'_j\} \cap V(P))$. Let $a \in \Sigma$ be an action. A transition $(s, a, s') \in T$ exists iff there exists a concrete transition $(\theta, a, \theta') \in \Omega$ such that $\theta \in \Theta(Prog)_s$ and $\theta' \in \Theta(Prog)_{s'}$.

Note that the LTSE does not explicitly build an LKS model. Though it applies the mapping described above to obtain an abstract representation of a concrete system, the LKS model is only used as an intermediate structure that allows us to store the information contained in context traces and, subsequently, produce an LTS model from it. Transition labels in the LKS model are explicit and correspond to the names of actions happening between contexts in a context trace. State labels, on the other hand, are implicit and used to uniquely identify different contexts when converting traces into context traces.

3.4   Mapping the LKS into an LTS Model

Essentially, an LKS is an LTS where states are labelled with values of attributes using a state-labelling function. Therefore, an LTS $M = (S', s'_i, \Sigma', T')$ can be obtained from an LKS $K = (S, s_i, P, \Gamma, \Sigma, T)$ simply by ignoring the values of the state labels of K. In this state-label elimination (SLE) process, every state $s' \in S'$ corresponds to a state $s \in S$, such that s' is the same as s but without its label, i.e., $\Gamma(s') = \Gamma(s) \setminus P$. The alphabet and the transition relation do not change after the mapping. Hence, $\Sigma' = \Sigma$ and $T' = T$.

If we associate propositions with actions [11,17], LTL formulas [20] can be defined on behaviours of a model. Hence, a model K satisfies an LTL property ϕ over Σ iff, for all $\pi \in L(K)$, $\pi \models \phi$.

Theorem 1. *Let $K = (S, s_i, P, \Gamma, \Sigma, T)$ be an LKS. Applying the SLE process to K results in an LTS $M = (S', s'_i, \Sigma', T')$ such that, given an LTL property ϕ over Σ, if $K \models \phi$ then $M \models \phi$.*

Therefore, this mapping is property-preserving when we consider LTL properties that only refer to actions in Σ. Note that we build an implicit LKS and, therefore, the elimination of state labels in practice only means that we no longer use the CT, but analyse directly the context traces.

The generated LTS can be visualised using the LTSA tool. This tool also allows the specification of LTL properties over actions and supports the checking of such properties against extracted models to detect possible violations.

For a complete description of the model extraction process and of the formal proofs of Theorem 1 and the theorems presented in the next section, refer to [9].

4   Model Faithfulness

Completeness of the generated models depends on the coverage provided by the set of traces used to build them. If the set of traces provides full coverage of the system behaviour, then it is possible to identify all reachable concrete states of the system and all valid transitions. However, this is normally not the case and, therefore, the model is generally an under-approximation of the behaviour of the system, i.e., $L(M) \subset L(Prog)$. Thus, it represents only the part of the behaviour observed during the generation of traces.

Correctness of the models depends essentially on the selection of the attributes to form the system state, used to define contexts. An empty set defines the most abstract model. By including more attributes to the set, the level of abstraction of the generated model can be decreased. Therefore, changing the attributes in the system state directly affects the correctness of the model.

Ideally, if a property ϕ holds in a behaviour model M, then it should also hold in the program $Prog$ represented by M. Nevertheless, this cannot always be guaranteed unless M is complete and correct. If a model is complete, then if a property ϕ holds in the model, it is guaranteed to hold in the system, irrespective of the model being correct or not. However, if the model is incorrect, detected violations can be real or just false negatives. If the model is correct but incomplete, then the absence of violations in the model does not necessarily mean that the property holds in the system. This only ensures that behaviours in $L(M) \cap L(Prog)$ preserve the property. Behaviours in $L(Prog) \setminus L(M)$ cannot be guaranteed to not violate the property.

4.1   Model Refinement

False negatives can usually be eliminated from the model using an abstraction refinement process. In our approach, this process corresponds to the addition of more attributes to the system state, thus decreasing the level of abstraction and improving correctness.

In a refinement process, an original model is said to be an *abstraction* of a refined model, as it includes just part of the information included in its refined version. In [2], the following definition is presented for an abstraction relation considering LKS models:

Definition 7 Abstraction. *Let $K = (S, s_i, P, \Gamma, \Sigma, T)$ and $K_A = (S_A, s_{i_A}, P_A, \Gamma_A, \Sigma_A, T_A)$ be two LKS. K_A is an* abstraction *of K, denoted by $K \sqsubseteq K_A$, iff*

1. *$P_A \subseteq P$,*
2. *$\Sigma_A = \Sigma$, and*
3. *For every path $\lambda = \langle s_1, a_1, ... \rangle \in \Lambda(K)$ there exists a path $\lambda' = \langle s'_1, a'_1, ... \rangle \in \Lambda(K_A)$ such that, for each $n \geq 1$, $a'_n = a_n$ and $\Gamma_A(s'_n) = \Gamma(s_n) \cap P_A$.*

Hence, K_A is an abstraction of K if the propositional language accepted by K_A contains the propositional language accepted by K when the language is restricted to the set of propositions of K_A. Ultimately, this means that K_A is an over-approximation of K, such that $L(K) \subseteq L(K_A)$. Remember that we consider this relation in terms of attributes, which just means that the set of values for each element of state labels may be different from $\{true, false\}$.

Theorem 2. *Let F_{Prog} be a set of log files recording traces of a program Prog. $K_A = (S_A, s_{i_A}, P_A, \Gamma_A, \Sigma_A, T_A)$ is an LKS model obtained from Prog following our mapping, using a set of traces $Tr(F_{Prog})$, collected from F_{Prog} during the CT construction, and a set of attributes $P_A \subseteq P_{Prog}$. If $Tr(F_{Prog})$ is used with a set of attributes $P \subseteq P_{Prog}$, such that $P_A \subseteq P$, then we obtain an LKS $K = (S, s_i, P, \Gamma, \Sigma, T)$ such that $K \sqsubseteq K_A$.*

In [2], the authors present a logic that is a superset of LTL, called SE-LTL. They show that, if a property ϕ is expressed in their logic and mentions only actions in the alphabet Σ_A, then if ϕ holds for K_A, then it also holds for K. Based on this and on Theorem 2, we can conclude that, for every LTL property ϕ over Σ_A, if $K_A \models \phi$, then $K \models \phi$.

Theorem 3. *Let $K_A = (S_A, s_{i_A}, P_A, \Gamma_A, \Sigma_A, T_A)$ and $K = (S, s_i, P, \Gamma, \Sigma, T)$ be two LKS models such that $K \sqsubseteq K_A$. If K_A is mapped into an LTS $M_A = (S'_A, s'_{i_A}, \Sigma'_A, T'_A)$ and K is mapped into an LTS $M = (S', s'_i, \Sigma', T')$, then, given an LTL property ϕ over Σ_A, if $M_A \models \phi$ then $M \models \phi$.*

Therefore, our refinement process between LKS models preserves LTL properties that consider only actions of the alphabet of the more abstract model. As a consequence, given that there is a property-preserving relation between two LKS models built with different sets of attributes, where one set is a subset of the other, and that the mapping from an LKS to an LTS model is also property-preserving, the generated LTS models have a property-preserving relation between them, which is also a refinement.

We will use again the buffer component mentioned in the previous section as an example. Following the mappings described before, and based on the traces collected, the LTSE generated the model presented in Fig. 1, where state E represents the final state. Note that it incorrectly allows action get.0 to happen repeatedly, even when the buffer is empty.

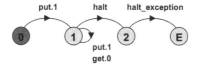

Fig. 1. LTS model of the buffer

Following our refinement approach, we attempt to remove this invalid behaviour by adding attributes to the system state. The problem seems to be connected with the fact that the model, at this level of abstraction, does not consider the status of the buffer. That is, the model does not show the behaviour of the buffer depending on the quantity of stored elements. Therefore, we add attribute `usedSlots` to the system state. This attribute controls the number of elements currently in the buffer.

Using the new system state to generate a model of the buffer results in the LTS shown in Fig. 2. This model does not include the possibility of a `get.0` happening when the buffer is empty.

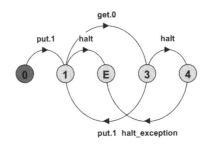

Fig. 2. Refined LTS model of the buffer

4.2   Improving Completeness

It is possible to improve completeness by adding new traces to the model. The addition of new traces increases the coverage of observed situations and may reveal unknown behaviours, which may violate the property being checked. One possible way of selecting relevant behaviours is to use a test suite. By choosing test cases, it is possible to control the inputs to the system and, this way, force it to exhibit some particular behaviours. Though testing is not directly connected with this work, the use of test cases to observe specific behaviours can help the construction of models tailored for the checking of properties of interest.

Regardless of the technique used to generate the traces (testing, profiling or monitoring), our approach allows new traces to be incrementally incorporated to the model. Therefore, missing traces can be added to provide information on executions not considered before. This way, it is possible to gradually improve completeness even if an initial model fails to include all the necessary behaviours to check a given property.

For instance, consider again the example discussed before. Even though the model in Fig. 2 seems a correct abstraction of the behaviour of the buffer, since it does not contain infeasible behaviours, it is incomplete. Note that, after the first occurrence of `put.1`, we reach state 1, where only actions `halt` and `get.0` are enabled. Therefore, the model does not permit the producer to store more than one element in the buffer at all times.

The absence of this behaviour does not affect the correctness of the model, but imposes a restriction that is not real. We improve completeness by adding a new trace. A delay for the initialisation of the consumer was introduced so that the producer could use the whole capacity of the buffer before the first attempt by the consumer to remove an element from it. This generates the new trace:

T4 = ⟨put.1 put.2 get.1 put.2 get.1 put.2 get.1 get.0 halt⟩

The addition of this trace leads to the construction of the model presented in Fig. 3, which includes the possibility of executing a second put before a get. Because we did not change the system state, this model preserves the correctness of the previous one.

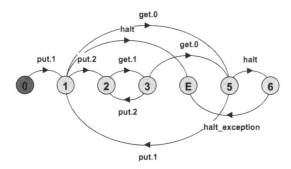

Fig. 3. More complete LTS model of the buffer

Note that the use of contexts not only allows us to combine multiple traces, as in this example, but also may result in the inclusion of additional behaviours to the model. These behaviours, though not observed in the individual traces, may be inferred based on the identification of similar contexts. Alternative paths may be included in the model even if these paths appear in different traces, provided that the context traces derived from them contain some common contexts. For instance, the sequence of actions ⟨put.1 put.2 get.1 get.0⟩ is a valid behaviour present in the model of Fig. 3 that does not appear in any of the traces. Hence, completeness may be automatically improved by the LTSE based on identified contexts, even without the addition of new traces.

5   Case Studies

Our approach has been applied to a variety of sequential and concurrent systems. Here, we discuss the results of two case studies. Detailed information can be found in [9].

5.1   Single-Lane Bridge

The first case study was based on the Single-Lane Bridge problem described in [19]. Though this system was quite simple, it helped us apply and evaluate our approach in a concurrent system. Moreover, manually created models are presented in [19], allowing the comparison of those models to our automatically generated models.

The traces generated in this example were a result of selecting options allowed by the interface of the system. We executed the system with one, two and three cars moving in either direction. We extracted the models for each component of the system and used model parallel composition [19] to generate a global model, which was checked against a property specification defined in [19]. A false negative was detected during this procedure, which was eliminated using the refinement process. The results of the analysis using the refined model in the LTSA tool confirmed those found by the authors.

5.2   Bully Algorithm

The Bully Algorithm [10] is a leader election algorithm where a new election starts whenever a process is detected to have failed or recovered. If a process that had failed recovers and its priority is higher than any of those of the processes still alive, then it becomes the leader.

For this case study, we used an implementation of the Bully Algorithm available on the Internet[2]. In order to reduce the complexity of the model to be generated and concentrate on the election procedure, we chose to analyse only the components involved in the process of electing a leader.

Election members were modelled using a parallel composition of models of six components, where each component represented the behaviour of a local thread. The models of each member were then also composed to generate a model of the entire system.

An interface was provided by the implementation which included operations *start*, *fail*, *recover* and *close* on election members. Using these operations, a set of test cases was created to collect traces from executions involving one, two and three members. The selected test cases were the following, where S represents *start*, F represents *fail*, R represents *recover*, C represents *close* and the numbers between brackets define the priorities of the members executing the operations[3]:

1. S(1), F(1), R(1), C(1)
2. S(1), F(1), R(1), F(1), C(1)
3. S(1,2), F(2), F(1), R(1), R(2), F(1), F(2), R(2), R(1), C(1,2)
4. S(1,2), F(1), F(2), C(1,2)
5. S(1,2,3), F(3), F(2), F(1), R(1), R(2), R(3), F(1), F(2), F(3), R(3), R(2), R(1), C(1,2,3)
6. S(1,2,3), F(2,3), R(2,3), F(1,3), R(1,3), F(1,2), R(1,2), F(1,2,3), C(1,2,3)

Each test case involved the abstract states of each executing member, which comprised its functional status (alive or down) and its membership status (normal or leader). These test cases were chosen with the purpose of producing traces where each member appears with different combinations of the values of these

---

two types of status. Note that when a member was down, it did not matter which was its member status. Therefore, tests with only one member involved the abstract states {alive,leader} and {down}. Tests with two members included the same abstract states for the member with priority 1 and the abstract states {alive,normal}, {alive, leader} and {down} for the member with priority 2. As for the tests with three members, we had the same abstract states mentioned before for the members with priorities 1 and 2. The member with priority 3 had the same abstract states as those of the member with priority 2.

A safety property was specified for the algorithm [9] stating that there could only be one leader at all times. We checked the property using the safety check provided by the LTSA tool. The detection of some false negatives led us to refine the models, resulting in the complete elimination of those invalid behaviours.

Even though the composite model could not be entirely generated due to lack of memory, it was still possible to check the property, as the safety check of the LTSA may not need to generate the whole composition to detect violations. Checking the property against the model with two members, the tool detected a violation.

The error trace indicated that if communication between members is too slow, the system might reach a state where there is more than one leader. The error found was not actually a problem in the code, but a result of the influence of the environment on the execution of the system. Although it may not be fixed by a simple modification in the code, the awareness of its existence allows users to be prepared for such a situation and strive to guarantee that the environment provides at least the minimum conditions to avoid the problem. Thus, the result of the analysis improved the knowledge about the system and correctly warned users about a possible violation of an essential property.

6   Related Work and Discussion

Techniques based only on traces, such as [6,21], share with our approach the dependence on the samples of execution to achieve completeness. However, they do not provide means of refining models to improve correctness. Moreover, though the work presented in [21] describes an incremental approach, the increase of completeness of an existing model usually causes the decrease of correctness. This is a consequence of the lack of information about how to combine different traces without creating infeasible behaviours. Context information provides us with the support for such an operation and, thus, improvement of completeness does not affect the correctness of the models.

Some techniques guarantee completeness by obtaining the complete CFG of the system [1,14,3]. As expected, this results in an over-approximated abstraction of the system, which can yield a number of false negatives, but which guarantees the absence of false positives. They rule out false negatives by applying an automatic refinement process based on predicate abstraction [12].

Based on the context information obtained from traces, we can use only partial control flow information to build our models. One could imagine our LTS models as partial representations of CFGs, as they contain only the sequences of actions defined by the behaviours described in the traces. This guarantees that every behaviour included in the model is a feasible behaviour at a certain level of abstraction, defined by the system state.

Though we do not provide automatic refinement, our refinement process has proved to successfully eliminate false negatives. This process is simple and, unlike the aforementioned related work, does not require the support of a theorem prover. However, the process still lacks well-defined heuristics as to how to select attributes to be used to refine models.

7   Conclusions and Future Work

Our model extraction process generates models based on traces containing context information. The completeness of these models depends on the quantity and quality of the observed behaviours and can be improved with the inclusion of more behaviours. The correctness of the models is affected by the set of attributes used as the system state. Improvement of correctness can be achieved by the addition of more attributes to contexts, thus ruling out false negatives. This refinement process is property-preserving provided that the properties only predicate over actions of the more abstract model.

Results of case studies applying our approach have demonstrated its usefulness for property checking. The refinement process has proved to effectively eliminate false negatives. Though completeness is not always possible to obtain, aiming to include only the necessary behaviours for checking a certain property reduces the possibility of false positives.

As future work, we intend to investigate techniques for the automatic selection of test cases based on a property specification. This would facilitate the identification of which behaviours can affect the property in order to choose an appropriate test suite. This investigation will also enhance our knowledge on how much results of an analysis using our models can improve and/or complement previous analyses based on testing outcomes.

Another possible path to be followed is to study the application of slicing to eliminate unnecessary parts of the code and allow the instrumentation and execution of a reduced version of the implementation. Using a property to be checked as the criterion to create the slice, we might be able to achieve completeness with respect to this property.

A definition of heuristics for the selection of attributes used as refinements will also be studied. These heuristics would possibly allow the implementation of an automatic refinement process. Though we have already identified that attributes used in control predicates are more likely to produce the expected results during the refinement process, we still need to find a more formal definition of the influence of these attributes regarding the checking of properties.

Acknowledgments. We thank Freeman Huang for providing the source code for the Bully Algorithm case study.

References

1. Ball, T., Rajamani, S.K.: The SLAM Project: Debugging System Software via Static Analysis. In: POPL, Portland, OR, USA, January 2002, pp. 1–3 (2002)
2. Chaki, S., Clarke, E.M., Ouaknine, J., et al.: State/Event-Based Software Model Checking. In: Boiten, E.A., Derrick, J., Smith, G.P. (eds.) IFM 2004. LNCS, vol. 2999, pp. 128–147. Springer, Heidelberg (2004)
3. Chaki, S., Clarke, E.M., Groce, A., et al.: Modular Verification of Software Components in C. IEEE TSE 30(6), 388–402 (2004)
4. Clarke, E.M., Wing, J.M.: Formal Methods: State of the Art and Future Directions. ACM Computing Surveys 28(4), 626–643 (1996)
5. Clarke, E.M., Grumberg, O., Peled, D.A.: Model Checking. The MIT Press, Cambridge (1999)
6. Cook, J.E., Wolf, A.L.: Discovering Models of Software Processes from Event-Based Data. ACM ToSEM 7(3), 215–249 (1998)
7. Corbett, J.C., Dwyer, M.B., Hatcliff, J., et al.: Bandera: Extracting Finite-State Models from Java Source Code. In: ICSE, Limerick, Ireland, June 2000, pp. 439–448 (2000)
8. Duarte, L.M., Kramer, J., Uchitel, S.: Model Extraction Using Context Information. In: Nierstrasz, O., Whittle, J., Harel, D., Reggio, G. (eds.) MoDELS 2006. LNCS, vol. 4199, pp. 380–394. Springer, Heidelberg (2006)
9. Duarte, L.M.: Behaviour Model Extraction using Context Information. Ph.D. thesis, Imperial College London, University of London (November 2007)
10. Garcia-Molina, H.: Elections in a Distributed Computing System. IEEE Trans. on Computers C-31(1), 48–59 (1982)
11. Giannakopoulou, D., Magee, J.: Fluent Model Checking for Event-Based Systems. In: ESEC/FSE, Helsinki, Finland, September 2003, pp. 257–266 (2003)
12. Graf, S., Saidi, H.: Construction of Abstract State Graphs with PVS. In: Grumberg, O. (ed.) CAV 1997. LNCS, vol. 1254, pp. 72–83. Springer, Heidelberg (1997)
13. Havelund, K., Pressburguer, T.: Model Checking Java Programs Using Java PathFinder. STTT 2(4), 366–381 (2000)
14. Henzinger, T.A., Jahla, R., Majumdar, R., et al.: Lazy Abstraction. In: POPL, Portland, OR, USA, January 2002, pp. 58–70 (2002)
15. Holzmann, G.J., Smith, M.H.: A Practical Method for Verifying Event-Driven Software. In: ICSE, Los Angeles, USA, May 1999, pp. 597–607 (1999)
16. Jackson, D., Damon, C.A.: Software Analysis: A Roadmap. In: ICSE, Limerick, Ireland, June 2000, pp. 133–145 (2000)
17. Leuschel, M., Massart, T., Currie, A.: How to Make FDR Spin: LTL Model Checking of CSP by Refinement. In: Oliveira, J.N., Zave, P. (eds.) FME 2001. LNCS, vol. 2021, pp. 99–118. Springer, Heidelberg (2001)
18. Ludewig, J.: Models in Software Engineering - An Introduction. SoSyM 2(1), 5–14 (2003)
19. Magee, J., Kramer, J.: Concurrency: State Models and Java Programming, 2nd edn. Wiley and Sons, Chichester (2006)
20. Manna, Z., Pnueli, A.: The Temporal Logic of Reactive and Concurrent Systems. Springer, New York (1992)
21. Mariani, L.: Behavior Capture and Test: Dynamic Analysis of Component-Based Systems. Ph.D. thesis, Università degli Studi di Milano Bicocca (2005)
22. Uchitel, S., Kramer, J., Magee, J.: Behaviour Model Elaboration Using Partial Labelled Transition Systems. In: ESEC/FSE, Helsinki, Finland, September 2003, pp. 19–27 (2003)

Leveraging Patterns on Domain Models to Improve UML Profile Definition

François Lagarde[1], Huáscar Espinoza[1], François Terrier[1], Charles André[2],
and Sébastien Gérard[1]

[1] CEA, LIST, Gif-sur-Yvette, F-91191, France
{francois.lagarde, huascar.espinoza, francois.terrier,
sebastien.gerard}@cea.fr
[2] I3S Laboratory,
BP 121,
06903 Sophia Antipolis Cédex,
France
charles.andre@unice.fr

Abstract. Building a reliable UML profile is a difficult activity that requires the use of complex mechanisms -stereotypes and their attributes,
OCL enforcement- to define a domain-specific modeling language (DSML).
Despite the ever increasing number of profiles being built in many domains, there is a little published literature available to help DSML designers. Without a clear design process, most such profiles are inaccurate
and jeopardize subsequent model transformations or model analyses. We
believe that a suitable approach to building UML based domain specific
languages should include systematic transformation of domain representations into profiles. This article therefore proposes a clearly-defined
process geared to helping the designer throughout this design activity.
Starting from the conceptual domain model, we identify a set of design
patterns for which we detail several profile implementations. We illustrate
our approach by creating a simplified profile that depicts elements belonging to a real-time system domain. The prototype tool supporting our approach is also described.

1 Introduction

Over the last few decades, domain-specific languages (DSLs) have proven efficient
for mastering the complexities of software development projects. The natural
adaptation of DSLs to the model-driven technologies has in turn established
domain-specific modeling languages (DSMLs) as vital tools for enhancing design
productivity.

A widespread approach to the design of a DSML is to make use of the so-called
profile mechanisms and to reuse the UML [1] metamodel as the base language.
By extending UML elements with stereotypes and their attributes, it is possible
to define new concepts to better represent elements of a domain. Despite the
ever-increasing number of profiles defined and successfully applied in many applications (Object Management Group (OMG) [2] has adopted thirteen profiles

J. Fiadeiro and P. Inverardi (Eds.): FASE 2008, LNCS 4961, pp. 116–130, 2008.
© Springer-Verlag Berlin Heidelberg 2008

covering a wide range of modeling domains), building a reliable profile is still an obscure process with very little literature available to help designers.

A study of the currently adopted profiles reveals two existing profile design methods. The first is a one-stage process: the profile is directly created to support concepts belonging to the targeted domain. This method has been adopted for instance by SysML [3] profile designers. The main drawback of such an approach is to narrow down the design space to the implementation level.

A second, more methodical process involves two stages. Stage one is intended to define the conceptual constructs required to cover a specific domain. The product of this stage is usually called the conceptual domain model. In stage two, this artifact is then mapped onto profile constructs. This was the approach used to design UML profiles such as the Schedulability, Performance and Time specification [4] and the QoS and Fault Tolerance specification [5]. Applying this second method allows designers to focus on domain concepts and their relationships before dealing with language implementation issues. The main disadvantage is the time it requires. Finding a correct profile construct to support a conceptual model domain is far from straightforward. Several profile implementations may support a concept, thus obliging the designer to apply cumbersome design heuristics to comply as much as possible with the conceptual model.

We believe that a suitable approach to building UML-based domain-specific languages entails systematic transformation of domain representations (captured in a metamodel) into profiles. For this purpose, we propose a clearly-defined process geared to help the designer. Transformation is based upon a set of design patterns occurring on the domain model for which we provide profile implementations. By doing so, we attempt to improve the accuracy of profiles and facilitate adoption of DSMLs based on UML profiles.

In a previous short-paper [6], we provided arguments in favor of a *staged* process. In the present paper, we give a thorough description of our process and present a set of preliminary results obtained from the prototype tool that we developed.

Most of the results given are based on experience acquired in defining various UML profiles [4, 7]. Among these, the UML profile for Modeling and Analysis of Real-Time and Embedded systems (MARTE) [7] required definition of a complex DSML that involved a significant collaborative effort by domain experts.

This paper is organized as follows: Section 2 explains the reasons for devising a DSML and advocates use of profiling mechanisms. Section 3 details the identified key stages of our process and progressively introduces a set of profile design guidelines. Section 4 presents the prototype. Section 5 describes related work and Section 6 gives our conclusions.

2   Why (How and When) to Create a DSML

Most of the reasons for creating DSLs are also valid for DSMLs. The expected benefits have been described in previous studies [8, 9]. The most widely shared of these advantages are that DSMLs:

- allow solutions to be expressed in the idiom and at the level of abstraction of the problem domain,
- embody domain knowledge and thus enable the conservation and reuse of this knowledge.

The easiest approach to design a DSML is to reuse an existing metamodel. A common approach is to develop libraries, also called domain-specific embedded languages (DSELs) [10], which are easy to integrate into almost all frameworks. In some cases, constraints may be expressed, to confine the use of an existing language to a specific domain. While both these options are applicable to almost all languages, model-driven technologies afford two novel approaches which are usually classified according to their mechanisms. They are:

heavyweight extension: this approach allows designers to extend and modify the source language as required to create a new DSML. In a recent paper [11], Alanen and Porres provide a comprehensive overview of available mechanisms, and outline the possibilities of subset and union properties in formal definition of new metamodels. This extension method is particularly suited to cases where there are few identifiable relationships to existing languages,

lightweight extension: this approach is restricted to the use and extension of an existing Meta-Object Facility (MOF) [12] based metamodel which cannot be modified. It is supported with the standard profiling mechanism.

Development of a DSML may lead to heavy investments, and recourse to such tool requires strategic decisions. Clearly, there are no systematic criteria for such decision making. A balanced rule would be to avoid creating a DSML wherever possible, by instead learning to better identify the design needs and recognize them in existing languages.

Unfortunately this rule cannot always be applied; and regardless of the mechanisms chosen, the following difficulties remain:

- designing and maintaining a DSML is a time-consuming task,
- it is hard to strike a suitable balance between domain-specific and general purpose language constructs,
- the costs of educating DSML users could be high.

Among the approaches available, standard mechanisms can be regarded as the most sustainable solutions. Such mechanisms benefit from the low cost of support tools and the limited investments involved in the learning process. We consequently advocate creation of metamodels with profiling mechanisms, since the latter are standard built-in mechanisms and present a more steeply downward-sloping learning curve for multiple and long term projects.

3 Design Activities Flow

This section discusses the four phases proposed for our process. Fig. 1 shows the process workflow with its different outputs, from conceptual domain definition to profile creation:

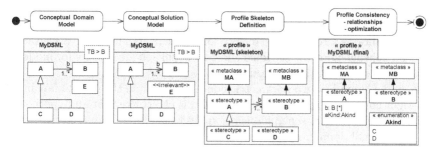

Fig. 1. Main workflow

1. The designer gives a coarse-grain description of the space problem using a UML class diagram. This first iteration is the conceptual domain model.
2. This model is then tailored to a conceptual solution model,
3. Solution entities are transformed into potential stereotypes and extensions to UML metaclasses are given. This operation results in a profile skeleton,
4. The profile skeleton is used as an analysis artifact. At this stage, profile designers decide how domain representations are to be supported in the final profile.

3.1   Conceptual Domain Model

Domain model definition is the initial phase of our process. It identifies the required concepts and their relationships in order to describe a problem area, also called problem space. This design activity is independent from technological solutions and thus lets the designer focus on domain constructs.

Much attention has been paid on domain analysis and many existing studies [13, 14] describe the techniques used to support this process. One of the central issues is how to manage the common concepts and variable concepts of a problem area to enable reuse assets for different projects.

One way of incorporating such flexibility into a modeling process is to make use of template mechanisms. These allow formal identification of parametric information that can subsequently be refined. Recourse to templates in the design work flow then makes it necessary to determine at what stage they can be included. While templates are frequently used for system modeling, few studies [15, 16] have examined their uses for metamodeling. We believe that to better meet the *design for reuse* criterion, we need to capture variability at the start of our process. We therefore introduce this facility at the conceptual domain definition stage.

We use the UML Class package to build the conceptual domain model. The advantages are that DSML designers are familiar with its concepts (e.g., inheritance, associations, and packages) and that the UML Class package has a support for template mechanisms.

To tangibly illustrate this discussion, we have created a simplified DSML for the real time domain, called Simple Real Time System, inspired by the profiles

SPT and MARTE. The SRTS package in the left panel of Fig. 2 is an excerpt of this conceptual model. A SchedulableResource depicts any resources to be scheduled and maintains a reference to exactly one Scheduler. The latter is characterized by its SchedulingPolicy. Schedule and SchedulingJob are entities for modeling a queue of jobs waiting to be executed.

The model embodies two parametric concepts shown in the dashed box in the upper right corner of Fig. 2. The reasons for this choice are that an hypothetical list of schedule policies or schedulable resources would have hampered reusability of the conceptual domain model.

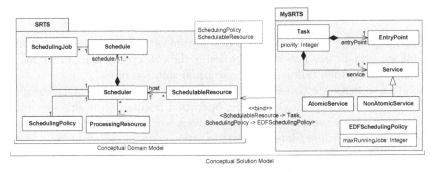

Fig. 2. Conceptual domain/solution model

3.2   Reducing the Problem Space: Building a Conceptual Solution Model

Some concepts may be required within the conceptual domain model to enhance the readability and completeness of a problem area description; these same concepts may not, however, be appropriate for solving a given problem. The subsequent stage in design consists of identifying the concepts which will serve as solution assets and to create bindings to the templates.

In order to indicate that a concept is merely present for description purposes, with respect to the targeted domain application, we introduce an *irrelevant concept* supported through a stereotype named Irrelevant.

The left and right panel in Fig. 2 together constitute the result of this stage (details have been omitted to preserve readability). It is then decided to identify ProcessingResource, SchedulingJob and Schedule as irrelevant concepts since their roles are limited to making the problem more understandable.

Templates bindings have been declared. The parameter SchedulableResource is substituted for Task. This concept is made up of one EntryPoint and a set of Services. The Service concept is further specialized into PremptibleService and NonPremptibleService. Scheduling policy is bound to the EDFSchedulingPolicy.

3.3   Profile Skeleton Definition

This phase initiates creation of the profile. Each conceptual solution entity is transformed into a stereotype; and all the relationships, such as generalizations and associations, are maintained. Note that the capability of stereotypes for participating in associations has only recently been included in version 2.1 of UML. Exceptions are the irrelevant concepts, since they are not intended for use in practical modeling situations.

At this point, the main design decision activity is mapping stereotypes to the UML metaclasses. A set of extension associations must therefore be manually established from the stereotypes to the UML metaclasses.

Fig. 3 is the profile skeleton. We have specialized the metaclass Class to support both Scheduler and Task, while considering that Operation metaclass is better suited to supporting EntryPoint and Service. EDFSchedulingPolicy reuses the DataType concept because it is a primitive type of our DSML.

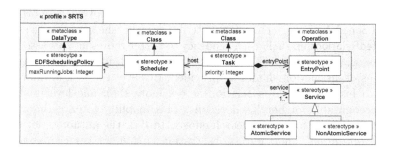

Fig. 3. Profile skeleton

3.4   Profile Consistency Analysis and Profile Optimization

To ensure definition of a well-formedness profile, a designer should ensure that none of the newly introduced concepts must conflict with the *semantics* of the extended metamodel. The term semantics must be interpreted in a broad sense. It namely encompasses the informal class description or class semantics of the UML metamodel, along with the structural definition of the metamodel (e.g., there is no possibility of creating additional meta-associations or meta-attributes). That is why, in [1, p.650], the reference metamodel is deemed to be *read-only*.

If this vital rule is usually satisfied in simple metamodel design, its strict application to a broader metamodel definition is difficult. The complexity of the UML metamodel, when combined with the (voluntary) ambiguities of UML semantics, means that there can be no guarantee of success other than the trust placed in the designer's skills.

Although a formal mechanism to assess well-formedness of profile and consistency with the reference metamodel seems hard to establish, in-depth exploration of the metamodel may help the designer select the most suitable profile implementation. The following section presents a set of formal guidelines enabling profile creation based on design patterns on the profile skeleton. We have divided these guidelines into two parts. First we identify all the patterns related to association/composition in the conceptual domain for which the profile solution is given, and, second, we provide detailed rules for profile optimization.

Dealing with Meta-association

It is common to create new meta-associations between concepts which must in some way be reflected in the profile.

The designer is then responsible for finding the implementation that best represents the meta-association. This mainly entails mapping onto two profile constructs; either a stereotype attribute is defined to maintain a reference to the associated concept or a submetaclass of a Relationship is made mandatory at level $M1$. Occasionally, the relationship may already be sufficiently represented in the metamodel and an OCL rule is enough to reinforce this intent. Even if these solutions express comparable information, they result in different profile applications scenarios that may affect its usability.

In our example, Scheduler has an association link with EDFSchedulingPolicy. The designer might choose the first solution, and the stereotype supporting the concept of Scheduler in turn embeds an attribute; or he/she might use a subclass of a DirectedRelationship such as Dependency to better represent this association.

Since associations at level $M2$ may be represented differently at level $M1$, some means of distinction should be provided. However the lack of information available to instantiate an association across more than one level makes the designer accountable for her/his decisions. This inability to carry information has already been the focus of research efforts. In [17], the authors refer to it as *shallow instantiation*. Their initial observation is that information concerning instantiation mechanisms is bound to one level. A recent study [18] formulates a similar diagnosis and its authors propose to recognize *induced associations* in models.

To provide a means for selecting the proper profile implementation, we identify different association patterns between concepts. Firstly, we detail the modeling case where the specialized metaclasses supporting the two associated concepts have an association. Secondly, we elaborate on the case in which no association is found. We then explore the constructs that make it possible to distinguish between a composite association and a non composite association. Fig. 4 summarizes the associations of interest here, along with the identified solutions.

Existing meta-association. In our example, Task is associated with EntryPoint and both extend the metaclasses Class and Operation. The first precaution is to make sure that this association does not violate the structure of the extended metamodel. Since there is at least one composite association from Class to Operation, the two introduced concepts satisfy this requirement. This meta-association may be mapped in three ways: attribute creation, directed relationship support or OCL enforcement.

We formally identify pattern recognition as follows:

Identification 1 (meta-association identification). *Let A and B be two stereotypes extending the metaclasses MA and MB respectively. If A has one (composite) association with B with member end rb (lower bound multiplicity n, upper bound multiplicity m) and if in MA there is at least one (composite) association with MB, then A and B are part of a meta-association pattern.*

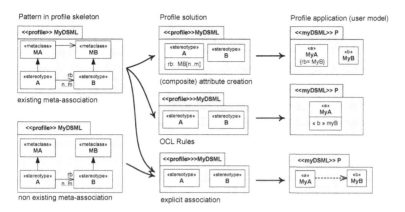

Fig. 4. Association patterns and profile solutions

An intuitive mapping solution is to declare an attribute in a stereotype to maintain information with the associated concept. In order to faithfully represent the information conveyed by the association: the type of the property must be that of the base class of the associated stereotype, and OCL rule enforcement must ensure correct application of stereotypes to the associated elements. We have generalized these considerations via the following profile solution:

Solution 1.1 (attribute creation). The property rb is used to create an attribute in A:

- the attribute rb is created with a multiplicity equal to the multiplicity of rb,
- attribute type is MB,
- stereotype «A» becomes a context for an OCL rule ensuring that values of rb are stereotyped «b»:

```
context A inv:
  self.rb->forAll(e:MB | not(e.extension_B.oclIsUndefined()))
```

Use of a relationship such as Dependency or Abstraction provides a flexible means for modeling references between DSML elements. A typical example of this is the allocation concept of SysML. The advantage of this approach is that relationships are readily recognizable, since they are represented with an explicit element.

In order to ensure that elements stereotyped «a» have DirectedRelationship links with enough elements stereotyped «b» we need to create an OCL constraint in the context of the stereotype «A». Because the base class supporting A is not affected by the DirectedRelationship, navigating to linked elements is difficult and involves exploring the namespace of the element stereotyped «A». We have only given a fragment of the OCL rule ensuring the lower bound multiplicity of property rb.

Solution 1.2 (explicit association). OCL constraints must be created to make sure that are enough DirectedRelationship links with element stereotyped «b» to comply with the multiplicity of rb.

```
context A inv:
self.base_MA.namespace.ownedMember->select(e: NamedElement |
  (e.oclIsTypeOf(uml::DirectedRelationship)) and
  (not(e.oclAsTypeOf(uml::DirectedRelationship))
      .target.extension_B.oclIsUndefined()))->size()>=n
```

The above two solutions either create a stereotype attribute or make explicit use of a subclass relationship metaclass. Alternatively we can consider that the association is sufficiently represented in the metamodel. In that case, we must ensure stereotypes application.

For instance, based on the association from Task to EntryPoint, we may decide that a profile application is correct as long as a Class stereotyped «task» owns enough Operation stereotyped «entryPoint».

The following OCL expression gives the generic profile solution (as illustration, only the lower bound multiplicity is verified). Note that this solution narrows down the scope of the associated elements to the owned members of MA.

Solution 1.3 (OCL rules). A becomes a context for an OCL declaration in charge of ensuring compliance with the multiplicity constraint obtained from property rb.

```
context A inv:
self.base_MA.ownedElement->select(e: Element |
  (e.oclIsTypeOf(MB)) and
  (not(e.extension_B.oclIsUndefined()))))->size()>=n
```

Non-existing meta-association. This subsection considers failure of the previous meta-association pattern identification, i.e stereotypes having associations that are not in the metamodel. The profile requirement that none of the introduced elements conflicts with the semantics (in this case the structure) of the extended metamodel is then not met.

Strict application of this requirement leads to the conclusion that there is a modeling *error* and to rejection of the offending association in the profile. The solution is to identify another metaclass to support one of the two stereotypes. For example, the designer may look at the parents of one of the base metaclasses, which are higher concepts with fewer constraints (the metaclass Element can be virtually used to support any extensions: it can also be part of any association with any other element, since Element has a cyclic composition with Element).

However, recourse to another metaclass may affect the semantics of the concept and not be a faithful support. To strike a balance between flexibility and adherence to the guideline, we suggest solutions that do not affect the base metaclass. Among the formerly identified patterns, the explicit use of a DirectedRelationship meets this requirement.

Handling composite concepts. Thus far, we have formulated no hypothesis about the kind of aggregation involved in the associations in the profile skeleton. However, this characteristic plays a key role in domain modeling and requires a reliable profile support.

The semantics of a composite association, also known as an *aggregation* or *containment relationship* have a common meaning in traditional programming language. They indicate that the aggregated object's lifecycle is controlled by the aggregating object. In models, composition is used to denote hierarchy and ownership. Composition between metaelements results in a deletion constraint between instances of the metaelements. In profiles, this definition has no straightforward interpretation. Stereotypes are statically applied to model elements and their application cannot therefore be coerced.

We have identified two possible solutions to support this design intent. The first, confines the use of composite association to concepts that extend metaclasses already having a composite relationship. In this situation, the attribute pattern solution and OCL solution comply with the composition constraint. Nevertheless, this approach raises much the same issues as already mentioned for the OCL solution and implies that composite elements are owned members of the aggregating element. By doing so, deletion of the base class supporting the aggregating concept results in deletion of the aggregated concepts.

To overcome this limitation, we opt for the attribute pattern solution and the aggregation kind meta-attribute of the stereotype attribute. This solution involves a support tool (discussed in section 4) to ensure correct deletion. When a base class supporting a stereotype is deleted, their attributes are inspected, if the kind of aggregation is composite then the referenced model elements are deleted.

Solution 1.4 (composite attribute creation). The same scheme is used as for the attribute creation solution. Additionally, composition information is reflected in the meta-attribute aggregation kind.

Optimization

The next identified subtask in profile creation is profile optimization for the purpose of minimizing the number of stereotypes. This is intended to preclude a proliferation of stereotypes and resulting applications that may be detrimental to the readability and understandability of models.

We propose two reduction patterns, as illustrated in Fig. 5. The first of these entails hiding a concept in an already existing UML concept with a stereotype attribute, and the second subsumes domain concepts in enumeration data types.

Hiding an existing concept. In our example, the Task concept is made up of EntryPoints. One alternative is to keep both concepts as stereotypes. However, we might consider that the EntryPoint entity, which is considered equivalent to a behavioral feature concept, is sufficiently represented by UML operation elements, and thus save one stereotype declaration. Based on this reasoning, we

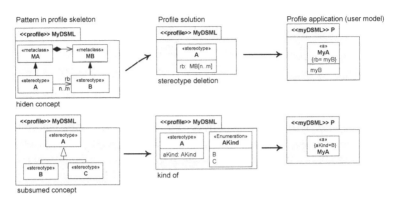

Fig. 5. Optimization patterns

can create a «Task» stereotype and use the association end named entryPoint to create an attribute typed as UML Operation. Obviously, this pattern only succeeds if the aggregated stereotype does not embed an attribute or participate in another association or generalization.

Identification 2 (hidden concept). *Let A and B be stereotypes complying with conditions expressed in the meta-association pattern. If A does not have additional stereotype attributes or additional stereotype association/generalization relationships, then B can be hidden in the target profile.*

Solution 2 (stereotype deletion). The attribute solution is reused with the difference that stereotype «B» is no longer required.

Subsuming a concept. This pattern occurs in inheritance relationships when the specialized concepts are used to describe taxonomies and do not carry any information (domain attributes or associations) except the concept itself.

In our example, Service is further specialized into AtomicService and NonAtomicService. The profile skeleton assigns one stereotype to each. As a reduction strategy, we might wish to replace the specialized concepts by an enumeration named ServiceKind, with a set of literals named NonAtomicService and AtomicService (see final profile in 6). Service thus contains an attribute named serviceKind, to indicate which kind of service we are referring to.

Identification 3 (subsumed concept). *If a set of stereotypes (e.g., B and C) specializes another stereotype A, and if the former do not embed any property or participate in any association or generalization relationship, then the substereotypes could potentially be reduced.*

Solution 3 (kind of). An enumeration AKind is created with literals matching the reduced substereotypes (e.g., C and D). An attribute in A allows reference to the enumeration data type: AKind.

Final Profile

6 is one final profile resulting from consecutive application of the identified transformation patterns to the initial profile skeleton. It embodies a set of OCL rules associated with the selected patterns. The derived profile clearly outlines the difference between the conceptual domain model and its implementation. Every association has been translated either into a stereotype attribute or into proper OCL constraints. The immediate result is that the profile can no longer be considered the main support for conveying how concepts are related to each other. However, this side effect has no impact on understanding of the DSML since we consider the domain model as the main artifact for declaring concepts.

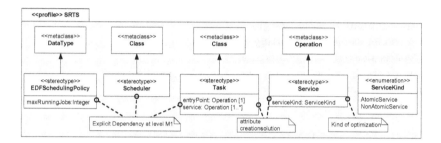

Fig. 6. One final profile

4   Tool Prototype and Evaluations

4.1   Tool Prototype

Our methodology involves several model manipulations which may be error-prone if they are performed manually. This is especially true for writing OCL enforcements and exploring metaclasses relationships.

Since we have identified profile design patterns for which we then identified pattern solutions, it is possible to partially automate our proposed approach. We have evaluated its viability by developing an Eclipse plug-in for the Papyrus UML tool as a means for partially automating the process. The plug-in's user interface is a sequence of dialogues corresponding to each of the identified key steps.

The main difficulty arises from the several profile implementation possibilities for an identified pattern. The designer is responsible for selecting the most appropriated solution and the transformation must take place interactively.

To provide a flexible support for describing rules we have defined a metamodel (not presented here due to limited space). Elements of this metamodel describe concepts for running **diagnoses** on models. This is done by a **protocol** definition that can execute **tests** on the model. Each such test associates a **recognition** concept, which is a context for declaring OCL helpers in charge of detecting a pattern in the model (like code smells for models), with the corresponding solutions. A solution is broken down into elementary fix. If a test succeeds, then one or more solutions are suggested to the designer with an order of preference.

Once a pattern is identified and a solution has been selected, the following operation is to process it with the relevant fix. We used Epsilon Object Language (EOL) [19] as an imperative OCL language for model manipulations. The Fix becomes a place to declare theses expressions.

Fig. 7 shows the dialog box that indicates which solutions may be applied to the Task. For each of these solutions, basic model transformations are also given.

As part of this prototype, we also defined mechanisms to handle the composite attribute creation solution. When a model element supporting a stereotype is deleted, if a composite attribute exists, a dialog box appears to confirm deletion of the composed elements.

Fig. 7. Dialog box for selecting a profile implementation

4.2 Evaluation and Feedback

This plug-in has made it possible to evaluate our approach on the MARTE profile. We have considered the final adopted MARTE profile (realtime/07-05-02) as the profile skeleton. The presented patterns/solutions have been described with a model that conforms to the protocol metamodel. In addition, new tests have been defined to take into account additional rules (e.g., naming convention, optimization of stereotype extensions). This led us to define more than 15 tests. The accuracy of the resulting profile is enhanced by the OCL constraints declared in each stereotype and some modeling design mistakes (stereotypes extending a metaclass and one of its sub-metaclass e.g. Class and Classifier) were identified.

5 Related Work

As already stated earlier, very little published material is available on design of domain-specific UML profiles.

In [20], Fuentes and Vallecillo pointed to the need for first defining a domain metamodel (using UML itself as the language) to clearly define the domain of the problem. In more recent work [21], Bran Selic has described a similar staged development of UML profiles and gives useful guidelines for mapping domain constructs to UML. The initial version of the SPEM [22] profile, presents general guidelines for transforming a metamodel into a profile. Our proposal also leverages use of a conceptual model but attempts to go a step further by identifying patterns on the conceptual model as a means for inferring a reliable profile.

Concerning conceptual modeling, Gerti Kappel et al described in [23] a process for "lifting metamodels into ontology models". A metamodel is considered here as an implementation-specific artifact that makes concepts hard to understand. It identifies a collection of patterns that help to transform metamodels into equivalent ontology constructs. Our research entails the opposite approach, i.e. transforming conceptual domain models into well-formedness profiles.

A precedent for our type of approach was established by the AUTOSAR (AUTomotive Open System ARchitecture) project, whose modeling framework defines an interesting mechanism for building templateable metamodels. This entails a special "language", defined by the UML profile for Templates. This language identifies a set of common patterns occurring in (meta)modeling (e.g., types, prototypes, instances). In our approach, we attempt to define a more systematic and flexible approach to designing the conceptual model and its implementation.

6   Conclusion

This paper presents a systematic approach to the design of UML profiles by leveraging use of the conceptual domain model. For this purpose, we have elaborated on a staged process that helps the designer throughout the profile design process. Starting from the conceptual domain we, determine a set of regularly occurring design pattern for which we identify profile solutions in terms of stereotypes as well as OCL constraints.

Our approach is illustrated by a running example for which we define concepts for depicting a simple real-time system domain. These domain concepts are transformed step-by-step into an equivalent profile.

To evaluate the viability of our approach, we present the Eclipse plug-in developed for this purpose. This plugin is a promising development that appears to have other potential applications. It could be used whenever a model transformation requires intervention from the designer to select a rule transformation from among several possibilities.

We are currently completing our plug-in to handle traceability requirements. This would allow designers to easily navigate between the different representations of an element: from conceptual domain to profile and vice versa. It would also allow storage of designer's decisions and permit profile regeneration.

References

1. Object Management Group: Unified Modeling Language, Superstructure Version 2.1.1 formal/-02-03 (2007)
2. Object Management Group: OMG, http://www.omg.org
3. Object Management Group: Systems Modeling Language (SysML), Specification, Adopted version, ptc/06-05-04 (2007)
4. Object Management Group: UML Profile for Schedulability, Performance and Time (SPT) formal/2005-01-02
5. Object Management Group: UML Profile for Modeling Quality of Service and Fault Tolerance Characteristics and mechanisms formal/06-05-02

6. Lagarde, F., Espinoza, H., Terrier, F., Gérard, S.: Improving UML Profile Design Practices by Leveraging Conceptual Domain Models. In: Automated Software Engineering (November 2007) (short paper)
7. Object Management Group: UML Profile for Modeling and Analysis of Real-Time and Embedded Systems (MARTE) 1.0 finalization underway
8. van Deursen, A.v., Klint, P., Visser, J.: Domain-specific languages: an annotated bibliography. SIGPLAN Not. 35(6), 26–36 (2000)
9. Consel, C., Marlet, R.: Architecturing software using a methodology for language development. In: Symposium on Programming Language Implementation and Logic Programming, vol. 1490, pp. 170–194 (1998)
10. Mernik, M., Heering, J., Sloane, A.M.: When and how to develop domain-specific languages. ACM Comput. Surv. 37(4), 316–344 (2005)
11. Alanen, M., Porres, I.: A metamodeling language supporting subset and union properties. Software and Systems Modeling (June 2007)
12. Object Management Group: Meta-Object Facility formal/2006/01-01
13. Frakes, W.B., Kang, K.: Software reuse research: Status and future. Software Engineering, IEEE Transactions on 31(7), 529–536 (2005)
14. Czarnecki, K.: Overview of Generative Software Development. Unconventional Programming Paradigms, 313–328 (2004)
15. Cuccuru, A., Mraidha, C., Terrier, F., Gérard, S.: Enhancing UML Extensions with Operational Semantics - Behaviored Profiles with Templates. In: Model Driven Engineering Languages and Systems (November 2007)
16. Emerson, M., Sztipanovits, J.: Techniques for Metamodel Composition. In: OOPSLA, 6th Workshop on Domain Specific Modeling, pp. 123–139 (2006)
17. Atkinson, C., Kühne, T.: Reducing accidental complexity in domain models. In: Software and Systems Modeling (2007)
18. Burgués, X., Franch, X., Ribó, J.: Improving the accuracy of UML metamodel extensions by introducing induced associations. Software and Systems Modeling (July 2007)
19. Kolovos, D., Paige, R., Polack, F.: The epsilon object language (eol), 128–142 (2006)
20. Fuentes-Fernández, L., Vallecillo-Moreno, A.: An Introduction to UML Profiles. UML and Model Engineering V(2) (April 2004)
21. Selic, B.: A Systematic Approach to Domain-Specific Language Design Using UML. In: International Symposium on Object and Component-Oriented Real-Time Distributed Computing, vol. 00, pp. 2–9 (2007)
22. Object Management Group: Software Process Engineering Metamodel (SPEM) formal/2005-01-06
23. Kappel, G., Kapsammer, E., Kargl, H., Kramler, G., Reiter, T., Retschitzegger, W., Schwinger, W., Wimmer, M.: Lifting Metamodels to Ontologies: A Step to the Semantic Integration of Modeling Languages. In: Model Driven Engineering Languages and Systems, pp. 528–542 (2006)

When Things Go Wrong: Interrupting Conversations

Juliana Bowles[1] and Sotiris Moschoyiannis[2]

[1] School of Computer Science, University of St Andrews
Jack Cole Building, North Haugh, St Andrews KY16 9SX, UK
jkfb@st-andrews.ac.uk
[2] Department of Computing, University of Surrey
Guildford, Surrey GU2 7XH, UK
s.moschoyiannis@surrey.ac.uk

Abstract. This paper presents a true-concurrent approach to formalising integration of Small-to-Medium Enterprises (SMEs) with Web services. Our approach formalises common notions in service-oriented computing such as *conversations* (interactions between clients and web services), *multi-party conversations* (interactions between multiple web services) and *coordination protocols*, which are central in a transactional environment. In particular, we capture long-running transactions with recovery and compensation mechanisms for the underlying services in order to ensure that a transaction either commits or is successfully compensated for.

1 Introduction

Business transactions between open communities of SMEs have been highlighted as a key area within the emerging Digital Economy [1]. A business transaction can be a simple usage of a service (rare in Business-to-Business (B2B) relationships) or a mixture of different levels of composition of services from various providers. Within the database community the conventional definition of a transaction [2] is based on ACID (Atomicity, Consistency, Isolation, Durability) properties. However, in advanced distributed applications these properties often present considerable limitations and in many cases are in fact undesirable.

Business transactions typically involve interactions and coordination between multiple partners. The specification of a transaction comprises a number of *sub-transactions* or *activities* which involve the execution of several underlying services from different providers, some of which take minutes, hours or even days to complete - hence the term *long-running* transaction. Indeed a wide range of B2B scenarios correspond to long-lived business activities and may have a long execution period.

It is often the case that internal activities need to share results before the termination of the transaction (commit). More generally, dependencies may arise between activities inside a transaction due to the required ordering on the service invocations or, simply, due the sharing of data [3]. Further, many B2B scenarios

J. Fiadeiro and P. Inverardi (Eds.): FASE 2008, LNCS 4961, pp. 131–145, 2008.
© Springer-Verlag Berlin Heidelberg 2008

require a transaction to release some results to another transaction, before it commits. That is to say, dependencies may exist across transactions due to the need for releasing *partial results* outside a transaction. Failure to accommodate this may lead to unacceptable delays in related transactions and, even worse, leave a service provider open to denial of service attacks (as data may be locked indefinitely in a non-terminating transaction). Thus, the Isolation property must be relaxed and this poses further challenges with regard to keeping track of the dependencies that arise between the corresponding service executions.

The multi-service nature of transactions makes Service-Oriented Computing (SOC) [4,5], whose goal is to enable applications from different providers to be offered as services that can be used, composed and coordinated in a loosely-coupled manner, the prevalent computing paradigm in a transactional environment. The actual architectural approach of SOC, called SOA, is a way of reorganising software applications and supporting infrastructure into an interconnected set of services, each accessible through standard interfaces and messaging (coordination) protocols.

In this paper we are concerned with modelling long-running transactions, and in particular the coordination of the underlying service executions. The challenges in exploiting the promise of SOA in a transactional environment requires a thorough understanding of the dependencies that arise from the complex interactions between services and the valid sequences of service invocations.

We have seen that business transactions involve interactions between multiple service providers which need to be orchestrated. Business transactions also need to deal with faults that arise at any stage of execution. In fact, a long-running transaction should either complete successfully (commit) or not take place at all. This means that there must be some mechanism/procedure in place, which in the event of a failure (service unavailable, network/platform disconnection, etc.) makes it possible to undo parts of the transaction that have actually happened so far. Therefore, in addition to formalising conversations in a transactional environment we also provide constructs for compensating (earlier parts of) conversations, in case some failure later on makes this necessary.

Our approach uses a true-concurrent model (labelled prime event structures) which can be obtained directly from UML 2.0 sequence diagrams describing multi-party conversations. The model is extended to capture possible faults that result in interrupting a conversation and taking compensating action. We show how our formal framework orchestrates conversations and associated compensations in order to achieve the desired effect - a transaction either commits or is successfully compensated for.

This paper is structured as follows. Section 2 outlines the use of sequence diagrams for modelling conversations within a transaction. Section 3 describes the formal model used for long-running transactions, and Section 4 extends it to describe interruptions and compensation whereby we distinguish between *rollback with memory* and *forgetful rollback*. A brief discussion on related work is included in Section 5 and the paper finishes with some ideas for future work given in Section 6.

2   Example

We consider a simple multi-party conversation within a long-running transaction and show how it can be modelled using UML2.0 [6]. The example has been simplified somewhat but still contains enough complexity to illustrate the key ideas behind our formal modelling approach.

We use sequence diagrams to represent conversations within long-running (multi-party service) transactions. We only model the participants of the conversations (web services) without explicitly representing a distinction between the initiator and a participant of a transaction. In sequence diagrams, we can indicate any exchange with a client or coordinator using *gates*. Gates correspond to the environment which we are not interested in capturing explicitly. Notice that this means that we are deliberately ignoring a choice of central or distributed coordination in our model. Indeed, our formalism works with both architectures. The choice of architecture very much depends on the target application - for example, in a digital business ecosystem involving SMEs a fully distributed solution may be most appropriate since the use of a centralised coordinator would violate local autonomy, as is the case with existing transaction models (e.g., BTP[13], WS-Tx[12] are briefly discussed in Section 5), and this is a barrier for the adoption of SOA by SMEs.

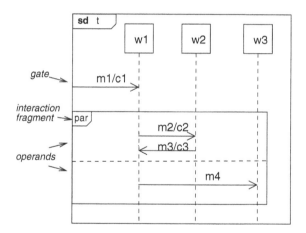

Fig. 1. A multi-party conversation

Fig. 1 shows three participants and the messages exchanged between them for transaction t. All messages are exchanged asynchronously. The **par** fragment indicates that the operands are executed in paralell. If a particular operation invocation needs to be compensated for in a specific way this is given by the application developer and is written after the name of the operation. For instance, the construct **m1/c1** indicates that **m1** is the operation being invoked and **c1** is the corresponding compensation. The compensation for an operation invocation can be complex and impose a sequence of message exchanges between services and the environment. For example, a lock mechanism might be required to ensure consistency of data used in the conversation during recovery (e.g. see [3]). If this is the case, c1 can itself be represented by a sequence diagram with the same name (and similarly for all compensations).

We use sequence diagrams to model conversations showing only protocol-specific message exchanges (e.g., m1, m2, and so on, in Fig. 1) and ignore initial activation and registration exchanges to initiate the execution of a conversation. However, within the duration of a long-running transaction there are other messages that can be sent between the participating web services and a coordinator. These messages are sent to indicate the status of the execution of the transaction and allow for compensating action to be taken whenever necessary. It may be instructive to note that in a distributed solution, each service provider will have its own coordinator that is responsible for the services it offers and has knowledge of their dependencies (on other coordinators' services that execute immediately before or after its own). An overview of a transaction model with local coordination can be found in [7]. In a transaction model with centralised coordination, services from each service provider communicate through the central coordinator which is typically controlled by the network provider.

Messages used for providing a transaction processing system with compensating capability include faulted, compensate and forget. A web service may fail the execution of its invoked operation in which case it sends a message faulted to the coordinator (or, its coordinator). All other participants need to be informed in the next step as they will need to compensate or forget their parts of the execution of the conversation so far. If a web service participating in the conversation receives a message compensate, then the normal flow of messages should stop immediately and all its previous actions (effects of previous message exchanges) within the conversation need to be undone. This compensation does not necessarily leave the web service in exactly the same state it had at the beginning of the conversation (we call it *rollback with memory*). By contrast, if a participant receives a forget message, again the normal flow of messages is interrupted abruptly, but this time the participating service returns to the same state as in the beginning of the conversation and all its previous actions are simply ignored (we call it *forgetful rollback*).

We do not represent these additional messages when modelling the (multi-party) conversation in Fig. 1 as it would complicate the model unnecessarily. All possible faults and consequences are, however, considered in our formal model as we will see in Section 4.

One example of a possible faulted scenario leading to the abortion of the long-running transaction of our example is given in Fig. 2. In this case, w3 fails whilst executing m4 and sends a faulted message to the corresponding coordinator. This leads to two further messages being sent from the coordinator, namely a forget to w3 and a compensate to w1 (the later one will possibly trigger a further compensate message to w2 depending on the state of the execution of the interaction in the first operand). Notice that in this particular scenario the

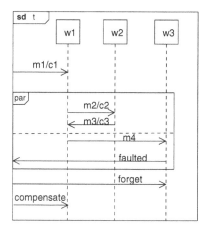

Fig. 2. A multi-party conversation with faults

`faulted` message is sent in parallel to the conversation between w1 and w2 and it is therefore possible that this sub-interaction has not happened and does not need to be compensated for. This can be made explicit in our formal model of conversations, which is described in the following sections.

3   The Model

We have used labelled event structures as an underlying model for sequence diagrams in UML 2.0[8,9]. In this paper, we use labelled event structures to capture conversations and coordination protocols.

3.1   Event Structures: Basic Notions

We recall some basic notions on the model we use, namely *labelled prime event structures* [10].

Prime event structures, or event structures for short, allow the description of distributed computations as event occurrences together with relations for expressing causal dependency and nondeterminism. The first relation is called *causality*, and the second *conflict*. The causality relation implies a (partial) order among event occurrences, while the conflict relation expresses how the occurrence of certain events excludes the occurrence of others. Consider the following definition of event structures.

Event Structure. An *event structure* is a triple $E = (Ev, \to^*, \#)$ where Ev is a set of events and $\to^*, \# \subseteq Ev \times Ev$ are binary relations called *causality* and *conflict*, respectively. Causality $\to^*$ is a partial order. Conflict $\#$ is symmetric and irreflexive, and propagates over causality, i.e., $e\#e' \wedge e' \to^* e'' \Rightarrow e\#e''$ for all $e, e', e'' \in Ev$. Two events $e, e' \in Ev$ are *concurrent*, $e \; co \; e'$ iff $\neg(e \to^* e' \vee e' \to^* e \vee e\#e')$.

From the two relations defined on the set of events, a further relation is derived, namely the *concurrency* relation *co*. As stated, two events are concurrent if and only if they are completely unrelated, i.e., neither related by causality nor by conflict.

In our approach to inter-object behaviour specification, we will consider a restriction of event structures sometimes referred to as *discrete* event structures. An event structure is said to be *discrete* if the set of previous occurrences of an event in the structure is finite.

Discrete Event Structure. Let $E = (Ev, \rightarrow^*, \#)$ be an event structure. E is a *discrete event structure* iff for each event $e \in Ev$, the *local configuration* of e given by $\downarrow e = \{e' \mid e' \rightarrow^* e\}$ is finite.

The finiteness assumption of the so-called local configuration is motivated by the fact that system computations always have a starting point, which means that any event in a computation can only have finitely many previous occurrences.

Consequently, we are able to talk about immediate causality in such structures. Two events e and e' are related by *immediate* causality if there are no other event occurrences in between. Formally, if $\forall_{e'' \in Ev}(e \rightarrow^* e'' \rightarrow^* e' \Rightarrow (e'' = e \lor e'' = e'))$ holds. If $e \rightarrow^* e'$ are related by immediate causality then e is said to be an *immediate predecessor* of e' and e' is said to be an *immediate successor* of e. We may write $e \rightarrow e'$ instead of $e \rightarrow^* e'$ to denote immediate causality. Furthermore, we also use the notation $e \rightarrow^+ e'$ whenever $e \rightarrow^* e'$ and $e \neq e'$.

Hereafter, we only consider discrete event structures.

Configuration. Let $E = (Ev, \rightarrow^*, \#)$ be an event structure and $C \subseteq Ev$. C is a *configuration* in E iff it is both (1) conflict free: for all $e, e' \in C$, $\neg(e \# e')$, and (2) downwards closed: for any $e \in C$ and $e' \in Ev$, if $e' \rightarrow^* e$ then $e' \in C$. A maximal configuration denotes a run. A run is sometimes called life cycle.

Finally, in order to use event structures to provide a denotational semantics to languages, it is necessary to link the event structures to the language they are supposed to describe. This is achieved by attaching a labelling function to the set of events. A generic labelling function is as defined next.

Labelling Function. Let $E = (Ev, \rightarrow^*, \#)$ be an event structure, and L be an arbitrary set. A *labelling function* for E is a total function $l : Ev \rightarrow L$ mapping each event into an element of the set L.

An event structure together with a labelling function defines a so-called labelled event structure.

Labelled Event Structure. Let $E = (Ev, \rightarrow^*, \#)$ be an event structure, L be a set of labels, and $l : Ev \rightarrow L$ be a labelling function for E. A *labelled event structure* is a pair $(E, l : Ev \rightarrow L)$.

Usually, events model the occurrence of actions, and a possible labelling function maps each event into an action symbol or a set of action symbols. In this paper, we use labelled event structures in the context of long-running transactions. As we will see, in our case, and since we use UML models of conversations within a transaction, the labelling function indicates whether an event represents sending or receiving a message, the beginning or end of an interaction fragment.

3.2   Event Structures for Transactions

In this paper, we use sequence diagrams to model transactions. We first need to understand how to obtain a labelled event structure for the sequence diagram (without faults), and then can move to show how compensation mechanisms can be integrated. In [8] we have shown how labelled event structures can be used to provide a model for sequence diagrams. Here we only provide the general idea.

To obtain the corresponding event structure model, we want to associate events to the *locations* of the diagram and determine the relations between those events to reflect the meaning of the diagram. Fig. 3 shows the relation between the locations in a simple sequence diagram (which could for example correspond to the interaction between a client and a service) and the corresponding event structure model (where we depict immediate causality). Asynchronous communication is captured as immediate causality as well, hence the two locations for sending and receiving message m2/c2 are captured by two consecutive events. The labels become clearer later when we define the labelling function used.

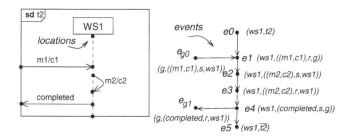

Fig. 3. A simple sequence diagram and its corresponding model

However, for more complex diagrams with fragments the correspondence between locations and events is not always so obvious.

The locations within different operands of an **alt** fragment are naturally associated to events in conflict. However, the end location of an **alt** fragment is problematic. If it corresponded to one event then this event would be in conflict with itself due to the fact that in a prime event structure conflict propagates over causality. This would, however, lead to an invalid model since conflict is irreflexive. We are therefore forced to copy events for locations marking the end of **alt** fragments, as well as for all locations that follow. Events associated to locations that fall within a **par** fragment are concurrent. Synchronous communication is denoted by a shared event whereas asynchronous communication is captured by immediate causality between the send event and receive event.

As mentioned earlier, for representing sequence diagrams we use a labelling function to indicate whether an event represents sending or receiving a message, a condition, the beginning or end of an interaction fragment. The only considered fragments in this paper is **par** and **alt**. For more details on further fragments please see [8,9].

Let D be a set of diagram names corresponding to conversations, transactions or the detailed description of compensations, W_t be the set of web services participating in the interaction described by $t \in D$, and g denote a gate or the environment (i.e., a client or coordinator) with $g \in W_t$ for all $t \in D$. Let $C_t \subset D$ be the set of compensations associated to messages in $t \in D$. Let $F_t = \{t, par, alt\} \cup C_t$ with $t \in D$ and $\overline{F_t} = \{\bar{t}, \overline{par}, \overline{alt}\} \cup \overline{C_t}$ where $\overline{C_t} = \{\bar{c} \mid c \in C_t\}$. We use par (or $\overline{par}$) as a label of an event associated to the location marking the beginning (or end) of a **par** fragment. In particular, events associated to initial (or end) locations of a diagram t have labels t (or $\bar{t}$). Similarly for compensation diagrams (i.e., diagrams representing the behaviour of compensations). Let M_{web} be the set of messages exchanged between web services and/or the environment, and M_{env} be a predefined set of messages exchanged only between a service and the environment. M_{env} consists of messages such as exited, completed, faulted (sent by a web service to the environment), and close, complete, compensate and forget (sent by the environment to a web service). Let $Mes_t = M_{web_t} \times (C_t \cup \{-\}) \cup M_{env_t}$ be the complete set of message labels for $t \in D$. The labelling function for diagram t is a total function defined over events as follows:

$$\mu_t : Ev \to W_t \times (Mes_t \times \{s, r\} \times W_t \cup F_t \cup \overline{F_t})$$

Each event is associated to a unique web service involved in t and can denote sending a message, receiving a message or indicating the beginning/end of a fragment. This labelling function has been simplified to capture only asynchronous messages as this is the only form of communication we use in this paper. In the example of Fig. 3, event e_1 has label $(ws1, ((m_1, c_1), r, g))$ indicating it belongs to service $ws1$ and corresponds to the receipt of message m_1 with compensation c_1 from g. Certain operation invocations may not have a compensation defined in case of failure, in which case the label is written $(s_1, ((m, -), r, s_2))$. An example of a label for predefined messages is $(ws1, (completed, s, g))$. We write $(\mu_t(e))_1$ to indicate the first projection of the label for e (e.g., associated service).

Finally, for $t \in D$, a model is a labelled event structure $M_t = (E_t, \mu_t)$.

4   Modelling Interruptions

In the previous section, we have seen how for a (multi-party) conversation of a long-running transaction captured as a sequence diagram, we can obtain the underlying formal model as a labelled event structure. In this section, we are going to see how the model can be extended to incorporate possible faults in transaction executions.

Recall the sequence diagram of Fig. 1 showing the interaction between three web services w1, w2 and w3. The labelled event structure that models the behaviour represented in the sequence diagram is given by Fig. 4. This model only takes into account the correct behaviour of all parties involved in the interaction. However, any of the operations invoked (m1, m2, m3 or m4) could possibly fail during execution, for example, as in the scenario of Fig. 2. If that happens, the corresponding service would need to inform its coordinator (in Fig. 2, w3

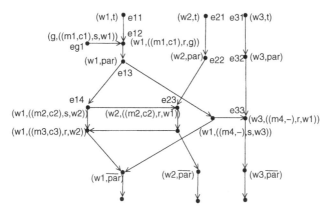

Fig. 4. LES for the multi-party conversation of Fig. 1

sends a message `faulted` to the environment) which would need to inform all parties of the correct compensation mechanism (in Fig. 2, the environment sends a message `forget` to w3, and `compensate` to w1). Consequently, we need to be able to represent the faults that can occur during an interaction and as well as their effects.

Initial Configuration. Let $M_t = (E_t, \mu_t)$ be a model for a transaction t. An initial configuration for M_t is $Q_0 = \{e \in Ev_t \mid \mu_t(e) = (w, t), w \in W_t\}$.

The initial configuration basically corresponds to the set of events associated to the initial location of every web service participating in the interaction. In Fig. 4, the initial configuration corresponds to the set of events $\{e_{11}, e_{21}, e_{31}\}$.

Immediate Configurations. Let $M_t = (E_t, \mu_t)$ be a model for a transaction t. For any two configurations $Q_1 \neq Q_2$ in E_t, we say that Q_1 and Q_2 are *immediate configurations* (or Q_2 is an *immediate postconfiguration* for Q_1, and Q_1 is an *immediate preconfiguration* of Q_2) iff (1) $Q_1 \subset Q_2$ and for any $e_1, e_2 \in Q_2 \setminus Q_1$ e_1 co e_2, and (2) if $(\mu_t(e))_1 = w$ for $w \in W_t$ and $e \in Q_2 \setminus Q_1$, then there is a maximal event $e' \in Q_1$ such that $e' \to e$ and $(\mu_t(e'))_1 = w$.

A configuration can have more than one possible immediate postconfiguration due to conflict or the possible concurrency between events corresponding to different services (for example, events e_{22}, e_{32} and e_{g1}). From one configuration to the next we can add either a single event or a set of events in concurrency. If two or more concurrent events appear in the same immediate postconfiguration we say they occur *simultaneously*. Otherwise their occurrence is effectively being interleaved. The initial configuration in Fig. 4 has seven immediate postconfigurations given by $\{e_{g1}, e_{11}, e_{21}, e_{31}\}$, $\{e_{11}, e_{21}, e_{22}, e_{31}\}$, $\{e_{11}, e_{21}, e_{31}, e_{32}\}$, $\{e_{g1}, e_{11}, e_{21}, e_{22}, e_{31}\}$, $\{e_{g1}, e_{11}, e_{21}, e_{31}, e_{32}\}$, $\{e_{11}, e_{21}, e_{22}, e_{31}, e_{32}\}$ and finally $\{e_{g1}, e_{11}, e_{21}, e_{22}, e_{31}, e_{32}\}$. Notice that $\{e_{11}, e_{12}, e_{21}, e_{31}\}$ is not a configuration (it does not satisfy the condition of being downwards closed) and can thus not be an immediate postconfiguration for the initial configuration. For the same reason, we know that receiving a message can never happen before the corresponding send.

Configuration Path. Let $M_t = (E_t, \mu_t)$ be a model for a transaction t. A *configuration path* in M_t is a sequence of immediate configurations $Q_0 \cdot Q_1 \cdot Q_2 \cdots Q_n$ in E_t starting with the initial configuration and ending in a maximal configuration or run.

Given our definition of immediate configurations and provided there is concurrency in the model, we always have several paths starting from an initial configuration and leading to a maximal configuration. In our example of Fig. 4 we have several paths but only one maximal configuration and consequently all paths lead to the same final configuration. If a model has conflict (due to alternatives given as **alt** fragments in the sequence diagram) we have as many maximal configurations as there are alternatives.

Models M_t for transactions that have more than one maximal configuration can be useful for providing *forward recovery* - that is, including capability for completing the transaction following an alternative path of execution rather than aborting in the event of a failure in some service of the corresponding conversation. We return to this discussion in the concluding section of the paper.

The difference between two immediate configurations is given by a set of events which corresponds to the occurrence of some action, i.e., sending/receiving a message or entering/exiting an interaction fragment. This can be seen as a transition between the two configurations labelled by the set of occurring action(s).

Configuration Transitions. Let $M_t = (E_t, \mu_t)$ be a model for a transaction t, and Q_1, Q_2 be immediate configurations in E_t with Q_1 the preconfiguration of Q_2. Let $Q_2 \setminus Q_1 = \{e_1, e_2, \ldots, e_n\}$ and $\mu_t(e_i) = l_i$ with $1 \leq i \leq n$. A *transition* from Q_1 to Q_2 is labelled by $\langle l_1, l_2, \ldots, l_n \rangle$ and written $Q_1 \xrightarrow{\langle l_1, l_2 \ldots l_n \rangle} Q_2$.

Consider the model of Fig. 4. The transition between $Q_0 = \{e_{11}, e_{21}, e_{31}\}$ and $Q_1 = \{e_{g1}, e_{11}, e_{21}, e_{31}\}$ is labelled by $\langle (g, ((m_1, c_1), s, w_1)) \rangle$. To simplify the label notation, we sometimes write $(w, m/c!, q)$ to denote w sending message m/c to q, and $(q, m/c?, w)$ to denote q receiving message m/c from w. Labels denoting entering/exiting fragments are often omitted (written $\langle - \rangle$). A possible path in the model of Fig. 4 could be given by the following transitions:

$$Q_0 \xrightarrow{\langle (g, m_1/c_1!, w_1) \rangle} Q_1 \xrightarrow{\langle (w1, m_1/c_1?, g) \rangle} Q_2 \xrightarrow{\langle - \rangle} Q_3 \xrightarrow{\langle (w1, m_4!, w_3) \rangle} Q_4$$

$$Q_4 \xrightarrow{\langle (w_3, m_4?, w_1) \rangle} Q_5 \xrightarrow{\langle (w_1, m_2/c_2!, w_2) \rangle} Q_6 \xrightarrow{\langle (w_2, m_2/c_2?, w_1) \rangle} Q_7$$

$$Q_7 \xrightarrow{\langle (w_2, m_3/c_3!, w_1) \rangle} Q_8 \xrightarrow{\langle (w_1, m_3/c_3?, w_2) \rangle} Q_9 \xrightarrow{\langle - \rangle} Q_{10} \xrightarrow{\langle - \rangle} E_t$$

We now want to add to the model possible faults that can happen in the execution of transactions. This corresponds to adding transitions labelled by the predefined messages seen earlier between a web service and the environment or vice versa (e.g., faulted, compensate, forget).

The execution of a message m for a web service w can only fail after m was invoked (the message was received), and before a subsequent message is sent by w. For the path in our example, m_4 could fail after configuration Q_5. The question now is what is the result of such a transition, namely what immediate postconfiguration(s) do we get for Q_5 that satisfy $Q_5 \xrightarrow{\langle (w_3, faulted!, g) \rangle} Q_6' \xrightarrow{\langle (g, faulted?, w_3) \rangle} Q_7'$. We assume that faulted messages have priority and thus the send is always followed by the receipt. Moreover, once a path is faulted no further normal transitions are allowed. Notice, that after a faulted message occurs the configurations are no longer configurations in M_t but in an extended model for t with fault events.

Faulted Transitions and Faulted Path. Let $M_t = (E_t, \mu_t)$ be a model for a transaction t, and $Q_0 \cdot Q_1 \cdot Q_2 \cdots Q_n$ in E_t be a configuration path in M_t. Let $Q_i \xrightarrow{\langle\langle w_2, m/c?, w_1 \rangle\rangle} Q_{i+1}$ be a transition. The *faulted transitions* associated to message $(w_2, m/c?, w_1)$ at Q_{i+1} correspond to $Q_{i+1} \xrightarrow{\langle\langle w_2, faulted!, g \rangle\rangle} Q'_{i+2} \xrightarrow{\langle\langle g, faulted?, w_2 \rangle\rangle} Q'_{i+3}$ where the new configurations are defined as follows $Q'_{i+2} = Q_{i+1} \cup \{e_2 \mid e_2 \notin Q_{i+1}, \mu_t(e_2) = (w_2, (faulted, s, g))\}$ with $e_1 \rightarrow e_2$ where e_1 is the maximal event in Q_{i+1} with $(\mu_t(e_1))_1 = w_2$; and $Q'_{i+3} = Q_{i+2} \cup \{e_3 \mid e_3 \notin Ev_t \cup \{e_2\}, \mu_t(e_3) = (g, (faulted, r, w_2))\}$ with $e_2 \rightarrow e_3$. The sequence $Q_0 \cdot Q_1 \cdot Q_2 \cdots Q_i \cdot Q_{i+1} \cdot Q'_{i+2} Q'_{i+3}$ is a *faulted path* for extended M_t.

Once a faulted message has been sent to and received by the environment (in effect the coordinator of the failed web service), the environment can respond with one or more forget or compensate. Similarly to faulted messages, sending and receiving a forget or compensate always happen successively. The definitions below reflect that a forget/compensate does not have to happen immediately after a faulted transition (there can be j pairs of configurations in between).

Forget Transitions. Let $M_t = (E_t, \mu_t)$ be a model for a transaction t, and $Q_0 \cdot Q_1 \cdot Q_2 \cdots Q_{i-1} \cdot Q_i \cdot Q_{i+1}$ be a faulted path for extended M_t where the faulted transitions are $Q_{i-1} \xrightarrow{\langle\langle w, faulted!, g \rangle\rangle} Q_i \xrightarrow{\langle\langle g, faulted?, w \rangle\rangle} Q_{i+1}$. The pair of *forget transitions* associated to the faulted transitions at Q_{i+1} correspond to $Q_{i+2j-1} \xrightarrow{\langle\langle g, forget!, w \rangle\rangle} Q_{i+2j} \xrightarrow{\langle\langle w, forget?, g \rangle\rangle} Q_{i+2j+1}$ where $j \in \mathbb{N}$ and the new configurations are defined as follows $Q_{i+2j} = Q_{i+2j-1} \cup \{e_2 \notin Q_{i+2j-1} \mid \mu_t(e_2) = (g, (forget, s, w))\}$ with $e_1 \rightarrow e_2$ where e_1 is an event in Q_{i+2j-1} with $\mu_t(e_1) = (g, (faulted, r, w))$. Let $O = \{w_1, \ldots, w_n \in W_t \mid \exists_{e_{w_k}, e'_{w_k} \in Q_i} (\mu_t(e_{w_k}))_1 = w_k, (\mu_t(e'_{w_k}))_1 = w$ and $e'_{w_k} \rightarrow^* e_{w_k}$ for all $1 \le k \le n\}$. $Q_{i+2j+1} = Q_{i+2j} \cup \{p_1, \ldots, p_n \notin Q_{i+2j} \mid \mu_t(p_k) = (w_k, t), w_k \in O$ for all $1 \le k \le n\}$ and $e_2 \rightarrow p_k$ for all $1 \le k \le n$.

After a service w receives a forget message, all its previous executions are undone and it returns to the configuration it had at the beginning. The other services remain unaffected, unless a service w' received a request from w during the conversation ($w' \in O$). If that is the case it also needs to reverse to its initial configuration. Further services that were not in (direct or indirect) interaction with w are unaffected and wait for a forget or compensate message from the environment. For space reasons, we omit the proof that the obtained configuration Q_{i+2j+1} after the forget transitions is a valid immediate configuration for Q_{i+2j}.

We now describe how to deal with compensation.

Compensate Transitions. Let $M_t = (E_t, \mu_t)$ be a model for a transaction t, and $Q_0 \cdot Q_1 \cdot Q_2 \cdots Q_{i-1} \cdot Q_i \cdot Q_{i+1}$ be a faulted path for extended M_t where the faulted transitions are $Q_{i-1} \xrightarrow{\langle\langle w1, faulted!, g \rangle\rangle} Q_i \xrightarrow{\langle\langle g, faulted?, w1 \rangle\rangle} Q_{i+1}$. A pair of *compensate transitions* correspond to a sequence of configurations $Q_{i+2j} \cdot$

$Q_{i+2j+1} \cdot Q'_{k_j} \cdots Q'_{k_0}$ where $Q_{i+2j-1} \xrightarrow{\langle(g,compensate!,w2)\rangle} Q_{i+2j} \xrightarrow{\langle(w2,compensate?,g)\rangle}$
Q_{i+2j+1}, $j \in \mathbb{N}$ and the new configurations are defined as follows:

- $Q_{i+2j} = Q_{i+2j-1} \cup \{e_2 \notin Q_{i+2j-1} \mid \mu_t(e_2) = (g, (compensate, s, w_2))\}$ with
  $e_1 \rightarrow^* e_2$ for $e_1 \in Q_{i+1}$ with $\mu_t(e_1) = (g, (faulted, r, w_1))$.
- $Q_{i+2j+1} = Q_{i+2j} \cup \{e_3 \notin Q_{i+2j} \mid \mu_t(e_3) = (w2, c)\}$ with $e \rightarrow e_3$ where e is the
  maximal event in Q_{i+2j} satisfying $(\mu_t(e))_1 = w_2$, and where e' is the maximal
  event in Q_k for the largest $k \leq i - 1$ satisfying $\mu_t(e') = (w_2, ((m, c), r, w))$
  for some $w \in W_t$ and $(m, c) \in Mes_t$.
- Let $\{Q_{k_0}, \dots, Q_{k_p} \mid$ for every Q_{k_m} with $1 \leq k_m < i$ and $0 \leq m \leq p$ such that
  there is a maximal event e_{k_m} with $\mu_t(e_{k_m}) = (w_2, ((m, c_{k_m}), r, w))$ for some
  $w \in W_t$ and $(m, c_{k_m}) \in Mes_t\}$. We define $Q'_{k_m} = Q'_{k_{m+1}} \cup \{e_{k_m} \notin Q'_{k_{m+1}} \mid$
  $\mu_t(e_{k_m}) = (w_2, c_{k_m})\}$ with $e_{k_{m+1}} \rightarrow e_{k_m}$ and where $Q'_{k_{p+1}} = Q_{i+2j+1}$.

If instead of a forget message the environment responds with a compensate
message, then the affected service needs to undo all its actions in reverse order
by doing all associated compensation actions. We obtain a succession of new
configurations for each compensation performed. We omit the proof that the
obtained sequence is a valid sequence of configurations in an extended model
M_t. Furthermore, if the compensations denote complex behaviour described in
another sequence diagram, we can obtain the refined model by applying the
categorical construction of [9].

If we go back to the example configuration path given earlier for the example
of Fig. 4, we can obtain the faulted path in accordance with the scenario of Fig. 2
as follows. A fault can happen after the invocation of m_4 at configuration Q_5,
namely after

$$Q_0 \xrightarrow{\langle(g,m_1/c_1!,w_1)\rangle} Q_1 \xrightarrow{\langle(w_1,m_1/c_1?,g)\rangle} Q_2 \xrightarrow{\langle-\rangle} Q_3 \xrightarrow{\langle(w_1,m_4!,w_3)\rangle} Q_4 \xrightarrow{\langle(w_3,m_4?,w_1)\rangle} Q_5$$

leading to

$$Q_5 \xrightarrow{\langle(w_3,faulted!,g)\rangle} Q'_6 \xrightarrow{\langle(g,faulted?,w_3)\rangle} Q'_7 \xrightarrow{\langle(g,forget!,w_3)\rangle} Q'_8 \xrightarrow{\langle(w_3,forget?,g)\rangle} Q'_9$$

and further

$$Q'_9 \xrightarrow{\langle(g,compensate!,w1)\rangle} Q'_{10} \xrightarrow{\langle(w1,compensate?,g)\rangle} Q'_{11}$$

In this case, only message m_1 for w_1 needs to be compensated and the faulted
path thus finished at Q'_{11} where a new event e_{11} has a label $\mu(e_{11}) = (w_1, c_1)$.

Once faults and associated forget/compensate mechanisms are done for all
configuration paths over M_t, we can derive a complete model from both configuration paths and faulted paths for the conversation t.

5   Related Work

We have seen that the need for releasing *partial results* outside a transaction may
not happen as often as sharing results inside a transaction, but is nevertheless

a primary requirement if long-running transactions are to cover a wide range of business models. Conventional transaction models such as *Sagas* [11] or the more recent models targeting web services such as *Web Services Transactions* (WS-Tx) [12] and *Business Transaction Protocol* (BTP) [13] do not provide capability for partial results and inevitably make it the business process designer's responsibility. This often means that new transactions are added that do not reflect the exact needs of the business activity itself but rather are added to get round the problem. Further, existing transaction models seem to be geared towards centralised control (WS-Coordination framework [12]) which means that, especially during compensation, access to the local state of service execution is required. This violates the primary requirement of SOA for loosely-coupled services and may not be possible or acceptable in a business environment as it does not respect the local autonomy of participating SMEs. Further, there is no capability for forward recovery and no provision for covering omitted results.

Part of the problem seems to be that multi-party conversations are involved and such frameworks are lacking a formal model for the coordination of the underlying interactions between services. It is only recently that long-running transactions have received the attention of the formal methods community.

The authors in [14] define a set of primitives for long-running transactions in flow composition languages concerned with structured control flows, given in terms of sequencing and branching. Their approach to modelling long-running transactions is driven by the understanding of long-running transactions as in *Sagas* [11]. The Sagas model is a point of reference for long-lived database transactions, nevertheless its applicability in conducting long-running business transactions is questioned (e.g. see [15]).

Furthermore, the basic idea is that a long-running transaction is modelled using CSP sequential processes. The fact there is no communication between sequential processes that are composed in parallel in [14] means that the parallel composition operator simply generates all nondeterministic interleavings of the actions from each process, and this may cause unnecessary overhead in compensating for parallel processes. In fact, the extension of CSP with compensations to produce the so-called *compensating* CSP (cCSP) [16] appeals to a non-interleaving semantics [17] when performing the compensations for sequential processes that are composed in parallel.

In the approach taken in [16] a long-running transaction is modelled as a sequential process, with the usual operators for sequential composition, choice of action, parallel composition. The authors incorporate constructs for writing compensable processes and then introduce a cancellation semantics for compensable processes. The resulting cCSP framework provides a blueprint for a process algebra that models long-running transactions. The notion of a long-running transaction considered however draws upon the concept found in Sagas, and this comes with potential pitfalls, as mentioned before.

In cCSP transactions are understood as sequences of isolated activities and no communication is allowed between internal activities of a transaction. The only communication allowed is that of synchronising on terminal events of sequential processes that have been composed in parallel. As a result of prohibiting communication, there is no provision for partial results but also it is not possible to trigger the compensating procedure in one process as soon as a failure occurs in some other process. This is not remotely satisfactory when modelling real problems which require activities within a transaction to be executed in parallel, since it may result in a situation where one process fails early on in its execution and the other processes have to complete their execution until they reach their terminal event in order to be notified (via synchronisation) that they need to compensate the activities performed due to a failure in the other process.

6   Conclusions

We have described a formal model for the coordination of multi-party conversations in the context of long-running transactions. In particular, we showed how to model interrupting conversations in the presence of faults and described the compensating sequences of operation invocations that are required to undo the (forward) operation invocations or conversations. We considered two ways in which to model interruptions: forgetful rollback and rollback with memory. Moreover, our approach allows communication between web services (multi-party conversation) of a transaction and these interactions may happen concurrently. The corresponding compensations, in case the conversation is interrupted, also take place concurrently.

The abortion of a transaction, even if it is successfully compensated for, can be very costly especially in a business environment where accountability and trust are major concerns. Rolling back the whole system may lead to chains of compensating activities that are time-consuming and impact on network traffic. For this reason it is important to add diversity into the system and allow for alternative paths of execution in cases where the path chosen originally encountered a failure. Our approach can be extended to handle *forward recovery* by examining the runs (maximal configurations) of a conversation and working out the extent to which a faulted path should be compensated until it reaches another configuration path that can lead to a run which allows the transaction to commit.

In previous work [18], which draws upon the translation of sequence diagrams in [8] outlined in this paper, we have looked at reasoning about scenario-based specifications using *vector languages* [17] and have shown how this can uncover additional scenarios which are potentially faulty (e.g. due to race conditions) or simply unthought in the initial design [19]. This provides interesting perspectives with regard to identifying the complete set of behaviours of a given multi-party conversation, and on that basis determine alternative scenarios of execution for the transaction.

Finally, we are currently extending our distributed temporal logic interpreted over labelled event structures (cf. [8]) to be able to express properties about (interrupted) conversations. The distributed nature of the logic is crucial in a context of loosely-coupled web services. With the logic we will also be able to analyse whether our extended models with faults are complete and possibly reveal further faulted paths.

References

1. Digital Business Ecosystem (DBE), EU-FP6 IST Integrated Project No 507953 (2006), http://www.digital-ecosystem.org
2. Date, C.J.: An Introduction to Database Systems, 5th edn. Addison-Wesley, Reading (1996)
3. Razavi, A., Moschoyiannis, S., Krause, P.: Concurrency Control and Recovery Management in Open e-Business Transactions. In: Proc. WoTUG Communicating Process Architectures (CPA 2007), pp. 267–285. IOS Press, Amsterdam (2007)
4. Papazoglou, M.P., Georgakopoulos, D.: Service-Oriented Computing. Communications of the ACM 46(10), 24–28 (2003)
5. Papazoglou, M.P., Traverso, P., Dustdar, S., Leymann, F., Kramer, B.J.: Service-Oriented Computing Research Roadmap. In: Dagstuhl Seminar Proc. 05462, Service-Oriented Computing (SOC), pp. 1–29 (2006)
6. O.M.G.: UML 2.0 Superstructure Specification. document ptc/04-10-02 (2004), http://www.uml.org
7. Razavi, A., Moschoyiannis, S., Krause, P.: A Coordination Model for Distributed Transactions in Digital Business Ecosystems. In: Digital Ecosystems and Technologies (DEST 2007), IEEE Computer Society Press, Los Alamitos (2007)
8. Küster-Filipe, J.: Modelling concurrent interactions. Theoretical Computer Science 351(2), 203–220 (2006)
9. Bowles, J.K.F.: Decomposing Interactions. In: Johnson, M., Vene, V. (eds.) AMAST 2006. LNCS, vol. 4019, pp. 189–203. Springer, Heidelberg (2006)
10. Winskel, G., Nielsen, M.: Models for Concurrency. In: Handbook of Logic in Computer Science, vol. 4, pp. 1–148. Oxford Science Publications (1995)
11. Garcia-Molina, H., Salem, K.: Sagas. In: ACM SIGMOD, pp. 249–259 (1987)
12. Cabrera, F.L., Copeland, G., Johnson, J., Langworthy, D.: Coordinating Web Services Activities with WS-Coordination, WS-AtomicTransaction, and WS-BusinessActivity (January 2004), http://msdn.micorsoft.com/webservices/default.aspx
13. Furnis, P., Dalal, S., Fletcher, T., Green, A., Ceponkus, A., Pope, B.: Business Transaction Protocol, version 1.1.0 (November 2004), http://www.oasis-open.org/committees/download.php/9836
14. Bruni, R., Melgatti, H., Montanari, U.: Theoretical Foundations for Compensations in Flow Composition Languages. In: Principles of Programming Languages (POPL 2005), pp. 209–220. ACM Press, New York (2005)
15. Furnis, P., Green, A.: Choreology Ltd. Contribution to the OASIS WS-Tx Technical Committee relating to WS-Coordination, WS-AtomicTransaction, and WS-BusinessActivity (November 2005), http://www.oasis-open.org/committees/download.php/15808
16. Butler, M., Hoare, A.C.R., Ferreira, C.: Trace Semantics for Long-Running Transactions. In: Abdallah, A.E., Jones, C.B., Sanders, J.W. (eds.) Communicating Sequential Processes. LNCS, vol. 3525, pp. 133–150. Springer, Heidelberg (2005)
17. Shields, M.W.: Semantics of Parallelism. Springer, London (1997)
18. Moschoyiannis, S., Krause, P., Shields, M.W.: A True Concurrent Interpretation of Behavioural Scenarios. In: FESCA 2007. ENTCS, Elsevier, Amsterdam (to appear)
19. Moschoyiannis, S.: Specification and Analysis of Component-Based Software in a Concurrent Setting. PhD thesis, University of Surrey (2005)

Distributed Behavioural Adaptation for the Automatic Composition of Semantic Services[*]

Tarek Melliti[1], Pascal Poizat[1,2], and Sonia Ben Mokhtar[2]

[1] IBISC FRE 2873 CNRS – Université d'Évry Val d'Essonne, France
tarek.melliti@ibisc.univ-evry.fr
[2] INRIA/ARLES project-team, France
{pascal.poizat,sonia.ben_mokhtar}@inria.fr

Abstract. Services are developed separately and without knowledge of all possible use contexts. They often mismatch or do not correspond exactly to the end-user needs, making direct composition without mediation impossible. In such a case, software adaptation can support composition by producing semi-automatically new software pieces called adaptors. Adaptation proposals have addressed the signature and behavioural service interface levels. Yet, taking also into account the semantic level is mandatory to enable the fully-automatic retrieval of adaptors from service interfaces. We propose a new adaptation technique that, compared to related work, supports both behavioural and semantic service interface levels, works system-wide, and generates automatically distributed adaptors.

Keywords: Model-Based Adaptation, Behavioural Adaptation, Semantic Adaptation, Services, Input Output Labelled Transition Systems.

1 Introduction

Service Oriented Architectures (SOA) [22] have introduced a new organizing of software, based on *services*, self describing and loosely coupled interacting software components that support the rapid and low-cost composition of distributed applications. An important issue in SOA is *service composition and its automation* [22,16], either to fulfill a user task or to have services collaborating in added-value composite services. Techniques that support the composition in component or service based systems rely on four interface description levels: signature (operations), behaviour (protocols), non functional (time, QoS) and semantics [23]. In SOA, *service composition* takes place after services have been discovered. It is often assumed that discovered services conform at the different interface levels, and first, at the signature one where syntactic matching is used to put in correspondence required and provided functionalities. Approaches that support the behavioural (called *conversation*) and semantics levels assume one-to-one functionality correspondences [5,3]. These assumptions do not yield

---

[*] This work is supported by the project "PERvasive Service cOmposition" (PERSO) of the French National Agency for Research, ANR-07-JCJC-0155-01.

J. Fiadeiro and P. Inverardi (Eds.): FASE 2008, LNCS 4961, pp. 146–162, 2008.
© Springer-Verlag Berlin Heidelberg 2008

in practice in open heterogeneous environments where services are developed by different organizations.

Software adaptation [11] has provided solutions for component interoperability through the computation – from component interfaces and user-defined adaptation specifications called *mappings* – of *adaptors* that operate in-between components to ensure their correct[1] composition at the signature and behavioural levels [11,6,2,19], and more recently at the non-functional level [25]. Yet, while *automatic adaptation* is highly desirable for SOA where systems are composed from dynamically discovered services, component adaptation techniques do not support the semantic level and therefore require a mapping to be given by a designer to deal for example with message name mismatch between services. Moreover, distributed adaptation is an important issue in domains such as pervasive computing, due to the use of small-resource devices and ad-hoc networks (no centralized server being available to execute the adaptor). Our objective is to overcome limitations of both semantic service composition – supporting complex dependencies between services or functionalities – and software adaptation – enabling one to obtain automatically distributed (local) adaptor models directly from service interface models, without requiring some mapping to be given, by supporting the semantic level in the adaptation process.

In the sequel, we present first a formalizing of service behavioural interfaces with associated semantic information (Sect. 2). We then develop our automatic service composition and adaptation technique (Sect. 3). Related work is discussed in Section 4 and we end with conclusions, including limitations of our work and perspectives.

2   A Model of Semantic Service Specifications

In this section we present our service model including service interfaces and service conversations. It is then extended with semantic information to enable automatic composition and adaptation.

Example 1 (Presentation). In the sequel we consider a simple pervasive system with four services. PDA is a service on top of a PDA which stores music files (mp3 or ogg). It is used to transmit music to be played at a given volume. dBMeter is a sensor which is used to transmit (in dB) the noise level in the room. HF is a Hi-Fi system which can play ogg files at a given volume which is adjusted according to the required one and the ambient noise level. Finally, Trans is a service that translates mp3 files into ogg files at a certain compression level, depending on the ambient noise level.

2.1   Service Interfaces (Interface Signature Level)

Service interfaces are used to advertise service provided functionalities to potential service clients. They are described, in the case of Web services, using WSDL[2]

---

[1] In the sense of deadlock freeness.
[2] http://www.w3.org/TR/wsdl for WSDL 1.1

as a set of *provided operations*, each described using a signature, *i.e.*, typed in/out arguments, as well as the corresponding XML messages carrying them. We abstract the WSDL elements we use for adaptation in our model as follows. We define M as the set of XML messages and *opNames* as the set of operation names, over which we range respectively using $m, m_1, \ldots$ and op. The symbols "?" and "!" used with messages denote respectively input and output, *e.g.*, $?m$ means receiving a message of type m. O is the set of operations, over which we range using o. An operation $o \in O$ can be either one-way $o = opName[?m]$ (solicitation) or $o = opName[!m]$ (notification); or two-way $o = opName[?m, !m]$ (request-response) or $o = opName[!m, ?m]$ (notification-response). Ω is the set of service names, over which we range using ω, w or w depending of the context. $\perp$ denotes an undefined message. $Input : O \rightarrow M \cup \{\perp\}$ returns the input message of an operation: $Input(o) = m$ if $o = op[?m]$, $o = op[?m, !m']$ or $o = op[!m', ?m]$); $\perp$ otherwise. $Output : O \rightarrow M \cup \{\perp\}$ returns the output message of an operation: $Output(o) = m$ if $o = op[!m]$, $o = op[?m', !m]$ or $o = op[!m, ?m']$; $\perp$ otherwise.

Example 2 (Service Interfaces). dBMeter (w1) has an operation to give the dB level, infodB$[?m11_a, !m11_b]$. HF (w2) has an operation play$[?m21]$ to play music. It also has an operation over which the ambient noise level can be given, ambiance$[?m22]$. Finally, an operation output$[!m23]$ outputs sound and volume. Trans (w3) has an operation, trans$[?m31_a, !m31_b]$ to translate music files. PDA (w4) provides no operation. This kind of pure client is used to model some user task the service composition is built for. It is implemented with additional operations corresponding to the interaction with (usually) a user interface. We name messages in correspondence with the service they correspond to, *e.g.*, $m\underline{31}_a$ for Trans (w$\underline{3}$), see also the operations on the left of Figure 1.

2.2 Service Conversations (Interface Behavioural Level)

In addition to the set of operations specified in the service interface, an elementary service described using BPEL4WS[3] (or BPEL for short) defines a long-run interaction protocol, called *business protocol*, where operations are invoked according to ordering and time constraints. These protocols mix both internal and external behaviours, while only the latter ones (conversations) are relevant for automatic composition: they constitute the service behavioural interface. Our solution relies on the derivation of Abstract BPEL[3] conversations from BPEL processes. This process, which abstracts from the service internal activities, is automated by a tool [18] and only briefly presented here since, for our present purpose, only its Abstract BPEL end-result is important.

Basic activities. The most relevant activities for service composition are *communication activities*: *invoke*[o] (invocation of operation o), *receive*[o] (reception of an operation o invocation, forbidden for notification), and *reply*[o] (response sending for an operation o invocation, forbidden for solicitation). They specify the communication constraints between a service and its *partners*, *i.e.*, the set

---

[3] http://www.ibm.com/developerworks/library/specification/ws-bpel for BPEL 1.1

of services/clients that interact with it. We distinguish two kinds of invocations: if the operation owner is known or if it has to be instantiated at run time. In the first case, invocation is assumed to be internal and is hidden. In the second case, we rely on a set of free variables $\overline{X} = \{x_1, x_2, \ldots\}$ to refer to service owners, with a fresh variable for each *invoke*, written $invoke[o](x_i)$. Moreover, as a composition involves several services, we ensure disjointness of fresh variables by indexing them with the service name, *e.g.*, $invoke[o](x_{i\omega})$. *Time activities* are used for example to define timeouts or watchdogs. They can be reduced to a time passing activity (which we will denote *time*) and the use of *scope* [20]. Finally, *empty* represents a void activity and *terminate* a terminated one. All other BPEL basic activities – *e.g.*, those locally executed by services, mainly providing data handling facilities – are hidden in interfaces.

Structured activities are control flow constructors. Each one defines an order with which activities are activated or executed, and can be applied to either basic or structured activities (both over which we range using $P, Q, R, \ldots$). We support here a simple subset of BPEL: parallel execution $(flow[\{P_{i,i\in\{1,\ldots,n\}}\}])$ with joint links ignored for simplicity, conditional execution $(switch[\{(\_, P_i)_{i\in\{1,\ldots,n\}}\}])$ and loops $(while(\_, P))$ where we assimilate conditions to internal non-deterministic choice (choice is performed internally, without external control over it). Other constructs could be supported provided it is possible to translate them into Timed Input Output Labelled Transition System (TIOLTS) as in Section 2.4 (see [20] for the additional support for time, fault and event handlers).

We may now introduce our formal definition of a service.

Definition 1 (Service). *A service is a tuple $\langle \omega, O^\bullet, O^\circ, B(\overline{X}) \rangle$ where $\omega \in \Omega$ is the service name (used as an abstraction of, e.g., XML name spaces), $O^\bullet \subseteq O$ is a WSDL interface that defines the service's set of provided operations, $O^\circ \subseteq O$ is a set of required operations, and $B(\overline{X}) \in ABP$, where ABP denotes the set of Abstract BPEL processes, is the service conversation, defined over a set of free variables $\overline{X} = \{x_1, \ldots, x_n\}$. Moreover, $B(\overline{X})$ respects: $o \in O^\circ$ for every $invoke[o](x)$ and $o \in O^\bullet$ for every $receive[o]$ and every $reply[o]$.*

Due to the assumed uniqueness of services names, we do not distinguish service names from the corresponding service definition, *i.e.*, for a service $\langle \omega, O^\bullet, O^\circ, B(\overline{X}) \rangle$ we may write $\omega = \langle O^\bullet, O^\circ, B(\overline{X}) \rangle$. We further define for a service ω: $O_\omega = O^\bullet \cup O^\circ$, $In_\omega = (\bigcup_{o \in O_\omega} \{Input(o)\}) \setminus \{\bot\}$, $Out_\omega = (\bigcup_{o \in O_\omega} \{Output(o)\}) \setminus \{\bot\}$, $M_\omega = In_\omega \cup Out_\omega$, and $M_\omega^{IO} = \{?m \mid m \in In_\omega\} \cup \{!m \mid m \in Out_\omega\}$.

Example 3 (Service Specifications). We can now give more detail about our services. dBMeter and HF have no required operations, and their behavioural interfaces are respectively receive[infodB] ; reply[infodB] ; empty and receive[play] ; receive[ambiance] ; reply[output] ; empty. Trans has a required operation, getNoise[?m32$_a$,!m32$_b$] and its behaviour is switch[(_,receive[trans] ; invoke [getNoise](x_{1w3}) ; reply[trans] ; empty), (_,terminate)] (it may terminate directly if not used). Finally, PDA has one required operation for each kind of music file, mp3Play[?m41$_a$,!m41$_b$] and oggPlay[?m42$_a$,!m42$_b$], and its behaviour is switch[(_,invoke[mp3Play](x_{1w4})),(_,invoke[oggPlay](x_{2w4}))] ; empty.

2.3   Semantic Information (Interface Semantic Level)

To support automatic composition, service descriptions must be extended with descriptive semantic information. A number of research efforts have been conducted for Web service semantic annotation, but SAWSDL[4] has become the W3C recommendation for the semantic annotation of WSDL documents. In this section we introduce a formal model for representing the descriptive semantics of a service described using SAWSDL complemented with BPEL. This integrated formal model allows reasoning on service compatibility at three levels at the same time (signature, behavioural and semantic levels).

Definition 2 (Semantic Structure). *A semantic structure $\mathcal{I}$ is a couple $(\mathcal{U}, \mathcal{R})$ where $\mathcal{U}$ is a set of units of sense (UoS), over which we range using u, and $\mathcal{R} \subseteq 2^{\mathcal{U}} \times \mathcal{U}$ is a relation where $(U, u) \in \mathcal{R}$ denotes that given a set U of UoS, one can obtain u.*

These structures support partner collaboration and can be related to concrete ontologies referenced in the SAWSDL service description, where units of sense correspond to the ontology concepts and properties, while $\mathcal{R}$ can be used to encapsulate relations such as the "subclassOf" one, *i.e.*, $\forall u, u' \in \mathcal{U}$, u' subclassOf $u \Rightarrow (\{u'\}, u) \in \mathcal{R}$. A semantic structure may result from ontology integration, *e.g.*, following [7], and support different semantic structures for different partners.

Example 4 (Semantic Structure). Elements of $\mathcal{U}$ are mfile (music file), ogg (ogg file), mp3 (mp3 file), vol (volume), noise (noise information), dB (noise in dB), sound (sound return), and info (information feedback). The relations between them are: ($\{$ogg$\}$,mfile) and ($\{$mp3$\}$,mfile) (ogg and mp3 are music files), ($\{$dB$\}$, noise) (noise information can be retrieved from dB), and ($\{$sound,vol$\}$,info) (sound and volume build an information).

A service receives requests, process them and sends answers back. Yet, to process a request, behind its representation (the message format), a set of information, UoS, is required. In turn, replies contain (possibly new) UoS. For instance, in order to play music, the HF service requires an ogg file and a volume, and outputs sound and volume. Moreover, for Web services, this information has to be XML-formatted (and published in the service SAWSDL interface). To support the automatic use of such a service by a partner, one has to ensure that all required information is known by the partner, format the request message and package the information into it, call the service, get the response, and finally process it to extract the set of information that is returned back. This principle is at the core of our adaptor behaviours and is first supported through semantic matching functions and a formal definition of partnership.

Definition 3 ((Semantic) Matching Function). *A matching function for a service ω over a semantic structure $\mathcal{I} = (\mathcal{U}, \mathcal{R})$ is a function $SM_{\omega, \mathcal{I}} : M_{\omega} \to 2^{\mathcal{U} \times Xpath(M_{\omega})}$ with $Xpath(M_{\omega})$ the set of Xpath expressions defined over M_{ω}.*

---

[4] http://www.w3.org/TR/sawsdl/

These functions are used to associate to each message the set of UoS it corresponds to, together with a syntactic expression ($Xpath$) that makes it possible to relate these UoS with the message XML tree.

Example 5 (Matching Functions). We have dbMeter: $(m11_a,\emptyset)$ and$(m11_b, \{(dB,\_)\})$ for infodB (dB output) – HF: $(m21,\{(ogg,\_),(vol,\_)\})$ and $(m23, \{(sound,\_),(vol,\_)\})$ for play and output (inputs ogg file and volume, outputs sound and volume), $(m22,\{(dB,\_)\})$ for ambiance (inputs ambient noise level) – Trans: $(m31_a,\{(mp3,\_)\})$ and $(m31_b,\{(ogg,\_)\})$ for trans (inputs mp3, outputs ogg), $(m32_a,\emptyset)$ and $(m32_b,\{(noise,\_)\})$ for getNoise (noise returned back) – PDA: $(m41_a,\{(mp3,\_),(vol,\_)\})$ and $(m41_b,\{(info,\_)\})$ for mp3Play, $(m42_a,\{(ogg,\_), (vol,\_)\})$ and $(m42_b,\{(info,\_)\})$ for oggPlay (file and volume sent, information expected in the end). Xpath information is omitted (_) due to lack of place.

We introduce hereafter the formal definition of *partners* and *partnerships* as a set of services collaborating on top of a semantic structure. We suppose an enumerable set Id over which partners are indexed (it can be naturals or the set of partners' names).

Definition 4 (Partner and Partnership). *A* partner *over a semantic structure $\mathcal{I}$ is a tuple $\rho_\omega = \langle \omega, \mathcal{I}, SM_{\omega,\mathcal{I}} \rangle$ where ω is a service and $SM_{\omega,\mathcal{I}}$ is a matching function for ω over $\mathcal{I}$. A* partnership *over a semantic structure $\mathcal{I}$ is a set of partners $\Upsilon_{Id} = \{\langle \omega_i, \mathcal{I}, SM_{\omega_i,\mathcal{I}} \rangle_{i \in Id}\}$ over $\mathcal{I}$. When clear, suffixes are omitted.*

2.4   Operational Semantics of Semantic Services

We present now the formal semantics of partners using operational semantics to favor operational issues such as algorithms and tools.

Configurations. To support automatic semantic composition, the operational semantics of a partner $\langle \omega, (\mathcal{U}, \mathcal{R}), SM \rangle$ should be defined through its evolution over time, directed by its behaviour, of hypotheses on the UoS it holds. This can be described using *configurations* $(P, \mathcal{H})$ where $P \in ABP$ is the current process representing the partner and $\mathcal{H} \in 2^{\mathcal{U}}$ is its current semantic environment. $\mathcal{H}^{\mathcal{R}^*}$ denotes the closure of $\mathcal{H}$ over $\mathcal{R}$ and $\mathcal{H} \leadsto_{\mathcal{R}} u$ that the u UoS can be obtained from $\mathcal{H}$: $\mathcal{H} \leadsto_{\mathcal{R}} u$ iff $u \in \mathcal{H}^{\mathcal{R}^*}$. When clear from the context (remind that all partners in a partnership share a common $\mathcal{R}$) this is simply noted $\mathcal{H} \leadsto u$. We also suppose that a UoS belongs to a partner configuration until it terminates.

Events. The semantics depends on message communication which is modelled using events ($!m$ and $?m$). We also introduce several specific events. As services may evolve in an unobservable way (*e.g.*, due to a condition abstraction), tau is used to denote internal actions. The termination event, $/$, enables the detection of service termination. Time is supported by χ that denotes the passing of one time unit (which stands for any delay). This is compatible with the fact that the time constraints of a Web service are generally soft, thus this discretization of time is a valid abstraction [18]. We define $!M = \{!m \mid m \in M\}$, $?M = \{?m \mid m \in M\}$

and $Event = !M \cup ?M \cup \{tau, /, \chi\}$. Moreover, we define *complementarity* as $(?m)^c = !m$, $(!m)^c = ?m$, and $a^c = a$ for all $a \in Event \backslash (!M \cup ?M)$. We introduce hereafter a structural operational semantics (SOS) for our semantic services. In this semantics, we are in the context of a given partner $\rho_\omega = \langle \omega, \mathcal{I}, SM_{\omega,\mathcal{I}} \rangle$.

Basic Activities are denoted by basic processes which are *terminate*, *empty*, *time*, *receive*[o], *reply*[o] and *invoke*[o].

time has one axiom, and **empty** can only terminate:

$$(time, \mathcal{H}) \xrightarrow{\chi} (time, \mathcal{H}) \qquad\qquad (empty, \mathcal{H}) \xrightarrow{/} (terminate, \emptyset).$$

receive[o]. Upon reception of the corresponding message, its UoS are augmented with the message ones (also for *invoke*, below):

$$(receive[o], \mathcal{H}) \xrightarrow{?\omega.Input(o)} (empty, \mathcal{H} \cup SM(Input(o)))$$

reply[o]. The UoS needed to build the message corresponding to a reply have to be obtainable from the ones in the configuration (also for *invoke*, below):

$$(reply[o], \mathcal{H}) \xrightarrow{!\omega.Output(o)} (empty, \mathcal{H}) \text{ if } \mathcal{H} \rightsquigarrow SM(Output(o))$$

invoke[o](x) semantics depends on the form of o:

$$(invoke[o](x), \mathcal{H}) \xrightarrow{!x.Input(o)} (empty, \mathcal{H}) \text{ if } \mathcal{H} \rightsquigarrow SM(Input(o))$$
$$\text{when } o = op[?m]$$

$$(invoke[o](x), \mathcal{H}) \xrightarrow{?x.Output(o)} (empty, \mathcal{H} \cup SM(Output(o)))$$
$$\text{when } o = op[!m]$$

$$(invoke[o](x), \mathcal{H}) \xrightarrow{!x.Input(o)} (invoke[op[!m_2]](x), \mathcal{H}) \text{ if } \rightsquigarrow SM(Output(o))$$
$$\text{when } o = op[?m_1, !m_2]$$

$$(invoke[o](x), \mathcal{H}) \xrightarrow{?x.Output(o)} (invoke[op[?m_2]](x), \mathcal{H} \cup SM(Output(o)))$$
$$\text{when } o = op[!m_1, ?m_2]$$

For one-way operations the process executes the event related to the operation signature and becomes *empty*. For two-way operations, the first event is executed and then the process becomes an *invoke* corresponding to the remaining (now one-way) operation. If *invoke* operates on a partner operation that starts with an input message then the associated event is an output message and *vice versa*. Events are prefixed by partner names.

Structured Activities are supported in a structured way as usual in process algebraic SOS for Web services. Due to lack of place, and since the basic activities are the main ones for this work, structured activity rules are presented in [20]. The modular application of basic and structured rules associates a TIOLTS to each ABP process.

Definition 5 (Partner External Behaviour). *The external behaviour of a partner* $\rho = \langle \omega = \langle O^\bullet, O^\circ, B(\overline{X}) \rangle, (\mathcal{U}, \mathcal{R}), SM \rangle$ *is a TIOLTS* $\mathcal{L}_\rho = \langle A, S, s_0, F,$

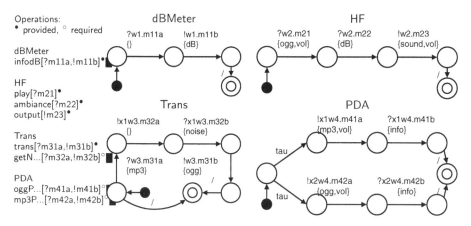

Fig. 1. Partners TIOLTS

$T(\overline{X})\rangle$ where $A = M_\omega^{IO} \cup \{tau, /, \chi\}$ is the alphabet, $S \subseteq ABP \times 2^{\mathcal{U}}$ is the set of configurations, $s_0 = (B(\overline{X}), \emptyset)$ is the initial state $(s_0 \in S)$, $F = \{(s_f, \mathcal{H}_f) \in S \mid \exists (s, \mathcal{H}) \in S \wedge (s, \mathcal{H}) \xrightarrow{\quad/\quad} (s_f, \mathcal{H}_f) \in T\}$ is the set of final states, and $T(\overline{X}) \subseteq S \times A \times S$ is the transition relation obtained from the SOS rules ($\overline{X}$ is the set of the free variables used in the transitions).

Based on this definition, we develop techniques operating on TIOLTS. Hence, in service and partner structures, TIOLTS will be used for ABP processes.

Example 6. Partners TIOLTS are given in Figure 1.

3   Automatic Composition Using Adaptation

To be compatible, two partners have to share complementary operations, messages and matching functions, *i.e.*, the UoS sent by one must correspond to UoS required by the second. Moreover, their two behaviours should also be compatible to ensure deadlock freedom. We reuse a relation defined in [18] which intuitively states that to be compatible (denoted using $\sim^c$), two behaviours must be such that (i) at each step of the interaction, each sent message can be received, and (ii) each expected message possibly corresponds to a sent one, regarding the history of past exchanged messages. This is related to bisimulation, yet taking into account the difference between sent and received messages. This is also related to the compatibility relation for interface automata [14] but with support for internal actions and time.

It is not realistic to suppose that compatibility yields from scratch in a context where services are designed by different parties. To release these strict composition constraints, a one-to-one correspondence between names could be supported parameterizing the compatibility relation by a name correspondence mapping (hence solving simple name mismatch), *i.e.*, for two services ω_1 and ω_2, defined

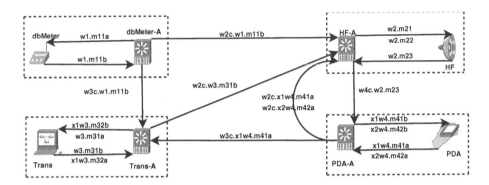

Fig. 2. Adapted System Architecture

over $M_{\omega_1} \times M_{\omega_2}$. However, it is not straightforward to support in such a way more complex correspondences and semantic information, as the UoS required for a partner's received message may correspond to several partners' sent messages. For example, ogg and vol for m21 in HF may come either directly from PDA (using m42$_a$) or using both PDA (m41$_a$) and Trans (m31$_b$). The possible need for message reordering and cyclic dependencies between required/produced UoS are also important locks. Recent advances in software adaptation [6,19] may help there, provided they are extended to support semantic information.

To solve these issues, we propose an approach were an adaptor is generated for each partner, which will only communicate through it. We process in three steps: (i) the generation of a compatible (correct) service client (CSC) for each partner, which allows to interact with the partner without changing its protocol, (ii) using the CSCs, the definition of a central global adaptor that defines all the valid interactions between partners, and finally (iii) the transformation of CSCs into local adaptors using the global adaptor protocol. The final desired architecture (adapted system, see Fig. 2) is such that there is compatibility (i) between each partner and its local adaptor (hiding its communications with the other adaptors) and (ii) between the adaptors (hiding their communications with their partners). This yields the deadlock freedom of the global system.

3.1   Step i: Generation of the Correct Service Clients (CSCs)

We compute, for each partner, a CSC which acts as a perfect environment for it and ensures compatibility by construction. This means that the CSC acts for its partner as if it provides all required operations and is always ready to consume (resp. send) its partner sent (resp. received) messages. This idea originates from controller synthesis and has been applied both in software adaptation [2] and in service compatibility checking [18]. We reuse the latter as step (i) is independent from the semantic information. Two tasks are performed on a partner TIOLTS to build its CSC TIOLTS: messages are complemented (exchanging directions) and the resulting TIOLTS is determinized. We fail when the CSC TIOLTS is

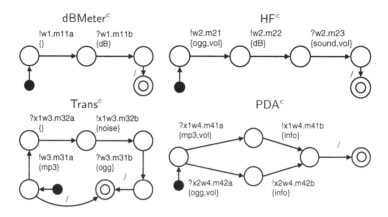

Fig. 3. CSC TIOLTS

non-deterministic on *tau* transitions or message sending as this ambiguity yields non implementable behaviours [18].

Definition 6 (Correct Service Client (CSC)). *The correct service client (CSC) for a partner* $\rho = \langle \omega = \langle O^{\bullet}, O^{\circ}, \mathcal{L}_{\omega} = \langle A, S, s_0, F, T(\overline{X}) \rangle \rangle, (\mathcal{U}, \mathcal{R}), SM \rangle$ *is a partner* $\rho^c = \langle \omega^c = \langle O^{\circ}, O^{\bullet}, \mathcal{L}_{\omega}^c \rangle, (\mathcal{U}, \mathcal{R}), SM \rangle$ *where* $\mathcal{L}_{\omega}^c$ $(\mathcal{L}_{\omega} \sim^c \mathcal{L}_{\omega}^c)$ *is computed using the [18] synthesis algorithm. When clear,* $\mathcal{L}_{\omega}^c$ *is also written* $\mathcal{L}_{\rho}^c$.

Example 7. The CSC TIOLTSs are given in Figure 3.

At the time, a CSC does not really provide the required operations to its partner, but only the corresponding received and/or send messages. The CSC must now be *extended* with implementations in terms of calls (resp. replies) to the other CSCs. Take Trans^c in Figure 3 for example. Its provided operation for noise information (getNoise, called with message m32$_a$ and noise result returned with message m32$_b$) should be implemented by getting this noise UoS from some other CSC (here, dBMeter^c, using the relation between dB and noise). Moreover, the extension of a CSC should also support additional message exchanges for some messages sent with UoS by this CSC (*e.g.*, for Trans^c, this means getting the mp3 UoS from some other CSC (here, PDA^c) before sending it to Trans using m31$_a$). All these extensions correspond to the message exchanges in between local adaptors in Figure 2. This is the objective of the next steps, where a global structure (called global adaptor) is first built (step ii) before being used to extend the CSCs into local adaptors (step iii).

3.2 Step ii: Generation of a Global Adaptor (GA)

Composing partners correctly in a partnership means to have them exchange messages in a way that guarantees that each partner fulfills its role in the composition until all terminate. The global adaptor (GA) is a composition of the CSC defined such that the orderings imposed by CSC protocols are respected,

The GA is ready to receive a message from any CSC at any time (augmenting correspondingly its UoS, Def. 7,(1)), and can only send a message when it has all the required information at its disposal (Def. 7,(2)). From one partner's point of view, this ensures that a given operation is run only when the other partners have sent all required information. Moreover, / is synchronized to ensure correct termination and time passing is weakly synchronized. The GA corresponds to a form of free product of the CSCs restricted by constraints over UoS.

The GA has access to UoS originating from different messages of different partners. We need to distinguish them in order to support step (iii): when adaptation is distributed, we must be able to detect which messages were used to obtain a UoS. Therefore, for a partnership $\Upsilon_{Id} = \{\langle \omega_i, \mathcal{I}, SM_{\omega_i} \rangle_{i \in Id}\}$, in the GA configurations the semantic information will be taken in $2^{\mathcal{E}}$ with $\mathcal{E} = \bigcup_{i \in Id} \{(m, u) \mid m \in M_{\omega_i} \wedge u \in SM_{\omega_i}(m)\}$. Given some $E \subseteq \mathcal{E}$, we also define projections on the message, $\pi^{msg}(E) = \{m \mid (m, u) \in E\}$, and on the UoS, $\pi^{uos}(E) = \{u \mid (m, u) \in E\}$.

Definition 7 (Global Adaptor Generation). *Let* $\Upsilon_{Id} = \{\rho_{i,i \in Id}\}$ *be a partnership with a corresponding set of CSC,* $\{\rho_i^c = \langle \omega_i = \langle O_i^\bullet, O_i^\circ, \mathcal{L}_i \rangle \rangle, (\mathcal{U}, \mathcal{R}),$ $SM_i \rangle_{i \in Id}\}$ *where for each i in Id,* $\mathcal{L}_i = \langle A_i, S_i, s_{0_i}, F_i, T_i \rangle$. *The global adaptor for Υ_{Id} is the TIOLTS* $\mathcal{A}_{\Upsilon_{Id}} = \langle A, S, s_0, F, T \rangle$ *where* $A = \bigcup_{i \in Id} A_i$, $S \subseteq (\Pi_{i \in Id}(S_i)) \times 2^{\mathcal{E}}$, $s_0 = (\Pi_{i \in Id}(s_{0_i}), \emptyset)$, $F = \{(s_1, ..., s_n) \in S \mid \forall i \in Id, s_i \in F_i\}$, *and T is defined as:* $\forall s = ((s_1, \ldots, s_n), E) \in S$,

- *if* $\exists j \in Id, (s_j, ?m, s_j') \in T_j$ *then* $(s, ?m, s') \in T$ *with* $s' = ((s_1, \ldots, s_j', \ldots, s_n), E \cup \{(m, u) \mid u \in SM_i(m)\})$; $\qquad(1)$
- *if* $\exists j \in Id, (s_j, !m, s_j') \in T_j$ *and* $\pi^{uos}(E) \leadsto SM_i(m)$ *then* $(s, !m, s') \in T$ *with* $s' = ((s_1, \ldots, s_j', \ldots, s_n), E)$; $\qquad(2)$
- *if* $\exists j \in Id, (s_j, tau, s_j') \in T_j$ *then* $(s, tau, s') \in T$ *with* $s' = ((s_1, \ldots, s_j', \ldots, s_n), E)$;
- *if* $\forall j \in Id, (s_j, /, s_j') \in T_j$ *then* $(s, /, s') \in T$ *with* $s' = ((s_1', \ldots, s_n'), \emptyset)$;
- *let* $J = \{j \in Id \mid \exists (s_j, \chi, s_j') \in T_j\}$, *if* $J \neq \emptyset$ *then* $(s, \chi, s') \in T$ *with* $s' = ((s_1', \ldots, s_j', \ldots, s_n'), E)$ *where for every* $j \in Id$, $(s_j, \chi, s_j') \in T_j$ *if $j \in J$ and $s_j' = s_j$ otherwise.*

Postprocessing is performed on the GA removing recursively transitions leading to deadlock states (non-final states without outgoing transitions). In such a case, compatibility will only yield on a subset of partners' interactions. The alternative is to abort the adaptation process.

Example 8. The GA is given in Figure 4 where states are labelled with UoS initials (*e.g.*, d for dB) and transitions with messages and corresponding UoS initials (obtained by receptions and needed for emissions). To understand postprocessing, let us suppose Trans had not been available. The grey states would not have been computed and the three bold states would have been removed (in three steps), being deadlocks. Compatibility between PDA and its adaptor would then only yield for the lower (ogg) branch in Figure 1. Arrow shapes and colors are used in the sequel to explain step (iii).

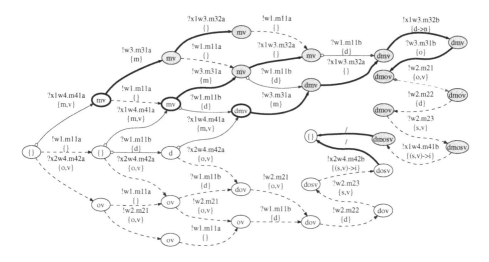

Fig. 4. The GA TIOLTS

The GA computation is exponential. Yet, additional criteria (wrt deadlock freedom) could be used to filter *on-the-fly* the GA during its computation and have a better complexity, as discussed in perspectives (Sect. 5).

3.3 Step iii: Generation of the Local Adaptors

The GA defines all valid interactions. Using it, we can generate for each partner ρ a *local adaptor* (hereafter adaptor for short) by extending its CSC ρ^c in three steps: (a) defining, for each message m sent by ρ^c to ρ, the set of potential messages from other CSC used to construct m, and receiving in ρ^c these potential messages; (b) defining, for each message m received from ρ in ρ^c, the set of interested CSC that need UoS from m to send some message to their own partner, and sending in ρ^c the UoS to these interested CSC; (c) updating the ρ^c alphabet and operations. In the sequel, we are in the context of $\rho_i^c = \langle \omega_i = \langle O_i^\bullet, O_i^\circ, \mathcal{L}_i^c \rangle \rangle, (\mathcal{U}, \mathcal{R}), SM_i \rangle$, the CSC of a partner ρ_i in a partnership $\Upsilon_{Id} = \{\rho_{i,i \in Id}\}$ and with the associated GA $\mathcal{A}_{\Upsilon_{Id}} = \langle A, S, s_0, F, T \rangle$.

(a) Reception of required messages from other adaptors. For all m such that $!m \in A_i^c$, we define $Const_m$, the set of messages involved (directly or by means of $\mathcal{R}$) in the construction of m according to $\mathcal{A}_{\Upsilon_{Id}}$, as follows: $Const_m = \{?m' \in A \backslash A_i^c \mid \exists (s, \mathcal{H}) \in S, u \in \mathcal{U}, \text{ with } (m', u) \in \mathcal{H} \wedge \exists ((s, \mathcal{H}), !m, -) \in T \wedge u \in SM(m) \cup \biguplus_{u' \in SM(m)} \mathcal{R}^{-1}(u')\}$. This corresponds to a form of GA backward analysis, from the sending of m by ρ_i^c to ρ_i, back to the messages that made the UoS (u) required for building m available. Yet, it is possible to look only one step back thanks to UoS union in Def. 7,(1). Note that when a UoS may come from several messages (and/or several CSC) then we non-deterministically choose one (*i.e.*, at most one application of (c2) in Def. 8 for each transition).

Example 9. Trans^c sends two messages to Trans: m31$_a$ (the initial call to Trans, requiring a mp3 UoS) and m32$_b$ (the sending of the noise UoS required by Trans to encode mp3 into ogg). In the GA (see the bullet/blue transitions), we see that the mp3 UoS for m31$_a$ comes from m41$_a$ ($Const_{w3.m31_a}$={?x1w4.m41$_a$}) and that the noise UoS for m32$_b$ is obtained from a dB UoS which comes from m11$_b$ ($Const_{x1w3.m32_b}$={?w1.m11$_b$}). See [20] for details on the construction of the other adaptors.

We define the ρ_i^c reception-extended alphabet as $\mathcal{AL}_i = A_i^c \cup \underset{!m \in A_i^c}{\uplus} Const_m$. From it, we can derive the expected behaviour of ρ_i^c. It corresponds to the ρ_i^c role in the GA, and therefore, to the projection of the GA on $\mathcal{AL}_i$. The projection must be selective, to avoid useless interactions. For example, let us consider a version of dBMeter (w1) with an operation (infodB[!m11$_b$]) that sends the dB UoS periodically. ?w1.m11$_b$ belongs to the Trans^c (w3^c) reception-extended alphabet. Yet, Trans^c should receive an instance of this message only if it is useful in a future state. Therefore, we first define for a TIOLTS $\langle A, S, s_0, F, T \rangle$ a precedence relation over states, $\preceq = \{(s, s') \mid (s, a, s') \in T\}^+$. Then we may define the projection that enables to retrieve the required receptions to be added in an adaptor.

Definition 8. *Let $\mathcal{A}_{\Upsilon_{Id}} = \langle A, S, s_0, F, T \rangle$ be a global adaptor TIOLTS of a partnership $\Upsilon_{Id} = \{\rho_{i,i \in Id}\}$ and $\mathcal{AL}_i \subseteq A$ be the alphabet of the ith (local) adaptor. The projection of $\mathcal{A}_{\Upsilon_{Id}}$ over $\mathcal{AL}_i$ is a TIOLTS $Pr(\mathcal{A}_{\Upsilon_{Id}})_{\mathcal{AL}_i} = \langle \mathcal{AL}_i \cup \{tau\}, S, s_0, F, T_{\mathcal{AL}_i} \rangle$ where $T_{\mathcal{AL}_i}$ is defined as $\forall(s, a, s') \in T$:*

- *(c1) if $a \in A_i^c$ then $(s, a, s') \in T_{\mathcal{AL}_i}$;*
- *(c2) if $a = ?m \in \mathcal{AL}_i \setminus A_i^c, \exists!m' \in A_i^c, \exists(s'', !m', -) \in T, a \in Const_{m'}, s' \preceq s''$, then $(s, ?\rho_i^c.m, s') \in T_{\mathcal{AL}_i}$*   *(prefixing by ρ_i^c ensures new private name)*
- *(c3) otherwise, $(s, tau, s') \in T_{\mathcal{AL}_i}$*   *(removed using tau-reduction)*

Example 10. Due to lack of place it is not possible to give the projection figures. Yet, projection may be explained on Trans^c using Figures 4 and 5 (without the diamond/red transition). Case c1 (bold transitions) corresponds to the original CSC messages. Case c2 (bullet/blue transitions) corresponds to receptions added in $\mathcal{AL}_i$, provided they are useful in the future, *e.g.*, not all ?w1.m11$_b$ transitions are in this case. *Wrt* the GA, in projections case c2 labels are prefixed with the CSC identifier (w3c for Trans^c) to ensure private communication between adaptors. Finally, case c3 (dashed transitions) corresponds to non useful messages (*taus*). In the projection they are reduced.

(b) Emission of messages to interested adaptors. An adaptor ρ_i^c must forward any message m received from its partner ρ_i to the adaptors that need it. These may change for each instance of m. For each $(s, ?m, s') \in T_{\mathcal{AL}_i}$ such that $?m \in A_i^c$, we define a set of Interested Adaptors $IA_{(m,s)} = \{\rho_j^c \mid i \neq j \land \exists !m' \in !A_j^c$ with $m \in Const_{m'} \land \exists s''(s'', !m', -) \in T \land s' \preceq s''\}$. This corresponds to a GA forward analysis, from the reception of m by ρ_i^c, to the messages m' of other adaptors (ρ_j^c) that need an UoS in m ($m \in Const_{m'}$). For each $(s, ?m, s') \in T_{\mathcal{AL}_i}$

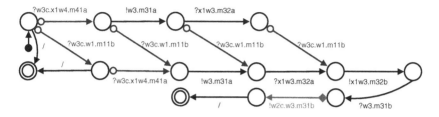

Fig. 5. Trans Adaptor TIOLTS

such that $?m \in A_i^c$, we add in the adaptor $Pr(A_{\Upsilon_{Id}})_{\mathcal{AL}_i}$ TIOLTS the interleaving of emissions to the elements of $IA_{(m,s)}$ as follows. Let $l = |IP(m,s)|$. First we add states, $S = S \cup \underset{j \in \{1,\dots,l\}}{\times} \{s'_{0j}, s'_{1j}\}$, then, transitions, $T_{\mathcal{AL}_i} = T_{\mathcal{AL}_i} \setminus (s, ?m, s') \cup (s, ?m, s'_0 = (s'_{01}, \dots, s'_{0l})) \cup \underset{j \in \{1,\dots,l\}}{\times} (s'_{0j}, !\rho_j^c.m, s'_{1j})$. Finally, we unify s' and $(s'_{10}, \dots, s'_{1l})$. This would correspond to flow branches in a BPEL implementation.

Example 11. Trans^c receives m32$_a$ (no UoS) and m31$_b$ (ogg) from its partner. We see in the GA that only HF^c (with m21, reading an ogg file) is interested in m31$_b$. The adding of emissions (diamond/red transitions) is demonstrated on the Trans adaptor (Fig. 5). Bullet/blue transitions were added in step iii(a). The final architecture with the exchanged messages is given in Figure 2 and the other adaptors in [20].

(c) Updating the adaptors alphabet and operations. The initial alphabet of an adaptor ρ_i^c (A_i^c) is extended in previous steps with messages for receptions (the $?\rho_i^c.m$) and emissions (the $!\rho_j^c.m$). As far as operations are concerned, we proceed as follows. For each reception $?\rho_i^c.m$ added in step iii(a), we add in $O_i^\bullet$ an operation $op_{\rho_i^c.m}[?m]$. For each emission $!\rho_j^c.m$ added in step iii(b), we add in O_i° an operation $op_{\rho_j^c.m}[!m]$. The adding of receptions and emissions in CSCs is transparent for their partners thanks to prefixing by CSC identifiers. Moreover, the fact that the added emissions are deterministic (*i.e.*, leads to the same state) preserves in adaptors the CSC correctness by construction. Our approach does not impose any constraint on resulting adaptors but for communication, data extraction from messages, and message construction (the latter two being supported by the Xpath part in matching functions), which makes our approach realistic for Web services adaptation.

4   Related Work

Behavioural component adaptation is now mature, but its application to SOA is recent. Mismatch patterns [4] or adaptation operators [15] may support adaptation but are not fully automatic as adaptation contracts must be defined. There are few fully automatic adaptation techniques. Service adaptation is performed using matching between service execution trees of BPEL processes in [8]. The matching process generates a workflow in an intermediary language (YAWL) which is then translated into BPEL. A form of adaptation may also be supported using ontology crossing [7]. Ontology matching is used in [21] to obtain behavioural correspondences and to compute a client-side adaptor that supports service replacement. Workflow analysis is used in [9] to build server-side adaptors that can be deployed as new services. All these approaches work with one client and (one or) several services, not system-wide. Yet, they build local adaptors and contrast with the centralized ones in most adaptation works [11,19].

A technique for the distribution of a centralized orchestrator into different topologies of decentralized orchestrators is presented in [17] and extended in [12] to support data flow constraints and a filtering mechanism to select the topologies that satisfy the constraints. These techniques do not address adaptation and require a centralized orchestrator to be given while our goal is to obtain distributed orchestrators (in our case, adaptors) directly from the service descriptions. In [24,1,2], the authors extend their earlier works on component adaptation to support respectively incremental local adaptation and the distribution of centralized adaptors. They do not support the semantic interface level and therefore either require a mapping to be given or cannot deal with message name mismatch between services.

5 Conclusion

Automatic service composition at run-time is one of the most challenging issues, as it enables to provide the end-users with added-value functionalities composed out of services existing in their environment. Automatic service composition approaches usually assume that services have been previously developed to be integrated, and the proposed composition processes are limited to simple correspondences between service functionalities. To overcome these limitations, we have proposed an approach which integrates solutions from behavioural adaptation into the service composition process. The distinctive features of this approach are possibly complex correspondences between service functionalities, the integration of descriptive semantics in the adaptation process, and distributed adaptors as opposed to a centralized one.

As explained before, the adaptation process is exponential due to the GA computation. To increase scalability, a first perspective concerns the *on-the-fly* filtering of the GA using a composition specification. This may be achieved by translating first this specification into an LTS and then taking this LTS into account in the GA computation [2,19]. Filtering with data flow constraints [12] could also be used to enhance the GA computation.

We have made the hypothesis that services are equipped with semantic annotations. This common assumption in semantic (Web) services enables the automatic composition and adaptation. Yet, semantic annotation may be difficult and error prone and may lead to the impossibility to compose and adapt services correctly. This is a general issue in adaptation, *e.g.*, in semi-automatic adaptation where a mapping is used to replace the semantic annotations and where wrong mappings yield empty adaptors. The solutions that have been proposed consist in performing verification using the service and the adaptor models [19], or to build interactive tools that help building correct mappings [10]. While the later one is not compatible with automatic adaptation, the first one would, provided composition properties are given. The approach we have presented is compatible with this as it is based on related formal models (LTS).

Another perspective concerns the automation of adaptor implementation. Some results are available for centralized adaptors in BPEL [8] or WF/.NET [13]. An issue is to restrict the services from engaging in a forbidden communication. A solution could be to rely on additional middleware messages [1].

References

1. Autili, M., Flammini, M., Inverardi, P., Navarra, A., Tivoli, M.: Synthesis of Concurrent and Distributed Adaptors for Component-Based Systems. In: Gruhn, V., Oquendo, F. (eds.) EWSA 2006. LNCS, vol. 4344, Springer, Heidelberg (2006)
2. Autili, M., Inverardi, P., Navarra, A., Tivoli, M.: SYNTHESIS: a tool for automatically assembling correct and distributed component-based systems. In: Proc. of ICSE 2007 (2007)
3. Ben Mokhtar, S., Georgantas, N., Issarny, V.: COCOA: COnversation-based Service Composition in PervAsive Computing Environments with QoS Support. Journal of Systems and Software 80(12) (2007)
4. Benatallah, B., Casati, F., Grigori, D., Motahari Nezhad, H.R., Toumani, F.: Developing Adapters for Web Services Integration. In: Pastor, Ó., Falcão e Cunha, J. (eds.) CAiSE 2005. LNCS, vol. 3520, Springer, Heidelberg (2005)
5. Benatallah, B., Sheng, Q.Z., Dumas, M.: The Self-Serv Environment for Web Services Composition. IEEE Internet Computing 7(1), 40–48 (2003)
6. Bracciali, A., Brogi, A., Canal, C.: A Formal Approach to Component Adaptation. Journal of Systems and Software 74(1) (2005)
7. Brogi, A., Corfini, S., Aldana, J.F., Navas, I.: Automated Discovery of Compositions of Services Described with Separate Ontologies. In: Dan, A., Lamersdorf, W. (eds.) ICSOC 2006. LNCS, vol. 4294, Springer, Heidelberg (2006)
8. Brogi, A., Popescu, R.: Automated Generation of BPEL Adapters. In: Dan, A., Lamersdorf, W. (eds.) ICSOC 2006. LNCS, vol. 4294, Springer, Heidelberg (2006)
9. Brogi, A., Popescu, R.: Service Adaptation through Trace Inspection. Int. J. Business Process Integration and Management 2(1), 9–16 (2007)
10. Cámara, J., Salaün, G., Canal, C.: Clint: A Composition Language Interpreter. In: Proc. of FASE 2008. LNCS, vol. 4961, pp. 423–427. Springer, Heidelberg (2008)
11. Canal, C., Murillo, J.M., Poizat, P.: Software Adaptation. L'Objet, Special Issue on Software Adaptation 12(1), 9–31 (2006)
12. Chafle, G., Chandra, S., Mann, V., Gowri Nanda, M.: Orchestrating Composite Web Services Under Data Flow Constraints. In: Proc. of ICWS 2005 (2005)
13. Cubo, J., Salaün, G., Canal, C., Pimentel, E., Poizat, P.: A Model-Based Approach to the Verification and Adaptation of WF/.NET Components. In: Proc. of FACS 2007 (2007)
14. de Alfaro, L., Henzinger, T.A.: Interface Automata. In: Proc. of ESEC/FSE 2001 (2001)

15. Dumas, M., Spork, M., Wang, K.: Adapt or Perish: Algebra and Visual Notation for Service Interface Adaptation. In: Dustdar, S., Fiadeiro, J.L., Sheth, A.P. (eds.) BPM 2006. LNCS, vol. 4102, Springer, Heidelberg (2006)
16. Dustdar, S., Schreiner, W.: A Survey on Web services Composition. Int. J. Web and Grid Services 1(1), 1–30 (2005)
17. Gowri Nanda, M., Chandra, S., Sarkar, V.: Decentralizing Execution of Composite Web Services. In: Proc. of OOPSLA 2004 (2004)
18. Haddad, S., Melliti, T., Moreaux, P., Rampacek, S.: Modelling Web Services Interoperability. In: Proc. of ICEIS 2004 (2004)
19. Mateescu, R., Poizat, P., Salaün, G.: Behavioral Adaptation of Component Compositions based on Process Algebra Encodings. In: Proc. of ASE 2007 (2007)
20. Melliti, T., Poizat, P., Ben Mokhtar, S.: Distributed Behavioural Adaptation for the Automatic Composition of Semantic Services (long version) (available from P. Poizat Web pages)
21. Motahari Nezhad, H.R., Benatallah, B., Martens, A., Curbera, F., Casati, F.: Semi-Automated Adaptation of Service Interactions. In: Proc. of WWW 2007 (2007)
22. Papazoglou, M.P., Georgakopoulos, D.: Service-Oriented Computing. Communications of the ACM 46(10), 25–28 (2003)
23. Poizat, P., Royer, J.-C., Salaün, G.: Formal Methods for Component Description, Coordination and Adaptation. In: Proc. of WCAT 2004 (2004)
24. Poizat, P., Salaün, G.: Adaptation of Open Component-based Systems. In: Bonsangue, M.M., Johnsen, E.B. (eds.) FMOODS 2007. LNCS, vol. 4468, Springer, Heidelberg (2007)
25. Tivoli, M., Fradet, P., Girault, A., Goessler, G.: Adaptor Synthesis for Real-Time Components. In: Hermanns, H., Palsberg, J. (eds.) TACAS 2006. LNCS, vol. 3920, Springer, Heidelberg (2006)

Engineering Service Oriented Applications: From StPowla Processes to SRML Models*

Laura Bocchi[1], Stephen Gorton[1,2], and Stephan Reiff-Marganiec[1]

[1] Department of Computer Science, University of Leicester
University Road, Leicester LE1 7RH, UK
{bocchi,smg24,srm13}@mcs.le.ac.uk
[2] ATX Technologies Ltd, MLS Business Centres,
34-36 High Holborn, London WC1V 6AE, UK

Abstract. Service Oriented Computing is a paradigm for developing software systems as the composition of a number of services. Services are loosely coupled entities, can be dynamically published, discovered and invoked over a network. The engineering of such systems presents novel challenges, mostly due to the dynamicity and distributed nature of service-based applications. In this paper, we focus on the modelling of service orchestrations. We discuss the relationship between two languages developed under the SENSORIA project: SRML as a high level modelling language for Service Oriented Architectures, and STPOWLA as a process-oriented orchestration approach that separates core business processes from system variability at the end-user's level, where the focus is towards achieving business goals. We also extend the current status of STPOWLA to include workflow reconfigurations. A fundamental challenge of software engineering is to correctly align business goals with IT strategy, and as such we present an encoding of STPOWLA to SRML. This provides a formal framework for STPOWLA and also a separated view of policies representing system variability that is not present in SRML.

1 Introduction

Service Oriented Computing (SOC) is a paradigm for developing software systems as the composition of a number of services, that are loosely coupled entities that can be dynamically published, discovered and invoked over a network. A service is an abstract resource whose invocation triggers a possibly interactive activity (i.e. a session) and that provides some functionality meaningful from the perspective of the business logic [8]. A Service Oriented Architecture (SOA) allows services with heterogeneous implementations to interact relying on the same middleware infrastructure. Web Services and the Grid are the most popular implementations of SOA. Exposing software in this way means that applications may outsource some functionalities and be dynamically assembled, leading to massively distributed, interoperable and evolvable systems.

The engineering of service-oriented systems presents novel challenges, mostly due to this dynamicity [20]. In this paper we focus on the modelling of orchestrations. An orchestration is the description of the executable pattern of service invocations/interactions to follow in order to achieve a business goal.

* This work has been partially sponsored by the project SENSORIA, IST-2005-016004.

J. Fiadeiro and P. Inverardi (Eds.): FASE 2008, LNCS 4961, pp. 163–178, 2008.
© Springer-Verlag Berlin Heidelberg 2008

We discuss the relationship between two modelling languages for service oriented systems developed in the context of SENSORIA, an IST-FET Integrated Project on Software Engineering for Service-Oriented Overlay Computers: the SENSORIA Reference Modelling Language (SRML) [5,1] and STPOWLA: the Service-Targeted, Policy-Oriented WorkfLow Approach [6]. We also discuss the advantages of their combined usage.

SRML is a high-level modelling language for SOAs whose goal is "to provide a set of primitives that is expressive enough to model applications in the service-oriented paradigm and simple enough to be formalized" [5]. SRML aims at representing, in a technology agnostic way, the various foundational aspects of SOC (e.g. service composition, dynamic reconfiguration, service level agreement, etc.) within one integrated formal framework.

STPOWLA is an approach to process modelling for service-oriented systems. It has three ingredients: workflows to express core processes, services to perform activities and policies to express variability. Workflows are expressed using a graphical notation, such as in [7]. Policies can make short-lived changes to a workflow instance, i.e. they last for the duration of the workflow instance and usually will be made during the execution of the instance, rather than applied to the overall workflow model.

So far, STPOWLA has been limited to non-functional changes to a workflow. In this paper, we extend the concept of workflow change to include reconfigurations: short lived structural changes to a workflow instance. We substantiate this extension by defining a further encoding of these advanced control flow aspects into SRML.

The encoding of STPOWLA into SRML provides a formal framework to STPOWLA. Business processes modelled in STPOWLA can be represented as SRML models and either analyzed alone or as part of more complex modules, where they are composed with other SRML models with heterogeneous implementations (e.g. SRML models extracted from existing BPEL processes [3]).

A second reason for the encoding is providing a higher layer to the modelling of orchestrations in SRML that includes a process-based approach to the definition of a workflow schedule, a separated view of policies, that had not been yet considered in SRML, and the inter-relation between workflow and policies.

In this paper, we give an overview of the STPOWLA approach, including the extension for workflow reconfigurations in section 2. We describe the main concepts of SRML, with respect to STPOWLA in section 3. We then provide an encoding of basic workflow control flow constructs in section 4, and proceed to describe STPOWLA reconfigurations as advanced control flow encodings in section 5. We describe related work and thus our position relative to these efforts in section 6, before discussing and concluding in sections 7 and 8.

2   Specifying and Reconfiguring StPowla Workflows

In this section, we give a brief introduction to the main concepts of STPOWLA. In addition, we present the concept of workflow reconfiguration, which is an extension to the current state of STPOWLA.

```
policyName
appliesTo task_id
     when task_entry
          do req(main, Inv, SLA)
```

Fig. 1. A STPOWLA task's default policy. The semantics of the req function are essentially to execute the processing of the task, as specified with functional requirements described in the main argument, in accordance with invocation parameters in the second argument and keeping to default SLA constraints in the third argument.

2.1 Overview

STPOWLA has three ingredients: workflows, SOA and policies. Workflows specify core business processes, in which all task requirements are satisfied by services. Each workflow task has a default policy as in Fig. 1.

We describe a workflow, according to [7], with the following grammar to show how complex processes can be composed:

$$
\begin{array}{ll}
WF ::= start; P; end & \text{root process} \\
P ::= T & \text{simple task} \\
\quad | \ P; P & \text{sequence} \\
\quad | \ \lambda^? P : P & \text{condition and simple (XOR) join} \\
\quad | \ FJ(m, \{P, \mathcal{B}\}, ..., \{P, \mathcal{B}\}) & \text{split and complex (AND) join} \\
\quad | \ SP(T, ..., T) & \text{strict preference} \\
\quad | \ RC(T, ..., T) & \text{random choice}
\end{array}
$$

We describe the semantics of each construct with a description of the relevant SRML transition in section 4.

Policies are either Event-Condition-Action (ECA) rules (in which case they require a trigger), or goals (essentially ECAs without triggers). The purpose of policies is to express system variability. Policies are written in APPEL [14], a policy description language with formal semantics via a mapping to $\Delta DSTL$ [10]. They are written by the end (business) user and are added and removed at any time to the workflow. In addition to default policies, other policies can be added to the workflow to express system variability in terms of refinement and reconfiguration. The former type express constraints over runtime execution and service selection, but is out of the scope of this paper.

We have mentioned in an earlier paper [6] that the choice of workflow notation in STPOWLA is of small significance. What is of interest is the identification of a common set of triggers for ECA policies. We have identified the following as valid triggers:

- Workflow entry/success/failure/abort;
- Task entry/success/failure/abort;
- Service entry/success/failure.

Note that in STPOWLA, we view services as a black box, i.e. we cannot intervene in their processing between invocation and (possible) response.

Table 1. Policy reconfiguration functions

Function Syntax	Informal Description
fail()	Declare the current task to have failed, i.e. discard further task processing and generate the task_failure event.
abort()	Abort the current task and progress to the next task, generating the task_abort event.
block(s, p)	Wait until predicate p is true before commencing scope s.
insert(x, y, z)	Insert task or scope y into the current workflow instance after task x if z is true, or in parallel with x if z is false.
delete(x)	Delete scope x from the current workflow instance.

2.2 Reconfiguring Workflows with Policies

A workflow reconfiguration is the structural change of a workflow instance. In STPOWLA, a policy can express a reconfiguration rule based on a number of available functions, as described in Table 1. These changes are short-lived, i.e. they only affect the workflow instance and not the overall workflow model.

As an example, consider a supplier whose business process is to receive an order from a registered customer, and then to process that order (which includes collecting, packing and shipping the items, plus invoicing the client). There are no extra constraints on each task, therefore the default task policies are effectively "empty".

Now consider that under certain conditions (e.g. financial pressure), a financial guarantee is required from all customers whose order is above a certain amount. We may have the following policy:

```
GetDepositIfLargeOrder
      appliesTo receiveOrder
          when task_completion
              if receiveOrder.orderValue > £250000
              do insert(requestDeposit, receiveOrder, false)
```

Intuitively, this policy (named *GetDepositIfLargeOrder*) applies to the *receiveOrder* task. It says that when the task completes successfully and the attribute *orderValue* (bound to that task) is above £250000, then there should be an action. The action in this case is the insertion of a task *requestDeposit* into the workflow instance after (not in parallel to) the *receiveOrder* task. The workflow instance thus undergoes the transformation as shown in Fig. 2.

3 Encoding of StPowla to SRML - Foundational Concepts

In SRML, composite services are modelled through *modules*. A module declares one or more components, that are tightly bound and defined at design time, a number of requires-interfaces that specify services, that need to be provided by external parties, and (at most) one provides-interface that describes the service that is offered by the

Fig. 2. A simple reconfiguration example where a core business process is transformed via the insertion of the *getDeposit* task after the *receiveOrder* task. The transformation rule comes from a policy.

module. A number of wires establish interaction protocols among the components and between the components and the external interfaces.

Components, external interfaces and wires are specified in terms of Business Roles, Business Protocols and Interaction Protocols, respectively. The specifications define the type of the nodes.

In this paper we provide an encoding to derive, from a business process specified in STPOWLA, an SRML component that we call BP, of type $businessProcess$ and a second component PI, of type $policyInterface$ that is connected to BP and represents the interface through which it is possible to trigger policies that modify the control flow. PI supports the set of interactions used to trigger a workflow modification in the component BP. Fig. 3 illustrates the structure of the SRML module representing the workflow and policies in the procurement example described earlier in this section.

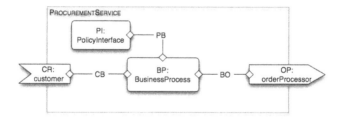

Fig. 3. The structure of a SRML module for the procurement service example

Components are instances of Business Roles specified in terms of (1) the set of supported interactions, (2) the way in which the interactions are orchestrated. We provide in the rest of this section an overview of Business Roles. The overview will not involve the other types of specification as they are not concerned in the encoding.

Business Roles: the Interactions. SRML supports asynchronous two-way conversational interactions: **s&r** denotes interactions that are initiated by the co-party, which expects a reply, **r&s** denotes interactions that are initiated by the party, which expects a reply from its co-party. SRML supports also asynchronous one-way and synchronous interactions that are not discussed here as they are not involved in the encoding.

It follows the specification of the interactions supported by *policyInterface*, corresponding each to one of the STPOWLA functions in Table 1. The Business Role *businessProcess* supports the complementary interactions (i.e. **r&s** instead of **s&r**). Each interaction can have ⌂-parameters for transmitting data when the interaction is initiated and ⊠-parameters for carrying a reply (the example below does not make use of the latter). The index i represents a key-parameter that allows us to handle occurrences of multiple interactions of the same type (as in SRML every interaction event must occur at most once). In this case, we allow PI to trigger more instances of policy functions of the same type.

```
INTERACTIONS
    s&r delete[i:natural]              s&r block[i:natural]
        ⌂ task:taskId                      ⌂ task:taskId
    s&r insert[i:natural]                      c:condition
        ⌂ task:taskId                  s&r fail[i:natural]
           newTask:taskId                  ⌂ task:taskId
           c:condition                 s&r abort[i:natural]
                                           ⌂ task:taskId
```

Business Roles: the Orchestration. The way the declared interactions are orchestrated is specified through a set of variables that provide an abstract view of the state of the component, and a set of transitions that model the way the component interacts with its co-parties. For instance, the local state of the orchestrator is defined as follows:

```
local start[root],start[x],start[ro],...:boolean, ...
state[root],state[x],state[ro],...:[toStart,running,exited]
```

An initialisation condition may define a specific initial state such as:

```
initialization start[root]=true
∧ start[x]=start[ro]=...=false
∧ state[root]=state[x]=state[ro]=...=toStart ∧ ...
```

Similarly, a termination condition may specify the situations in which the component has terminated any activity. The behaviour of components is described by transition rules. Each transition has a name, and a number of other features:

```
transition policyHandlerExample
    triggeredBy samplePolicy⌂[i]?
    guardedBy state[samplePolicy⌂[i].task] = toStart
    effects policy[samplePolicy⌂[i].task]' ∧ ......
    sends samplePolicy⊠[i]!
```

1. A trigger is a condition: typically, the occurrence of a receive-event or a state condition. In the example we engage in the *policyHandlerExample* transition when we receive the initiation of the interaction *samplePolicy*.
2. A guard is a condition that identifies the states in which the transition can take place. For instance, the *policyHandlerExample* transitions should only be taken when the involved task is in state *toStart* (i.e. it is neither in execution, nor has it completed execution). The involved task is identified by the parameter task of the interaction samplePolicy (i.e., *samplePolicy⌂[i].task*).
3. The effects concern changes to the local state. We use *var'* to denote the value the state variable *var* has after the transition.

4. The sends sentence describes the events that are sent and the values taken by their parameters. In the example we invoke the *samplePolicy* reply event to notify the correct management of the policy.

4   Basic Control Flow Encoding

In this section we present an encoding from the control constructs of STPOWLA to SRML orchestrations. Our focus is on the control constructs and we abstract from the interactions of the service and from the semantics of the simple activities of the workflow tasks.

STPOWLA represents a business process as the composition of a number of tasks, either simple (e.g. interactions with services) or complex (e.g. coordinating other tasks by executing them in sequence, parallel, etc.). In SRML we associate an identifier, of type $taskId$, to any task. We denote with T the set of all the task indexes in the workflow schedule.

For every task identifier x we define the following local variables, used to handle the control flow and coordinate the execution of the tasks:

- $start[x]$ is a boolean variable that, when true, triggers the execution of x;
- $done[x]$ is a boolean variable that signals the successful termination of x and triggers the continuation of the workflow schedule;
- $fail[x]$ is a boolean variable that signals the termination with failure of x and triggers the failure handler.

In general, the next activity in the control flow is executed when the previous one terminates successfully. In case of task failure the flow blocks (i.e. the next task is waiting for a signal of successful termination from the previous task) and the failure signal is collected by a failure handler that possibly involves a number of policies. According to the failure handler, the execution of the process can be terminated, resumed, altered, etc. We leave the specification of the failure handling mechanisms as a future work. Anyway, the constructs of strict preference and random choice, that try a number of alternative tasks until one terminates with success, handle the failure signal directly within the workflow.

We will introduce in section 5 a set of transitions, as a part of the orchestration of BP that model the policy handler. The policy handler has the responsibility to enact the modifications of the control flow induced by the policies triggered by PI. The policy handler blocks the normal flow by setting the variable $policy[x] = true$, where x is the identifier of the first task involved in the modification. The variable $policy[x]$ is a guard to the execution of x. We will describe the policy handler more later in this paper, but now it is important to know that when a policy function has to be executed on a task, the task has to be blocked. It is responsibility of the policy handler to reset the flow of execution.

Some policies can be applied only on running processes (e.g. abort) and some others only on tasks that have not started yet (e.g. delete). A local variable $state[x]$ identifies the state of the execution of x by taking the values $toStart$ (i.e. the execution of the task has not started yet), $running$ (i.e. the task is in execution) and $exited$ (i.e. x has terminated). The state variable $state[x]$ will be used to ensure that policies act on a task in the correct state of execution.

We consider the simple tasks as black boxes: we are not interested in the type of activity that they perform but only on the fact that a task, for example task x, is activated by $start[x]$, signals its termination along either $done[x]$ or $failed[x]$ and notifies its state along $state[x]$.

The execution of the workflow is started by a special transition *root* that sets $start[x] = true$ where x is the first task in the workflow schedule. The local variables are initialized as follows: $\forall i \in T \setminus root, start[i] = false \wedge start[root] = true$, $\forall i \in T, done[i] = failed[i] = policy[i] = false$ and $\forall i \in T, state[i] = toStart$.

It follows the encoding of the workflow template $start; P; end$ where P is associated to the task identifier x:

```
transition root
    triggeredBy start[root] ∨ done[x]
    guardedBy ¬ policy[root]
    effects start[root] ⊃ ¬ start[root]' ∧ state[root]'=running ∧ start[x]'
    ∧ done[x] ⊃ ¬ done[x]' ∧ done[root]' ∧ state[root]'=exited
```

Sequence. The sequence operator $P_1; P_2$, illustrated in Fig. 4, first executes P_1 and, after the successful termination of P_1, executes P_2. We remark that failures are not handled in this document and will be addressed in the future.

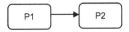

Fig. 4. The sequence control construct in STPOWLA

The encoding of the sequence construct in SRML is as follows. The sequence activity triggers the execution of the first task, with task identifier $p1$, then collects the termination signal from $p1$ and triggers the execution of the second subprocess, with task identifier $p2$. The sequence is encoded in the following SRML transition, with task identifier x:

```
transition X
    triggeredBy start[x] ∨ done[p1] ∨ done[p2]
    guardedBy ¬ policy[x]
    effects start[x] ⊃ ¬ start[x]' ∧ state[x]'=running ∧ start[p1]'
    ∧ done[p1] ⊃ ¬ done[p1]' ∧ start[p2]'
    ∧ done[p2] ⊃ ¬ done[p2]' ∧ done[x]' ∧ state[x]'=exited
```

Condition and Simple Join (XOR). The condition and simple join construct $\lambda? P_1 : P_2$, illustrated in Fig. 5(a), consists of the combination of the flow junction, that diverts the control flow down one of two branches P_1 and P_2, represented by the task identifiers $p1$ and $p2$, respectively, according to a condition λ, and the flow merge of a number of flows where synchronization is not an issue.

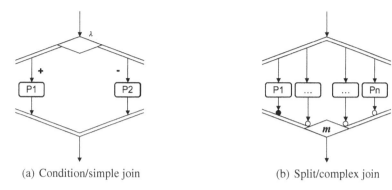

(a) Condition/simple join   (b) Split/complex join

Fig. 5. Multiple branches constructs in STPOWLA

The condition and simple join are encoded into the following SRML transition:

```
transition X
    triggeredBy start[x] ∨ done[p1] ∨ done[p2]
    guardedBy ¬ policy[x]
    effects start[x] ⊃ ¬ start[x]' ∧ state[x]'=running
        ∧ (λ ⊃ start[p1]') ∧ (¬ λ ⊃ start[p2]')
    ∧ done[p1] ⊃ ¬ done[p1]' ∧ done[x]' ∧ state[x]'=exited
    ∧ done[p2] ⊃ ¬ done[p2]' ∧ done[x]' ∧ state[x]'=exited
```

Split and Complex Join (AND). The split and complex join construct $FJ(m, \{P_1, \mathcal{B}_1\}, \ldots, \{P_n, \mathcal{B}_n\})$ consists of the combination of the flow split, that splits the control flow over many branches, and the conditional merge, that synchronizes two or more flows into one. The value of m, that is statically determined, represents the minimum number of branches that have to be synchronized. Furthermore, any branch is associated to a boolean $\mathcal{B}_i$ that determines whether the $i - th$ branch is mandatory in the synchronization. The graphical notation of the construct is illustrated in Fig. 5(b).

The encoding is as follows: Let S be the set, with cardinality n, of the task indexes associated to the branches of the split/join. Let the identifiers for the subtasks of x to range over $p1, \ldots, pn$. Let N be the set of indexes of the necessary tasks and $m \in \mathbb{N}$ be the minimum number of branches that have to be synchronized. We assume that $m \leq |N|$. The complex join is encoded in the following SRML transition, where $Kcomb$ is the set of $(m - |N|) - subsets$ of $S \setminus N$:

```
transition X
    triggeredBy start[x] ∨ (∧_{i∈N}done[pi]∧(∨_{K∈Kcomb}(∧_{k∈K}done[pj])))
    guardedBy ¬ policy[x]
    effects start[x] ⊃ ¬ start[x]' ∧ state[x]'=running ∧_{i∈[1,...,n]} start[pi]'
    ∧ ¬ start[x] ⊃ done[x]' ∧ state[x]'=exited ∧_{i:[1..n]}(¬ done[pi]')
```

The transition is executed: (1) when the task x is triggered or (2) in case of successful termination of all the necessary subtasks (i.e. $\wedge_{i \in N} done[pi]$) and of a number of tasks greater or equal to m (i.e. $\vee_{K \in Kcomb}(\wedge_{k \in K} done[pj])$).

Strict Preference. The strict preference $SP(P_1, \ldots, P_n)$, illustrated in Fig. 6(a), attempts the tasks $P_1, \ldots, P_n$ one by one, in a specific order, until one completes successfully. In this case, with no loss of generality we consider the tasks ordered by increasing index numbers.

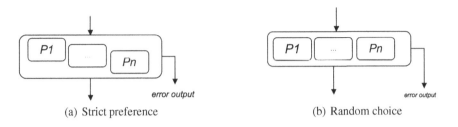

(a) Strict preference   (b) Random choice

Fig. 6. Other constructs in STPOWLA

The strict preference is encoded in the following SRML transition:

```
transition X
    triggeredBy  start[x] V_{i:[1..n]}(done[pi] V failed[pi])
    guardedBy ¬ policy[x]
    effects start[x] ⊃ ¬ start[x]' ∧ state[x]'=running ∧ start[p1]'
    ∧_{i:[2..n-1]}failed[pi] ⊃ ¬ failed[pi]' ∧ start[p(i+1)]'
∧ failed[pn] ⊃ ¬ failed[pn]' ∧ failed[x]' ∧ state[x]'=exited
∧ V_{i:[1..n]}done[pi] ⊃ done[x]' ∧  state[x]'=exited ∧_{i:[1..n]}done[pi]'
```

Random Choice. The random choice $RC(P_1, \ldots, P_n)$, illustrated in Fig. 6(b), attempts the tasks $P_1, \ldots, P_n$ simultaneously and completes when one completes successfully.

The random choice is encoded in the following SRML transition:

```
transition X
    triggeredBy start[x] V_{i:[1..n]}(done[pi])V (∧_{i:[1..n]}(failed[pi]))
    guardedBy ¬ policy[x]
    effects start[x] ⊃ ¬ start[x]' ∧ state[x]=running ∧_{i:[1..n]}start[pi]'
    ∧ (∧_{i:[1..n]}failed[pi])⊃ failed[x]'∧ state[x]'=exited ∧_{i:[1..n]}¬ failed[pi]'
    ∧ (V_{i:[1..n]}done[pi]) ⊃ done[x]' ∧ state[x]'=exited
    ∧_{i:[1..n]}(¬ done[pi]' ∧ ¬ failed[pi]')
```

5   Advanced Control Flow Encoding

One of the aims of this paper is to illustrate how policies can influence the control flow and how this can be modelled in SRML. In this section we discuss the encoding of policies, as described in STPOWLA, into SRML orchestrations. Each interaction is handled, in the orchestration of BP, by one or more transitions that model the policy handler. We will see such transitions in detail when discussing individual interactions, in the rest of this section.

A policy related to a task can have effect (1) on the state prior to the task execution (i.e. *delete*, *block* and *insert*) or (2) during the execution of a task (i.e. *fail* and *abort*). The state of a task is notified along the variable $state[y]$. The policy handler must check that the task is in the correct state according to the specific policy that has to be enacted. The policy handler prevents the execution of either (1) the task or (2) the rest of the task by using the variable $policy[x]$: the condition $\neg policy[x]$ guards the transition(s) corresponding to the execution of task. Notice that with most of the control constructs it is not possible to trigger policies of this second type on atomic tasks whose state changed directly from *toStart* to *done*.

Delete Task. The deletion of task (i.e. delete(x) in STPOWLA) skips the execution of x. The policy manager prevents the execution of x by signaling a policy exception (i.e. $policy[x] = true$). When the signal for the execution of x is received, the policy handler signals the successful termination of x. The condition $P\_delete[i]$⊖? is $true$ when the event $delete[i]$⊖? occurred in the past.

```
transition policyHandler_delete_1
    triggeredBy delete[i]⊖?
    guardedBy state[delete[i]⊖.task] = toStart
    effects policy[delete[i]⊖.task]'

transition policyHandler_delete_2
    triggeredBy start[x]
    guardedBy P_delete[i]⊖? ∧ delete[i]⊖.task=x
    effects ¬ start[x]' ∧ done[x]' ∧ state[x]' = done
    sends delete[i]✉!
```

Block Task. The function block(x, p) in STPOWLA blocks a task x until p is $true$. In SRML the policy handler prevents x from executing (i.e. $policy[x]$ becomes $true$) temporarily until p is $true$. The policy handler notifies the enactment of the policy to the environment and after that the task has been unblocked.

```
transition policyHandler_block_1
    triggeredBy block[i]⊖?
    guardedBy state[block[i]⊖.task] = toStart
    effects policy[block[i]⊖.task]'

transition policyHandler_block_2
    triggeredBy block[i]⊖?.condition
    guardedBy P_block[i]⊖?
    effects ¬ policy[block[i]⊖.task]'
    sends block[i]✉!
```

Insert Task. The insertion of a task, represented by the function insert(x, y, z) in STPOWLA, inserts the task y in sequence or in parallel with respect to x depending on the value of the boolean variable z. In SRML the insertion is triggered by the interaction $insert[i]$✉? with parameter $insert[i]$✉.$task$ representing the task x, $insert[i]$✉.$insertedTask$ representing the task y and $insert[i]$✉.$condition$ representing the condition z. We assume that the set of tasks available for insertion is determined a priori, in this way we assume that the SRML encoding has a set of transitions for each possible task, including the task to possibly insert, that is executed by setting $start[y]$ to $true$. We introduce in this way a limitation on the number of task types that we can insert and on the fact that a task can be inserted only once (we will manage multiple insertions in the future, when we will encode looping constructs) but we do not provide any limitation on the position of the insertion.

We rely on a function $next : taskId \rightarrow taskId$ that returns, given a task, the next task to execute in the workflow. Such a function can be defined by induction on the syntax of STPOWLA defined in section 2.1.

The transition $policyHandler\_insert\_1$ prevents the execution of the task on which the policy applies (i.e. $insert[i]$✉.$task$) and of the successive one. The transition $policyHandler\_insert\_2$ starts the execution of the task on which the policy applies (in parallel with the inserted task if $insert[i]$✉.$condition = true$). The

transitions *policyHandler_insert_sequence* and *policyHandler_insert_parallel*
coordinate the execution of the tasks (the one on which the policy applies and the inserted one) in sequence or in parallel, according to the condition.

```
transition policyHandler_insert_1
    triggeredBy insert[i]⌂?
    guardedBy  state[insert[i]⌂.task]=toStart
    effects policy[insert[i]⌂.task]'

transition policyHandler_insert_2
    triggeredBy start[x]
    guardedBy P_insert[i]⌂? ∧ insert[i]⌂.task=x
    effects insert[i]⌂?.condition ⊃ ¬ policy[insert[i]⌂.task]'
    ∧ ¬ insert[i]⌂?.condition ⊃ policy[insert[i]⌂.task]'
    ∧ start[insert[i]⌂.insertedTask]'

transition policyHandler_insert_sequence
    triggeredBy done[x] ∨ done[y]
    guardedBy P_insert[i]⌂? ∧ insert[i]⌂.condition
    ∧ (insert[i]⌂.task=x ∨ insert[i]⌂.insertedTask=y)
    effects done[x] ⊃ ¬ done[x]' ∧ start[y]' ∧ done[y] ⊃
    ¬ done[y]' ∧ start[next(x)]'

transition policyHandler_insert_parallel
    triggeredBy done[x] ∧ done[y]
    guardedBy P_insert[i]⌂? ∧ ¬ insert[i]⌂.condition
    ∧ insert[i]⌂.task=x ∧ insert[i]⌂.insertedTask=y
    effects ¬ done[x]' ∧ ¬ done[y]' ∧ start[next(block[i]⌂.task)]'
```

Fail Task. The failure of a task must occur during the execution of the task (it has no effect otherwise). The failure can be triggered autonomously, within the task or induced externally by the execution of the policy *fail*. We consider here the second case.

```
transition policyHandler_fail
    triggeredBy fail[i]⌂?
    guardedBy state[fail[i]⌂.task]=running
    effects policy[i][fail[i]⌂.task]' ∧ state[fail[i]⌂.task]'=failed
    sends fail[i]✉!
```

Abort Task. The abortion of a task is similar to a deletion, but it involves a running task. Aborting a task that has neither started or has already completed has no effect.

```
transition policyHandler_abort
    triggeredBy abort[i]⌂?
    guardedBy state[abort[i]⌂.task]=running
    effects policy[abort⌂.task]' ∧ state[abort[i]⌂.task]'=done
    sends abort[i]✉!
```

5.1   An Example: The Reconfiguration of the Procurement Scenario

The orchestration of the Business Role *businessProtocol* would consist of the sequence of the tasks request order (i.e. task *ro*) and process order (i.e. task *po*).

```
transition X
    triggeredBy start[x] ∨ done[ro] ∨ done[po]
    guardedBy policy[x]
    effects start[x] ⊃ ¬ start[x]' ∧ state[x]'=running ∧ start[ro]'
    ∧ done[ro] ⊃ ¬ done[ro]' ∧ start[po]'
    ∧ done[po] ⊃ ¬ done[po]' ∧ done[x]' ∧ state[x]'=exited
```

In the case of a receive event of type $insert[i]\boxtimes?$, triggered by the component PI, with parameter $task$ equal to po, parameter $insertedTask$ equal to gbd (i.e. get deposit), and the parameter $condition$ equal to $true$. The policy handler would: (1) block the execution of ro (preventing in this way ro to trigger its continuation $po = next(ro)$) by setting $policy[ro] = policy[po] = true$, (2) wait for the condition $start[ro] = true$ that is triggered by transition X, (3) since the parameter $condition$ is $true$, the policy handler would unblock ro, (4) the transition $policyHandler\_insert\_sequence$ would handle the execution of gd after ro and, finally, trigger po by setting $start[po] = true$.

6 Related Work

SRML is inspired by the Service Component Architecture (SCA) [9]. SCA is a set of specifications, proposed by an industrial consortium, that describe a middleware-independent model for building over SOAs.

Similarly to SCA, SRML provides primitives for modelling, in a technology agnostic way, business processes as assemblies of (1) tightly coupled components that may be implemented using different technologies (including wrapped-up legacy systems, BPEL, Java, etc.) and (2) loosely coupled, dynamically discovered services.

Differently from SRML, SCA is not a modelling language but a framework for modelling the structure of a service-oriented software artifact and for its deployment. SCA abstracts from the business logic provided by components in the sense that it does not provide a means to model the behavioural aspects of services. SRML is, instead, a modelling language that relies on a mathematical framework and that provides the primitives to specify such behavioural aspects.

Process modelling at a business level is generally achieved using graphical languages such as BPMN [19] or UML Activity Diagrams. However, they do not cater for all workflow patterns [17], as described in [21] and [15], respectively. YAWL [16] caters for all workflow patterns and has a graphical syntax with formal semantics, based on petri nets, so it is a good candidate for the process notation. As we have previously mentioned, the syntax is not significant, but rather the places where a policy can interact is. We have used the language of [7] for its simplicity, expressive power and our familiarity with it. At a lower business level, languages such as BPEL or WS-CDL are capable of expressing business processes, but with a code-based approach that is not high level enough for the end user.

Policies have generally been used as an administration technique in system management (e.g. access control [11] or Internet Telephony [13]). In addition, a methodology has been proposed to extract workflows from business policies [18]. However, we are not aware of policies being used as a variability factor in service-targeted processes.

Dynamic processes that are based on the end-user's needs are more difficult to find. The closest we know of are AgentWork [12], which is dynamic only because of the choice of rules to follow under failure, and Worklets [2], the YAWL module for dynamic processes. Worklets though are based on a set of processing rules that are predefined, and of which one is selected.

7 Discussion

The benefits of this work are twofold. The mapping from STPOWLA to SRML creates a formal framework for the former (which previously only benefitted from a formal semantics for the APPEL policy language). Since applications are often designed based on the business process, STPOWLA is the ideal vehicle for this step. Transformation to SRML modules allows for analysis of the modules, either on their own or as part of more complex modules. Looking at the encoding bottom-up, STPOWLA adds a higher level of modelling to SRML modules in the form of a process-oriented workflow schedule, with system variability separated from the core business concerns.

To exemplify the benefits, we describe an application scenario from an industrial case study, provided by a partner in the SENSORIA PROJECT. The scenario describes the interaction between a VoIP telephony provider and their internal service network, based on a pre-delivery state.

The trigger of the workflow is the supplier receiving an order from a customer. Under normal operating circumstances, this proceeds to a testing phase, where the customer can choose to accept or decline the test results. If they accept the results, then the supplier will proceed to identifying an offer proposal. In order to do this, legal assistance is required from a legal service. This assistance is then received and embedded into a Service Level Agreement between the customer and the supplier. The contract is created and the workflow is then complete.

There are two policies that affect how the workflow is executed. Firstly, if the order is sufficiently small and the customer's order is of sufficiently small value, then the initial testing phase should be bypassed. Secondly, if the order is of sufficiently small value, then no legal assistance should be sought. If both these policies were applied to the workflow, then it would essentially be represented as *ReceiveOrder → IdentifyOffer → CreateContract*.

All tasks inside the workflow are handled by services, either internal to the supplier or external (e.g. in the case of legal assistance and getting customer acceptance or refusal). The service composition and configuration can then be modelled formally in SRML. The effect of the policies can also be incorporated and through the application to the SRML model, the effects can be analysed and reasoned about.

Any method suggested for software engineering must be considered with respect to its scalability. The term can be interpreted in two different ways here, namely does the encoding mechanism itself scale and also do the STPOWLA and SRML methods scale. To answer the former, it can be said that it scales as every opeartor of STPOWLA is mapped into a relatively straight forward transition in SRML. The only exception is the random choice operator, where the matching transition is slightly more complex. As for the latter aspect, and in our opinion this is more crucial for practical purposes, we actually gain scalability. This is achieved by using the high-level STPOWLA notation to capture the business process in a more abstract and more easily understandable way than one would achieve by using SRML directly. However reasoning for e.g. validation can make use of the formality of SRML in addition of course to SRML being a step towards implementation.

8   Summary and Conclusion

The engineering of Service Oriented applications, as opposed to more traditional application development, is faced with novel challenges arising from the dynamicity of component selection and assembly, leading to massively distributed, interoperable and evolvable systems. Furthermore, a continuing challenge is to correctly align business goals with IT strategy. As such, the development approach must change to accommodate these factors.

In this paper, we have presented a mapping from STPOWLA to SRML. SRML is a high level modelling language for service-based applications, based on a formal framework. SRML can model service compositions and configurations. The orchestration of the services is modelled by a central agent in each SRML module. However, the business process aspect is less clear. STPOWLA is an SOA aware approach that combines workflows and policies. It allows to define the orchestration according to a business process.

The main contributions of this report are 1) to encode basic STPOWLA workflow constructs in SRML, 2) to extend STPOWLA with workflow reconfiguration functions, and 3) to encode these reconfiguration functions in SRML.

Future work includes the application of this work to some larger case studies and consider mapping STPOWLA refinement policies into SRML.

References

1. Abreu, J., Bocchi, L., Fiadeiro, J.L., Lopes, A.: Specifying and Composing Interaction Protocols for Service-Oriented System Modelling. In: Derrick, J., Vain, J. (eds.) FORTE 2007. LNCS, vol. 4574, pp. 358–373. Springer, Heidelberg (2007)
2. Adams, M., ter Hofstede, A.H.M., Edmond, D., van der Aalst, W.M.P.: Worklets: A service-oriented implementation of dynamic flexibility in workflows. In: Meersman, R., Tari, Z. (eds.) OTM 2006. LNCS, vol. 4275, pp. 291–308. Springer, Heidelberg (2006)
3. Bocchi, L., Hong, Y., Lopes, A., Fiadeiro, J.L.: From BPEL to SRML: A Formal Transformational Approach. In: Proc.of 4th International Workshop on Web Services and Formal Methods (WSFM 2007). LNCS, Springer, Heidelberg (2007)
4. Dustdar, S., Fiadeiro, J.L., Sheth, A.P. (eds.): BPM 2006. LNCS, vol. 4102. Springer, Heidelberg (2006)
5. Fiadeiro, J.L., Lopes, A., Bocchi, L.: A Formal Approach to Service Component Architecture. Web Services and Formal Methods 4184, 193–213 (2006)
6. Gorton, S., Montangero, C., Reiff-Marganiec, S., Semini, L.: StPowla: SOA, Policies and Workflows. In: Proceedings of 3rd International Workshop on Engineering Service-Oriented Applications: Analysis, Design, and Composition, Vienna, Austria, September 17, 2007 (2007)

7. Gorton, S., Reiff-Marganiec, S.: Towards a task-oriented, policy-driven business requirements specification for web services. In: Dustdar,, et al. (eds.) [4], pp. 465–470
8. Haas, H., Brown, A.: Web Services Glossary. W3C Working Group Note, World Wide Web Consortium (W3C) (2004), http://www.w3.org/TR/ws-gloss/
9. Beisiegel, M., Blohm, H., Booz, D., Dubray, J., Colyer, A., Edwards, M., Ferguson, D., Flood, B., Greenberg, M., Kearns, D., Marino, J., Mischkinsky, J., Nally, M., Pavlik, G., Rowley, M., Tam, K., Trieloff, C.: Building Systems using a Service Oriented Architecture. Whitepaper, SCA Consortium (2005), http://www.oracle.com/technology/tech/webservices/standards/sca/pdf/SCA_White_Paper1_09.pdf
10. Montangero, C., Reiff-Marganiec, S., Semini, L.: Logic–Based Detection of Conflicts in Appel Policies. In: Arbab, F., Sirjani, M. (eds.) FSEN 2007. LNCS, vol. 4767, pp. 257–271. Springer, Heidelberg (2007)
11. Moses, T.: extensible access control markup language specification (2005), www.oasis-open.org
12. Müller, R., Greiner, U., Rahm, E.: Agentwork: a workflow system supporting rule-based workflow adaptation. Data Knowl. Eng. 51(2), 223–256 (2004)
13. Reiff-Marganiec, S.: Policies: Giving users control over calls. In: Ryan, M.D., Meyer, J.-J.C., Ehrich, H.-D. (eds.) Objects, Agents, and Features, Dagstuhl Seminar 2003. LNCS, vol. 2975, pp. 189–208. Springer, Heidelberg (2004)
14. Reiff-Marganiec, S., Turner, K.J., Blair, L.: APPEL: the ACCENT project policy environment/language. Technical Report TR-161, University of Stirling (2005)
15. Russell, N., van der Aalst, W.M.P., ter Hofstede, A.H.M., Wohed, P.: On the suitability of uml 2.0 activity diagrams for business process modelling. In: Stumptner, M., Hartmann, S., Kiyoki, Y. (eds.) APCCM. CRPIT, vol. 53, pp. 95–104. Australian Computer Society (2006)
16. van der Aalst, W.M.P., ter Hofstede, A.H.M.: Yawl: yet another workflow language. Inf. Syst. 30(4), 245–275 (2005)
17. van der Aalst, W.M.P., ter Hofstede, A.H.M., Kiepuszewski, B., Barros, A.P.: Workflow patterns. Distributed and Parallel Databases 14(1), 5–51 (2003), Information, www.workflowpatterns.com
18. Wang, H.J.: A Logic-based Methodology for Busines Process Analysis and Design: Linking Business Policies to Workflow Models. PhD thesis, University of Arizona (2006)
19. White, S.A.: Business process modelling notation. Object Management Group (OMG) and Business Process Management Initiative (2004), www.bpmn.org
20. Wirsing, M., Bocchi, L., Clark, A., Fiadeiro, J.L., Gilmore, S., Hölzl, M., Koch, N., Pugliese, R.: SENSORIA: Engineering for Service-Oriented Overlay Computers, June 2007. MIT, Cambridge (submitted 2007)
21. Wohed, P., Aalst, W.M.P.v.d., Dumas, M., Hofstede, A.H.M.t., Russell, N.: On the suitability of bpmn for business process modelling. In: Dustdar, et al. (eds.) [4], pp. 161–176

A Logic of Graph Constraints

Fernando Orejas[1], Hartmut Ehrig[2], and Ulrike Prange[2]

[1] Dpto de L.S.I., Universitat Politècnica de Catalunya, Campus Nord, Mòdul Omega, Jordi
Girona 1-3, 08034 Barcelona, Spain
orejas@lsi.upc.edu
[2] Fak. IV, Technische Universität Berlin, Franklinstrasse 28/29, 10587 Berlin, Germany
{ehrig,uprange}@cs.tu-berlin.de

Abstract. Graph constraints were introduced in the area of graph transformation, in connection with the notion of (negative) application conditions, as a form to limit the applicability of transformation rules. However, we believe that graph constraints may also play a significant role in the area of visual software modelling or in the specification and verification of semi-structured documents or websites (i.e. HTML or XML sets of documents). In this sense, after some discussion on these application areas, we concentrate on the problem of how to prove the consistency of specifications based on this kind of constraints. In particular, we present proof rules for three classes of (increasingly more powerful) graph constraints and show that our proof rules are sound and (refutationally) complete for each class.

1 Introduction

Graph constraints were introduced in the area of graph transformation, together with the notion of (negative) application conditions, as a form to limit the applicability of transformation rules [7,9,12,6,10,11]. More precisely, a graph constraint is the graphical description of some kind of pattern that must be present (or must not be present) on the graphs that we are transforming. In particular, a transformation would be illegal if the resulting graph would violate any of the given constraints. Graph constraints have been studied mainly in connection with negative application conditions. These conditions are constraints that are associated to the left-hand side or the right-hand side of a graph transformation rule. Then, one such rule would be applicable to a given graph if the left-hand side application conditions are satisfied by the given graph (or rather by the rule matching) and the right-hand side application conditions are satisfied by the result of the transformation. In this context, most of the above-mentioned work has been related to the extension of the basic graph transformation concepts and results to the use of application conditions and constraints and to show how one can transform a set of constraints into application conditions for the given transformation rules. Other work related to these notions has studied the detection of conflicts for graph transformation with application conditions [15], or the expressive power of some kinds of graph constraints [17].

We believe that graph constraints can go beyond their use in connection to graph transformation. More precisely, there are two areas in which we think that graph

J. Fiadeiro and P. Inverardi (Eds.): FASE 2008, LNCS 4961, pp. 179–198, 2008.
ⓒ Springer-Verlag Berlin Heidelberg 2008

constraints may play an interesting role. The first one is the area of visual software modelling. The second one is the specification and verification of classes of semi-structured documents, including the specification and verification of websites (i.e. HTML or XML sets of documents).

In the area of visual modelling, especially in the context of UML modelling, models are designed using different kinds of diagrams. However, if we have to impose some specific constraints on the models then we have to use a textual notation as OCL. We consider that this situation is quite inconvenient. Especially in the case when we want to express constraints on the structure of the model, we think that using a graphical notation which is close to the visual description of the model is much more clear and intuitive than using some textual expression where one has to previously code or represent that structure.

On the other hand, we know two kinds of approaches for the specification and verification of semi-structured documents. The first one [2,8] is based on extending a fragment of first-order logic allowing us to refer to the components of the given class of documents (in particular, using XPath notation). This approach, in our opinion, poses two kinds of problems. On one hand, from a technical point of view, the extension of first-order logic to represent XML patterns has to make use of associative-commutative operators. This may make deduction difficult to implement efficiently, since using unification in inference rules may be very costly (in general, two arbitrary atoms may have a doubly exponential amount of most general unifiers). As a consequence, the approaches presented in [2,8] present specification languages that allow us to specify classes of documents and tools that allow us to check if a given document (or a set of documents) follows a specification. However, they do not consider the problem of defining deductive tools to analyze specifications, for instance for looking for inconsistencies. On the other hand, from a pragmatic point of view, XPath expressions can be quite verbose and this may make the resulting specifications unpleasant to read and to write.

The other approach that we know [13], which we consider especially interesting, has a more practical nature. Schematron is a language and a tool that is part of an ISO standard (DSDL: Document Schema Description Languages). The language allows us to specify constraints on XML documents by describing directly XML patterns (using XML) and expressing properties about these patterns. Then, the tool allows us to check if a given XML document satisfies these constraints. However, we consider that there are two problems with this approach. The most important one is that this work lacks proper foundations. The other one is that the kind of patterns that can be expressed in the Schematron language could be a bit limited. On the other hand, as in the approaches mentioned above, Schematron provides no deductive capabilities.

In this paper we start the study of graph constraints as a specification formalism. In particular, we study their underlying logic, providing inference rules that would allow us to prove the consistency (or satisfiability) of specifications. Actually, we show that these rules are sound and refutationally complete for the class of constraints considered. It must be noted that, as it is well-known, the fact that our inference rules are refutationally complete means that we have a complete method to prove consequences of our specifications. In particular, if we want to check if a given property is a consequence of a specification then it is enough to see if the given specification, together with the negation of the property, is inconsistent.

It must also be noted that the results that we present are quite more general than what they actually may seem. Following recent work on algebraic graph transformation (see, e.g., cite [5]), our results apply not only to plain graphs, but generalize to a large class of structures including typed and attributed graphs (we discuss this issue in more detail in the conclusion). In particular, instead of a logic of *graph* constraints we could speak of a logic of *pattern* constraints, since our results would also apply to reasoning about constraints based on other kinds of patterns, like XML patterns. In this sense, we consider that the work that we present in this paper provides the basis for defining the logical foundations of Schematron, and for extending it with more powerful constraints and with deduction capabilities. In particular, the XML patterns that are used in Schematron can be seen just as the textual representation (or, rather, the XML representation) of a subclass of the graph constraints that we consider. In particular, our work could be used to provide deductive capabilities to analyze the consistency of Schematron specifications.

The work that we present is not the first logic to reason about graphs. In particular, with different aims, Courcelle in a series of papers has studied in detail the use of monadic second-order logic (MSOL) to express graph properties (for a survey, see [4]). That logic is quite more powerful than the one that we study in this paper. For instance, we cannot express global properties about graphs (e.g that a graph is connected), but using MSOL we can. Actually, we think that MSOL is too powerful for the kind of applications that we have in mind. On the other hand, in [3] Courcelle's logic is extended with temporal operators. In this case, the intention is to present a logic that can be used for the verification of graph transformation systems. Again, this logic goes far beyond our aims.

The paper is organized as follows. In the following section we present the kind of graph constraints that we consider in this paper and present a small example to motivate their use in connection with visual modelling or website specification. This example will be used as a running example in the rest of the paper. The following section is the core of the paper. It presents inference rules for three classes of graph constraints with increasing expressive power, showing, for all cases, their soundness and completeness. Finally, in the conclusion we discuss several issues concerning the results that we present, in particular, their generality and different issues concerning the possible implementation of a deductive tool.

2 Graphs and Graph Constraints

In this section we present the basic notions that are used in this paper. First we present some notation and terminology needed, and then, in the second subsection we introduce the kind of graph constraints that we consider. For simplicity, we present our definitions in terms of plain directed graphs, although in some examples, for motivation, we deal with typed or attributed graphs. Anyhow, following the approach used in [5], it is not difficult to show that our results generalize to a large class of (graphical) structures, including typed, labelled or attributed graphs. In Section 4 we discuss this issue in more detail.

2.1 Graphs

As said above, all our notions and results will be presented in terms of plain directed graphs, i.e.:

Definition 1 (Graphs). *A graph $G = (G_V, G_E, s, t)$ consists of a set G_V of nodes, a set G_E of edges, a source function $s : G_E \to G_V$, and a target function $t : G_E \to G_V$.*

It may be noted that we do not explicitly state that the sets of nodes and edges of a graph are finite sets. That is, according to our definition, unless it is explicitly stated, graphs may be infinite. This issue is discussed in some detail in Section 3.

All over the paper we will have to express that a certain graph G_1 is included into another graph G_2. Obviously, we could have done this through a subgraph relationship. However, G_2 may include several instances of G_1. For this reason, in order to be precise when specifying the specific instance in which we may be interested, we will deal with these inclusions using the notion of graph monomorphism:

Definition 2 (Graph morphisms). *Given the graphs $G = (G_V, G_E, s, t)$ and $G' = (G'_V, G'_E, s', t')$, a graph morphism $f : G \to G'$ is a pair of mappings, $f_V : G_V \to G'_V, f_E : G_E \to G'_E$ such that f commutes with the source and target functions, i.e. the diagrams below are commutative.*

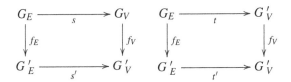

A graph morphism $f : G \to G'$ is a monomorphism *if f_V and f_E are injective mappings.*

In several results of the paper, given two graphs G, G' we will need to put them together in all possible ways. This will be done using the construction $G \otimes G'$:

Definition 3 (Jointly surjective morphisms). *Two graph morphisms $m : H \to G$ and $m' : H' \to G$ are* jointly surjective *if $m_V(H_V) \cup m'_V(H'_V) = G_V$ and $m_E(H_E) \cup m'_E(H'_E) = G_E$.*

Given two graphs G and G', the set of all pairs of jointly surjective monomorphisms from G and G' is denoted $G \otimes G'$, that is:

$$G \otimes G' = \{m : G \to H \leftarrow G' : m' \mid m \text{ and } m' \text{ are jointly surjective monomorphisms}\}.$$

The definition of $G \otimes G'$ in terms of sets of pairs of monomorphisms may look a bit more complex than needed but, as in the case of the inclusions, we often need to identify the specific instances of G and G' inside H. However, in many occasions it is enough to consider that $G \otimes G'$ is the set of all graphs that can be seen as the result of putting together G and G'.

Note that if G and G' are finite graphs then $G \otimes G'$ is a also finite set. This is needed because in several inference rules (see Section 3) the result is a clause involving a disjunction related to a set of this kind. In particular, if $G \otimes G'$ is infinite so would be the corresponding disjunction.

The above operation can be extended for putting together arbitrary (finite) sequences of graphs.

2.2   Graph Constraints

The underlying idea of a graph constraint is that it should specify that certain structures must be present (or must not be present) in a given graph. For instance, the simplest kind of graph constraint, $\exists C$, specifies that a given graph G should include (a copy of) C. For instance, the constraint:

$$\exists \left(\bigcirc \!\!\!-\!\!\!\!-\!\!\!\!-\!\!\!\!\longrightarrow\!\!\bigcirc \right)$$

specifies that a graph should include at least one edge. Obviously, $\neg \exists C$ specifies that a given graph G should not include (a copy of) C. For instance, the constraint:

$$\neg \exists \left(\bigcirc \!\!\!\Longrightarrow\!\!\bigcirc \right)$$

specifies that a given graph G should not include two different edges between any two nodes. A slightly more complex kind of graph constraints are atomic constraints of the form $\forall (c : X \rightarrow C)$ where c is a monomorphism (or, just, an inclusion). This constraint specifies that whenever a graph G includes (a copy of) the graph X it should also include (a copy of) its extension C. However, in order to enhance readability (the monomorphism arrow may be confused with the edges of the graphs), in our examples we will display this kind of constraints using an **if - then** notation, where the two graphs involved have been labelled to implicitly represent the given monomorphism. For instance, the constraint:

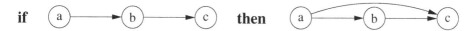

specifies that a graph must be transitive, i.e. the constraint says that for every three nodes, a, b, c if there is an edge from a to b and an edge from b to c then there should be an edge from a to c.

Obviously, graph constraints can be combined using the standard connectives $\vee$ and $\neg$ (as usual, $\wedge$ can be considered a derived operation). In addition, in [6,17] a more complex kind of constraints, namely nested constraints, is defined, but we do not consider them in this paper.

Definition 4 (Syntax of graph constraints). *An* atomic graph constraint $\forall (c : X \rightarrow C)$ *is a graph monomorphism* $c : X \rightarrow C$. *An atomic graph constraint* $\forall (c : X \rightarrow C)$, *where* $X = \emptyset$, *is called a basic atomic constraint (or just a basic constraint) and will be denoted* $\exists C$.

Graph constraints *are logic formulas defined inductively as usual:*

- *Every atomic graph constraint is a graph constraint.*

- *If α is a graph constraint then $\neg\alpha$ is also a graph constraint.*
- *If α_1 and α_2 are graph constraints then $\alpha_1 \vee \alpha_2$ is also a graph constraint.*

Satisfaction of constraints is defined inductively following the intuitions described above.

Definition 5 (Satisfaction of graph constraints). *A graph G satisfies a constraint α, denoted $G \models \alpha$ if:*

- *$G \models \forall(c : X \to C)$ if for every monomorphism $h : X \to G$ there is a monomorphism $f : C \to G$ such that $h = f \circ c$.*
- *$G \models \neg\alpha$ if G does not satisfy α.*
- *$G \models \alpha_1 \vee \alpha_2$ if $G \models \alpha_1$ or $G \models \alpha_2$.*

In this paper, for simplicity, we will assume that our specifications consist only of atomic constraints and negated atomic constraints (negative constraints). However, our results should extend straightforwardly to clausal specifications, i.e. sets of formulas of the form $L_1 \vee \cdots \vee L_n$, where each *literal* L_i is either an atomic constraint (a *positive literal*) or a negative atomic constraint (a *negative literal*). Actually, this would mean that we could deal with arbitrary formulas since they could always be transformed into clausal form.

It may be noted that in the case of basic constraints the above definition specializes as expected:

Fact 1 (Satisfaction of basic constraints)
$G \models \exists C$ *if there is a monomorphism $f : C \to G$.*

It may also be noted that, according to these definitions, the constraint $\exists\emptyset$, where $\emptyset$ denotes the empty graph, is satisfied by any graph, i.e. $\exists\emptyset$ may be considered the trivial *true* constraint.

Remark 1. Atomic constraints can be generalized by allowing its definition in terms of arbitrary morphisms. That is, we could have defined atomic graph constraints $\forall(c : X \to C)$ where c is an arbitrary morphism. However, with our notion of satisfaction, this generalization does not add any additional power to our logic, since it can be proved [10] that if c is not a monomorphism then the constraint $\forall(c : X \to C)$ is logically equivalent to the constraint $\neg\exists X$. For instance, the two constraints below are equivalent. In particular, both constraints specify that there can not be two different edges between any two nodes.

(1)   if then   (2) $\neg\exists$ ( )

Analogously, we could have also generalized our notion of satisfaction by allowing h and f to be also arbitrary morphisms and not just monomorphisms. This generalized form of satisfaction has been studied in [11], where it is called $\mathcal{A}$-satisfaction in contrast with the notion of satisfaction that we use, which is called $\mathcal{M}$-satisfaction in that paper.

In particular, in [11], it is shown how to transform constraints such that $\mathcal{A}$-satisfiability for a certain constraint is equivalent to $\mathcal{M}$-satisfiability for the transformed constraint (and vice versa). This would mean that, again, working with $\mathcal{A}$-satisfaction would not add any additional power. Moreover, we believe that $\mathcal{A}$-satisfaction is not very intuitive implying that it may be not very appropriate for specification purposes.

As pointed out above, these notions can be defined not only for plain graphs but for other classes of structures. In this sense, in the example below we will use typed attributed graph constraints.

Example 1. Let us suppose that we want to model an information system describing the lecturing organization of a department. Then the type graph of (part of) our system could be the following one:

This means that in our system we have three types of nodes: Rooms including two attributes, the room number and a time slot, and Subjects and Lecturers, having its name as an attribute. We also have two types of edges. In particular, an edge from a Subject S to a Lecturer L means, obviously, that L is the lecturer for S. An edge from a Subject S to to a Room means that the lecturing for S takes place on that room for the given time slot. Now for this system we could include the following constraints:

$$\textbf{(1)} \quad \exists \left(\begin{array}{|c|} \hline Subject \\ \hline Name=CS1 \\ \hline \end{array} \right) \qquad\qquad \textbf{(2)} \quad \exists \left(\begin{array}{|c|} \hline Subject \\ \hline Name=CS2 \\ \hline \end{array} \right)$$

meaning that the given system must include the compulsory subjects Computer Science 1 and Computer Science 2. Moreover we may have a constraint saying that every subject included in the system must have some lecturer assignment and some room assignment:

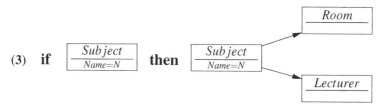

Then, we may also have constraints expressing some negative conditions. For instance, that a room is not assigned at the same time to two subjects or that two different rooms are assigned at the same time to the same subject:

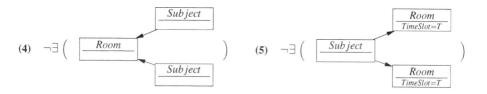

or, similarly, that a lecturer does not have to lecture on two different subjects in two different rooms at the same time:

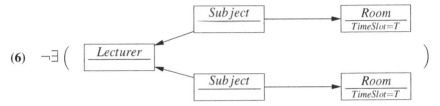

(6)

Finally, perhaps we may want to specify that not every lecturer has a teaching assignment, so that every semester there may be someone on sabbatical:

(7)

It may be noticed that the system that we are describing with these graphical constraints may be not an information system, but the set of web pages of a department, where an arrow from a node of type t_1 to a node of type t_2 may mean that there is a link between two web pages (for instance from the web page of a subject to the web pages of the lecturers), or it may mean that the information of type t_2 is a subfield of the information of type t_1 (for instance the room assignment may be a field of the subjects web pages). In this case, we could have displayed our constraints not in terms of graphs, but as HTML or XML expressions.

3   Satisfiability of Sets of Graph Constraints

In this section we will present several inference systems that provide sound and complete refutation procedures for checking satisfiability for different classes of graph constraints. More precisely, after defining some standard basic concepts about refutation procedures, we will study the case of (positive and negative) basic constraints. In particular, in this case the inference rules define a sound and complete procedure for checking satisfiability that always terminate. Then, in the third subsection we will study the case where we have positive and negative basic constraints and positive atomic constraints. Finally, we consider the satisfiability problem for specifications consisting of arbitrary positive and negative atomic constraints. In this case, the inference rules deal with a more general notion of constraint, which we call *contextual literals* consisting of a positive literal with an associated context. In particular, this context is a finite set of negative atomic constraints together with monomorphisms binding the conditional part of each constraint to the corresponding literal. Using these contextual clauses, we prove that our inference system defines a refutation procedure which is sound and complete. In the last two cases, our refutation procedures may not terminate, which means that the procedures are just refutationally complete. Moreover, in these two cases our procedures check satisfiability with respect to the class of finite and infinite graphs. In fact, we show an example of a specification whose only models are infinite graphs. As a consequence, we guess that satisfiability for this class of constraints is already undecidable (but semi-decidable).

3.1 Basic Concepts

As it is often done in the area of automatic reasoning, the refutation procedures that we present in this paper are defined by means of some inference rules. More precisely, as usual, each rule tells us that if certain premises are satisfied then a given consequence will also hold. In this context, a refutation procedure can be seen as a (possibly nonterminating) nondeterministic computation where the current state is given by the set of formula that have been inferred until the given moment and where a computation step means adding to the given state the result of applying an inference rule to that state.

More precisely, in our case, we assume that the inference rules have the form:

$$\frac{\Gamma_1 \quad \alpha}{\Gamma_2}$$

where Γ_1 and Γ_2 are clauses of the form $\exists G_1 \vee \cdots \vee \exists G_n$, where $\exists G_1, \exists G_n$ are basic positive constraints and where α is an atomic constraint. Moreover, Γ_1 is assumed to belong to the current set of inferred clauses and α is assumed to belong to the original specification. Then a *refutation procedure* for a set of constraints $\mathcal{C}$ is a sequence of inferences:

$$C_0 \Rightarrow_C C_1 \Rightarrow_C \cdots \Rightarrow_C C_i \Rightarrow_C \cdots$$

where the initial state just includes the *true* clause (i.e. $C_0 = \{\exists \emptyset\}$) and where we write $C_i \Rightarrow_C C_{i+1}$ if there is an inference rule like the one above such that $\Gamma_1 \in C_i$, $\alpha \in C$, and $C_{i+1} = C_i \cup \{\Gamma_2\}$. Moreover, we will assume that $C_i \subset C_{i+1}$, i.e. $\Gamma_2 \notin C_i$, to avoid useless inferences.

It may be noted that our refutation procedures are *linear*, which means that no inferences from derived clauses are needed. If we would generalize our approach, allowing C to be a set of arbitrary graph constraints, then we would lose the linearity of the refutation procedures.

In this framework, proving the unsatisfiability of a set of constraints means inferring the *false* clause (which is represented by the empty clause, i.e. the empty disjunction, denoted $\square$), provided that the procedure is sound and complete. Since the procedures are nondeterministic, there is the possibility that we never apply some key inference. To avoid this problem we will always assume that our procedures are *fair*, which means that if at any moment i, there is a possible inference $C_i \Rightarrow_C C_i \cup \{\Gamma\}$, for some clause Γ, then at some moment j we have that $\Gamma \in C_j$.

Then, a refutation procedure for C is *sound* if whenever the procedure infers the empty clause we have that C is unsatisfiable. And a procedure is *complete* if, whenever C is unsatisfiable, we have that the procedure infers. $\square$

It may be noted that if a refutation procedure is sound and complete then we may know in a finite amount of time if a given set of constraints is unsatisfiable. However, it may be impossible to know in a finite amount of time if the set of constraints is satisfiable. For this reason, sometimes the above definition of completeness is called refutational completeness, using the term completeness when both satisfiability and unsatisfiability are decidable.

As usual, for proving soundness of a refutation procedure it is enough to prove the soundness of the inference rules. This means that for every rule as the one above and every graph G, if $G \models \Gamma_1$ and $G \models \alpha$ then $G \models \Gamma_2$.

3.2   Basic Constraints

In this section we study the case where specifications consist only of positive and negative basic constraints. This means that specifications are assumed to be sets of literals of the form $\exists C_1$ or $\neg\exists C_1$. However, as said above, in the deduction process we will deal with clauses of the form $\exists G_1 \vee \cdots \vee \exists G_n$. Now, for this case, satisfiability will be based on two rules that can be found below (obviously, we assume disjunction to be commutative and associative, which means that the literal $\exists C_1$ in the premises of the rules is not necessarily the leftmost literal in the given clause).

$$\frac{\exists C_1 \vee \Gamma \quad \neg\exists C_2}{\Gamma} \quad \textbf{(R1)}$$

if there exists a monomorphism $m : C_2 \to C_1$

$$\frac{\exists C_1 \vee \Gamma \quad \exists C_2}{(\bigvee_{G \in \mathcal{G}} \exists G) \vee \Gamma} \quad \textbf{(R2)}$$

if there is no monomorphism $m : C_2 \to C_1$, where $\mathcal{G} = \{G \mid \langle f_1 : C_1 \to G \leftarrow C_2 : f_2 \rangle \in (C_1 \otimes C_2)\}$ and where $(\bigvee_{G \in \mathcal{G}} \exists G)$ denotes the (finite) disjunction $\exists G_1 \vee \cdots \vee \exists G_n$, if $\mathcal{G} = \{G_1, \ldots, G_n\}$.

The first rule is, in some sense, similar to resolution and is the rule that may allow us to infer the empty clause. The reason is that it is the only rule that generates clauses with fewer literals. The second one can be seen as a rule that, given two constraints, builds a new constraint that subsumes them. More precisely, the graphs involved in the new literals in the clause, i.e. the graphs $G \in \mathcal{G}$ satisfy both constraints $\exists C_1$ and $\exists C_2$. This means that if we apply this rule repeatedly, using all the positive constraints in the original set C, we would build (minimal) graphs that satisfy all the positive constraints in C.

Example 2. If we consider the basic constraints that are included in the Example 1 (i.e. the constraints (1), (2), (4), (5), and (6)) then it would only be possible to infer the constraint below as follows. First, using rule (R2) on the trivial clause $\exists 0$ and constraint (1) we obtain a clause including only constraint (1). Then, using again rule (R2) on this clause and constraint(2) we obtain the clause:

$$\textbf{(8)} \quad \exists \left(\begin{array}{|c|} \hline Subject \\ \hline Name{=}CS1 \\ \hline \end{array} \qquad \begin{array}{|c|} \hline Subject \\ \hline Name{=}CS2 \\ \hline \end{array} \right)$$

meaning that the graph representing the system must include at least two Subject nodes (with attributes CS1 and CS2). No further inference rule can be applied, which means that these constraints are satisfiable, and indeed this constraint represents a (minimal) model satisfying the constraints (1), (2), (4), (5), and (6).

These two rules are sound and complete. The soundness of the first rule is quite obvious. If a graph G satisfies both premises and in addition we know that C_2 is included in C_1 then G cannot satisfy $\exists C_1$. Therefore, it should satisfy Γ. The soundness of the second rule is based on the so-called *pair factorization property*: Given two (mono)morphisms, $f_1 : G_1 \to G$, $f_2 : G_2 \to G$, with the same codomain G there exists a graph H and monomorphisms $g_1 : G_1 \to H$, $g_2 : G_2 \to H$ and $h : H \to G$ such that g_1 and g_2 are jointly surjective and the diagram below commutes:

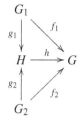

Then, if a graph G satisfies $\exists C_1$ and $\exists C_2$ the pair factorization property will tell us that G will also satisfy $\exists H$, where H is a graph in $\mathcal{G}$.

It may be noted that in the proof of soundness of rule (R2) we have not used the condition that there is no monomorphism $m : C_2 \to C_1$. The reason for such condition is to limit the number of possible inferences, i.e. to make the refutation procedure a bit more efficient since we do not lose completeness with this restriction.

Now, in this case, as said above, we can ensure not only the completeness of any fair refutation procedure, but also its termination. The key property for proving completeness and termination, related to the observation made above about the second inference rule, is that if $C_0 \Rightarrow_C^* C'$ and $\exists C$ is an atom (different from the trivial constraint $\exists \emptyset$) included in a clause in C' then $C \in \{G \mid \langle f_1 : H_1 \to G \leftarrow H_2 : f_2 \rangle \in (\bigotimes_{C_i \in L} C_i)\}$, where L is a subset of C consisting only of positive constraints. Then, since there is a finite number of these graphs, we can be sure that there is a finite number of clauses involving these graphs and, hence, only a finite number of sets of clauses can be inferred using the two rules. This ensures termination. On the other hand, if we know that the refutation procedure terminates on the set of clauses C_k it is easy to see that either it includes the empty clause or there is a clause involving a graph G that satisfies all the constraints in C. Therefore, we have:

Theorem 1 (Termination, Soundness and Completeness). *Given a set of basic (positive and negative) constraints C, any fair refutation procedure defined over C based on the rules (R1) and (R2) will always terminate, i.e. there is an k such that $C \Rightarrow_C C_1 \Rightarrow_C C_2 \Rightarrow_C \cdots \Rightarrow_C C_k$ and no rule can be applied on C_k. Moreover, C is unsatisfiable if and only if the empty clause is in C_k.*

3.3 Basic Constraints and Positive Atomic Constraints

In this section we extend the case studied in the previous subsection by allowing specifications including positive atomic constraints. This means that the given specifications are assumed to consist of literals of the form $\exists C_1$, $\neg \exists C_1$, or $\forall(c : X \to C_2)$. In this case, satisfiability is based on the two rules presented in the previous subsection plus the following new rule:

$$\frac{\exists C_1 \vee \Gamma \quad \forall(c : X \to C_2)}{(\bigvee_{G \in \mathcal{G}} \exists G) \vee \Gamma} \quad \textbf{(R3)}$$

if there is a monomorphism $m : X \to C_1$ such that there is no monomorphism $h : C_2 \to C_1$ such that $m = h \circ c$ and where $\mathcal{G}$ is the set consisting of all the graphs G such that there

are two jointly surjective monomorphisms $f_1 : C_1 \rightarrow G$ and $f_2 : C_2 \rightarrow G$ such that the
diagram below commutes:

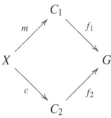

This new rule is similar to rule (R2) in the sense that given a positive basic constraint
and a positive atomic constraint it builds a disjunction of literals representing graphs
that try to satisfy both constraints. However, in this case the satisfaction of the constraint
$\forall(c : X \rightarrow C_2)$ is not ensured. In particular, the idea of the rule is that if we know that
X is included in C_1 then we build all the possible extensions of C_1 which also include
C_2 (each G would be one of such extensions). However, in this case we cannot be sure
that G satisfies $\forall(c : X \rightarrow C_2)$, because G may include an instance of X which was not
included in C_1. For instance, suppose that we have the following constraints:

(1) $\exists \left(\bigcirc \right)$ (2)   **if**   ⓐ   **then**   ⓐ ⟶ ⓑ

where the first one specifies that the given graph must include a node and where the
second one specifies that every node must have an outgoing edge. Then applying rule
(R3) to these constraints would yield a clause one of whose subterms is the constraint:

$$\exists \left(\text{ⓐ} \longrightarrow \text{ⓑ} \right)$$

Now, in this graph node a has an outgoing edge, but node b does not have it, so the
graph still does not satisfy the second constraint. If we would apply again the third rule,
then we would infer a clause including a graph with three nodes and two edges, and so
on. This is the reason why, in this case, a refutation procedure may not terminate. Moreover, as we will also see, if the procedure does not refute the given set of constraints
then the completeness proof ensures that there will be a model that satisfies this set of
constraints, but this model may be an infinite graph built by an infinite colimit. One may
wonder whether there will also exist a finite model of that specification. In the case of
this example such a finite graph exists. Actually, the resulting clause after applying for
the second time the third rule to the graph above, would also include the graph below
that satisfies both constraints.

However, in general, we do not know if an arbitrary set of basic constraints and
positive atomic constraints which is satisfiable by an infinite graph, is also satisfied by
some finite graph. Nevertheless, in the general case (when dealing with positive and
negative atomic constraints) there are sets of constraints whose only models are infinite

graphs, as we will see in the following subsection. For this reason we conjecture that in this case the answer to this question will also be negative.

Example 3. Let us consider the basic constraints and the positive atomic constraints that are included in Examples 1 and 2 (i.e. the constraints (1), (2), (3), (4), (5), (6), and (8)). If we apply the third rule on constraints (8) and (3), and again on the resulting clause and on constraint (3) then we would infer the following clause:

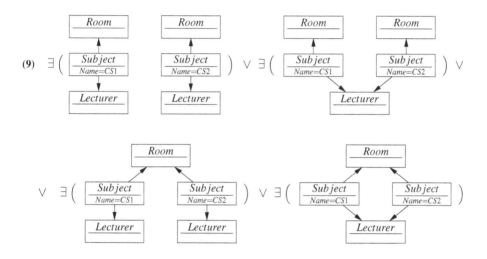

This clause states that the graph should include two subjects (CS1 and CS2) and these subjects may be assigned to two different rooms and to either two different lecturers, or to the same lecturer, or they may be assigned to the same room, and to either different lecturers, or the same lecturer. Obviously, the last two constraints in this clause violate constraint (4), which means that we can eliminate them using twice rule (R1), yielding the following clause:

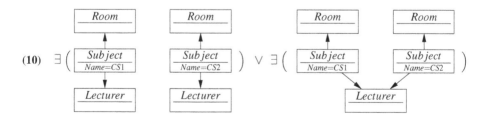

Then, no further inferences can be applied, which means that this set of constraints is satisfiable. Actually, the two graphs occurring in clause (10) would be (minimal) models of the set of constraints (except constraint (7) which is considered in the following subsection).

The proof of soundness of the new rule (R3) is very similar to the proof for rule (R2). If G satisfies $\exists C_1$ and $\forall (c : X \to C_2)$, using pair factorization we get the diagram below:

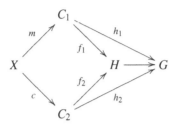

then, G will also satisfy $\exists H$, where H is a graph in $\mathcal{G}$.

In this case, the proof of completeness is a bit more involved as a consequence of the possible nontermination of the refutation procedure. The underlying idea is inspired by a technique called *model construction* used for proving completeness of some inference systems for first-order logic with equality [16]. According to this technique, we see the inference rules as steps for building a model of the given set of constraints. In particular, given a set of constraints C, we consider sequences of graphs $\emptyset \prec C_1 \prec \cdots \prec C_i \prec \ldots$, where $C_i \prec C_{i+1}$ if (a) $\exists C_{i+1}$ is a literal in the clause inferred after applying rules (R2) or (R3) to $\exists C_i$ and to some positive constraint in C (this means that C_i is included in C_{i+1}) ; and (b) C_{i+1} satisfies all the negative constraints in C. Each of these sequences can be seen as a path for building a possible model of C. In this sense, condition (b) is needed because if C_{i+1} does not satisfy a negative constraint in C then it is useless to continue this path. Moreover, we require these sequences to be fair, which means that if we can have $C_i \prec C'_{i+1}$ via some inference an the sequence is infinite, then there would be some j such that C_j includes C'_{i+1}. Then, we have three cases:

- All maximal sequences of this kind are finite, and in all cases the last graph C_i in each sequence does not satisfy all positive constraints in C. This means that no path is useful for building a model. Then we can show that a fair procedure would generate the empty clause for C.
- There is a finite sequence whose last graph C_i satisfies all the constraints in C. Then we have built a finite model for C.
- There is an infinite fair sequence. Then we show that if we take the union of all the graphs in the sequence (the colimit of the sequence) the result is a model for C.

As a consequence, we have:

Theorem 2 (Soundness and Completeness). *Let $C \Rightarrow_C C_1 \Rightarrow_C \cdots \Rightarrow_C C_k \ldots$ be a fair refutation procedure defined over a set of basic constraints and positive atomic constraints C, based on the rules (R1), (R2), and (R3). Then, C is unsatisfiable if and only if there is a j such that the empty clause is in C_j.*

3.4 Atomic Constraints

In this section we study the case of general specifications including arbitrary positive and negative atomic constraints. In this case, in order to ensure completeness, the inference rules are defined over a generalized notion of clause, consisting of *contextual literals*, which are positive basic constraints with an associated context. More precisely, given a constraint $\exists C$, a context for this constraint is a set of negative atomic constraints $\neg \forall (g : X \rightarrow C_1)$ such that X is included in C. Actually, C has to satisfy this negative constraint. However, as usual, we need to know not only that X is a subgraph of C, but also to identify the specific instance X that cannot be extended to C_1. For this reason we consider that a context is a finite set of negative atomic constraints together with monomorphisms binding the conditional part of each constraint to the corresponding literal. Below, when sketching the completeness proof, we will explain the need for these contexts.

Definition 6 (Contextual Constraints). *A contextual constraint $\exists C[Q]$ is a pair consisting of a basic constraint, $\exists C$, and a set Q consisting of pairs $\langle \neg \forall (g : X \rightarrow C_1), h : X \rightarrow C \rangle$, where $\neg \forall (g : X \rightarrow C_1)$ is a negative atomic constraint and h is a monomorphism such that there is no monomorphism $h' : C_1 \rightarrow C$ such that $h = h' \circ g$.*

Now, we have to define satisfaction for this kind of contextual constraints. The idea is that a graph satisfies a contextual constraint $\exists C[Q]$ if it satisfies $\exists C$ and all the constraints in its context:

Definition 7 (Satisfaction of Contextual Constraints). *A graph G satisfies a contextual constraint $\exists C[Q]$ via a monomorphism $f : C \rightarrow G$, $G \models_f \exists C[Q]$, if for every $\langle \neg \forall (g : X \rightarrow C_1), h : X \rightarrow C \rangle \in Q$ there is no monomorphism $h' : C_1 \rightarrow G$ such that $f \circ h = h' \circ g$. G satisfies $\exists C[Q]$, $G \models \exists C[Q]$, if there is a monomorphism $f : C \rightarrow G$ such that $G \models_f \exists C[Q]$.*

Finally, given a contextual constraint $\exists C[Q]$ and a graph G that satisfies it via a monomorphism $f : C \rightarrow G$, in our inference rules we need to be able to build a contextual constraint whose left-hand side is $\exists G$ and whose context includes the same negative constraints as $[Q]$. In order to do this we need to define the new binding of the negative constraints in $[Q]$ with G:

Definition 8. *Given a contextual constraint $\exists C[Q]$ and a monomorphism $g : C \rightarrow G$, we define the context $g\langle Q \rangle$ as the set $\{\langle \neg \forall (g : X \rightarrow C_1), g \circ h : X \rightarrow G \rangle \mid \langle \neg \forall (g : X \rightarrow C_1), h : X \rightarrow C \rangle \in Q\}$.*

In this case, satisfiability is based on four rules. The first three rules are a reformulation (in terms of contextual constraints) of the rules defined in the previous sections. In addition, a new rule describes the kind of inferences that can be done using negative atomic constraints. The four rules are:

$$\frac{\exists C_1[Q] \vee \Gamma \quad \neg \exists C_2}{\Gamma} \quad \textbf{(R1')}$$

if there exists a monomorphism $m : C_2 \rightarrow C_1$

$$\frac{\exists C_1[Q] \vee \Gamma \quad \exists C_2}{(\bigvee_{G \in \mathcal{G}} \exists G[f_1\langle Q \rangle]) \vee \Gamma} \quad \textbf{(R2')}$$

if there is no monomorphism $m : C_2 \to C_1$ and where $\mathcal{G} = \{G \mid \langle f_1 : C_1 \to G \leftarrow C_2 : f_2 \rangle \in (C_1 \otimes C_2), \text{ such that } G \models_{id} \exists G[f_1 \langle Q \rangle]\}$.

$$\frac{\exists C_1[Q] \vee \Gamma \quad \forall(c : X \to C_2)}{(\bigvee_{G \in \mathcal{G}} \exists G[f_1 \langle Q \rangle]) \vee \Gamma} \quad \textbf{(R3')}$$

if there is a monomorphism $m : X \to C_1$ and there is no monomorphism $h : C_2 \to C_1$ such that $m = h \circ c$ and where $\mathcal{G}$ is the set consisting of all the graphs G such that there are two jointly surjective monomorphisms $f_1 : C_1 \to G$ and $f_2 : C_2 \to G$ such that $G \models_{id} \exists G[f_1 \langle Q \rangle]\}$ and the diagram below commutes:

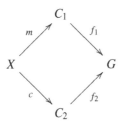

$$\frac{\exists C_1[Q] \vee \Gamma \quad \neg\forall(g : X \to C_2)}{(\bigvee_{G \in \mathcal{G}} \exists G[Q']) \vee \Gamma} \quad \textbf{(R4)}$$

if $(\neg\forall(g : X \to C_2)) \notin Q$ and where $\mathcal{G} = \{G \mid \langle f_1 : C_1 \to G \leftarrow X : f_2 \rangle \in (C_1 \otimes X), \text{ such that } G \models_{id} \exists G[Q']\}$, and $Q' = f_1 \langle Q \rangle \cup \{\langle \neg\forall(g : X \to C_2), f_2 \rangle\}$.

This new rule is similar to (the reformulation of) rule (R2). The reason is that a negative atomic constraint $\neg\forall(c : X \to C_2)$ (partly) specifies that there must be a copy of X in the given graph, as it happens with the constraint $\exists X$. The main difference to rule (R2') is that, in the new rule, the negative constraint is added to the context of the new constraints introduced in the clause inferred by the rule.

It may be noticed that with any of these four rules we may generate the empty clause, since all the rules may delete a literal from a rule because of the contexts. In the previous cases only rule (R1) would eliminate literals. However, in this case, in rules (R2'), (R3') and (R4) it may happen that no $G \in \mathcal{G}$ satisfies the resulting context. As a consequence, in this situation, the resulting clause would be Γ.

Example 4. Let us consider all the constraints and clauses from Examples 1, 1, and 3. If we apply twice the fourth rule on clause (10) and constraint (7) then we would infer the following clause:

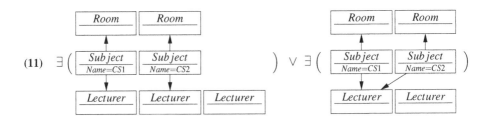

where the context associated to both literals (not displayed above) would consist of constraint (7). Again, no further inferences can be applied, which means that this set of constraints is satisfiable, and the two graphs occurring in clause (11) would be (minimal) models of the set of constraints.

Now, with this new formulation, again we are able to show soundness and completeness of our inference rules. In particular, the proofs of soundness for rules (R1')-(R3') are very similar to the proofs for rules (R1)-(R3). The only difference is that we have to take into account the contexts. Then the proof of soundness for rule (R4) also follows the same pattern. In particular, if $G \models_{h_1} \exists C_1[Q]$ and $G \models \neg \forall (c : X \to C_2)$ then using again the property of pair factorization we have:

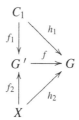

where $f_1 : C_1 \to G'$ and $f_2 : X \to G'$ are jointly surjective. In this context, it is routine to prove that, on one hand, $G' \models_{id} \exists G'[Q']$ (so, $G' \in \mathcal{G}$) and, on the other, $G \models_f G'[Q']$.

The proof of completeness in this case is very similar to the previous completeness proof. The main difference is in the key role played by the contexts. The idea in the previous proof was to consider sequences of graphs $\emptyset \prec C_1 \prec \cdots \prec C_i \prec \ldots$, where every C_i is included in C_{i+1}, that could be seen as the construction of a model for C, if the empty clause was never inferred. In particular, these sequences were associated to the given inferences. Moreover, an important property in that proof is that it was assumed that every graph in these sequences would satisfy all the negative constraints in C. In particular, given a graph C_i, if a possible successor C_{i+1} does not satisfy a negative constraint $\neg \exists C$ in C then we know that a sequence $\emptyset \prec C_1 \prec \cdots \prec C_i \prec C_{i+1} \prec \ldots$ would never yield a model of C. The reason is that any graph including C_{i+1} will neither satisfy $\neg \exists C$. However, this is not true for negative atomic constraints. If C_{i+1} does not satisfy $\neg \forall (g : X \to C)$ then some graphs G including C_{i+1} may satisfy $\neg \forall (g : X \to C)$. For this reason it would be wrong to prune a sequence $\emptyset \prec C_1 \prec \cdots \prec C_i \prec \ldots$, if we know that C_i does not satisfy a constraint $\neg \forall (g : X \to C)$, because some graph C_k, with $k > i$, may satisfy it. However, in this situation it is impossible to say if this sequence, in the limit (or, rather, in the colimit) would yield a model of C and, especially, if it would satisfy that constraint.

The use of contexts solves this problem. In particular, if $C_i[Q]$ does not satisfy a constraint $\neg \forall (g : X \to C)$ in its context Q then no larger graph would satisfy it. Then, in a similar manner as in the previous completeness proof, we can define sequences $\emptyset[\emptyset] \prec C_1[Q_1] \prec \cdots \prec C_i[Q_i] \prec C_{i+1}[Q_{i+1}] \prec \ldots$, where each C_i satisfies all the negative basic constraints in C and all the negative constraints in Q_i. Then, fairness of the sequences ensure that for every sequence there is an i such that Q_i includes all the negative atomic constraints in C. This ensures that a fair sequence will yield a model of C, provided that the empty clause cannot be inferred from C.

As a consequence, we have:

Theorem 3 (Soundness and Completeness). *Let* $C \Rightarrow_C C_1 \Rightarrow_C \cdots \Rightarrow_C C_k \ldots$ *be a fair refutation procedure defined over a set of atomic constraints* C, *based on the rules* *(R1'), (R2'), (R3') and (R4). Then,* C *is unsatisfiable if and only if there is a* j *such that the empty clause is in* C_j.

As discussed above, our completeness results show that a set of constraints is satisfiable then a fair refutation procedure will never infer an empty clause from the given set of constraints. However, in the proof of completeness, the model constructed to show the satisfiability of the constraints is an infinite graph. One could wonder whether in this situation it would always be possible to find an alternative finite model for these constraints. The answer is no. As we can see in the counter-example below, there are sets of atomic constraints which do not have finite models.

Example 5. The set of constraints below is not satisfied by any finite graph, but only by infinite graphs:

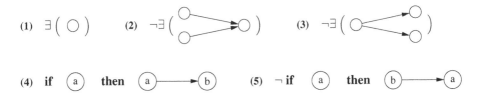

Let n be the number of nodes of a graph satisfying the constraints and e its number of edges. The first constraint specifies that the graph must have at least a node, i.e. $n \geq 1$. The second and third constraints specify that every node must have at most one incoming edge and one outgoing edge, i.e. $n \geq e$. The fourth constraint specifies that every node has an outgoing edge, , i.e. $n \leq e$ and, finally, the fifth constraint specifies that not every node has an incoming edge, i.e., $n > e$. Now, obviously no finite graph would satisfy these constraints. However the graph below does satisfy them:

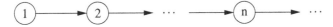

4   Conclusion

In this paper we have shown how we can use graph constraints as a specification formalism to define constraints associated to visual modelling formalisms or to specify classes of semi-structured documents. In particular, we have shown how we can reason about these specifications, providing inference rules that are sound and complete. Moreover, as can be seen in our examples, the completeness proofs (only sketched in the paper) show that our inference rules can also be used for the construction of minimal models for the given sets of constraints.

As pointed out above, our results apply not only to plain graphs, but generalize to a large class of structures including typed and attributed graphs. In this sense, in [6,5] the constraints that we consider have been defined for any adhesive HLR-category [14,5]. However, to be precise, to generalize our results we would need that the underlying category of structures satisfies two properties that are not considered in [6,5]. On one hand, we would need that $G_1 \otimes G_2$ is finite provided that G_1 and G_2 are finite. It may be noticed that this may be not the case if G_1 and G_2 are arbitrary attributed graphs. However, if we restrict ourselves to the class of monomorphisms which are the identity on the attributes then the property would hold. On the other hand, the second condition that we need is the existence of infinite colimits (together with some additional technical property).

We have not yet implemented these techniques, although it would not be too difficult to implement them on top of the AGG system [1], given that the basic construction that we use in our inference rules (i.e. building $G_1 \otimes G_2$) is already implemented there. However we think that, before doing this kind of implementation, it may be worth to make our approach more "efficient". In particular, in this paper we have defined our rules caring mainly about completeness. However there are some other rules that, although they do not help in ensuring completeness, may help to prove more rapidly the (un)satisfiability of a set of constraints. In a different sense, in our refutation procedures we never eliminate any clause from the given proof state. However, we know that we can use some other rules for eliminating clauses, which means that we would reduce the search space of the procedure.

Acknowledgements. This work has been partially supported by the CICYT project FORMALISM (ref. TIN2007-66523) and by the AGAUR grant to the research group ALBCOM (ref. 00516).

References

1. AGG.: The AGG, httptfs.cs.tu-berlin.de/agg
2. Alpuente, M., Ballis, D., Falaschi, M.: Automated Verification of Web Sites Using Partial Rewriting. Software Tools for Technology Transfer 8, 565–585 (2006)
3. Baldan, P., Corradini, A., Kšnig, B., Lluch-Lafuente, A.: A Temporal Graph Logic for Verification of Graph Transformation Systems. In: Recent Trends in Algebraic Development Techniques, 18th International Workshop, WADT 2006. LNCS, vol. 4409, pp. 1–20. Springer, Heidelberg (2007)
4. Courcelle, B.: The expression of Graph Properties and Graph Transformations in Monadic Second-Order Logic. In: [18], pp. 313–400 (1997)
5. Ehrig, H., Ehrig, K., Prange, U., Taentzer, G.: Fundamentals of Algebraic Graph Transformation. Springer, Heidelberg (2006)
6. Ehrig, H., Ehrig, K., Habel, A., Pennemann, K.-H.: Constraints and Application Conditions: From Graphs to High-Level Structures. In: Ehrig, H., Engels, G., Parisi-Presicce, F., Rozenberg, G. (eds.) ICGT 2004. LNCS, vol. 3256, pp. 287–303. Springer, Heidelberg (2004)
7. Ehrig, H., Habel, A.: Graph Grammars with Application Conditions: From Graphs to High-Level Structures. In: Rozenberg, G., Salomaa, A. (eds.) The Book of L, pp. 87–100. Springer, Heidelberg (1986)
8. Ellmer, E., Emmerich, W., Finkelstein, A., Nentwich, C.: Flexible Consistency Checking. ACM Transaction on Software Engineering and Methodology 12(1), 28–63 (2003)
9. Habel, A., Heckel, R., Taentzer, G.: Graph Grammars with Negative Application Conditions. Fundam. Inform. 26(3/4), 287–313 (1996)

10. Habel, A., Pennemann, K.-H.: Nested Constraints and Application Conditions for High-Level Structures. In: Kreowski, H.-J., Montanari, U., Orejas, F., Rozenberg, G., Taentzer, G. (eds.) Formal Methods in Software and Systems Modeling. LNCS, vol. 3393, pp. 293–308. Springer, Heidelberg (2005)
11. Habel, A., Pennemann, K.-H.: Satisfiability of High-Level Conditions. In: Corradini, A., Ehrig, H., Montanari, U., Ribeiro, L., Rozenberg, G. (eds.) ICGT 2006. LNCS, vol. 4178, pp. 430–444. Springer, Heidelberg (2006)
12. Heckel, R., Wagner, A.: Ensuring Consistency of Conditional Graph Grammars - A Constructive Approach. In: Proceedings SEGRAGRA 1995. Electr. Notes Theor. Comput. Sci., vol. 2, pp. 118–126 (1995)
13. Jelliffe, R.: "Schematron", Internet Document (May 2000), http://xml.ascc.net/resource/schematron/
14. Lack, S., Sobocinski, P.: Adhesive Categories. In: Walukiewicz, I. (ed.) FOSSACS 2004. LNCS, vol. 2987, pp. 273–288. Springer, Heidelberg (2004)
15. Lambers, L., Ehrig, H., Orejas, F.: Conflict Detection for Graph Transformation with Negative Application Conditions. In: Corradini, A., Ehrig, H., Montanari, U., Ribeiro, L., Rozenberg, G. (eds.) ICGT 2006. LNCS, vol. 4178, pp. 61–76. Springer, Heidelberg (2006)
16. Nieuwenhuis, R., Rubio, A.: Paramodulation-Based Theorem Proving. In: Robinson, A., Voronkov, A. (eds.) Handbook of Automated Reasoning, Elsevier Science and MIT Press (2001)
17. Rensink, A.: Representing First-Order Logic Using Graphs. In: Ehrig, H., Engels, G., Parisi-Presicce, F., Rozenberg, G. (eds.) Graph Transformations, Second International Conference, ICGT 2004. LNCS, vol. 3256, pp. 319–335. Springer, Heidelberg (2004)
18. Rozenberg, G. (ed.): Handbook of Graph Grammars and Computing by Graph Transformation, vol. 1. World Scientific, Singapore (1997)

A Generic Complete Dynamic Logic for Reasoning About Purity and Effects

Till Mossakowski[1,2], Lutz Schröder[1,2], and Sergey Goncharov[2]

[1] DFKI Laboratory, Bremen
[2] Department of Computer Science, University of Bremen

Abstract. For a number of programming languages, among them Eiffel, C, Java and Ruby, Hoare-style logics and dynamic logics have been developed. In these logics, pre- and postconditions are typically formulated using potentially effectful programs. In order to ensure that these pre- and postconditions behave like logical formulae (that is, enjoy some kind of referential transparency), a notion of purity is needed. Here, we introduce a generic framework for reasoning about purity and effects. Effects are modeled abstractly and axiomatically, using Moggi's idea of encapsulation of effects as monads. We introduce a dynamic logic (from which, as usual, a Hoare logic can be derived) whose logical formulae are pure programs in a strong sense. We formulate a set of proof rules for this logic, and prove it to be complete with respect to a categorical semantics. Using dynamic logic, we then develop a relaxed notion of purity which allows for observationally neutral effects such writing on newly allocated memory.

1 Introduction

Design and programming by contract reduces software errors by providing specifications of Hoare-style pre- and postconditions and invariants along with the program. Originating in the Eiffel language [12], this paradigm has become a guiding design principle for a number of languages, including Sather [17], Lisaac [24], Nice [3], and D [4]. Moreover, for many existing languages, among them C, C++, Java, JavaScript, Scheme, Perl, Python, and Ruby, libraries, preprocessors and other tools have been developed that support programming by contract; for example, the Java modeling language JML comes with extended static analysis [5] and verification [26] tools. [6] treats contracts in a higher-order functional setting.

Unlike Hoare's original logic [8] and unlike some known formalisations of Hoare-logics in theorem provers like Isabelle and PVS [9, 27, 16], most of these languages do not have a separate language for expressing pre- and postconditions. Instead, these are expressed in a *pure subset* of the programming language itself. The restriction to a pure subset is necessary since specifications should not have side-effects; this serves both conceptual clarity and the possibility of run-time testing (which could easily yield wrong results if specifications could change the behaviour of a program).

Purity in this sense is closely related to referential transparency. Informally, pure programs have the following properties:

1. discardability: pure computations can be left out from a sequence of computation steps without changing its behaviour;

J. Fiadeiro and P. Inverardi (Eds.): FASE 2008, LNCS 4961, pp. 199–214, 2008.
© Springer-Verlag Berlin Heidelberg 2008

2. determinism: pure programs always return the same value;
3. interchangeability: pure programs can be interchanged with each other, that is, the order does not matter.

Of course, these properties depend on a suitable notion of observational equivalence of programs that explains the term "without changing its behaviour". The observational equivalence in turn depends on the specific set of possible operations; for example, allocating a new memory cell and writing a value into it will not be observable in Java, while in C, it can be observed if the integer representation of the memory cell's address is guessed or known by chance and converted from an integer to a pointer. By contrast, the latter operation is not available in Java.

It becomes clear that the Hoare logics for the above mentioned languages, while all following essentially the same style, may vary in subtle but important details. This greatly complicates the study of properties of such logics. Consequently, the goal of this paper is to formalize these notions and provide logical rules for Hoare-style reasoning in a way that abstracts from the details of the particular languages. The abstraction is achieved by encapsulating notions of effect and computation as monads, as originally suggested by Moggi [13] and used in the design of the functional programming language Haskell [18] as well as in programming semantics, e.g. for Java [10]. In earlier work [21, 23], we have developed a dynamic logic for generic side effects whose semantics is defined in terms of monads; in particular, we have given a sound proof calculus for this logic.[1] Here, we extend the proof calculus to a calculus which is strongly complete for the generic part of the calculus and linear sequential programs[2]. This setting is sufficient for our treatment of observational purity. Our logic is related to Pitts' evaluation logic [19], which in turn essentially puts the language-specific logic of [2] on a generic basis. Both these logics omit loops, like the restricted logic considered here, but unlike the full logic of [23].

In more detail, the definition of our dynamic logic is based on a strict notion of purity where the above requirements for referential transparency (discardability, determinism, interchangeability) are postulated to hold as actual equalities. Once we have the logic available, we can define a weaker notion of *observational purity* where referential transparency holds only up to observational equivalence in the logic. We thus arrive at a practically usable notion of purity, which in particular allows harmless side-effects such as creating and writing on new references. This generic concept of observational purity is related to the programming language specific notion put forward in [15]. An interesting point here is that as a byproduct of our completeness proof, we obtain the existence of fully abstract categorical models, where observational equalities hold on the nose, and in particular all observationally pure functions are pure in the original strict sense.

Besides the specification and verification of monadic programs, our logic serves also the *specification* of monads, i.e. notions of side effect and purity. That is, effects may

---

[1] There are two dynamic logics for Java, one for the KIV prover [25], and on in the KeY project [1]. However, they neither address purity, nor are they generic.

[2] The original calculus does feature generic loop constructs; however, absolute completeness results such as the one proved here are impossible for dynamic logics over Turing complete languages: this would entail recursive enumerability of the set of non-terminating programs.

be described in an axiomatic manner, which abstracts away from particular details of the implementation, and moreover allows for loose specifications that deliberately leave open particular design decisions.

2   Monads for Computations

The presence of computational effects, e.g. state, store, exceptions, input, output, non-determinism, or backtracking, substantially complicates reasoning about programs. Dealing with such features has in the past typically required dedicated logics, designed specifically for a particular combination of effects. In seminal work by Moggi [13], monads have been established as a unifying framework for modeling computational effects (including in particular all effects mentioned above) in an elegant way.

Intuitively, a monad associates to each type A a type TA of computations of type A; a function with side effects that takes inputs of type A and returns values of type B is, then, just a function of type $A \rightarrow TB$. This approach abstracts from particular notions of computation such as store, non-determinism, non-termination etc.; a surprisingly large amount of reasoning can be carried out without commitment to a particular type of side effect.

A monad on a given category $\mathbf{C}$ can be defined as a *Kleisli triple* $\mathbb{T} = (T, \eta, \_^*)$, where $T : \mathrm{Ob}\,\mathbf{C} \rightarrow \mathrm{Ob}\,\mathbf{C}$ is a function, the *unit* η is a family of morphisms $\eta_A : A \rightarrow TA$, and $\_^*$ assigns to each morphism $f : A \rightarrow TB$ a morphism $f^* : TA \rightarrow TB$ such that

$$\eta_A^* = id_{TA}, \quad f^*\eta_A = f, \quad \text{and} \quad g^*f^* = (g^*f)^*.$$

This description is equivalent to the more familiar one [11].

In order to support a language with finitary operations and multi-variable contexts (see below), one needs a further ingredient: a monad is called *strong* if it is equipped with a natural transformation

$$t_{A,B} : A \times TB \rightarrow T(A \times B)$$

called *strength*, subject to certain coherence conditions (see e.g. [13]).

Example 1 ([13]). Computationally relevant monads on **Set** (all monads on **Set** are strong [23, 13]) include the following.

1. *Stateful computations with non-termination:* $TA = S \rightarrow? (A \times S)$, where S is a fixed set of states and $\_ \rightarrow? \_$ denotes the partial function type.

2. *Non-determinism:* $TA = \mathcal{P}(A)$, where $\mathcal{P}$ is the covariant power set functor.

3. *Exceptions:* $TA = A + E$, where E is a fixed set of exceptions.

4. a) *Interactive input:* TA is the smallest fixed point of $\gamma \mapsto A + (U \rightarrow \gamma)$, where U is a set of input values. b) *Interactive output:* TA is the smallest fixed point of $\gamma \mapsto A + (U \times \gamma)$, where U is a set of output values.

5. *Non-deterministic stateful computations:* $TA = (S \rightarrow \mathcal{P}(A \times S))$, where, again, S is a fixed set of states (here, we can use the total function arrow since the binding operator can treat undefinedness as the empty set of results).

6. These monads can also be combined. E.g. non-deterministic stateful computations are obtained as $TA = S \to \mathcal{P}(A \times S)$. A monad for Java has been defined as follows [10]

$$JA - S \to (A \times S + E \times S + 1),$$

with S the set of states and E the set of exceptions. A state typically will comprise a stack, a heap, and a heap pointer, that is,

$$S = V^* \times (Loc \mapsto V) \times Loc \times \cdots$$

where V is a set of values and Loc a set of locations. While Java will provide an operation $new : J\ Loc$ that allocates a new location, C will additionally provide a coercion operation $int2loc : Int \to Loc$ (written e.g. as "(*char)" in C, if characters are stored).

3   Monad-Based Dynamic Logic

In program specification, dynamic logic as introduced in [20] and extended to monadic computations in [23] has a number of advantages over less expressive formalisms such as Hoare logic, among them the ability to express both partial and total correctness in a natural way and the possibility of reusing a state, say for statements of the nature 'what would happen if'. Here, we examine the infrastructure that is needed in order to develop generic monad-based dynamic logic, and illustrate that this does indeed make sense when instantiated to typical concrete computational monads.

3.1   Syntax

We begin by fixing the syntax of *monad-based dynamic logic (MDL)*. Given a set *Sort* of *basic types*, the set of *types* over *Sort* is generated by

$$A ::= 1 \mid \Omega \mid PA \mid TA \mid A \times A \mid Sort.$$

A *signature* $\Sigma = (Sort, F)$ consists of a set *Sort* of basic types and a set F of operation symbols $f : A \to B$, where A and B are types over *Sort*. Examples of such operation symbols are $new : T\ Loc$ and $int2loc : Int \to Loc$ as explained above. We make the general assumption that the operations in the signature have T-*free* argument types, more precisely, types containing neither T nor P. The term language over a signature Σ and a context Γ of typed variables is given in Fig. 1. $\Gamma \rhd t : A$ means that from context Γ, one can drive that term t has type A. $\top$ stands for *true*, $\bot$ for *false*. We let metavariables t etc. range over terms, a and b over normal formulas (i.e. terms of type Ω), φ, ψ, χ over monadic formulas (i.e. terms of type $P\Omega$), and p, q etc. over programs, i.e. terms whose type is of the form $T A$. ret t is an effectless computation that just returns the value t. In the term do $x \leftarrow p; q$, the variable x is locally bound in q (but not in p), the interpretation is "perform computation p, bind the result to x and then perform computation $q(x)$". Repeated bindings such as do $x_1 \leftarrow p_1, \ldots, x_n \leftarrow p_n; q$ are somewhat inaccurately denoted in the form do $\bar{x} \leftarrow \bar{p}; q$. Term fragments of the form $\bar{x} \leftarrow \bar{p}$ are called *program sequences*.

$$\text{(var)} \ \frac{x : A \in \Gamma}{\Gamma \rhd x : A} \qquad \text{(app)} \ \frac{f : A \to B \in \Sigma \ \ \Gamma \rhd t : A}{\Gamma \rhd f(t) : B} \qquad \text{(1)} \ \frac{}{\Gamma \rhd * : 1}$$

$$\text{(pair)} \ \frac{\Gamma \rhd t : A \ \ \Gamma \rhd u : B}{\Gamma \rhd \langle t, u \rangle : A \times B} \qquad \text{(fst)} \ \frac{\Gamma \rhd t : A \times B}{\Gamma \rhd \text{fst}(t) : A} \qquad \text{(snd)} \ \frac{\Gamma \rhd t : A \times B}{\Gamma \rhd \text{snd}(t) : A}$$

$$\text{(}\top\text{)} \ \frac{}{\Gamma \rhd \top : \Omega} \quad \text{(}\bot\text{)} \ \frac{}{\Gamma \rhd \bot : \Omega} \quad \text{(}\neg\text{)} \ \frac{\Gamma \rhd a : \Omega}{\Gamma \rhd \neg a : \Omega} \ \ \text{similarly for} \ \wedge, \vee, \Rightarrow, \Longleftrightarrow$$

$$\text{(do)} \ \frac{\Gamma \rhd p : TA \ \ \Gamma, x : A \rhd q : TB}{\Gamma \rhd \text{do} \ x \leftarrow p; q : TB} \qquad \text{(doP)} \ \frac{\Gamma \rhd p : PA \ \ \Gamma, x : A \rhd q : PB}{\Gamma \rhd \text{do} \ x \leftarrow p; q : PB}$$

$$\text{(ret)} \ \frac{\Gamma \rhd t : A}{\Gamma \rhd \text{ret} \ t : PA} \quad \text{(}\Box\text{)} \ \frac{\Gamma \rhd p : T\Omega}{\Gamma \rhd \Box p : P\Omega} \quad \text{(P)} \ \frac{\Gamma \rhd p : PA}{\Gamma \rhd p : TA}$$

Fig. 1. Term language for monad-based dynamic logic

The operations fst and snd are the projection functions for binary products. We treat n-ary products as iterated binary products; then projections π_i^n can easily be defined in terms of fst and snd.

The type TA contains the monadic programs over A; PA is a subtype of TA containing pure programs. The type of Booleans is denoted Ω; consequently, we take $P\Omega$ as the type of formulae of monad-based dynamic logic. The term forming operation $\Box : T\Omega \to P\Omega$ is a closure operator. The formula $\Box p$ intuitively expresses that all terminating runs of p return $\top$. Note that $\Box$ does not behave like a modal operator; in particular, for $\varphi : P\Omega$, we will have $\varphi \Longleftrightarrow \Box\varphi$. However, $\Box$ serves to define modalities: For $\varphi : P\Omega$, we let $[\bar{x} \leftarrow \bar{p}]\,\varphi$ abbreviate the formula $\Box \, \text{do} \ \bar{x} \leftarrow \bar{p}; \varphi$, and omit $\bar{x}$ if it does not occur in φ. The formula $\langle \bar{x} \leftarrow \bar{p} \rangle \varphi$ abbreviates $\neg[\bar{x} \leftarrow \bar{p}]\,\neg\varphi$. Both in do-*terms and within modal operators, we implicitly identify terms up to α-equivalence.*

Besides the specification and verification of monadic programs, MDL serves also the (potentially loose) *specification* of monads, i.e. notions of side effect.

The running example of [21, 23] involves references and non-determinism; numerous further examples can be found in [28], including the Java monad and a parsing monad, as well as a queue monad over a fixed set U of entries. Here, we present the specification of a monad for dynamic references. It is axiomatized using Hoare triples for total correctness

$$[\varphi] \ p \ [\psi]$$

by interpreting them as partial correctness plus termination:

$$\varphi \Rightarrow (\langle p \rangle \top \wedge [p] \, \psi).$$

The implication $\varphi \Rightarrow \langle p \rangle \top$ is called the termination part, and the implication $\varphi \Rightarrow [p] \, \psi$ is called the partial correctness part of the Hoare triple.

Example 2. We assume, for any basic type a, a (basic) type $Ref\ a$ of references to objects of type a. The specification of dynamic references is then as follows.

$$*\_\_ : Ref\ a \to P\ a$$
$$\_\_ := \_\_ : (Ref\ a) \times a \to T\ 1$$
$$new : a \to T(Ref\ a)$$

$$[\,]r := x\ [x = *r] \qquad\qquad\qquad\qquad\qquad \text{read-write}$$
$$[x = *r]\ s := y\ [x = *r \vee r = s] \qquad\qquad \text{read-write-other}$$
$$[\,]\ r \leftarrow new\ x\ [x = *r] \qquad\qquad\qquad\quad \text{read-new}$$
$$[x = *r]\ s \leftarrow new\ y\ [x = *r \vee \neg r = s] \qquad \text{read-new-other}$$
$$[\,]\ r \leftarrow new\ x; p; s \leftarrow new\ y\ [\neg r = s] \qquad \text{new-distinct}$$

The operation $*\_\_$ reads the value from the location specified by the reference, while $\_\_ := \_\_$ assigns a new value to the location, and new creates a new location.

Note that the profile of $*\_\_$ ensures that reading is pure. The first axiom expresses that after assignment, the assigned value can be read; the second one that assignment for a particular location does not affect the other locations. The next two axioms state similar properties for the new operation, and the last axiom ensures that two newly created locations are distinct.

$$\textbf{(var)} \quad \frac{}{[\![x_1 : A_1, \ldots, x_n : A_n \rhd x_i : A_i]\!] = \pi_i^n}$$

$$\textbf{(app)} \quad \frac{f : A \to B \in \Sigma \quad [\![\Gamma \rhd t : A]\!] = h}{[\![\Gamma \rhd f(t) : B]\!] = [\![f]\!] \circ h} \qquad \textbf{(1)} \quad \frac{}{[\![\Gamma \rhd * : 1]\!] =\,!}$$

$$\textbf{(pair)} \quad \frac{[\![\Gamma \rhd t : A]\!] = h_1 \quad [\![\Gamma \rhd u : B]\!] = h_2}{[\![\Gamma \rhd \langle t, u \rangle : A \times B]\!] = \langle h_1, h_2 \rangle}$$

$$\textbf{(fst)} \quad \frac{[\![\Gamma \rhd t : A \times B]\!] = h}{[\![\Gamma \rhd \text{fst}(t) : A]\!] = \pi_1 \circ h} \qquad \textbf{(snd)} \quad \frac{[\![\Gamma \rhd t : A \times B]\!] = h}{[\![\Gamma \rhd \text{snd}(t) : A]\!] = \pi_2 \circ h}$$

$$\textbf{($\top$)} \quad \frac{}{[\![\Gamma \rhd \top : \Omega]\!] = \top} \qquad \textbf{($\bot$)} \quad \frac{}{[\![\Gamma \rhd \bot : \Omega]\!] = \bot}$$

$$\textbf{($\neg$)} \quad \frac{[\![\Gamma \rhd a : \Omega]\!] = h}{[\![\Gamma \rhd \neg a : \Omega]\!] = \neg(h)} \quad \text{similarly for } \wedge, \vee, \Rightarrow, \Longleftrightarrow$$

$$\textbf{(do)} \quad \frac{[\![\Gamma \rhd p : TA]\!] = h_1 \quad [\![\Gamma, x : A \rhd q : TB]\!] = h_2}{[\![\Gamma \rhd \text{do } x \leftarrow p; q : TB]\!] = h_2^* \circ t_{[\![\Gamma]\!], [\![A]\!]} \circ \langle id, h_1 \rangle}$$

$$\textbf{(ret)} \quad \frac{[\![\Gamma \rhd t : A]\!] = h}{[\![\Gamma \rhd \text{ret } t : PA]\!] = \eta_{[\![A]\!]} \circ h}$$

$$\textbf{($\Box$)} \quad \frac{[\![\Gamma \rhd p : T\Omega]\!] = h}{[\![\Gamma \rhd \Box p : P\Omega]\!] = \Box \circ h} \qquad \textbf{(P)} \quad \frac{[\![\Gamma \rhd p : PA]\!] = h}{[\![\Gamma \rhd p : TA]\!] = \iota_A \circ h}$$

Fig. 2. Semantics of monad-based dynamic logic

3.2 Semantics

MDL is interpreted over a strong monad $\mathbb{T}$ on a cartesian category $\mathbf{C}^3$ with additional structure as follows. There is a distinguished object Ω such that hom-sets into Ω coherently carry a Boolean algebra structure; i.e. the hom-functor $\hom(\_, \Omega)$ factors through Boolean algebras. In order to enforce a Boolean logic, we additionally require that $(id_A \times \top : A \times 1 \to A \times \Omega, id_A \times \bot : A \times 1 \to A \times \Omega)$ is an episink. Moreover, $\mathbb{T}$ needs to be equipped with a strong submonad $\mathbb{P}$, with functor part P (the inclusion is denoted $\iota : P \to T$); we require that PA consists of pure computations as defined further below.[4] Finally, we need a left inverse $\square : T\Omega \to P\Omega$ of the inclusion $\iota : P\Omega \hookrightarrow T\Omega$. It will be axiomatized uniquely later on (cf. Prop. 11).

Remark 3. In a distributive category, one obtains the Boolean algebra structure by defining Ω as $1 + 1$. E.g., every topos is distributive, and in a classical topos, the subobject classifier is just $1 + 1$. In a category with equalizers, there is also a canonical choice for the subfunctor P, namely to take PA as the subobject of TA determined by purity as defined below. Then the $\square$ arrow is uniquely determined if it exists (see Prop. 11 below).

We then interpret the basic sorts as objects in $\mathbf{C}$. This is easily extended to all types, giving an interpretation $[\![A]\!]$ for each type A. Basic operations $f : A \to B$ are interpreted as morphisms $[\![A]\!] \to [\![B]\!]$, and terms $x_1 : A_1, \ldots, x_n : A_n \rhd t : A$ as morphisms $[\![t]\!] : [\![A_1 \times \cdots \times A_n]\!] \to [\![A]\!]$, using the cartesian structure for pairing and projections, the monad for do and ret, and the Boolean algebra structure on Ω for the Boolean connectives as shown in Fig. 2. (Note that there is no particular rule for sequential composition within P: the fact that $\mathbb{P}$ is a submonad guarantees closedness under sequential composition). Observe, that logical connectives are also applicable to $P\Omega$. For instance $p \wedge q$ is an alias for $(do\ x \leftarrow p; y \leftarrow q; ret\ x \wedge y)$. The fact that $P\Omega$ inherits Boolean algebra structure from Ω strongly relies on the definition of P [23]. Equations between terms are interpreted as equations between the corresponding morphisms; this will be used in a series of definitions below (we often leave the context implicit).

3.3 Purity

MDL formulae will be interpreted as computations of type $P\Omega$ (i.e. morphisms from the object interpreting the context into the object $P\Omega$). They are expected to have no side-effect, although they may e.g. read the state (if a notion of state is present in the monad). The three conditions for purity listed in Sect. 1 are abstractly captured as follows.

Definition 4. In a monad given as above, a program $p : TA$ is called *discardable* if

$$(do\ y \leftarrow p; ret\ *) = ret\ *,$$

and *copyable* if

$$(do\ x \leftarrow p; y \leftarrow p; ret\ (x, y)) = do\ x \leftarrow p; ret\ (x, x).$$

---

[3] $\times$ is product with projections π_1, π_2, 1 the terminal object with $!_A : A \to 1$ the unique arrow.
[4] One obvious possibility is to let PA consist of *all* pure computations; this always gives a strong submonad. We will use this possibility in the examples below.

Finally, p is *pure* if it is both discardable and copyable, and *commutes* with all such programs q, that is,

$$(\mathrm{do}\ x \leftarrow p; y \leftarrow q; \mathrm{ret}\,(x, y)) = \mathrm{do}\ y \leftarrow q; x \leftarrow p; \mathrm{ret}\,(x, y).$$

The last condition follows from the first two for simple monads, on which we focus here; cf. Prop. 18.

For the monads described in Example 1, purity of p means the expected things:

1. State monad: p possibly reads the state, but does not change it;
2. Non-determinism: p is deterministic (i.e. returns precisely one value);
3. Exceptions: p terminates normally;
4. In-/Output: p does not read/write;
5. Nondeterministic state monad: p is deterministic and only reads the state, but does not change it.
6. Java monad: p only reads the state and terminates normally

The equation for discardability can be interpreted as a pair of arrows dis_0, dis_1 : $T[\![A]\!] \rightarrow T[\![1]\!]$; we require that $\iota_{[\![A]\!]} : P[\![A]\!] \rightarrow T[\![A]\!]$ equalizes this pair. (We do *not* require that $\iota_{[\![A]\!]}$ is the equalizer, for the reconstruction of this equalizer in the term model would require a coercion of provably pure terms of type TA to type PA, which means that term formation rules would need to interact with proof rules.) A similar requirement holds for copyability; i.e. we require that PA contains only pure programs.

3.4   The Logic

We will want to regard programs that return truth values as formulae with side effects in a modal logic setting. A basic notion we need for such formulae is that of global validity, which we denote explicitly by a 'global box' $\boxed{G}$:

Definition 5. Given a term $p : T\Omega$, $\boxed{G}p$ abbreviates the equation

$$p = \mathrm{do}\ p; \mathrm{ret}\ \top.$$

If p is discardable, then $\boxed{G}p$ simplifies to $p = \mathrm{ret}\ \top$; otherwise, the equation above ensures that the right hand side has the same side-effect as p. We say that an MDL formula φ is *valid* in a model $\mathbb{T}$, and write $\mathbb{T} \models \varphi$, if $\boxed{G}\varphi$; this is usually expressed by just writing φ. As usual, by $\mathbb{T} \models \Phi$ for a set Φ of MDL formulae we mean that $\mathbb{T} \models \varphi$ for all $\varphi \in \Phi$, and by $\Phi \models \psi$ that $\mathbb{T} \models \Phi$ implies $\mathbb{T} \models \psi$ for all $\mathbb{T}$.

A related notion is that of *global dynamic judgements* of the form $[\bar{x} \leftarrow \bar{p}]\,a$, which intuitively state that a holds after $\bar{x} \leftarrow \bar{p}$, where $a : \Omega$ is a truth-valued term in variables $\bar{x}$. The idea is to work with formulae that have all side effects shoved to the outside, so that the usual logical rules apply to the remaining part.

Definition 6. Given a program sequence $\bar{x} \leftarrow \bar{p}$ and a formula a of type Ω, the notation $[\bar{x} \leftarrow \bar{p}]\,a$ abbreviates the equation

$$(\mathrm{do}\ \bar{x} \leftarrow \bar{p}; \mathrm{ret}\,\langle \bar{x}, a\rangle) = \mathrm{do}\ \bar{x} \leftarrow \bar{p}; \mathrm{ret}\,\langle \bar{x}, \top\rangle.$$

Definition 7. A monad is called *simple* if Ⓔ do $\bar{x} \leftarrow \bar{p}$; ret a implies $[\bar{x} \leftarrow \bar{p}]\, a$. (The converse implication holds universally.) Roughly, an algebraic monad [11] is simple if, in each of its equations, the two sides contain the same variables. All monads of Example 1 are simple. The continuation monad and the abelian group monad are not simple. *In the sequel, all monads are assumed to be simple.*

We adapt the axiomatic definition of the dynamic modal operators from [23] to the simplified setting of simple monads:

Definition 8. $\mathbb{T}$ is said to *admit dynamic logic*, if for each $q : T\Omega$ and each $\bar{x} \leftarrow \bar{p}$ containing $x_i : \Omega$,

$$[\bar{x} \leftarrow \bar{p}; a \leftarrow \Box q]\,(x_i \Rightarrow a) \text{ iff } [\bar{x} \leftarrow \bar{p}; a \leftarrow q]\,(x_i \Rightarrow a).$$

This definition essentially axiomatizes $\Box$ via its interaction with global dynamic judgements. In order to gain some intuitive understanding, let us assume that we are working in a non-deterministic state monad. Note that purity of $\Box q$ is enforced by its type; this means that in a given state, $\Box q$ returns either $\top$ or $\bot$ (but not both — it is deterministic). Hence, the above definition expresses that in any given state ($\bar{p}$ can be used to move to that state), $\Box q$ holds iff all executions of q (starting from the given state) return true.

For the next proposition, it is important to recall the difference between the *local box* $[\bar{x} \leftarrow \bar{p}]\,\varphi$ (a monadic value of type $P\Omega$ that may be used in formation of monadic terms) and the *global box* $[\bar{x} \leftarrow \bar{p}]\,a$ (a global equation between certain monadic terms).

Proposition 9. *If a simple monad $\mathbb{T}$ admits dynamic logic, then*

$$[\bar{x} \leftarrow \bar{p}; a \leftarrow [\bar{y} \leftarrow \bar{q}]\,\varphi]\,(x_i \Rightarrow a) \text{ iff } [\bar{x} \leftarrow \bar{p}; \bar{y} \leftarrow \bar{q}; a \leftarrow \varphi]\,(x_i \Rightarrow a),$$

i.e. $\mathbb{T}$ admits dynamic logic in the sense of [23].

Thus, the operator $[\bar{y} \leftarrow \bar{q}]$ in a sense serves to predict all *positive* statements to be made about the result $\bar{y}$ after executing the computations $\bar{q}$ *in a given state*; the formal content of the latter phrase is reflected in the quantification over program sequences $\bar{x} \leftarrow \bar{p}$ to be executed before $\bar{q}$.

Example 10. All monads described in Example 1 admit dynamic logic, with the meaning of the dynamic modal operators made explicit below. A typical example that fails to admit dynamic logic is the continuation monad $\lambda X.\,(X \rightarrow R) \rightarrow R$ [23].

1. *Stateful computations with non-termination* $(TA = (S \rightarrow? (A \times S)))$: Elements of $P\Omega$ are state-dependent truth values, i.e. functions $S \rightarrow \Omega$. A state s satisfies $[x \leftarrow p]\,\varphi$ if the value x, if any, returned by p after terminating execution starting in state s satisfies φ.

2. *Non-determinism* $(TA = \mathcal{P}(A))$: $P\Omega$ is isomorphic to the set Ω of truth values; $[x \leftarrow p]\,\varphi$ holds if all $x \in p$ satisfy φ.

3. *Exceptions* $(TA = A + E)$: $P\Omega$ is essentially Ω; $[x \leftarrow p]\,\varphi$ holds if p is either an exception or a value x satisfying φ.

4. *Interactive input* $(TA = \mu\gamma. A + (U \to \gamma))$: $P\Omega$ is essentially Ω; $[x \leftarrow p]\,\varphi$ holds if the value returned by p after reading a number of inputs satisfies φ. *Interactive output* $(TA = \mu\gamma. A + (U \times \gamma))$: again, $P\Omega$ is essentially Ω, and $[x \leftarrow p]\,\varphi$ holds if the value returned by p satisfies φ (the output is ignored).

5. *Non-deterministic stateful computations* $(TA = \mathcal{P}(S \to (A \times S)))$: Elements of $P\Omega$ are state-dependent truth values $S \to \Omega$. A state s satisfies $[x \leftarrow p]\,\varphi$ if all values x possibly returned by p after terminating execution starting in state s satisfy φ.

6. *Java monad* $(TA = S \to (A \times S + E \times S + 1))$: again, $P\Omega$ is $S \to \Omega$, and also $[x \leftarrow p]\,\varphi$ means that all values x returned by p after a terminating execution satisfy φ.

While at first sight, items 2–4 look uninteresting from the perspective of dynamic logic, it should be kept in mind that all these monads may be combined with 'dynamic' monads such as the state monad, as exemplified for the cases of the non-determinism monad in item 5 and the Java monad in item 6.

For $\varphi, \psi : P\Omega$, let $\varphi \leq \psi$ if

$$[a \leftarrow \varphi; b \leftarrow \psi]\,(a \Rightarrow b)$$

This is easily seen to be a partial order. The following two claims are proved similarly as in [23].

Proposition 11. *The formula $\Box p$ is the greatest formula $\varphi : P\Omega$ such that*

$$[a \leftarrow \varphi; b \leftarrow p]\,(a \Rightarrow b).$$

Proposition 12. $[\bar{x} \leftarrow \bar{p}]\,a$ *iff* $\boxed{c}[\bar{x} \leftarrow \bar{p}]\,\mathrm{ret}\,a$

Proposition 11 implies that $\Box p$ is uniquely determined if it exists. Proposition 12 relates global dynamic judgements and local modal formulae. Note the difference between *global* dynamic judgements $[\bar{x} \leftarrow \bar{p}]\,a$ and the similar-looking MDL formulae $[\bar{x} \leftarrow \bar{p}]\,\varphi$ involving a *local* modality. From a technical point of view, a global dynamic judgement is an equation between terms (and the component formula a has type Ω), while a local modal formula is a term (and the component formula φ has type $P\Omega$). But the difference is more fundamental: local modalities can be nested, and e.g. in the state monad one can think of them as being evaluated relative to a local state. This is not possible with global dynamic judgements: they always quantify over *all* states.

4   A Calculus for Dynamic Logic

Figure 3 shows a proof calculus for MDL. The calculus differs from the one in [23] in that the rules for the diamond are omitted, because in classical logic, $\Diamond$ can be defined as $\neg\Box\neg$. Moreover, Axioms ($\Box$) (resembling the implicit definition of $\Box$ in the formula for admission of dynamic logic), (dis) and (copy) (expressing purity of terms of type PA), (unit) and (CC) have been added. The axiom schema (CC) throws in all equations $CC \vdash t = u$ derivable using only the standard equations for tupling, projections, and

*, i.e. the internal equations of cartesian categories. The usual logical connectives are lifted to $P\Omega$ by defining e.g.

$$\varphi \Rightarrow \psi := [a \leftarrow \varphi; b \leftarrow \psi] \, \text{ret} \, (a \Rightarrow b) : P\Omega,$$

which by ($\square$MDL) below is equivalent to

$$\text{do } a \leftarrow \varphi; b \leftarrow \psi; \text{ret} \, (a \Rightarrow b).$$

We write $\Phi \vdash \psi$ if a formula is derivable in the calculus from a set Φ of axioms.

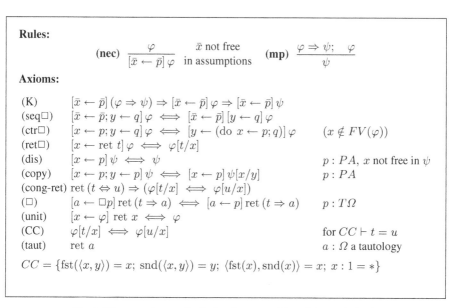

Fig. 3. The generic proof calculus for monad-based dynamic logic

Proposition 13 (Soundness of MDL). *If $\Phi \vdash \psi$, then $\Phi \models \psi$.*

We now discuss some structural properties of the calculus.

Definition 14. A term is in *product β-normal form* if it does not contain subterms of the form $\text{fst}\langle t, u \rangle$ or $\text{snd}\langle t, u \rangle$.

Theorem 15. *The system of reduction rules*

$$\begin{array}{lcl}
\text{fst}(\langle t, u \rangle) & \longmapsto & t \\
\text{snd}(\langle t, u \rangle) & \longmapsto & u \\
\text{do } x \leftarrow \text{ret } t; p & \longmapsto & p[t/x] \\
\text{do } x \leftarrow (\text{do } y \leftarrow p; q); r & \longmapsto & \text{do } y \leftarrow p; x \leftarrow q; r \\
\square\square p & \longmapsto & \square p
\end{array}$$

is confluent and strongly normalizing.

In the sequel, the terms *rewriting* and *normal form* will always refer to the above rule system.

Proposition 16. *Let φ be a formula in product β-normal form having a sub-term $r : TA$. Then there is a provably equivalent formula ψ with $\varphi \longmapsto \psi$ (ψ is even a subformula of φ) such that ψ has one of the following forms:*
1. p, where $p : P\Omega$,   2. $\Box p$, where $p : T\Omega$,
3. do $\bar{x} \leftarrow \bar{p}; q$,   4. $\Box(\text{do } \bar{x} \leftarrow \bar{p}; q)$.

Using this result, we can apply a leftmost-outermost reduction strategy to obtain

Proposition 17. *An MDL formula φ is provably equivalent to its normal form.*

This result in turn leads to further admissible rules:

Proposition 18. *The following rules are admissible:*

$$\textbf{(cong)} \quad \frac{\varphi \Leftrightarrow \psi}{\chi[\varphi/x] \Leftrightarrow \chi[\psi/x]} \qquad \textbf{(subst)} \quad \frac{\varphi}{\varphi[t/x]}.$$

The following equivalence is derivable:

$$\textbf{(comm)} \quad [x \leftarrow \varphi; y \leftarrow \psi]\,\chi \iff [y \leftarrow \psi; x \leftarrow \varphi]\,\chi.$$

For a tautology a, ret a can be derived.

5   Observational Purity

Our notion of purity has some practical limitations: The program do $r \leftarrow new\ x$; ret r is *not* pure, since it modifies the state. In particular, it is not discardable, since it generally makes a difference whether a new memory cell is allocated or not. However, we generally cannot *observe* whether a memory cell is allocated (unless we program in C, where a function *int2loc* is available). This leads to the following notions:

Given a background MDL theory Φ (that axiomatizes a given combination of effects), two programs p and q are *observationally equivalent*, $p \approx q$, iff for all φ,

$$\Phi \vdash [x \leftarrow p]\,\varphi \iff [x \leftarrow q]\,\varphi.$$

A program is *observationally pure*, if the equations for discardability, copyability and commutation hold up to observational equivalence. For example, in the case of discardability, this means that

$$\Phi \vdash [x \leftarrow (\text{do } y \leftarrow p; \text{ret } *)]\,\varphi \iff [x \leftarrow \text{ret } *]\,\varphi,$$

which amounts to $\Phi \vdash \varphi \iff [p]\,\varphi$.

For the monads described in Example 1, observational purity of p of course depends on the observational equivalence, that is, on the number of observations that can be made. We have:

1. State monad: p possibly reads the state, and moreover possibly makes changes to the state *none of which are observable*. In particular, this means that operations such as *new* are observationally pure as long as there is no possibility to directly observe memory cells.

2. Non-determinism: p is deterministic (i.e. returns precisely one value) *up to observational equivalence*.

3. Exceptions: p terminates normally (note that non-termination is always observable, because $[p] \top$ holds for non-terminating p).

4. In-/Output: any p is observationally pure—this is caused by the non-observability of input and output (assuming there is no feedback between input and output). Informally, this means that setting breakpoints and outputting trace information is harmless.

5. Nondeterministic state monad: p is deterministic up to observational equivalence and changes the state only to an observationally equivalent one.

6. Java monad: p changes the state only to an observationally equivalent one and terminates normally.

6   Completeness

The completeness proof for MDL is based on a term model construction. Given a signature Σ and a set Φ of MDL formulae over Σ, we construct a category $\mathbf{C}_{\Sigma,\Phi}$ as follows: the objects of $\mathbf{C}_{\Sigma,\Phi}$ are the types of Σ, and morphisms $t : A \to B$ are terms in context

$$x : A \rhd t : B,$$

taken modulo *contextual equivalence*

$$t \sim u \text{ iff for all MDL formulae } \varphi, \ \Phi \vdash \varphi[t/x] \iff \varphi[u/x] \qquad (*)$$

(this is obviously a congruence). Identities are given by variables $[x : A \rhd x : A]_\sim$, and composition by substitution

$$[y : B \rhd u : C]_\sim \circ [x : A \rhd t : B]_\sim := [x : A \rhd u[t/y] : C]_\sim.$$

Using axiom (ret□), one easily proves that this is well-defined and obeys the identity and associativity laws of a category. The basic types of Σ are interpreted as themselves, and so are the basic operations:

$$[\![f : A \to B]\!] := [x : A \rhd f(x) : B]_\sim.$$

The category $\mathbf{C}_{\Sigma,\Phi}$ comes with a canonical cartesian structure, which on objects is just given by taking product types as categorical products, and the unit type as the terminal object. Projections are $\pi_1 := [x : A \times B \rhd \mathrm{fst}(x) : A]_\sim$ and $\pi_2 := [x : A \times B \rhd \mathrm{snd}(x) : B]_\sim$, pairing of morphisms is $\langle [t]_\sim, [u]_\sim \rangle := [\langle t, u \rangle]_\sim$, and the unique morphism into the terminal object is $!_A := [x : A \rhd * : 1]_\sim$. Axiom (CC) ensures that this does define a cartesian structure.

The problem with contextual equivalence is that, although its definition is simple and intuitive, it can be quite hard to prove that given monadic programs are contextually equivalent. The key result is

Theorem 19. *For terms of type TA, contextual equivalence $\sim$ coincides with observational equivalence $\approx$.*

We are now ready to complete the term model construction by constructing a monad $\mathbb{T}_{\Sigma,\Phi}$ on $\mathbf{C}_{\Sigma,\Phi}$. It is given by the following data:

$$\mathbb{T}_{\Sigma,\Phi}\,A := T\,A, \qquad \eta_A := [x : A \rhd \mathrm{ret}\ x : T A]_\sim,$$

and given $x : A \rhd q : TB$,

$$[x : A \rhd q : TB]^*_\sim := [p : TA \rhd \mathrm{do}\ x \leftarrow p; q : TB]_\sim$$

Well-definedness follows easily by Theorem 19. Finally, the strength is given by

$$t_{A,B} := [p : A \times TB \rhd \mathrm{do}\ x \leftarrow \mathrm{snd}(p); \mathrm{ret}\ \langle \mathrm{fst}(p), x \rangle : T(A \times B)]_\sim$$

In $\mathbf{C}_{\Sigma,\Phi}$, $Hom(A, \Omega)$ is coherently turned into a Boolean algebra by defining e.g.

$$[x : A \rhd t : \Omega]_\sim \wedge [x : A \rhd u : \Omega]_\sim = [x : A \rhd t \wedge u : \Omega]_\sim$$

Lemma 20. *In $\mathbf{C}_{\Sigma,\Phi}$, $(id_A \times \top : A \times 1 \to A \times \Omega, id_A \times \bot : A \times 1 \to A \times \Omega)$ is an episink.*

To complete the construction of the term model, we put $\iota_A : PA \to TA := [p : PA \rhd p : TA]_\sim$, and $\Box : T\Omega \to P\Omega := [p : T\Omega \rhd \Box p : P\Omega]_\sim$.

Corollary 21 (Full abstractness). *In $\mathbb{T}_{\Sigma,\Phi}$, $[\![t]\!] = [\![u]\!]$ iff $t \sim u$.*

By Theorem 19, we also have

Corollary 22. *In $\mathbb{T}_{\Sigma,\Phi}$, for $p, q : TA$, $[\![p]\!] = [\![q]\!]$ iff $p \approx q$.*

The crucial properties of the term model construction are summarized in the next two results.

Proposition 23. $\mathbb{T}_{\Sigma,\Phi}$ *is a fully abstract simple strong monad admitting dynamic logic.*

Lemma 24 (Truth Lemma). $\mathbb{T}_{\Sigma,\Phi} \models \varphi$ *iff* $\Phi \vdash \varphi$.

The main result now follows straightforwardly:

Theorem 25 (Completeness of MDL). *If $\Phi \models \psi$, then $\Phi \vdash \psi$.*

7   Conclusion and Future Work

Inspired by the logics of design by contract languages, we have introduced monad-based dynamic logic (MDL) as a means of handling with effects, purity and observational equivalence in an abstract way that avoids the development of a specific theory for each language. Our generic notion of observational purity captures the same intuition as Naumann's notion of observational purity [15] when instantiated to his specific imperative language. However, besides state, store and non-termination, our logic can also handle effects like non-determinism, input/output, and many others. Moreover, our notions of observational and contextual equivalence (which coincide in the term model) come out of the logic in a more natural way, compared with the variety of notions in [15]. The sound and complete calculus allows for reasoning about Hoare style and dynamic logic assertions as well as about observational purity in a uniform way.

MDL is similar to Pitts' evaluation logic [19], but equipped with a different semantics which is induced directly by the underlying monad — rather than relying on an extra hyperdoctrine structure, which must in all likelihood be considered additional data (e.g. in the case of the state monad, the interpretation of formulae as state predicates is explicitly imposed by the chosen hyperdoctrine). Existing completeness results for monad-based logics rely on a *global* semantics [14, 7], which e.g. for the state monad means that a sequence of nested modalities leads to universal quantification over all states at each new nesting level - the (implicit) state is not passed across nesting levels. By contrast, our logic allows for reasoning in a truly local way about changes of state. So far, no completeness result has been proved for such logics.

A Hoare calculus has been built on top of MDL [21] and extended to a treatment of Java-style abrupt termination [22, 29]. Practical applications of MDL include reasoning about Haskell and the imperative fragment of Java. Numerous examples and a coding in the theorem prover Isabelle can be found in [28].

The completeness result now guarantees closedness of the deduction system (after the extension w.r.t. [23]) and paves the way for the future development of decision procedures. Of course, one cannot expect a decision procedure for arbitrary equational theories. In this respect, our calculus (unlike similar calculi [19, 14, 7]) has the advantage that it makes use only of a rather limited and efficiently decidable equational theory. In particular, equations between programs are avoided; instead, properties of programs are expressed in terms of their observable behaviour.

More practical experience is needed for evaluating how practical actual proofs of purity and observational purity are. Typically, such proofs will not be semantical like those of the claims made in Sect. 5, but rather rely on the types of basic operations that deliver pure results, and on suitable axioms. Indeed, our calculus can be instantiated with a variety of different effects by *axiomatizing* these effects; we have provided one sample axiomatization for the dynamic reference monad.

The generalization to non-simple monads is an important open question. Another important extension will be the treatment of control structures such as while loops (which currently happens at the meta-level) as well as of datatypes in the calculus proper.

Acknowledgements. This work forms part of the DFG-funded project HASCASL (KR 1191/7-1 and KR 1191/7-2). The authors wish to thank the anonymous referees for useful comments, and Erwin R. Catesbeiana for pointing out various pitfalls.

References

[1] Beckert, B.: A dynamic logic for the formal verification of Java Card programs. In: Attali, I., Jensen, T. (eds.) JavaCard 2000. LNCS, vol. 2041, pp. 6–24. Springer, Heidelberg (2001)

[2] Boehm, H.-J.: Side effects and aliasing can have simple axiomatic descriptions. ACM Trans. Program. Lang. Syst 7, 637–655 (1985)

[3] Bonniot, D., Keller, B.: The Nice user's manual (2003), http://nice.sourceforge.net

[4] Bright, W.: The D programming language. Dr. Dobb's Journal of Software Tools 27(2), 36–40 (2002)

[5] Cok, D.R., Kiniry, J.R.: ESC/Java2: Uniting ESC/Java and JML. In: Barthe, G., Burdy, L., Huisman, M., Lanet, J.-L., Muntean, T. (eds.) CASSIS 2004. LNCS, vol. 3362, pp. 108–128. Springer, Heidelberg (2005)

[6] Findler, R.B., Felleisen, M.: Contracts for higher-order functions. In: ICFP, pp. 48–59 (2002)

[7] Goncharov, S., Schröder, L., Mossakowski, T.: Completeness of global evaluation logic. In: Královič, R., Urzyczyn, P. (eds.) MFCS 2006. LNCS, vol. 4162, pp. 447–458. Springer, Heidelberg (2006)

[8] Hoare,: An axiomatic basis for computer programming. CACM 12 (1969)

[9] Huisman, M.: Java program verification in higher order logic with PVS and Isabelle. PhD thesis, University of Nijmegen (2001)

[10] Jacobs, B., Poll, E.: Coalgebras and Monads in the Semantics of Java. Theoret. Comput. Sci. 291, 329–349 (2003)

[11] Mac Lane, S.: Categories for the Working Mathematician. Springer, Heidelberg (1997)

[12] Meyer, B.: Eiffel: The Language. Prentice-Hall, Englewood Cliffs (1992)

[13] Moggi, E.: Notions of computation and monads. Inform. and Comput. 93, 55–92 (1991)

[14] Moggi, E.: A semantics for evaluation logic. Fund. Inform. 22, 117–152 (1995)

[15] Naumann, D.A.: Observational purity and encapsulation. Theoret. Comput. Sci 376, 205–224 (2007)

[16] Nipkow, T.: Hoare logics in Isabelle/HOL. In: Schwichtenberg, H., Steinbrüggen, R. (eds.) Proof and System-Reliability, pp. 341–367. Kluwer Academic Publishers, Dordrecht (2002)

[17] Omohundro, S.M.: The Sather language. Technical report, International Computer Science Institute, Berkeley (1991)

[18] Peyton-Jones, S. (ed.): Haskell 98 Language and Libraries — The Revised Report, Cambridge (2003), also: J. Funct. Programming 13 (2003)

[19] Pitts, A.: Evaluation logic. In: Higher Order Workshop, Workshops in Computing, pp. 162–189. Springer, Heidelberg (1991)

[20] Pratt, V.: Semantical considerations on Floyd-Hoare logic. In: Foundations of Conputer Science, FOCS 1976, pp. 109–121. IEEE, Los Alamitos (1976)

[21] Schröder, L., Mossakowski, T.: Monad-independent Hoare logic in HASCASL. In: Pezzè, M. (ed.) FASE 2003. LNCS, vol. 2621, pp. 261–277. Springer, Heidelberg (2003)

[22] Schröder, L., Mossakowski, T.: Generic Exception Handling and the Java Monad. In: Rattray, C., Maharaj, S., Shankland, C. (eds.) AMAST 2004. LNCS, vol. 3116, pp. 443–459. Springer, Heidelberg (2004)

[23] Schröder, L., Mossakowski, T.: Monad-independent dynamic logic in HASCASL. J. Logic Comput. 14, 571–619 (2004)

[24] Sonntag, B., Colnet, D.: Lisaac: the power of simplicity at work for operating system. In: Technology of Object-Oriented Languages and Systems, TOOLS Pacific 2002. CRPIT, vol. 10, pp. 45–52. ACS (2002)

[25] Stenzel, K.: A formally verified calculus for full Java Card. In: Rattray, C., Maharaj, S., Shankland, C. (eds.) AMAST 2004. LNCS, vol. 3116, pp. 491–505. Springer, Heidelberg (2004)

[26] van den Berg, J., Jacobs, B.: The LOOP compiler for Java and JML. In: Margaria, T., Yi, W. (eds.) TACAS 2001. LNCS, vol. 2031, pp. 299–312. Springer, Heidelberg (2001)

[27] von Oheimb, D.: Hoare logic for Java in Isabelle/HOL. Concurrency and Computation: Practice and Experience 13, 1173–1214 (2001)

[28] Walter, D.: Monadic dynamic logic: Application and implementation. Master's thesis, University of Bremen (2005), http://www.cs.chalmers.se/~denniswa

[29] Walter, D., Schröder, L., Mossakowski, T.: Parametrized exceptions. In: Fiadeiro, J.L., Harman, N.A., Roggenbach, M., Rutten, J. (eds.) CALCO 2005. LNCS, vol. 3629, pp. 424–438. Springer, Heidelberg (2005)

Modelling and Verification
of
Timed Interaction and Migration

Gabriel Ciobanu[1] and Maciej Koutny[2]

[1] Faculty of Computer Science
A.I.Cuza University of Iasi
700483 Iasi, Romania
gabriel@info.uaic.ro
[2] School of Computing Science
Newcastle University
Newcastle upon Tyne, NE1 7RU, United Kingdom
maciej.koutny@newcastle.ac.uk

Abstract. We present a process algebra where timeouts of interactions and adaptable migrations in a distributed environment with explicit locations can be defined. Timing constraints allow to control the interaction (communication) between co-located mobile processes, and a migration action with variable destination supports flexible movement from one location to another. We define an operational semantics, and outline a structural translation of the proposed process algebra into operationally equivalent finite high level timed Petri nets. The purpose of such a translation is twofold. First, it yields a formal semantics for timed interaction and migration which is both compositional and allows to deal directly with concurrency and causality. Second, it should facilitate the use of simulation and verification tools developed within the area of Petri nets.

Keywords: mobility, timers, process algebra, high-level Petri nets, compositional translation, behavioural consistency.

1   Introduction

The increasing complexity of mobile applications means that the need for their effective analysis and verification is becoming critical. Our aim here is to explore formal modelling of mobile distributed systems where one can also specify time-related aspects of migrating processes. To this end, we first introduce the TiMo (Timed Mobility) model which is a simple process algebra for mobile systems where, in addition to process mobility and interaction, it is possible to add timers to the basic actions. Processes are equipped with input and output capabilities which are active up to pre-defined time deadline and, if not taken, another continuation for the process behaviour is chosen. Another timing constraint allows to specify the earliest and latest time for moving a process from one location to another. We provide the syntax and operational semantics of TiMo which is

J. Fiadeiro and P. Inverardi (Eds.): FASE 2008, LNCS 4961, pp. 215–229, 2008.
© Springer-Verlag Berlin Heidelberg 2008

a discrete time semantics incorporating maximally concurrent executions of the basic actions.

The time model defined for TiMo is similar to that considered in the theory of compositional timed Petri nets [21]. Therefore, in the second part of the paper we outline a structural translation of process algebra terms into behaviourally equivalent finite high-level timed Petri nets, similar to those considered in [12].

Such a dual development yields a formal semantics for explicit mobility and time which is compositional, and at the same time, allows one to deal directly with concurrency and causality which can easily be captured in the Petri net domain. The Petri net representation should also be useful for automatically verifying behavioural properties using suitable model-checking techniques and tools.

To introduce the basic concepts of TiMo, we use the *simple e-shops* running example (*SES*). In this scenario, we have a client process which initially resides in the *home* location, and wants to find an address of an e-shop where different kinds of electronic items (e-items) can be purchased. To find out the address of a suitable e-shop, the client waits for a couple of time units and then, within 5 time units, moves to the location *info* in order to acquire the relevant address. After 7 time units the e-item loses its importance and the client is no longer interested in acquiring it. The location *info* contains a broker who knows all about the availability of the e-shops stocking the desired e-item. In the first 5 time units the right e-shop is the one at the location *shopA*, and after that for 7 time units that at location *shopB*. It is important to point out that we assume that any interaction between processes can only happen within the same location, and so it is necessary for the client to move to the broker location in order to find out about the i-item. The timers can define a coordination in time and space of the client, and take care of the relative time of interaction of the processes residing at the same location.

The paper is structured in the following way. We first describe the syntax and semantics of TiMo. After that we outline the net algebra used in the translation from TiMo expressions to Petri nets, and then describe the translation itself. We also explain the nature of behavioural equivalence of the resulting Petri net model and the original expression.

We assume that the reader is familiar with the basic concepts of process algebras [19], high-level Petri nets [9,17], and timed Petri nets [22].

2   A Calculus for Timed Mobility

We start by giving the syntax and semantics of TiMo which uses timing constraints allowing, for example, to specify what is the time window for a mobile process to move to another location. In TiMo, waiting for a communication on a channel or a movement to new location is no longer indefinite. If an action does not happen before a predefined deadline, the waiting process switches its operation to an alternate mode. This approach leads to a method of sharing of the channels over time. A timer (such as $\Delta 7$) of an output action $a^{\Delta 7}$! makes it available for communication only for the period of 7 time units. We use timers for both input and output actions. The reason for having the latter stems from the fact that in a distributed system there are both multiple clients and multiple servers, and so clients may decide to switch from one server to another depending on the waiting time.

2.1 Syntax

We assume that $Chan$ is a set of channels, Loc is a set of locations, Var is a set of location variables, and $Ident$ is a finite set of process identifiers (each identifier $I \in Ident$ has a fixed arity $m_I \geq 0$). The syntax of TiMo is given below:

$$
\begin{aligned}
P, Q \ ::= \ & a^{\Delta t} \,!\, \langle v \rangle \,\text{then}\, P \,\text{else}\, Q \quad | \\
& a^{\Delta t} \,?\, (u) \,\text{then}\, P \,\text{else}\, Q \quad | \\
& \mathbf{go}^{t \Delta t'} \, v \,\text{then}\, P \,\text{else}\, Q \quad | \\
& 0 \ | \ I(v_1, \dots, v_{m_I}) \quad | \\
& P \,|\, Q \ | \ \#P \qquad\qquad\qquad\qquad \text{(processes)}
\end{aligned}
$$

$$
M, N \ ::= \ l[\![P]\!] \ | \ M \,|\, N \qquad \text{(networks of located processes)}
$$

In the above description, it is assumed that:

- $a \in Chan$ is a channel,
- $t, t' \in \mathbb{N}$ are integers ($t \leq t'$),
- $v, v_1, \dots, v_{m_I} \in Loc \cup Var$ are locations and/or location variables,
- $l \in Loc$ is a location, and u is a variable.

Moreover, for each process identifier $I \in Ident$, there is a unique definition of the form

$$
I(u_1, \dots, u_{m_I}) = P_I \,, \tag{1}
$$

where $u_i \neq u_j$ (for $i \neq j$) are variables acting here as parameters. Given a network of located processes of the form

$$
\dots \quad l[\![\ \dots \ | P | \ \dots \ ]\!] \quad \dots
$$

we call P a *top-level* expression if it does not contain any occurrences of the special symbol $\#$. To improve readability, we will often denote expressions like $\alpha \,\text{then}\, 0 \,\text{else}\, 0$ and $\alpha \,\text{then}\, P \,\text{else}\, 0$ by α and $\alpha \,.\, P$, respectively.

Note that since we allow v in the $\mathbf{go}^{t \Delta t'} \, v \,\text{then}\, P \,\text{else}\, Q$ construct to be a variable and so its value is assigned dynamically though communication with other processes, migration actions support a flexible scheme for movement of processes from one location to another.

Process $a^{\Delta t} \,!\, \langle v \rangle \,\text{then}\, P \,\text{else}\, Q$ attempts to send the location given by v over the channel a for t time units. If this happens, then it continues as process P, and otherwise it continues as the alternate process Q. Similarly, process $a^{\Delta t} \,?\, (u) \,\text{then}\, P \,\text{else}\, Q$ attempts for t time units to input a location and substitute it for the variable u within its body.

Table 1. Rules of the structural equivalence

(EQ1)	$M \mid N \equiv N \mid M$
(EQ2)	$(M \mid N) \mid N' \equiv M \mid (N \mid N')$
(EQ3)	$l[\![P]\!] \equiv l[\![P|0]\!]$
(EQ4)	$l[\![I(l_1, \ldots, l_{I_A})]\!] \equiv l[\![\{l_1/u_1, \ldots, l_{m_I}/u_{m_I}\}P_I]\!]$
(EQ5)	$l[\![P|Q]\!] \equiv l[\![P]\!] \mid l[\![Q]\!]$

Mobility is implemented using processes like $\mathbf{go}^{t \Delta t'} u \, \mathbf{then} \, P \, \mathbf{else} \, Q$. It first waits for t time units doing nothing and after that it can move within $t' - t$ time units to the location u and behave as process P. If the move is not carried out in the allowed time window, the process continues as Q at its current location.

Processes are further constructed from the (terminated) process 0 and parallel composition $(P|Q)$. A located process $l[\![P]\!]$ is a process running at location l. Finally, process expressions of the form $\#P$ represent a purely technical notation which is used in our formalisation of structural operational semantics of TIMO; intuitively, it specifies a process P which is temporarily blocked and so cannot execute any action.

The construct $a^{\Delta t} \, ? \, (u) \, \mathbf{then} \, P \, \mathbf{else} \, Q$ binds the location variable u within P (but *not* within Q), and $fv(P)$ are the free variables of a process P (and similarly for networks of located processes). Processes are defined up to the alpha-conversion, and $\{l/u, \ldots\}P$ is obtained from P by replacing all free occurrences of u by l, etc, possibly after alpha-converting P in order to avoid clashes. For a process definition as in (1), we assume that $fv(P_I) \subseteq \{u_1, \ldots, u_{m_I}\}$ and so the free variables of P_I are parameter bound.

A network of located processes is *well-formed* if no variable used in both the network definition and process identifier definitions (1) is both free and bound, no variable ever generates more than one binding, there are no free variables in the network, and there are no occurrences of the special blocking symbol $\#$.

The specification of the running example which captures the essential features of the scenario described in the introduction can then be written down in the following way:

$$SES \;=\; home[\![Client]\!] \mid info[\![Broker]\!]$$

where

$$Client \;=\; \mathbf{go}^{2\Delta 5} \, info \;.\; (a^{\Delta 2} \, ? \, (shop) \, \mathbf{then} \, \mathbf{go}^{0\Delta 0} \, shop \, \mathbf{else} \, \mathbf{go}^{0\Delta 0} \, home \,)$$

$$Broker \;=\; a^{\Delta 5} \, ! \, \langle shopA \rangle \, \mathbf{then} \, 0 \, \mathbf{else} \, a^{\Delta 7} \, ! \, \langle shopB \rangle$$

Table 2. Rules of the operational semantics, where $\beta \neq \sqrt{}$

(MOVE)	$k[\![\mathbf{go}^{0\vartriangle t}\, l\, \mathbf{then}\, P\, \mathbf{else}\, Q]\!] \xrightarrow{k:l} l[\![\#P]\!]$

(WAIT) $k[\![\mathbf{go}^{0\vartriangle t}\, l\, \mathbf{then}\, P\, \mathbf{else}\, Q]\!] \xrightarrow{\tau} k[\![\#\mathbf{go}^{0\vartriangle t}\, l\, \mathbf{then}\, P\, \mathbf{else}\, Q]\!]$

(COM) $k[\![a^{\vartriangle t}\, !\, \langle l\rangle\, \mathbf{then}\, P\, \mathbf{else}\, Q \mid a^{\vartriangle t'}\, ?\, (u)\, \mathbf{then}\, P'\, \mathbf{else}\, Q']\!]$

$$\xrightarrow{k:a(l)}$$
$$l[\![\#P \mid \#\{l/u\}P']\!]$$

(PAR)
$$\frac{N \xrightarrow{\beta} N'}{N \mid M \xrightarrow{\beta} N' \mid M}$$

(STRUC)
$$\frac{N \equiv N' \quad N \xrightarrow{\beta} M \quad M \equiv M'}{N' \xrightarrow{\beta} M'}$$

(TIME)
$$\frac{N \not\rightarrow}{N \xrightarrow{\sqrt{}} \phi(N)}$$

2.2 Operational Semantics

The first component of the operational semantics of TIMO is the structural equivalence $\equiv$ on networks, similar to that used in [7]. It is the smallest congruence such that the equalities in Table 1 hold (note that $\{l_1/u_1, \ldots, l_{m_I}/u_{m_I}\}$ there denotes simultaneous substitution).

The action rules of the operational semantics are given in Table 2. They are based on the structural equivalence defined in Table 1 and two kinds of transition rules:

$$M \xrightarrow{\beta} N \quad \text{and} \quad M \xrightarrow{\sqrt{}} N$$

where the former is recording an execution of an action β, and the latter is a time step. The action β can be $k : l$ or $k : a(l)$ or τ, where k is the location where the action is executed and l is either the location a process has moved to, or the location name communicated between two processes over the channel a. Moreover, τ indicates that a process which could have moved to another location decided to wait in the same location for another time unit.

In the rule (TIME), $N \nrightarrow$ denotes the fact that no other rule in Table 2 can be applied. Moreover, $\phi(N)$ is obtained from N in the following *consecutive* stages:

- Each top-level expression $I(l_1, \ldots, l_{I_A})$ is replaced by the corresponding definition $\{l_1/u_1, \ldots, l_{m_I}/u_{m_I}\}P_I$.
- Each top-level expression of the form

$$a^{\Delta 0} \ldots \text{then } P \text{ else } Q \quad \text{or} \quad \mathbf{go}^{0\Delta 0} \ldots \text{then } P \text{ else } Q$$

  is replaced by $\#Q$.
- Each top-level expression of the form $a^{\Delta t} ! \langle l \rangle \text{ then } P \text{ else } Q$ is replaced by $a^{\Delta(t-1)} ! \langle l \rangle \text{ then } P \text{ else } Q$.
- Each top-level expressions of the form $a^{\Delta t} ? (u) \text{ then } P \text{ else } Q$ is replaced by $a^{\Delta(t-1)} ? (u) \text{ then } P \text{ else } Q$.
- Each top-level expression of the form $\mathbf{go}^{t\Delta t'} \text{ then } P \text{ else } Q$ is replaced by $\mathbf{go}^{t''\Delta(t'-1)} \text{ then } P \text{ else } Q$ where $t'' = \max\{0, t-1\}$.
- All occurrences of the special symbol $\#$ are deleted.

Note that $\phi(N)$ is a well-formed network of located processes provided that we started from a well-formed network in the first place (see below). For the running example, a possible execution corresponding is given in Table 3.

The way networks of located processes evolve can be regarded as conforming to the maximally concurrent paradigm. If we start with a well-formed network, execution proceeds through alternating executions of time steps and contiguous sequences of actions making up what can be regarded as a maximally concurrent

Table 3. An execution for the running example

$$SES \xrightarrow{\checkmark} \xrightarrow{\checkmark} \xrightarrow{home:info}$$

$$info[\![\#P \mid a^{\Delta 3} ! \langle shopA \rangle \text{ then } 0 \text{ else } a^{\Delta 7} ! \langle shopB \rangle]\!] \xrightarrow{\checkmark}$$

$$info[\![P \mid a^{\Delta 2} ! \langle shopA \rangle \text{ then } 0 \text{ else } a^{\Delta 7} ! \langle shopB \rangle]\!] \xrightarrow{info:a(shopA)}$$

$$info[\![\#\mathbf{go}^{0\Delta 0} shopA \mid \#0]\!] \xrightarrow{\checkmark}$$

$$info[\![\mathbf{go}^{0\Delta 0} shopA \mid 0]\!] \xrightarrow{info:shopA}$$

$$shopA[\![\#0]\!] \mid info[\![0]\!] \xrightarrow{\checkmark}$$

$$shopA[\![0]\!] \mid info[\![0]\!]$$

where $\quad P = a^{\Delta 2} ? (shop) \text{ then } \mathbf{go}^{0\Delta 0} shop \text{ else } \mathbf{go}^{0\Delta 0} home$

step (note the role of the special blocking symbols #). Now, if N is a well-formed networks and we have

$$N \xrightarrow{\beta_1} \cdots \xrightarrow{\beta_k} \xrightarrow{\checkmark} M$$

then M is also a well-formed network. Moreover, we write $N \xrightarrow{\Gamma} M$, where Γ is the multiset comprising all β_i's different from τ, and call M *directly reachable* from N. In other words, we capture the cumulative effect of execution.

Then the labelled transition system $\mathsf{ts}(N)$ of a well-formed network of located processes N has as its states all well-formed networks directly and indirectly reachable from N together with all possible arcs labelled by the multisets of observed actions. The initial state is itself the network N.

We can define a barbed (observation) predicate $N \downarrow_l$ for networks of located processes expressing that N has as component a (non-zero) process located at l. For timed mobile ambients we have defined a barbed predicate $\downarrow_{n@k}$ and a global predicate $\downarrow_n$ in [2]. However here we have only locations, and so we cannot define a global predicate. Also, the definition of $N \downarrow_l$ is rather trivial; it only describes something which can be immediately seen from the description of N.

3   An Algebra of Nets

We now outline an algebra of high-level timed Petri nets which we will then use to render TiMo networks of located processes. We focus on nets modelling finite networks, as this translation still includes all the essential novel features, and the case of networks involving process identifiers (more precisely, recursive process identifiers, as any non-recursive network specification can be transformed so that no process identifier is used) can be treated similarly as in [12]. The current development, resulting in *tm-nets*, has been inspired by the box algebra [5,6,13] and timed box algebra [21].

We use coloured tokens and read-arcs allowing any number of transitions to simultaneously check for the presence of a resource stored in a place [9]. The latter feature is crucial as we aim at defining a step semantics for tm-nets based on their maximally concurrent executions.

There are two kinds of places in tm-nets:

- *Control flow places*
  These model control flow and are labelled by their status symbols: (i) the *internal* places by i; (ii) the *entry* places by e; and (iii) the *exit* places by x and x'. The status of a control flow place is used to specify its initial marking and to determine its role in the net composition operations describe later on. The tokens carried by control flow places are of the form $l{:}t$ where l is the current location of the thread represented by the token, and t is the age of the token.

- *Location places*
  Each such place is labelled by a location (or location variable) and is used as a store for process locations which can then be accessed by process threads.

There are two kinds of arcs used in tm-nets, the standard directed arcs and read arcs used for token testing, which can be labelled by one of the following annotations: $L{:}T$, $L{:}T'$, L', $L{:}0$, $L'{:}0$, where L, L' are (Petri net) location variables and T, T' are time variables.

An (unmarked) *tm-net* is a triple $\Sigma = (S^{flow} \uplus S^{loc}, Tr, \iota)$, where: S^{flow} and S^{loc} are finite disjoint sets of, respectively, control-flow and location *places*; Tr is a finite set of *transitions* disjoint from S^{flow} and S^{loc}; ι is an *annotation function* defined for the places, transitions, and arcs between places and transitions. The arcs may be either directed (transferring tokens) or undirected (checking for the presence of tokens). We assume that:

- For every s in S^{flow}, $\iota(s) \in \{\mathsf{e}, \mathsf{i}, \mathsf{x}, \mathsf{x}'\}$ is a label giving the status of the place, determining its role during the application of composition operators. In what follows, $°\Sigma$ is the set of all entry places of Σ (forming its entry interface).
- For every s in S^{loc}, $\iota(s)$ is a location or location variable. At most one location place with a given label is allowed to be present in Σ.
- For every tr in Tr, $\iota(tr)$ is a pair $(\lambda(tr), \gamma(tr))$ where $\lambda(tr)$ is its *label* (a term with variables representing what is visible from the outside when the transition fires) and $\gamma(tr)$ is a *guard* (giving a timing constraint for the executability of the transition).
- For every arc $\mathfrak{a}$, either undirected ($\mathfrak{a} = \{s, tr\}$) or directed from a place to a transition ($\mathfrak{a} = (s, tr)$) or from a transition to a place ($\mathfrak{a} = (tr, s)$), $\iota(\mathfrak{a})$ is an annotation which is a set of terms with variables.[1]

As usual, if V are the variables occurring in the annotation of a transition tr and on the arcs adjacent to tr, we shall denote by $\flat$ a *binding* assigning to each variable in V a value in its domain. We shall only consider *legal bindings*, i.e., such that for each arc $\mathfrak{a}$ between t and s, if $\hbar \in \iota(\mathfrak{a})$, the evaluation of $\hbar$ under the binding $\flat$ (denoted $\flat(\hbar)$) delivers a value allowed in s. The observed label of a transition fired under binding $\flat$ is $\flat(\lambda(tr))$.

A *marking* $\mathcal{M}$ of a tm-net Σ is a function assigning to each place s a multiset of tokens.[2] Below we use $\oplus$ and $\ominus$ to denote respectively multiset sum and difference. Moreover, if $\mathcal{M}$ and $\mathcal{M}'$ are multisets over the same set of elements Z then $\mathcal{M} \geq \mathcal{M}'$ means that $\mathcal{M}(z) \geq \mathcal{M}'(z)$, for all $z \in Z$.

In what follows, a *marked* tm-net is a pair $(\Sigma, \mathcal{M})$ where Σ is a tm-net and $\mathcal{M}$ is its *initial* marking.

3.1   Firing Rule for tm-Nets

Let $\mathcal{M}$ be a marking of a tm-net Σ. As usual for Petri nets, we first need to say what it means for a transition of Σ to be enabled at the marking $\mathcal{M}$.

---

[1] In the nets resulting from the translation, all such sets are either empty or singletons.
[2] Even though all the markings in the nets resulting from translation have at most one token on any place at all times, it is easier to treat them as multisets.

Given a transition tr of Σ and a binding $\flat$ for tr, we denote by $\mathcal{M}^\flat_{tr,in}$ and $\mathcal{M}^\flat_{tr,out}$ two markings of Σ defined in such a way that, for every place s,

$$\mathcal{M}^\flat_{tr,in}(s) = \bigoplus_{\hbar\in\iota((s,tr))} \{\flat(\hbar)\} \quad \text{and} \quad \mathcal{M}^\flat_{tr,out}(s) = \bigoplus_{\hbar\in\iota((tr,s))} \{\flat(\hbar)\} .$$

Intuitively, $\mathcal{M}^\flat_{tr,in}$ represents all the tokens which are consumed by the firing of tr under the binding $\flat$, and $\mathcal{M}^\flat_{tr,out}$ represents all the tokens which are produced by the firing of tr under the same binding.

A transition tr is *enabled* under the binding $\flat$ at marking $\mathcal{M}$ if the following are satisfied:

- $\flat(\gamma(tr))$ evaluates to *true*,
- for every place s, $\mathcal{M}(s) \geq \mathcal{M}^\flat_{tr,in}(s)$,
- for every place s and every $\hbar \in \iota(\{s,tr\})$, $\flat(\hbar) \in \mathcal{M}(s)$.

An enabled transition tr may then be *fired*, which transforms $\mathcal{M}$ into a new marking $\mathcal{M}'$ in such a way that, for each place s:

$$\mathcal{M}'(s) = \mathcal{M}(s) \ominus \mathcal{M}^\flat_{tr,in}(s) \oplus \mathcal{M}^\flat_{tr,out}(s) .$$

This is denoted by $(\Sigma, \mathcal{M}) \xrightarrow{\flat(\lambda(tr))} (\Sigma, \mathcal{M}')$. Actions of this type will be used in the generation of the labelled transition system generated by a tm-net executed from its initial marking.

To define the desired labelled transition system, we still need to incorporate two aspects: maximally concurrent execution of actions, and the timing aspects. The first one is captured using the step semantics of Petri nets. More precisely, a *computational step* of $(\Sigma, \mathcal{M})$ is derived in the following way:

- We select a set of transitions U such that they form a valid *step* of transitions in the usual Petri net sense (i.e., each transition can be fired in isolation, and there are enough resources for all of them to be executed simultaneously). Moreover, none of the transitions is labelled by τ, and one cannot extend U by adding a transition labelled by $L{:}a(L')$ and still have a valid step for the marking $\mathcal{M}$. The firing of U results in an intermediate marking $\mathcal{M}''$.
- We change $\mathcal{M}''$ by replacing each token of the form $l{:}t$ by $l{:}(t + 1)$ which gives a new marking $\mathcal{M}'''$.
- We take the set U' of all enabled τ-labelled transitions (in the tm-nets resulting from the translation described below, U' is always a valid step). The firing of U' results in a marking $\mathcal{M}'$.

We then denote $(\Sigma, \mathcal{M}) \xrightarrow{\Gamma} (\Sigma, \mathcal{M}')$ where Γ is the multiset comprising all the labels generated by the transitions in U.

Note that the above definition treats some transitions as urgent, and the other as non-urgent to reflect the fact that in the process algebra some of the actions can be postponed while the others cannot.

We then can form the transition system $\mathsf{ts}(\Sigma, \mathcal{M})$ of a tm-net $(\Sigma, \mathcal{M})$ in the usual way, using the Γ-labelled executions based on the last definition.

3.2   Composing tm-Nets

Among the various operations which can be defined for the tm-nets, two are needed for the translation of a relatively simple TIMO process algebra. The first is a ternary *action* operation (Σ_1 then Σ_2 else Σ_3), and the other one a binary *parallel composition* ($\Sigma_1 | \Sigma_2$). We now assume that

$$\Sigma_i = (S_i^{flow} \uplus S_i^{loc}, Tr_i, \iota_i) \qquad (i = 1, 2, 3)$$

are unmarked tm-nets with disjoint sets of places and transitions (note that one can always rename the identities of the nodes of different tm-nets to make sure that this condition is satisfied).

action composition. The composition Σ_1 then Σ_2 else Σ_3 is defined if Σ_1 has a unique e-place, a unique x-place s_1, and a unique x'-place r_1. It is obtained in the following:

- Σ_1, Σ_2 and Σ_3 are put side by side.
- For every $s_2 \in {}^\circ\Sigma_2$, we create a new place s_2' with the status i and such that each arc a between s_i and $tr \in Tr_i$, for $i \in \{1, 2\}$, is replaced by an arc of the same kind (directed to or from, or undirected) and with the same annotation, between s_2' and tr. Then s_1 and the e-places of Σ_2 are deleted. The same is then done for r_1 and the e-places of Σ_3.
- Location places with the same label are 'merged' into a location place with the same label, and with all the arcs and annotations linking them to the transitions in Σ_1, Σ_2 and Σ_3 being inherited by the new location place.

parallel composition. The composition $\Sigma_1 | \Sigma_2$ is obtained through the following procedure:

- Σ_1 and Σ_2 are put side by side.
- Location places with the same label are merged as in the previous case.

4   From Networks of Located Processes to Nets

We translate the following well-formed network of located processes:

$$N \ = \ l_1[\![P_1]\!] \ | \ \ldots \ | \ l_n[\![P_n]\!]$$

The translation is carried out in the following three phases:

Phase I. For each $i \leq n$, we first translate P_i compositionally into $\mathbb{K}(P_i)$, assuming that actions are translated as follows:

$$\mathbb{K}(\alpha \text{ then } P \text{ else } Q) = \mathbb{K}(\alpha) \text{ then } \mathbb{K}(P) \text{ else } \mathbb{K}(Q) \ .$$

where $\mathbb{K}(\alpha)$ is given in Figure 1. Moreover, the translation for the terminated process 0 consists of just two isolated control flow places, one e-place and one x-place.

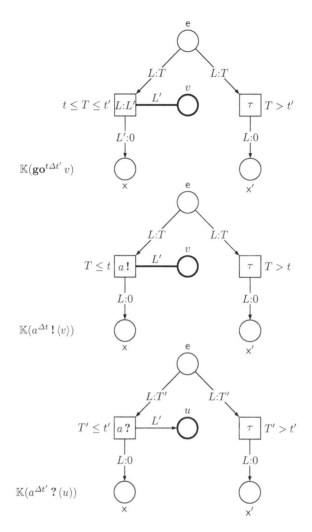

Fig. 1. Basic translations. Note that location places and read arcs are represented by thicker lines.

Phase II. We take the parallel composition of all the $\mathbb{K}(P_i)$'s, and then insert the initial marking, in the following way:

- into each e-labelled place originating from $\mathbb{K}(P_i)$ we insert a single token $l_i{:}0$,
- into each l-labelled location place (where l is a location rather than a location variable) we insert a single token l.

Phase III. For each pair of transitions, tr and tr', respectively labelled by a ! and a ? , we create a new synchronisation transition which inherits the connectivity of the both tr and tr'. The guard of the new transition is the conjunction of the guards of tr and tr', and the label is $L{:}a(L')$. After that all transitions labelled by $a!$ or $a?$ are deleted, yielding the result of the whole translation denoted by $\mathbb{PN}(N)$.

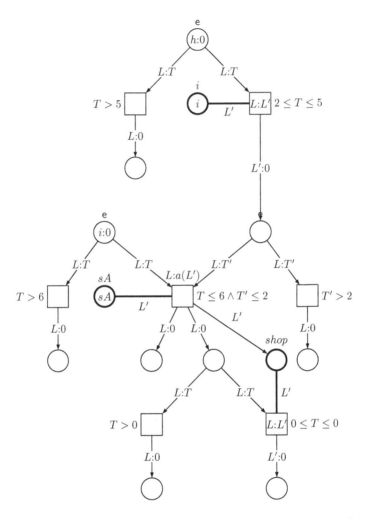

Fig. 2. An example of translation from TiMo to tm-nets. To improve readability, the exit places are not shown (they are all isolated and unmarked), and the labels of the internal places as well as τ labels are omitted.

Figure 2 shows the result of the three-phrase translation for a slightly simplified version of the running example:

$$h[\mathbf{go}^{2\Delta 5}\,i\,.\,(a^{\Delta 2}\,?\,(shop)\,\mathbf{then}\,\mathbf{go}^{0\Delta 0}\,shop\,\mathbf{else}\,0\,)]\mid i[a^{\Delta 6}\,!\,\langle sA\rangle]$$

The soundness of the above translation is given by the following result.

Theorem 1. *The transition system of* $\mathbb{PN}(N)$ *is strongly bisimilar in the sense of [18] to the transition system of* N.

As a consequence, the evolutions of process expressions and the corresponding tm-nets can simulate each other. It is therefore possible to conduct behavioural analyses for each of the two representations, and their results are applicable after suitable interpretations to the other representation as well. For example, by analysing the control flow tokens in a given marking of the tm-net representation, we can easily detect whether any process currently resides in a given network location.

The proof of Theorem 1 has similarities with the proof of a result of [12]. The main idea is to observe that the way translation from process expressions to Petri nets has been defined ensures that for every (individual or synchronised) action in the former, one can find a corresponding transition in the latter. It is then a matter of case by case analysis to conclude that two corresponding specifications simulate each other very closely. A notable difference is the fact that in the tm-net model the fact that the second branch of the action construct has been taken is signified by a τ-transition, whereas in the process algebra a rewriting is applied. Therefore, firing of such a τ-transition is not recorded in the labelled transition system generated by the tm-net semantics.

5 Conclusions and Related Work

Process algebras have long been used to model and study distributed concurrent systems in an algebraic framework. A number of highly successful models have been formulated within this framework, including ACP [4], CCS [18], CSP [16], distributed π-calculus [15], and mobile ambients [8]. However, none was able to capture properties of timing in distributed systems in a natural way. Process algebras with timing features were presented in [1,11,14,20], but without being able to express process mobility. Mobility can be expressed by other formalisms, such as the timed π-calculus [3], timed distributed π-calculus [10], and timed mobile ambients [2]. Timed distributed π-calculus uses a relative time of interaction given by timers, and a global clock which decrements the timers [10]. Timers are used to restrict the interaction between components, and both typing and timers are used to control the availability of resources. In the timed distributed π-calculus, the notion of space is flat. A more realistic account of physical distribution is obtained using a hierarchical representation of space, and this is given in [2] by the timed mobile ambients.

In this paper we introduced a simple TiMo process algebra where we have explicit mobility and can specify timers for the basic actions. We succeeded in translating finite TiMo specifications into the class of tm-nets which are high level Petri nets with time. In the future work, we plan to treat other salient features of distributed systems, including general data transfer and typing of channels.

Acknowledgement

We would like to thank the anonymous referees for their very helpful and constructive comments. This research was supported by the EC IST grant 511599 (RODIN), the NSFC project 60433010, and the CEEX grant Idei 402/2007.

References

1. Aceto, L., Murphy, D.: Timing and Causality in Process Algebra. Acta Informatica 33, 317–350 (1996)
2. Aman, B., Ciobanu, G.: Mobile Ambients with Timers and Types. In: Jones, C.B., Liu, Z., Woodcock, J. (eds.) ICTAC 2007. LNCS, vol. 4711, pp. 50–63. Springer, Heidelberg (2007)
3. Berger, M.: Basic Theory of Reduction Congruence forTwo Timed Asynchronous π-Calculi. In: Gardner, P., Yoshida, N. (eds.) CONCUR 2004. LNCS, vol. 3170, pp. 115–130. Springer, Heidelberg (2004)
4. Bergstra, J.A., Klop, J.W.: Process Theory based on Bisimulation Semantics. In: de Bakker, J.W., de Roever, W.-P., Rozenberg, G. (eds.) Linear Time, Branching Time and Partial Order in Logics and Models for Concurrency. LNCS, vol. 354, pp. 50–122. Springer, Heidelberg (1989)
5. Best, E., Fraczak, W., Hopkins, R.P., Klaudel, H., Pelz, E.: M-nets: an Algebra of High Level Petri Nets, with an Application to the Semantics of Concurrent Programming Languages. Acta Informatica 35, 813–857 (1998)
6. Best, E., Devillers, R., Koutny, M.: Petri Net Algebra. In: EATCS Monographs on TCS, Springer, Heidelberg (2001)
7. Bettini, L., et al.: The KLAIM Project: Theory and Practice. In: Priami, C. (ed.) GC 2003. LNCS, vol. 2874, Springer, Heidelberg (2003)
8. Cardelli, L., Gordon, A.: Mobile Ambients. Teoretical Computer Science 240, 170–213 (2000)
9. Christensen, S., Hansen, N.D.: Coloured Petri Nets Extended with Place Capacities, Test Arcs and Inhibitor Arcs. In: Ajmone Marsan, M. (ed.) ICATPN 1993. LNCS, vol. 691, Springer, Heidelberg (1993)
10. Ciobanu, G., Prisacariu, C.: Timers for Distributed Systems. Electronic Notes in Theoretical Computer Science 164, 81–99 (2006)
11. Corradini, F.: Absolute Versus Relative Time in Process Algebras. Information and Computation 156, 122–172 (2000)
12. Devillers, R., Klaudel, H., Koutny, M.: A Petri Net Semantics of a Simple Process Algebra for Mobility. Electronic Notes in Theoretical Computer Science 154, 71–94 (2006)
13. Devillers, R., Klaudel, H., Koutny, M., Pommereau, F.: Asynchronous Box Calculus. Fundamenta Informaticae 54, 295–344 (2003)
14. Gorrieri, R., Roccetti, M., Stancampiano, E.: A Theory of Processes with Durational Actions. Theoretical Computer Science 140, 73–94 (1995)
15. Hennessy, M., Regan, T.: A Process Algebra for Timed Systems. Information and Computation 117, 221–239 (1995)
16. Hoare, C.A.R.: Communicating Sequential Processes. Prentice Hall, Englewood Cliffs (1985)
17. Jensen, K., Rozenberg, G. (eds.): High-level Petri Nets. Theory and Application. Springer, Heidelberg (1991)

18. Milner, R.: Communication and Concurrency. Prentice Hall, Englewood Cliffs (1989)
19. Milner, R.: Communicating and Mobile Systems: the π-calculus. Cambridge University Press, Cambridge (1999)
20. Moller, F., Tofts, C.: A temporal Calculus of Communicating Systems. In: Groote, J.F., Baeten, J.C.M. (eds.) CONCUR 1991. LNCS, vol. 527, pp. 401–415. Springer, Heidelberg (1991)
21. Niaouris, A.: An Algebra of Petri Nets with Arc-Based Time Restrictions. In: Liu, Z., Araki, K. (eds.) ICTAC 2004. LNCS, vol. 3407, pp. 447–462. Springer, Heidelberg (2005)
22. Starke, P.: Some Properties of Timed Nets under the Earliest Firing Rule. In: Rozenberg, G. (ed.) APN 1989. LNCS, vol. 424, Springer, Heidelberg (1990)

A Model Checking Approach for Verifying COWS Specifications*

Alessandro Fantechi[1], Stefania Gnesi[2], Alessandro Lapadula[1], Franco Mazzanti[2],
Rosario Pugliese[1], and Francesco Tiezzi[1]

[1] Dipartimento di Sistemi e Informatica, Università degli Studi di Firenze
[2] Istituto di Scienza e Tecnologie dell'Informazione "A. Faedo", ISTI - CNR, Pisa

Abstract. We introduce a logical verification framework for checking functional properties of service-oriented applications formally specified using the service specification language COWS. The properties are described by means of SocL, a logic specifically designed to capture peculiar aspects of services. Service behaviours are abstracted in terms of Doubly Labelled Transition Systems, which are used as the interpretation domain for SocL formulae. We also illustrate the SocL model checker at work on a bank service scenario specified in COWS.

1 Introduction

Service-oriented computing (SOC) is an emerging paradigm for developing loosely coupled, interoperable, evolvable applications, which exploits the pervasiveness of the Internet and its related technologies. SOC systems deliver application functionality as services to either end-user applications or other services. Current software engineering technologies for SOC, however, remain at the descriptive level and do not support analytical tools for checking that services enjoy desirable properties and do not manifest unexpected behaviors. On the other end, logics have been since long proved able to reason about such complex software systems as SOC applications, because they only provide abstract specifications of these systems and can thus be used for describing system properties rather than system behaviours. Indeed, in the last twenty years, several modal, temporal and, more recently, spatial logics have been proposed as suitable means for specifying properties of concurrent and distributed systems owing to their ability of expressing notions of necessity, possibility, eventuality, etc.

In this paper, we introduce a logical verification framework for checking functional properties of services by abstracting away from the computational contexts in which they are operating. In what follows, services are abstractly considered as entities capable of accepting requests, delivering corresponding responses and, on-demand, cancelling requests. Thus, we will say that a service is

1. *available:* if it is always capable to accept a request.
2. *reliable:* if, when a request is accepted, a final successful response is guaranteed.
3. *responsive:* if it always guarantees a response to each received request.
4. *broken:* if, after accepting a request, it does not provide the (expected) response.

---

* This work has been partially funded by the EU project SENSORIA (IST-2005-016004).

J. Fiadeiro and P. Inverardi (Eds.): FASE 2008, LNCS 4961, pp. 230–245, 2008.
© Springer-Verlag Berlin Heidelberg 2008

5. *unavailable:* if it refuses all requests.
6. *fair:* if it is possible to cancel a request before the response.
7. *non-ambiguous:* if, after accepting a request, it provides no more than one response.
8. *sequential:* if, after accepting a request, no other requests may be accepted before giving a response.
9. *asynchronous:* if, after accepting a request, other requests may be accepted before giving a response.
10. *non-persistent:* if, after accepting a request, no other requests can be accepted.

Albeit not exhaustive, this list contains many common properties that express desirable attributes of services and SOC applications (see, e.g., the SENSORIA ontology [5] or [2]).

To formalize the properties above, we introduce SocL, a logic specifically designed to capture peculiar aspects of services. SocL is a variant of the logic UCTL [3], originally introduced to express properties of UML statecharts. UCTL and SocL have many commonalities: they share the same temporal logic operators, they are both state and event based branching-time logics, they are both interpreted on Doubly Labelled Transition Systems (L^2TSs, [9]) by exploiting the same on-the-fly model-checking engine. The two logics mainly differ for the syntax and semantics of state-predicates and action-formulae, and for the fact that SocL also permits to specify parametric formulae.

As specification language for the services and SOC applications of interest we use COWS (*Calculus for Orchestration of Web Services*, [14]), a recently proposed process calculus for specifying and combining services, while modelling their dynamic behaviour. The design of the calculus has been influenced by the principles underlying WS-BPEL [16], an OASIS standard language for orchestration of web services, and in fact COWS supports service instances with shared states, allows a same process to play more than one partner role and permits programming stateful sessions by correlating different service interactions. COWS has also taken advantage of previous work on process calculi. Indeed, it combines in an original way constructs and features borrowed from well-known process calculi, e.g. not-binding input activities, asynchronous communication, polyadic synchronization, pattern matching, protection, delimited receiving and killing activities, while however resulting different from any of them.

To check if a COWS term enjoys some abstract properties expressed as SocL formulae, the following four steps must be performed. Firstly, the semantics of the COWS term is defined by using a Labelled Transition System (LTS). Secondly, this LTS is transformed into an L^2TS by labelling each state with the set of actions the COWS term is able to perform immediately from that state. Thirdly, by applying a set of application-dependent abstraction rules over the actions, the concrete L^2TS is abstracted into a simpler L^2TS. Finally, the SocL formulae are checked over this abstract L^2TS. To assist the verification process, we have developed CMC, an on-the-fly model checker for SocL formulae over L^2TS.

The rest of the paper is organized as follows. Section 2 introduces SocL, while Section 3 presents syntax and main features of COWS; this is done in a step-by-step fashion while modelling a bank service scenario, used for illustration purposes in the rest of the paper. Section 4 demonstrates how to transform the original LTS of a COWS term into an abstract L^2TS by using suitable abstraction rules. Section 5 presents CMC and illustrates the results of the verification of the bank service scenario. Section 6 touches upon related work and directions for future works.

2   The Logic SocL

In this section, we introduce the *action* and *state-based* branching time temporal logic SocL that is interpreted over L^2TSs [9]. SocL combines the action paradigm, classically used to describe systems via LTS, with predicates that are true over states, as usually exploited when using Kripke structures as semantic model. The advantage of *action and state-based* logics lies in the ease of expressiveness of properties that in pure action-based or pure state-based logics can be quite cumbersome to write down. Indeed in recent years, several logics that allow one to express both action-based and state-based properties have been introduced, for many different purposes (see for example [3,7,8,6,13]).

Before presenting the syntax of SocL, we report some basic definitions and notations used in the sequel.

Definition 1 (Doubly Labelled Transition System, L^2TS). *An L^2TS is a tuple* $\langle Q, q_0, Act, R, AP, L \rangle$, *where:*

- *Q is a set of states;*
- *$q_0 \in Q$ is the initial state;*
- *Act is a finite set of observable events (actions) with α ranging over 2^{Act} and ϵ denoting the empty set;*
- *$R \subseteq Q \times 2^{Act} \times Q$ is the transition relation[1]; instead of $(q, \alpha, q') \in R$ we may also write $q \xrightarrow{\alpha} q'$.*
- *AP is a set of atomic propositions with π ranging over AP;*
- *$L : Q \longrightarrow 2^{AP}$ is a labelling function that maps each state in Q to a subset of AP.*

Basically, an L^2TS is an LTS (defined as the quadruple $\langle Q, q_0, Act, R \rangle$), extended with a labelling function from states to sets of atomic propositions. By means of an L^2TS, a system can be characterized by states and state changes and by the events (actions) that are performed when moving from one state to another.

In the interpretation domain of SocL, *Act* and *AP* are defined as follows.

- *Act* is a finite set of observable actions, ranged over by *a*, such as: *request(i, c)*, *response(i, c)*, *cancel(i, c)* and *fail(i, c)*, where the name *i* indicates the interaction to which the operation performed by a service belongs[2], and *c* denotes a tuple of correlation values that identifies a particular invocation of the operation. The meaning of actions is as follows: *request(i, c)* indicates that the performed operation corresponds to the initial request of the interaction *i* and its invocation is identified by the correlation tuple *c*; similarly, *response(i, c)*, *cancel(i, c)* and *fail(i, c)* characterise operations that correspond to a response, a cancellation and a failure notification, respectively, of the interaction *i*.

---

[1] Notice that this definition differs from the classical one [9] for the labelling of the transitions: we label transitions by sets of events rather than by single (un)observable events. This extension allows to model the occurrence of more than one action at the same time. Unobservable actions are rendered by the empty set.

[2] See Section 5 for an explanation of the mapping between service operations and interactions.

- *AP* is a finite set of atomic propositions, parameterized by interactions and correlation tuples, like *accepting_request(i)* and *accepting_cancel(i, c)*, that can be true over a state of an L^2TS.

To define the auxiliary logic of observable actions $\mathcal{AF}(Act\$)$, we extend *Act* to include the possibility that the correlation tuples refer variables. Let *var* be a correlation variable name, we use $\$var$ to indicate the binder of the occurrences $\%var$. For example, *request(i, $var)* denotes a request action for the interaction *i* that is uniquely identified through the correlation variable $\$var$. This way, subsequent actions, corresponding e.g. to response to that specific request, can unambiguously refer it through $\%var$. We denote the extended set by $Act\$$ and let *a$* to range over it. We will use *a%* to range over actions of $Act\$$ whose correlation tuple does not contain variables of the form $\$var$. Note that $Act \subset Act\$$.

Definition 2 (Action formulae). *Given a set of observable actions Act$, the language $\mathcal{AF}(Act\$)$ of the action formulae on Act$ is defined as follows:*

$$\gamma ::= a\$ \mid \chi \qquad\qquad \chi ::= tt \mid a\% \mid \tau \mid \neg\chi \mid \chi \wedge \chi$$

As usual, *ff* abbreviates $\neg tt$ and $\chi \vee \chi'$ abbreviates $\neg(\neg\chi \wedge \neg\chi')$.

The introduction of variables to express correlation requires the notion of *substitution*, that in its turn requires that of pattern-matching function.

Definition 3 (Substitutions and the pattern-matching function)

- Substitutions, *ranged over by ρ, are functions mapping correlation variables to values and are written as collections of pairs of the form var/val.*
- *The empty substitution is denoted by $\emptyset$.*
- *Application of substitution ρ to a formula ϕ, written $\phi \cdot \rho$, has the effect of replacing every occurrence $\%var$ in ϕ with val, for each var/val $\in \rho$.*
- *The partial function $m(\_, \_)$ from pairs of actions to substitutions, that permits performing pattern-matching, is defined by the following rules:*

$$m(request(i, c), request(i, c')) = m(c, c') \qquad m(\$var, val) = \{var/val\}$$
$$m(response(i, c), response(i, c')) = m(c, c') \qquad m(val, val) = \emptyset$$
$$m(cancel(i, c), cancel(i, c')) = m(c, c') \qquad m(fail(i, c), fail(i, c')) = m(c, c')$$
$$m((e_1 \cdot c_1), (e_2 \cdot c_2)) = m(e_1, e_2) \cup m(c_1, c_2)$$

where notation $e \cdot c$ stands for a tuple with first element e.

Definition 4 (Action formulae semantics). *The satisfaction relation $\models$ for action formulae is defined over sets of observable actions in Act$ and over a substitution.*

- $\alpha \models a\$ \rhd \rho$ *iff* $\exists! b \in \alpha$ *such that* $m(a\$, b) = \rho$;
- $\alpha \models \chi \rhd \emptyset$ *iff* $\alpha \models \chi$, *where the relation* $\alpha \models \chi$ *is defined as follows:*
  - $\alpha \models tt$ *holds always;*
  - $\alpha \models a\%$ *iff* $\exists! b \in \alpha$ *such that* $m(a\%, b) = \emptyset$;

- $\alpha \models \tau$ *iff* $\alpha = \epsilon$;
- $\alpha \models \neg\chi$ *iff not* $\alpha \models \chi$;
- $\alpha \models \chi \wedge \chi'$ *iff* $\alpha \models \chi$ *and* $\alpha \models \chi'$.

The notation $\alpha \models \gamma \triangleright \rho$ means: the formula γ is satisfied over the set of observable actions α (only) under substitution ρ. Notably, in the above definition we require that an observable action $a\$$ or $a\%$ matches only and only one action in α. This is a consequence of the assumption that inside a single evolution step two or more actions with the same type and interaction do not occur. Thus, e.g., the transition label $\{request(i, \langle 1 \rangle), request(i, \langle 2 \rangle)\}$ never appears in SocL interpretation models. Notice also that actions containing correlation variable occurrences like $\%var$ (that have not yet been replaced by values) cannot be assigned a semantics; indeed, the case $\alpha \models a\%$ requires that $\mathsf{m}(a\%, b) = \emptyset$ that, according to the rules defining the pattern-matching function, means that $a\% \in Act$, i.e. $a\%$ does not contain variables.

Definition 5 (SocL syntax). *The syntax of SocL formulae is defined as follows:*

| (state formulae) | ϕ | $::=$ | $true$ | $\mid$ | π | $\mid$ | $\neg\phi$ | $\mid$ | $\phi \wedge \phi'$ | $\mid$ | $E\Psi$ | $\mid$ | $A\Psi$ |
| (path formulae) | Ψ | $::=$ | $X_\gamma\phi$ | $\mid$ | $\phi_\chi U \phi'$ | $\mid$ | $\phi_\chi U_\gamma \phi'$ | $\mid$ | $\phi_\chi W \phi'$ | $\mid$ | $\phi_\chi W_\gamma \phi'$ |

We comment on salient points of the grammar above. $\pi \in AP$ are atomic propositions, A and E are *path quantifiers*, and X, U and W are indexed *next*, *until* and *weak until* operators drawn on from those firstly introduced in [9]. The next operator says that in the next state of the path, reached by an action satisfying γ, the formula ϕ holds; the meaning of the until operators is that ϕ' holds at the current or at a future state (reached by an action satisfying γ or without any specific behaviour), and ϕ has to hold until that state is reached and the actions executed satisfy χ or are unobservable; finally, the weak until operators hold either if the corresponding strong until operators hold or if for all states of the path the formula ϕ holds (by executing actions satisfying χ or unobservable). A peculiarity of SocL is that the satisfaction relation of the next and until operators may define a substitution which is propagated to subformulae. Notably, in the left side of until operators we use χ instead of γ, to avoid formulae like the following $\phi_{request(i,\langle \$v \rangle)} U_\gamma \phi'$, where the satisfaction relation for $request(i, \langle \$v \rangle)$ could produce a different substitution for each state that comes before the one where ϕ' holds.

To define the semantics of SocL, we first formalise the notion of *path* in an L^2TS.

Definition 6 (Path). *Let $\langle Q, q_0, Act, R, AP, L \rangle$ be an L^2TS and let $q \in Q$.*

- *σ is a path from q if $\sigma = q$ (the empty path from q) or σ is a (possibly infinite) sequence $(q_0, \alpha_1, q_1)(q_1, \alpha_2, q_2) \cdots$ with $q_0 = q$ and $(q_{i-1}, \alpha_i, q_i) \in R$ for all $i > 0$.*
- *The concatenation of paths σ_1 and σ_2, denoted by $\sigma_1\sigma_2$, is a partial operation, defined only if σ_1 is finite and its final state coincides with the first state of σ_2.*
- *If $\sigma = (q_0, \alpha_1, q_1)(q_1, \alpha_2, q_2) \cdots$ then the ith state in σ, i.e. q_i, is denoted by $\sigma(i)$.*
- *We write $path(q)$ for the set of all paths from q.*

Definition 7 (SocL semantics). *The satisfaction relation of closed SocL formulae, i.e. formulae without unbound variables, over an L^2TS is defined as follows:*

- *$q \models true$ holds always;*
- *$q \models \pi$ iff $\pi \in L(q)$;*

- $q \models \neg\phi$ iff not $q \models \phi$;
- $q \models \phi \wedge \phi'$ iff $q \models \phi$ and $q \models \phi'$;
- $q \models E\Psi$ iff $\exists \sigma \in path(q)$ such that $\sigma \models \Psi$;
- $q \models A\Psi$ iff $\forall \sigma \in path(q)$ $\sigma \models \Psi$;
- $\sigma \models X_\gamma\phi$ iff $\sigma = (q, \alpha, q')\sigma'$, $\alpha \models \gamma \triangleright \rho$, and $q' \models \phi \cdot \rho$;
- $\sigma \models \phi\,_\chi U\phi'$ iff there exists $j \geq 0$ such that $\sigma(j) \models \phi'$ and for all $0 \leq i < j$:
    $\sigma = \sigma'(\sigma(i), \alpha_{i+1}, \sigma(i+1))\sigma''$ implies $\sigma(i) \models \phi$ and $\alpha_{i+1} = \epsilon$ or $\alpha_{i+1} \models \chi$;
- $\sigma \models \phi\,_\chi U_\gamma\phi'$ iff there exists $j \geq 1$ such that $\sigma = \sigma'(\sigma(j-1), \alpha_j, \sigma(j))\sigma''$
    and $\alpha_j \models \gamma \triangleright \rho$ and $\sigma(j) \models \phi' \cdot \rho$ and $\sigma(j-1) \models \phi$, and for all $0 < i < j$:
    $\sigma = \sigma'_i(\sigma(i-1), \alpha_i, \sigma(i))\sigma''_i$ implies $\sigma(i-1) \models \phi$, and $\alpha_i = \epsilon$ or $\alpha_i \models \chi$;
- $\sigma \models \phi\,_\chi W\phi'$ iff either
    there exists $j \geq 0$ such that $\sigma(j) \models \phi'$ and for all $0 \leq i < j$:
    $\sigma = \sigma'(\sigma(i), \alpha_{i+1}, \sigma(i+1))\sigma''$ implies $\sigma(i) \models \phi$ and $\alpha_{i+1} = \epsilon$ or $\alpha_{i+1} \models \chi$
    or for all $0 \leq i$:
    $\sigma = \sigma'(\sigma(i), \alpha_{i+1}, \sigma(i+1))\sigma''$ implies $\sigma(i) \models \phi$, and $\alpha_{i+1} = \epsilon$ or $\alpha_{i+1} \models \chi$;
- $\sigma \models \phi\,_\chi W_\gamma\phi'$ iff either
    there exists $j \geq 1$ such that $\sigma = \sigma'(\sigma(j-1), \alpha_j, \sigma(j))\sigma''$ and
    $\alpha_j \models \gamma \triangleright \rho$ and $\sigma(j) \models \phi' \cdot \rho$ and $\sigma(j-1) \models \phi$, and for all $0 < i < j$:
    $\sigma = \sigma'_i(\sigma(i-1), \alpha_i, \sigma(i))\sigma''_i$ implies $\sigma(i-1) \models \phi$, and $\alpha_i = \epsilon$ or $\alpha_i \models \chi$
    or for all $0 \leq i$:
    $\sigma = \sigma'_i(\sigma(i-1), \alpha_i, \sigma(i))\sigma''_i$ implies $\sigma(i-1) \models \phi$, and $\alpha_{i+1} = \epsilon$ or $\alpha_{i+1} \models \chi$.

Other useful operators can be derived as usual. In particular, the ones that we use in the sequel are: *false* stands for $\neg true$; $< \gamma > \phi$ stands for $EX_\gamma\phi$; $[\gamma]\phi$ stands for $\neg < \gamma > \neg\phi$; $EF\phi$ stands for $E(true\,_{tt}U\phi)$; $EF_\gamma true$ stands for $E(true\,_{tt}U_\gamma true)$; $AF_\gamma true$ stands for $A(true\,_{tt}U_\gamma true)$; $AG\phi$ stands for $\neg EF\neg\phi$.

We end this section by showing how the abstract properties presented in the Introduction can be expressed as generic patterns in SocL. For the sake of readability, here we consider correlation tuples composed of only one element and use notations $v and %v instead of the more cumbersome notations $\langle \$v \rangle$ and $\langle \%v \rangle$, respectively.

1. *Available* service: $AG(accepting\_request(i))$.
   This formula means that in every state the service may accept a request; a weaker interpretation of service availability, meaning that the server accepts a request infinitely often, is given by the formula $AGAF(accepting\_request(i))$.
2. *Reliable* service: $AG[request(i, \$v)]AF_{response(i,\%v)}\,true$.
   Notably, the response belongs to the same interaction i of the accepted request and they are correlated by the variable v.
3. *Responsive* service: $AG[request(i, \$v)]\,AF_{response(i,\%v)\vee fail(i,\%v)}\,true$.
4. *Broken* service: $\neg AG[request(i, \$v)]\,AF_{response(i,\%v)\vee fail(i,\%v)}\,true$.
   This formula means that the service is *temporarily broken*; instead, the formula $AG[request(i, \$v)]\neg EF_{response(i,\%v)\vee fail(i,\%v)}\,true$ means that the service is *permanently broken*.
5. *Unavailable* service: $AG[request(i, \$v)]\,AF_{fail(i,\%v)}\,true$.
6. *Fair* service:
   $AG[request(i, \$v)]\,A(accepting\_cancel(i, \%v)\,_{tt}W_{response(i,\%v)\vee fail(i,\%v)}true)$.

Table 1. COWS syntax

$s ::=$ **kill**(k) | $u \cdot u'!\bar{e}$ | $\sum_{i=0}^{l} p_i \cdot o_i?\bar{w}_i.s_i$	(kill, invoke, receive-guarded sum)
| $s \mid s$ | $\{s\}$ | $[d] s$ | $* s$	(parallel, protection, delimitation, replication)

This formula means that the server is ready to accept a cancellation required by the client (fairness towards the client); instead the formula $AG[response(i, \$v)] \neg EF < cancel(i, \%v) > true$ means that the server cannot accept a cancellation after responding to a request (fairness towards the server).

7. *Non-ambiguous* service:
   $AG[request(i, \$v)] \neg EF < response(i, \%v) > EF < response(i, \%v) > true$.
8. *Sequential* service:
   $AG[request(i, \$v)] A(\neg accepting\_request(i) {}_{tt} U_{response(i,\%v)\lor fail(i,\%v)} true)$.
9. *Asynchronous* service:
   $AG[request(i, \$v)] EF < response(i, \%v) \lor fail(i, \%v) > true$.
10. *Non-persistent* service: $AG[request(i, \$v)] AG \neg accepting\_request(i)$.

The SocL formulation of the properties 1–10 shows that their natural language description can sometimes be interpreted in different ways: hence, formalization within the logic enforces a choice among different interpretations.

3   COWS: Calculus for Orchestration of Web Services

In this section, we report the syntax of COWS and explain the semantics of its primitives in a step-by-step fashion while modelling a bank service scenario, that will be used in the rest of the paper for illustration purposes. Due to lack of space, here we only provide an informal account of the semantics of COWS and refer the interested reader to [14,15] for a formal presentation, for examples illustrating its peculiarities and expressiveness, and for comparisons with other process-based and orchestration formalisms.

The syntax of COWS is presented in Table 1. It is parameterized by three countable and pairwise disjoint sets: the set of *(killer) labels* (ranged over by $k, k', \ldots$), the set of *values* (ranged over by $v, v', \ldots$) and the set of 'write once' *variables* (ranged over by $x, y, \ldots$). The set of values is left unspecified; however, we assume that it includes the set of *names*, ranged over by $n, m, o, p, \ldots$, mainly used to represent partners and operations. The language is also parameterized by a set of *expressions*, ranged over by e, whose exact syntax is deliberately omitted. We just assume that expressions contain, at least, values and variables, but do not include killer labels (that, hence, are *not* communicable values).

We use w to range over values and variables, u to range over names and variables, and d to range over killer labels, names and variables. Notation $\bar{\cdot}$ stands for tuples of objects, e.g. $\bar{x}$ is a compact notation for denoting the tuple of variables $\langle x_1, \ldots, x_n \rangle$ (with $n \geq 0$ and $x_i \neq x_j$ for each $i \neq j$). In the sequel, we shall use $+$ to abbreviate binary choice and write $[d_1, \ldots, d_n] s$ in place of $[d_1] \ldots [d_n] s$. We will write $Z \triangleq W$ to assign a symbolic name Z to the term W.

The COWS specification of the bank service is composed of two persistent subservices: *BankInterface*, that is publicly invocable by customers, and *CreditRating*, that is an 'internal' service that can only interact with *BankInterface*. The scenario also involves the processes $Client_1$ and $Client_2$ that model requests for charging the customer's credit card with some amount. Thus, the COWS term representing the scenario is

$$[o_{check}, o_{checkOK}, o_{checkFail}] \, (\, * \, BankInterface \mid * \, CreditRating \,) \mid Client_1 \mid Client_2$$

The main operator is the *parallel composition* $\_ \mid \_$ that allows the different components to be concurrently executed and to interact with each other. The *delimitation* operator $[\_]\_$ is used here to declare that o_{check}, $o_{checkOK}$ and $o_{checkFail}$ are (operation) names known to the bank services, and only to them. Moreover, the *replication* operator $*\_$, that spawns in parallel as many copies of its argument term as necessary, is exploited to model the fact that *BankInterface* and *CreditRating* can create multiple instances to serve several requests simultaneously. Now, *BankInterface* and *CreditRating* are defined as follows:

$$BankInterface \triangleq [x_{cust}, x_{cc}, x_{amount}, x_{id}]$$
$$p_{bank} \cdot o_{charge}?\langle x_{cust}, x_{cc}, x_{amount}, x_{id} \rangle.$$
$$(\, p_{bank} \cdot o_{check}!\langle x_{id}, x_{cc}, x_{amount} \rangle$$
$$\mid p_{bank} \cdot o_{checkOK}?\langle x_{id} \rangle. \, x_{cust} \cdot o_{chargeOK}!\langle x_{id} \rangle$$
$$+ \, p_{bank} \cdot o_{checkFail}?\langle x_{id} \rangle. \, x_{cust} \cdot o_{chargeFail}!\langle x_{id} \rangle \,)$$

$$CreditRating \triangleq [x_{id}, x_{cc}, x_a]$$
$$p_{bank} \cdot o_{check}?\langle x_{id}, x_{cc}, x_a \rangle.$$
$$[p, o] \, (\, p \cdot o!\langle \rangle \mid p \cdot o?\langle \rangle. \, p_{bank} \cdot o_{checkOK}!\langle x_{id} \rangle$$
$$+ \, p \cdot o?\langle \rangle. \, p_{bank} \cdot o_{checkFail}!\langle x_{id} \rangle \,)$$

We only comment on *BankInterface*; *CreditRating* is similar and its description is omitted. The *receive-guarded prefix* operator $p_{bank} \cdot o_{charge}?\langle x_{cust}, x_{cc}, x_{amount}, x_{id} \rangle._{-}$ expresses that each interaction with the bank starts with a *receive* activity of the form $p_{bank} \cdot o_{charge}?\langle x_{cust}, x_{cc}, x_{amount}, x_{id} \rangle$ corresponding to reception of a request emitted by $Client_1$ or $Client_2$. Receives, together with *invokes*, written as $p \cdot o!\langle e_1, \ldots, e_m \rangle$, are the basic communication activities provided by COWS. Besides input parameters and sent values, they indicate an *endpoint*, i.e. a pair composed of a partner name p and an operation name o, through which communication should occur. $p \cdot o$ can be interpreted as a specific implementation of operation o provided by the service identified by the logic name p. An inter-service communication takes place when the arguments of a receive and of a concurrent invoke along the same endpoint do match, and causes substitution of the variables arguments of the receive with the corresponding values arguments of the invoke (within the scope of variables declarations). For example, variables x_{cust}, x_{cc}, x_{amount} and x_{id}, declared local to *BankInterface* by means of the delimitation operator, are initialized by the receive leading the charge activity with data provided by either $Client_1$ or $Client_2$.

Once prompted by a request, *BankInterface* creates one specific instance to serve that request and is immediately ready to concurrently serve other requests. Notably, each instance uses the *choice* operator $\_ + \_$ and exploits communication with *CreditRating* on 'internal' operations o_{check}, $o_{checkOK}$ and $o_{checkFail}$ to model a conditional choice

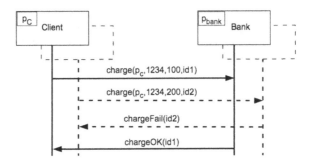

Fig. 1. Graphical representation of the bank scenario

(for the sake of simplicity, the choice between approving or not a request for charging the credit card is here completely non-deterministic). Thus, if after some invocations the service receives a message along the endpoints $p_{bank} \cdot o_{checkOk}$ or $p_{bank} \cdot o_{checkFail}$, a certain number of service instances could be able to accept it. However, the message is routed to the proper instance by exploiting the customer data stored in the variable x_{id} as a correlation value.

To illustrate, define the customer processes as follows:

$$Client_1 \triangleq p_{bank} \cdot o_{charge}!\langle p_C, 1234, 100, id_1 \rangle \mid p_C \cdot o_{chargeOK}?\langle id_1 \rangle + p_C \cdot o_{chargeFail}?\langle id_1 \rangle$$

$$Client_2 \triangleq p_{bank} \cdot o_{charge}!\langle p_C, 1234, 200, id_2 \rangle \mid p_C \cdot o_{chargeOK}?\langle id_2 \rangle + p_C \cdot o_{chargeFail}?\langle id_2 \rangle$$

The processes perform two requests in parallel for charging the credit card 1234 with the amounts 100 and 200. Two different correlation values, id_1 and id_2, are used to correlate the response messages to the corresponding requests. A customized UML sequence diagram depicting a possible run is shown in Figure 1.

The specification of the scenario does not exploit all COWS operators. In particular, the remaining two operators are especially useful when modelling fault handling and compensation behaviours, that, for the sake of simplicity, are not considered in this paper. In fact, *kill* activities of the form **kill**(k), where k is a killer label, can be used to force termination of all unprotected parallel terms inside the enclosing $[k]$, that stops the killing effect. Kill activities run *eagerly* with respect to the other parallel activities but critical code, such as e.g. fault/compensation handlers, can be protected from the effect of a forced termination by using the *protection* operator $\{\_\}$.

4   L²TS Semantics for COWS Terms

The semantics of COWS associates an LTS to a COWS term. We have seen instead that SocL is interpreted over L²TSs. We need therefore to transform the LTS associated to a COWS term into an L²TS by defining a proper labelling for the states of the LTS. This is done by labelling each state with the set of actions that each active subterm of the COWS term would be able to perform immediately. Of course, the transformation preserves the structure of the original COWS LTS. For example, the concrete L²TS obtained by applying this transformation to the bank scenario is shown in Figure 2.

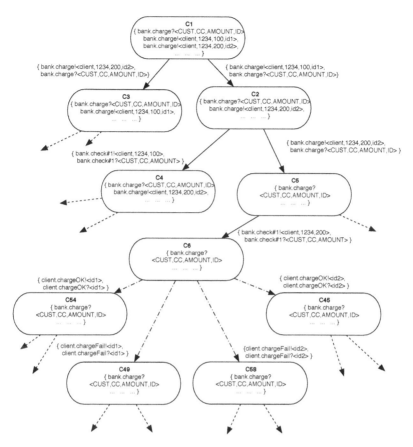

Fig. 2. Excerpt of the L²TS for the bank scenario with concrete labels

Both in the original LTS and in the L²TS obtained as explained before, transitions
are labelled by 'concrete' actions, i.e. those actions occurring in the COWS term. Notice also that labels corresponding to communications retain all information contained
in the two synchronising invoke and receive activities. However, since we are interested in verifying abstract properties of services, such as those shown in Section 2,
we need to abstract away from unnecessary details by transforming concrete actions in
'abstract' ones. This is done by applying a set of suitable abstraction rules to the concrete actions. Specifically, these rules replace concrete labels on the transitions with actions belonging to the set *Act*, i.e. *request(i, c)*, *response(i, c)*, *cancel(i, c)* and *fail(i, c)*,
that better represent their semantics meaning. This way, different concrete actions can
be mapped into the same SocL action. Moreover, the rules replace the concrete labels on the states with predicates belonging to the set *AP*, e.g. *accepting_request(i)*
and *accepting_cancel(i, c)*, that say if the service is able to accept a specific request
or a cancellation of a previous request. The transformation only involves the concrete
actions we want to observe. Indeed, concrete actions that are not replaced by their abstract counterparts cannot be observed.

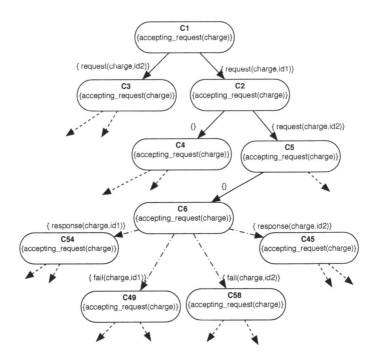

Fig. 3. Excerpt of the COWS specification of the banking example (abstract model)

For example, the abstract L^2TS of the bank scenario shown in Figure 3 is obtained by applying to the concrete L^2TS of Figure 2 the following abstraction rules:

$$
\begin{aligned}
Action: \ & charge\langle *, *, *, \$1\rangle \ && \rightarrow \ request(charge, \langle \$1\rangle) \\
Action: \ & chargeOK\langle \$1\rangle \ && \rightarrow \ response(charge, \langle \$1\rangle) \\
Action: \ & chargeFail\langle \$1\rangle \ && \rightarrow \ fail(charge, \langle \$1\rangle) \\
State: \ & charge \ && \rightarrow \ accepting\_request(charge)
\end{aligned}
$$

The first rule prescribes that whenever a concrete action $bank.charge!\langle v_1, v_2, v_3, v_4\rangle$ matching $charge\langle *, *, *, \$1\rangle$ and producing the substitution $\{\$1/v_4\}$ occurs in the label of a transition, then it is replaced by the abstract SocL action $request(charge, \langle v_4\rangle)$. Variables "$\$n$" (with n natural number) can be used to defined generic (templates of) abstraction rules. Also the wildcard " $*$ " can be used for increasing flexibility. The last rule applies to concrete labels of states instead of transitions and acts similarly. Notably, (internal) communications between the bank subservices are not transformed and, thus, become unobservable.

Of course, the set of "$Action:$" and "$State:$" rules is not defined once and for all, but is application-dependent and, thus, must be defined from time to time. Indeed, it embeds information, like the intended semantics of each action and the predicates on the states, that are not coded into the COWS specification.

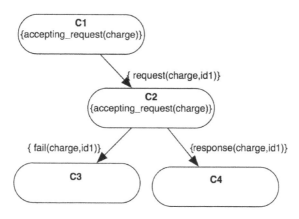

Fig. 4. An example of L^2TS

5 Model Checking COWS Specifications

To assist the verification process of SocL formulae over L^2TS, we are developing CMC, an efficient model checker for SocL that can be used to verify properties of services specified in COWS. A prototypical version of CMC can be experimented via a web interface available at the address http://fmt.isti.cnr.it/cmc/.

CMC is implemented by exploiting an on-the-fly algorithm which permits to achieve in many cases the 'linear' complexity typical of on-the-fly model checking algorithms. Indeed, depending on the formula to be checked, only a fragment of the overall state space might need to be generated and analyzed in order to produce the correct result [4,11,17]. Moreover, in case of parametric formulae, only a subset of their possible instantiations will be generated as requested by the on-the-fly evaluation.

The basic idea behind CMC is that, given a state of an L^2TS, the validity of a SocL formula on that state can be established by checking the satisfiability of the state predicates, by analyzing the transitions allowed in that state, and by establishing the validity of some subformula in some of the next reachable states. This schema has been extended with appropriate data-collection activities in order to be able to produce, in the end, also a clear and detailed explanation of the returned results (i.e. a *counterexample*), and with appropriate formula instantiation activities in order to deal with parametric formulae.

To show the peculiarity of our framework with respect to parametric formulae evaluation, we illustrate the process of establishing the satisfiability of the SocL formula

$$\phi = EX_{request(charge,\langle \$id \rangle)} AX_{response(charge,\langle \%id \rangle)} true$$

on the abstract L^2TS of Figure 4. We have therefore to check if the following holds:

$$C1 \models EX_{request(charge,\langle \$id \rangle)} AX_{response(charge,\langle \%id \rangle)} true$$

Table 2. Verification results

Property	Result	States
Available	TRUE	274
Reliable	FALSE	37
Responsive	TRUE	274
Permanently Broken	FALSE	12
Temporarily Broken	FALSE	274
Unavailable	FALSE	18

Property	Result	States
Fair 1	FALSE	3
Fair 2	TRUE	274
Non-ambiguous	TRUE	274
Sequential	FALSE	3
Asynchronous	TRUE	274
Non-persistent	FALSE	3

Thus, the model checking algorithm tries to find a next state reachable with an action matching $request(charge, \langle \$id \rangle)$. Since $C1 \xrightarrow{request(charge,\langle id1 \rangle)} C2$, then, for the semantics of action formulae, we have:

$$request(charge, \langle id1 \rangle) \models request(charge, \langle \$id \rangle) \rhd \rho$$

where the produced substitution ρ is

$$\rho = \mathsf{m}\,(request(charge, \langle \$id \rangle), request(charge, \langle id1 \rangle)) = \mathsf{m}\,(\$id, id1) = \{id/id1\}$$

It remains then to check if $C2 \models AX_{response(charge,\langle \%id \rangle)} \, true \cdot \rho$ that is, by applying the substitution, if

$$C2 \models AX_{response(charge,\langle id1 \rangle)} \, true$$

Since $C2 \xrightarrow{response(charge,\langle id1 \rangle)} C4$, by a trivial matching between the action formula and the action on the transition, we get that the subformula $X_{response(charge,\langle \%id \rangle)} \, true \cdot \rho$ is satisfied on this path. But if we take the other path, i.e. $C2 \xrightarrow{fail(charge,\langle id1 \rangle)} C3$, we fail to find a matching, hence the same subformula is not satisfied on this path. Therefore, since the subformula is under a universal quantification, we conclude that ϕ is not satisfied.

Coming back to the abstract properties introduced in Section 1 – and formalized in SocL in Section 2 – the results of the verification on the bank service scenario are summarized in Table 2, where we also report the number of states considered during the evaluation. The instantiation of the generic patterns of formulae of Section 2 over the bank service has been obtained by just replacing any occurrence of i with $charge$. Thus, e.g., the formula predicating responsiveness of the bank service becomes:

$$AG\,[request(charge, \$v)]\,AF_{response(charge,\%v) \lor fail(charge,\%v)} \, true$$

The results show that the bank service exhibits the desired characteristics to be responsive, not broken, available, non ambiguous, and to admit parallel and iterated requests. Reliability is a too strong request for our service which can explicitly fail: indeed, responsiveness is sufficient to guarantee the expected behavior. Fairness properties are not significant for this service, that does not offer the possibility to cancel a request. Finally, the service is persistent, and we can understand why just looking at the counterexample generated when verifying the corresponding property:

```
-------------------------------------------
The formula:  AG  [ request ] AG  not (accepting_request(charge))
   is FOUND_FALSE in State C1
because
 the formula:  [ request ] AG  not (accepting_request(charge))
   is FOUND_FALSE in State C1
because
 C1  --> C2 { bank.charge!,bank.charge? } {{ request(charge,id1)}}
 and the formula:  AG  not accepting_request(charge)
   is FOUND_FALSE in State C2
because
 the formula:  not accepting_request(charge)
   is FOUND_FALSE in State C2
because
 the formula: ASSERT(accepting_request(charge))
   is FOUND_TRUE in State C2
-------------------------------------------
```

6   Concluding Remarks

We have introduced a logical verification framework for checking functional properties of service-oriented applications specified using COWS. Our approach consists in: first, singling out a set of abstract properties describing desirable peculiar features of services; then, expressing such properties as SocL formulae; finally, verifying satisfaction of these properties by a COWS service specification by exploiting the model checker CMC. We refer the interested reader to the full version [10] of this paper for additional details on our logical verification framework and for further case studies.

One advantage of our approach is that, since the logic interpretation model (i.e. L^2TSs) is independent from the service specification language (i.e. COWS), it can be easily tailored to be used in conjunction with other SOC specification languages. To this aim, one has to define first an LTS-based operational semantics for the language of interest and then a suitable set of abstraction rules mapping the concrete actions of the language into the abstract actions of SocL. Another advantage is that SocL permits expressing properties about any kind of interaction pattern, such as *one–way, request–response, one request–multiple responses, one request-one of two possible responses,* etc. Indeed, properties of complex interaction patterns can be expressed by correlating SocL observable actions using interaction names and correlation values.

With respect to pure action-based or pure state-based temporal logics, action/state-based temporal logics facilitate the task of formalizing properties of concurrent systems, where it is often necessary to specify both state information and evolution in time by actions. Moreover, the use of L^2TSs as model of the logic helps to reduce the state space and, hence, the memory used and the time spent for verification. In [3], we have introduced the action/state-based branching time temporal logic UCTL that was originally tailored to express properties over UML statecharts. UCTL has been already used in [1] to describe some properties of services specified in SRML [12]. The main difference of SocL with respect to UCTL is that the former permits specifying parametric formulae, allowing correlation between service requests and responses to be expressed.

We leave for future work the extension of our framework to support a more compositional verification methodology. In fact, we are currently only able to analyse systems of services 'as a whole', i.e. we cannot analyse isolated services (e.g. a provider service without a proper client). This is somewhat related to the original semantics of COWS that follows a 'reduction' style; we are now defining an alternative operational semantics that should permit to overcome this problem.

Acknowledgements. We thank the anonymous referees for their useful comments.

References

1. Abreu, J., Bocchi, L., Fiadeiro, J., Lopes, A.: Specifying and composing interaction protocols for service-oriented system modelling. In: Derrick, J., Vain, J. (eds.) FORTE 2007. LNCS, vol. 4574, pp. 358–373. Springer, Heidelberg (2007)
2. Alonso, G., Casati, F., Kuno, H., Machiraju, V.: Web Services. Springer, Heidelberg (2004)
3. ter Beek, M.H., Fantechi, A., Gnesi, S., Mazzanti, F.: An action/state-based model-checking approach for the analysis of communication protocols for Service-Oriented Applications. In: FMICS 2007. LNCS, vol. 4916, Springer, Heidelberg (to appear)
4. Bhat, G., Cleaveland, R., Grumberg, O.: Efficient on-the-fly model checking for ctl*. In: LICS, pp. 388–397. IEEE Computer Society Press, Los Alamitos (1995)
5. Bocchi, L., Fantechi, A., Gönczy, L., Koch, N.: Prototype language for service modelling: Soa ontology in structured natural language. In: Sensoria deliverable D1.1a (2006)
6. Chaki, S., Clarke, E.M., Grumberg, O., Ouaknine, J., Sharygina, N., Touili, T., Veith, H.: State/event software verification for branching-time specifications. In: Romijn, J.M.T., Smith, G.P., van de Pol, J. (eds.) IFM 2005. LNCS, vol. 3771, pp. 53–69. Springer, Heidelberg (2005)
7. Chaki, S., Clarke, E.M., Ouaknine, J., Sharygina, N., Sinha, N.: State/event-based software model checking. In: Boiten, E.A., Derrick, J., Smith, G.P. (eds.) IFM 2004. LNCS, vol. 2999, pp. 128–147. Springer, Heidelberg (2004)
8. Chaki, S., Clarke, E.M., Ouaknine, J., Sharygina, N., Sinha, N.: Concurrent software verification with states, events, and deadlocks. Form. Asp. Comp. 17(4), 461–483 (2005)
9. De Nicola, R., Vaandrager, F.: Three logics for branching bisimulation. J. ACM 42(2), 458–487 (1995)
10. Fantechi, A., Gnesi, S., Lapadula, A., Mazzanti, F., Pugliese, R., Tiezzi, F.: A model checking approach for verifying COWS specifications. Technical report, Dipartimento di Sistemi e Informatica, Univ. Firenze (2007), http://rap.dsi.unifi.it/cows
11. Fernandez, J., Jard, C., Jéron, T., Viho, C.: Using on-the-fly verification techniques for the generation of test suites. In: Alur, R., Henzinger, T.A. (eds.) CAV 1996. LNCS, vol. 1102, pp. 348–359. Springer, Heidelberg (1996)
12. Fiadeiro, J., Lopes, A., Bocchi, L.: A formal approach to service component architecture. In: Bravetti, M., Núñez, M., Zavattaro, G. (eds.) WS-FM 2006. LNCS, vol. 4184, pp. 193–213. Springer, Heidelberg (2006)
13. Huth, M., Jagadeesan, R., Schmidt, D.A.: Modal transition systems: A foundation for three-valued program analysis. In: Sands, D. (ed.) ESOP 2001. LNCS, vol. 2028, pp. 155–169. Springer, Heidelberg (2001)

14. Lapadula, A., Pugliese, R., Tiezzi, F.: A Calculus for Orchestration of Web Services. In: De Nicola, R. (ed.) ESOP 2007. LNCS, vol. 4421, pp. 33–47. Springer, Heidelberg (2007)
15. Lapadula, A., Pugliese, R., Tiezzi, F.: A Calculus for Orchestration of Web Services (full version). Technical report, Dipartimento di Sistemi e Informatica, Univ. Firenze (2007), http://rap.dsi.unifi.it/cows
16. OASIS WSBPEL TC. Web Services Business Process Execution Language Version 2.0. Technical report, OASIS (April 2007), http://docs.oasis-open.org/wsbpel/2.0/OS/wsbpel-v2.0-OS.html
17. Stirling, C., Walker, D.: Local model checking in the modal μ-calculus. In: Díaz, J., Orejas, F. (eds.) TAPSOFT 1989. LNCS, vol. 351, pp. 369–383. Springer, Heidelberg (1989)

Contextual Integration Testing of Classes*

Giovanni Denaro[1], Alessandra Gorla[2], and Mauro Pezzè[1,2]

[1] University of Milano-Bicocca, Dipartimento di Informatica, Sistemistica e
Comunicazione, Via Bicocca degli Arcimboldi 8, 20126, Milano, Italy
denaro@disco.unimib.it
[2] University of Lugano, Faculty of Informatics,
via Buffi 13, 6900, Lugano, Switzerland
alessandra.gorla@lu.unisi.ch, mauro.pezze@unisi.ch

Abstract. This paper tackles the problem of structural integration testing of stateful classes. Previous work on structural testing of object-
oriented software exploits data flow analysis to derive test requirements
for class testing and defines contextual def-use associations to characterize inter-method relations. Non-contextual data flow testing of classes
works well for unit testing, but not for integration testing, since it misses
definitions and uses when properly encapsulated. Contextual data flow
analysis approaches investigated so far either do not focus on state dependent behavior, or have limited applicability due to high complexity.

This paper proposes an efficient structural technique based on contextual data flow analysis to test state-dependent behavior of classes that
aggregate other classes as part of their state.

1 Introduction

Object-oriented programs are characterized by classes and objects, which enforce
encapsulation and behave according to their internal state. Object-oriented features discipline programming practice, and reduce the impact of some critical
classes of faults, for instance those that derive from excessive use of non-local
information or from unexpected access to hidden details. However, they introduce new behaviors that cannot be checked satisfactorily with classic testing
techniques, which assume procedural models of software [1]. In this paper, we
focus on structural testing of state-based behavior, which impacts on both unit
and integration testing of classes.

The most promising structural approaches to testing object oriented software
exploit data flow analysis to implicitly capture state-based interactions. Harrold and Rothermel proposed data flow analysis for structural testing of classes
in 1994 [2]. In their early work, Harrold and Rothermel define a class control
flow graph to model data flow interactions within classes, and apply data flow
analysis to characterize such interactions in terms of flow relations of class state

---

* This work has been partially funded by the European Commission through the
project SHADOWS, by the Italian Government through the project COMMUTA
and by the Swiss National Fund through the project PerSeoS.

J. Fiadeiro and P. Inverardi (Eds.): FASE 2008, LNCS 4961, pp. 246–260, 2008.
© Springer-Verlag Berlin Heidelberg 2008

variables. This analysis supports well unit testing, but does not apply satisfactorily to integration testing of classes. In fact, when accesses to state variables are properly encapsulated, standard data flow analysis does not distinguish chains of interactions that flow through different methods, thus missing several integration dependencies, and in particular dependencies of classes that aggregate other classes as part of their state. In 2003, Souter and Pollock proposed a contextual data flow analysis algorithm for object oriented software [3]. Souter and Pollock's algorithm distinguishes accesses to the same variables through different chains of method invocations, and thus captures inter-method interactions even when variables are encapsulated in classes. Differently from our work, the work of Souter and Pollock does not focus on state dependent behavior. Moreover, Souter and Pollock's algorithm is very accurate, but quite expensive ($O(N^4)$ in the size of the program). The complexity of the algorithm limits the scalability of the approach and the development of efficient tools.

This paper proposes an approach to state based integration testing of classes that properly extends the early approach by Harrold and Rothermel: We use contextual information about method invocations to analyze state-dependent behavior of classes that can aggregate other classes as part of their state. We share the main concept of contextual def-use associations with Souter and Pollock, but with different goals: Souter and Pollock pursue exhaustive analysis of single methods, while we focus on state based interactions between methods that can be independently invoked from outside the classes. Moreover, differently from Souter and Pollock, we extend the algorithm proposed by Harrold and Soffa to capture inter-procedural propagations of definitions and uses by including contextual information [4]. Our algorithm for contextual data flow analysis is more efficient, albeit less accurate, than the algorithm of Souter and Pollock: it is quadratic in the size of the program in the worst case, and more efficient in many practical cases.

This paper describes an efficient contextual data flow analysis approach for object oriented software, discusses the computational complexity, and proposes structural coverage criteria for class integration testing (Sect. 2). It introduces a prototype implementation that we used for evaluating the suitability of the proposed approach (Sect. 3). It presents empirical data that support the applicability of the proposed coverage, and discusses the limits of the approach (Sect. 4). It surveys the main related work, and acknowledges the contribution of previous research (Sect. 5). It concludes by summarizing the contribution of the paper, and by describing ongoing research work (Sect. 6).

2   Contextual Data Flow Testing of Classes

A class is a (possibly) stateful module that encapsulates data and exports operations (aka methods). At runtime, a method takes a class instance (aka an object) as part of its input, and reads and manipulates the object state as part of its action. Thus in general, the behavior of the methods depends on the state of the objects, and the set of reachable states of the objects depends on the

```
1   public class Msg {                    18   public void setStored(byte b){
2     private byte info;                  19     stored = b;
3     public Msg(){info = 0;}             20   }
4     public void setInfo(byte b){        21   public byte getStored(){
5       info=b;                           22     return stored;
6     }                                   23   }
7     public byte getInfo(){              24   public void recvMsg(Msg m){
8       return info;                      25     byte recv = m.getInfo();
9     }                                   26     msg.setInfo(recv);
10  }                                     27   }
11  public class Storage {                28   public void storeMsg(){
12    private Msg msg;                    29     byte b = msg.getInfo();
13    private byte stored;                30     setStored(b);
14    public Storage(){                   31   }
15      msg = new Msg();                  32 }
16      stored = 0;
17    }
```

Fig. 1. A sample Java program

methods. The states of the classes are often composed of instances of other classes. To thoroughly test classes, we need to identify test cases, i.e., sequences of method calls, that exercise the relevant state dependencies of the methods in the reachable (composed) states.

Data flow analysis can assist testing of classes: it identifies the relevant dependencies between methods by capturing definitions and uses of state variables across methods [2]. Section 2.1 briefly recaps the minimal background on data flow testing. Section 2.2 discusses the limits of classic data flow analysis in identifying chains of interactions that flow through different classes. As a consequence, classic data flow analysis misses interactions through structured variables properly encapsulated in classes, which are extremely relevant during integration testing. Section 2.3 introduces our approach that leverages previous work on data flow testing of classes, making it amenable for the purpose of class integration testing.

2.1 Def-Use Associations

Given a program variable v, a standard (context-free) def-use association (d, u) is a pair of program locations, definition (d) and use (u) locations for v, where v is assigned a new value at d, and has its value read and used at u. Testing a def-use association (d, u) executes a program path that traverses first d and then u, without traversing statements that define v between d and u (the subpath between d and u is *def-free*). Def-use associations lead to many testing criteria [5].

Methods of a class interact through local variables, parameters, state variables and global objects. Def-use associations capture such interactions by identifying methods that use values set by other methods. For example the def-use association for variable `stored` at lines (19, 22) of Fig. 1 captures the dependency between methods `setStored()` and `getStored()`.

Def-use associations that involve local variables and parameters characterize method interactions through these elements, and are exploited by many tools, e.g., Coverlipse [6], and are not further considered in this paper.

2.2   Contextual Def-Use Associations

Contextual def-use associations extend def-use associations with the *context* of the method invocations. A context is the chain of (nested) method invocations that leads to the definition or the use [3][1]. A contextual def-use association for a variable v is a tuple (d, u, cd, cu), where (d, u) is a def-use association for v, and cd and cu are the contexts of d and u, respectively. This concept is illustrated in Fig. 1: The context-free def-use association for variable `stored` at lines (19,22) corresponds to two contextual def-use associations ($\rightarrow$ indicates method calls):
(19, 22, `Storage::setStored()`, `Storage::getStored()`) and
(19, 22, `Storage::storeMsg()` $\rightarrow$ `Storage::setStored()`, `Storage::getStored()`)

In general, in absence of context information, def-use associations are satisfied by test cases that focus on trivial rather than complex interactions, while context information identifies a more thorough set of test cases. For example, the context-free def-use associations at lines (19, 22) can be satisfied with a simple test case that invokes methods `setStored()` at line 18 and `getStored()` at line 21, while the corresponding contextual def-use associations illustrated above require also the (more interesting) invocations of methods `storeMsg()` at line 28 and `getStored()` (line 21). We clarify the concept through some common design practice: accessor methods and object aggregation.

Accessor methods are used to guarantee controlled access to state variables. A common design style is to define *get* methods (e.g., `getStored()`) to access state variables, and *set* methods (e.g., `setStored()`) to define state variables. Context-free definitions and uses of variables with accessors are always located within the accessor methods themselves, by construction. Thus, all state interactions that involve these variables are characterized by the few (context-free) def-use associations that derive from the accessor methods, while the many interactions mediated by the accessors are not captured. A test suite that covers all (context-free) def-use associations involving accessors would focus on trivial interactions only, missing the relevant ones. Contextual def-use associations distinguish between direct and mediated invocations of accessors, thus capturing also interactions between methods that access state variables through accessors. In the previous example the test cases derived from context-free def-use associations would focus on the trivial interaction between `setStored()` and `getStored()` only, missing the more relevant interaction between `storeMsg()` and `getStored()`, while the test cases derived from contextual def-use associations would capture all interactions through variable `stored`.

Object aggregation indicates the use of an object as part of the data structure of another object. Since it is a good practice to encapsulate the state of an aggregated object within its methods, definitions and uses of the internal state variables are located within these methods. State interactions that involve internal variables of aggregated objects are then characterized by context-free def-use associations that involve methods of the aggregated object only. Test

---

[1] In presence of multiple invocations from the same method, context may or may not distinguish the different invocation points. For the goals of this paper we do not need to distinguish different invocation points in the same method.

Table 1. Definitions and uses computed for the sample program in Fig. 1

Method	Line (state var)	Context
	Defs@exit	
Msg::Msg	3 (info)	Msg::Msg
Msg::setInfo	5 (info)	Msg::setInfo
Storage::Storage	16 (stored)	Storage::Storage
Storage::setStored	19 (stored)	Storage::setStored
Storage::storeMsg	19 (stored)	Storage::storeMsg→Storage::setStored
Storage::Storage	15 (msg)	Storage::Storage
Storage::Storage	3 (msg.info)	Storage::Storage→Msg::Msg
Storage::recvMsg	5 (msg.info)	Storage::recvMsg→Msg::setInfo
	Uses@entry	
Msg::getInfo	8 (info)	Msg::getInfo
Storage::getStored	22 (stored)	Storage::getStored
Storage::recvMsg	26 (msg)	Storage::recvMsg
Storage::storeMsg	29 (msg)	Storage::storeMsg
Storage::storeMsg	8 (msg.info)	Storage::storeMsg→Msg::getInfo

cases that cover context-free def-use associations focus on single objects and not the aggregated ones, thus missing complex and usually semantically more relevant interactions, while contextual def-use associations identify interactions of simple as well as aggregated objects and lead to a more thorough set of test cases. For example the context-free def-use association for variable info at lines (5, 8) in Fig. 1 characterizes both the interaction between methods setInfo() and getInfo() in class Msg, and the interaction between methods recvMsg() and storeMsg() in class Storage (which aggregates a Msg object as part of its state).

2.3   Deriving Contextual Associations

We compute state-based def-use associations by first identifying contextual definitions and uses that reach method boundaries, and then pairing definitions and uses of the same state variables across methods. In this phase, our main contribution is the redefinition of the classic algorithms for data flow testing: Differently from Harrold and Rothermel, we compute contextual information of definitions and uses, and thus we capture important inter-procedural properties of object oriented software; We adapt the classic Harrold and Soffa's inter-procedural algorithm to contextual definitions and uses in the context of object oriented software; We borrow the definitions of contextual information by Souter and Pollock, but we use a more efficient algorithm that focuses on definitions and uses of state variables that reach method boundaries as illustrated in the next paragraphs.

We illustrate the algorithm through the example of Fig. 1. In the first step, we statically analyze the methods of the classes under test, and we compute two sets of data, *defs@exit* and *uses@entry*. The *defs@exit* set includes all contextual definitions of state variables that can reach the end of the method, i.e., for which there exists at least a (statically identified) def-free path from the definition to an exit of the method. The *uses@entry* set includes all contextual uses of state variables that can be reached from the entry of the method, i.e., for which there

Table 2. Def-use associations for the sample program in Fig. 1

Class (state var)	Assoc.	Def context	Use context
Msg (info)	(3, 8)	Msg::Msg	Msg::getInfo
Msg (info)	(5, 8)	Msg::setInfo	Msg::getInfo
Storage (stored)	(16, 22)	Storage::Storage	Storage::getStored
Storage (stored)	(19, 22)	Storage::setStored	Storage::getStored
Storage (stored)	(19, 22)	Storage::storeMsg→Storage::setStored	Storage::getStored
Storage (msg)	(15, 26)	Storage::Storage	Storage::recvMsg
Storage (msg)	(15, 29)	Storage::Storage	Storage::storeMsg
Storage (msg.info)	(3, 8)	Storage::Storage→Msg::Msg	Storage::storeMsg→Msg::getInfo
Storage (msg.info)	(5, 8)	Storage::recvMsg→Msg::setInfo	Storage::storeMsg→Msg::getInfo

exists at least one def-free path from the entry of the method to the use. For each element in the two sets, we record location, related state variable, and context information. Table 1 shows the *defs@exit* and *uses@entry* sets for the code in Fig. 1.

In the second step, we match the information computed in the first step by combining definitions in *defs@exit* and uses in *uses@entry* that relate to same state variables. In this way, we compute the set of contextual def-use associations for the class under analysis. Table 2 shows the complete set of def-use associations for the classes in Fig. 1.

Our data flow analysis implements intra-procedural analysis according to the classic reaching definition algorithm [7,8]. We then compute inter-procedural relationships by elaborating the inter-procedural flow graph (IFG), as proposed by Harrold and Soffa [4]. We extended the algorithm to propagate the context information on the control-flow edges that represent inter-procedural relationships.

Context tracking in presence of recursive calls and programs with recursive data structures requires specific handling. Recursion of method calls may generate infinitely many new contexts, which may cause the algorithm to diverge. To avoid divergence, at each node of the IFG our algorithm distinguishes only one level of nested calls, by merging contexts that contain repeated subsequences of method calls. Recursive data structures define aggregations of possibly infinite state variables, which may generate unbounded sets of definitions and uses. Our algorithm expands recursive data structures up to one level of recursion. While limiting the depth of recursion and recursive data structures may threaten the completeness of the analysis, we conjecture that one level of depth is enough to test at least once all interactions between distinct modules, and thus this limit should not impact significantly on integration testing.

The extended algorithm works with the same number of propagation steps as the original rapid data flow algorithm, and thus has a temporal complexity of the same order of magnitude as the original one ($O(n^2)$ worst case complexity and linear in most practical situations[4,7,8], while Souter and Pollock's algorithm is $O(n^4)$.) Space complexity slightly increases because of the extra space for memorizing context information, and because definitions and uses that reach IFG nodes through different contexts are now tracked as distinct items. The details of the algorithm, omitted here for space limitations, are discussed in [9].

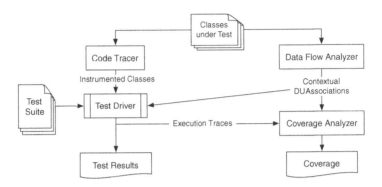

Fig. 2. Logical structure of the **DaTeC** prototype

In our experiments, we completed static data flow analysis in few minutes, even for large programs (see Sect. 4 for details.)

3   Evaluation Framework

Contextual def-use analysis captures many non-trivial object interactions that depend on program state. Thus testing all contextual def-use associations should increase the possibility of revealing state-dependent faults, and the confidence in the proper behavior of the program. However, complex interaction patterns may result in many contextual def-use associations, which may be expensive to compute. Moreover, the contextual information may increase the amount of infeasible associations, thus weakening the strength of testing all contextual def-use associations.

To empirically evaluate our approach, we built a prototype. Fig. 2 illustrates the fundamental components of the **DaTeC** (Data flow Testing of Classes) prototype and the information flow to and from a classic testing environment. In a classic testing environment, a *test driver* (for instance *JUnit*), executes a set of *test cases* for the *classes under test*, and produces a set of *test results*. **DaTeC** extends a classic testing environment by computing the contextual def-use associations of the classes under test, and by identifying the contextual def-use associations exercised during testing. The prototype is composed of a *data flow analyzer* that statically computes the contextual def-use associations for the classes under test, a *code tracer* that inserts probes into the classes under test to identify the executed definitions, uses and contexts, and a *coverage analyzer* that identifies the associations executed by a test suite. The *code tracer* has been implemented by instantiating a general purpose monitor. In the next paragraphs, we describe the data flow and the coverage analyzers.

The *Data Flow Analyzer* instantiates contextual data flow analysis for analyzing Java bytecode. Our implementation relies on the JABA API (Java Architecture for Bytecode Analysis [10]) for exploring the control flow graphs of the methods. Following the schema presented in Sect. 2.3, we adapted the traditional algorithms (reaching definitions and its inter-procedural counterpart) to compute contextual def-use associations of state variables for given sets of classes under test.

The *Coverage Analyzer* computes the contextual def-use associations that belong to a set of program traces. A trace T is a sequence of program locations that correspond to a program execution. For each location, a trace records the class and the object involved in the execution at that point.[2] A specific trace $\overline{T}$ covers a contextual def-use association $(\overline{d}, \overline{u}, \overline{cd}, \overline{cu})$ for a state variable $\overline{v}$ if and only if:

- the locations $\overline{d}$ and $\overline{u}$ occur in $\overline{T}$ in this order;
- the variable $\overline{v}$ is instantiated within the same object;
- no killing definition for $\overline{v}$ occurs in $\overline{T}$ between $\overline{d}$ and $\overline{u}$;
- the trace $\overline{T}$ satisfies the contexts $\overline{cd}$ and $\overline{cu}$ at locations $\overline{d}$ and $\overline{u}$, respectively. A generic trace T satisfies a context c at a location l, if, in T, l is reached through a chain c of method invocations. Notice that if T satisfies c at l, it satisfies also all contexts obtained by considering the tails of c.

The algorithm for coverage analysis is computation intensive. The trivial algorithm that scans all traces and checks all def-use associations for each trace has a complexity linear in the product of the number of traces, the length of the traces, and the number of def-use associations. To reduce the execution time and memory consumption, we compare contexts incrementally, and we index the def-use associations by the traversed locations. In this way, we consider only the associations related to the locations in the trace currently analyzed, thus reducing the impact of the total number of associations on the complexity. In our experiments, we processed programs with traces containing up to 10^8 entries, and a total of up to 10^5 contextual def-use associations without problems.

Although the technique is applicable to general Java programs, the prototype does not currently handle exceptions and polymorphism; it does not statically analyze the code for aliases; and it treats arrays with some imprecision. Here we briefly discuss the impact of these limits on the experiments.

Exceptions require special treatment as discussed by Sinha and Harrold [11], Chatterjee and Ryder [12], and Chatterjee et al. [13]. Exceptions are part of the plans for the next release of our prototype. In the current release, the data flow analyzer ignores exception handlers and the coverage analyzer does not report the related coverage.

Polymorphism and dynamic binding can cause an exponential explosion of combinations. Rountev et al. propose a technique to efficiently treat polymorphism based on class analysis that can be integrated with our approach [14]. The current prototype does not solve the bindings, but considers the ones indicated by the user.

Aliases widen the set of possible interactions. We are currently evaluating alias analysis algorithms for inclusion in the next release [15,16].

---

[2] Object identifiers are ignored for **static** methods.

Table 3. Statistics of our contextual data flow analysis on a set of sample programs

	Number of classes	SLOC	State vars	Max assoc. for 95% of classes	Time (in sec)
Jedit	910	92,213	2,975	381	70
Ant	785	80,454	4,081	331	60
BCEL	383	23,631	929	792	24
Lucene	287	19,337	1,013	410	17
JTopas	63	5,359	196	49	8
NanoXML	25	3,279	39	4	5
Siena	27	2,162	66	35	5

SLOC indicates the number of lines of source code, excluding blank and comment lines. SLOC has been computed using SLOCCount (under Linux).

All benchmarks are public open-source software: Ant, BCEL and Lucene are available at apache.org; JEdit is available at jedit.org; Siena, NanoXML and JTopas are available from the SIR repository [19].

Data flow analysis, as most static analysis techniques, cannot handle well arrays, since array elements are often accessed through indexes whose values are computed dynamically. The Java dynamic initialization of arrays worsen the problem. Forgács and Hamlet et al. present some techniques for handling arrays efficiently [17,18]. The current prototype approximates arrays as a whole, without distinguishing accesses to single element.

The limitations discussed in this section characterize most static analysis techniques, but none of them prevents the applicability of data flow analysis.

4   Empirical Data

We tested the technique proposed in this paper to check for efficiency (the ability of dealing with large programs), feasibility (the portion of infeasible contextual def-use associations), and effectiveness (the ability of revealing failures).

4.1   Scalability

The size of the programs that can be analyzed may be limited by the complexity of data flow and coverage analysis. As discussed in Sects. 2 and 3, our data flow analysis is quadratic in the worst case and linear in many practical cases, while coverage analysis depends on both the length of the analyzed traces and the amount of contextual def-use associations.

To appreciate the impact of the complexity of data flow and coverage analysis, we analyzed a set of sample open-source programs of increasing complexity with our prototype. Table 3 reports the amount of associations and the time for computing them. The first four columns identify the analyzed programs and their complexity (program name, number of classes, lines of code and number of state variables). Column *Time* indicates the overall time for completing the analysis with our prototype running on a Dell PowerEdge 2900 server with two 3.0 GHz Dual-Core Intel Xeon processors and 8 GB of RAM.

Column *Max Assoc. for 95% of classes* indicates the maximum amount of associations computed for a single class, excluding the outliers (the 5% of the classes with the highest number of contextual def-use associations.) We decided to exclude the outliers because most classes present a relatively small number of contextual def-use associations with few exceptions, as illustrated in Fig. 3 that plots the relation between the lines of code and the number of associations in a class for all the sample programs. In the cases considered so far, the outliers are algorithm intensive classes, *tokenizers* or *parsers* for Jedit, BCEL, Lucene and JTopas, which use state variables for storing intermediate results of the computation. Most of these classes are automatically produced with parser generators, and are of little interest from the class testing viewpoint. Thus, we can obtain good testing results even ignoring the associations of these classes.

As shown in the example of Sect. 3, a single test case may cover several associations, thus we can cover the associations with a number of test cases smaller than the amount of associations.

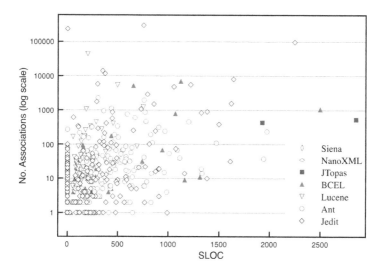

Fig. 3. SLOC and number of associations for all sample programs classes

4.2   Feasibility

Testing criteria may not be effective when they statically identify too many infeasible elements, thus resulting in highly variable coverages. Typical industrially-relevant criteria, such as statement, branch and MC/DC coverage, result in 75% to 95% of feasible elements [1]. To evaluate the impact of infeasible associations, we inspected all contextual def-use associations derived from the packages junit.framework of JUnit and a lucene.document of Lucene (all the details can be found in [9]). The package junit.framework presents a total of 102 contextual def-use associations, and only 3 of them are infeasible. Thus 96% contextual def-use associations are feasible in junit.framework. Three associations are infeasible because they involve uses in unreachable code, and none is infeasible due to data flow limitations. The classes of the Lucene package that we inspected contain a total of 354 contextual def-use associations, 280 (80%) of which are feasible. All the infeasible contextual def-use associations derive from the impossibility of executing all associations in all possible contexts, since some classes invoke some methods with a subset of parameter values that restrict the amount of code that can be executed in the specific contexts.

4.3 Effectiveness

We studied the ability of exposing failures by comparing the performance of standard test suites with test suites that guarantee coverage of feasible contextual def-use associations. We ran the experiments on the 3.8.1 distribution of the package junit.framework of JUnit, since it is distributed with a standard test suite. We first augmented the test suite provided with the distribution with additional test cases that guarantee 100% coverage of the feasible contextual def-use associations. We then compared the effectiveness of the standard and the augmented test suites by measuring the ability of revealing a set of seeded faults.

The 58 test cases of the standard test suite cover only 52% of the contextual def-use associations (54 out of a total of 102 associations, 99 of which are feasible). We augmented the default test suite with 19 additional test cases to cover all 99 feasible associations. Neither of the suites find any faults, as expected, since JUnit is a mature tool, and the package junit.framework, which we analyzed, is the core of the tool.

A qualitative inspection of the additional test cases indicates that the original test suite omits some relevant checks: The test cases of the original suite (1) do not check for the consistency of the initial state of most objects, (2) do not check some functionalities, and (3) do not check the behavior of some methods when invoked in states that violate the preconditions of the methods. For example, in JUnit, test suites can be given a name, but no original test case checks for the correct treatment of this case. Moreover JUnit requires test cases to be defined in public classes, but the behavior in presence of test suites included in private classes is not checked by the standard test suite.

To further assess the performance of the augmented test suite, we evaluated the original and the augmented suites with respect to a set of 83 mutants generated with mutant operators applied to constructs involving the state of the classes. The original suite identifies only 56 out of 83 seeded faults, the original suite augmented with 9 test cases to reach 100% coverage of the feasible statements identifies 65 seeded faults, while the test suite augmented to cover all feasible contextual def-use associations identifies all 83 faults.

This preliminary result suggests that the increment of test cases required to execute all feasible contextual def-use associations is less than the increment in the number of revealed faults. To execute all feasible contextual def-use associations we ran 77 test cases, 33% more than the original suite (58) and 15% more than the suite that executes all statements (67), but we revealed all 83 seeded faults, 48% more than the seeded faults revealed by the original suite, and 28% more than the suite that covers all feasible statements.

4.4   Limitations and Threats to Validity

The main threats to the validity of the empirical results reported in this section derive from the limitations of the prototype used in the experimental work: the language issues that are not addressed by the prototype (exception handling, polymorphism, and reference aliasing) might affect the precision of the computed sets of contextual def-use associations, thus biasing our figures. Alias analysis algorithms, such us the ones proposed by Liang, Pennings and Harrold [15] and Milanova, Rountev and Ryder [16] should improve the precision of the results. We are currently evaluating such algorithms to include alias analysis in the next release of the prototype. Exception handlers may worsen the problem of infeasible associations, but we believe that they should be addressed independently.

The results on fault-detection effectiveness based on mutation analysis may be biased by the set of injected faults, even if they confirm the preliminary feedback from comparing different test suites. We are currently experimenting with known faults in publicly available applications to further confirm the preliminary results of mutation analysis.

Additional validity threats may derive from having experimented only with open-source software, which could not adequately represent software produced in industrial settings. We are working with our industrial partners to confirm the preliminary results obtained with open-source software.

5   Related Work

The problem of testing state-dependent behavior has been originally addressed in the domain of communication protocols, and then further extended to cope with object oriented software [1,20]. Most work on testing the state-dependent behavior of object oriented software has focused on deriving test cases from state-based specifications, often UML (e.g., [21,22]).

The most relevant code-based approaches to testing the state-dependent behavior of object-oriented software have exploited data flow analysis techniques. Harrold and Rothermel first, and Souter and Pollock later laid down the foundations [2,3,4].

Harrold and Rothermel introduced a suitable data flow model of class interactions, and defined intra- and inter-class testing. We based our analysis on this model, and our prototype on the JABA library [10], which extracts the model from Java bytecode. Our work properly extends Harrold and Rothermel's approach by computing contextual information of definitions and uses.

Souter and Pollock introduced contextual def-use associations for better characterizing the interactions within object-oriented software, and proposed an algorithm that analyzes method interactions by examining complete chains of method invocations. Our framework adapts the notion of contextual def-use associations defined by Souter and Pollock, to provide a framework for defining intra-class integration testing strategies.

Souter and Pollock instantiated their approach in the tool TATOO [23] that analyzes inter-method interactions, and used this tool to explore the use contexts of different granularity. TATOO was not publicly available at the time of writing, thus we could not make a direct comparison with our prototype. Based on what published in the literature [3,23], our prototype seems to scale up better than TATOO: uses of TATOO are reported for programs up to 10 KLOC and 100 classes, while we have successfully analyzed programs up to 100 KLOC and 1,000 classes. On the other hand, our static analysis for building contextual def-use associations is less precise than Pollock and Souter's one. Their algorithm analyzes each method separately for each context in which it can be invoked, and partially accounts for reference aliasing that can differ across different contexts. We ignore aliasing for the moment.

Other tools that address data flow coverage for Java programs, e.g., Coverlipse [6] and JaBUTi [24], consider only intra-method interactions, thus they are not suitable for integration testing.

Several papers propose approaches to increase the precision of the data flow analysis for Java by accounting for reference aliasing, exception handling and polymorphism [13,14,15,16,25,26]. We are currently extending our prototype to include alias analysis, and improve the precision of the results.

The presence of libraries or components available without source code impacts on the precision of data flow analysis. Rountev et al. propose an approach to inter-procedural data flow analysis that relies on summary information provided with external libraries, and does not require access to the source code [27]. Since our analysis works at the bytecode level, we face this problem only in presence of native code in Java libraries.

6   Conclusions

Classic structural testing approaches do not adequately address subtle failures that may depend on state-dependent behavior of object-oriented classes. Data flow analysis techniques have been recently extended to capture dependencies from instance variables that determine the state of the classes, taking into account the context in which methods that access instance variables are invoked.

In this paper, we propose a framework that adapts and extends previous results to structural integration testing of classes [2], aiming to better support integration testing of classes. Our approach exploits contextual def-use associations defined by Souter and Pollock, but differently from them focuses on state dependent behavior and proposes a more efficient algorithm, thus improving scalability. We report a preliminary set of empirical data obtained though a prototype implementation of the approach on a set of open-source programs.

The analysis proposed in this paper can be performed incrementally on single classes, since definition and use sets can be combined at integration time, while Souter and Pollock's analysis combines the points-to-graphs of the different methods for each method invocation, and thus gains precision at the expense of scalability. Souter and Pollock's approach applies well to the analysis of complete programs and single methods, while our approach fits better the analysis of the interactions of methods that can be invoked independently from outside the class.

The empirical results confirm the complexity results and suggests that the technique proposed in this paper scales up well to mid-size programs (we analyzed programs of up to 100,000 lines of code and 1000 classes in few minutes). The results indicate also a high percentage of feasible contextual def-use associations, thus sustaining the usefulness of the proposed structural coverage. Finally, the results suggest that the coverage proposed in this paper includes relevant state-dependent behavior that are ignored by classic structural coverage criteria.

References

1. Pezzè, M., Young, M.: Software Test and Analysis: Process, Principles and Techniques. John Wiley and Sons, Chichester (2008)
2. Harrold, M.J., Rothermel, G.: Performing data flow testing on classes. In: Proceedings of the 2nd ACM SIGSOFT Symposium on Foundations of Software Engineering, pp. 154–163. ACM Press, New York (1994)
3. Souter, A.L., Pollock, L.L.: The construction of contextual def-use associations for object-oriented systems. IEEE Transaction on Software Engineering 29(11), 1005–1018 (2003)
4. Harrold, M.J., Soffa, M.L.: Efficient computation of interprocedural definition-use chains. ACM Transactions on Programming Languages and Systems 16(2), 175–204 (1994)
5. Rapps, S., Weyuker, E.J.: Selecting software test data using data flow information. IEEE Transactions on Software Engineering SE-11(4), 367–375 (1985)
6. Kempka, M.: Coverlipse: Eclipse plugin that visualizes the code coverage of JUnit tests Open source project on SourceForge.net,
   http://coverlipse.sourceforge.net
7. Kildall, G.A.: A unified approach to global program optimization. In: Proceedings of the 1st annual ACM SIGACT-SIGPLAN Symposium on Principles of Programming Languages, pp. 194–206. ACM Press, New York (1973)
8. Muchnick, S.S.: Advanced Compiler Design and Implementation. Morgan Kaufmann, San Francisco (1997)
9. Denaro, G., Gorla, A., Pezzè, M.: An empirical evaluation of data flow testing of Java classes. Technical Report 2007/03, University of Lugano, Faculty of Informatics (2007)
10. JABA: Aristotele Research Group. Java Architecture for Bytecode Analysis (2005)
11. Sinha, S., Harrold, M.J.: Analysis and testing of programs with exception handling constructs. IEEE Transactions on Software Engineering 26(9), 849–871 (2000)
12. Chatterjee, R., Ryder, B.G.: Data-flow-based testing of object-oriented libraries. Technical Report DCS-TR-433, Department of Computer Science, Rutgers University (2001)
13. Chatterjee, R., Ryder, B.G., Landi, W.: Complexity of points-to analysis of Java in the presence of exceptions. IEEE Transactions on Software Engineering 27(6), 481–512 (2001)
14. Rountev, A., Milanova, A., Ryder, B.G.: Fragment class analysis for testing of polymorphism in Java software. IEEE Transactions on Software Engineering 30(6), 372–387 (2004)

15. Liang, D., Pennings, M., Harrold, M.J.: Evaluating the impact of context-sensitivity on Andersen's algorithm for Java programs. In: Proceedings of the ACM Workshop on Program Analysis For Software Tools and Engineering, pp. 6–12. ACM Press, New York (2005)

16. Milanova, A., Rountev, A., Ryder, B.G.: Parameterized object sensitivity for points-to analysis for Java. ACM Transactions on Software Engineering and Methodology 14(1), 1–41 (2005)

17. Forgács, I.: An exact array reference analysis for data flow testing. In: Proceedings of the 18th International Conference on Software Engineering, pp. 565–574. IEEE Computer Society Press, Los Alamitos (1996)

18. Hamlet, D., Gifford, B., Nikolik, B.: Exploring dataflow testing of arrays. In: Proceedings of the 15th International Conference on Software Engineering, pp. 118–129. IEEE Computer Society Press, Los Alamitos (1993)

19. Do, H., Elbaum, S., Rothermel, G.: Supporting controlled experimentation with testing techniques: An infrastructure and its potential impact. Empirical Software Engineering: An International Journal 10(4), 405–435 (2005)

20. Binder, R.V.: Testing Object-Oriented Systems, Models, Patterns, and Tools. Addison-Wesley, Reading (2000)

21. Briand, L.C., Penta, M.D., Labiche, Y.: Assessing and improving state-based class testing: A series of experiments. IEEE Transactions on Software Engineering 30(11), 770–793 (2004)

22. Hartmann, J., Imoberdorf, C., Meisinger, M.: Uml-based integration testing. In: Proceedings of the 2000 International Symposium on Software Testing and Analysis, pp. 60–70. ACM Press, New York (2000)

23. Souter, A., Wong, T., Shindo, S., Pollock, L.: TATOO: Testing and analysis tool for object-oriented software. In: Margaria, T., Yi, W. (eds.) TACAS 2001. LNCS, vol. 2031, Springer, Heidelberg (2001)

24. Vincenzi, A.M.R., Maldonado, J.C., Wong, W.E., Delamaro, M.E.: Coverage testing of Java programs and components. Science of Computer Programming 56(1-2), 211–230 (2005)

25. Liang, D., Pennings, M., Harrold, M.J.: Extending and evaluating flow-insensitive and context-insensitive points-to analyses for Java. In: Proceedings of the ACM SIGPLAN-SIGSOFT Workshop on Program Analysis For Software Tools and Engineering, pp. 73–79. ACM Press, New York (2001)

26. Rountev, A., Milanova, A., Ryder, B.G.: Points-to analysis for Java using annotated constraints. In: Proceedings of the 16th ACM SIGPLAN Conference on Object Oriented Programming, Systems, Languages, and Applications, pp. 43–55. ACM Press, New York (2001)

27. Rountev, A., Kagan, S., Marlowe, T.: Interprocedural dataflow analysis in the presence of large libraries. In: Mycroft, A., Zeller, A. (eds.) CC 2006. LNCS, vol. 3923, pp. 2–16. Springer, Heidelberg (2006)

An Automatic Verifier for Java-Like Programs Based on Dynamic Frames

Jan Smans[1], Bart Jacobs[1], Frank Piessens[1], and Wolfram Schulte[2]

[1] Katholieke Universiteit Leuven, Belgium
{jans,bartj,frank}@cs.kuleuven.be
[2] Microsoft Research Redmond, USA
schulte@microsoft.com

Abstract. Data abstraction is crucial in the construction of modular programs, since it ensures that internal changes in one module do not propagate to other modules. In object-oriented programs, classes typically enforce data abstraction by providing access to their internal state only through methods. By using method calls in method contracts, data abstraction can be extended to specifications. In this paper, methods used for this purpose must be side-effect free, and are called pure methods.

We present an approach to the automatic verification of object-oriented programs that use pure methods for data abstraction. The cornerstone of our approach is the solution to the framing problem, i.e. client code must be able to determine whether state changes affect the return values of pure methods. More specifically, we extend each method contract with a method footprint, an upper bound on the memory locations read or written by the corresponding method. Footprints are specified using dynamic frames, special pure methods that return sets of memory locations. Thanks to this abstraction, implementations can evolve independently from specifications, loosely coupled only by pure functions.

We implemented this approach in a custom build of the Spec# program verifier, and used it to automatically verify several challenging programs, including the iterator and observer patterns. The verifier itself and the examples shown in this paper can be downloaded from the authors' homepage [1].

1 Introduction

The principle of data abstraction is a central concept in object-oriented programming. That is, a class typically hides its implementation details from clients, and instead offers methods to access its internal state. Adherence to the principle of data abstraction ensures that client code remains independent of the implementation of classes it is using, and as a consequence that changing the implementation of a class (within the boundaries described by its contract) does not affect clients. For example, consider the class *Cell* shown in Figure 1. Each *Cell* object holds an integer value which is stored in the private field x. Client code can only access x through the getter *getX* and the setter *setX*. Since clients only depend

J. Fiadeiro and P. Inverardi (Eds.): FASE 2008, LNCS 4961, pp. 261–275, 2008.
© Springer-Verlag Berlin Heidelberg 2008

on the getter and setter, changing *Cell*'s internal representation does not affect them. In particular, changing the implementation will not affect the correctness of the client program of Figure 1(b).

To preserve data abstraction within specifications, specifications must be written in an implementation-independent manner. In particular, specifications should not expose the private fields of a class. One way to achieve this independence is to use method calls within specifications. In this paper, methods used for this purpose must be side-effect free, and are called pure methods. Non-pure methods are called mutators. For example, the behavior of the mutator *setX* is specified by describing its effect on the pure method *getX*. The specification of *Cell* never mentions the field x. Using pure methods within specifications

```
class Cell {
    private int x;

    Cell()
        writes ∅;
        ensures getX() = 0;
        ensures footprint().isFresh();
    { }

    pure int getX()
        reads footprint();
    { return x; }

    void setX(int value)
        writes footprint();
        ensures getX() = value;
        ensures footprint().newElemsFresh();
    { x := value; }

    pure set footprint()
        reads footprint();
    { return { &x }; }
}
```
(a)

```
Cell c₁ := new Cell();
c₁.setX(5);

Cell c₂ := new Cell();
c₂.setX(10);

assert c₁.getX() = 5;
```
(b)

Fig. 1. A class *Cell* and a client program

gives rise to a framing problem [2, Challenge 3], i.e. client code must be able to determine the effect of heap changes on the return values of pure methods. For instance, to show that $c_1.getX()$ equals 5 at the end of the code snippet in Figure 1(b), we must be able to deduce that creating and modifying c_2 does not affect the state of c_1. This deduction should not rely on *Cell*'s implementation, since doing so would break information hiding.

Recently, Kassios [3,4] proposed a promising solution to the framing problem. More specifically, he proposes using dynamic frames, specification variables (similar to pure methods) that return sets of memory locations, to specify the effect of mutators and the dependencies of specification variables in an abstract manner. However, his solution is formulated in the context of an idealized, higher-order logical framework. For example, it does not show how to apply the approach to Java-like inheritance. Furthermore, the proposed approach is not applied in the context of an automatic program verifier for first-order logic.

In this paper, we propose an approach to the automatic verification of annotated Java-like object-oriented programs that combines pure methods to achieve data abstraction with Kassios' solution to the framing problem. More specifically, to solve the framing problem, we extend each method contract with a method footprint which specifies an upper bound on the memory locations read or written by the corresponding method. A memory location is an (object identifier, field name) pair. The footprint of a pure method (**reads** annotation) specifies an upper bound on the memory locations the pure method depends on, while a mutator's footprint (**writes** annotation) specifies an upper bound on the locations writable by the method. To prove that a heap change (i.e. a field update or mutator invocation) does not affect the return value of a pure method, one simply has to show that the footprint of the state change is disjoint from the pure method's footprint.

In our running example, the method footprint of both $getX$ and $setX$ is the singleton containing the receiver's field x. However, saying so explicitly in the method contract would expose the field x to clients and break information hiding. To specify method footprints in an implementation-independent manner, we allow developers to define dynamic frames, special pure methods that return a set of memory locations. These dynamic frames can then be used to abstractly specify method footprints. The method *footprint* is an example of a dynamic frame, and it is used to specify the footprint of all of *Cell*'s methods.

Given *Cell*'s specification, we can now prove the assertion at the end of the code snippet in Figure 1(b). Informally, the reasoning goes as follows. The specification of *Cell* guarantees that the constructor only writes to locations that were unallocated in the method pre-state, and that the new object's footprint contains only such locations. Since footprints of existing objects contain only allocated locations, the assignment $c_1 := $ **new** $Cell()$; creates a new object whose footprint is disjoint from any existing object's footprint. $setX$'s postcondition ensures that $c_1.getX()$ equals 5 after the call statement $c_1.setX(5)$;. Furthermore, the mutator's specification ensures that it only modifies unallocated locations and locations in receiver's pre-state footprint, and that it only adds newly allocated objects to that footprint. The next assignment $c_2 := $ **new** $Cell()$; creates a new footprint for c_2 disjoint from any other footprint. Because of this disjointness, the following statement $c_2.setX(10)$; affects neither $c_1.getX()$ nor $c_1.footprint()$. It follows that the assertion $c_1.getX()$ equals 5 *still* holds despite the intervening creation of and update to c_2.

In summary, the *contributions* of this paper are the following:

- We propose an approach to the automatic verification of Java-like object-oriented programs that combines the use of pure methods for data abstraction

with Kassios' approach to solve the framing problem. In particular, we show how Kassios' solution applies to Java-like inheritance [3, Future Work].
- We implemented our approach in a tool [1], and used it to automatically verify challenging examples, such as the iterator and observer patterns.

The remainder of this paper is structured as follows. In Section 2, we explain how programs such as the one shown in Figure 1 can be verified automatically. In Section 3, we demonstrate the expressive power of our approach by showing how it verifies various object-oriented programming and specification patterns. Section 4 extends the solution of Section 2 with support for inheritance. Finally, we discuss our experience with the verifier prototype, compare with related work and conclude in Sections 5, 6 and 7.

2   Solution

SJava. In this paper we restrict our attention to a small Java-like language, called SJava. SJava does not include features such as exceptions and multi-threading. However, SJava extends regular Java in three ways:

(1) SJava introduces a new primitive type **set**. An expression of type **set** represents a set of memory locations. A memory location is an (object reference, field name) pair, and the location corresponding to $e.f$ is denoted by $\&e.f$. The standard mathematical set operations such as $\cup$, $\cap$, and $\in$ can applied to expressions of type set. In addition, postconditions can apply *isFresh* and *newElemsFresh* to expressions of type set: $s.isFresh()$ is a two-state predicate expressing that s contains only fresh locations (i.e. locations corresponding to objects that were not allocated in the method pre-state), and $s.newElemsFresh()$ is a two-state predicate denoting that only fresh locations are added to s. *universe* denotes the set of all locations. **elems**(a) denotes the locations corresponding to the elements of the array a.

(2) A method in an SJava program can be marked with a **pure** annotation, indicating that it can be used in specifications. The body of a pure method consists of a single return statement returning a side-effect free expression. An expression is side-effect free if it does not contain object or array creations, simple or compound assignments, increment or decrement operators, and only calls pure methods. Non-pure methods are called *mutators*. Pure methods with return type **set** are called *dynamic frames*.

(3) Each method has a corresponding method contract, consisting of preconditions, a method footprint and postconditions. Preconditions and postconditions are boolean side-effect free expressions. The former define valid method pre-states, while the latter define valid method post-states. A method footprint is a side-effect free expression of type **set**. The footprint of a pure method (**reads** annotation) specifies the locations that can potentially be be read by the method, while a mutator's footprint (**writes** annotation) specifies the locations that can be modified by the method. More specifically, a mutator can only modify $o.f$ if $\&o.f$ is in the method's footprint or if o was unallocated at the start of the method. Pure methods have no need for writes clauses, since by definition they

are not allowed to modify any location. Mutators have no need for reads clauses, and can read any location. Indeed, the effect of heap changes on the return values of mutators is not relevant in our approach (no axiom is generated to frame the return value of mutators) as only pure methods can be used in specifications. Only parameters and the variable **this** may occur free in preconditions and footprints. Postconditions can additionally mention the variable **result**, denoting the return value of the method. Furthermore, postconditions may contain old expressions **old**(e), denoting the value of the expression e in the method's pre-state.

In this section, we consider only SJava without inheritance. Section 4 explains how inheritance can be supported.

Verification. Our verifier takes an SJava program as input and generates, via a translation into an intermediate verification language, a set of verification conditions. The verification conditions are first-order logical formulas whose validity implies the correctness of the program. The formulas are analyzed automatically by satisfiability-modulo-theory (SMT) solvers. Our approach is based on a general approach described in [5]. In this subsection, we focus on novel aspects of our approach: namely the way pure methods and their contracts are modeled in the verification logic and the way method footprints are enforced.

Notation. Heaps are modeled in the verification logic as maps from object references and field names to values. For example, the expression $h[o, f]$ denotes the value of the field f of object o in heap h. The function wf returns whether a given heap is well-formed, i.e. whether the fields of allocated objects point to allocated objects. $\$Heap$ denotes the current value of the global heap. Allocatedness of objects is tracked by means of a special boolean field named $\$allocated$.

$[\![E]\!]_{h_1,h_2,r}$ denotes the translation of the side-effect free expression E to first-order logic, where h_1 denotes the heap, h_2 denotes the pre-state heap (used in the translation of old expressions), and r denotes the term to be substituted for the variable **result**. We will omit the second and third parameter for single-state predicates.

Pure Methods. We treat pure methods as follows. For every pure method

$$\textbf{pure } t\ m(t_1\ x_1, \ldots, t_n\ x_n)$$
$$\textbf{requires } P;\ \textbf{reads } R;\ \textbf{ensures } Q;$$
$$\{\ \textbf{return } E;\ \}$$

defined in a class C, a function symbol $\#C.m$ is introduced in the verification logic that takes a heap, the receiver and the method parameters as its formal parameters. To define the function symbol's meaning, three kinds of axioms are generated: an implementation axiom, a framing axiom, and a postcondition axiom.

(1) The *implementation axiom* declares that the result of the function $\#C.m$ is equal to evaluating the method body.

$$\forall heap, o, x_1, \ldots, x_n \bullet wf(heap) \wedge heap[o, \$allocated] \wedge [\![P]\!]_{heap} \Rightarrow$$
$$\#C.m(heap, o, x_1, \ldots, x_n) = [\![E]\!]_{heap}$$

The implementation axiom can only be used within the module where C is defined.

(2) The *framing axiom* states that the function $\#C.m$ only depends on locations in m's footprint R. More specifically, a state change does not affect the return value of m if m's precondition holds in the pre and post-state and if locations in m's footprint have equal values.

$$\forall heap_1, heap_2, o, x_1, \ldots, x_n \bullet wf(heap_1) \wedge wf(heap_2) \wedge$$
$$heap_1[o, \$allocated] \wedge heap_2[o, \$allocated] \wedge [\![P]\!]_{heap_1} \wedge [\![P]\!]_{heap_2} \wedge$$
$$(\forall q, f \bullet (q, f) \in [\![R]\!]_{heap_1} \Rightarrow heap_1[q, f] = heap_2[q, f]) \Rightarrow$$
$$\#C.m(heap_1, o, x_1, \ldots, x_n) = \#C.m(heap_2, o, x_1, \ldots, x_n)$$

The framing axiom can only be used by modules that use the module where C is defined.

(3) The *postcondition axiom* axiomatizes the pure method's postcondition.

$$\forall heap, o, x_1, \ldots, x_n \bullet wf(heap) \wedge heap[o, \$allocated] \wedge [\![P]\!]_{heap} \Rightarrow$$
$$[\![Q]\!]_{heap, heap, \#C.m(heap, o, x_1, \ldots, x_n)}$$

m's postcondition axiom can only be used by modules that use the module where C is defined. For each dynamic frame, a default postcondition axiom is added stating that the dynamic frame only contains allocated objects. This axiom holds because of the well-formedness of the heap which implies that only allocated objects are reachable from allocated objects.

Our verifier prototype determines automatically which modules are being used within a certain method implementation by looking at the declared type of fields, parameters and local variables. A module is never considered to use itself.

Footprints. Method footprints are enforced differently for mutators and for pure methods. For a pure method m with footprint R, we check that every location (directly or indirectly) read by the method body is an element of R. More specifically, we check at each field access and method invocation within the body that the set of objects read by the subexpression is a subset of R. For a field access $o.f$, the set of read locations equals the singleton $\{(o, f)\}$. To determine the set of locations read by a callee, we rely on the callee's reads annotation.

The footprint W of a mutator m is checked by means of an additional postcondition: for each location (o, f), either m does not affect the value of the (o, f), or o was not allocated in the method pre-state, or the location was an element of W.

$$\forall o, f \bullet \mathbf{old}(\$Heap[o, f]) = \$Heap[o, f] \vee$$
$$\neg\mathbf{old}(\$Heap[o, \$allocated]) \vee$$
$$(o, f) \in [\![W]\!]_{\mathbf{old}(\$Heap)}$$

This postcondition is used to enforce the footprint and to verify client code.

Soundness. The soundness of our approach rests on two pillars: (I) the consistency of the verification logic and (II) the property that the value of a pure method is preserved by a state change, provided the footprint of the state change is disjoint from the pure method's footprint.

To satisfy the former component, we must ensure that the axioms generated based on user-defined pure methods are consistent. One way to enforce this consistency is to impose two restrictions: the module usage relation is acyclic and pure methods only call pure methods in used modules. Enforcing these restrictions guarantees termination of pure methods, which ensures (1) that implementation axioms are consistent, (2) that postconditions and reads clauses have to be proven (as there is always a path leading to the post-state), and (3) that the proof of a postcondition/framing axiom cannot rely on itself.

To show (II) we argue informally as follows. The postcondition of a mutator ensures that the method cannot modify allocated locations outside of its footprint. Similarly, by checking that every subexpression of the body of a pure method reads a subset of the method's footprint, we know that the value of a pure method depends only on locations within its footprint. Suppose the mutator m writes X, that the pure method p reads Y, and that X and Y are disjoint. Since method footprints can only contain allocated locations, m cannot modify locations within Y, since doing so would violate its writes clause. Hence, the value of p is preserved. Note that p is preserved, even if X and Y are no longer disjoint in m's post-state, since m can only write to the pre-state footprint X.

3   Invariants, Aggregates and Peers

In this section, we demonstrate how various object-oriented programming and specification patterns can be handled using our approach. More specifically, we focus on object invariants, aggregate objects and peer objects. It is important to note that supporting these patterns does *not* require any additional methodological machinery. All the examples shown in this paper have been verified automatically using our verifier prototype. Both the prototype and the examples can be downloaded from the authors' homepage [1].

Object Invariants. An object invariant describes what it means for an object to be in a consistent state. For example, consider class *ArrayList* in Figure 2. An *ArrayList* object o is consistent if $o.items$ points to a non-null array, and if $o.count$ is a valid index in the array.

Some other approaches such as [6,7] treat object invariants differently from regular predicates, thereby introducing additional complexity. In our approach an object invariant is just another pure, boolean method. For instance, in class *ArrayList* the method *invariant* specifies the object invariant. To assume/assert the object invariant, it suffices to assume/assert that the invariant method returns *true*.

Some readers may have noticed the peculiar, conditional form of *invariant*'s footprint. If $o.invariant()$ returns true, then it is framed by $o.footprint()$; otherwise, $o.invariant()$ may depend on any location (*universe* denotes the set of all locations). It suffices to frame $o.invariant()$ only when it returns true, since client code that relies on the reads clause typically only "sees" valid *ArrayList* objects. Instead of using a conditional reads clause, one could frame *invariant* by *footprint*(). However, one would also have to remove *footprint*'s precondition, and modify *footprint*'s body to take into account invalid object states, thereby essentially duplicating the part of the invariant.

Aggregate Objects. Many objects internally use other objects to help represent their internal state. Such objects are sometimes called aggregate objects. Typically, the consistency of an aggregate object implies the consistency of all its helper objects, and an aggregate object's footprint includes the footprint of all its helper objects. Consider the class *Stack* shown in Figure 2. A *Stack* object internally uses an *ArrayList* object to represent its internal state, and can therefore be considered an aggregate object. A stack's footprint includes its arraylist's footprint, and a *Stack* object's invariant implies the invariant of the internal *ArrayList* object.

Our approach does not impose any (built-in) aliasing restrictions. In particular, it does not forbid an aggregate object from leaking references to its internal helper objects. For example, a *Stack* is allowed to pass a reference to its internal *ArrayList* to client code. However, in that case client code will not be able to establish disjointness between the aggregate object's footprint and the helper object's footprint. As a consequence, updating the helper object causes the client to lose all information (given by the return values of its pure methods) about the aggregate object, and as a result clients cannot falsely assume that the state of the aggregate object is preserved when one of the helper objects is modified.

The return value of pure methods can change over time. In particular, locations can be added to or removed from an object's footprint. For example, the method *Switch* (in class *Stack*) shown below exchanges the internal *ArrayList* of the receiver and the parameter *other*. Again, our approach does not impose special methodological rules to ensure this "ownership transfer" takes place safely.

void *Switch*(*Stack other*)
   requires *other* $\neq$ *null* $\wedge$ *other.invariant*();
   requires *invariant*() $\wedge$ *footprint*() $\cap$ *other.footprint*() $= \emptyset$;
   writes *footprint*() $\cup$ *other.footprint*();
   ensures *invariant*() $\wedge$ *other.invariant*();
   ensures *size*() $=$ **old**(*other.size*()) $\wedge$ *other.size*() $=$ **old**(*size*());
   ensures *footprint*() $\cap$ *other.footprint*() $= \emptyset$;
   ensures (*footprint*() $\cup$ *other.footprint*()).*newElemsFresh*();
   { *ArrayList tmp* = *contents*; *contents* = *other.contents*; *other.contents* = *tmp*; }

Peer Objects. The examples considered so far can be verified using traditional ownership-based solutions, since the object graph has an hierarchical, tree-like structure. However, many object-oriented programming patterns, including the observer and iterator pattern, do not follow this structure. For example, consider class *iterator* in Figure 3. No single iterator uniquely "owns" the list, and similarly the list does not own its iterators.

Modifying a list while iterators are iterating over it can give rise to unexpected exceptions. For example, removing elements from a list can cause an

```
class ArrayList {
  int count;
  Object[] items;

  ArrayList()
    writes ∅;
    ensures invariant() ∧ size() = 0;
    ensures footprint().isFresh();
  { items := new Object[10]; }

  void add(Object o);
    requires invariant();
    writes footprint();
    ensures invariant();
    ensures size() = old(size() + 1);
    ensures get(size() − 1) = o;
    ensures ∀i ∈ (0 : size() − 1) • get(i) = old(get(i));
    ensures footprint().newElemsfresh();
  { ... }

  pure Object get(int i);
    requires invariant() ∧ 0 ≤ i < size();
    reads footprint();
  { return items[i]; }

  pure int size();
    requires invariant();
    reads footprint();
    ensures 0 ≤ result;
  { return count; }

  pure bool invariant()
    reads invariant()?footprint() : universe;
  { return items ≠ null ∧ 0 ≤ count ≤ items.length; }

  pure set footprint()
    requires invariant();
    reads footprint();
  { return {&count, &items} ∪ elems(items); }
}
```

```
class Stack {
  ArrayList contents;

  Stack()
    writes ∅;
    ensures invariant() ∧ size() = 0;
    ensures footprint().isFresh();
  { contents := new ArrayList(); }

  void Push(Object o)
    requires invariant();
    writes footprint();
    ensures invariant();
    ensures size() = old(size()) + 1;
    ensures footprint().newElemsFresh();
  { contents.add(o); }

  pure int size()
    requires invariant();
    reads footprint();
  { return contents.size(); }

  pure bool invariant()
    reads invariant()?footprint() : universe;
  {
    return contents ≠ null∧
      contents.invariant()∧
      &contents ∉ contents.footprint();
  }

  pure set footprint()
    requires invariant();
    reads footprint();
  { return {&contents} ∪ contents.footprint(); }
}
```

Fig. 2. A class *ArrayList* and a class *Stack*. *Stack* objects internally use *ArrayList* objects.

ArrayOutOfBoundsException in a corresponding iterator's *next* method. However, since the reads clause of an iterator's invariant includes the footprint of the corresponding list, any modification to the list immediately invalidates its corresponding iterators, making it impossible to use an iterator which is "out of sync" with its list.

```
class Iterator {
  ArrayList list;
  int index;

  Iterator(ArrayList l)                      pure ArrayList list()
    requires l ≠ null ∧ l.invariant();         requires invariant();
    writes ∅;                                  reads footprint();
    ensures invariant();                     { return list; }
    ensures list() = l;
    ensures footprint().isFresh();           pure bool invariant()
  { list := l; }                               reads invariant()?
                                                 (footprint() ∪ list().footprint()) : universe;
  Object next()                              { return list ≠ null ∧ list.invariant()∧
    requires invariant() ∧ hasNext();          0 ≤ index ≤ list.count∧
    writes footprint();                        &list ∉ list.footprint()∧
    ensures invariant() ∧ list() = old(list()); &index ∉ list.footprint();  }
    ensures footprint().newElemsFresh();
  { return list.items[index + +]; }          pure set footprint()
                                               requires invariant();
  pure bool hasNext()                          reads footprint();
    requires invariant();                    { return {&list, &index}; } }
    reads footprint() ∪ list().footprint();
  { return index < list.count; }
```

Fig. 3. The iterator pattern

4   Inheritance

Adding inheritance to SJava complicates the handling of pure methods, since inheritance allows binding method calls statically and dynamically, depending on the method itself and on the calling context. More specifically, an abstract method is always dynamically bound, while a private or final method is always statically bound. Non-abstract, non-private methods can either be statically or dynamically bound: a super call to such a method is statically bound, but any other call is dynamically bound.

To model the fact that a call to a pure method m in a class C can be both statically and dynamically bound, we introduce two function symbols for every pure method in the verification logic (instead of only one): $\#C.m$ and $\#C.m_D$ (similar to [7,8]). The former function symbol represents statically bound calls to m, and is axiomatized as described in Section 2. The latter function symbol represents dynamically bound calls is axiomatized by relating it to the former symbol using the following axiom.

$$\forall heap, o, x_1, \ldots, x_n \bullet typeof(o) = C \Rightarrow$$
$$\#C.m_D(heap, o, x_1, \ldots, x_n) = \#C.m(heap, o, x_1, \ldots, x_n)$$

That is, given that the dynamic type of some object o (denoted by $typeof(o)$) is C, one may assume that dynamically bound calls to the object equal statically bound calls to C's method m. In addition, whenever a method $D.m$ overrides a method $A.m$, the following axiom is added: two dynamically bound calls of m yield the same result whenever the receiver's dynamic type is a subtype (denoted by $<:$) of D.

$$\forall heap, o, x_1, \ldots, x_n \bullet typeof(o) <: D \Rightarrow$$
$$\#A.m_D(heap, o, x_1, \ldots, x_n) = \#D.m_D(heap, o, x_1, \ldots, x_n)$$

Calls on the receiver object in method contracts are treated differently from such calls in code. If a method call is dynamically bound, then calls on the receiver object in the method contract are treated as dynamically bound; otherwise calls in the contract on the receiver are treated as statically bound. Methods themselves are verified assuming they are called statically, i.e. calls in the contract on the receiver are bound statically. Doing so is sound, provided every subclass overrides each method. Indeed, if a method is called statically, then the caller and callee agree on the method contract. If a method is called dynamically, then the dynamic type of the receiver equals the static type, and therefore the static contract equals the dynamic one.

To ensure Liskov's substitution principle, we impose the restriction that overriding methods must inherit the contract of overridden methods as is. The only exception to this rule are postconditions. More specifically, an overriding method may extend the contract of the overridden method with additional postconditions. More flexible approaches to ensure proper subtyping exist (e.g. [9]), and combining them with our approach is part of future work.

5 Discussion

Defaults. The examples shown in this paper contain on about 2 lines of specification for every line of code, where we consider the invariant and footprint methods to be part of the specification. To reduce this annotation overhead, we propose using defaults for common programming and specification patterns. More specifically, we propose generating footprint and invariant methods based on field modifiers, and adding default contracts to methods. Using these defaults reduces the number of annotation in class *Stack* of Figure 2 from 17 to 3.

The scheme is as follows. The footprint and invariant methods in a class C are generated based on C's fields. That is, the footprint method includes locations corresponding to C's fields. Moreover, fields may be marked with a **rep** modifier. The footprint of an object referenced from one of C's rep fields is also included in the footprint. Finally, C's footprint method includes the footprint of the superclass. C's invariant method states that rep fields are non-null, that the footprints of rep objects and of the superclass do not contain locations corresponding to fields of C, and that those footprints are mutually disjoint. The footprint method requires the invariant and reads itself. The invariant method reads the footprint, provided it returns true.

Each method is given a default method contract. Pure methods require the invariant and read the footprint. Constructors write the new object's footprint, ensure the invariant, and ensure that the footprint contains only fresh locations. Other mutators require and ensure the invariant, write the pre-state footprint, and ensure that the footprint is only extended with fresh locations.

Experience. Table 1 lists the time taken to discharge the verification conditions generated for each program. The experiments have been carried out on a regular desktop pc with a Pentium 4 3.00 Ghz CPU and 512 Mb of RAM.

The verifier prototype is a custom build of the Spec# program verifier [10], and uses 2 theorem provers: Z3 and Simplify. The latter prover is only used if the former fails to verify a verification condition. Z3 is typically faster than Simplify, but is sometimes unable to prove the constructor's postcondition stating that elements in the new object's footprint are fresh.

Table 1. Table showing the time taken (in seconds) to verify the examples. Examples not shown in this paper can be downloaded from [1].

	cell	fraction	list, stack & iterator	observer	masterclock
# lines	20	52	138	85	74
time taken	0.6	1.6	25.2	15.1	11.4

6   Related Work

The approach presented in this paper was inspired by the work of Kassios [3,4]. Kassios uses specification variables, similar to our pure methods, to achieve data abstraction. To solve the framing problem, he proposes using dynamic frames to abstractly specify the footprint of specification variables and the effect of mutator methods. Dynamic frames are specification variables that hold sets of memory locations. However, Kassios' solution is presented in the context of an idealized, higher-order logical framework. We show how Kassios' ideas can be incorporated in a program verifier for a Java-like language based on first-order logic, and demonstrate that many interesting examples can be verified automatically. Moreover, we extend his solution to deal with Java-like inheritance.

In the basic Boogie methodology [6], data abstraction is limited to object invariants. More specifically, each object has a ghost field inv, and the methodology ensures that the invariant of an object o holds whenever $o.inv$ is true. To ensure the soundness of the approach, the Boogie methodology imposes several restrictions: inv can only be updated using special operations called **pack** and **unpack**, updating a field $o.f$ requires $o.inv$ to be false, and finally the invariant itself can only mention fields within the object's ownership cone. The dynamic frames approach can be considered to be conceptually simpler than the Boogie methodology (and its extensions), since it does not impose any methodological restrictions.

In [11] and [12], the authors extend the basic Boogie methodology to deal with non-hierarchical object structures. In particular, they allow invariants to mention fields outside of the object's ownership cone provided certain visibility requirements are met. More specifically, if the invariant of class C mentions a field f of a non-owned object, then C must be visible in the the class declaring f. No such restriction is present in our approach.

[7,13] and [14] both extend the basic Boogie methodology with support for data abstraction using pure methods. Similarly to our approach, they model pure methods as functions in the verification logic. Both approaches essentially solve the framing problem by encoding in the verification logic that these functions depend only on a number of ownership cones instead of on the entire heap. To ensure the consistency of the verification logic (regardless of the addition of axioms generated based on pure methods), [7] and [14] enforce the termination of pure methods. The former approach does so by checking the acyclicity of the call-graph at load-time. The latter approach relies on a heuristic for finding a well-founded order. One of the major differences between their approach and ours is that we allow pure methods to depend on any location, as long as the location is an element of the method's footprint (which can be any expression of type set), and it is up to client code to track disjointness of method footprints, while they only allow pure methods to depend on objects in a limited number of ownership cones (indicated by means of rep modifiers on fields).

Leino and Müller [15] extend the basic Boogie methodology with model fields to achieve data abstraction. A model field declaration consists of a type, a name, and a constraint. A model field cannot be assigned to within the program text; instead the model field is assigned a random value satisfying the constraint whenever the object is being packed. To prevent unsound reasoning arising from unsatisfiable constraints, Leino and Müller require the theorem prover to come up with a witness before assuming the constraint holds. However, experience shows that theorem provers (in particular Simplify) are unable to find witnesses even in simple cases, and as such it is unlikely that their approach is suitable for use within an automatic program verifier.

Parkinson and Bierman [16,17] extend separation logic to the Java programming language, introducing abstract predicates to attain data abstraction. Their solution has not been implemented in an automatic program verifier, and the feasibility of automatic verification has not been shown. Furthermore, Parkinson's abstract predicates are not part of the programming language itself, while pure methods are. This might make it easier for programmers to use pure methods.

In [18], the authors propose using data groups to specify side-effects. A data group represents a set of variables (similarly to our footprint methods), and mutator methods can abstractly specify their footprint using a modifies clause in terms of these data groups (similarly to our writes clauses which use footprint methods). However, to ensure the soundness, their approach imposes two methodological restrictions: the pivot uniqueness and owner exclusion restriction. Our approach requires no such restrictions, and as a consequence it can handle programs that [18] cannot. For example, the former restriction rules out sharing of representation objects, as is the case in the iterator example shown in Figure 3.

Banerjee, Naumann and Rosenberg [19] propose using regions, state-dependent expressions similar to our method footprints, to specify the effect of mutators. They develop a Hoare-style calculus and proof its soundness. However, the logic is not implemented and, in effect, there are some challenges to do so when one would target SMT solvers, e.g. they use ghost state and "recursion" to express reachability, and they use frame subsumption, which should only be applied on demand.

Müller [8]'s thesis combines model fields with an ownership type system called Universes. Model fields are similar to pure methods that have no parameters. Model fields may depend on the fields of owned objects and the fields of peer objects, i.e. objects with the same owner as the receiver. However, model fields can only depend on peers if a model field is visible within the peer. For example, if the pure method *hasNext* from Figure 3 were a model field, then *hasNext* would have to be visible to the class ArrayList. Our approach has no such restriction.

7 Conclusion

In summary, this paper proposed an approach to the automatic verification of Java-like programs that combines the use of pure methods to achieve data abstraction with Kassios' solution to the framing problem [3,4]. More specifically, we solve the framing problem by extending each method contract with a method footprint, an upper bound on the set of memory locations read or written by the corresponding method. Thanks to the use of dynamic frames, pure methods that return a set of memory locations, these method footprints can be specified without breaking information hiding. The approach has been implemented in a prototype [1], which has been used to automatically verify several challenging programs, including the iterator and observer pattern. We plan to extend our approach to concurrent programs, and apply our approach in a larger case-study.

Acknowledgments

The authors thank Rustan Leino and David Naumann for helpful comments and discussions. Jan Smans is a research assistant of the Fund for Scientific Research - Flanders (FWO). Bart Jacobs is a postdoctoral fellow of the Fund for Scientific Research - Flanders (FWO).

References

1. http://www.cs.kuleuven.be/~jans/DFJ
2. Leavens, G.T., Leino, K.R.M., Müller, P.: Specification and verification challenges for sequential object-oriented programs. In: Formal Aspects of Computing

3. Kassios, Y.: A Theory of Object Oriented Refinement. PhD thesis, University of Toronto (2006)
4. Kassios, Y.T.: Dynamic frames: Support for framing, dependencies and sharing without restrictions. In: Formal Methods (2006)
5. Leino, K.R.M., Schulte, W.: A verifying compiler for a multi-threaded object-oriented language. In: Marktoberdorf Summer School Lecture Notes (2006)
6. Barnett, M., DeLine, R., Fahndrich, M., Leino, K.R.M., Schulte, W.: Verification of object-oriented programs with invariants. Journal of Object Technology 3(6) (2004)
7. Jacobs, B., Piessens, F.: Verification of programs with inspector methods. In: FT-FJP (2006)
8. Müller, P.: Modular Specification and Verification of Object-Oriented Programs. PhD thesis, FernUniversität Hagen (2001)
9. Dhara, K.K., Leavens, G.T.: Forcing behavioral subtyping through specification inheritance. In: ICSE (1996)
10. Barnett, M., Leino, K.R.M., Schulte, W.: The spec# programming system: An overview. In: Barthe, G., Burdy, L., Huisman, M., Lanet, J.-L., Muntean, T. (eds.) CASSIS 2004. LNCS, vol. 3362, Springer, Heidelberg (2005)
11. Leino, K.R.M., Müller, P.: Object invariants in dynamic contexts. In: Odersky, M. (ed.) ECOOP 2004. LNCS, vol. 3086, Springer, Heidelberg (2004)
12. Barnett, M., Naumann, D.A.: Friends need a bit more: Maintaining invariants over shared state. In: Kozen, D. (ed.) MPC 2004. LNCS, vol. 3125, Springer, Heidelberg (2004)
13. Jacobs, B., Piessens, F.: Inspector methods for state abstraction. Journal of Object Technology 6(5) (2007)
14. Darvas, A., Leino, K.R.M.: Practical reasoning about invocations and implementations of pure methods. In: Dwyer, M.B., Lopes, A. (eds.) FASE 2007. LNCS, vol. 4422, Springer, Heidelberg (2007)
15. Leino, K.R.M., Müller., P.: A verification methodology for model fields. In: Sestoft, P. (ed.) ESOP 2006. LNCS, vol. 3924, Springer, Heidelberg (2006)
16. Parkinson, M.: Local Reasoning for Java. PhD thesis, University of Cambridge (2005)
17. Parkinson, M., Bierman, G.: Separation logic and abstraction. In: POPL (2005)
18. Leino, K.R.M., Poetzsch-Heffter, A., Zhou, Y.: Using data groups to specify and check side effects. In: PLDI (2002)
19. Banerjee, A., Naumann, D.A., Rosenberg, S.: Regional logic for local reasoning about global invariants. (Unpublished, 2007)

A Domain Analysis to Specify Design Defects and Generate Detection Algorithms

Naouel Moha[1,2], Yann-Gaël Guéhéneuc[1],
Anne-Françoise Le Meur[2], and Laurence Duchien[2]

[1] Ptidej Team – GEODES, DIRO
University of Montreal, Quebec, Canada
{mohanaou,guehene}@iro.umontreal.ca
[2] Adam Team – INRIA Futurs, LIFL
Université des Sciences et Technologies de Lille, France
{Laurence.Duchien,Anne-Francoise.Le-Meur}@lifl.fr

Abstract. Quality experts often need to identify in software systems design defects, which are recurring design problems, that hinder development and maintenance. Consequently, several defect detection approaches and tools have been proposed in the literature. However, we are not aware of any approach that defines and reifies the process of generating detection algorithms from the existing textual descriptions of defects. In this paper, we introduce an approach to automate the generation of detection algorithms from specifications written using a domain-specific language. The domain-specific is defined from a thorough domain analysis. We specify several design defects, generate automatically detection algorithms using templates, and validate the generated detection algorithms in terms of precision and recall on XERCES v2.7.0, an open-source object-oriented system.

Keywords: Design defects, antipatterns, code smells, domain-specific language, algorithm generation, detection, Java.

1 Introduction

Software quality is an important goal of software engineering because software systems are pervasive and realise vital functions in our societies. It is assessed and improved mainly by quality experts during formal technical reviews, which objective is to detect errors and defects early, before they are passed on to subsequent software engineering activities or released to customers [23].

During the reviews, the experts track design defects, which are "bad" solutions to recurring design problems in object-oriented systems. Design defects are problems resulting from bad design practices [21]. They include problems ranging from high-level and design problems, such as antipatterns [3], to low-level or local problems, such as code smells [9]. They make adding, debugging, and evolving of features difficult. These defects are at a higher-level than Halstead or Fenton's defects, which are "deviations from specifications or expectations

J. Fiadeiro and P. Inverardi (Eds.): FASE 2008, LNCS 4961, pp. 276–291, 2008.
© Springer-Verlag Berlin Heidelberg 2008

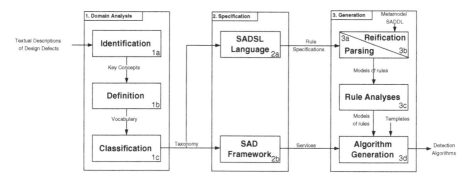

Fig. 1. Generation Process

which might lead to failures in operation" [8,15]. Code smells are symptoms of antipatterns.

Several approaches have been proposed in the literature to specify and detect design defects, for example [16,20,28]. Although showing interesting precisions, these approaches are, to the best of our knowledge, all based on detection algorithms that are defined programmatically and implemented by hand: (1) The detection algorithms are defined at the code level by developers rather than at the domain level by quality experts; (2) The implementation of the algorithms is guided by the services of the underlying detection framework rather than by a study of the textual descriptions of the defects. Thus, it is difficult for quality experts to evaluate the choices made by the developers, to adapt the algorithms to different contexts, and to compare the results of different implementations.

In this paper, we follow the principle of domain analysis to propose a domain-specific language to specify design defects at the domain level and generate automatically detection algorithms from these specifications. Our domain-specific language, SADSL (*Software Architectural Defects Specification Language*), offers the following benefits with respect to previous work: (1) The language is based on the key concepts found in the textual descriptions of the defects rather than on the underlying detection framework; (2) The specifications are used to generate automatically detection algorithms rather than implementing algorithms by hand. Thus, quality experts can specify defects using domain-related abstractions, taking into account the context and characteristics of the analysed systems, and generate traceable detection algorithms.

The new aspects presented in this paper compared with our previous work [18,19] are threefold. First, we present a domain analysis of the key concepts defining design defects and its resulted and enhanced domain-specific language to specify defects, SADSL. However, we re-present the underlying detection framework, SAD (*Software Architectural Defects*) for the sack of clarity. Second, we propose a explicit process for generating detection algorithms automatically using templates. Third, we present the validation of this process including the first study of both precision and recall on a large open-source software system, XERCES v2.7.0. Figure 1 relates the different contributions.

Table 1. List of Design Defects

The *Blob* (called also God class [25]) corresponds to a large controller class that *depends on data* stored in surrounded data classes. A large class declares many fields and methods with a low cohesion. A controller class monopolises most of the processing done by a system, takes most of the decisions, and closely directs the processing of other classes [30]. We identify controller classes using suspicious names such as 'Process', 'Control', 'Manage', 'System', and so on. A data class contains only data and performs no processing on these data. It is composed of highly cohesive fields and accessors.
The *Functional Decomposition* antipattern may occur if experienced procedural developers with little knowledge of object-orientation implement an object-oriented system. Brown describes this antipattern as "a 'main' routine that calls numerous subroutines". The Functional Decomposition design defect consists of a main class, *i.e.*, a class with a procedural name, such as 'Compute' or 'Display', in which inheritance and polymorphism are scarcely used, that is *associated with small classes*, which declare many private fields and implement only *few* methods.
The *Spaghetti Code* is an antipattern that is characteristic of procedural thinking in object-oriented programming. Spaghetti Code is revealed by classes with no structure, declaring *long methods* with *no parameters*, and utilising *global variables* for processing. *Names of classes and methods* may suggest *procedural* programming. Spaghetti Code does not exploit and prevents the use of object-orientation mechanisms, *polymorphism* and *inheritance*.
The *Swiss Army Knife* refers to a tool fulfilling a wide range of needs. The Swiss Army Knife design defect is a complex class that offers a high number of services, for example, a complex class implementing a high number of interfaces. A Swiss Army Knife is different from a Blob, because it exposes a high complexity to address all foreseeable needs of a part of a system, whereas the Blob is a singleton monopolising all processing and data of a system. Thus, several Swiss Army Knives may exist in a system, for examples utility classes typically.

In the rest of this paper, Section 2 presents the domain analysis performed on the literature pertaining to design defects. Section 3 presents SADSL and SAD. Section 4 describes the generation process of detection algorithms. Section 5 validates our contributions with the specification and detection of four design defects: Blob, Functional Decomposition, Spaghetti Code, and Swiss Army Knife, on the open-source system XERCES v2.7.0. Section 6 surveys related work. Section 7 concludes and presents future work.

2   Domain Analysis of Design Defects

"Domain analysis is a process by which information used in developing software systems is identified, captured, and organised with the purpose of making it reusable when creating new systems" [24].

In the context of design defects, *information* relates to the defects, *software systems* are detection algorithms, and the information on design defects must be *reusable* when specifying new design defects. Thus, we have studied the textual descriptions of design defects in the literature to identify, define, and organise the key concepts of the domain, Steps 1a–1c in Figure 1.

2.1   Identification of the Key Concepts

The first step of the domain analysis consists of reviewing the literature on design defects, in particular books and articles, for example these cited in the related work in Section 6, to identify essential key concepts. This step is performed manually so its description would be necessarily narrative. Therefore, to illustrate this step, we use the example of the Spaghetti Code antipattern. We summarise the textual description of the Spaghetti Code [3, page 119] in Table 1 along with these of the Blob [3, page 73], Functional Decomposition [3, page 97], and Swiss Army Knife [3, page 197].

In the textual description of the Spaghetti Code, we identify the key concepts (highlighted) of classes with long methods, procedural names and with methods with no parameter, of classes defining global variables, and of classes not using inheritance and polymorphism.

We perform this first step iteratively: for each description of a defect, we extract all key concepts, compare them with existing concepts, and add them to the set of key concepts avoiding synonyms, a same concept with two different names, and homonyms, two different concepts with the same name. We study 29 defects, which included 8 antipatterns and 21 code smells. These 29 defects are representative of the whole set of defects described in the literature and include about 60 key concepts.

2.2 Definition of the Key Concepts

The key concepts include metric-based heuristics as well as structural and lexical information. In the second step, we define the key concepts precisely and form a unified vocabulary of reusable concepts to describe defects. For lack of space, we cannot present the definitions of each key concept but introduce a classification of the key concepts according to the types of properties on which they apply: measurable, lexical, and structural properties.

Measurable properties pertain to concepts expressed with measures of internal attributes of the constituents of systems (classes, interfaces, methods, fields, relationships, and so on). A measurable property defines a numerical or an ordinal value for a specific metric. Ordinal values are defined with a 5-point Likert scale: very high, high, medium, low, very low. Numerical values are used to define thresholds whereas ordinal values are used to define values relative to all the classes of a system under analysis.

These properties also related to a set of metrics identified during the domain analysis, including Chidamber and Kemerer metric suite [6]: depth of inheritance DIT, lines of code in a class LOC_CLASS, lines of code in a method LOC_METHOD, number of attributes declared in a class NAD, number of methods declared in a class NMD, lack of cohesion in methods LCOM, number of accessors NACC, number of private fields NPRIVFIELD, number of interfaces NINTERF, number of methods with no parameters NMNOPARAM.

Lexical Properties relate to the concepts pertaining to the vocabulary used to name constituents. They characterise constituents with specific names, defined in a list of keywords. In future work, we plan to use the WORDNET lexical database of English to deal with synonyms.

Structural Properties pertain to concepts related to the structure of the constituents of systems. For example, the property USE_GLOBAL_VARIABLE is used to check if a class uses global variables, and the property NO_POLYMORPHISM to check if a class does not/prevents the use of polymorphism. System classes and

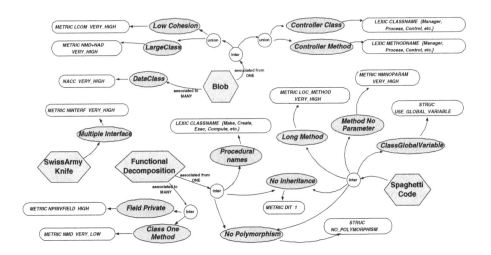

Fig. 2. Taxonomy of Design Defects. (Hexagons are antipatterns, gray ovals are code smells, white ovals are properties, and circles are set operators.)

interfaces characterised by the previous properties may be, in addition, linked with one another with three types of relationships: association, aggregation, and composition. Cardinalities define the minimum and the maximum numbers of instances of rules that participate in a relationship.

In the example of the Spaghetti Code, we obtain the following classification: measurable properties include the concepts of *long methods*, *methods with no parameter*, *inheritance*; lexical properties include the concepts of *procedural names*; structural properties include the concepts of *global variables*, *polymorphism*. Structural properties and relationships among constituents appear in the Blob and Functional Decomposition (see the key concepts *depends on data* and *associated with small classes*).

We also observe during the domain analysis that properties can be combined using **set operators**, such as intersection and union. For example, all properties must be present to characterise a class as Spaghetti Code.

2.3   Classification of the Key Concepts

Using the key concepts and their definitions, we build a taxonomy of defects by using all relevant key concepts to relate code smells and antipatterns on a single map and clearly identify their relationships.

We produce a map organising consistently defects and key concepts. This map is important to prevent misinterpretation by clarifying and classifying defects. It is similar in purpose to Gamma *et al*'s Pattern Map [12, inside back cover]. For lack of space, we only show in Figure 2 the taxonomy from the domain analysis of the four design defects in Table 1.

The taxonomy shows the structural relationships or set combinations among antipatterns (hexagons) and code smells (ovals in gray), and their relation with

```
1   CODESMELL   define   LongMethod      as  METRIC LOC_METHOD with   VERY_HIGH and 10.0;
2   CODESMELL   define   NoParameter     as  METRIC NMNOPARAM with    VERY_HIGH and 5.0;
3   CODESMELL   define   NoInheritance   as  METRIC DIT        with   1 and 0.0;
4   CODESMELL   define   NoPolymorphism  as  STRUC  NO_POLYMORPHISM;
5   CODESMELL   define   ProceduralName  as  LEXIC  CLASS_NAME with   (Make, Create, Exec);
6   CODESMELL   define   UseGlobalVariable as STRUC USE_GLOBAL_VARIABLE;
7   CODESMELL   define   ClassOneMethod  as  METRIC NMD        with   VERY_LOW and 10.0;
8   CODESMELL   define   FieldPrivate    as  METRIC NPRIVFIELD with   HIGH and 10.0;
9   ANTIPATTERN define   SpaghettiCode   as  {
              ((LongMethod INTER NoParameter) INTER (NoInheritance INTER NoPolymorphism))
              INTER
              (ProceduralName INTER UseGlobalVariable) };
10  ANTIPATTERN define   FunctionalDecomposition as {
              ASSOC FROM (ProceduralName INTER (NoInheritance INTER NoPolymorphism)) ONE
              TO (ClassOneMethod UNION FieldPrivate) MANY };
```

Fig. 3. Specifications of the Spaghetti Code and Functional Decomposition

measurable, structural, and lexical properties (ovals in white). It gives an overview of all key concepts that characterise the four defects and differentiates the key concepts as either structural relationships between code smells or their properties (measurable, structural, lexical). It also makes explicit the relationships among high- and low-level defects.

3 Specification of Design Defects

The domain analysis performed in the previous section provides a set of key concepts, their definition, and a classification. Then, following Steps 2a and 2b in Figure 1, we design SADSL, a domain-specific language (DSL) [17] to specify defects in terms of their measurable, structural and lexical properties, and SAD, a framework providing the services required to make operational computation of the properties, set operations, and so on.

We build SADSL and SAD using and only using the identified key concepts, thus they both capture domain expertise. Therefore, SADSL and SAD differ from general purpose languages and their runtime environments, which are designed to be universal [7]. They also differ from previous work on design defect detection, which did not define *explicitly* a DSL and in which the detection framework drove the specification of the detection algorithms.

Thus, with SADSL and SAD, it is easier for quality experts to understand design defect specifications and to specify new defects because these are expressed using domain-related abstractions and focus on *what* to detect instead of *how* to detect it [7].

3.1 SADSL

With SADSL, quality experts specify defects as sets of rules. Rules are expressed using key concepts. They can specify code smells, which correspond to measurable, lexical, or structural properties, or express antipatterns, which correspond

```
1   rulespec         ::= (codesmell)⁺ (antipattern)⁺
2   codesmell        ::= CODESMELL   define codesmellName   as   csContent ;
3   antipattern      ::= ANTIPATTERN define antipatternName as  { apContent };

4   csContent        ::= property
5   apContent        ::= codesmellName | (apContent operator apContent) | relationship
6   operator         ::= INTER | UNION | DIFF

7   property         ::= METRIC metricID with  metricValue and fuzziness
8                       | LEXIC lexicID   with  ((lexicValue,)⁺)
9                       | STRUC structID
10  metricID         ::= DIT | NINTERF | NMNOPARAM | LCOM | LOC_METHOD
11                      | LOC_CLASS | NAD | NMD | NACC | NPRIVFIELD
12                      | metricID + metricID
13                      | metricID - metricID
14  metricValue      ::= VERY_HIGH | HIGH | MEDIUM | LOW | VERY_LOW | NUMBER
15  lexicID          ::= CLASS_NAME | INTERFACE_NAME | METHOD_NAME | FIELD_NAME | PARAMETER_NAME
16  structID         ::= USE_GLOBAL_VARIABLE | NO_POLYMORPHISM
17                      | ABSTRACT_CLASS | IS_DATACLASS | ACCESSOR_METHOD
18                      | FUNCTION_CLASS | FUNCTION_METHOD | STATIC_METHOD
19                      | PROTECTED_METHOD | OVERRIDDEN_METHOD
20                      | INHERITED_METHOD | INHERITED_VARIABLE

21  relationship     ::= relationshipType FROM apContent cardinality TO apContent cardinality
22  relationshipType ::= ASSOC | AGGREG | COMPOS
23  cardinality      ::= ONE | MANY | ONE_OR_MANY

24  codesmellName, antipatternName, lexicValue ∈ string
25  fuzziness ∈ double { 0...100 }
```

Fig. 4. BNF Grammar of Design Defect Rule Specifications

to combinations of code smells using set operators or structural relationships. Figure 3 shows the specifications of the Spaghetti Code and Functional Decomposition antipatterns and their code smells. These two antipatterns shared some code smells as shown in the taxonomy in Figure 2.

A Spaghetti Code is specified using the intersection of two rules, which are intersections of two other rules (line 9). A class is Spaghetti Code if it declares methods with a very high number of lines of code (measurable property, line 1), with no parameter (measurable property, line 2); if it does not use inheritance (measurable property, line 3), and polymorphism (structural property, line 4), and has a name that recalls procedural names (lexical property, line 5), while declaring/using global variables (structural property, line 6). The float value after the keyword 'and' in measurable properties corresponds to the degree of fuzziness, which is the margin acceptable in percentage around the numerical value (line 3) or around the threshold relative to the ordinal value (lines 1-2). We further explain the ordinal values and the fuzziness in Section 4.

We formalise specifications with a Backus-Naur Form (BNF) grammar, shown in Figure 4. A specification lists first a set of code smells and then a set of antipatterns (Figure 4, line 1). A code smell is defined as a property. A property can be of three different kinds: measurable, structural, or lexical, and define pairs of identifier–value (lines 7–9). The BNF grammar specifies only a subset of possible structural properties, other can be added as new domain analyses are performed. The antipatterns are combinations of the code smells defined in the specification using set operators (lines 5–6). The antipatterns can also be linked to these code smells using relationships such as the composition, aggregation or association(lines 5, 21–23). Each code smell is identified by a name (line 2) and can be reused in the definition of antipatterns. Thus, the specification of the code smells, which can be viewed as a repository of code smells, can be reused or modified for the specification of different antipatterns.

3.2   SAD

The SAD framework provides services that implement operations on the relationships, operators, properties, and ordinal values. It also provides services to build, access, and analyse systems. Thus, with SAD, it is possible to compute metrics, analyse structural relationships, perform lexical and structural analyses on classes, and apply the rules. The set of services and the overall design of the framework are directed by the key concepts and the domain analysis. SAD represents a super-set of previous detection frameworks and therefore could delegate part of its services to exiting frameworks.

SAD is built upon the PADL meta-model (*Pattern and Abstract-level Description Language*), a language-independent meta-model to represent object-oriented systems, including binary class relationships [13] and accessors, and on the POM framework (*Primitives, Operators, Metrics*) for metric computation [14]. PADL offers a set of constituents from which we can build models of systems. It also offers methods to manipulate these models easily and generate other models, using the Visitor design pattern. We choose PADL because it is mature with 6 years of active development and is maintained in-house.

3.3   Discussions

The defect specifications are self-documenting and express naturally the textual descriptions of the defects. They can be modified by quality experts either to refine them by adding new rules or modifying existing ones to take into account the contexts of the systems. For example, in small applications, a domain expert could consider as defects classes with a high DIT but not in large systems. In a management application, a domain expert could also consider different keywords as indicating controller classes. Thus, specifications can be modified easily at the domain level without any knowledge of the underlying detection framework.

4   From Specifications to Detection Algorithms

The problem that we solve is the automatic transition from the specifications to detection algorithms to avoid the manual implementation of algorithms, which is costly and not reusable, and to ensure the traceability between specifications and occurrences of defects detected. Thus, the automatic generation of detection algorithms spares the experts or developers of implementing by hand the detection algorithms and allows them to save time and resources.

The generation process consists of four fully automated steps, starting from the specifications through their reification to algorithm generation, as shown in Figure 1, Steps 3a–3d, and detailed below.

4.1 Parsing and Reification

The first step consists of parsing the design defect specifications. A parser is built using JFLEX and JAVACUP (cf. http://www2.cs.tum.edu/projects/cup/) from the BNF grammar, extended with appropriate semantic actions.

Then, as a specification is parsed, the second step consists of reifying the specifications based on the dedicated SADDL meta-model (*Software Architectural Defects Definition Language*). The meta-model is a representation of the abstract syntax tree generated by the parser. The meta-model SADDL defines constituents to represent specifications, rules, set operators, relationships among rules, and properties. The result of this reification is a SADDL model of the specification, instance of class `Specification` defined in SADDL. An instance of `Specification` is composed of objects of type `IRule`, which describes rules that can be either simple or composite. A composite rule, `CompositeRule`, is a rule composed of other rules (`Composite` design pattern). Rules are combined using set operators defined in class `Operators`. Structural relationships are enforced using methods defined in class `Relationships`. The SADDL meta-model also implements the `Visitor` design pattern.

4.2 Rule Analyses

This step consists of visiting the models of specifications and applying some consistency and domain-specific analyses. These analyses aim to identify incoherent or meaningless rules before generating the detection algorithms. Consistency analyses consist of verifying that specifications are not inconsistent, redundant, or incomplete. An inconsistent specification is, for example, two code smells defined with identical names but different properties. A redundant specification corresponds, for example, to two code smells defined with different names but identical properties. An example of an incomplete specification is a code smell referenced in the rule of an antipattern but not defined in the rule set of code smells. Domain-specific analyses consist of verifying that the rules are conform to the domain. For example, the value associated to a metric has a meaning in the domain : typically, a measurable property with the metric number of methods declared `NMD` equal to a float has no meaning in the domain.

4.3 Algorithm Generation

The generation of the detection algorithms is implemented as a set of visitors on models of specifications. The generation targets the services of the SAD framework and is based on templates. Templates are excerpts of Java code source with well-defined tags to be replaced by concrete code. We use templates because our previous studies [18,19] showed that detection algorithms have recurring structures. Thus, we aggregate naturally all common structures of detection algorithms into templates. As we visit the model of a specification, we replace the tags with the data and values appropriate to the rules. The final source code generated for a specification is the detection algorithm of the corresponding design defect and this code is directly executable without any manual interventions.

We detail in the following the generation of the detection algorithms of the set operators and the measurable properties. We do not present the generation of the lexical properties, structural properties, and structural relationships because they are similar to the ones presented here.

Measurable Properties. The template given in Figure 5(e) is a class called `<CODESMELL>Detection` that extends the class `CodeSmellDetection` and implements `ICodeSmellDetection`. It declares the method `performDetection()`, which consists of computing the specified metric on each class of the system. All the metric values are compared with one another with a boxplot, a statistical technique [4], to identify ordinal values, *i.e.*, outlier or normal values. Then, the boxplot returns only the classes with metric values that verify the ordinal values. Figure 5(c) presents the process of generating code to verify a measurable property defined in the specification of the Spaghetti Code on a set of constituents. When the rule is visited in the model of the specification, we replace the tag `<CODESMELL>` by the name of the rule, *LongMethod*, tag `<METRIC>` by the name of the metric, `LOC_METHOD`, tag `<FUZZINESS>` by the value 10.0, and tag `<ORDINAL_VALUES>` by the method associated with the ordinal value `VERY_HIGH`. Figure 5(g) presents the code generated for the rule given in Figure 5(a).

Set Operators. The rules can be combined using set operators such as the intersection (Figure 5(b). The code generation for set operators is quite different from the generation of properties. The template given in Figure 5(f) contains also a class called `<CODESMELL>Detection` that extends the class `CodeSmellDetection` and implements `ICodeSmellDetection`. However, the method `performDetection()` consists of combining with a set operator the list of classes in each operand of the rule given in Figure 5(b) and returning classes that satisfy this combination. Figure 5(d) presents the process related to the code generation for set operators in the specification of the Spaghetti Code. When an operator is visited in the model of the specification, we replace the tags associated to the operands of the rule, `operand1: LongMethod`, `operand2: NoParameter`, and the tag `<OPERATION>` by the type of set operator specified in the specification, *i.e.*, intersection. The operands correspond to detection classes generated when visiting other rules (Figure 5(h)).

Discussion. The generated algorithms are by construct deterministic. We do not need to revise manually the code because the generation process ensures the correctness of the code source with respect to the specifications. This generated code tends sometimes itself towards Spaghetti Code and could be improved using polymorphism, yet it is automatically generated and is not intended to be read by quality experts and it will be improved in future work. We do not report the generation times because it takes only few seconds.

5   Validation

We validate our contributions by specifying and detecting four design defects and computing the precision and recall of the generated algorithms. We use XERCES

```
CODESMELL   define  LongMethod as
METRIC  LOC_METHOD  with  VERY_HIGH and 10.0;
```

(a) Excerpt of the Spaghetti Code.

```
ANTIPATTERN  define  SpaghettiCode as {
    ((LongMethod ∩ NoParameter) ...
```

(b) Excerpt of the Spaghetti Code.

```
1   public void visit(IMetric aMetric) {
2     replaceTAG("<CODESMELL>", aRule.getName());
3     replaceTAG("<METRIC>", aMetric.getName());
4     replaceTAG(<FUZZINESS>,
5       aMetric.getFuzziness());
6     replaceTAG(<ORDINAL_VALUE>,
7       aMetric.getOrdinalValue());
8   }
9   private String getOrdinalValue(int value) {
10    switch (value) {
11      case VERY_HIGH :
12        "getHighOutliers";
13      case HIGH :
14        "getHighValues";
15      case MEDIUM :
16        "getNormalValues";
17      ...
18  }
```

(c) Visitor.

```
1   public void visit(IOperator anOperator) {
2     replaceTAG("<OPERAND1>",
3       anOperator.getOperand1());
4     replaceTAG("<OPERAND2>",
5       anOperator.getOperand2());
6     switch (anOperator.getOperatorType()) {
7       case OPERATOR_UNION :
8         operator = "union";
9       case OPERATOR_INTER :
10        operator = "intersection";
11      ...
12    }
13    replaceTAG("<OPERATION>", operator);
```

(d) Visitor.

```
1   public class <CODESMELL>Detection
2     extends CodeSmellDetection
3     implements ICodeSmellDetection {
4     public Set performDetection() {
5       IClass c = iteratorOnClasses.next();
6       LOCofSetOfClasses.add(
7         Metrics.compute(<METRIC>, c));
8       ...
9       BoxPlot boxPlot = new BoxPlot(
10        <METRIC>ofSetOfClasses, <FUZZINESS>);
11      Map setOfOutliers =
12        boxPlot.<ORDINAL_VALUE>();
13      ...
14      suspiciousCodeSmells.add( new CodeSmell(
15        <CODESMELL>, setOfOutliers));
16      ...
17      return suspiciousCodeSmells;
18  }
```

(e) Template.

```
1   public class <CODESMELL>Detection
2     extends CodeSmellDetection
3     implements ICodeSmellDetection {
4     public void performDetection() {
5       ICodeSmellDetection cs<OPERAND1> =
6         new <OPERAND1>Detection();
7       op1.performDetection();
8       Set set<OPERAND1> =
9         cs<OPERAND1>.listOfCodeSmells();
10      ICodeSmellDetection cs<OPERAND2> =
11        new <OPERAND2>Detection();
12      op2.performDetection();
13      Set set<OPERAND2> =
14        cs<OPERAND2>.listOfCodeSmells();
15      Set setOperation = Operators.getInstance().
16        <OPERATION>(set<OPERAND1>, set<OPERAND2>);
17      this.setSetOfSmells(setOperation);
18  }
```

(f) Template.

```
1   public class LongMethodDetection
2     extends CodeSmellDetection
3     implements ICodeSmellDetection {
4     public Set performDetection() {
5       IClass c = iteratorOnClasses.next();
6       LOCofSetOfClasses.add(
7         Metrics.compute("LOC_METHOD", c));
8       ...
9       BoxPlot boxPlot = new BoxPlot(
10        LOC_METHODofSetOfClasses, 10.0);
11      Map setOfOutliers =
12        boxPlot.getHighOutliers();
13      ...
14      suspiciousCodeSmells.add( new CodeSmell(
15        LongMethod, setOfOutliers));
16      ...
17      return suspiciousCodeSmells;
18  }
```

(g) Generated Code.

```
1   public class Inter1
2     extends CodeSmellDetection
3     implements ICodeSmellDetection {
4     public void performDetection() {
5       ICodeSmellDetection csLongMethod =
6         new LongMethodDetection();
7       csLongMethod.performDetection();
8       Set setLongMethod =
9         csLongMethod.listOfCodeSmells();
10      ICodeSmellDetection csNoParameter =
11        new NoParameterDetection();
12      csNoParameter.performDetection();
13      Set setNoParameter =
14        csNoParameter.listOfCodeSmells();
15      Set setOperation = Operators.getInstance().
16        intersection(setLongMethod, setNoParameter);
17      this.setSetOfSmells(setOperation);
18  }
```

(h) Generated Code.

Fig. 5. Code Generation for Measurable Properties (left) and Set Operators (right)

v2.7.0, a framework for building XML parsers in Java. XERCES contains 71,217 lines of code, 513 classes, and 162 interfaces. We seek to obtain a recall of 100% because quality experts need all design defects to improve software quality and ease formal technical reviews. We are not aware of any other work reporting both precision and recall for design defect detection algorithms and will gratefully provide our data for comparison with other work.

5.1 Validation Process

First, we build a model of XERCES. This model is obtained by reverse engineering. Then, we apply the generated detection algorithms on the model of the system and obtain all suspicious classes that have potential design defects. The list of suspicious classes is returned in a file. We validate the results of the detection algorithms by analysing the suspicious classes in the context of the complete model of the system and its environment.

We recast the validation in the domain of information retrieval and use the measures of precision and recall, where precision assesses the number of true identified defects, while recall assesses the number of true defects missed by the algorithms [10]. The computation of precision and recall is performed using independent results obtained manually because only quality experts can assess whether a suspicious class is *indeed* a defect or a false positive, depending on the specifications and the context and characteristics of the system. We asked three master students and two independent software engineers to analyse manually XERCES using only Brown and Fowler's books to identify design defects and compute the precision and recall of the algorithms. Each time a doubt on a candidate class arose, they considered the books as reference in deciding by consensus whether or not this class was actually a design defect. This task is tedious, some design defects may have been missed by mistake, thus we have asked other software engineers to perform this same task to confirm our findings and on other systems to increase our database.

5.2 Results

Table 2 reports detection times, numbers of suspicious classes, and precisions and recalls. We perform all computations on a Intel Dual Core at 1.67GHz with 1Gb of RAM. Computation times do not include building the models of the system but include accesses to compute metrics and check structural relationships and lexical and structural properties.

The recalls of the generated algorithms are 100% for each defect. Precisions are between 41.07% to more than 80%, providing between 5.65% and 14.81% of the total number of classes, which is reasonable for quality experts to analyse by hand, with respect to analysing the entire system, 513 classes, manually.

For the Spaghetti Code, we found 76 suspicious classes. Out of these 76 suspicious classes, 46 are indeed Spaghetti Code previously identified in XERCES manually by software engineers independent of the authors, which leads to a precision of 60.53% and a recall of 100.00% (see third line in Table 2). The result file

Table 2. Precision and Recall in XERCES v2.7.0. (In parenthesis, the percentage of classes affected by a design defect.). The number of classes in XERCES v2.7.0 is 513.

Design Defects	Numbers of Known True Positives	Numbers of Detected Defects	Precision	Recall	Time
Blob	39 (7.60%)	44 (8.58%)	88.64%	100.00%	2.45s
Functional Decomp.	15 (2.92%)	29 (5.65%)	51.72%	100.00%	0.91s
Spaghetti Code	46 (8.97%)	76 (14.81%)	60.53%	100.00%	0.23s
Swiss Army Knife	23 (4.48%)	56 (10.91%)	41.07%	100.00%	0.08s

contains all suspicious classes, including class `org.apache.xerces.impl.xpath.regex.RegularExpression` declaring 57 methods. Among these 57 methods, method `matchCharArray(...)` is typical of Spaghetti Code: it does not use inheritance and polymorphism, uses 18 class variables, and weighs 1,246 LOC.

5.3   Discussion

The validation shows that the specifications of the design defects lead to generated detection algorithms with expected recalls and good precisions. Thus, it confirms that: (1) The language allows describing several design defects. We described four different design defects, composed of 15 code smells; (2) The generated detection algorithms have a recall of 100%, *i.e.*, all known design defects are detected, and an average precision greater than 40%, *i.e.*, the detection algorithms report less than 2/3 of false positives with respect to the number of true positives; and, (3) The complexity of the generated algorithms is reasonable, *i.e.*, the generated algorithms have computation times of few seconds. Computation is fast because the complexity of our detection algorithms depends only on the number of classes in the system, n, and on the number of properties to verify. The complexity of the generated detection algorithms is $(c + op) \times \mathcal{O}(n)$, where c is the number of properties and op of operators.

The results depend on the specifications of the defects. The specifications must be neither too loose, not to detect too many suspicious classes, nor too constraining, and miss design defects. With SADSL, quality experts can refine the specifications of the design defects easily, according to the detected suspicious classes and their knowledge of the system through iterative refinement.

6   Related Work

Several defect detection approaches and tools have been proposed in the literature. We only present approaches and tools that are directly related to design defects. We are not aware of any approach that is based on an explicit domain analysis and the resulting domain-specific language.

Several books provide in-breadth views on pitfalls [29], heuristics [25], code smells [9], and antipatterns [3] aimed at a wide audience for educational purposes. However, they describe *textually* design defects and thus, it is difficult to build detection algorithms from their textual descriptions because they lack precision and are prone to misinterpretation. Travassos *et al.* [27] introduced a process based on manual inspections to identify design defects. No attempt was made to automate this process and thus it does not scale to large systems easily. Also, it only covers the manual detection of defects, not their specification.

Several semi-automatic approaches for the detection of defects exist. Among these, Marinescu [16] presented a metric-based approach to detect code smells with *detection strategies*, implemented in a tool called IPLASMA. This approach introduces metric-based strategies capturing deviations from good design principles. This process is simplistic and does not provide enough details to reproduce the declaration of detection strategies in other tools or to guide the definition of new strategies. However, detection strategies are a step towards precise specifications of code smells. As our tool, IPLASMA implements the technique of the boxplot. However, the mapping from the relative values of the boxplot with the metrics is not explicit. In our approach, we not only explicit this technique but also we enhance it with fuzzy logic and, thus, alleviates the problem related to the definition of thresholds. It is difficult to compare our approach with this approach because its detection algorithms are ad hoc and black box. Finally, the IPLASMA tool was only evaluated in terms of precision, no recall was computed. Munro [20] also noticed the limitations of the textual descriptions and proposed a template to describe code smells more systematically. It is a step towards more precise specifications of code smells but code smells remain nonetheless textual descriptions subject to misinterpretation. Munro also proposed metric-based heuristics to detect code smells, which are similar to Marinescu's detection strategies. Alikacem and Sahraoui proposed a description language of quality rules to detect violations of quality principles and low-level defects [1].

Tools such as PMD [22], CHECKSTYLE [5], and FXCOP [11] detect problems related to coding standards, bugs patterns or unused code. Thus, they focus on implementation problems but do not address higher-level design defects such as antipatterns. CROCOPAT [2] provides an efficient language to manipulate relations of any arity with a simple and expressive query and manipulation language. However, this language is at a low-level of abstraction and requires quality experts to understand the implementation details of its underlying model.

7   Conclusion and Future Work

In this paper, we introduced a domain analysis of the key concepts defining design defects; a domain-specific language to specify defects, SADSL, and its underlying detection framework, SAD; and a process for generating detection algorithms automatically. We implemented SADSL, SAD and the generation process and studied the precision and recall of four generated algorithms on XERCES v2.7.0. We showed that the detection algorithms are efficient and precise, and have 100% recall. With SADSL, SAD, and the generation process, quality experts can specify defects at the domain level using their expertise, generate detection algorithms, and detect defects during formal technical reviews.

The validation in terms of precision and recall sets a landmark for future quantitative comparisons. Thus, we plan to perform such a comparison of our work with previous approaches. We also plan to integrate the WORDNET lexical database of English into SAD, to improve the generated code in terms of quality and reusability, and to compute the precision and recall on more systems. We will assess the flexibility of the code generation offered when using XML technologies [26]. We will also perform usability studies of the language with quality experts.

Acknowledgments. We thank Giuliano Antoniol, Kim Mens, Dave Thomas, and Stéphane Vaucher for fruitful discussions. We also thank the master students and software engineers who performed the manual analysis and Duc-Loc Huynh and Pierre Leduc for their help in building SAD.

References

1. Alikacem, E.H., Sahraoui, H.: Détection d'anomalies utilisant un langage de description de règle de qualité. In: actes du 12e colloque LMO, pp. 185–200 (2006)
2. Beyer, D., Noack, A., Lewerentz, C.: Efficient relational calculation for software analysis. Transactions on Software Engineering 31(2), 137–149 (2005)
3. Brown, W.J., Malveau, R.C., Brown, W.H., McCormick III, H.W., Mowbray, T.J.: Anti Patterns: Refactoring Software, Architectures, and Projects in Crisis, 1st edn (1998)
4. Chambers, J.M., Clevelmd, W.S., Kleiner, B., Tukey, P.A.: Graphical methods for data analysis (1983)
5. CheckStyle (2004), http://checkstyle.sourceforge.net
6. Chidamber, S.R., Kemerer, C.F.: A metrics suite for object oriented design. IEEE Transactions on Software Engineering 20(6), 476–493 (1994)
7. Consel, C., Marlet, R.: Architecturing software using: A methodology for language development. In: Palamidessi, C., Meinke, K., Glaser, H. (eds.) ALP 1998 and PLILP 1998. LNCS, vol. 1490, pp. 170–194. Springer, Heidelberg (1998)
8. Fenton, N.E., Neil, M.: A critique of software defect prediction models. Software Engineering 25(5), 675–689 (1999)
9. Fowler, M.: Refactoring – Improving the Design of Existing Code, 1st edn. Addison-Wesley, Reading (1999)
10. Frakes, W.B., Baeza-Yates, R.: Information Retrieval: Data Structures and Algorithms. Prentice-Hall, Englewood Cliffs (1992)
11. FXCop (2006), http://www.gotdotnet.com/team/fxcop/
12. Gamma, E., Helm, R., Johnson, R., Vlissides, J.: Design Patterns – Elements of Reusable Object-Oriented Software, 1st edn. Addison-Wesley, Reading (1994)
13. Guéhéneuc, Y.-G., Albin-Amiot, H.: Recovering binary class relationships: Putting icing on the UML cake. In: Proceedings of the 19th OOSPLA Conference, pp. 301–314 (2004)
14. Guéhéneuc, Y.-G., Sahraoui, H., Zaidi, F.: Fingerprinting design patterns. In: Proceedings of the 11th WCRE Conference, pp. 172–181 (2004)
15. Halstead, M.H.: Elements of Software Science. Operating and programming systems series. Elsevier Science Inc., New York (1977)
16. Marinescu, R.: Detection strategies: Metrics-based rules for detecting design flaws. In: Proceedings of the 20th ICSM Conference, pp. 350–359 (2004)
17. Mernik, M., Heering, J., Sloane, A.M.: When and how to develop domain-specific languages. ACM Computing Surveys 37(4), 316–344 (2005)

18. Moha, N., Guéhéneuc, Y.-G., Leduc, P.: Automatic generation of detection algorithms for design defects. In: Proceedings of the 21st ASE Conference (2006)
19. Moha, N., Huynh, D.-L., Guéhéneuc, Y.-G.: Une taxonomie et un métamodèle pour la détection des défauts de conception. In: actes du 12e colloque LMO, pp. 201–216 (2006)
20. Munro, M.J.: Product metrics for automatic identification of "bad smell" design problems in java source-code. In: Proceedings of the 11th Metrics Symposium (2005)
21. Perry, D.E., Wolf, A.L.: Foundations for the study of software architecture. Software Engineering Notes 17(4), 40–52 (1992)
22. PMD (2002), http://pmd.sourceforge.net/
23. Pressman, R.S.: Software Engineering – A Practitioner's Approach, 5th edn. McGraw-Hill Higher Education (2001)
24. Prieto-Díaz, R.: Domain analysis: An introduction. Software Engineering Notes 15(2), 47–54 (1990)
25. Riel, A.J.: Object-Oriented Design Heuristics. Addison-Wesley, Reading (1996)
26. Swint, G.S., Pu, C., Jung, G., Yan, W., Koh, Y., Wu, Q., Consel, C., Sahai, A., Moriyama, K.: Clearwater: extensible, flexible, modular code generation. In: Proceedings of the 20th IEEE/ACM International Conference on Automated Software Engineering, pp. 144–153 (2005)
27. Travassos, G., Shull, F., Fredericks, M., Basili, V.R.: Detecting defects in object-oriented designs: using reading techniques to increase software quality. In: Proceedings of the 14th OOSPLA Conference, pp. 47–56 (1999)
28. Trifu, A., Marinescu, R.: Diagnosing design problems in object oriented systems. In: Proceedings of the 12th WCRE Conference (2005)
29. Webster, B.F.: Pitfalls of Object Oriented Development. M & T Books (1995)
30. Wirfs–Brock, R., McKean, A.: Object Design: Roles, Responsibilities and Collaborations. Addison-Wesley Professional, Reading (2002)

Automated Analysis of
Permission-Based Security Using UMLsec

Jan Jürjens[1,*], Jörg Schreck[2], and Yijun Yu[1]

[1] Computing Department, The Open University, GB
http://www.jurjens.de/jan
[2] O_2 (Germany), Munich

Abstract. To guarantee the security of computer systems, it is necessary to define security permissions to restrict the access to the systems' resources. These permissions enforce certain restrictions based on
the workflows the system is designed for. It is not always easy to see if
workflows and the design of the security permissions for the system fit
together. We present research towards a tool which supports embedding
security permissions in UML models and model-based security analysis
by providing consistency checks. It also offers an automated analysis of
underlying mechanisms for managing security-critical permissions using
Prolog resp. automated theorem provers for first-order logic.

A commonly used security concept is permission-based access control, i.e. associ-
ating entities (e.g. users or objects) in a system with permissions and allowing an
entity to perform a certain action on another entity only if it has been assigned
the necessary permissions. Designing and enforcing a correct permission-based
access control policy (with respect to the general security requirements) is very
hard, considering the complex interplay between the system entities. This is ag-
gravated by the fact that permissions can also be delegated to other objects for
actions to be performed on the delegating object's behalf.

In this tool demonstration, we present a tool which supports the integration of permissions into early design models, in particular for object-oriented
design using UML. We describe both static modelling aspects, where we introduce owned and required permissions and capabilities for their delegation into
class diagrams, and dynamic modelling aspects. Dynamic modelling aspects are
characterized by the use and delegation of permissions within an interaction of
the system objects, modelled as a sequence diagram. To gain confidence in the
correctness of the permission-based access control policy, we define checks for
the consistency of the permission-related aspects within the static and dynamic
models and between these models. Using a translation from the UML models
to Prolog resp. to the input notation of a first-order predicate logic automated
theorem prover, based on a formal semantics for the UML diagrams used, these
permissions can then be verified for security properties, for example, the analysis
of the correctness of authorization chains.

---

* This work was partially performed when this author was at TU Munich and is partly
funded by the Royal Society through an international joint project with TU Munich
on model-based security analysis of crypto-protocol implementations.

J. Fiadeiro and P. Inverardi (Eds.): FASE 2008, LNCS 4961, pp. 292–295, 2008.
© Springer-Verlag Berlin Heidelberg 2008

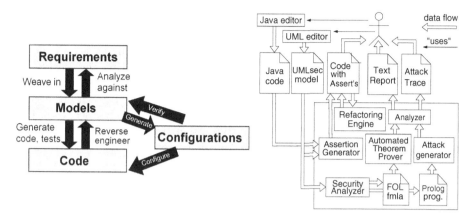

Fig. 1. a) Model-based Security Engineering; b) Model-based Security Tool Suite

Security Analysis using UMLsec: Model-based Security Engineering (MBSE, [Jür04,Jür05]) is a soundly based approach for developing security-critical software where recurring security requirements (such as secrecy, integrity, authenticity) and security assumptions on the system environment can be specified either within a UML specification or within the source code as annotations (cf. Fig. 1a). Analysis plugins in the associated UMLsec tool framework [Too07] (Fig. 1b) generate logical formulas formalizing the execution semantics and the annotated security requirements. Automated theorem provers (ATPs) and model checkers automatically establish whether the security requirements hold. If not, a Prolog-based tool automatically generates an attack sequence violating the security requirement, which can be examined to determine and remove the weakness. Thus we encapsulate knowledge on prudent security engineering and make it available to developers who may not be security experts. Since the analysis that is performed is too sophisticated to be done manually, it is also valuable to security experts. Part of the MBSE approach is the UML extension UMLsec for secure systems development which allows the evaluation of UML specifications for vulnerabilities using a formal semantics of a simplified fragment of the UML. The UMLsec extension is given in form of a UML profile using the standard UML extension mechanisms. *Stereotypes* are used together with *tags* to formulate the security requirements and assumptions. *Constraints* give criteria that determine whether the requirements are met by the system design by referring to a precise semantics of the used fragment of UML.

The UMLsec tool-support in Fig. 1b) can then be used to check the constraints associated with UMLsec stereotypes mechanically, based on XMI output of the diagrams from the UML drawing tool in use [Too07,Jür05]. There is also a framework for implementing verification routines for the constraints associated with the UMLsec stereotypes. Thus advanced users of the UMLsec approach can use this framework to implement verification routines for the constraints of self-defined stereotypes. The semantics for the fragment of UML used for UMLsec is defined in [Jür04] using so-called *UML Machines*, which is a kind of state machine with input/output interfaces and UML-type communication mechanisms.

On this basis, important security requirements such as secrecy, integrity, authenticity, and secure information flow are defined.

Security permissions in UMLsec: The objects to which the access should be secured by permissions (which is for example supported by the Java Security Architecture, making use of the concept of Guarded Objects) are identified by marking classes in the class diagram at hand that define or own permission objects with the stereotype « permission − secured ». Whether an object owns certain permissions on other objects at instantiation time is stated as follows: A tagged value is associated with the « permission − secured » stereotype consisting of a list of pairs structured as follows: {permission = [(*class*, permission)]}. The first element of the pair indicates the class on which the permission is valid, the second names the permission. Methods and public attributes to which access is restricted are marked with the stereotype « permissioncheck » and an associated tagged value containing the list of permissions needed for access ({permission = [permission]}). The association to classes is given by the class implementing the method or containing the attribute. To allow objects of certain classes classified as reliable unrestricted access to particular methods and public variables, one can associate a second tag to the stereotype « permission_check ». The tagged value {no_permission_needed = [*class*]} indicates that objects of the named classes need no permissions for access. A permission is implemented as a message consisting of *permission* and *identifier* (of the object the permission is valid on). The object owning the permission will be specified by appending the object's public key. Therefore it is impossible for any other object to use this permission. A *certificate* is defined as a triple consisting of the identifier followed by the permission and the public key of the user of the *certificate*. For signing the permissions, there is a trusted instance in the system called security authority (SA). This instance releases all permissions and passes them on to the objects at their instantiation time. It is not possible to change the definition of a permission once signed by this authority. So a certificate defining a permission will be formally defined as follows: $Sign(identifier::permission::K_{legit}, K_{SA}^{-1})$.

For the specification of the workflow, a sequence diagram is created, allowing one to specify the connection between permissions and messages by regarding the exchange of messages between objects. First, we define which of the objects are permission-secured objects, using the same stereotype « permission − secured » as in the class diagram. To this stereotype, we attach the permissions the object owns on other objects, utilizing tagged values. These tags are defined the same way as in the class diagrams, by {permission = [(*object*, permission)]}. In contrast to the class diagram, here the first element of the pair means no longer a class but a concrete object on which the permission is valid. Permissions which are needed for executing a method are attached directly to the message which is to be protected by these permissions. If a message is protected by permissions, it is marked with the stereotype « permission_check », where the permissions are named as tagged values: {permission = [permission]}.

Delegation of permissions is stated by a tag as well: {delegation=[(class, permission, role/class)]}. It is executed by passing on certificates, which are formally defined as 7-tuples certificate $= (e, d, c, o, p, x, s)$ with emittent e, delegate d, class c of the delegate, object o, permission p which is valid on o, expiration timestamp x and sequence number s. In the sequence diagram, messages where permission certificates are sent are marked by the stereotype « certification », where a 7-tuple representing a certificate will be directly attached as a tagged value. The parameters of this tag correspond to the definition above. To implement the delegation of permissions, passing on the permission is not enough. The delegating object must issue a certificate containing the permission and restrictions for its use. In addition, the certificate contains the public key of the owner of the permission. This allows other objects to prove that this object originally was the owner of the permission. The certificate is signed with the private key of the permission's owner: $Sign(K_{legit}:: Sign(object :: permission :: K_{legit}, K_{SA}^{-1}):: [properties], K_{legit}^{-1})$.

Checking the UML model: One can then use the UMLsec tool-support to check properties regarding the security permissions. The following are examples for properties which can be captured using the UMLsec notation and then checked by the tool.

- A permission certificate must be received before the corresponding action can be executed.
- The emittent of a certificate must own the permission to create the certificate, and the permission must be released for delegation.

The analysis is carried out by translating the permission-relevant information from the sequence diagrams to Prolog resp. first-order logic (depending on the property to be checked) and giving it as input to a Prolog compiler resp. an automated theorem prover for first-order logic (SPASS or e-SETHEO).

Conclusion: We presented a tool for the security analysis of permissions specified in UML models, using Prolog resp. automated theorem provers for first-order logic. It allows one to define security permissions to restrict the access to the systems' resources based on the workflows the system is designed for. Using the associated tool, one can automatically see if workflows and the design of the security permissions for the system are consistent and satisfy the overall security requirements on the system. The tool is mature and has been used in industrial projects, such as [BJN07,JSB08].

References

BJN07. Best, B., Jürjens, J., Nuseibeh, B.: Model-based security engineering of distributed information systems using UMLsec. In: 29th Int. Conf. on Softw. Engineering (ICSE), pp. 581–590. ACM Press, New York (2007)

JSB08. Jürjens, J., Schreck, J., Bartmann, P.: Model-based security analysis for mobile communications. In: 30th Int. Conf. on Softw. Engineering (ICSE), ACM Press, New York (2008)

Jür04. Jürjens, J.: Secure Systems Development with UML. Springer, Heidelberg (2004)

Jür05. Jürjens, J.: Sound methods and effective tools for model-based security engineering with UML. In: 27th Int. Conf. on Softw. Engineering (ICSE), pp. 322–331. IEEE, Los Alamitos (2005)

Too07. UMLsec Tool, 2001-07,
        http://computing-research.open.ac.uk/jj/umlsectool

Software Quality Improvement Via Pattern Matching

Radu Kopetz and Pierre-Etienne Moreau

INRIA & LORIA
{Radu.Kopetz,Pierre-Etienne.Moreau}@loria.fr

Abstract. Nested *if-then-else* statements is the most common programming schema in applications like data transformation or data analysis. In most cases, these can be replaced by higher level pattern matching constructs, rendering the code more readable and easier to maintain. We present a tool that integrates strong semantically grounded pattern matching features in JAVA via a plug-in for the Eclipse platform.

1 Introduction

Software systems tend to be bigger and more complex every day. Consequently, software maintenance grows in importance, stressing the need for code that is more readable and easier to maintain. In domains like simplifications of formulae or query optimizations, an important percent of the code is concerned with deciding if we are in a case or another, decisions that are usually implemented using sequences of nested *if-then-else* statements. E-commerce applications are also perfect examples where data retrieval and data analysis play a central role. In many cases they use persistence APIs, such as JPA [3], to map a database on an object-relational model. Then, the analysis and the transformation (to adapt an online catalog to different devices for examples) are performed in JAVA, using a combination of *getters* and *if-then-else* statements.

Nesting *if*-s, along with *else* statements and negations renders the code quite illegible. The use of pattern matching, a well known feature that exists in functional programming languages, is an interesting alternative to improve the quality and reduce the maintenance cost of software. In this paper we propose a seamless integration of advanced pattern matching features in new or already existing JAVA projects, using a plug-in for the Eclipse platform [2].

2 Matching Java Objects

Tom language. TOM[1] [1] is an extension of JAVA which adds support for algebraic data-types and pattern matching. An important construct is %match, which is parameterized by a list of objects, and contains a list of rules. The left-hand side of the rules are pattern matching conditions (build upon JAVA class

---

[1] http://tom.loria.fr/

J. Fiadeiro and P. Inverardi (Eds.): FASE 2008, LNCS 4961, pp. 296–300, 2008.
© Springer-Verlag Berlin Heidelberg 2008

names and variables), and the right-hand side are JAVA statements. Like standard `switch/case` construct, patterns are evaluated from top to bottom, firing each action (*i.e.* right-hand side) whose corresponding left-hand side *matches* the list of objects given as arguments.

For instance, suppose that we have a hierarchy of classes composed of `Account`, from which inherit `CCAccount` (credit card account) and `SAccount` (savings account), each with a field `owner` of type `Owner`. Given two objects `s1` and `s2`, if they are of type `CCAccount`, respectively `SAccount`, and have the same owner's name we want to print this name. If they are both of type `CCAccount`, just print the text `"CCAccount"`:

```
%match(s1,s2) {
  CCAccount(Owner(name)),SAccount(Owner(name)) -> { print(name); }
  CCAccount(_),CCAccount(_) -> { print("CCAccount"); }
}
```

In the above example, `name` is a variable. Using the same variable more than once in the left-hand side of a rule is called *non-linearity*, and denotes that the same value is expected. The _ is an anonymous variable that stands for anything. The equivalent JAVA code would be:

```
if (s1 instanceof CCAccount) {
  if (s2 instanceof SAccount) {
    Owner o1=((CCAccount)s1).getOwner();
    Owner o2=((SAccount)s2).getOwner();
    if (o1 != null && o2 != null) {
      if ((o1.getName()).equals(o2.getName())) {
        print(o1.getName());
      }
    }
  } else { if (s2 instanceof CCAccount) { print("CCAccount"); } }
}
```

Besides matching simple objects, TOM can also match lists of objects. For instance, given a list of accounts (`List<Account> list`), the following code prints all the names of the credit card accounts' owners:

```
%match(list) {
 AccountList(X*,CCAccount(Owner(name)),Y*) -> { print(name); }
}
```

`AccountList` is a variadic list operator, the variables suffixed by * are instantiated with lists (possibly empty), and can be used in the action part: here `X*` is instantiated with the beginning of the list up to the matched object, whereas `Y*` contains the tail. The action is executed for each pattern that matches the subject (assigning different values to variables). Patterns can be non-linear: `AccountList(X*,X*)` denotes a list composed of two identical sublists, whereas `AccountList(X*,x,Y*,x,Z*)` denotes a list that has twice the same element. Another feature of TOM patterns that's worth mentioning is the possibility to embed negative conditions using the complement symbol ' ! ' [4]. For instance, !AccountList(X*,CCAccount(_),Y*) denotes a list of accounts that does not contain a credit card account. Similarly, !AccountList(X*,x,Y*,x,Z*) stands for a list with only distinct elements, and AccountList(X*,x,Y*,!x,Z*) for one that has at least two distinct elements. There is no restriction on patterns, including complex nested list operators combined with negations. This allows the expression of different algorithms in a very concise and safe manner.

Eclipse plug-in for Tom. Since TOM is a conservative extension of JAVA, to make it easier to use, we have developed an Eclipse plug-in that provides most of the functionalities available for JAVA (wizards for new files and projects, edition with coloring and completion, automatic compilation, errors and warnings, *etc.*), making the edition of TOM files (*.t) transparent. A TOM program is an alternation between JAVA code and TOM code. When saving a .t file, the compilation is launched automatically, producing a JAVA file. Actually, the TOM parts are replaced with equivalent JAVA code, leaving untouched the rest of the code. After editing and saving a .t file, the eventual errors and warnings (both TOM and JAVA ones) are reported in the classical Problem View of Eclipse, as well as in the editor (similar to editing plain JAVA files). Given any hierarchy of JAVA classes, the plug-in also provides the necessary support to match against JAVA objects, as exemplified previously.

3   Behind the Scene

Until now, we briefly exposed the matching capabilities of TOM without giving any details on how the %match can be transformed into JAVA code. Actually, the %match construct can be used with any JAVA object, given that some additional information about the structure of the object is provided. Therefore, for any object that we intend to match on, we have to provide a *mapping* — a piece of code that gives TOM the information he needs to test the JAVA type of the object, the equality between two objects of the same type as well as how to decompose it.

Writing the mappings is not difficult, but involves some prior knowledge about how they work. As we advocate for an effortless integration of pattern matching in JAVA, the plug-in embeds a *mapping generator* that produces mappings for any set of compiled java classes. We integrated the generator as a two-step wizard: a right click on a .class file (or on a folder) and choosing the option *Generate mappings*, opens a window to choose the destination folder and the name of the file that will contain the mappings; pressing *Finish* launches the generator and creates the file. If the user selected a folder to generate the mappings for, then the generator traverses recursively the folder and its sub-folders producing mappings for all .class files. Then, all we have to do is to add %include{mapping_file.tom} in the TOM files where we want to use it.

There are two important characteristics of the generated mappings that are worth mentioning: first of all, for all the classes the generator also produces the necessary mappings for matching lists of objects of that kind. For instance, given the class CCAccount, this allows to write the following code:

```
CCAccount cc = new CCAccount(...);   List ccList = getCCAccountList();
%match(cc) {                         %match(ccList) {
 CCAccount(_) -> { ... }                 CCAccountList(X*,CCAccount(_),Y*) -> { ... }
 ...                                     ...
}                                    }
```

The second important characteristic of the generated mappings is that they offer the full support of the JAVA polymorphism. Actually, the type of a class is specified in the mappings as the type of the highest class in its hierarchy (the one before Object). This is very useful, for instance, when using polymorphic queries in JPA. In our case, CCAccount and SAccount inherit from the class Account, that has a field accNum of type String. We can write the code:

```
List accounts = getAccountList(); // retrieves all accounts from DB
%match(accounts) {
  AccountList(X*,a@Account(accNum),Y*) -> {
    print(accNum); //prints the number of any account (CCAccount or SAccount)
    %match(a) {
      SAccount(Owner(name)) -> { print("SAccount:" + name); }
      CCAccount(_)          -> { print("CCAccount"); }
    }
}}
```

The notation @ denotes an alias which stores in a the Account that is matched.

4   Application Scenarios and Related Work

We presented the %match construct that is well suited for integrating pattern-matching facilities in new or already existing projects. TOM is a lot richer, and most important, it offers the possibility to clearly separate the notions of transformation rules, expressed with %match, from their application control, encoded using *strategies*. This is more generally a software development methodology, which reduces both the development time and maintenance costs through its flexibility.

TOM is an environment for defining transformations. Compared to other term rewriting based languages, like ASF+SDF, MAUDE, ELAN, STRATEGO an important advantage of TOM is its seamless integration in any JAVA project, which enables its usage in an industrial context. TOM is used in several companies to develop applications that range from query optimizers for Xquery, non-trivial transformations of SQL and OLAP queries, to simplifications of logic formulae. Recently, users report also the use of TOM for statical analysis of JSP pages.

It is also used in academia for the development of proof assistants for instance, for encoding and verification of security policies, and other different rewrite-based applications. TOM is a perfect environment for defining DSLs and compilers. For instance, the TOM compiler is developed in TOM. Most of the work of the TOM compiler, as of any preprocessor as a matter of fact, is to perform transformations on an AST (Abstract Syntax Tree) initially produced by the parser, until the TOM code parts are completely transformed into JAVA ones. Therefore, most of the code is concerned with matching different parts of the AST, and is written entirely using %match blocks combined with strategies.

Other languages provide pattern-matching extensions for JAVA: SCALA, PIZZA, JMATCH. To our knowledge, they only provide a basic pattern-matching. More specifically, they lack the list-matching, as well as the negative conditions. Other rule-based languages like JRULES, JBOSS RULES or JESS have *business rules* as their application domain, and not program transformation.

5   Conclusion

We have presented a tool for a smooth integration of pattern matching in JAVA. It is a mature implementation, used both in academia and industry.

Using such an approach is quite straightforward, even in an existing project: only a few clicks and an include have to be done. After a short learning curve, the use of pattern matching greatly improves the quality of the implementations. By separating the retrieval of data from its transformation, and by making explicit the structure of objects that are manipulated, the code becomes easier to read, to understand, and to maintain. The use of high-level constructs such as list matching or complement symbols also renders the code safer.

While actively working on the integration of graph matching facilities to handle data-structures with cycles, we also study the possibility to make the integration simpler, by automatically generating the mappings and the inclusion statement. This would even require less effort from the programmer to use TOM.

Acknowledgments. We sincerely thank the anonymous referees for their valuable remarks and suggestions.

References

1. Balland, E., Brauner, P., Kopetz, R., Moreau, P.-E., Reilles, A.: Tom: Piggybacking rewriting on java. In: Baader, F. (ed.) RTA 2007. LNCS, vol. 4533, pp. 36–47. Springer, Heidelberg (2007)
2. Gamma, E., Beck, K.: Contributing to Eclipse: Principles, Patterns, and Plugins. Addison Wesley Longman Publishing Co., Inc, Redwood City (2003)
3. Keith, M., Schincariol, M.: Pro EJB 3: Java Persistence API (Pro). Apress, Berkely (2006)
4. Kirchner, C., Kopetz, R., Moreau, P.-E.: Anti-pattern matching. In: De Nicola, R. (ed.) ESOP 2007. LNCS, vol. 4421, pp. 110–124. Springer, Heidelberg (2007)

Object Composition in Scenario-Based Programming*

Yoram Atir, David Harel, Asaf Kleinbort, and Shahar Maoz

The Weizmann Institute of Science, Rehovot, Israel
{yoram.atir,dharel,asaf.kleinbort,shahar.maoz}@weizmann.ac.il

Abstract. We investigate the classical notion of object composition in the framework of scenario-based specification and programming. We concentrate on live sequence charts (LSC), which extend the classical partial order semantics of sequence diagrams with universal/existential and must/may modalities. In order to tackle object composition, we extend the language with appropriate syntax and semantics that allow the specification and interpretation of scenario hierarchies – trees of scenarios – based on the object composition hierarchy in the underlying model. We then describe and implement a composition algorithm for scenario hierarchies, and discuss a trace-based semantics and operational semantics (play-out) for the extension. The extension has been fully implemented, and the ideas are demonstrated using a small example application.

1 Introduction

Building upon the preliminary (unpublished) work in [3], we integrate object composition with scenario-based specification and programming. Object composition, that is, the 'part-of' hierarchical relation, is a fundamental concept in object oriented analysis and design [5]. We consider strong composition, for which part-objects are intrinsically associated with their whole, and do not exist independently. Scenarios, depicted using variants of sequence diagrams, are popular means for specifying the inter-object behavior of reactive systems (see, e.g, [8,12,18,20]), are included in the UML standard [19], and are supported by many modeling tools. To specify scenarios we use a UML2 compliant variant of *live sequence charts* (LSC) [7,10], a visual formalism that extends classical message sequence charts (MSC) [13], mainly by making a distinction between possible and mandatory behavior. The LSC language has an executable (operational) semantics (play-out) [11], and thus may be used not only for requirements and specification but also as a programming language.

We define an appropriate extension of the syntax and semantics of LSC, which allows the specification and interpretation of a scenarios hierarchy that is based

---

* This research was supported in part by The John von Neumann Minerva Center for the Development of Reactive Systems at the Weizmann Institute of Science and by a Grant from the G.I.F., the German-Israeli Foundation for Scientific Research and Development.

J. Fiadeiro and P. Inverardi (Eds.): FASE 2008, LNCS 4961, pp. 301–316, 2008.
© Springer-Verlag Berlin Heidelberg 2008

on the object composition hierarchies in the model. Combining object composition with scenario-based specifications supports information hiding together with a scalable and decentralized design, where high level scenarios are refined by specifying the inner behavior of their participating objects modulo the scenario-based context.

The main mechanism we introduce is *LSC-trees*; hierarchies of modal scenarios induced by the system model's object composition hierarchy. LSC-trees are created by allowing lifelines to be decomposed into *part-scenarios*. Semantically, part-scenarios are indeed *parts*; i.e., not only do they specify the interaction between part-objects, but in addition their lifespan (as scenario instances) and scope (in terms of binding and unification) are restricted by the parent scenario. We define syntactic rules and (operational) semantics for LSC-trees and present a composition algorithm that checks the consistency of a given LSC-tree and outputs a semantically equivalent (implicit) annotated *flat-LSC*. The semantics of LSC-trees and the composition algorithm handle the classical partial order semantics of sequence diagrams and the must/may modalities of LSC.

An implementation of LSC play-out using aspects was presented in [16] and has been implemented in the S2A compiler [9]. In way of implementing the ideas of the present paper, we have implemented object composition in S2A by supporting the compilation of LSC-trees. The implementation is compliant with the UML2 standard notion of part-decomposition ([19], pp. 496–499) and the *modal* profile as defined in [10].

Combining object composition with scenario-based specifications has been studied before (see, e.g., [12,15]). The main contributions of our work are these: we explicitly describe and implement a composition algorithm; we focus on the operational semantics and the execution of the composed scenarios; and, finally, we not only handle the classical partial order semantics of sequence diagrams but consider the part-decomposition extension in the context of the more expressive must/may (hot/cold) modal semantics of LSC. We consider the extended semantics along with the concepts presented in Sec. 4 and Sec. 5, as the main contributions of this paper.

The paper is organized as follows. In Sec. 2 we briefly discuss LSC and object composition. Sec. 3 presents syntax and semantics for the integration of the two, and defines *LSC-trees*. Sec. 4 describes the lifeline composition algorithm and discusses its complexity. Some more advanced issues are discussed in Sec. 5. In Sec. 6, we illustrate our work using a simple example. Sec. 7 discusses related work and Sec. 8 concludes. Additional technical details, proof sketches, an optimized version of the basic composition algorithm, and an extended example appear in [4].

2   Preliminaries

2.1   Live Sequence Charts and Play-Out

Live Sequence Charts. We use a UML2 compliant variant of live sequence charts (LSC) [7,10,11], a visual formalism for scenario-based inter-object specifications which extends the partial order semantics of classical message sequence charts (MSC) [13] with universal and existential modalities. LSC is defined as a proper UML profile that extends UML2 Interactions [19] with a <<modal>> stereotype consisting of two attributes: *mode* and *execution mode*. Each element in an LSC, e.g., a message, a constraint, has a *mode* attribute which can be either *hot* (universal) or *cold* (existential), and an *execution mode*, which can be either *monitor* or *execute*. Thus, LSC allows not only to specify traces that "may happen", "must happen", or "should never happen", but also to divide the responsibility for execution between the environment, the participating objects, and the coordination mechanism. Notice that this LSC variant is a proper extension of the original LSC language. For example the notion of prechart is generalized, since cold fragments inside universal interactions serve prechart-like purposes: a cold fragment does not have to be satisfied in all runs but if and when it is satisfied it necessitates the satisfaction of its subsequent hot fragment; and this is true in all runs. LSC notation extends the classical sequence chart notation as follows: hot (resp. cold) elements are colored red (resp. blue), execution (resp. monitoring) elements use solid (resp. dashed) lines.

Play-out. An operational semantics for LSC, termed *play-out*, was presented in [11]. Each event in a chart includes a number of locations and *covers* (visually and logically) one or more lifelines. The covered lifelines are those that participate in the execution of the event or need to synchronize on it. A *minimal event* in a chart is an event, which no other event precedes it in the partial order of event induced by the chart. Minimal events are important in our execution mechanism: whenever an event e occurs, a new copy of each chart that features e as a minimal event is instantiated and start being monitored/executed. Each active LSC, instantiated following the occurrence of a *minimal event*, has a *cut*, which is a mapping from each lifeline to one of its locations. Roughly, the execution mechanism reacts to events that are statically referenced in one or more of the LSCs; for each LSC instance the mechanism checks whether the event is *enabled* with regard to the current cut; if it is, it advances the cut accordingly; if it is *violating* and the current cut is cold (a cut is cold if all its elements are cold and is hot otherwise), it discards this LSC instance; if it is violating and the current cut is hot, an exception is thrown; if the event does not appear in the LSC, it is ignored (an LSC does not restrict the occurrence of events not explicitly appearing in it). Conditions (UML2 state-invariants), are evaluated as soon as they are enabled in a cut; if a condition evaluates to true, the cut advances accordingly; if it evaluates to false and the current cut is cold, the LSC instance is discarded; if it evaluates to false and the current cut it hot, an appropriate exception is thrown. If the cut of an LSC instance reaches maximal locations on all lifelines, the instance is discarded. Once all the cuts have been updated, the execution mechanism chooses an event to execute from among the execution-enabled methods that are not violating any chart, if any exist.

Play-out requires careful event unification and dynamic binding mechanism. Roughly, two methods are unifiable if their senders (receivers) are concrete instance-level (or are already bound) and equal, or are symbolic class-level of the same class and at least one is still unbound. When methods with arguments are considered, an additional condition requires that corresponding arguments have equal concrete values, or that at least one of them is free.[1]

The LSC MVCSetState (Fig. 1), specifies an interaction between 3 objects: view, controller and model of types: IView, IController, and IModel respectively. The three lifelines in the chart are interface-level, i.e, each of them can represent any instance that implements the corresponding interfaces. This LSC specifies part of a variant of the behavior of the classic *Model-View-Controller* design pattern (MVC): *Whenever the view informs the controller that the user has input, and the input is not null, then a series of actions must eventually occur: the controller should eventually set the model's state[2]; the model should eventually inform the view that the state has changed, and then the view should eventually update itself according to the new state. Finally, the controller should order the view to start listening for new input.*

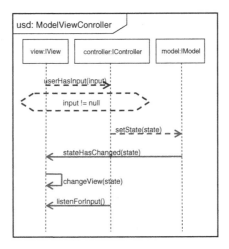

Fig. 1. The LSC MVCSetState

Scenario aspects and S2A. An implementation of play-out using aspects was suggested in [16], and has been implemented in the S2A compiler [9]. Each LSC is translated into a *scenario aspect*, which simulates a small automaton whose states correspond to the LSC cuts. S2A exploits the inherent similarity between the scenario-based approach and the aspect-oriented approach to software specification: in both cases part of the system's behavior is specified in a way that explicitly crosses the boundaries between objects. The compilation scheme takes advantage of the similar unification semantics of play-out and AspectJ pointcuts. The work described in the present paper was implemented in S2A, see Sec. 4.

---

[1] Full definitions of the play-out algorithm for LSCs, including unification, can be found in [11].

[2] This method is marked as 'monitored' so this LSC is not responsible for executing it.

2.2   Object Composition

Object composition, that is, a 'part-of' hierarchical relation, is a fundamental concept in object oriented analysis and design [5]. We consider composition to imply strong ownership, that is, part-objects are intrinsically associated with their whole, and do not exist independently (in the UML standard this is termed *composite aggregation* in contrast to other types of aggregation). A part instance is included in at most one composite ('whole') at a time. The composite object (the 'whole') has the responsibility for the existence and storage of its part objects. If a composite is deleted, all of its parts are deleted with it [6,19].

We assume that a system is equipped with a directed acyclic graph (DAG) of objects (representing the *part-of* binary relation). The DAG has a transitive deletion characteristics; deleting an object results in the deletion of the subgraph below it (i.e, deleting its parts). The graph can be symbolic, with objects being replaced by classes. Notice that since a part object can be included in at most one composite, the object graph is actually a forest (at the class level, we allow classes to be part-of more than one class – the single owner restriction applies only for instances – hence the use of a DAG rather than a tree).

We use the directed acyclic graph of objects (or classes) in order to answer relation queries about objects (at run-time) or classes (statically, during LSC compilation). We say that a class (object) A is a *part-of* a class (object) B iff there is a direct edge from B to A in the DAG. B *has-a* A iff A is *part-of* B. We say that A is *recursively part-of* B if there is a directed path from B to A. Thus, 'recursively part-of' is a strict partial order (transitive, antisymmetric, and irreflexive) between objects (classes).

The package `PhoneBook` in Figure 4 displays a simple part-of graph. For example, in the figure, the class `InputPane` is part-of the class `PhoneBookView`.

3   Object Composition in Scenario-Based Programming

We are now ready to present our integration of object composition and scenario-based programming. We use UML2 terminology.

3.1   The Basics

Syntactically, we use *PartDecomposition* as the main mechanism to introduce object composition into a scenario-based specification. In every scenario, each lifeline may be decomposed into a new set of lifelines, which collectively form a new scenario. Thus, a forest-like hierarchical structure is created.

More formally, Let L be an LSC with a set of lifelines $I = \{I_1, \ldots, I_n\}$. Each lifeline I_i has a property $I_i.decomposedAs$, which can either be null (and then we call I a *flat* lifeline) or hold a reference to another LSC L_{I_i}, which specifies the inner behavior of I_i's parts modulo the scenario described in L. We call L a *parent-LSC* and L_{I_i} a *part-LSC*. Lifelines of part-LSCs may be further decomposed and an LSC may have several non-flat lifelines, giving rise to the depth and width of the hierarchical structure. An LSC is *flat* if all its lifelines are flat. The *part-of* relation defined between objects in the model is naturally extended to scenarios. An LSC L_1 is *part-of* an LSC L_2 iff L_2 contains a lifeline I s.t. $I.decomposedAs = L_1$. We call the resulting hierarchical structure an *LSC-tree*. In the following we adopt tree terminology and use *parent*-LSC, LSC-*node*, LSC-*leaf* (necessarily flat), and LSC-*root*.

We require two basic syntactic constraints on the part-of relation between LSCs, as follows (we refine these rules in Sec. 5):

R1. Lifelines of a part-LSC may only represent classes (objects) that are part-of the class (object) represented by the decomposed lifeline.

R2. Given a lifeline I decomposed into part-LSC L, all events covering I must appear in L and induce the same partial order.

A specification that violates the above rules is considered inconsistent.

Fig. 2 shows an example LSC-tree. The LSC-root, MVCSetState, has two non flat lifelines. The view lifeline is decomposed into the part-LSC ViewDetailed and the model lifeline is decomposed into the part-LSC ModelDetailed. The restrictions described above hold for both part-LSCs. In the following we refer to this LSC-tree by its root's name.

The second restriction above induces a natural correspondence relation between the events that appear in a parent-LSC and cover the decomposed lifeline and (some of) the events that appear in its part-LSC. We call these *corresponding events*. For example, the method changeView(state) in the part-LSC ViewDetailed *corresponds to* the method with the same signature in the parent-LSC MVCSetState. For the time being we require that corresponding events preserve temperature and execution modes. In Sec. 5 we present a setting where this rule is refined, and we discuss additional issues regarding corresponding events.

3.2 Operational Semantics

The notions of cuts, enabled/violating events, and minimal events, are carried over from the semantics of flat LSC to the semantics of the LSC-tree. The differences manifest themselves mainly by modifications in the definitions of minimal-events, violating-events, and most importantly lifeline bindings and event unification rules.

We start by adding restrictions to the lifeline binding rules. Consider an LSC L and a lifeline I in L that is decomposed into a part-LSC L_I. Lifelines in L_I can only be bound to objects that are indeed parts-of the object (class) represented by I in L. During execution, for a given instance of L, once I binds to an object O, all the lifelines in L_I that represent its parts may be bound to O's parts only. Bindings may occur in the other direction too: when a lifeline in an instance of L_I binds to a (part) object P, I binds to the owner of P.

Message unification rules are also extended in a natural way. Messages that are unifiable in the flat setting are still unifiable. In addition, instead of requiring identical callers (receivers) or unifiable types, we also allow a setting where one caller (receiver) is (recursively) part-of the other (specifically, corresponding events are unifiable). Note that this still allows identical lifeline bindings and

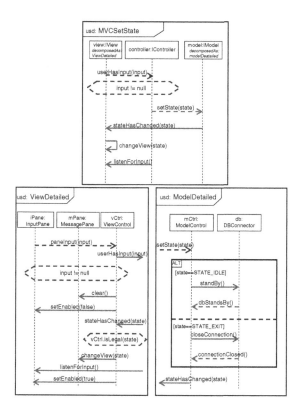

Fig. 2. The `MVCSetState` LSC-tree; the tree is composed of a root (`MVCSetState`) and two part-LSCs, (`ViewDetailed` and `ModelDetailed`)

message unification across different LSCs in the specification, including between different LSC-trees (see the examples in [4]).

The set of minimal events must be considered with regard to the partial order induced by the LSC-tree as a whole. Thus, a minimal event of an LSC-node might not be minimal for the tree. When a minimal event with regard to the tree occurs, an active instance of the whole tree is created (see the examples in [4]). Allowing part-LSCs to introduce new minimal events has its advantages and disadvantages. In Sec. 5.5 we discuss a setting where part-LSCs are not allowed to introduce new minimal events.

Recall that a cut of an LSC induces a set of violating events and a set of enabled events. When dealing with LSC-trees, each LSC-node in an instance of an LSC-tree has its own (local) cut, and hence its own sets of enabled and violating events. The rule for enabled events does not change: when an enabled event in an LSC-node occurs, the cut of this node advances accordingly. As usual, due to event unification, a single event might cause several cuts in several LSCs in the same tree to advance simultaneously.

When an event that violates one of the LSCs in an LSC-tree occurs, we interpret it as violating the tree. The violation is hot if one of the LSCs in the tree (not necessarily the one where the local violation 'occurred') was in a hot cut when the violation occurred, and it is cold otherwise. When a cold violation occurs in an instance of an LSC-tree, the entire instance is discarded; when a hot violation occurs an appropriate exception is thrown, as in the flat LSC setting.

4   Lifeline Composition Algorithm

The composition algorithm receives as input a single LSC-tree and if the LSC-tree is consistent it outputs an annotated (implicit) flat-LSC that captures exactly the behavior specified by the tree. If the LSC-tree is inconsistent, i.e., it violates rules R1, R2 defined in Section 3.1, an appropriate output message is given. For example, Fig. 3 displays the (implicit) flat-LSC created as a result of running the algorithm on the LSC-tree MVCSetState (of Fig. 2).

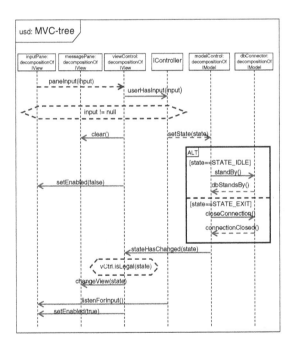

Fig. 3. The (implicit) composed flat-LSC

The basic procedure used by the algorithm merges two LSCs, a part-LSC and its parent-LSC, into a single annotated flat-LSC. We use a DAG to represent the partial order of events of each LSC, and merge the two DAGs using a merging algorithm inspired by the classic way to merge sorted lists [14].

By applying the merging procedure recursively from leaves to root, the algorithm collapses the tree into a single flat-LSC. The resulting LSC's set of lifelines is the union of all the LSC-node's sets of lifelines, where we (recursively) replace each decomposed lifeline with the lifelines of its corresponding part-LSC. The pseudo-code for the (essence of the) merging procedure appears in Proc. 1. A proof of correctness and a detailed explanation of the algorithm are given in [4].

---

procedure 1. $composeLSCs$(LSC L_{parent},LSC L_{part})

1: let I be the lifeline in L_{parent} that is decomposed into L_{part}
2: create new LSC L_{flat}
3: set L_{flat} lifelines to be L_{parent}'s lifelines but replace I with L_{part}'s lifelines
4: let E_{parent} be L_{parent}'s event graph
5: let E_{part} be L_{part}'s event graph
6: **while** $E_{parent} \neq \emptyset$ **do**
7:     let e be a minimal event in E_{parent}
8:     $E_{parent} \leftarrow E_{parent} \setminus \{e\}$
9:     **if** e does not cover I **then**
10:         append e to L_{flat}
11:     **else** {//e covers I}
12:         $addPartLSCEvents(E_{part}, e, L_{flat})$
13:     **end if**
14: **end while**
15: $addPartLSCEvents(E_{part}, null, L_{flat})$
16: return L_{flat}

---

procedure 2. $addPartLSCEvents$(Event graph E_{part},Event e_{parent},LSC L_{flat})

1: **while** $E_{part} \neq \emptyset$ **do**
2:     let e_{part} be a minimal event in E_{part}
3:     **if** e_{part} corresponds to e_{parent} **then**
4:         $E_{part} \leftarrow E_{part} \setminus \{e_{part}\}$
5:         let e_u be the static unification of e_{part} and e_{parent}
6:         append e_u to L_{flat}
7:         return
8:     **else if** e_{part} corresponds to another event in L_{parent} **then**
9:         **if** there are more minimal events in E_{part} **then**
10:             choose another minimal event and continue the loop with it.
11:         **else** {//no more minimal events}
12:             throw 'Error: Violation of the partial order'
13:         **end if**
14:     **else** {// e_{part} does not correspond to any event in the parent-LSC}
15:         append e_{part} to L_{flat}
16:     **end if**
17: **end while**
18: **if** $e_c == null$ **then**
19:     return $\emptyset$
20: **else**
21:     throw 'Error: No corresponding event for e_{parent} in the part-LSC'
22: **end if**

Complexity. The $composeLSCs$ procedure runs in time linear in the total number of events in the two input LSCs, since it traverses each event in the two DAGs only once. We assume that operations such as static event unification and adding an event to a list take constant time. To allow extraction of minimal events in constant time we keep a dynamic set of sources for each DAG.

Let T be an LSC-tree with n LSC-nodes. Denote the set of events of an LSC L by E_L. Let $k = \max \{|E_L| : L \in T\}$. The complexity of the composition algorithm is $O(n^2 k)$. The report in [4] contains a detailed analysis of the algorithm's complexity and suggests a simple optimization (already used in our implementation), which results in a running time of $O(nk)$.

4.1 Implementation

We have implemented the algorithm in the S2A compiler [9] by adding the ability to compile LSC-trees. S2A uses the optimized version of the composition algorithm presented above to reduce each LSC-tree in the specification to a single annotated flat-LSC. It then translates this implicit flat-LSC into a *scenario aspect* [16]. Some modifications of the original scenario aspect code are required in order to support the extended lifeline binding and unification rules.

5 Advanced Issues

We now discuss several advanced issues that arise in our work.

5.1 Lifeline Bindings and Scope

Integrating object composition into scenario-based specifications introduces a new notion of scope, which materializes in lifelines binding and event unification rules. Consider a parent-LSC L_1 with lifeline I_1 of type C_1, decomposed into a part-LSC L_2. Let I_2 be a symbolic lifeline in L_2 representing a class C_2. I_2 cannot be bound to any object of type C_2. Rather, it may be bound only to an object of type C_2 that is also *part-of* an object of type C_1. The part-LSC scenario is thus considered only within the scope of its parent.

5.2 The Partial Order

In general, the events covering a decomposed lifeline must all appear in the part-LSC and must induce the same partial order. It is possible, however, that the total order of events along a decomposed lifeline is relaxed in the corresponding part-LSC. For example, in the LSC `ViewDetailed`, the methods `changeView(state)` and `listenforInput()` are unordered, while in the parent-LSC `MVC` the corresponding methods are ordered (see Fig. 2).

We consider two possible design intentions. The designer may have intended to indeed specify a total order between the events but could not express this in the part-LSC due to the disjoint sets of covered lifelines. Alternatively, the designer may have intended an explicit partial order but could not express it in the parent-LSC because the events share a covered lifeline.

The S2A compiler produces a warning when this issue occurs in an LSC-tree. In our current work and its implementation, we support the first design intention by default. That is, in addition to compiling the composed annotated implicit flat-LSC, each LSC-node in the tree is compiled separately. This allows monitoring the order specified in any parent-LSC, and enforcing the total order of execution (or reacting otherwise in case this order is violated).

The second design intention can be supported by allowing the user to use the *co-region* operator, which relaxes the total order along a single lifeline (see [3,7,19]). Our current implementation does not support this.

5.3   Identifying Corresponding Events

Our composition algorithm depends on the ability to decide whether two events on different levels of the tree correspond. This assumption, however, is not obvious. For example, a given method in a parent-LSC may have several legal corresponding methods in the part-LSC. The use of conditions and symbolic parameters may create similar complex situations. One may consider this as a form of under-specification.

In practice, this problem can be partly addressed by requiring the designer to statically mark corresponding events, or, as in our current implementation, when more than one possibility exists, the composition algorithm could emit an appropriate warning message and make a non-deterministic choice.

5.4   Hot/Cold Modalities in an LSC-Tree

Recall that LSCs are modal scenarios. Each event has a temperature attribute: cold events *may* eventually occur, while hot events *must* eventually occur (see [7,10]). These modalities should also be considered in the semantics of LSC-trees. The simplest approach is to require that corresponding events be given identical temperatures. This constraint, however, is neither sufficient nor necessary. To see that it is not sufficient consider a cold event added in the part-LSC in between two hot events that have corresponding parent-LSC events (e.g., Fig. 2, the cold condition vCtrl.isLegal(state) in the ViewDetailed part-LSC) . A cold violation that occurs at this part-LSC when this cold event is enabled will always result in a hot violation for the LSC-tree. Thus, in terms of trace languages (see [10]), a run accepted by the composed flat-LSC may not be accepted by the parent-LSC.

Therefore, to carry over the modal characteristics of the language from the single LSC to the LSC-tree, we define the following rules, which ensure the consistency between a part-LSC and its parent in terms of accepted runs:

R3. Hot events in a parent-LSC must remain hot in the part-LSC. (Cold events in a parent-LSC can be either cold or hot in the part-LSC)

R4. For any event that appears in a part-LSC and does not appear in the parent-LSC, if there is a next (minimal) event after it that has a corresponding hot event in the parent-LSC, then the new event must be hot.

Roughly, these additional rules ensure that a finite trace inducing a hot cut in the parent-LSC, will also induce a hot cut in the LSC-tree (that is, in the composed flat-LSC). In [4] we show that they are indeed necessary for the soundness of our work. Note that a check for these restrictions can be easily integrated into our composition algorithm. Indeed, our implementation checks these conditions and outputs an appropriate warning if necessary.

5.5 Minimal Events in an LSC-Tree

Recall that minimal events have a special role in LSC semantics: whenever a minimal event of a chart occurs, an instance of the chart is created and becomes active. Thus, every occurrence of a minimal event must be followed eventually by a successful completion of the chart. Accordingly, whenever a minimal event in the partial order induced by an LSC-tree (essentially, its corresponding composed flat-LSC) occurs, an instance of the LSC-tree is created and becomes active.

Note, however, that if part-LSCs introduce new minimal events with respect to their parent, a run accepted by the composed flat-LSC may not be accepted by the parent-LSC. Depending on the context and usage of LSC-trees (e.g., formal verification, testing, execution), this may or may not be considered problematic. Thus, to ensure trace containment between an LSC-tree and its root-LSC, we suggest restricting part-LSCs from introducing new minimal events:

R5. Every minimal event in a part-LSC must have a corresponding event in the parent-LSC.

In [4] we give the formal definition of R5 and show that it is necessary for the trace containment property. Still, we believe that deciding whether or not to apply R5 should depend on the specific application.

5.6 Existential LSC-Trees

The language of LSC defines two types of charts, universal and existential [7,10]. We have concentrated on universal LSCs here, since they are the ones involved in play-out. The lifeline decomposition extension, however, may be applied to existential LSCs too (which can be used, e.g., for testing and monitoring), creating existential LSC-trees that specify, as usual, scenarios that must be satisfied by at least one possible run of the system model. Existential LSCs do not use the hot/cold modalities and their minimal events have no special semantic significance. Hence, the basic rules defined in Sec. 3.1 (R1 and R2) suffice to ensure the consistency of an existential LSC-tree. Specifically, the composition algorithm checks the consistency of existential LSCs too and outputs a corresponding existential flat-LSC. Thus, our implementation works for existential LSCs and indeed checks the consistency of 'classical' UML2 sequence diagrams that use part-decomposition with an existential interpretation and no modalities.

6 Example: Phone Book Application

We demonstrate the key features of our work using a small example of a Phone Book application[3]. It has a simple user interface, allowing a user to add

---

[3] The example was partly inspired by an IBM tutorial for Rational Software Architect written by Tinny Ng, available from http://www.ibm. com/developerworks/.

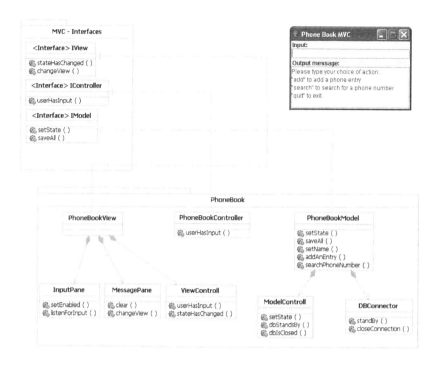

Fig. 4. The Phone Book application's class diagram and GUI

name/number pairs to the phone book, search a number by name, etc. A detailed description appears in [4]. The example UML model and code are available for download from the S2A website [1].

Fig. 4 displays the class diagram of the application and the application's GUI. The application uses the MVC design pattern. The classes in the diagram are implemented in Java. The code for the interactions between these classes, however, was generated from a UML2 compliant LSC specification using the S2A compiler.

The application uses three interfaces, IView, IController, and IModel, implemented by the classes PhoneBookView, PhoneBookController, and PhoneBookModel respectively. The generic interaction between the three interfaces is specified in the MVCSetState LSC (Fig. 1) mentioned earlier. The behavior described in MVCSetState is relevant for many applications that are based on this design pattern; i.e, it is reusable. In order to use it in the phone book application we apply the part-of decomposition mechanism to two lifelines: the IView lifeline is decomposed into the ViewDetailed part-LSC, and the IModel lifeline is decomposed into the ModelDetailed part-LSC (for additional LSCs used in the application, see [4]).

The class PhoneBookView is responsible for the phone book's GUI (Fig. 4), consisting of two visible parts, the MessagePane (which is where the messages for the user are displayed), and the InputPane (which is where the user enters textual input). In addition, `PhoneBookView` has another (logical) part, the `ViewController`, which coordinates between the GUI parts and is used as a gateway object. The inner behavior of the `PhoneBookView` with respect to `MVCSetState` is specified in the `ViewDetailed` part-LSC (Fig. 2).

The class `PhoneBookModel` is responsible for the phone book's storage and holds the current state of the application. Its inner behavior (with respect to the `MVCSetState` scenario) is specified in the `ModelDetiled` LSC (Fig. 2), which reveals the events that take place 'inside' the `PhoneBookModel` after its state is changed. The specific behavior depends on the new state.

Note that while the `MVCSetState` LSC describes the behavior of general interfaces that can be implemented in different applications, the decomposed part-LSCs are application specific. This shows the power of symbolic instances [17] and their implementation in S2A in creating *reusable* behavioral specifications.

Also note the flexibility and modularity that object-composition adds to the scenario-based specification. For example, we have created another implementation of the `IView` interface, replacing the class `PhoneBookView` with a new class `PhoneBookExtendedView` of enhanced GUI. The inner behavior of the latter (in the context of this scenario!) is specified in a new LSC `ExtendedViewDetailed` which by itself is not flat; i.e., it contains a lifeline that is decomposed into another LSC, involving the new GUI elements. We were able to change the application's behavior by simply replacing a subtree in the original LSC-tree.

The complete example, including UML model and code is available from the S2A website [1]. Additional details including a snippet from the generated code appear in [4].

7 Related Work

The notion of lifeline decomposition appears already in [13] and in the UML2 standard [19], which includes syntactic restrictions for part-decomposition. These were used as a basis for our basic syntactic rules.

STAIRS [12] is an approach for the compositional development of UML interactions. Among the refinement relations formally defined in STAIRS is *detailing*, which is based on lifeline decomposition.

Krüger [15] defines various refinement relations between MSCs, one of which is *structural refinement*, which relates object refinement in the system model with MSC refinement. Krüger suggests syntactic rules for the substitution of one MSC with another, based on the object composition in the system model.

The Rhapsody tool [2] allows the user to define a 'decomposed-as' reference from a lifeline to a sequence diagram. However, no syntactic rules are checked by the tool.

Our work uses the part-decomposition mechanism presented in the standard and defines similar syntactic restrictions for part-LSCs. We explicitly describe and implement a composition algorithm that reduces an LSC-tree into a flat-LSC and checks the consistency of the LSC-tree with respect to the basic rules adopted from the standard (R1, R2) and the more advanced rules (R3, R4); we not only handle a trace-based semantics but focus on the operational semantics and the execution of the composed scenarios. Also, we handle both the classical partial order semantics of sequence diagrams and the part-decomposition extension in the context of the more expressive must/may (hot/cold) modal semantics of LSC. Most of our work is applicable to the aforementioned work too.

8   Discussion and Future Work

We have extended the LSC language to allow the specification and interpretation of scenario hierarchies — trees of scenarios — based on an object composition hierarchy in the underlying model. The present paper grew out of previous work done in our group [3], in which LSC was extended with support for object composition by defining LSC-trees. Here we have decided to omit some of the more complicated issues dealt with in [3].

Composition and inheritance are two complementary concepts in OOD. Partial support for inheritance was introduced to LSC using symbolic instances in [17], and was implemented in the Play-Engine tool [11]. In [9,16] this was explicitly extended to support class inheritance and interface implementation in Java. The present paper integrates object composition into the scenario-based context, and thus may be viewed as complementing this previous work.

While we focus on LSCs and their direct execution, the presented ideas are applicable to UML2 sequence diagrams in general, and to their use throughout the development cycle. Planned future work includes the development of design methodologies that will take advantage of our work, the implementation of additional case studies using the S2A compiler, and related compiler optimizations.

References

1. S2A Website, http://www.wisdom.weizmann.ac.il/~maozs/s2a/
2. Telelogic Rhapsody, http://www.telelogic.com/
3. Atir, Y.: Object Refinement and Composition in Scenario-Based Programming: An LSC Extension. Master's thesis, The Weizmann Institute of Science (2005)
4. Atir, Y., Harel, D., Kleinbort, A., Maoz, S.: Object Composition in Scenario-Based Programming. Technical report, The Weizmann Institute of Science (2007)
5. Booch, G.: Object-Oriented Analysis and Design with Applications. Benjamin/Cummings (1994)
6. Booch, G., Rumbaugh, J., Jacobson, I.: The Unified Modeling Language User Guide, 2nd edn. Addison-Wesley, Reading (2005)
7. Damm, W., Harel, D.: LSCs: Breathing Life into Message Sequence Charts. J. on Formal Methods in System Design 19(1), 45–80 (2001)
8. Harel, D.: From Play-In Scenarios To Code: An Achievable Dream. IEEE Computer 34(1), 53–60 (2001)
9. Harel, D., Kleinbort, A., Maoz, S.: S2A: A compiler for multi-modal UML sequence diagrams. In: Dwyer, M.B., Lopes, A. (eds.) FASE 2007. LNCS, vol. 4422, pp. 121–124. Springer, Heidelberg (2007)
10. Harel, D., Maoz, S.: Assert and Negate Revisited: Modal Semantics for UML Sequence Diagrams. Software and Systems Modeling (2007)

11. Harel, D., Marelly, R.: Come, Let's Play: Scenario-Based Programming Using LSCs and the Play-Engine. Springer, Heidelberg (2003)
12. Haugen, Ø., Husa, K.E., Runde, R.K., Stølen, K.: STAIRS towards formal design with sequence diagrams. Software and Systems Modeling 4(4), 355–357 (2005)
13. ITU. Recommendation Z.120: Message Sequence Charts. Technical report, (1996)
14. Knuth, D.E.: The Art of Computer Programming. Sorting and Searching, vol. III. Addison-Wesley, Reading (1998)
15. Krüger, I.: Distributed System Design with Message Sequence Charts. PhD thesis, Institut für Informatik, Ludwig-Maximilians-Universität München (2000)
16. Maoz, S., Harel, D.: From Multi-Modal Scenarios to Code: Compiling LSCs into AspectJ. In: Proc. 14th Int. ACM/SIGSOFT Symp. Foundations of Software Engineering (FSE-14), Portland, Oregon (November 2006)
17. Marelly, R., Harel, D., Kugler, H.: Multiple Instances and Symbolic Variables in Executable Sequence Charts. In: Proc. 17th ACM Conf. on Object-Oriented Prog., Systems, Lang. and App. (OOPSLA 2002), Seattle, WA, pp. 83–100 (2002)
18. Uchitel, S., Kramer, J., Magee, J.: Synthesis of behavioral models from scenarios. IEEE Trans. Software Eng. 29(2), 99–115 (2003)
19. UML. Unified Modeling Language Superstructure Specification, v2.0. OMG spec., OMG (August 2005), http://www.omg.org
20. Whittle, J., Kwan, R., Saboo, J.: From scenarios to code: An air traffic control case study. Software and Systems Modeling 4(1), 71–93 (2005)

Regular Inference for State Machines Using Domains with Equality Tests

Therese Berg[1], Bengt Jonsson[1], and Harald Raffelt[2]

[1] Department of Computer Systems, Uppsala University, Sweden
{thereseb,bengt}@it.uu.se
[2] Chair of Programming Systems and Compiler Construction, University of
Dortmund, Germany
harald.raffelt@cs.uni-dortmund.de

Abstract. Existing algorithms for regular inference (aka automata learning) allows to infer a finite state machine by observing the output that the machine produces in response to a selected sequence of input strings. We generalize regular inference techniques to infer a class of state machines with an infinite state space. We consider Mealy machines extended with state variables that can assume values from a potentially unbounded domain. These values can be passed as parameters in input and output symbols, and can be used in tests for equality between state variables and/or message parameters. This is to our knowledge the first extension of regular inference to infinite-state systems. We intend to use these techniques to generate models of communication protocols from observations of their input-output behavior. Such protocols often have parameters that represent node adresses, connection identifiers, etc. that have a large domain, and on which test for equality is the only meaningful operation. Our extension consists of two phases. In the first phase we apply an existing inference technique for finite-state Mealy machines to generate a model for the case that the values are taken from a small data domain. In the second phase we transform this finite-state Mealy machine into an infinite-state Mealy machine by folding it into a compact symbolic form.

1 Introduction

Model-based techniques for verification and validation of reactive systems, such as model checking and model-based test generation [1] have witnessed drastic advances in the last decades. They depend on the availability of a formal model, specifying the intended behavior of a system or component, which ideally should be developed during specification and design. However, in practice often no such model is available, or becomes outdated as the system evolves over time, implying that a large effort in many model-based verification and test generation projects is spent on manually constructing a model from an implementation. It is therefore important to develop techniques for automating the task of generating models of existing implementations. A potential approach is to use program analysis to construct models from source code, as in software verification

J. Fiadeiro and P. Inverardi (Eds.): FASE 2008, LNCS 4961, pp. 317–331, 2008.
© Springer-Verlag Berlin Heidelberg 2008

(e.g., [2,3]). However, many system components, including peripheral hardware components, library modules, or third-party components do not allow analysis of source code. We will therefore focus on techniques for constructing models from observations of their external behavior.

The construction of models from observations of component behavior can be performed using regular inference (aka automata learning) techniques [4, 5, 6, 7, 8, 9, 10]). This class of techniques has recently started to get attention in the testing and verification community, e.g., for regression testing of telecommunication systems [11, 12], and for combining conformance testing and model checking [13, 14]. They describe how to construct a finite-state machine (or a regular language) from the answers to a finite sequence of *membership queries*, each of which observes the component's output in response to a certain input string. Given "enough" membership queries, the constructed automaton will be a correct model of the system under test (SUT). Angluin [4] and others introduce *equivalence queries*, queries to whether a hypothesized automaton is a correct model of the SUT, they can be seen as idealizing some procedure for extensively verifying (e.g., by conformance testing) whether the learning procedure is completed. The reply to an equivalence query is either *yes* or a counterexample, an input string on which the constructed automaton and the SUT respond with different output.

We intend to use regular inference to construct models of communication protocol entities. Such entities typically communicate by messages that consist of a protocol data unit (PDU) type with a number of parameters, each of which ranges over a sometimes large domain. Standard regular inference can only construct models with a moderately large finite alphabet. In previous work [15], we presented an optimization of regular inference to cope with models where the domain over which parameters range is large but finite. But, in order to fully support the generation of models with data parameters, we must consider a general theory for inference of infinite-state state machines with input and output symbols from potentially infinite domains.

In this paper, we present the first extension of regular inference to infinite-state state machines. We consider Mealy machines where input and output symbols are constructed from a finite number of message types that can have parameters from a potentially infinite domain. These parameters can be stored in state variables of the machine for later use. The only allowed operation on parameter values is a test for equality. The motivation is to handle parameters that, e.g., are identifiers of connections, objects, etc. This class of systems is similar to, and slightly more expressive than, the class of "data-independent" systems, which was the subject of some of the first works on model checking of infinite-state systems [16, 17].

In standard regular inference states and transitions are infered, and counterexamples to a hypothesized automaton are only used to add more states to the automaton. In this paper, we also infer state variables and operations on them, and counterexamples to a hypothesized model are used to extend the model with either more states or more state variables.

In our approach, we first observe the behavior of the protocol when the parameters of input messages are from a small domain. Using the regular inference algorithm by Niese [18] (which adapts Angluin's algorithm to Mealy machines), we generate a finite-state Mealy machine, which describes the behavior of the component on this small domain. We thereafter fold this finite-state Mealy machine into a smaller *symbolic* model.

Organization. The paper is organized as follows. In the next section, we review the Mealy machine model and in Section 3 we introduce the model for state machines using domains with equality tests. In Section 4 we review the inference algorithm for Mealy machines by Niese [18], and the adaptation required for our setting. In Section 5 we present our algorithm to map Mealy machines to Symbolic Mealy machines. Correctness and complexity of our algorithm is discussed in Section 6, and conclusions and future work are presented in Section 7.

Related Work. Regular inference techniques have been used for verification and test generation, e.g., to create models of environment constraints with respect to which a component should be verified [19], for regression testing to create a specification and a test suite [11,12], to perform model checking without access to code or to formal models [14,13], for program analysis [20], and for formal specification and verification [19]. Li, Groz, and Shahbaz [21,22] extend regular inference to Mealy machines with a finite subset of input and output symbols from the possible infinite set of symbols. This work resembles the intermediate model, in our earlier work [15], used to construct a symbolic model. In this work we handle infinite sets of parameter values, and can also generate infinite-state models with both control states and state variables that range over potentially infinite domains.

2   Mealy Machines

A *Mealy machine* is a tuple $\mathcal{M} = \langle \Sigma_I, \Sigma_O, Q, q_0, \delta, \lambda \rangle$ where Σ_I is a finite nonempty set of *input symbols*, Σ_O is a finite nonempty set of *output symbols*, Q is a nonempty set of *states*, $q_0 \in Q$ is the *initial state*, $\delta : Q \times \Sigma_I \to Q$ is the *transition function*, and $\lambda : Q \times \Sigma_I \to \Sigma_O$ is the *output function*. Elements of Σ_I^* and Σ_O^* are (input and output, respectively) *strings* or *words*. Given $u, v \in \Sigma_I^*$, u is said to be a *prefix* of v if $v = uw$ for some $w \in \Sigma_I^*$.

An intuitive interpretation of a Mealy machine is as follows. At any point in time, the machine is in one state $q \in Q$. It is possible to give inputs to the machine, by supplying an input symbol a. The machine responds by producing an output string $\lambda(q, a)$ and transforming itself to the new state $\delta(q, a)$.

We extend the transition and output functions from input symbols to sequences of input symbols, by defining:

$$\delta(q, \varepsilon) = q \qquad\qquad \lambda(q, \varepsilon) = \varepsilon$$
$$\delta(q, ua) = \delta(\delta(q, u), a) \qquad\qquad \lambda(q, ua) = \lambda(q, u)\lambda(\delta(q, u), a)$$

The Mealy machines that we consider are *completely specified*, meaning that at every state the machine has a defined reaction to every input symbol in Σ_I, i.e., δ and λ are total. They are also *deterministic*, meaning that for each state q and input a exactly one next state $\delta(q, a)$ and output string $\lambda(q, a)$ is possible.

Let q and q' be two states of the same Mealy machine, or two states in different machines. The states q and q' are *equivalent* if $\lambda(q, u) = \lambda(q', u)$ for each input string $u \in \Sigma_I^*$. That is, for each input string the machine starting in q will produce the same output string as the machine starting in q'. A Mealy machine $\mathcal{M}$ is *minimized* if there are no pair of states q and q' of $\mathcal{M}$, where $q \neq q'$, that are equivalent. There are well-known algorithms for efficiently minimizing a given Mealy machine [23]. Given a Mealy machine $\mathcal{M}$ with input alphabet Σ_I and initial state q_0 we define $\lambda_{\mathcal{M}}(u) = \lambda(q_0, u)$, for $u \in \Sigma_I^*$. Two Mealy machines $\mathcal{M}$ and $\mathcal{M}'$ with input alphabets Σ_I are *equivalent* if $\lambda_{\mathcal{M}} = \lambda_{\mathcal{M}'}$.

3   Symbolic Mealy Machines

In this section, we introduce Symbolic Mealy machines. They extend ordinary Mealy machines in that input and output symbols are messages with parameters, e.g., as in a typical communication protocol. We will specialize to the case when these parameters are from a large (in practice "infinite") domain $\mathcal{D}$, on which the only permitted operation is test for equality. In general, we could have several such domains, but let us here assume that all parameters are from one domain.

Let I and O be finite sets of *actions*, each of which has a nonnegative arity. Let $\mathcal{D}$ be a (finite or infinite) domain of data values. Let $\Sigma_I^{\mathcal{D}}$ be the set of *input symbols* of form $\alpha(d_1, \ldots, d_n)$, where $\alpha \in I$ is an action of arity n, and $d_1, \ldots, d_n \in \mathcal{D}$ are parameters from $\mathcal{D}$. The set of *output symbols* $\Sigma_O^{\mathcal{D}}$ is defined analogously.

We assume a set of *location variables*, ranged over by $v, v_1, v_2, \ldots$, and a set of *formal parameters*, ranged over by $p, p_1, p_2, \ldots$. A *symbolic value* is either a location variable or a formal parameter. We use y or z to range over symbolic values. A *parameterized input action* is a term of form $\alpha(p_1, \ldots, p_n)$, where α is an input action of arity n, and $p_1, \ldots, p_n$ are formal parameters. A *parameterized output action* is a term of form $\beta(z_1, \ldots, z_k)$, where $\beta \in O$ is an output action of arity k and each z_i is a symbolic value. We write $\overline{v}$ for $v_1, \ldots, v_m$, $\overline{y}$ for $y_1, \ldots, y_m$, $\overline{p}$ for $p_1, \ldots, p_n$, and $\overline{z}$ for $z_1, \ldots, z_k$. A *guard* over the location variables $\overline{v}$ and formal parameters $\overline{p}$ is a conjunction of equalities and inequalities between the symbolic values in $\overline{v}, \overline{p}$. A *guarded action* is of the form

$$\alpha(\overline{p}); g/\overline{v} := \overline{y}; \beta(\overline{z})$$

where $\alpha(\overline{p})$ is a parameterized input action, g is a guard over location variables and the formal parameters $\overline{p}$, where $\overline{v} := \overline{y}$ is the assignment $\langle v_1, \ldots, v_m \rangle := \langle y_1, \ldots, y_m \rangle$, meaning that $v_i := y_i$, in which each y_i is a location variable or a formal parameter, and $\beta(\overline{z})$ is a parameterized output action over symbolic values. An example of a guarded action is $\alpha(p_1, p_2); true/v_1 := p_1; \beta(p_2)$, where the first input parameter value is stored in a location variable, and the second input parameter value is output.

Let a *valuation function* ρ be a mapping from a (possibly empty) set $Dom(\rho)$ of location variables to data values in $\mathcal{D}$. We let ρ_0 denote the valuation function with an empty domain. We extend valuation functions to operate on vectors of location variables by defining $\rho(v_1, \ldots, v_m)$ as $\rho(v_1), \ldots, \rho(v_m)$. For an input symbol $\alpha(\overline{d})$, a valuation function ρ, and guard g such that $v_i \in Dom(\rho)$ for all v_i occurring in g, we let $(\alpha(\overline{d}), \rho) \models g$ denote that $g[\overline{d}/\overline{p}, \rho(\overline{v})/\overline{v}]$ is true, i.e., that g is true when the formal parameters $\overline{p}$ assume the data values $\overline{d}$ and the location variables $\overline{v}$ assume the data values $\rho(\overline{v})$.

Definition 1 (Symbolic Mealy machine). *A Symbolic Mealy machine is a tuple* $\mathcal{SM} = (I, O, L, l_0, \longrightarrow)$, *where*

- *I is a finite set of* input actions,
- *O is a finite set of* output actions,
- *L is a finite set of* locations, *each of which has a nonnegative* arity *representing the number of location variables in that location,*
- *$l_0 \in L$ is the* initial location *with arity 0, and*
- *$\longrightarrow$ is a finite set of* transitions. *Each transition is a tuple* $\langle l, \alpha(\overline{p}), g, \overline{v} := \overline{y}, \beta(\overline{z}), l' \rangle$, *where* $l, l' \in L$ *are locations and* $\alpha(\overline{p}); g/\overline{v} := \overline{y}; \beta(\overline{z})$ *is a guarded action respecting constrains given by arities of l and l'.* □

We write $l \xrightarrow{\alpha(\overline{p}); g/\overline{v}:=\overline{y}; \beta(\overline{z})} l'$ to denote $\langle l, \alpha(\overline{p}), g, \overline{v} := \overline{y}, \beta(\overline{z}), l' \rangle \in \longrightarrow$. We require that Symbolic Mealy machines are completely specified and deterministic, i.e., for each reachable $\langle l, \rho \rangle$ and symbol $\alpha(\overline{d})$, there is exactly one transition $\langle l, \alpha(\overline{p}), g, \overline{v} := \overline{y}, \beta(\overline{z}), l' \rangle$ from l such that $(\alpha(\overline{d}), \rho) \models g$.

Example. An example of a Symbolic Mealy machine is shown in Figure 1. The Symbolic Mealy machine has one input action α with arity two, two output actions β and β' both with arity one, one location l_0 with arity zero and a second location l_1 with arity one.

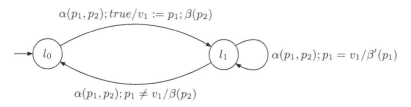

$\alpha(p_1, p_2); true/v_1 := p_1; \beta(p_2)$

$\alpha(p_1, p_2); p_1 = v_1/\beta'(p_1)$

$\alpha(p_1, p_2); p_1 \neq v_1/\beta(p_2)$

Fig. 1. Example of a Symbolic Mealy machine

Let $\mathcal{D}$ be a (finite or infinite) domain of data values. A Symbolic Mealy machine $\mathcal{SM} = (I, O, L, l_0, \longrightarrow)$ acting on the domain $\mathcal{D}$ is the (possibly infinite-state) Mealy machine $\mathcal{SM}_\mathcal{D} = \langle \Sigma_I^\mathcal{D}, \Sigma_O^\mathcal{D}, Q, \langle l_0, \rho_0 \rangle, \delta, \lambda \rangle$, where

- $\Sigma_I^\mathcal{D}$ is the set of input symbols,
- $\Sigma_O^\mathcal{D}$ is the set of output symbols,

- Q is the set of pairs $\langle l, \rho \rangle$, where $l \in L$ and ρ is a valuation function,
- $\langle l_0, \rho_0 \rangle$ is the initial state, and
- δ and λ are defined as follows. Whenever $l \xrightarrow{\alpha(\overline{p}); g / \overline{v} := \overline{y}; \beta(\overline{z})} l'$ and $(\alpha(\overline{d}), \rho) \models g$ then
  - $\delta(\langle l, \rho \rangle, \alpha(\overline{d})) = \langle l', \rho' \rangle$, where $\rho'(v_i)$ is
    * $\rho(v_j)$ if y_i is a location variable v_j,
    * d_j if y_i is a formal parameter p_j, and
  - $\lambda(\langle l, \rho \rangle, \alpha(\overline{d})) = \beta(d'_1, \ldots, d'_k)$, where d'_i is
    * $\rho(v_j)$ if z_i is a location variable v_j,
    * d_j if z_i is a formal parameter p_j.

Note that δ is well-defined since $\mathcal{SM}$ is completely specified and deterministic.

If $\mathcal{D}$ is finite, then $\mathcal{SM}_\mathcal{D}$ is a finite-state Mealy machine with at most $\sum_{l \in L} |\mathcal{D}|^{arity(l)}$ states, where $arity(l)$ is the arity of location l.

4   Inference of Symbolic Mealy Machines

In this section, we present our algorithm for inference of Symbolic Mealy machines. It is formulated in the same setting as Angluin's algorithm [4], in which a so called *Learner*, who initially knows nothing about $\mathcal{SM}$, is trying to infer $\mathcal{SM}$ by asking queries to a so called *Oracle*. The queries are of two kinds.

- A *membership query* consists in asking what the output is on a word $w \in (\Sigma_I^{\mathcal{E}})^*$.
- An *equivalence query* consists in asking whether a hypothesized Symbolic Mealy machine $\mathcal{H}$ is correct, i.e., whether $\mathcal{H}$ is equivalent to $\mathcal{SM}$. The *Oracle* will answer *yes* if $\mathcal{H}$ is correct, or else supply a *counterexample*, which is a word $u \in (\Sigma_I^{\mathcal{D}})^*$ such that $\lambda_{\mathcal{SM}_\mathcal{D}}(u) \neq \lambda_{\mathcal{H}_\mathcal{D}}(u)$.

The typical behavior of a *Learner* is to start by asking a sequence of membership queries until she can build a "stable" hypothesis from the answers. After that she makes an equivalence query to find out whether $\mathcal{H}$ is equivalent to $\mathcal{SM}$. If the result is successful, the *Learner* has succeeded, otherwise she uses the returned counterexample to revise $\mathcal{H}$ and perform subsequent membership queries until converging at a new hypothesized Symbolic Mealy machine, etc.

In our algorithm for the *Learner*, we build a hypothesis $\mathcal{H}$ in two phases: In the first phase we supply input from a small finite domain $\mathcal{E}$, and infer a hypothesis $\mathcal{M}$ for the Mealy machine $\mathcal{SM}_\mathcal{E}$ using an adaptation of Angluin's algorithm due to Niese [18]. There is an optimal smallest size of $\mathcal{E}$ which is still large enough to be able to exercise all tests for equalities between parameter values in $\mathcal{SM}$, but we do not *a priori* know this size. Therefore, we start with a small domain $\mathcal{E}$ that can be gradually extended when feedback from equivalence queries makes it necessary.

To characterize the "optimal smallest size", let $\mathcal{M}$ be $\langle \Sigma_I^{\mathcal{E}}, \Sigma_O^{\mathcal{E}}, Q, q_0, \delta, \lambda \rangle$, where I, O are the input and output action alphabet, respectively. We say that a data value $d \in \mathcal{E}$ is *fresh* in a state $q \in Q$ if there exists an input string $u \in (\Sigma_I^{\mathcal{E}})^*$ which leads to $\delta(q_0, u) = q$ such that d does not occur as a data value in u. We say that $\mathcal{M}$ is *fresh* if for each state $q \in Q$, there are n data values in $\mathcal{E}$ which are fresh in q, where n is the maximal arity of input actions in I. A sufficient condition on $\mathcal{E}$ is given by the following Lemma 1.

Lemma 1. *Let* $\mathcal{SM} = (I, O, L, l_0, \longrightarrow)$ *be a Symbolic Mealy machine,* $\mathcal{E}$ *be a domain of data values,* m *be the maximal arity of the locations in* L*, and* n *be the maximal arity of the input actions in* I*. Then if the size of* $\mathcal{E}$ *is bigger than* $m + n$*, the Mealy machine* $\mathcal{SM}_{\mathcal{E}}$ *is fresh.*   □

Returning to our inference algorithm, if the hypothesis $\mathcal{M}$ generated by Niese's algorithm is not fresh, we do not make any equivalence query, but instead enlarge $\mathcal{E}$ by one, and continue Niese's algorithm with the new enlarged $\mathcal{E}$. If $\mathcal{M}$ is fresh, we transform $\mathcal{M}$ into a Symbolic Mealy machine $\mathcal{H}$ such that $\mathcal{H}_{\mathcal{E}}$ is equivalent to $\mathcal{M}$: this transformation is presented in Section 5. Thereafter $\mathcal{H}$ is supplied in an equivalence query, to find out whether $\mathcal{H}$ is equivalent to $\mathcal{SM}$. If the result is successful, the algorithm terminates. Otherwise, the counterexample returned needs to be analyzed, since it may contain values outside of $\mathcal{E}$. Let the counterexample be input string $u \in \Sigma_I^{\mathcal{D}}$, with data values from domain $\mathcal{D}$.

In the case that $|\mathcal{D}| \leq |\mathcal{E}|$, we apply any injective mapping from $\mathcal{D}$ to $\mathcal{E}$, on the data values in the counterexample, and use the mapped counterexample in Niese's algorithm.

In the case that $|\mathcal{D}| > |\mathcal{E}|$, we try to find a mapping from $\mathcal{D}$ to a subset $\mathcal{D}' \subseteq \mathcal{D}$ which is as small as possible, but such that the mapped counterexample is still a counterexample to $\mathcal{H}$. To find such a mapping, one can either use an exhaustive search or a heuristic search guided by $\mathcal{H}$. The search involves asking more membership queries. We then extend $\mathcal{E}$ to the same size as $\mathcal{D}'$, and continue Niese's algorithm with the mapped counterexample.

5   Transforming Mealy Machines to Symbolic Mealy Machines

In this section, we present the transformation from a Mealy machine $\mathcal{M}$ to a Symbolic Mealy machine $\mathcal{SM}$. Throughout this section, we will use the Symbolic Mealy machine in Figure 1 as a running example to illustrate the steps in our algorithm. We assume that we used the domain $\mathcal{E} = \{1, 2, 3\}$ of size 3, which is the smallest domain to make $\mathcal{SM}_{\mathcal{E}}$ fresh, and that we obtained the hypothesis Mealy machine shown in Figure 2.

In the second phase, we transform the Mealy machine $\mathcal{M}$ into a Symbolic Mealy machine $\mathcal{SM}$, which must "simulate" $\mathcal{M}$ in the sense that $\mathcal{SM}_{\mathcal{E}}$ is equivalent to $\mathcal{M}$. The transformation algorithm has four steps.

- In the first step, the algorithm figures out for each state of n $\mathcal{M}$ which data values must be remembered by a corresponding Symbolic Mealy machine in order to produce its future behavior. These data values are the basis for

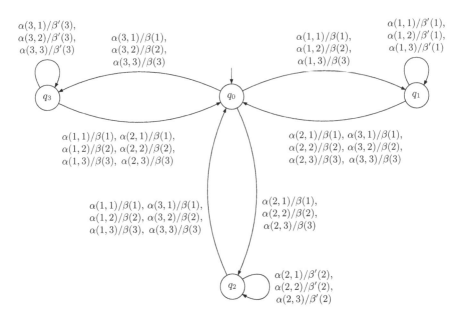

Fig. 2. A Mealy machine constructed with the inference algorithm applied to the example in Figure 1. All transitions that have the same start and target state are depicted with one edge.

constructing the location variables required in the corresponding location in the Symbolic Mealy machine. In the running example of Figure 2, the algorithm figures that, e.g., in state q_1 the data value 1 must be remembered.

- In the second step, we use the data values inferred in the first step to transform transitions of $\mathcal{M}$ into a so called symbolic normal form, which is especially designed to capture exactly the equalities and inequalities between formal parameters and location variables. In the running example, the transition on $\alpha(1,2)/\beta'(1)$ from, e.g., location q_1, will be transformed into $\alpha(v_1, p_1)/v_1 := v_1; \beta'(v_1)$.
- In the third step, we merge states of $\mathcal{M}$ into locations of $\mathcal{SM}$, if the symbolic forms of their future behavior are the same, using an adaptation of a standard partition-refinement algorithm. In the running example, states q_1, q_2, and q_3 will be merged into one location.
- In the fourth and final step, we transform transitions from symbolic normal form to the standard form used in Definition 1, and merge transitions when possible. The result of the first part of this step is shown in Figure 4.

Step One. The first step in our algorithm is to compute a *state-value function* $V : Q \mapsto 2^{\mathcal{E}}$ from states in $\mathcal{M}$ to sets of data values, which for each state gives the set of data values that $\mathcal{M}$ must remember for its future behavior. We first observe that if the data value d is fresh in a state q, then obviously d should not be in $V(q)$. Furthermore, if a data value d' is not remembered by $\mathcal{M}$ in q, then the future behavior from q remains unchanged if we swap the roles of d and d' (note that d and d' will occur in future input symbols). Let u be the input string which takes $\mathcal{M}$ from its initial state to q and does not contain d. The input string u', obtained by replacing all occurrences of d' by d in u will, by symmetry, take $\mathcal{M}$ from its initial state to a state q' whose future behavior has swapped the roles of d and d' as compared with q. Since $\mathcal{M}$ is minimized, q must be the same state as q'. Thus d' is also in fresh in q. In summary, $V(q)$ should contain all data values that are not fresh in q.

The calculation of the state-value function in the example in Figure 2 yields that $V(q_0)$ is the empty set $\emptyset$, $V(q_1)$ is $\{1\}$, $V(q_2)$ is $\{2\}$, and $V(q_3)$ is $\{3\}$.

Step Two. In the second step, we transform transition labels into a symbolic form. Intuitively, the transition $q \xrightarrow{\alpha(\overline{d}^I)/\beta(\overline{d}^O)} q'$ will be transformed into a symbolic transition $q \xrightarrow{\alpha(\overline{p});g/\overline{v}:=\overline{y};\beta(\overline{z})} q'$ where g is as strong as possible. We will use a different representation for such a symbolic transition, which we call *symbolic normal form*, which does not use guards: instead each data value in $\overline{d}^I$ and $\overline{d}^O$ will be replaced by v_i if it occurs as the ith data value stored in state q, otherwise by an appropriate input parameter symbol p_j. Furthermore, different symbolic values are implicitly required to be different. A problem is that we cannot know in which "order" the data values in $V(q)$ will be mapped to location variables, so therefore the transformation will depend on a specific ordering $\overline{d}$ of the data values in $V(q)$ and a specific ordering $\overline{d}'$ of the data values in $V(q')$.

Let us define precisely the symbolic normal form. For each ordering $\overline{d}$ of the data values in $V(q)$, for each vector $\overline{d}^I$ of data values received in an input symbol, and for each data value d in $\overline{d} \cup \overline{d}^I$, define $SV_{\overline{d},\overline{d}^I}(d)$ as

- v_i if there exists $d_i \in \overline{d}$ such that $d = d_i$, or else
- p_k if j is the smallest index such that $d_j \in \overline{d}^I$ is $d_j = d$, and k is the number of unique data values $d_l \in \overline{d}^I$ with index $l \leq j$, such that d_l does not appear in $\overline{d}$,

We extend $SV_{\overline{d},\overline{d}^I}$ to vectors of data values, by defining $SV_{\overline{d},\overline{d}^I}(d_1,\ldots,d_n)$ as $SV_{\overline{d},\overline{d}^I}(d_1),\ldots,SV_{\overline{d},\overline{d}^I}(d_n)$.

For each ordering $\overline{d}$ of the data values in $V(q)$ and each ordering $\overline{d}'$ of the data values in $V(q')$, the *symbolic normal form* of $q \xrightarrow{\alpha(\overline{d}^I)/\beta(\overline{d}^O)} q'$ is defined as

$$(q,\overline{d}) \xrightarrow{\alpha(SV_{\overline{d},\overline{d}^I}(\overline{d}^I))/\overline{v}:=\overline{y};\beta(SV_{\overline{d},\overline{d}^I}(\overline{d}^O))} (q',\overline{d}'),$$

where $\overline{v}:=\overline{y}$ is an assignment in which y_i is

- $SV_{\overline{d},\overline{d}^I}(d_j)$ if $d'_i = d_j$, for some $d'_i \in \overline{d}'$ and $d_j \in \overline{d}$, or else
- $SV_{\overline{d},\overline{d}^I}(d^I_j)$ if $d'_i = d^I_j$, for some $d'_i \in \overline{d}'$ and $d^I_j \in \overline{d}^I$.

As an example, the symbolic normal form of $q_0 \xrightarrow{\alpha(1,2)/\beta(2)} q_1$, a transition in the Mealy machine in Figure 2, calculates to $(q_0, [])\xrightarrow{\alpha(p_1,p_2)/v_1:=p_1;\beta(p_2)}(q_1, 1)$, where $[]$ is the empty vector of data values.

Step Three. In the third step, we merge states of $\mathcal{M}$ if the symbolic forms of their future behaviors are equivalent. As explained in the description of Step two, the symbolic normal form of the behavior from a state q is defined only with respect to a given ordering $\bar{d}$ of the data values in $V(q)$, meaning that for each state q we must fix some ordering of the stored data values. However, since some combinations of orderings allow to merge more states and obtain smaller machines than others, we shall not fix this ordering *a priori*. Instead, we create several copies of each q, one for each possible ordering of the data values in $V(q)$, and thereafter perform the merging starting with all these copies. Since at the end, we need only one pair of form $(q, \bar{d})$ for each q, we will prune copies of q that will create additional states, as long as at least one copy of each q remains.

Thus, our partitioning algorithm partitions pairs $(q, \bar{d})$ of states and data-value vectors into blocks $\mathcal{B}_1, \ldots, \mathcal{B}_m$, representing potential locations in a Symbolic Mealy machine. Each block $\mathcal{B}_i$ is a set of pairs $(q, \bar{d})$, where $q \in Q$ and $\bar{d}$ is some ordering of the data values $V(q)$. To break the symmetry between different orderings of data values, we pick for each block $\mathcal{B}_i$ an arbitrary pair $(q, \bar{d}) \in \mathcal{B}_i$ which is called *representative* for $\mathcal{B}_i$, to represent how the symbolic transitions from $\mathcal{B}_i$ will look like. The goal of the partitioning is that each block should be consistent, as defined in the following definition.

Definition 2 (Block consistency for a block $\mathcal{B}$). *Let $(q, \bar{d}) \in \mathcal{B}$ be the representative for block $\mathcal{B}$. Block $\mathcal{B}$ is consistent if whenever $(r, \bar{e}) \in \mathcal{B}$ there is a transition $(r, \bar{e}) \xrightarrow{\alpha(\bar{z})/\bar{v}:=\bar{y};\beta(\bar{z}')} (r', \bar{e}')$ (on symbolic normal form) iff there is a symbolic transition $(q, \bar{d}) \xrightarrow{\alpha(\bar{z})/\bar{v}:=\bar{y};\beta(\bar{z}')} (q', \bar{d}')$ (on symbolic normal form) with the same label, such that $(r', \bar{e}')$ and $(q', \bar{d}')$ are in the same block.* □

We find a partitioning of pairs into consistent blocks by fix-point iteration, using a variation of the standard partition-refinement algorithm, as follows.

- Initially, for each i which is the size of $V(q)$ for some $q \in Q$, there is a block $\mathcal{B}_i$ with all pairs $(q, \bar{d})$ such that $\bar{d}$ has exactly i data values.
- Repeat the following step until convergence.
  - Pick a block $\mathcal{B}_i$ and let $(q, \bar{d})$ be the representative for $\mathcal{B}_i$.
  - Split $\mathcal{B}_i$ by letting a pair $(r, \bar{e})$ in $\mathcal{B}_i$ remain in the block if for all $\alpha(\bar{z})$ there is a symbolic transition $(q, \bar{d}) \xrightarrow{\alpha(\bar{z})/\bar{v}:=\bar{y};\beta(\bar{z}')} (q', \bar{d}')$ from the representative $(q, \bar{d})$ iff there is a symbolic transition $(r, \bar{e}) \xrightarrow{\alpha(\bar{z})/\bar{v}:=\bar{y};\beta(\bar{z}')} (r', \bar{e}')$ from $(r, \bar{e})$ with the same label, such that $(q', \bar{d}')$ and $(r', \bar{e}')$ are in the same block. Let $\mathcal{B}_i'$ be the set of all pairs $(r, \bar{e})$ that were originally in $\mathcal{B}_i$ but did not pass this test.
  - Delete from $\mathcal{B}_i'$ all pairs $(r, \bar{e})$ for which some other pair $(r, \bar{e}')$ with the same state r remains in $\mathcal{B}_i$. It should be noted that this deletion of copies

is safe due to the strong symmetry between different orderings of data values $\bar{e}$ in pairs of form $(r, \bar{e})$.

- If $\mathcal{B}'_i$ is thereafter non-empty, we let $\mathcal{B}'_i$ be a new block, and choose an arbitrary member in $\mathcal{B}'_i$ as its representative,
- The algorithm terminates when all blocks are consistent. Let $\{\mathcal{B}_1, \ldots, \mathcal{B}_f\}$ denote the final set of blocks.

From the example in Figure 2 we create two consistent blocks, $\mathcal{B}_0$ and $\mathcal{B}_1$, see Figure 3. Block $\mathcal{B}_0$ contains the pair $(q_0, [])$, and block $\mathcal{B}_1$ contains the pairs $(q_1, 1)$, $(q_2, 2)$, and $(q_3, 3)$. Let us choose $(q_0, [])$ as the representative for block $\mathcal{B}_0$, and $(q_1, 1)$ as the representative for block $\mathcal{B}_1$. In the figure, from block $\mathcal{B}_1$ only the labels on the outgoing transitions from one of the pairs is drawn, since all pairs have the same labels on outgoing transitions.

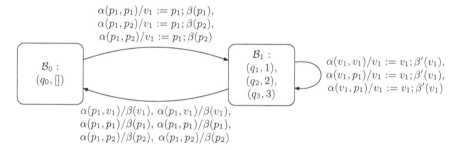

Fig. 3. The set of consistent blocks constructed from the example in Figure 2

Step Four. In the fourth step, we complete the transformation of the Mealy machine $\mathcal{M}$ by creating a Symbolic Mealy machine $\mathcal{SM}$ from the result of step three. This also involves transforming the symbolic normal form of transitions into the form used in Definition 1, and merging transitions. The locations of $\mathcal{SM}$ correspond to the blocks resulting from the third step. When creating the transitions of $\mathcal{SM}$, we can select an arbitrary member $(q, \bar{d})$ in each block $\mathcal{B}_i$, and use only these selected members and the transitions between them to construct $\mathcal{SM}$. It is possible to select only one member since, by block consistency, all members are equivalent. For simplicity we let the block representative be the selected member.

Each transition between representatives must be transformed from symbolic normal form to the form used in Definition 1. As an example, consider the self-loop from the representative $(q_1, 1)$ in Figure 3 labeled by $\alpha(v_1, p_1)/v_1 := v_1; \beta'(v_1)$. It states that if an input symbol $\alpha(d_1, d_2)$ is received where d_1 is equal to the current value of the location variable v_1, and d_2 is different from the value of any location variable, then the location variable is unchanged, and $\beta'(d_1)$ is generated. It should obtain the label $\alpha(p_1, p_2) : (p_1 = v_1 \wedge p_2 \neq v_1)/v_1 := v_1; \beta'(v_1)$, to conform with Definition 1. To define this transformation precisely, for a vector $\overline{z}$ of symbolic values, let $T_{\overline{z}}$ be a mapping from symbolic values to symbolic values, defined as

- $T_{\overline{z}}(v_j) = v_j$ for any location variable v_j,
- $T_{\overline{z}}(p_j) = p_i$ if p_j is a formal parameter which occurs in $\overline{z}$, and i is the smallest value such that p_j is the ith element z_i in $\overline{z}$.

$T_{\overline{z}}$ is extended to vectors of symbolic values, by defining $T_{\overline{z}}(y_1, \ldots, y_n)$ as $T_{\overline{z}}(y_1), \ldots, T_{\overline{z}}(y_n)$. For example $T_{p_1,p_1,v_1,p_2}(p_2, v_1, p_1, p_1) = p_4, v_1, p_1, p_1$.

For a vector $\overline{z}$ of symbolic values and vector $\overline{v}$ of location variables, define the guard $g_{\overline{z},\overline{v}}$ over formal parameters $\overline{p}$ and location variables $\overline{v}$ as the conjunction of the following conjuncts:

- for each formal parameter p_j which is the ith element z_i in $\overline{z}$:
  - $p_i \neq v_k$ for all location variables v_k in $\overline{v}$,
  - $p_i = p_k$ whenever p_j is both the ith and the kth element of $\overline{z}$, and k is the largest index such that p_j is the kth element of $\overline{z}$,
  - $p_i \neq p_k$ whenever the kth element z_k in $\overline{z}$ is a formal parameter different from p_j and $i < k$,
- for each location variable v_j which is the ith element z_i in $\overline{z}$:
  - $p_i = v_j$.

From the set of consistent blocks $\{\mathcal{B}_1, \ldots, \mathcal{B}_f\}$ resulting from the third step, starting from $\mathcal{M} = \langle \Sigma_I^{\mathcal{E}}, \Sigma_O^{\mathcal{E}}, Q, q_0, \delta, \lambda \rangle$, we can now construct a Symbolic Mealy machine $\mathcal{SM} = (I, O, L, l_0, \longrightarrow)$, where

- I is the set of input actions,
- O is the set of output actions,
- L is the set of blocks $\{\mathcal{B}_1, \ldots, \mathcal{B}_f\}$; the arity of each location $\mathcal{B}_i \in L$ is the size of $\overline{d}$, where $(q, \overline{d})$ is the representative of $\mathcal{B}_i$,
- $l_0 \in L$ is the block among $\mathcal{B}_1, \ldots, \mathcal{B}_f$ that contains the pair $(q_0, [])$,
- $\longrightarrow$ contains for each symbolic normal form $(q, \overline{d}) \xrightarrow{\alpha(\overline{z})/\overline{v}':=\overline{y};\beta(\overline{z}')} (q', \overline{d}')$ of a transition between representative q of block $\mathcal{B}$ and representative q' of $\mathcal{B}'$, the transition

$$\mathcal{B} \xrightarrow{\alpha(\overline{p}) \; ; \; g_{\overline{z},\overline{v}} \; / \; \overline{v}':=T_{\overline{z}}(\overline{y}) \; ; \; \beta(T_{\overline{z}}(\overline{z}'))} \mathcal{B}' \quad ,$$

where $\overline{v}$ is the location variables of $\mathcal{B}$, and $\overline{p}$ is the vector $p_1, \ldots, p_n$ of formal parameters where n is the size of $\overline{z}$.

In general, the resulting Symbolic Mealy machine in general has "too small" transitions, since each guard completely characterizes equalities and inequalities between the formal input parameter $\overline{p}$ and the location variables. To get a final Symbolic Mealy machine, we merge transitions that differ only in their guards, by taking the disjunction of their guards, whenever the new guard is still a conjunction.

In the final step in our work with our example, we create a Symbolic Mealy machine from the set of consistent blocks shown in Figure 3. The initial construction, after transforming transitions from symbolic normal form is the Symbolic

Mealy machine shown in Figure 4. We thereafter merge the two self loops in Figure 4 into $\alpha(p_1, p_2) : p_1 = v_1/v_1 := v_1; \beta'(v_1)$. On the other edges, the parameterized output actions can be replaced by $\beta(p_2)$ without altering the output behavior, then we merge transitions, obtaining the Symbolic Mealy machine in Figure 1.

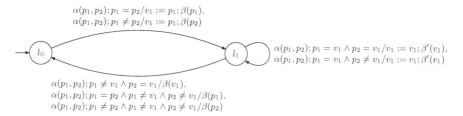

$\alpha(p_1, p_2); p_1 = p_2/v_1 := p_1; \beta(p_1),$
$\alpha(p_1, p_2); p_1 \neq p_2/v_1 := p_1; \beta(p_2)$

$\alpha(p_1, p_2); p_1 = v_1 \wedge p_2 = v_1/v_1 := v_1; \beta'(v_1),$
$\alpha(p_1, p_2); p_1 = v_1 \wedge p_2 \neq v_1/v_1 := v_1; \beta'(v_1)$

$\alpha(p_1, p_2); p_1 \neq v_1 \wedge p_2 = v_1/\beta(v_1),$
$\alpha(p_1, p_2); p_1 = p_2 \wedge p_1 \neq v_1 \wedge p_2 \neq v_1/\beta(p_1),$
$\alpha(p_1, p_2); p_1 \neq p_2 \wedge p_1 \neq v_1 \wedge p_2 \neq v_1/\beta(p_2)$

Fig. 4. Intermediate Symbolic Mealy machine constructed from the blocks in Figure 3

6 Correctness and Complexity

The correctness of our transformation from a Mealy machine $\mathcal{M}$ to a Symbolic Mealy machine $\mathcal{SM}$ follows from the following two theorems.

Theorem 1. *Let $\mathcal{E}$ be a finite domain, and let $\mathcal{M} = \langle \Sigma_I^{\mathcal{E}}, \Sigma_O^{\mathcal{E}}, Q, q_0, \delta, \lambda \rangle$ be a finite-state (minimized) Mealy machine. If $\mathcal{SM} = (I, O, L, \longrightarrow, l_0)$ is the result of the transformation described in Section 5, then $\mathcal{M}$ and $\mathcal{SM}_{\mathcal{E}}$ are equivalent (i.e., they produce the same output for all input strings $u \in (\Sigma_I^{\mathcal{E}})^*$).*   □

Theorem 2. *Let $\mathcal{SM}$ and $\mathcal{SM}'$ be Symbolic Mealy machines with the same set of input actions I and output actions O. Let m be the maximal arity of the locations in $\mathcal{SM}$ and $\mathcal{SM}'$, and let n be the maximal arity of the input actions in I. If the size of $\mathcal{E}$ is bigger than $m + n$, and if $\mathcal{SM}_{\mathcal{E}}$ and $\mathcal{SM}'_{\mathcal{E}}$ are equivalent, then for any data-value domain $\mathcal{D}$ the Mealy machines $\mathcal{SM}_{\mathcal{D}}$ and $\mathcal{SM}'_{\mathcal{D}}$ are equivalent.*   □

The two preceding theorems imply that if $\mathcal{SM}$ is the Mealy machine which we attempt to learn, and $\mathcal{SM}'$ is the machine we construct, then $\mathcal{SM}_{\mathcal{E}}$ is equivalent to $\mathcal{SM}'_{\mathcal{E}}$ for any domain $\mathcal{E}$.

An upper bound on the number of membership queries can be obtained from the corresponding bound on the number of membership queries needed to infer a Mealy machine $\mathcal{M} = \langle \Sigma_I^{\mathcal{E}}, \Sigma_O^{\mathcal{E}}, Q, q_0, \delta, \lambda \rangle$, which is $\mathcal{O}(|\Sigma_I^{\mathcal{E}}| \times |Q| \times \max(|\Sigma_I^{\mathcal{E}}|, |Q|) \times C)$, where

- $|\Sigma_I^{\mathcal{E}}| = \sum_{\alpha \in I} |\mathcal{E}|^{actarity(\alpha)}$, where $actarity(\alpha)$ is the arity of α,
- $|Q| = \sum_{l \in L} |\mathcal{E}|^{arity(l)},$
- C is the length of the longest counterexample returned in equivalence queries.

where $|\mathcal{E}|$ can be chosen as $m + n + 1$ (in the notation of Lemma 1) to make sure that $\mathcal{SM}_\mathcal{E}$ is fresh. The maximum number of equivalence queries required by the algorithm is $|Q| + |\mathcal{E}|$. To infer our example in Figure 2 we performed 333 membership queries and 1 equivalence query.

A way to reduce the number of membership queries required to infer the Mealy machine is to use a symmetry filter which deduces answers to membership queries from already answered membership queries [12]. The symmetry filter will filter out membership queries which have the same differences and equalities between parameter values as an already answered membership query.

7   Conclusions and Future Work

We have extended regular inference to a class of state machines with infinite state-spaces and infinite alphabets. Our motivation is to develop techniques for inferring models of entities in communication protocols by observing test executions. It would be interesting to try to extend our approach to data domains with more complex operations, such as counters, time-stamps, etc.

Our two-phase approach implies that the intermediate finite-state Mealy machine may get rather large, in comparison with the final Symbolic Mealy machine. This problem might be mitigated by developing an algorithm where the generation of the intermediate machine and the compacting transformation are performed "in parallel". Next on our agenda is to apply the results of this paper in a case study on realistic communication protocols.

Acknowledgement. We thank B. Steffen and J. Parrow for helpful discussions.

References

1. Broy, M., Jonsson, B., Katoen, J.-P., Leucker, M., Pretschner, A. (eds.): Model-Based Testing of Reactive Systems. LNCS, vol. 3472. Springer, Heidelberg (2005)
2. Ball, T., Rajamani, S.: The SLAM project: Debugging system software via static analysis. In: Proc. 29th ACM Symp. on Principles of Programming Languages, pp. 1–3 (2002)
3. Henzinger, T., Jhala, R., Majumdar, R., Sutre, G.: Lazy abstraction. In: Proc. 29th ACM Symp. on Principles of Programming Languages, pp. 58–70 (2002)
4. Angluin, D.: Learning regular sets from queries and counterexamples. Information and Computation 75, 87–106 (1987)
5. Balcázar, J., Díaz, J., Gavaldá, R.: Algorithms for learning finite automata from queries: A unified view. In: Advances in Algorithms, Languages, and Complexity, pp. 53–72. Kluwer Academic Publishers, Dordrecht (1997)
6. Dupont, P.: Incremental regular inference. In: Miclet, L., de la Higuera, C. (eds.) ICGI 1996. LNCS, vol. 1147, pp. 222–237. Springer, Heidelberg (1996)
7. Gold, E.M.: Language identification in the limit. Information and Control 10, 447–474 (1967)
8. Kearns, M., Vazirani, U.: An Introduction to Computational Learning Theory. MIT Press, Cambridge (1994)

9. Rivest, R., Schapire, R.: Inference of finite automata using homing sequences. Information and Computation 103, 299–347 (1993)
10. Trakhtenbrot, B.A., Barzdin, J.M.: Finite automata: behaviour and synthesis. North-Holland, Amsterdam (1973)
11. Hagerer, A., Hungar, H., Niese, O., Steffen, B.: Model generation by moderated regular extrapolation. In: Kutsche, R.-D., Weber, H. (eds.) FASE 2002. LNCS, vol. 2306, pp. 80–95. Springer, Heidelberg (2002)
12. Hungar, H., Niese, O., Steffen, B.: Domain-specific optimization in automata learning. In: Proc. 15th Int. Conf. on Computer Aided Verification (2003)
13. Peled, D., Vardi, M.Y., Yannakakis, M.: Black box checking. In: Wu, J., Chanson, S.T., Gao, Q. (eds.) Formal Methods for Protocol Engineering and Distributed Systems, FORTE/PSTV, Beijing, China, pp. 225–240. Kluwer Academic Publishers, Dordrecht (1999)
14. Groce, A., Peled, D., Yannakakis, M.: Adaptive model checking. In: Katoen, J.-P., Stevens, P. (eds.) TACAS 2002. LNCS, vol. 2280, pp. 357–370. Springer, Heidelberg (2002)
15. Berg, T., Jonsson, B., Raffelt, H.: Regular inference for state machines with parameters. In: Baresi, L., Heckel, R. (eds.) FASE 2006. LNCS, vol. 3922, pp. 107–121. Springer, Heidelberg (2006)
16. Wolper, P.: Expressing interesting properties of programs in propositional temporal logic (extended abstract). In: Proc. 13th ACM Symp. on Principles of Programming Languages, pp. 184–193 (1986)
17. Jonsson, B., Parrow, J.: Deciding bisimulation equivalences for a class of non-finite-state programs. Information and Computation 107(2), 272–302 (1993)
18. Niese, O.: An integrated approach to testing complex systems. Technical report, Dortmund University, Doctoral thesis (2003)
19. Cobleigh, J.M., Giannakopoulou, D., Pasareanu, C.S.: Learning assumptions for compositional verification. In: Garavel, H., Hatcliff, J. (eds.) TACAS 2003. LNCS, vol. 2619, pp. 331–346. Springer, Heidelberg (2003)
20. Ammons, G., Bodik, R., Larus, J.: Mining specificatoins. In: Proc. 29th ACM Symp. on Principles of Programming Languages, pp. 4–16 (2002)
21. Li, K., Groz, R., Shahbaz, M.: Integration testing of distributed components based on learning parameterized I/O models. In: Najm, E., Pradat-Peyre, J.-F., Donzeau-Gouge, V.V. (eds.) FORTE 2006. LNCS, vol. 4229, pp. 436–450. Springer, Heidelberg (2006)
22. Shahbaz, M., Li, K., Groz, R.: Learning and integration of parameterized components through testing. In: Petrenko, A., Veanes, M., Tretmans, J., Grieskamp, W. (eds.) TestCom/FATES 2007. LNCS, vol. 4581, pp. 319–334. Springer, Heidelberg (2007)
23. Kohavi, Z.: Switching and Finite Automata Theory: Computer Science Series. McGraw-Hill Higher Education (1990)

COMP-REF: A Technique to Guide the Delegation of Responsibilities to Components in Software Systems

Subhajit Datta and Robert van Engelen

Department of Computer Science and School of Computational Science
Florida State University, Tallahassee, FL 32306, USA
sd05@fsu.edu, rvaneng@fsu.edu

Abstract. In software systems, components collaborate to collectively fulfill requirements. A key concern of software design is the delegation of responsibilities to components such that user needs are most expediently met. This paper presents the COMP-REF technique based on a set of metrics and Linear Programming (LP) to guide the allocation of responsibilities of a system's components. We define the metrics *Aptitude Index*, *Requirement Set*, and *Concordance Index* to extract some design characteristics and use these metrics in an optimization algorithm. Results from experimental validation of the COMP-REF technique across a range of software systems are reported. We also discuss future directions of work in extending the scope of technique.

1 Introduction

Larman has called the ability to assign responsibilities as a "desert-island skill" [22], highlighting its criticality in the software development process. Indeed, deciding which component does what remains an important challenge for the software designer. Ideally, each component should perform a specialized task and cooperate with other components to deliver the system's overall functionality. But very often responsibilities are delegated to components in an ad-hoc manner, resulting in components that try to do almost everything by themselves or those that depend extensively on other components for carrying out their primary tasks. During initial design, it is not unusual to spawn a new component for every new bit of functionality that comes to light. As design matures, many of these components are best combined to form a compact set of components, whose each member is strongly focused on its task and interacts closely with other components to deliver the overall system functionality. The intrinsically iterative nature of software design offers opportunities for such re-organization of components.

However, this kind of design refinement usually depends on intuition, experience, and nameless "gut-feelings" of designers. In this paper we introduce the COMP-REF technique to guide such refinement of components using a set of metrics and a Linear Programming based optimization algorithm. Upon its

J. Fiadeiro and P. Inverardi (Eds.): FASE 2008, LNCS 4961, pp. 332–346, 2008.
© Springer-Verlag Berlin Heidelberg 2008

application, the technique recommends *merging* of certain components, whose current roles in the system warrant their responsibilities be delegated to other components, and they be de-scoped. Recognizing the deeply reflective nature of software design, COMP-REF seeks to *complement* a designer's judgment by abstracting some basic objectives of component interaction and elucidating some of the design choices.

Before going into the details of our approach it will be helpful to clarify the meaning of certain terms in the context of this paper.

- A *requirement* is described as "... a design feature, property, or behavior of a system" by Booch, Rumbaugh, and Jacobson [5]. These authors call the statement of a system's requirements the assertion of a contract on what the system is expected to do. How the system does that is essentially the designer's call.
- A *component* carries out specific responsibilities and interacts with other components through its interfaces to collectively deliver the system's functionality (of course, within acceptable non-functional parameters).
- A *collaboration* is described in the *Unified Modeling Language Reference Manual, Second Edition* as a "... society of cooperating objects assembled to carry out some purpose" [26]. Components collaborate via messages to fulfill their tasks.
- "Merging" of a particular component will be taken to mean distributing its responsibilities to other components in the system and removing the component from the set of components fulfilling a given set of requirements. So *after* merging, a set of components will be *reduced* in number, but will be fulfilling the same set of requirements as before.
- In this paper "compact" in the context of a set of components will be taken to mean "designed to be small in size ...". [1]

We also assume COMP-REF technique is applicable in an iterative development scenario. This is a reasonable assumption, since even if the iterative and incremental model is not officially being followed, it is widely accepted that software design is an iterative activity.

In the next sections, we present a model for the software development space as a basis for the COMP-REF technique, introduce the ideas of *aptitude* and *concordance*, formally define our set of metrics, discuss the background and intuition behind the COMP-REF technique and present its steps. We then report results of experimental validation of the technique, highlight some related work and conclude with a discussion of open issues and directions of future work.

2   A Model for the Software Development Space

In order to examine the dynamics of software systems through a set of metrics, a *model* is needed to abstract the essential elements of interest.

---

[1] http://dictionary.reference.com/browse/compact

The development space consists of the set requirements $Req = \{R_1, ..., R_x\}$ of the system, which are fulfilled by the set of components $Comp = \{C_1, ..., C_y\}$.

We take *fulfillment* to be the satisfaction of any user defined criteria to judge whether a requirement has been implemented. Fulfillment involves delivering the *functionality* represented by a requirement. A set of mapping exists between requirements and components, we will call this *relationships*. At one end of a relationship is a requirement, at the other ends are all the components needed to fulfill it. Requirements also mesh with one another – some requirements are linked to other requirements, as all of them belong to the same system, and collectively specify the overall scope of the system's functionality. The links between requirements are referred to as *connections*. From the designer's point of view, of most interest is the interplay of components. To fulfill requirements, components need to collaborate in some optimal ways, this is referred to as the *interaction* of components.

Thus one aspect of the design problem may be viewed as: *given a set of connected requirements, how to devise a set of interacting components, such that the requirements and components are able to forge relationships that deliver the system's functionality within given constraints?*

Based on this model, the COMP-REF technique uses metrics to examine the interaction of components and suggest how responsibilities can be re-aligned. Before the metrics are formally defined, we introduce the notions of *aptitude* and *concordance* in the next section.

3   The Ideas of *Aptitude* and *Concordance*

Every software component exists to perform specific tasks, which may be called its *responsibilities*. The canons of good software design recommend that each component be entrusted with one primary responsibility. In practicality, components may end up being given more than one task, but it is important to try and ensure they have one primary responsibility. Whether components have one or more responsibilities, they can not perform their tasks entirely by themselves, without any interaction with other components. This is specially true for the so-called *business objects* – components containing the business logic of an application. The extent to which a component has to interact with other components to fulfill its core functionality is an important consideration. If a component's responsibilities are strongly focused on a particular line of functionality, its interactions with other components can be expected to be less disparate. Let us take *aptitude* to denote the quality of a component that reflects how coherent its responsibilities are. Intuitively, the *Aptitude Index* measures the extent to which a component (one among a set fulfilling a system's requirements) is coherent in terms of the various tasks it is expected to perform.

As reflected upon earlier, the essence of software design lies in the collaboration of components to collectively deliver a system's functionality within given constraints. While it is important to consider the responsibility of individual components, it is also imperative that inter-component interaction be clearly understood. Software components need to work together in a spirit of harmony if they have to fulfill requirements through the best utilization of resources. Let us take *concordance* to denote such cooperation amongst components. How do we recognize such cooperation? It is manifested in the ways components share the different tasks associated with fulfilling a requirement. Some of the symptoms of less than desirable cooperation are replication of functionality – different components doing the same task for different contexts, components not honoring their interfaces (with other components) in the tasks they perform, one component trying to do everything by itself etc. The idea of concordance is an antithesis to all such undesirable characteristics – it is the quality which delegates the functionality of a system across its set of components in a way such that it is evenly distributed, and each task goes to the component most well positioned to carry it out. Intuitively, the metric *Concordance Index* measures the extent to which a component is concordant in relation to its peer components in the system.

How do these ideas relate to cohesion and coupling? Cohesion is variously defined as "... software property that binds together the various statements and other smaller modules comprising the module" [16] and "... attribute of a software unit or module that refers to the relatedness of module components" [4]. (In the latter quote, "component" has been used in the sense of part of a whole, rather than a unit of software as is its usual meaning in this paper.) Thus cohesion is predominantly an *intra-component* idea – pointing to some feature of a module that closely relates its constituents to one another. But as discussed above, concordance carries the notion of concord or harmony, signifying the spirit of successful collaboration amongst components towards collective fulfillment of a system's requirements. Concordance is an *inter-component idea*; the concordance of a component can only be seen in the light of its interaction with other components.

Coupling has been defined as "... a measure of the interdependence between two software modules. It is an intermodule property" [16]. Thus coupling does not take into account the reasons for the so called "interdependence" – that modules (or components) need to cooperate with one another as they must together fulfill a set of connected requirements. In the same vein as concordance, aptitude is also an intra-component idea, which reflects on a component's need to rely on other components to fulfill its primary responsibility/responsibilities.

Cohesion and coupling are legacy ideas from the time when software systems were predominantly monolithic. In the age of distributed systems, successful software is built by carefully regulating the interaction of components, each of which are entrusted with clearly defined responsibilities. The perspectives of aptitude, and concordance – explored intuitively in this section, with metrics based on them formally defined in the next section – complement cohesion and coupling in helping recognize, isolate, and guide design choices that will lead to the development of usable, reliable, and evolvable software systems.

4 Defining the Metrics

Considering a set of requirements $Req = \{R_1, ..., R_x\}$ and a set of components $Comp = \{C_1, ..., C_y\}$ fulfilling it, we define the metrics in the following subsections:

4.1 Aptitude Index

The *Aptitude Index* seeks to measure how coherent a component is in terms of its responsibilities.

To each component C_m of $Comp$, we attach the following *properties* [12]. A *property* is a set of zero, one or more components.

- *Core* - $\alpha(m)$
- *Non-core* - $\beta(m)$
- *Adjunct* - $\gamma(m)$

$\alpha(m)$ represents the set of component(s) required to fulfill the primary responsibility of the component C_m. As already noted, sound design principles suggest the component itself should be in charge of its main function. Thus, most often $\alpha(m) = \{C_m\}$.

$\beta(m)$ represents the set of component(s) required to fulfill the secondary responsibilities of the component C_m. Such tasks may include utilities for accessing a database, date or currency calculations, logging, exception handling etc.

$\gamma(m)$ represents the component(s) that guide any conditional behavior of the component C_m. For example, for a component which calculates interest rates for bank customers with the proviso that rates may vary according to a customer *type* ("gold", "silver" etc.), an *Adjunct* would be the set of components that help determine a customer's type.

Definition 1. *The Aptitude Index $AI(m)$ for a component C_m is a relative measure of how much C_m depends on the interaction with other components for delivering its core functionality. It is the ratio of the number of components in $\alpha(m)$ to the sum of the number of components in $\alpha(m)$, $\beta(m)$, and $\gamma(m)$*

$$AI(m) = \frac{|\alpha(m)|}{|\alpha(m)| + |\beta(m)| + |\gamma(m)|} \tag{1}$$

4.2 Requirement Set

Definition 2. *The Requirement Set $RS(m)$ for a component C_m is the set of requirements that need C_m for their fulfillment.*

$$RS(m) = \{R_p, R_q, ...\} \tag{2}$$

where C_m participates in the fulfillment of R_p, R_q etc.

Evidently, for all C_m, $RS(m) \subseteq Req$.

4.3   Concordance Index

Definition 3. *The Concordance Index $CI(m)$ for a component C_m is a relative measure of the level of concordance between the requirements being fulfilled by C_m and those being fulfilled by other components of the same system.*

For a set of components $Comp = \{C_1, C_2, ..., C_n, ..., C_{y-1}, C_y\}$ let,
$W = RS(1) \cup RS(2) \cup ... \cup RS(y-1) \cup RS(y)$
   For a component C_m ($1 \leq m \leq y$), let us define,
$X(m) = (RS(1) \cap RS(m)) \cup ... \cup ((RS(m-1) \cap RS(m)) \cup$
$((RS(m) \cap (RS(m+1)) \cup ... \cup ((RS(m) \cap (RS(y))$
   Thus $X(m)$ denotes the set of requirements that are not only being fulfilled by C_m but also by some other component(s).
   Expressed as a ratio, the *Concordance Index $CI(m)$* for component C_m is:

$$CI(m) = \frac{|X(m)|}{|W|} \tag{3}$$

5   COMP-REF: A Technique to Refine the Organization of Components

COMP-REF is a technique to guide design decisions towards allocating responsibilities to a system's components. As in human enterprises, for a successful collaboration, software components are expected to carry out their tasks in a spirit of cooperation such that each component has clearly defined and specialized responsibilities, which it can deliver with reasonably limited amount of support from other components. *Aptitude Index* measures how self sufficient a component is in carrying out its responsibilities, and *Concordance Index* is a measure of the degree of its cooperation with other components in the fulfillment of the system's requirements. Evidently, it is desired that cooperation across components would be as high as possible, within the constraint that each requirement will be fulfilled by a limited number of components. This observation is used to formulate an objective function and a set of linear constraints whose solution gives a measure of how much each component is contributing to maximizing the concordance across the entire set of components. If a component is found to have low contribution (low value of the a_n variable corresponding to the component in the LP solution as explained below), *and* it is not significantly self-sufficient in carrying out its primary responsibility (low *Aptitude Index* value) the component is a candidate for being de-scoped and its tasks (which it was hardly executing on its own) distributed to other components. This results in a more compact set of components fulfilling the given requirements.
   The goal of the COMP-REF technique is identified as *maximizing* the *Concordance Index* across all components, for a given set of requirements, in a particular iteration of development, within the constraints of *not* increasing the number of components currently participating in the fulfillment of each requirement.
   A new variable a_n ($a_n \in [0, 1]$) is introduced corresponding to each component C_n, $1 \leq n \leq N$, where N = the total number of components in the system. The

values of a_n are arrived at from the LP solution. Intuitively, a_n for a component C_n can be taken to indicate the extent to which C_n contributes to maximizing the *Concordance Index* across all components. As we shall see later, the a_n values will help us decide which components to merge.

The LP formulation can be represented as:

$$\text{Maximize } \sum_{n=1}^{y} CI(n)a_n$$

Subject to: $\forall R_m \in Req, \sum_{n=1}^{y} a_n \le p_m/N$, a_n such that $C_n \in CS(m)$. $p_m = |CS(m)|$. (As defined in [13], the *Component Set* $CS(m)$ for a requirement R_m is the set of components required to fulfill R_m.)

So, for a system with x requirements and y components, the objective function will have y terms and there will be x linear constraints.

The COMP-REF technique is summarized as: Given a set of requirements $Req = \{R_1, ..., R_x\}$ and a set of components $Comp = \{C_1, ..., C_y\}$ fulfilling it in iteration I_z of development,

- STEP 0: Review *Req* and *Comp* for new or modified requirements and/or components compared to previous iteration.
- STEP 1: Calculate the *Aptitude Index* for each component.
- STEP 2: Calculate the *Requirement Set* for each component.
- STEP 3: Calculate the *Concordance Index* for each component.
- STEP 4: Formulate the objective function and the set of linear constraints.
- STEP 5: Solve the LP formulation for the values of a_n
- STEP 6: For each component C_n, check:
  - Condition 6.1: a_n has a low value compared to that of other components? (If yes, implies C_n is not contributing significantly to maximizing the concordance across the components.)
  - Condition 6.2: $AI(n)$ has a low value compared to that of other components? (If yes, implies C_n has to rely heavily on other components for delivering its core functionality.)
- STEP 7: **If** *both* conditions 6.1 and 6.2 hold TRUE, GOTO STEP 8, **else** GOTO STEP 10
- STEP 8: For C_n, check:
  - Condition 8.1: Upon merging C_n with other components, in the resulting set $\tilde{Comp}$ of q components (say), $CI(q) \ne 0$ for all q? (If yes, implies resulting set of q components has more than one component).
- STEP 9: **If** condition 8.1 is TRUE, C_n is a candidate for being merged; after merging components C_n GOTO STEP 0, starting with *Req* and $\tilde{Comp}$, **else** GOTO STEP 10.
- STEP 10: Wait for the next iteration.

6   Experimental Validation

In this section we present results from our experimental validation of the COMP-REF technique.

6.1   Validation Strategy

We have applied the COMP-REF technique on the following variety of scenarios to better understand its utility and limitations.

- **A "text-book" example** – *The Osbert Oglesby Case Study* is presented in Schach's software engineering textbook [27] as a software development project across life cycle phases and workflows. Using the Java and database components given as part of the design, we use the COMP-REF technique to suggest a reorganization of components and examine its implication on the design thinking outlined in the study.
- **The Financial Aid Application (FAA) project** – Florida State University's University Computing Services[2] is in charge of meeting the university's computing and networking goals. As a development project in 2006, existing paper based *Financial Aid Application* (FAA) was migrated to an online system. The development team took the previously used paper forms as the initial reference and built a system using JavaServer Pages (JSP), Java classes, and a back-end database to allow students to apply for financial aid over the Web. The COMP-REF technique is applied to suggest the merging of some of the components and its effect discussed on the overall design.
- **Morphbank: A Web-based Bioinformatics Application** – Morphbank[3] serves the biological research community as an open web repository of images. "It is currently being used to document specimens in natural history collections, to voucher DNA sequence data, and to share research results in disciplines such as taxonomy, morphometrics, comparative anatomy, and phylogenetics". The Morphbank system uses open standards and free software to store images and associated data and is accessible to any biologist interested in storing and sharing digital information of organisms. The COMP-REF technique investigates whether the overall design can be streamlined by a re-allocation of responsibilities across components and retiring some of them.
- **FileZilla: An open source project** – "FileZilla is a fast FTP and SFTP client for Windows with a lot of features. FileZilla Server is a reliable FTP server."[4] We use COMP-REF to examine FileZilla's allocation of component responsibilities.
- **The SCIT Workshop** – Symbiosis Center for Information Technology (SCIT)[5] is a leading academic institution in India, imparting technology and management education at the graduate level. Twenty five first-year students of the two year Master of Business Administration – Software Development and Management (MBA-SDM) graduate program participated in an workshop conducted by us. All the students had undergraduate degrees in science or engineering, and about half of them had prior industrial experience in software development. The students were divided into two groups with an even

---

[2] http://www.ucs.fsu.edu/
[3] http://www.morphbank.net
[4] http://sourceforge.net/projects/filezilla/
[5] http:///www.scit.edu

distribution of experience and exposure to software development ideas. Each group was in turn divided into two teams, *customer* and *developer*. The objective of the workshop was to explore how differently the same software system will be designed, with and without the use of the COMP-REF technique. Accordingly, each group was given the high level requirements of a contrived software project of building a Web application for a bank, where its customers can access different banking services. Within each group, the *developer* team interacted with the *customer* team to come up with a design in terms of interacting components that best met the requirements. The COMP-REF technique was applied in guiding the design choices of one group, which we will call Group A, while the other group, Group B, had no such facility. The workshop provided valuable insights into how COMP-REF can complement (and at times constrain) the intuition behind software design. We wish to thank Ms.Shaila Kagal, Director, SCIT for her help and support in conducting the study.

6.2   Presentation and Interpretation of the Results

Due to space constraints, we can not present each of the above validation scenarios in detail. Instead, we illustrate the application of COMP-REF in the FAA project in detail. The summary of all the validation scenarios are presented in Table 1.

Table 2 gives brief description of the requirements for the first iteration of the FAA project.

The $RS(m)$ column of Table 3 shows the *Requirement Set* for each component. Evidently, $W = \{R_1, R_2, R_3, R_4, R_5\}$ and $|W| = 5$. The $AI(m)$ and $CI(m)$ columns of Table 3 give the *Aptitude Index* and the *Concordance Index* values respectively for each component.

From the design artifacts, we noted that R_1 needs components C_1, C_5, C_{11} ($p_1 = 3$), R_2 needs $C_2, C_6, C_7, C_8, C_9, C_{11}$ ($p_2 = 6$), R_3 needs $C_3, C_6, C_7, C_8, C_9, C_{11}$ ($p_3 = 6$), R_4 needs $C_3, C_6, C_7, C_8, C_9, C_{11}$ ($p_4 = 6$), and R_5 needs C_4, C_6, C_7, C_{10}, C_{11} ($p_5 = 5$) for their respective fulfillment. Evidently, in this case $N = 11$.

Based on the above, the objective function and the set of linear constraints was formulated as:
Maximize
$$0.2a_1 + 0.2a_2 + 0.4a_3 + 0.2a_4 + 0.2a_5 + 0.8a_6 + 0.8a_7 + 0.4a_8 + 0.4a_9 + 0.2a_{10} + a_{11}$$
Subject to

$a_1 + a_5 + a_{11} \leq 0.27$
$a_2 + a_6 + a_7 + a_8 + a_9 + a_{11} \leq 0.55$
$a_3 + a_6 + a_7 + a_8 + a_9 + a_{11} \leq 0.55$
$a_3 + a_6 + a_7 + a_8 + a_9 + a_{11} \leq 0.55$
$a_4 + a_6 + a_7 + a_{10} + a_{11} \leq 0.45$

Using the automated solver, GIPALS (General Interior-Point Linear Algorithm Solver)[6], the above LP formulation was solved (values in the a_n column of Table 3).

---

[6] http://www.optimalon.com/

Table 1. Experimental Validation: A Snapshot

System	Scope and Technology	Parameters	Findings
Osbert Oglesby Case Study	A detailed case study across software development life cycle workflows and phases presented in [27], using Java and database components.	Three requirements, eighteen components.	COMP-REF suggested 27% of the components can be merged with other components.
FAA project	Migration of paper based student aid application system to a Web based system, using Java and database components.	Five requirements, eleven components.	COMP-REF suggested 18% of the components can be merged with other components. Detailed calculation and interpretation given in Section 6.2 of this paper.
Morphbank	A Web-based collaborative biological research tool using PHP and database components. We studied the *Browse* functional area.	Seven requirements, eighty-one components.	The results of applying COMP-REF were inconclusive. Almost all the components executing common tasks across functional areas (around 75% of the total number of components) are suggested to be potential candidates for merging.
FileZilla	A fast and reliable cross-platform FTP, FTPS and SFTP client using C/C++.	As this is a software product vis-a-vis a project, there are no user defined requirements; three major lines of functionality and around one thirty eight components (ignoring header files).	While applying COMP-REF, difficulties were faced in correlating requirements with components. Assuming very coarse-grained requirements, COM-REF did not find valid justification for merging a notable percent of components.
SCIT workshop	Two separate groups designed a contrived software system of a Web based banking application using Java and database components. One group (Group A) was allowed the use of the COMP-REF technique, while the other group (Group B) was not. Group A and Group B were oblivious of one another's design choices.	Three requirements; Group A had eight components, Group B had twelve.	Group A's components 33% fewer than Group B's, they also had cleaner interfaces and smaller number of inter-component method calls. It appears COMP-REF helped Group A deliver the same functionality through a more compact set of component by being able to use COMP-REF in intermediate stages of design.

Let us examine how the COMP-REF technique can guide design decisions. Based on the a_n values in Table 3, evidently components $C_5, C_7, C_8, C_9, C_{10}$ have the least contribution to maximizing the objective function. So the tasks performed by these components may be delegated to other components. However, as mandated by COMP-REF, another factor needs be taken into account

Table 2. Requirements for FAA: iteration I_1

Req ID	Brief Description
R_1	Display financial aid information to users.
R_2	Allow users to enter enrollment period and record the information after validation.
R_3	Allow users to enter FSU sessions and record the information after validation.
R_4	Allow users to enter expected summer resources and record the information after validation.
R_5	Display summary of the user's enrollment status.

Table 3. FAA case study: Metrics values and LP solution for iteration I_1

C_m	Component name	$RS(n)$	$\alpha(n)$	$\beta(n)$	$\gamma(n)$	$AI(n)$	$X(n)$	$CI(n)$	a_n
C_1	summary.jsp	R_1	C_1	C_5, C_{11}	-	0.33	1	0.2	0.25
C_2	summer_instructions.jsp	R_2	C_2	C_8, C_9, C_6,C_{11}	C_7	0.17	1	0.2	0.4
C_3	summer_app.jsp	R_3, R_4	C_3	C_8, C_9, C_6,C_{11}	C_7	0.17	2	0.4	0.4
C_4	alerts_summary.jsp	R_5	C_4	C_{10},C_6,C_{11}	C_7	0.2	1	0.2	0.3
C_5	RetrieveSummerData.java	R_1	C_5	C_8, C_{11}	-	0.33	1	0.2	0
C_6	SummerApplication.java	R_2, R_3, R_4, R_5	C_6	C_8, C_9	C_3	0.25	4	0.8	0.13
C_7	SummerApplicationUtils.java	R_2, R_3, R_4, R_5	C_7	-	-	1	4	0.8	0
C_8	ValidateSummerApplication.java	R_2, R_3, R_4	C_8	-	-	1	2	0.4	0
C_9	SaveSummerApplication.java	R_2, R_3, R_4	C_9	C_{10}, C_{11}	C_3	0.25	2	0.4	0
C_{10}	RetrieveSummerApplication	R_5	C_{10}	-	C_7	0.5	1	0.2	0
C_{11}	StuSummerApp	R_1, R_2, R_3, R_4, R_5	C_{11}	-	-	1	5	1	0.02

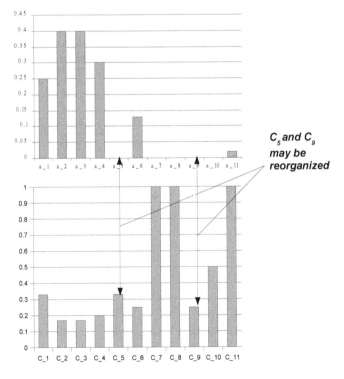

Fig. 1. a_n values from LP solution(top) and $AI(n)$ vs. C_n (bottom)

before deciding on the candidates for merging. How self-sufficient are the components that are sought to be merged? We next turn to $AI(n)$ values for the components in Table 3. We notice, $AI(5) = 0.33$, $AI(7) = 1$, $AI(8) = 1$, $AI(9) = 0.25$, and $AI(10) = 0.5$. Thus C_7, C_8 and C_{10} have the highest *Aptitude Index* values. These are components delivering functionalities of general utility, user input validation and database access logic respectively – facilities used across the application. Thus it is expedient to keep them localized. But C_5 and C_9, as their relatively low values of $AI(n)$ suggest, need to interact significantly with other components to carry out their task. And given their negligible contribution to maximizing concordance; a helpful design choice would be to merge them with other components. A smaller set of high concordance components is preferred over a larger set of low concordance ones, as the former has lesser inter-component interaction, thereby leading to better resilience to modification of particular components due to requirement changes. Figure 1 summarizes these discussions, suggesting reorganization of the two components through merging.

Thus one cycle of application of the COMP-REF technique suggests the reduction of the number of components from eleven to nine (18%) in fulfilling the set of requirements for the first iteration of the FAA project.

7 Related Work

Although it is common to use the terms *measure*, *measurement* and *metrics* in place of one another, some authors have underscored subtle distinctions [25], [2], [17]. For our discussion, we have taken *metrics* to mean "a set of specific measurements taken on a particular item or process" [3]. Metrics for analysis include the closely reviewed function point based approaches [1] and the Bang metric [15]. Card and Glass [6] have proposed software design complexity in terms of *structural complexity*, *data complexity* and *system complexity*. [23] identifies some important uses of complexity metrics. Fenton underscores the challenges of trying to formulate general software complexity measures [17]. Chidamber and Kemerer present a widely referenced set of object oriented software metrics in [7], [8]. Harrison, Counsell and Nithi have evaluated a group of metrics for calibrating object-oriented design [19].

Freeman's paper, *Automating Software Design*, is one of the earliest expositions of the ideas and issues relating to design automation [18]. Karimi et al. [21] report their experiences with the implementation of an automated software design assistant tool. Ciupke presents a tool based technique for analyzing legacy code to detect design problems [9]. O'Keeffe et al. [24] present an approach towards automatically improving Java design. Jackson's group are working on the *Alloy Analyzer* tool that employs "automated reasoning techniques that treat a software design problem as a giant puzzle to be solved" [20].

This current paper extends our ongoing research in understanding the effects of changing requirements on software systems, the role of metrics as design heuristics, and how the development life cycle can tune itself to the challenges of enterprise software development [13],[12], [11], [10], [14]. Particularly, [13] explores the relationship between requirements and components from another perspective.

8   Open Issues and Future Work

From the summary of the experimental results in Table 1, it is apparent COMP-REF is able to give conclusive recommendations in some of the validation scenarios. Let us reflect on the scenarios its suggestions are inconclusive. In the case of Morphbank, the system does not follow a clear separation of functionality in delegating responsibilities to its components. For FileZilla, it is difficult to extract clearly defined requirements and correlate them with corresponding components. This is not unusual for a software product, vis-a-vis a software development project, where a system is built to fulfill user given requirements. From the validation results so far, COMP-REF *appears* to work best for systems that have a clear set of requirements, follows the n-tier architecture paradigm and use object orientation to ensure a clear separation of concerns. We expect to scrutinize this conclusion further through ongoing case studies. The scalability of the technique also needs to be tested on very large scale systems and across many iterations of development.

COMP-REF suggests the merging of components. The in-built safeguards within the technique (STEP 8) ensures it will not lead to a single component *monolithic* system. The underlying assumption behind COMP-REF is that fewer components delivering the same functionality is better than a larger number of components, on grounds of more streamlined inter-component interaction, reduced communication overheads between members of the team developing the software, and better localization of the effects of inevitable changes in requirements [13]. In some cases there may be a need to *split* components instead of merging them. We plan to extend the technique to cover this aspect in future work. We are also working on developing an automated tool using the Eclipse platform [7] that will parse design artifacts (such as Unified Modeling Language diagrams), apply COMP-REF and present a set of recommendations. This tool integrates COMP-REF with our earlier work on a mechanism to track the effects of changing requirements on software systems [13]. Initial results from applying the tool are very promising.

9   Conclusions

In this paper we presented COMP-REF as a promising technique to guide the organization of components in software systems. COMP-REF is meant to complement, and certainly not replace, the intuitive and subjective aspects of software design. Results from applying the technique on a variety of systems were presented. Experimental data suggests COMP-REF works best for object-oriented

---

[7] http://www.eclipse.org/

systems using n-tiered architecture that fulfill user requirements. We plan to refine the technique through further validation and extend it into a fully automated framework for guiding analysis and design of software systems.

References

1. Albrecht, A.: Measuring Application Development Productivity. In: Proc. Joint SHARE/GUIDE/IBM Application Development Symposium, October 1979, pp. 83–92 (1979)
2. Baker, A.L., Bieman, J.M., Fenton, N., Gustafson, D.A., Melton, A., Whitty, R.: A philosophy for software measurement. J. Syst. Softw. 12(3), 277–281 (1990)
3. Berard, E.V.: Metrics for object-oriented software engineering (1995), http://www.ipipan.gda.pl/~marek/objects/TOA/moose.html
4. Bieman, J.M., Ott, L.M.: Measuring functional cohesion. IEEE Trans. Softw. Eng. 20(8), 644–657 (1994)
5. Booch, G., Rumbaugh, J., Jacobson, I.: The Unified Modeling Language User Guide, 2nd edn. Addison-Wesley, Reading (2005)
6. Card, D.N., Glass, R.L.: Measuring Software Design Quality. Prentice-Hall, Englewood Cliffs (1990)
7. Chidamber, S.R., Kemerer, C.F.: Towards a metrics suite for object oriented design. In: OOPSLA 1991: Conference proceedings on Object-oriented programming systems, languages, and applications, pp. 197–211. ACM Press, New York (1991)
8. Chidamber, S.R., Kemerer, C.F.: A metrics suite for object oriented design. IEEE Trans. Softw. Eng. 20(6), 476–493 (1994)
9. Ciupke, O.: Automatic detection of design problems in object-oriented reengineering. In: TOOLS 1999: Proceedings of the Technology of Object-Oriented Languages and Systems, Washington, DC, USA, p. 18. IEEE Computer Society Press, Los Alamitos (1999)
10. Datta, S.: Integrating the furps+ model with use cases - a metrics driven approach. In: Supplementary Proceedings of the 16th IEEE International Symposium on Software Reliability Engineering (ISSRE2005), Chicago, IL, November 7–11, 2005, pp. 4–51–4–52 (2005)
11. Datta, S.: Agility measurement index: a metric for the crossroads of software development methodologies. In: ACM-SE 44: Proceedings of the 44th annual southeast regional conference, pp. 271–273. ACM Press, New York (2006)
12. Datta, S.: Crosscutting score: an indicator metric for aspect orientation. In: ACM-SE 44: Proceedings of the 44th annual southeast regional conference, pp. 204–208. ACM Press, New York (2006)
13. Datta, S., van Engelen, R.: Effects of changing requirements: a tracking mechanism for the analysis workflow. In: SAC 2006, pp. 1739–1744. ACM Press, New York (2006)
14. Datta, S., van Engelen, R., Gaitros, D., Jammigumpula, N.: Experiences with tracking the effects of changing requirements on morphbank: a web-based bioinformatics application. In: ACM-SE 45: Proceedings of the 45th annual southeast regional conference, pp. 413–418. ACM Press, New York (2007)
15. DeMarco, T.: Controlling Software Projects. Yourdon Press (1982)
16. Dhama, H.: Quantitative models of cohesion and coupling in software. In: Selected papers of the sixth annual Oregon workshop on Software metrics, pp. 65–74. Elsevier Science Inc., New York (1995)

17. Fenton, N.: Software measurement: A necessary scientific basis. IEEE Trans. Softw. Eng. 20(3), 199–206 (1994)
18. Freeman, P.: Automating software design. In: DAC 1973: Proceedings of the 10th workshop on Design automation, Piscataway, NJ, USA, pp. 62–67. IEEE Computer Society Press, Los Alamitos (1973)
19. Harrison, R., Counsell, S.J., Nithi, R.V.: An evaluation of the mood set of object-oriented software metrics. IEEE Trans. Softw. Eng. 24(6), 491–496 (1998)
20. Jackson, D.: Software Abstractions: Logic, Language and Analysis. MIT Press, Cambridge (2006)
21. Karimi, J., Konsynski, B.R.: An automated software design assistant. IEEE Trans. Softw. Eng. 14(2), 194–210 (1988)
22. Larman, C.: Applying UML and Patterns. Prentice Hall, Englewood Cliffs (1997)
23. McCabe, T.: A software complexity measure. IEEE Trans. Softw. Eng. SE-2, 308–320 (1976)
24. O'Keeffe, M., Cinneide, M.M.O.: A stochastic approach to automated design improvement. In: PPPJ 2003: Proceedings of the 2nd international conference on Principles and practice of programming in Java, pp. 59–62. Computer Science Press, Inc., New York (2003)
25. Pressman, R.S.: Software Engineering: A Practitioners Approach. McGraw-Hill, New York (2000)
26. Rumbaugh, J., Jacobson, I., Booch, G.: The Unified Modeling Language Reference Manual, 2nd edn. Addison-Wesley, Reading (2005)
27. Schach, S.: Object-oriented and Classical Software Development, 6th edn., McGraw-Hill International Edition (2005)

Verification of Architectural Refactorings by Rule Extraction

Dénes Bisztray[1], Reiko Heckel[1], and Hartmut Ehrig[2]

[1] Department of Computer Science, University of Leicester
{dab24,reiko}@mcs.le.ac.uk
[2] Institut für Softwaretechnik und Theoretische Informatik,
Technische Universität Berlin
ehrig@cs.tu-berlin.de

Abstract. With the success of model-driven development as well as component-based and service-oriented systems, models of software architecture are key artefacts in the development process. To adapt to changing requirements and improve internal software quality such models have to evolve while preserving aspects of their behaviour.

To avoid the costly verification of refactoring steps on large systems we present a method which allows us to extract a (usually much smaller) rule from the transformation performed and verify this rule instead. The main result of the paper shows that the verification of rules is indeed sufficient to guarantee the desired semantic relation between source and target models. We apply the approach to the refactoring of architectural models based on UML component, structure, and activity diagrams, with using CSP as a semantic domain.

Keywords: Service Oriented Architecture, UML, Refactoring, Graph Transformation, CSP.

1 Introduction

Nothing endures but change, as the philosopher says [Lae25]. As much as anywhere else, this applies to the world of software. In order to improve the internal structure, performance, or scalability of software systems, changes may be required that preserve the observable behaviour of systems. In OO programming, such behaviour-preserving transformations are known as refactorings [FBB+99]. Today, where applications tend to be distributed and service-oriented, the most interesting changes take place at the architectural level. Even if these changes are structural, they have to take into account the behaviour encapsulated inside the components that are being replaced or reconnected. In analogy to the programming level we speak of architectural refactorings if preservation of observable behaviour is intended.

In this paper, refactoring is addressed at the level of models. Given a transformation from a source to a target model we would like to be able to verify their relation. In order to make this precise we have to fix three ingredients: the modelling language used, its semantics, and the relation capturing our idea of

J. Fiadeiro and P. Inverardi (Eds.): FASE 2008, LNCS 4961, pp. 347–361, 2008.
© Springer-Verlag Berlin Heidelberg 2008

behaviour preservation. Notice however that in the mathematical formulation of our approach, these parameters can be replaced by others, subject to certain requirements. For *modelling language* we use the UML, which provides the means to describe both structure (by component and static structure diagrams) and behaviour (by activity diagrams) of service-oriented systems [OMG06]. The *semantics* of the relevant fragment of the UML is expressed in a denotational style, using CSP [Hoa85] as semantic domain and defining the mapping from UML diagrams to CSP processes by means of graph transformation rules. As different UML diagrams are semantically overlapping, the mapping has to produce one single consistent semantic model [EKGH01]. The *semantic relation* of behaviour preservation can conveniently be expressed using one of the refinement and equivalence relations on CSP processes.

Based on these (or analogue) ingredients, we can formalise the question by saying that a model transformation $M_1 \rightarrow M_2$ is behaviour-preserving if $sem(M_1)$ $\mathcal{R}$ $sem(M_2)$ where sem represents the semantic mapping and $\mathcal{R}$ the desired relation on the semantic domain. However, the verification of relation $\mathcal{R}$ over sufficiently large M_1 and M_2 can be very costly, while the actual refactoring might only affect a relatively small fragment of the overall model. Hence, it would be advantageous if we could focus our verification on those parts of the model that have been changed, that is, verify the refactoring *rules* rather than the actual steps. This is indeed possible, as we show in this paper, if both semantic mapping sem and semantic relation $\mathcal{R}$ satisfy suitable compositionality properties. We satisfy these requirements by specifying the mapping sem by graph transformation rules of a certain format and choosing CSP refinements as semantic relations.

However, model-level architectural refactorings are unlikely to be created directly from semantics-preserving rules. Such rule catalogues as exist focus on object-oriented systems and are effectively liftings to the model level of refactoring rules for OO programs. Rather, an engineer using a modelling tool performs a manual model transformation $M_1 \rightarrow M_2$ from which a verifiable refactoring rule has to be extracted first. In this we follow the idea of *model transformation by example* [Var06] where model transformation rules expressed as graph transformations are derived from sample transformations.

The paper is structured as follows. In Sect. 3 we present our architectural models along with an example, on which a refactoring step is performed in Sect. 4. Section 5 introduces CSP as the semantic domain and describes the mapping and the semantic relation. The formal justification for rule-level verification is discussed in Sect. 6. It is demonstrated that the method is sound if the semantic mapping is compositional, which is true based on a general result which derives this property from the format of the mapping rules. Section 7 concludes the paper. A detailed exposition of all relevant definitions and proofs is given in [Bis08].

2   Related Work

After refactorings for Java were made popular by Fowler [FBB+99], several proposals for formalisation and verification based on first-order logics and invariants have been made [SPTJ01,LM04,MGB06]. The first formal approach to refactoring based on graph transformations is due to Mens [MDJ02], focussing on the analysis of conflicts and dependencies between rules.

Refactoring of architectural models has been studied formally in architectural description languages (ADLs) like WRIGHT [ADG98] or Darwin [MK96], using process calculi like CSP or π-calculus for expressing formal semantics. Our semantic mapping to CSP follows that of [EKGH01] for UML-RT [Sel98], an earlier component-based extension to the UML, but distinguishes type and instance level architectural models in UML 2.

A number of authors have studied instance level architectural transformations, or reconfigurations. For example, Taentzer [TGM00] introduces the notion of distributed graph transformation systems to allow architectural reconfiguration by means of two-level rules to express system-level and local transformations. The approach of [WF02] uses an algebraic framework to represent reconfigurations based on the coordination language Community. In [HIM98] the architecture is represented by hypergraphs, where the hyperedges are the components, and the nodes are the communication ports. Architectural reconfigurations are represented by synchronised hyperedge replacement rules.

Our approach combines the type level, typical of source code refactoring, which happens at the level of classes, with the instance level typical of architectural transformations.

3   Architectural Models

This section presents our choice of architectural modelling language by means of an example based on the *Car Accident Scenario* from the SENSORIA Automotive Case Study [WCG+06].

We use UML *component* and *composite structure diagrams* for representing the type and instance-level architecture of our system in conjunction with *activity diagrams* specifying the workflows executed by component instances [OMG06].

Briefly, the scenario is as follows. A car company is offering a service by which, in case one of the sensors in their car detects an accident, customers are contacted via their mobile phone to check if they require assistance. If they do, a nearby ambulance is dispatched. The system consists of three main parts: the agent in the car, the accident server, and the interface to the local emergency services. We present the architecture and behaviour of the accident server in detail.

Type-Level. Component diagrams specify the components, ports, interfaces that make up the building blocks of the system. Figure 1(a) shows the component diagram of the accident server.

The *AccidentManager* is the core component, responsible for receiving incoming alerts from cars through the *AlertRecv* port. In order to initiate a phone call it acquires the number of the driver from the *PersistentDatabase*, and passes it to the *PhoneService*, which calls the driver. In case the driver replies saying that assistance is not required, the alert is cancelled. Otherwise, the call is returned to

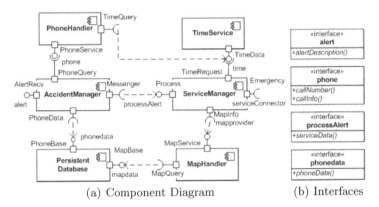

(a) Component Diagram   (b) Interfaces

Fig. 1. Architectural model of the accident server

the *AccidentManager*, which assesses the available data (including sensorial and location data from the car) and decides if the situation is a real emergency. In this case it passes the necessary data to the *ServiceManager*, which matches the GPS location of the car using the *MapHandler*, creates a service description, and contacts the *serviceConnector* interface that provides access to local emergency services.

In the diagram, components are represented by rectangles with a component icon and classifier name. Smaller squares on the components represent the *ports*, *provided interfaces* are represented by circles and *required interfaces* by a socket shape [OMG06]. Dashed arrows represent dependencies between the provided and required interfaces.

Instance-Level. The composite structure diagram specifying the configuration of the accident server is shown in Figure 2. Boxes named *instance : type* represent component instances. Ports are typed by interfaces defining the possible actions that can happen through that port. For instance, the possible actions of the *PhoneQuery* port are defined by the *phone* interface. Links between port instances represent connectors, enabling communication between component instances [OMG06].

Behaviour. The behaviours of the components are described by *activity diagrams*, like the one depicted in Figure 3 associated with the *AccidentManager* component. Apart from the obvious control flow constructs they feature *accept event actions*, denoted by concave pentagons, that wait for the occurrence of specific events triggered by *send signal actions*, shown as convex pentagons [OMG06]. They fit into the communication framework by representing functions calls from the corresponding *interface* through the relevant *port*. For instance, the *phoneData* send signal action in Fig. 3 represents the function call from *phone* interface through *PhoneQuery* port.

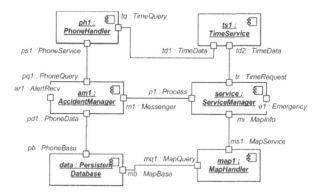

Fig. 2. Static Structure Diagram of the Accident Server

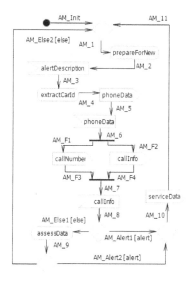

Fig. 3. Activity Diagram of the AccidentManager component

4 Model Refactoring

With the current architecture scalability issues may arise. Assuming that 70% of the incoming alerts are not real emergencies, the analysis of 'false alerts' consumes considerable resources. The *AccidentManager* may thus turn out to be a bottleneck in the system.

To address this scalability problem we extract the initial handling of alerts from the *AccidentManager* into an *AlertListener* component. The solution is depicted in Figure 4. The *AlertListener* receives alerts from cars, forwards them to the *AccidentManager* for processing while querying the database for the phone number and invoking the telephone service, which sends the results of its calls to the *AccidentManager*.

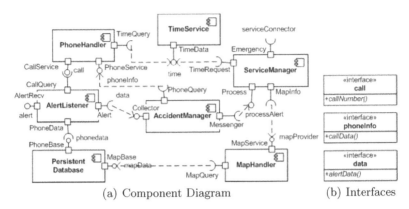

(a) Component Diagram   (b) Interfaces

Fig. 4. Architectural model of the refactored Accident Server

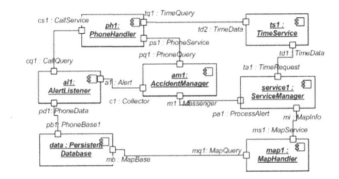

Fig. 5. Configuration after the refactoring

The behaviour of the new *AlertListener* component is given in Figure 6(a), while the updated behaviour of the *AccidentManager* is shown in Figure 6(b).

However, rather than comparing the semantics of the entire system model before and after the change, we focus on the affected parts and their immediate context. More precisely, we are proposing to extract a model transformation *rule* which, (1) when applied to the source model produces the target model of the refactoring and (2) is semantics preserving in the sense that its left-hand side is in the desired semantic relation with its right-hand side. We will demonstrate in Sect. 6 that this is indeed sufficient to guarantee the corresponding relation between source and target model. In the example present, such a rule is shown in Fig. 7 for the structural part only. The behaviour transformation is given by the new and updated activity diagrams associated with the components in the rule. The rule is applied by selecting in the source model an occurrence isomorphic to the left-hand side of the rule at both type and instance level. Thus, component C is matched by *AccidentManager* from Fig. 1(a), interface N corresponds to *phone*, M to *processAlert*, and J to *phoneData*. At instance level a similar correspondence is established.

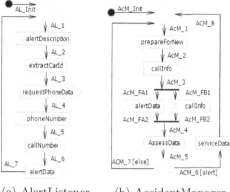

(a) AlertListener   (b) AccidentManager

Fig. 6. Owned behaviour after the refactoring

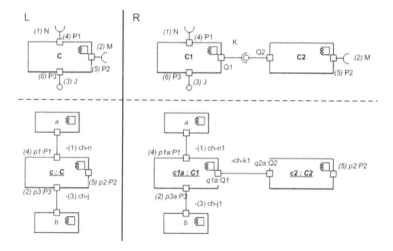

Fig. 7. Refactoring rule

A rule is extracted as follows: G denotes the original model while H denotes the refactored one. The smallest consistent submodel of G containing $G \setminus H$ would form the left-hand side L of the rule, while the smallest submodel of H containing $H \setminus G$ would form the right hand side R. In the algebraic approach to graph transformation, which provides the formal background of this work, this is known as Initial Pushout Construction [EEPT06].

Recently a similar construction has been used as part of the *model transformation by example* approach, where a transformation specification is derived inductively from a set of sample transformation rules [Var06]. Notice that while the rule thus obtained is known to achieve the desired transformational effect, it is not in general guaranteed that the semantic relation between L and R can indeed be verified, even if it holds between G and H. The reason is that additional context information present in G and H may be required to ensure semantic compatibility. It is the responsibility of the modeller to include this additional context into the rule. However, as in the example presented, a minimal rule might not be enough because some additional context may have to be taken into account in order to guarantee the preservation of the semantics. In the example this has led to the introduction into the rule of generic component instances a and b (the PhoneHandler and Database in the concrete model).

The example illustrates the potential complexity of the problem at hand, with changes in all three diagrams types to be coordinated in order to lead to an equivalent behaviour. In the following section we will see how the combined effect of these three models is reflected in the semantic mapping to CSP.

5   Semantic Mapping

In order to verify the semantic relation between source and target models, UML models are mapped to CSP processes. After introducing the relevant concepts, the mapping rules are sketched. Formally, the UML models are instances of metamodels represented by attributed typed graphs. Also, the mapping consists of rules of a triple graph grammar [Sch94] presented here using the concrete syntax of UML and CSP, rather than the abstract graph-based presentation. This relation has been explained at length in [BH07], where a similar technique is used to describe the mapping of activity diagrams to CSP.

Communicating Sequential Processes. Communicating Sequential Processes [Hoa85] is a process algebra providing for concurrent systems and supported by tools [FSEL05]. A *process* is the behaviour pattern of a component with an alphabet of events. Processes are defined using recursive equations based on the following syntax.

$$P ::= event \rightarrow P \mid P \sqcap Q \mid P \;\square\; Q \mid P \parallel Q \mid P \setminus a \mid SKIP \mid STOP$$

The prefix $a \rightarrow P$ performs action a and then behaves like P. The processes $P \sqcap Q$ and $P \;\square\; Q$ represent internal and external choice between processes P and Q, respectively. The process $P \parallel Q$ behaves as P and Q engaged in a lock-step synchronisation. Hiding $P \setminus a$ behaves like P except that all occurrences of event a are hidden. $SKIP$ represents successful termination, $STOP$ is a deadlock. Due to the distinction of type and instance level, in our application it is important to define groups of processes with similar behaviour. To this end, we use labelling: Each process within a group is labelled by a different name, which is also used to distinguish its events. A labelled event is a pair $l.x$ where l is a label, and x is the event. A process P labelled by l is denoted by $l : P$ [Hoa85].

The semantics of CSP is defined in terms of traces, failures, and divergences [Hoa85]. A trace of a process behaviour is a finite sequence of events in which the process has engaged up to some moment in time. The complete set of all possible traces of process P is denoted by $traces(P)$. For the three semantics domains, corresponding equivalence and refinement relations can be deducted. Two processes are trace equivalent, i.e. $P \equiv_T Q$ if the traces of P and Q are the same, i.e. $traces(P) = traces(Q)$. Trace refinement means that $P \sqsubseteq_T Q$ if $traces(Q) \subseteq traces(P)$. Hence, every trace of Q is also a trace of P. Analogously the equivalence and refinement relations based on failures and divergences can be defined. These relations shall be used to express behaviour preservation of refactoring rules and compatibility of system components.

Despite the existence of more expressive mathematical models, the compositional property and tool support are most important to our aim. FDR2 [FSEL05] enables the automatic verification of the above mentioned equivalence and refinement relations.

Type-Level Mapping. In Fig. 8 the mapping of a component and its ports are shown. The component is mapped to a process definition, where its owned behaviour (obtained from the activity diagram) and the derived processes of the contained ports are put in parallel.

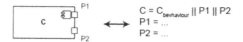

Fig. 8. Mapping of a Component and its Ports

The ports are then mapped to simple processes, allowing all send and receive events for messages declared in the interfaces that the port implements. In case of a provided interface, the port receives the messages, which is denoted by a $recv_{methodname}$ event. For required interfaces, the port sends the message, leading to a $send_{methodname}$ event.

Fig. 9. Mapping of an Interface

Instance-Level Mapping. In the mapping of component instances it is important to deal with multiple occurrences. Thus, components and port instances are labelled by their instance name from the diagram as shown in Fig. 10.

As channels describe communication, they contain events corresponding to messages sent and received. As shown in Figure 11, *send* and *recv* events are labelled by the corresponding port instances and put in a prefix relationship to ensure the correct order.

As behind the concrete syntax the rules are graph transformation rules, the mapping of events between LHS and RHS graphs are notated by a unique *map id*.

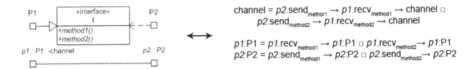

$c1{:}C = c1{:}C_{behaviour} \parallel p1{:}P1 \parallel p2{:}P2$
$p1{:}P1 = ...$
$p2{:}P2 = ...$

Fig. 10. Mapping of a Component Instance

channel = $p2.send_{methor1} \rightarrow p1.recv_{method1} \rightarrow$ channel $\Box$
$p2.send_{method2} \rightarrow p1.recv_{method2} \rightarrow$ channel

$p1{:}P1 = p1.recv_{method1} \rightarrow p1{:}P1 \Box p1.recv_{method2} \rightarrow p1{:}P1$
$p2{:}P2 = p2.send_{method1} \rightarrow p2{:}P2 \Box p2.send_{method2} \rightarrow p2{:}P2$

Fig. 11. Mapping of a Channel with Ports

Mapped objects bear the same *map id*. To make the mapped event names identical on both sides, these events are labelled on instance level by their *map id*, that overrides the structure based labelling presented above.

Application to the Rule. To verify the compatibility of the rule with a semantic relation, say trace refinement, we map the instance levels of both left- and right-hand side to their semantic representation and verify the relation between them. For the left-hand side, for example, this yields

$$sem(L) = a \| ch\text{-}n \| c{:}C \| ch\text{-}j \| b \setminus \{ \, unmapped_1 \,, unmapped_2, ... \}$$

by placing all component instances and connectors in parallel and hiding the unmapped events.

That means connectors and component behaviours are running in parallel. Since the parallel operator in CSP means lock-step synchronisation, whenever a *send* event happens at the component, the channel attached changes state to and waits for the corresponding *recv* event at the other end.

On the right hand side we hide all internal communication between instances of $C1$ and $C2$. For example, referring to our activity diagram in Fig. 6(a), the *alertData* and *callStarted* events are hidden because they serve the combination between the two parts of the newly split component C. To check if $sem(L) \sqsubseteq sem(R)$ we would take into account the CSP mappings of all activity diagrams of components involved in the transformation.

Implementation. The transformation was implemented using the Tiger EMF Transformer [Tig07] tool. It consists of 43 rules organised in 4 major groups (type-level, owned behaviour, instance-level, renaming). The production rules are defined by rule graphs, namely a left-hand side (LHS), a right-hand side (RHS) and possible negative application conditions (NACs). These rule graphs are object-structures that contain objects typed over EMF metamodels of UML diagrams as well as CSP expressions. These object-structures are also essentially attributed typed graphs.

The generated CSP code for the refactoring rule was 62 lines for the LHS, and 76 lines for the RHS. The trace refinement was verified with FDR2 through 24,168 states and 121,586 transitions.

6   Correctness of Rule-Level Verification

In this section we demonstrate that the method of verifying a transformation by verifying an extracted rule is indeed correct. The crucial condition is the compositionality of the semantic mapping, which guarantees that the semantic relation $\mathcal{R}$ (think refinement or equivalence) is preserved under embedding of models. We will first formulate the principle and prove that, assuming this property, our verification method is sound. Then we establish a general criterion for compositionality and justify why this applies to our semantic mapping.

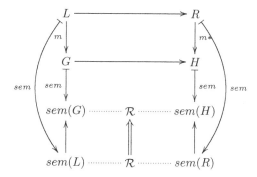

Fig. 12. CSP correspondence for behaviour verification

Correctness. The overall structure is illustrated in Fig. 12. The original model (component, composite structure and activity diagrams) is given by graph G. The refactoring results in graph H by the application of rule $p : L \to R$ at match m. Applying the semantic mapping *sem* (itself described by a graph transformation from models to CSP) to the rule's left- and right-hand side, we obtain the CSP processes $sem(L)$ and $sem(R)$. Whenever the relation $sem(L) \mathcal{R} sem(R)$ (say $\mathcal{R} = \sqsubseteq$ is trace refinement, so all traces of the left processes are also traces of the right), we would like to be sure that also $sem(G) \mathcal{R} sem(H)$ (traces of $sem(G)$ are preserved in $sem(H)$).

The main assumption is the compositionality of the semantic mapping *sem*. Intuitively, the mapping must be closed under context, i.e., the semantics of a model L is embedded within the semantics of an extension G of L. Embedding of CSP processes is expressed by the notion of context, i.e., a CSP expression with a single occurrence of a distinguished free variable.

Definition 1 (compositionality). *A mapping sem from graphs to CSP processes is compositional if for each injective graph morphisms* $m : L \to G$ *there* *exists a context E such that $sem(G) \equiv E(sem(L))$. Moreover, this context is uniquely determined by the part of G not in the image of L, i.e., given a pushout diagram as below with injective morphisms only, and a context F with $sem(D) \equiv F(sem(K))$, then E and F are equivalent.*

$$
\begin{array}{ccc}
K & \overset{l}{\longrightarrow} & L \\
\downarrow{\scriptstyle d} & & \downarrow{\scriptstyle m} \\
D & \underset{g}{\longrightarrow} & G
\end{array}
$$

Definition 1 applies particularly where L is the left hand side of a rule and G is the given graph of a transformation. In this case, the CSP expression generated from L contains the one derived from G up to *traces, failures or divergences* equivalence, while the context E is uniquely determined by $G \setminus m(L)$. The proof also relies on the fact that semantic relations $\mathcal{R}$ in CSP are closed under context.

Theorem 1. *Assume a compositional mapping sem from graphs to CSP processes. Then, for all transformations $G \overset{p,m}{\Longrightarrow} H$ via rule $p : L \to R$ with injective match m, it holds that $sem(L) \ \mathcal{R} \ sem(R)$ implies $sem(G) \ \mathcal{R} \ sem(H)$, where $\mathcal{R}$ may be any of $\{\equiv, \sqsubseteq, \sqsupseteq\}$ on traces, failures, or divergences.*

Proof. By assumption the match m, and therefore the comatch $m^* : R \to H$ are injective. Since the mapping *sem* is compositional, according to Definition 1 there are contexts E and F such that $sem(G) \equiv E(sem(L))$ and $sem(H) \equiv F(sem(R))$. Now, $E(sem(L)) \ \mathcal{R} \ E(sem(R))$ since $sem(L) \ \mathcal{R} \ sem(R)$ and $\mathcal{R}$ is closed under context. Finally, $E(sem(R)) \equiv F(sem(R))$ by the uniqueness of the contexts.

Thus, it remains to demonstrate that compositionality holds for the semantic mapping at hand. The proof is based on the embedding and extension theorem for double-pushout graph transformation [EHK01] and only sketched below. Full details are given in [Bis08].

Compositionality. In this section we present a proof sketch for the fact that our semantic mapping is compositional. The result is interesting by itself because it holds for a large class of mappings described by triple graph grammars [Sch94]. The idea is that triple graph grammars describe model transformations by creating the target from the source model and linking both by a relation model. Hence it is not necessary to remove the source model, and rules can be designed in such a way that also on the relation and target model rules are non-deleting.

For simple rules (without negative application conditions), compositionality then follows directly from the fact that the transformations realising the semantic mapping can be embedded into larger contexts.

Theorem 2. *Given a mapping sem from graphs to CSP described by graph transformation rules in the DPO approach. If all rules of sem are non-deleting and do not contain negative application conditions, then the mapping is compositional.*

Proof. (sketch) The main argument is based on the *Embedding Theorem* [EEPT06] applied to a transformation sequence $t = G_0 \overset{*}{\Rightarrow} G_n$ implementing the mapping. We assume a graph H_0 containing G_0 with inclusion morphism m_0. For a transformation t we create a boundary graph B and a context graph C. The boundary graph is the smallest subgraph of G_0 which contains the identification points and dangling points of m_0. Since (2) is a pushout, the context graph can be determined. If none of the productions of t deletes any item of B, then m_0 is consistent with t and there is an extension diagram over t and m_0. This means that H_n is the pushout complement of t and m_0, and can thus be determined without applying the transformation t on H_0. Hence, the compositionality condition holds for c.

$$
\begin{array}{ccccc}
B & \overset{b_0}{\longrightarrow} & G_0 & \overset{t}{\Longrightarrow} & G_n \\
\Big\downarrow & (2) & \Big\downarrow {\scriptstyle m_0}\ (1) & & \Big\downarrow {\scriptstyle m_n} \\
C & \longrightarrow & H_0 & \overset{t}{\Longrightarrow} & H_n
\end{array}
$$

Adding context and boundary graph to our picture, we get the extension diagram above.

The initial graph G_0 is either the left- or right-hand side of our refactoring rule. Graph G_n thus corresponds to either $sem(L)$ or $sem(R)$, i.e., our graph transformation t implements the mapping sem. The inclusion into H_0 is given by the match $m_0 : L \to G$ for the refactoring rule.

Negative application conditions (NAC) restrict the applicability of rules by forbidden patterns, i.e., structures which must not occur in the given graph in order for the transformation to be permitted. The definition of our mapping, as many realistic transformation systems, make heavy use of this feature. In order to extend Theorem 2, we require the notions of *created points* and *creational type*. Intuitively, *created points* are those nodes and edges in a graph production rule that are only present in the right-hand side, and are thus created during its application. The *creational type* is the set of all nodes and edges in the type graph (metamodel) that are never deleted during a transformation. Formal definitions are given in [Bis08], as well as the proof of the theorem.

Theorem 3. *A mapping sem from graphs to CSP is compositional if*

1. *All rules of sem are non-deleting;*
2. *All NACs defined for rules in sem only contain elements of created types;*
3. *Source models do not contain any elements of created types.*

These conditions are naturally satisfied in the case of triple graph grammars [Sch94]: Created types are elements of the target and relational metamodels, hence they do not occur in source models. The only real restriction is that no negative application conditions are allowed on the source model. Our mapping from UML architectural models to CSP satisfies these restrictions and is thus compositional.

7   Conclusion and Future Work

The results presented in this paper are spanning two levels of abstraction. At the level of architectural refactoring, we have developed a method for verifying transformations of UML architectural models based on a semantic mapping into CSP processes. More generally, we have shown that the correctness of such an approach depends on the compositionality of the semantic mapping, and that this property can be guaranteed by a structural condition on the form of the mapping rules which is easily satisfied, for example, by triple graph grammars.

Future work will continue to address both levels. At the concrete level we hope to be able to come up with a catalogue of verified refactoring rules, rather than relying on the extraction of rules from individual transformations as in this paper. It remains to be seen if a general catalogue comparable to OO refactorings is possible. In general, the approach of rule extraction needs to be supported by heuristics about which elements of a model, apart from those that are changed, should be included into the rule in order to verify its semantic compatibility.

References

ADG98.   Allen, R., Douence, R., Garlan, D.: Specifying and Analyzing Dynamic Software Architectures. In: Astesiano, E. (ed.) FASE 1998. LNCS, vol. 1382, Springer, Heidelberg (1998)

BH07.   Bisztray, D., Heckel, R.: Rule-level verification of business process transformations using csp. In: Proc. of 6th International Workshop on Graph Transformations and Visual Modeling Techniques (GTVMT 2007) (2007)

Bis08.   Bisztray, D.: Verification of architectural refactoring rules. Technical report, Department of Computer Science, University of Leicester (2008), http://www.cs.le.ac.uk/people/dab24/refactoring-techrep.pdf

EEPT06. Ehrig, H., Ehrig, K., Prange, U., Taentzer, G.: Fundamentals of Algebraic Graph Transformation. EATCS Monographs in Theoretical Computer Science. Springer, Heidelberg (2006)

EHK01.   Engels, G., Heckel, R., Küster, J.M.: Rule-based specification of behavioral consistency based on the UML meta model. In: Gogolla, M., Kobryn, C. (eds.) UML 2001. LNCS, vol. 2185, Springer, Heidelberg (2001)

EKGH01. Engels, G., Küster, J.M., Groenewegen, L., Heckel, R.: A methodology for specifying and analyzing consistency of object-oriented behavioral models. In: Gruhn, V. (ed.) Proc. European Software Engineering Conference (ESEC/FSE 2001), Vienna, Austria. LNCS, vol. 1301, pp. 327–343. Springer, Heidelberg (2001)

FBB⁺99. Fowler, M., Beck, K., Brant, J., Opdyke, W., Roberts, D.: Refactoring: Improving the Design of Existing Code, 1st edn. Addison-Wesley Professional, Reading (1999)

FSEL05. Formal Systems Europe Ltd. FDR2 User Manual (2005), http://www.fsel.com/documentation/fdr2/html/index.html

HIM98.   Hirsch, D., Inverardi, P., Montanari, U.: Graph grammars and constraint solving for software architecture styles. In: ISAW 1998: Proceedings of the third international workshop on Software architecture, pp. 69–72. ACM Press, New York (1998)

Hoa85.   Hoare, C.A.R.: Communicating Sequential Processes. Prentice Hall International Series in Computer Science. Prentice Hall, Englewood Cliffs (1985)

Lae25.   Laertius, D.: Lives of Eminent Philosophers, vol. 2. Loeb Classical Library (January 1925)

LM04.   Leino, K.R.M., Müller, P.: Object invariants in dynamic contexts. In: Odersky, M. (ed.) ECOOP 2004. LNCS, vol. 3086, pp. 491–516. Springer, Heidelberg (2004)

MDJ02.   Mens, T., Demeyer, S., Janssens, D.: Formalising behaviour preserving program transformations. In: Corradini, A., Ehrig, H., Kreowski, H.-J., Rozenberg, G. (eds.) ICGT 2002. LNCS, vol. 2505, pp. 286–301. Springer, Heidelberg (2002)

MGB06.   Massoni, T., Gheyi, R., Borba, P.: An approach to invariant-based program refactoring. In: Software Evolution through Transformations 2006, Electronic Communications of the EASST (2006)

MK96.   Magee, J., Kramer, J.: Dynamic structure in software architectures. In: SIGSOFT 1996: Proceedings of the 4th ACM SIGSOFT symposium on Foundations of software engineering, pp. 3–14. ACM Press, New York (1996)

OMG06.   OMG. *Unified Modeling Language, version 2.1.1* (2006), http://www.omg.org/technology/documents/formal/uml.htm

Sch94.   Schürr, A.: Specification of graph translators with triple graph grammars. In: Mayr, E.W., Schmidt, G., Tinhofer, G. (eds.) WG 1994. LNCS, vol. 903, pp. 151–163. Springer, Heidelberg (1995)

Sel98.   Selic, B.: Using uml for modeling complex real-time systems. In: Müller, F., Bestavros, A. (eds.) LCTES 1998. LNCS, vol. 1474, pp. 250–260. Springer, Heidelberg (1998)

SPTJ01.   Sunyé, G., Pollet, D., Le Traon, Y., Jézéquel, J.-M.: Refactoring uml models (2001)

TGM00.   Taentzer, G., Goedicke, M., Meyer, T.: Dynamic change management by distributed graph transformation: Towards configurable distributed systems. In: Ehrig, H., Engels, G., Kreowski, H.-J., Rozenberg, G. (eds.) TAGT 1998. LNCS, vol. 1764, pp. 179–193. Springer, Heidelberg (2000)

Tig07.   Tiger Developer Team. Tiger EMF Transformer (2007), http://www.tfs.cs.tu-berlin.de/emftrans

Var06.   Varró, D.: Model transformation by example. In: Nierstrasz, O., Whittle, J., Harel, D., Reggio, G. (eds.) MoDELS 2006. LNCS, vol. 4199, pp. 410–424. Springer, Heidelberg (2006)

WCG+06.   Wirsing, M., Clark, A., Gilmore, S., Hölzl, M., Knapp, A., Koch, N., Schroeder, A.: Semantic-Based Development of Service-Oriented Systems. In: Najm, E., Pradat-Peyre, J.-F., Donzeau-Gouge, V.V. (eds.) FORTE 2006. LNCS, vol. 4229, pp. 24–45. Springer, Heidelberg (2006)

WF02.   Wermelinger, M., Fiadeiro, J.L.: A graph transformation approach to software architecture reconfiguration. Sci. Comput. Program. 44(2), 133–155 (2002)

Formal Model-Driven Program Refactoring

Tiago Massoni[1], Rohit Gheyi[2], and Paulo Borba[2]

[1] Department of Computing Systems, University of Pernambuco
tlm@dsc.upe.br
[2] Informatics Center, Federal University of Pernambuco
{rg,phmb}@cin.ufpe.br

Abstract. Evolutionary tasks, specially refactoring, affect source code and object models, hindering correctness and conformance. Due to the gap between object models and programs, refactoring tasks get duplicated in commonly-used model-driven development approaches, such as Round-Trip Engineering. In this paper, we propose a formal approach to consistently refactor systems in a model-driven manner. Each object model refactoring applied by the user is associated with a sequence of behavior preserving program transformations, which can be semi-automatically performed to an initially conforming program. As a consequence, this foundation for model-driven refactoring guarantees behavior preservation of the target program, besides its conformance with the refactored object model. This approach is described in detail, along with its formal infrastructure, including a conformance relationship between object models and programs. A case study reveals evidence on issues that will surely recur in other model-driven development contexts.

1 Introduction

During development and maintenance activities, software evolution is acknowledged as a demanding task. The original software structure usually does not smoothly accommodate adaptations or additions. Evolution is further complicated by the adoption of models, for instance object models, which contain domain related structures and constraints that must be followed by the implementation. In this scenario, it is useful that abstractions in models and source code evolve consistently, for documentation or even development purposes, as seen in model-driven methodologies [1].

When evolving programs or models, maintaining those artifacts consistent is usually hard, requiring manual updates, even in state-of-the-art tool support. As a consequence, most projects abandon models early in the life cycle, adhering to code-driven approaches. A popular technique for dealing with a number of evolution-related problems is *refactoring* [2,3], which improves software structure while preserving behavior. Nevertheless, the same issues are observed when refactoring multiple artifacts.

We propose a formal approach to *semi-automatically refactor programs in a model-driven manner*. A sequence of formal behavior preserving program transformations is associated to each predefined model refactoring. Applying a model

J. Fiadeiro and P. Inverardi (Eds.): FASE 2008, LNCS 4961, pp. 362–376, 2008.
© Springer-Verlag Berlin Heidelberg 2008

refactoring triggers the corresponding sequence of program refactorings, which (1) update code declarations as refactored in the model and (2) adapt statements according to the modified declarations. This is accomplished with *invariants*, which are assumed throughout all program's executions, through a conformance relationship. Although developer only applies refactorings to object models, both artifacts get refactored, avoiding manual updates on source code.

Our approach is a formal investigation of evolution tasks, showing evidence about issues with keeping object models and their implementations in conformance during refactoring. We establish our approach on formal languages relying on previous work in object modeling and program refinement. For instance, object models in Alloy [4], which includes structures for expressing objects, relations and invariants equivalent to the core concepts of UML class diagrams. For programs, we consider a core language for Java, developed for reasoning on object-oriented programming [5].

Our solution differs from related approaches as it argues the application of transformations only on object model, and programs are made consistent by semi-automatic, independent transformations, while still maintaining some abstraction gap. Round-trip engineering, in contrast, generates changes to programs from models, which results in the need for manual updates. Alternatively, Model-Driven Architecture (MDA) [1] allows generation of platform-specific programs from a modeled description of the system. In this case, model abstraction is significantly compromised, as platform-independent program logic must be included into models for a complete executable generation. We developed a case study with our approach for illustrating evidence on issues that will surely recur in other Model-Driven Development contexts.

2   Motivating Example

An Alloy model contains a sequence of *paragraphs*; one kind of paragraph is a *signature*, which are used for defining new types. Instances of these signatures can be related by the *relations* declared in the signatures. As an example, we use a simple object model of a file system in Alloy, as implemented in commonly used operating systems. The following fragment defines signatures for FSObject and Name. The keyword sig declares a signature with a name. Signature Name is an empty signature, while FSObject declares two relations. For example, every instance of FSObject is related to exactly one instance of signature Name by the relation name – the keyword one denotes an injective relation. Also, file system objects may have contents; it is optional, and maybe more than one instance, since it is annotated with the set keyword, which establishes no constraints on the relation. Also, signature may extend another, with the extends keyword, establishing that the extended signature is a subset of the parent signature – File and Dir. In addition, Root is a subtype of Dir.

```
sig Name {}
sig FSObject {
  name: one Name,
```

```
    contents: set FSObject }
  sig File,Dir extends FSObject {}
  sig Root extends Dir {}
```

We may further constrain this object model with invariants, for establishing more complex domain rules concerning the declared signatures and relations. For this purpose, an Alloy model can be enriched with formula paragraphs called *fact*, which is used to package formulas that always hold for the model. The first formula in the following fact states that there can be exactly one Root instance in every file system, by the **one** keyword. Next, the second formula defines that from all file system objects, only directories may present contents. In the expression (FSObject-Dir).contents, the join operator (.) represents relational dereference (in this case, yielding contents from the set of instances resulting from FSObject instances that are not directories; the - symbol is equivalent to set difference). The **no** keyword establishes that the expression that follows results in an empty set, which gives the constraint the following meaning: only directories have contents in the file system.

```
  fact {
    one Root
    no (FSObject-Dir).contents }
```

The following code fragment shows a direct implementation for this file system in a formal Java-like language [5], which is used as basis for the formal investigation showed in this paper. Classes declare fields, methods and constructors. The **main** method, within the **Main** class reads a file system object from the user (with the input/output field **inout**), and in the case of a directory, adds a new File; otherwise, none is added. The keyword **is** corresponds to Java's **instanceof**. Also, a constructor can be declared with the **constr** keyword. The **set** modifier establish a collection variable (set of objects). Keywords **result** and **self** denote, respectively, method return and the current object. Following the invariant from the object model, only directories have contents.

```
class FSObject{
  pri Name name;
  pub Dir set contents;
  set Dir getContents() { result:= self.contents; }
  void setContents(set FSObject c) { self.contents:= c } }
class Dir extends FSObject{..}
class File extends FSObject{ constr {.. self.contents:= ∅ }
class Main{
    void main(){
      File f:= new File,currentFSObj:= null in ..
        currentFSObj:= (FSObject)self.inout;
        if (currentFSObj is Dir)
          then currentFSObj.setContents({f})
          else currentFSObj.setContents(∅) } }
```

The source code shows a situation for likely refactoring: there is a field in the superclass, contents, which is only useful in one of the subclasses – a "bad smell" [2]. The refactoring can be accomplished by moving contents down to Dir. Additional changes are needed for correctness, such as updating accesses to contents with casts to Dir. Issues with evolution arise as the object model is updated for conformance. Round-trip Engineering (RTE) [6] tools are popular choices for automation, applying reverse engineering for recovering object models from code. In this case, usually models become rather concrete, as *visualizations of source code, losing abstraction.*

On the other hand, the mentioned "bad smell" can be detected in the object model. The relation is then pushed down from FSObject to Dir. Likewise, conformance of the source code is desirable; in the context of RTE, a usual technique for automatic updates to the source code marks previously edited code fragments as immutable, in order to avoid loss of non-generated code that is marked by the tool. However, if the field is simply moved to Dir, *these immutable statements become incorrect*; for instance, accesses to the field with left expressions not exactly typed as Dir, as within FSObject and File, showed next.

```
class FSObject{ ..
    set Dir getContents() { result:= self.contents; }
    void setContents(set FSObject c) { self.contents:= c } }
class File extends FSObject{...
    constr {...self.contents:= ∅...} }
```

Due to the representation gap between object models and programs, the immutable code may rely on model elements that were modified, showing a recurring evolution problem in RTE-based tools. Manual updates must be applied, making evolution more expensive.

An alternative is employed in tools following the *Model-driven architecture* (MDA) [1]. Models in MDA include programming logic, written in a platform-independent fashion – for instance, action semantics in executable UML [7]. Tool support then generates source code for that logic in a specific implementation platform. Under such approach the model refactoring in this section's example would also include changes to the programming logic attached to models, maintaining source code up-to-date [8]. Although the MDA approach might be promising, it lacks a more abstract view of the domain given by object models, which is still useful for overall understanding. Our approach investigates model-driven refactorings in this context.

3   Model Transformations

As model refactoring must preserve semantics, and the task is usually accomplished in an *ad hoc* way, unexpected results are usually observed. We can improve safety by founding refactoring over semantics-preserving *primitive transformations*, which can be composed into refactorings preserving semantics by construction. Examples of these primitive transformations are showed in Section 3.1, while refactoring composition is explained in Section 3.2.

3.1   Primitive Transformations

For the Alloy language [4], a catalog of primitive transformations has been proposed [9]. Although the transformations are language specific, they can be leveraged to other object modeling notations, such as UML class diagrams, as we previously investigated [10].

These primitive transformations are presented as equivalences, which delimit two transformations; they are regarded as primitive since they cannot be derived from other transformations. In addition, syntactic conditions are defined as requirements for a correct application. Such conditions ensure that the transformation preserves the semantics of the object model, while maintaining its well-formedness. Soudness, completeness and compositionality have been proved for the catalog [9]. The equivalences use a flexible equivalence notion [11] as basis for comparing object models.

For instance, the catalog includes an equivalence for introducing and removing relations. Equivalence 1 states that we can introduce a new relation along with its definition, which is a formula of the form $r = exp$, establishing a value for the relation (a set of pair of objects). Likewise, we can remove a relation that is not being used, by applying the reverse transformation.

Equivalence 1. ⟨introduce relation and its definition⟩

$$
\begin{array}{ll}
\begin{array}{l}
ps \\
\textbf{sig } S \ \{ \\
\quad rs \\
\} \\
\textbf{fact } F \ \{ \\
\quad forms \\
\}
\end{array}
&
\begin{array}{l}
ps \\
\textbf{sig } S \ \{ \\
\quad rs, \\
\quad r : \textbf{set } T \\
\} \\
\textbf{fact } F \ \{ \\
\quad forms \ AND \ r \ = \ exp \\
\}
\end{array}
\end{array}
$$

provided
($\rightarrow$) (1) S's hierarchy in ps does not declare any relation named r; (2) r is not used in exp, or exp is r; (3) exp is a subtype of r;
($\leftarrow$) r is not used in ps.

We use ps to denote the remainder of the model (signatures, relations and facts). Each equivalence defines two templates of models on the left and the right side, with syntactic conditions. We write ($\rightarrow$), before the condition, to indicate that this condition is required when applying the left-to-right (L-R) transformation. Similarly, we use ($\leftarrow$) to indicate what is required when applying the opposite transformation (R-L).

Equivalence 2 introduces transformations for adding or removing a subsignature from an existing hierarchy. We can add an empty subsignature if declared with a fresh name. After this transformation, the supersignature becomes abstract (defining no direct instances), as denoted by the resulting constraint (S=U-T). Similarly, the subsignature can be removed if it is not being used elsewhere and there is no formula in the model with its type, in order to avoid type errors – $\leq$ denotes subtype.

Equivalence 2. ⟨introduce subsignature⟩

ps
sig U { rsU }
sig T **extends** U{ rsT }
fact F { $forms$ }
	$=$	ps
		sig U { rsU }
		sig T **extends** U{ rsT }
		sig S **extends** U{}
		fact F {
		 $forms$ AND $S = U - T$
		}

provided
($\rightarrow$) (1) ps does not declare any signature named S; (2) there is no signature in ps that is subsignature of U;
($\leftarrow$) (1) S does not appear in ps; (2) exp, where $exp \leq U$ and $exp \nleq T$, does not appear in ps.

3.2   Model Refactorings

The primitive Alloy transformations can be used as basis for several applications that require semantics-preserving transformations, for instance *model refactorings*. Since the primitive transformations are simpler – dealing with a few language constructs – they can be more easily proved to be semantics-preserving. By construction, a composition of correct primitive transformations is also correct, providing safe refactorings for object models [9].

Refactoring 1 depicts a formal rule for pushing down a relation, which can be done if the model presents an invariant stating that the relation's range is within subsignature S. Similarly, we can pull up a relation by adding this constraint to the model. This refactoring is derived by successive applications of transformations from the Equivalences 1 and 2. It must be clear that this derivation is carried out only once by a refactoring designer; once done, the refactoring is ready to be applied.

4   Laws of Programming

For establishing a formal basis for program refactoring, we use *laws of programming* [12]. An extensive set of laws of object-oriented programming has been defined for ROOL [13], a formal subset of Java. These laws, proved to be behavior-preserving according to a formal semantics, provide a formal basis for defining program refactorings. These laws have been proved, however, for a copy semantics, in which objects are *values*, not referenced by pointers. This decision simplified the semantics to the point in which certain laws – in special laws based on class refinement [13] – require simpler proofs, as *aliasing* can be ruled out, allowing direct modular reasoning. However, it is rather inconvenient to define

Refactoring 1. ⟨Push Down Relation⟩

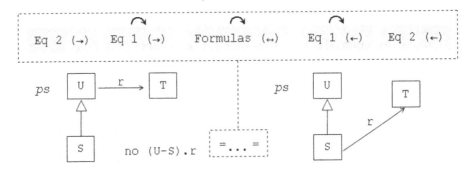

($\rightarrow$) $exp.r$, where $exp \leq U$ and $exp \nleq S$, does not appear in ps;
($\leftarrow$) S's family does not declare any relation named r.

refactoring on a language that is disconnected from the practice of OO programming. Therefore, we transferred the catalog to a reference-based language defined in the work of Banerjee and Naumann [5], since it guarantees modular reasoning by using *ownership confinement* as a requirement for programs; therefore, we require confinement in the programs to be refactored. Laws related to class refinement can be proved by showing a correct simulation, as showed in their work. Most laws used in our work are clearly still sound in the presence of reference semantics; even though, we developed proofs for a demonstrative number of laws in the new language.

For instance, the following law eliminates or introduces classes. Classes can be removed when they have no use anywhere in the program. Similar to model equivalences, laws denote two transformations (from left to right and vice-versa). The class to be eliminated or introduced is denoted by cd_1 – CT is a *class table*, the context of class declarations.

Law 1. ⟨*class elimination*⟩
$CT\ cd_1\ =\ CT$

provided
($\leftrightarrow$) $cd_1 \neq$ Main;
($\rightarrow$) cd_1 is not used in CT.
($\leftarrow$) (1) cd_1 is a distinct name; (2) field, method and superclass types within cd_1 are declared in CT.

In addition to equivalence laws, reasoning about classes usually requires a notion of class refinement, for changes of representation like addition and removal of private fields. The application of refinement changes the bodies of the methods in the target class, using a *coupling invariant* that relates the old and the new field declarations [13].

5   Model-Driven Refactoring

In this section, we present our model-driven approach to refactoring. The catalog
of primitive model transformations is used for model refactorings; the applied
primitive transformations form the basis for defining semi-automatic refactoring
in programs. The approach is delineated in Section 5.1, and the required notions
of conformance and confinement are showed in Section 5.2. The approach is
explained in detail in Section 5.3, as applied to the file system example.

5.1   The Approach

Our solution considers the context in which object models can be refactored
using the formal primitive transformations, directly or indirectly (in the latter
case, by using refactorings derived from primitive transformations). To each
primitive model transformation from the catalog, we associate a sequence of
program transformations – a *strategy* –, to be applied to a program, with no
user intervention, guided by laws of programming.

The approach is depicted in Figure 1, where OM represents an object model,
and P a program. In (a) we partially repeat the sequence of model transformations applied in Refactoring 1; after the model refactoring, all primitive transformations are *recorded* (for instance, in a CASE tool), for later association with
the strategies. We associate each primitive model transformation (depicted as
"corresponds" in Figure 1) with a specific strategy, which will semi-automatically
refactor the program in (b), resulting in a program consistent with the refactored program. Strategies are constructed as the automatic application of laws
of programming – ensuring behavior preservation –, denoted as L_k.

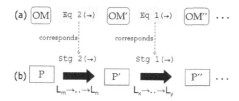

Fig. 1. Model-driven refactoring with strategies

A strategy performs program refactoring following a sequence of transformations on the assumption of conformance. Therefore, it is especially conceived to
exploit the model invariants that are known to be met by the program; hence,
program transformations can be more powerful with high-level assumptions
about program declarations, such as classes and fields. In this context, a strategy must rewrite programs for updating correspondent declarations that were
refactored in the object model and preserve program behavior. In an iterative
software process, this approach could be applied when refactoring models during analysis and design activities, and some source code is already implemented

from previous iterations. The user would have to ensure the conformance relationship between the source code and the object model, which is the precondition for applying the approach, by other conformance checking tool, since it is beyond the scope of this paper.

Regarding tool support, this approach could be implemented primarily as a modeling tool, which would include a built-in catalog of primitive model transformations, which could be composed into refactorings. The application of a refactoring could be recorded in terms of the primitive transformations composing this refactoring. Next, strategies correspondent to each applied primitive are applied to the attached source code, in the same order as the primitives were applied to the model. With such a supporting tool, our approach differs from Round-trip Engineering as it avoids generation of source code from models (or models from code) completely. In fact, object model and program refactorings take place independently. Similarly, MDA-based tools are different as they include programming logic information, which yields more concrete models.

5.2   The Required Conformance Relationship

In order to establish which changes each strategy is expected to carry out, we define assumptions that constrain programs that are amenable to model-driven refactoring. We assume *conformance* before applying transformations, and strategies guarantee its preservation. In this context, a definition of conformance must be established for defining which programs may be refactored by strategies associated to a model transformation.

Semantically, a program is in conformance with a object model if its states – heaps of linked objects – meet the modeled invariants. In the file system model in Section 2, a conforming program must create a single `Root` directory in the system, for example, for all possible execution states. Additionally, we assume a syntactic conformance between models and programs in which model structures (signatures and relations) strictly correspond to program structures (classes and fields). Also, relations with multiplicity (0..1) or (1) are implemented as single fields; differently, unconstrained multiplicities are implemented by set fields. Signature hierarchies must be maintained by classes, although additional abstract classes can be declared between two modeled classes. A deep discussion on other forms of implementing object models can be seen in our previous work on formal conformance between object models and programs [14].

Also, for ensuring that program transformations that employ some form of class refinement are correct, aliasing is partially restricted; for example, class invariants may be invalidated if other classes share references to internal elements of this class (representation exposure). Therefore we enforce that programs to be refactored with our approach present syntactic properties that guarantee ownership confinement. A related work presents some syntax directed static analysis rules for confinement [5], which we direct apply in our work.

5.3   Applying the Approach

Regarding the file system example, the object model invariant guarantees that the `contents` relation will be empty for any instance of `FSObject` subsignatures, except for `Dir`. In the required conformance relationship, the invariant is always valid in the program. This allows strategies to be semi-automatically applied for each primitive transformations carried out in the object model.

After the application of Refactoring 1, a number of primitive model transformations, have been applied, as showed in Section 3.2. First, Equivalence 2 was applied, from left to right; it is correspondent to the strategy *introduceSubclass*, according to Table 1. This table also presents all strategies from our approach.

Table 1. Strategies Corresponding to Model Equivalences

Model Equivalence	Strategy →	Strategy ←
Introduce Signature	*introduceClass*	*removeClass*
Introduce Generalization	*introduceSuperclass*	*removeSuperclass*
Introduce Subsignature	*introduceSubclass*	*removeSubclass*
Introduce Relation	*introduceField*	*removeField*
Remove Optional Relation	*fromOptionalToSetField*	*fromSetToOptionalField*
Remove Scalar Relation	*fromSingleToSetField*	*fromSetToSingleField*
Split Relation	*splitField*	*removeIndirectReference*

We formalize strategies using *refinement tactics*, based on the ArcAngel language [15], in order to add preciseness to the description for easier implementation in the transformation language of choice. We present the main constructs of the language while showing the *introduceSubclass* strategy. Law applications are denoted by the keyword **law**. Alternation (|) establishes that if the first application fails, the second one is executed; in the following strategy, we consider that the program may already have a class with the same name of the introduced subclass (C, in the example X), so we rename the existing class (C'). If it fails, the name is new; with **skip**, nothing else happens in this case. After introducing X, with `FSObject` as its superclass, we replace all commands of type `x:= new FSObject` by `x:= new X`, using a law of programming called *new superclass* [13]. Equivalence 2 establishes on the right-hand side the superclass as an abstract class, thus objects of `FSObject` may no longer exist.

Tactic *introduceSubclass*(C:Class,SC:Class)
   applies to program do
     (**law** *rename*(C,"C'") | **skip**);
     setExtends(C,SC);
     law *classElimination*(C,←);
     law *newSuperclass*(SC,C,→);
end

Then for each recorded model transformation, strategies are semi-automatically applied following the correspondence in Table 1. For instance, auxiliary fields contentsDir, contentsFile and contentsX are introduced with strategy *Introduce Field,* with invariant (self.contentsFile = self.contents ∧ (self is File)). Writings to self.contents are then extended with additional commands, as follows. In the outcome, the desired invariant is enforced.

```
class File { ..
      self.contents:= ∅;
      if (self is File) then ((File)self).contentsFile:=  self.contents }
```

Deduction of invariants, such as contents = contentsDir + contentsFile + contentsX, do not affect the source code, therefore no strategies are associated with these model transformations. The subsequent strategy removes the contents field based on a given invariant definition for the corresponding relation in the model; this strategy uses class refinement for removing a field after adjusting the code for replacing its occurrences with the equivalent expression from the invariant.

After removing the auxiliary subclass X and renaming the new contentsDir field to contents, a partial view of the resulting program is showed in the following program fragment.

```
class FSObject{ ..
   set Dir getContents() {
      if (self is Dir) then result:=  ((Dir)self).contents }
   void setContents(set FSObject c) {
      ((Dir)self).contents:= c } }
class Dir extends FSObject{ set Dir contents ;.. }
class File extends FSObject{ constr {..} }
class Main{ ..
   void main(){ ..
      if (currentFSObj is Dir)
         then currentFSObj.setContents({f})
         else currentFSObj.setContents(∅)  .. }
```

We previously mentioned that strategies are *semi-automatic*, as their automation is limited by a number of issues, mainly problems in strategies with class refinement steps, whose proofs are not automatic. These strategies involve changes in the internal representation of a class or hierarchy. For instance, this is crucial in strategies that introduce or change fields, implicating in changes to the methods internal to this class (as exemplified by strategy *introduceField*). First, the generation of a coupling invariant for the refinement is not straightforward, and even harder it is to prove the simulation for an arbitrary class. This problem is identified in this work, albeit we do not intend to provide a solution at this point.

For validating the correctness of our approach, we developed *soundness proofs* for each strategy, ensuring that they preserve program behavior, do not break confinement and the refactored program is in conformance with the refactored model. These proofs are not showed here due to space restrictions.

6   Case Study

In this section we apply our approach in a case study contemplating a recurring example for refactoring, taken from Fowler's book on refactoring [2]. From an initial object model of the video rental domain, we established three (3) refactorings; these refactorings are formed of primitive model transformations from the catalog. Next, program strategies can be semi-automatically applied to an original conforming program. Figure 2(a) shows the initial object model subject to refactoring, by means of a UML class diagram. The invariant states that a rental is never registered to both a customer and one of its dependents (# refers to set cardinality). The refactored model is depicted in Figure 2(b).

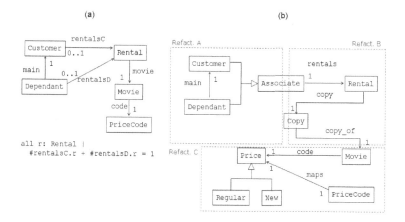

Fig. 2. Video Rental Object Model

The applied model refactorings are described as follows with results highlighted in Figure 2(b):

A extract a signature, `Associate`, defining a general structure for people who can rent movies. This refactoring is made of generalization introduction and a new relation (`rentals`), removing the original relations `rentalsC` and `rentalsD`;

B add a new signature – `Copy` – between `Rental` and `Movie`, since more than one copy is available for one movie. For this, we must split the relation `movie` into two new relations, before its removal;

C restructure the relationship between a movie and its current status – new or regular – based on the State Design Pattern. For this, we must introduce `New` and `Regular`, with the `Price` supersignature, and move `code` to Price.

Assuming that these primitive transformations have been recorded as a queue by a supporting tool, the matching strategies are semi-automatically applied, following the queue order. For the first refactoring, the opening strategy automatically introduces the `Associate` superclass. Other strategies include the new field `rentals`, replacing old references for the previous fields `rentalsC` and `rentalsD`; this replacement cannot be made automatically, due to the class refinement issue mentioned in Section 5.

For adding movie copies, the *splitField* strategy creates two fields `copy` and `copy_of`, besides a new class (`Copy`). The class refinement contained in this strategy can automatically duplicate writings using the old field, as exemplified in the next program fragment.

```
self.movie:= myMovie; self.copy.copy_of:= self.movie;
```

In the end, `movie` is eliminated. The refactored program presents an interesting aspect: even though the concept of copy is introduced, the program logic still considers movies to be "the copies". Therefore, although the resulting program has its behavior preserved, being also in conformance with the resulting model, but not reflecting the user intent. This aspect may be a limitation of model-driven refactorings from object models. We visualize two potential solutions: more concrete models with programming logic, as in MDA [1], or to consider behavioral models, in addition to object models (a possible future work). Furthermore, user interaction could be used here for application-specific transformations that could change this result.

Adding the State Design Pattern includes strategies for adding three new classes and moving the `code` field. The automatic application of the latter is only possible by explicitly defining a one-to-one relation between a `Code` to `Price` (`maps` field). This information is actually implicit in the Fowler's example in the book [2], but an analysis by means of model transformations made it evident.

7   Related Work

Opdyke proposes refactorings to which a number of preconditions are attached, which, if satisfied by the target program, ensure the preservation of behavior [3]. His work is similar to ours as it proposes a number of primitive refactorings, including creation, deletion and change of program entities. In contrast, semantics preservation is informally defined as a number of properties – related to inheritance, scope, type compatibility and semantic equivalence – that are required to hold after applying the refactoring.

A closely related approach was developed by Tip et al. [16]. They realized that some enabling conditions and modifications to source code, for automated refactorings, depend on relationships between types of variables, evident in refactorings involving subtypes. These type constraints enable the tool to selectively perform transformations on source code, avoiding type errors that would otherwise prohibit the overall application of the refactoring. This approach is similar to ours in the sense that both use additional information (in our case, model invariants) in order to achieve advanced refactorings. In fact, both approaches might be even integrated.

Co-evolution between models and programs is dealt with by several related approaches. For instance, Harrison et al. [17] show a method for maintaining conformance between models (UML class diagrams) and Java programs, by advanced code generation from models at a higher level of abstraction, compared to simple graphical code visualization. This approach is related to ours, as the relationship between model and source code avoids round-tripping. Their conformance relationship is more flexible, as we require a more strict structural similitude between the artifacts. No details are offered on how conformance mappings will consistently evolve.

Conformance is more specifically addressed by another work [18], aims at bridging the gap between object-oriented modeling and programming languages, in particular regarding binary associations, aggregations and compositions in UML class diagrams. They describe algorithms that detect automatically these relationships in code. As the semantics of such constructs is not well-defined, the authors provide their own interpretation from textual descriptions. This approach introduces a more flexible conformance relationship for relationships between objects, while still maintaining the model abstract, which may be applicable to our solution as well. However, further investigation is required for assessing potential benefits of this notion to model-driven refactoring based on algebraic laws.

8   Conclusions

In this paper, we propose a formal approach for program refactoring by refactoring only object models, maintaining program conformance by correct and semi-automatic refactorings corresponding to the applied model transformations. The approach is backed by a formal infrastructure of transformation laws, which are proved to be semantics preserving for both object models and programs, and a conformance relationship. We also exemplified the approach with a case study.

The Alloy laws can be directly leveraged for UML class diagrams [10], as well as the used programming language is similar to mainstream OO languages, as Java and C++. The investigation of model refactoring and its implications to source code in this work provides evidence over the challenges that effective model-driven methodologies will face in order to support evolution. In this context, the level of abstraction is a key aspect; in this research we ended up with a tighter conformance relationship than initially expected. First, for useful model refactoring, the main declarations often must be maintained. Second, less restrictions to the source code implementation imply in more transformations required to make the source code conforming to the refactored model, which would lower the quality of the outcome. Nevertheless, the required conformance relationship still preserves some abstraction: methods and additional classes can be freely implemented, and hierarchies can contain more classes then modeled.

Assumptions include reliance on the maturity of conformance checking tool support in practice – still incipient in practice – and a closed-world context in which we have access to the full source code of a program. Also, strategies involving class refinement may present limitations, in particular when an arbitrary formula must be translated to the coupling invariant for the refinement transformations. This situation reduces to the complex problem of generating code from a logical formula. However, we believe that automation can still be applied to some extent; interaction with users could be an alternative.

References

1. Kleppe, A., et al.: MDA Explained: the Practice and Promise of The Model Driven Architecture. Addison-Wesley, Reading (2003)
2. Fowler, M.: Refactoring—Improving the Design of Existing Code (1999)
3. Opdyke, W.: Refactoring Object-Oriented Frameworks. PhD thesis, University of Illinois at Urbana-Champaign (1992)
4. Jackson, D.: Software Abstractions: Logic, Language and Analysis (2006)
5. Banerjee, A., Naumann, D.A.: Ownership confinement ensures representation independence for object-oriented programs. Journal of the ACM 52(6), 894–960 (2005)
6. Sendall, S., Küster, J.: Taming Model Round-Trip Engineering. In: Workshop on Best Practices for Model-Driven Software Development (OOPSLA 2004) (2004)
7. Balcer, M.J., Mellor, S.J.: Executable UML: A Foundation for Model Driven Architecture (2002)
8. Hailpern, B., Tarr, P.: Model-driven development: The good, the bad, and the ugly. IBM Systems Journal 45(3), 451–461
9. Gheyi, R.: A Refinement Theory for Alloy. PhD thesis, Informatics Center – Federal University of Pernambuco (August 2007)
10. Massoni, T., Gheyi, R., Borba, P.: Formal Refactoring for UML Class Diagrams. In: 19th SBES, Uberlandia, Brazil, pp. 152–167 (2005)
11. Gheyi, R., Massoni, T., Borba, P.: An abstract equivalence notion for object models. ENTCS 130, 3–21 (2005)
12. Hoare, C.A.R., Hayes, I.J., Jifeng, H., Morgan, C.C., Roscoe, A.W., Sanders, J.W., Sorensen, I.H., Spivey, J.M., Sufrin, B.A.: Laws of Programming. Communications of the ACM 30(8), 672–686 (1987)
13. Borba, P., et al.: Algebraic Reasoning for Object-Oriented Programming. Science of Computer Programming 52, 53–100 (2004)
14. Massoni, T., Gheyi, R., Borba, P.: A Formal Framework for Establishing Conformance between Object Models and Object-Oriented Programs. In: SBMF, pp. 201–216 (2006)
15. Oliveira, M., Cavalcanti, A., Woodcock, J.: ArcAngel: a Tactic Language for Refinement. Formal Aspects of Computing 15(1), 28–47 (2003)
16. Tip, F., et al.: Refactoring for Generalization Using Type Constraints. In: 18th OOPSLA, pp. 13–26. ACM Press, New York (2003)
17. Harrison, W., et al.: Mapping UML Designs to Java. In: Proceedings of OOPSLA 2000, pp. 178–187. ACM Press, New York (2000)
18. Guéhéneuc, Y.G., Albin-Amiot, H.: Recovering Binary Class Relationships: Putting Icing on the UML Cake. In: Proceedings of the 19th OOPSLA, October 2004, pp. 301–314. ACM Press, New York (2004)

An Algebraic Semantics for MOF

Artur Boronat[1] and José Meseguer[2]

[1] Department of Computer Science, University of Leicester
aboronat@le.ac.uk
[2] Department of Computer Science, University of Illinois at Urbana-Champaign
meseguer@uiuc.edu

Abstract. Model-driven development is a field within software engineering in which software artifacts are represented as models in order to improve productivity, quality, and cost effectiveness. In this field, the Meta-Object Facility (MOF) standard plays a crucial role by providing a generic framework where the abstract syntax of different modeling languages can be defined. In this work, we present a formal, algebraic semantics of the MOF standard in membership equational logic (MEL). By using the Maude language, which directly supports MEL specifications, this formal semantics is furthermore *executable*, and can be used to perform useful formal analyses. The executable algebraic framework for MOF obtained this way has been integrated within the Eclipse Modeling Framework as a plugin. In this way, formal analyses, such as semantic consistency checks, become available within Eclipse to provide formal support for model-driven development processes.

Keywords: MOF, model-driven development, membership equational logic, metamodeling semantics, reflection.

1 Introduction

Model-driven development is a field in software engineering in which software artifacts are represented as models in order to improve productivity, quality, and cost-effectiveness. Models provide a more abstract description of a software artifact than the final code of the application. The Meta-Object Facility (MOF) standard [1] describes a generic framework in which the abstract syntax of modeling languages can be defined. This is done by specifying within MOF different metamodels for different modeling languages. Models in a modeling language are then conforming instances of their corresponding metamodel. The MOF standard aims at offering a good basis for model-driven development, providing some of the building concepts that are needed: what is a model, what is a metamodel, what is reflection in a MOF framework, etc. However, most of these concepts lack at present a formal semantics in the current MOF standard. This is, in part, due to the fact that metamodels can only be defined as data in the MOF framework.

In this paper, we define a reflective, algebraic, executable framework for precise metamodeling that supports the MOF standard. On the one hand, our formal framework provides a formal semantics of the following notions: *metamodel,*

J. Fiadeiro and P. Inverardi (Eds.): FASE 2008, LNCS 4961, pp. 377–391, 2008.
© Springer-Verlag Berlin Heidelberg 2008

model and *conformance* of a model to its metamodel. We clearly distinguish the different roles that the notion of *metamodel* usually plays in the literature: as *data*, as *type*, and as *theory*. In addition, we introduce two new notions: (i) *meta-model realization*, referring to the mathematical representation of a metamodel; and (ii) *model type*, allowing models to be considered as first-class citizens. In particular, our executable algebraic semantics for MOF generates in an automatic way the algebraic semantics of any MOF metamodel. This is a powerful and very useful form of *reflection*, in which metamodel MOF reflection is systematically related to logical reflection in MEL. The executable formal semantics of a meta-model obtained in this reflective way can then be used to automatically analyze the conformance of its model instances, which are characterized either as terms modulo structural axioms or, equivalently, as graphs. This makes the formal semantics particularly useful, since models can be directly manipulated as graphs in their term-modulo-axioms formal representation. Furthermore, our framework provides an executable environment that is plugged into the Eclipse Modeling Framework (EMF) [2] and that constitutes the kernel of a model management framework, supporting model transformations and formal analysis techniques.

The paper is structured as follows: Section 2 briefly describes the underlying formal background; Section 3 identifies important concepts that are not defined in the MOF standard, which are usually left unspecified in most of the MOF implementations; Section 4 gives a high level view of our algebraic framework, indicating how the algebraic semantics of MOF metamodels is defined; Section 5 presents some related work; and Section 6 summarizes the main contributions of this work and discusses future work.

2   Preliminaries: Membership Equational Logic

A membership equational logic (MEL) [3] *signature* is a triple (K, Σ, S) (just Σ in the following), with K a set of *kinds*, $\Sigma = \{\Sigma_{w,k}\}_{(w,k) \in K^* \times K}$ a many-kinded signature and $S = \{S_k\}_{k \in K}$ a K-kinded family of disjoint sets of sorts. The kind of a sort s is denoted by $[s]$. A MEL Σ-algebra A contains a set A_k for each kind $k \in K$, a function $A_f : A_{k_1} \times \cdots \times A_{k_n} \to A_k$ for each operator $f \in \Sigma_{k_1 \cdots k_n, k}$ and a subset $A_s \subseteq A_k$ for each sort $s \in S_k$, with the meaning that the elements in sorts are well-defined, while elements without a sort are *errors*. $T_{\Sigma, k}$ and $T_\Sigma(X)_k$ denote, respectively, the set of ground Σ-terms with kind k and of Σ-terms with kind k over variables in X, where $X = \{x_1 : k_1, \ldots, x_n : k_n\}$ is a set of kinded variables.

Given a MEL signature Σ, *atomic formulae* have either the form $t = t'$ (Σ-equation) or $t : s$ (Σ-membership) with $t, t' \in T_\Sigma(X)_k$ and $s \in S_k$; and Σ-*sentences* are conditional formulae of the form $(\forall X)\, \varphi \ \ if \ \ \bigwedge_i p_i = q_i \wedge \bigwedge_j w_j : s_j$, where φ is either a Σ-equation or a Σ-membership, and all the variables in φ, p_i, q_i, and w_j are in X.

A MEL theory is a pair (Σ, E) with Σ a MEL signature and E a set of Σ-sentences. The paper [3] gives a detailed presentation of (Σ, E)-algebras, sound and complete deduction rules, and initial and free algebras. In particular, given a MEL theory (Σ, E), its initial algebra is denoted $T_{(\Sigma/E)}$; its elements are E-equivalence classes of ground terms in T_Σ.

Order-sorted notation $s_1 < s_2$ can be used to abbreviate the conditional membership $(\forall x : k)\ x : s_2\ \ if\ \ x : s_1$. Similarly, an operator declaration $f : s_1 \times \cdots \times s_n \to s$ corresponds to declaring f at the kind level and giving the membership axiom $(\forall x_1 : k_1, \ldots, x_n : k_n)\ f(x_1, \ldots, x_n) : s\ \ if\ \ \bigwedge_{1 \le i \le n} x_i : s_i$. We write $(\forall x_1 : s_1, \ldots, x_n : s_n)\ t = t'$ in place of $(\forall x_1 : k_1, \ldots, x_n : k_n)\ t = t'\ \ if\ \ \bigwedge_{1 \le i \le n} x_i : s_i$.

We can use order-sorted notation as syntactic sugar to present a MEL theory (Σ, E) in a more readable form as a tuple $(S, <, \Sigma, E_0 \cup A)$ where: (i) S is the set of sorts; (ii) $<$ is the subsort inclusions, so that there is an implicit kind associated to each connected component in the poset of sorts $(S, <)$; (iii) Σ is given as an order-sorted signature with possibly overloaded operator declarations $f : s_1 \times \ldots \times s_n \to s$ as described above; and (iv) the set E of (possibly conditional) equations and memberships is quantified with variables having specific sorts (instead than with variables having specific kinds) in the sugared fashion described above; furthermore, E is decomposed as a disjoint union $E = E_0 \cup A$, where A is a collection of "structural" axioms such as associativity, commutativity, and identity. Any theory $(S, <, \Sigma, E_0 \cup A)$ can then be desugared into a standard MEL theory (Σ, E) in the way explained above.

The point of the decomposition $E = E_0 \cup A$ is that, under appropriate executability requirements explained in [4], such as confluence, termination, and sort-decreasingness modulo A, an MEL theory $(S, <, \Sigma, E_0 \cup A)$ becomes *executable* by rewriting with the equations and memberships E_0 *modulo* the structural axioms A. Furthermore, the initial algebra $T_{(\Sigma/E)}$ then becomes isomorphic to the *canonical term algebra* $Can_{\Sigma/E_0, A}$ whose elements are A-equivalence classes of ground Σ-terms that cannot be further simplified by the equations and memberships in E_0.

3   Presentation of the Problem

In this section, we give an informal description of the MOF standard by describing the MOF architecture and the main concepts in the MOF metamodel, which are then given a formal semantics in subsequent sections.

3.1   The MOF Modeling Framework

MOF is a semiformal approach to define modeling languages. It provides a four-level hierarchy, with levels M0, M1, M2 and M3. The entities $\widetilde{m}$ populating each level M_i, written $\widetilde{m} \in M_i$, are always *collections*, made up of constituent *data elements* $\widetilde{e}$. Each entity $M \in M_{i+1}$ at level i+1 metarepresents a *model*[1] M and is viewed as the metarepresentation of a collection of *types*, i.e., as a

---

[1] In the MOF framework, the concept of a *model* M is conceptually specialized depending on the specific metalevel, in which a model is located: *model* at level M1, *metamodel* at level M2 and *meta-metamodel* at level M3; as shown below.

metadata collection that defines a specific collection of types. Each *type* T is metarepresented as $\widetilde{T} \in \widetilde{M}$ and characterizes a collection of data elements, its *value domain*. We write that a data element $\widetilde{e} \in \widetilde{m}$ is *a value of* type $\widetilde{T} \in \widetilde{M}$ as $\widetilde{e} \;\stackrel{\sim}{:}\; \widetilde{T}$. A metarepresentation at level $i + 1$ of a collection $\widetilde{M} \in M_{i+1}$ of types characterizes collections of data elements $\widetilde{m} \in M_i$ at level i. A specific data collection $\widetilde{m} \in M_i$ is said to *conform to* model M, which is metarepresented by its collection of types $\widetilde{M} \in M_{i+1}$, iff for each data element $\widetilde{e} \in \widetilde{m}$ there exists a type $\widetilde{T} \in \widetilde{M}$ such that $\widetilde{e} \;\stackrel{\sim}{:}\; \widetilde{T}$. We write $\widetilde{m} \;\stackrel{\sim}{:}\; \widetilde{M}$ to denote this conformance relation for model M, which we call the *structural conformance relation*. The *isValueOf* relation $\widetilde{e} \;\stackrel{\sim}{:}\; \widetilde{T}$ and the *structural conformance relation* $\widetilde{m} \;\stackrel{\sim}{:}\; \widetilde{M}$ are summarized in Fig. 1.

$$
\begin{array}{ccc}
M_i & & M_{i+1} \\
\cup & & \cup \\
\widetilde{m} & \stackrel{\sim}{:} & \widetilde{M} \\
\cup & & \cup \\
\widetilde{e} & \stackrel{\sim}{:} & \widetilde{T}
\end{array}
$$

Fig. 1. *isValueOf* and *structural conformance* relations

Fig. 2 illustrates example collections at each level M1-M3 of the MOF framework. Each collection is encircled by a boundary and tagged with a name. For example, $rsPerson \in M_1$, which is a model corresponding to a relational schema. The *isValueOf* relation between elements $\widetilde{e}$ of a data collection and the metarepresentation of types $\widetilde{T}$ of a type collection, and the *structural conformance* relation between a data collection $\widetilde{m}$ and the metarepresentation $\widetilde{M}$ of a model M are depicted with dashed arrows. We consider levels M1–M3 out of the MOF hierarchy in this work, as illustrated in Fig. 2, which are:

M1 level. The M1 level contains metarepresentations of *models*. A model is a set of types that describe the elements of some physical, abstract or hypothetical reality by using a well-defined language. In addition, a model is suitable for computer-based interpretation, so that development tasks can be automated. For example, a model can define a relational schema describing the concepts, i.e., types, of *Person*, *Invoice* and *Item*. The type of *Person* is a table *Person*, with columns *name* and *age*; similarly, there is a table *Invoice*, with columns *date* and *cost*; and a table *Item*, with columns *name* and *price*; a foreign key *Invoice_Person_FK*; and a foreign key *Item_Invoice_FK*.

M2 level. The M2 level contains metarepresentations of *metamodels*. A metamodel is a model specifying a modeling language. As an example, we take a simple relational metamodel from the example of the QVT standard that contains the main concepts to define relational schemas, as shown in Fig. 2 in UML notation. The types of a relational schema are called *table*, *column*, *foreign key*, etc. Our example model, the relational schema with tables

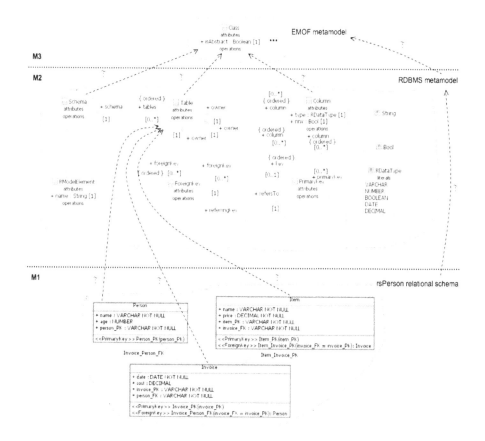

Fig. 2. The MOF framework

Person, Invoice and *Item* can be represented as a collection at level M1 that conforms to the relational metamodel at level M2.

M3 level. An entity at the M3 level is the metarepresentation of a *meta-metamodel*. A meta-metamodel specifies a *modeling framework*, which could also be called a *modeling space*. In MOF, there is only one such meta-metamodel, called the MOF meta-metamodel. Within the MOF modeling framework one can define many different metamodels. Such metamodels, when represented as data, must conform to the MOF meta-metamodel. In particular, the relational metamodel conforms to the MOF meta-metamodel. But in MOF one can likewise define many other metamodels, for example the UML metamodel to define UML models, the OWL metamodel to define ontologies, the AADL metamodel, and so on. The fact that all these meta-models are specified within the single MOF framework greatly facilitates systematic model/metamodel interchange and integration.

3.2 Discussion and Open Problems

At present, important MOF concepts such as those of metamodel, model and conformance relation do not have an explicit, *syntactically characterizable* status in their data versions. For example, we can syntactically characterize the correctness of the data elements in $\widetilde{M}$ for a metamodel $\mathcal{M}$, but there is no explicit type that permits defining $\widetilde{M}$ as a well-characterized value, which we call a *model type*. In addition, in the MOF standard and in current MOF-like modeling environments, such as Eclipse Modeling Framework or MS DSL tools, a metamodel $\mathcal{M}$ does not have a precise *mathematical* status. Instead, at best, a metamodel $\mathcal{M}$ is realized as a program in a conventional language, which may be generated from $\widetilde{\mathcal{M}}$, as, for example, the Java code that is generated for a metamodel $\widetilde{\mathcal{M}}$ in EMF. This informal implementation corresponds to what we call a *metamodel realization*. In these modeling environments, the *conformance relation* between a model definition $\widetilde{M}$ and its corresponding metamodel definition $\widetilde{\mathcal{M}}$ is checked by means of indirect techniques based on XML document validation or on tool-specific implementations in OO programming languages. Therefore, metamodels $\widetilde{\mathcal{M}}$ and models $\widetilde{M}$ cannot be explicitly characterized as first-class entities in their data versions, and the semantics of the *conformance relation* remains formally unspecified. This is due to the lack of a suitable reflective formal framework in which software artifacts, and not just their metarepresentations, can acquire a formal semantics.

In this work, we formalize the notions of: (i) model type, (ii) metamodel realization and (iii) conformance relation, by means of a reflective semantics that associates a mathematical metamodel realization to each metamodel definition $\widetilde{\mathcal{M}}$ in MOF.

4 An Algebraic Semantics for MOF

The practical usefulness of a formal semantics for a language is that it provides a rigorous standard that can be used to judge the correctness of an implementation. For example, if a programming language lacks a formal semantics, compiler writers may interpret the informal semantics of the language in different ways, resulting in inconsistent and diverging implementations. For MOF, given its genericity, the need for a formal semantics that can serve as a rigorous standard for any implementation is even more pressing, since many different modeling languages rely on the correctness of the MOF infrastructure. In this section, we propose an algebraic, mathematical semantics for MOF in membership equational logic (MEL).

4.1 A High-Level View of the MOF Algebraic Semantics

A metamodel definition $\widetilde{\mathcal{M}}$ describes a metamodel realization that contains a model type $\mathcal{M}$. What this metamodel definition describes is, of course, a *set* of models. We call this the *extensional* semantics of $\widetilde{\mathcal{M}}$, and denote this semantics by $[[\mathcal{M}]]_{\text{MOF}}$. Recall that we use the notation $\widetilde{M} : \mathcal{M}$ for the conformance relation. Using this notation, the extensional semantics can be informally defined as follows:

$$[[\mathcal{M}]]_{\text{MOF}} = \{\widetilde{M} \mid \widetilde{M} : \mathcal{M}\}.$$

We make the informal MOF semantics just described mathematically precise in terms of the *initial algebra semantics* of MEL. As already mentioned in Section 2, a MEL specification (Σ, E) has an associated initial algebra $T_{(\Sigma,E)}$. We call $T_{(\Sigma,E)}$ the *initial algebra semantics* of (Σ, E), and write

$$[[(\Sigma, E)]]_{IAS} = T_{(\Sigma,E)}.$$

Let $[[\text{MOF}]]_{\text{MOF}}$ denote the set of all MOF metamodel definitions $\widetilde{\mathcal{M}}$, and let *SpecMEL* denote the set of all MEL specifications. The reason why we define $[[\text{MOF}]]_{\text{MOF}}$ as a set of metamodel definitions $\widetilde{\mathcal{M}}$, instead than as a set of model types $\mathcal{M}$ is because, as already mentioned, the mathematical status of $\mathcal{M}$ is, as yet, undefined, and is precisely one of the questions to be settled by a mathematical semantics. Instead, well-formed metamodel definitions $\widetilde{\mathcal{M}}$ *are* data structures that can be syntactically characterized in a fully formal way. Therefore, the set $[[\text{MOF}]]_{\text{MOF}}$, thus understood, is a well-defined mathematical entity. Our algebraic semantics is then defined as a function

$$reflect_{\text{MOF}} : [[\text{MOF}]]_{\text{MOF}} \longrightarrow SpecMEL$$

that associates to each MOF metamodel definition $\widetilde{\mathcal{M}}$ a corresponding MEL specification $reflect_{\text{MOF}}(\widetilde{\mathcal{M}})$. Our informal semantics $[[\mathcal{M}]]_{\text{MOF}}$ is now made mathematically precise. Recall that any MEL signature Σ has an associated set S of sorts. Therefore, in the initial algebra $T_{(\Sigma,E)}$ each sort $s \in S$ has an associated set of elements $T_{(\Sigma,E),s}$. The key point is that in any MEL specification of the form $reflect_{\text{MOF}}(\widetilde{\mathcal{M}})$, there is always a sort called $ModelType\{\mathcal{M}\}$, which we also denote as $\mathcal{M}$ for short, whose data elements in the initial algebra are precisely the data representations of those models that conform to $\mathcal{M}$. That is, $\mathcal{M}$ is the *model type* associated to a metamodel definition $\widetilde{\mathcal{M}}$. Therefore, we can give a precise mathematical semantics to our informal MOF extensional semantics by means of the equation

$$[[\mathcal{M}]]_{\text{MOF}} = T_{reflect_{\text{MOF}}(\widetilde{\mathcal{M}}),ModelType\{\mathcal{M}\}}.$$

Note that our algebraic semantics gives a precise mathematical meaning to the entities lacking such a precise meaning in the informal semantics, namely, the notions of: (i) model type $\mathcal{M}$, (ii) metamodel realization $reflect_{\text{MOF}}(\widetilde{\mathcal{M}})$, and (iii) conformance relation $\widetilde{M} : \mathcal{M}$. Specifically, we associate to a metamodel definition $\widetilde{\mathcal{M}}$ a precise mathematical object, namely, the MEL theory $reflect_{\text{MOF}}(\widetilde{\mathcal{M}})$, constituting its *metamodel realization*. The *structural conformance* relation between a model and its metamodel is then defined mathematically by the equivalence

$$\widetilde{M} : \mathcal{M} \quad \Leftrightarrow \quad \widetilde{M} \in T_{reflect_{\text{MOF}}(\widetilde{\mathcal{M}}),ModelType\{\mathcal{M}\}}.$$

4.2   Algebraic Semantics of MOF Metamodels

As introduced above, the $reflect_{\mathrm{MOF}}$ function maps a MOF metamodel definition $\widetilde{\mathcal{M}}$ to a MEL theory $reflect_{\mathrm{MOF}}(\widetilde{\mathcal{M}})$ that constitutes its metamodel realization. In this section, we provide a high-level summary of the definition of the $reflect_{\mathrm{MOF}}$ function, whose complete definition is available in [5].

MOF as a MEL theory. We denote the metamodel definition that constitutes the meta-metamodel of the MOF framework by $\widetilde{\mathrm{MOF}}$. $\widetilde{\mathrm{MOF}}$ is itself a MOF metamodel definition, since $\widetilde{\mathrm{MOF}}$: MOF. We first define a MEL theory $reflect_{\mathrm{MOF}}(\widetilde{\mathrm{MOF}})$, that is, we first define $reflect_{\mathrm{MOF}}$ for a *single* metamodel, namely $\widetilde{\mathrm{MOF}}$. The $reflect_{\mathrm{MOF}}(\widetilde{\mathrm{MOF}})$ theory defines the $[\![\mathrm{MOF}]\!]_{\mathrm{MOF}}$ type as the set of metamodel definitions $\widetilde{\mathcal{M}}$, which can be viewed as both graphs and terms. This theory has been manually defined as a first step in the bootstrapping process needed to define the $reflect_{\mathrm{MOF}}$ function in general.

The $reflect_{\mathrm{MOF}}(\widetilde{\mathrm{MOF}})$ theory provides the algebraic representation for object types and model types for defining metamodel definitions $\widetilde{\mathcal{M}}$. In this theory, object types are used to describe a metamodel definition $\widetilde{\mathcal{M}}$: MOF as a set of objects. Objects are defined by using the following sorts: `Oid#MOF` for object identifiers; `Cid#MOF` for class names; and `PropertySet#MOF` for multisets of comma-separated pairs of the form `(property : value)`, which represent property values. Objects in a metamodel definition $\widetilde{\mathcal{M}}$ are then syntactically characterized by means of an operator

```
<_:_|_> : Oid#MOF Cid#MOF PropertySet#MOF -> Object#MOF.
```

These sorts, subsorts and operators are defined, in Maude notation, as follows:

```
sorts Oid#MOF Cid#MOF Property#MOF PropertySet#MOF Object#MOF .
subsort Property#MOF < PropertySet#MOF .
op noneProperty : -> PropertySet#MOF .
op _',_ : PropertySet#MOF PropertySet#MOF -> PropertySet#MOF
   [assoc comm id: noneProperty] .
op <_:_|_> : Oid#MOF Cid#MOF PropertySet#MOF -> Object#MOF .
```

In the $reflect_{\mathrm{MOF}}(\widetilde{\mathrm{MOF}})$ theory, a metamodel definition $\widetilde{\mathcal{M}}$ that conforms to the metamodel MOF, that is, such that $\widetilde{\mathcal{M}}$: MOF, can be represented as a collection of objects by means of a term of sort `ModelType{MOF}`. A term of sort `ModelType{MOF}` is defined by means of the following constructors, in Maude notation:

```
op __ : ObjectCollection{MOF} ObjectCollection{MOF} -> ObjectCollection{MOF} [assoc comm] .
op <<_>> : ObjectCollection{MOF} -> ModelType{MOF} .
```

where the `Object#MOF` sort is a subsort of the `ObjectCollection{MOF}` sort. That is, we first form a multiset of objects of sort `ObjectCollection{MOF}` using the associative and commutative multiset union operator $\_{}^2$ and then we *wrap* the set of objects by using the `<<_>>` constructor to get the desired term of sort `ModelType{MOF}`.

---

^{2} This binary operator symbol has empty syntax (juxtaposition).

Each of the modeling primitives that constitute the MOF metamodel is specified in the $reflect_{\text{MOF}}(\widetilde{\text{MOF}})$ theory by means of sorts, subsorts and operators. As an example, we focus on the CLASS and PROPERTY object types of the MOF metamodel.

CLASS *object type.* Object types are the central concept of MOF to model entities of the problem domain in metamodels. An object type is defined in a metamodel definition $\mathcal{M}$ as a CLASS instance $\widetilde{c}$ and a set of PROPERTY instances $\widetilde{p}$. The object type CLASS contains meta-properties like *name*, which indicates the name of the object type, *ownedAttribute*, which indicates the properties that belong to the CLASS instance, and *superClass*, which indicates that the object type is defined as a specialization of the object types that are referred to by means of this property. The CLASS object type is specified as a sort `Class`, such that `Class < Cid#MOF`, and a constant `Class : -> Class`. Each of the class properties is defined as a constructor for the sort `Property#MOF`. For example, to define the *name* property, we have the constructor `name':_ : String -> Property#MOF`, and to define the *package* property, we have the constructor `package':_ : Oid -> Property#MOF`[3].

In the relational metamodel definition, the CLASS instance that defines the object type TABLE in the metamodel $\widetilde{\text{RDBMS}}$ is defined as the term

```
< 'Foo : Class | name : "Table", package : ..., ownedAttribute : ...>,
```

where `'Foo` is an object identifier.

PROPERTY *object type.* A model can be viewed as a graph where the collection of nodes is constituted by the collection of attributed objects of the model and the edges are defined by means of directed references or links between objects. A PROPERTY object in a metamodel definition $\mathcal{M}$ enables the definition of an attribute in an object or a reference between objects in a model definition $M : \mathcal{M}$, one level down in the MOF framework. A PROPERTY object defines the type of the property, where the type can be a basic type definition, an enumeration type definition or an object type definition. Other meta-properties, such as *lower*, *upper*, *ordered* and *unique*, constitute the multiplicity metadata of a specific property.

The constructors that permit defining objects of the PROPERTY object type are defined, in Maude notation, as follows:

```
sort Property  . subsort Property < Cid#MOF .
op Property : -> Property .
op lower':_ : Int -> Property .     op upper':_ : Int -> Property .
op isOrdered':_ : Bool -> Property . op isUnique':_ : Bool -> Property .
```

The PROPERTY instance $\widetilde{p}$ that defines the metaproperty *name* of the object type RMODELELEMENT in the metamodel definition $\widetilde{\text{RDBMS}}$ is represented by the term

---

[3] Note that property operators can be typed with an object identifier (in the case of references) and with a data type (in the case of attributes).

```
< 'Foo : Property | name : "name", lower : 1, upper: 1, isOrdered = true, isUnique = false,
   isComposite = false, type : 'PrimitiveType0, class : 'Class0 >.
```

We have taken into account the modeling primitives that constitute the Essential MOF metamodel definition, including simple data types and enumeration types. A detailed specification is provided in [5].

Reflective Algebraic Semantics of MOF Metamodels. Once the $reflect_{\mathrm{MOF}}(\widetilde{\mathrm{MOF}})$ theory is defined, we focus on the $ModelType\{\mathrm{MOF}\}$ sort in this theory, whose carrier in the initial algebra defines the $[\![\mathrm{MOF}]\!]_{\mathrm{MOF}}$ type, i.e., the model type whose elements are metamodels:

$$[\![\mathrm{MOF}]\!]_{\mathrm{MOF}} = T_{reflect_{\mathrm{MOF}}(\widetilde{\mathrm{MOF}}),ModelType\{\mathrm{MOF}\}}.$$

Note that, since $[\![\mathrm{MOF}]\!]_{\mathrm{MOF}}$ is the set of all metamodel definitions $\widetilde{\mathcal{M}}$ in MOF, this means that

$$\widetilde{\mathrm{MOF}} \in [\![\mathrm{MOF}]\!]_{\mathrm{MOF}}.$$

We then define the value of the function $reflect_{\mathrm{MOF}}$ on *any* metamodel $\widetilde{\mathcal{M}}$, such that $\widetilde{\mathcal{M}} \in [\![\mathrm{MOF}]\!]_{\mathrm{MOF}}$, as its corresponding MEL theory $reflect_{\mathrm{MOF}}(\widetilde{\mathcal{M}})$. Given a metamodel definition $\widetilde{\mathcal{M}}$, the $reflect_{\mathrm{MOF}}(\widetilde{\mathcal{M}})$ theory defines the $[\![\mathcal{M}]\!]_{\mathrm{MOF}}$ semantics as the set of model definitions $\widetilde{M}$ that are constituted by a collection of typed objects, which can be viewed as both a graph and a term.

In the $reflect_{\mathrm{MOF}}(\widetilde{\mathcal{M}})$ theory, the algebraic notion of *object type* is generically given by means of the sort $Object\#\mathcal{M}$. Terms of sort $Object\#\mathcal{M}$ are defined by means of the constructor

$$< \_ : \_ | \_ > : Oid\#\mathcal{M} \ \ Cid\#\mathcal{M} \ \ PropertySet\#\mathcal{M} \to Object\#\mathcal{M},$$

which is analogous to the constructor for objects that has been presented in the $reflect_{\mathrm{MOF}}(\widetilde{\mathrm{MOF}})$ theory.

Model definitions $\widetilde{M} : \mathcal{M}$ are given as collections of objects, which are instances of a specific object type OT. Object types are defined in a metamodel definition $\widetilde{\mathcal{M}} : \mathrm{MOF}$, as a multiset of objects $\mathrm{OT} \subseteq \widetilde{\mathcal{M}}$. Defining the algebraic semantics of an object type involves the definition of the object identifiers and the properties that may be involved in the definition of a specific object in a model definition $\widetilde{M} : \mathcal{M}$. Object type specialization relationships must be also taken into account. Therefore, we need to define the carrier of the sorts $Oid\#\mathcal{M}$, $Cid\#\mathcal{M}$ and $PropertySet\#\mathcal{M}$ for a specific object type definition.

Consider, for example, the $\widetilde{\mathrm{RDBMS}}$ metamodel definition, where the TABLE object type, denoted by $\widetilde{\mathrm{TABLE}}$, is specified in Maude notation as

```
<< < 'Table : Class | name : "Table", isAbstract : false,
   ownedAttribute : OrderedSet{ 'prop0 ::'prop1 :: 'prop2 :: 'prop3},
   superClass : OrderedSet{ 'RModelElement } >
< 'prop0 : Property | name : "schema", lower : 1, upper: 1,
   isOrdered = true, isUnique = true, isComposite = true, type : 'Schema, class : 'Table >
< 'prop1 : Property | name : "column", lower : 0, upper: -1,
   isOrdered = true, isUnique = true, isComposite = false, type : 'Column, class : 'Table >
```

```
< 'prop2 : Property | name : "key", lower : 0, upper: 1,
  isOrdered = true, isUnique = true, isComposite = false, type: 'PrimaryKey, class : 'Table >
< 'prop3 : Property | name : "foreignKey", lower : 0, upper: -1, isOrdered = true,
  isUnique = true, isComposite = false, type : 'PrimaryKey, class : 'Table > >>.
```

where 'PrimaryKey is the object identifier for the CLASS instance of the PRIMA-RYKEY object type in the relational metamodel $\widetilde{\text{RDBMS}}$. In subsequent paragraphs, we use this example to obtain the theory that defines the TABLE object type.

Object Type Names. In the $reflect_{\text{MOF}}(\widetilde{\mathcal{M}})$ theory, each CLASS instance $\widetilde{cl}$ in $\widetilde{\mathcal{M}}$ is defined as a new sort and a constant, both of them with the name of the class. *Abstract classes* are defined as those that cannot be instantiated. The name of an abstract class C is *not* specified with a constant $C : C$, so that objects in a metamodel definition $\widetilde{\mathcal{M}}$ cannot have C as their type.

In the example of the RDBMS metamodel, the $reflect_{\text{MOF}}$ function generates a single sort and a single constant for the object type TABLE, specified in Maude notation as follows,

```
sort Table . subsort Table < Cid#rdbms . op Table : -> Table .
```

Object Type Properties. An object type OT is defined with a collection of PROPERTY instances describing its properties. A PROPERTY instance $\widetilde{p}$ in a metamodel definition $\widetilde{\mathcal{M}}$: MOF is given by an object $\widetilde{p}$, such that $\widetilde{p}$: PROPERTY and $\widetilde{p} \in \widetilde{\mathcal{M}}$. A Property instance $\widetilde{p}$ is associated with a specific type $\widetilde{t}$ in the metamodel definition $\widetilde{\mathcal{M}}$, which is defined as an object $\widetilde{t}$: TYPE. Depending on the type $\widetilde{t}$ of a property, we can distinguish two kinds of properties:

- *Value-typed Properties or Attributes.* Properties of this kind are typed with DATATYPE instances, which can represent either a simple data type or an numeration type. Value-typed properties define the attributes of the of nodes in a graph.
- *Object-typed Properties or References.* Properties of this kind are typed with object types. Model definitions $\widetilde{M}$ can then be viewed as graphs, where objects define graph nodes and object-typed properties define graph edges. For example, we can define a CLASS instance "Table" and a PROPERTY instance "name" that are related by means of their respective *ownedAttribute* and *class* properties:

```
< 'class0 : Class | name : "Table", ownedAttribute : OrderedSet{ 'prop0 } >
< 'prop0 : Property | name : "name", class : 'class0 >
```

The *type* meta-property together with the multiplicity metadata define a set of specific constraints on the acceptable values for the property type. These constraints are taken into account in the algebraic type that is assigned to the property by means of OCL collection types. In the example, the TABLE object type is specified in the theory $reflect_{\text{MOF}}(\widetilde{\text{RDBMS}})$, in Maude notation, as follows:

```
sorts Table . subsort Table < Cid#rdbms . op Table : -> Table .
op schema : Oid -> Property#rdbms . op column : OrderedSet{Oid} -> Property#rdbms .
op key : [Oid] -> Property#rdbms .  op foreignKey : OrderedSet{Oid} -> Property#rdbms .
```

Object Type Specialization Relation. A *specialization* is a taxonomic relationship between two object types. This relationship specializes a general object type into a more specific one. In the RDBMS example, we algebraically define the specialization relationship between the object types $\widetilde{RModelElement}$ and $\widetilde{Table}$ as the subsorts `Table < RModelElement`. The supersorts of the resulting subsort hierarchy are defined as subsorts of the `Cid#rdbms` sort, for object type name sorts and object identifier sorts, respectively. In this way, we can define a table instance as `< 'Foo : Table | name : "date", ...>`, where the `name` property is defined for the RModelElement object type.

Algebraic Semantics of Object Types. The algebraic semantics of an object type is then given by the set of all the objects that can be defined either as instances of the object type, i.e., a class, or as instances of any of its subtypes. The algebraic semantics of an object type definition $\widetilde{OT}$, such that $OT : MOF$, is defined as follows:

$$[\![OT]\!]_{\mathrm{MOF}} = \{\widetilde{o} \mid \widetilde{o} \in T_{reflect_{\mathrm{MOF}}(\widetilde{\mathcal{M}}), Object\#\mathcal{M}} \,\wedge\, class(\widetilde{o}) \in T_{reflect_{\mathrm{MOF}}(\widetilde{\mathcal{M}}), ClassSort(\widetilde{OT})}\}.$$

where *class* is an operator that obtains the type constant of a given object, and *ClassSort* is an operator that obtains the sort that corresponds to the object type constant in $reflect_{\mathrm{MOF}}(\widetilde{\mathcal{M}})$. The *isValueOf* relation $\widetilde{o} : OT$ indicates if an object $\widetilde{o}$ is instance of a given object type OT, is defined as follows:

$$\widetilde{o} : OT \;\Leftrightarrow\; \widetilde{o} \in [\![OT]\!]_{\mathrm{MOF}}.$$

Algebraic Semantics of MOF Metamodels. The $reflect_{\mathrm{MOF}}(\widetilde{\mathcal{M}})$ theory constitutes the metamodel realization of the metamodel definition $\widetilde{\mathcal{M}}$. This theory provides the model type $\mathcal{M}$, which is represented by the sort $ModelType\{\mathcal{M}\}$. $\mathcal{M}$ is the type of collections of typed objects that have both a graph and a term structure. The semantics of the $\mathcal{M}$ type is defined by the equation

$$[\![\mathcal{M}]\!]_{\mathrm{MOF}} = T_{reflect_{\mathrm{MOF}}(\widetilde{\mathcal{M}}), ModelType\{\mathcal{M}\}},$$

and the *structural conformance relation* between a model definition $\widetilde{M}$ and its corresponding model type $\mathcal{M}$ is then formally defined by the equivalence

$$\widetilde{M} : \mathcal{M} \Leftrightarrow \widetilde{M} \in [\![\mathcal{M}]\!]_{\mathrm{MOF}}.$$

Embedding MOF Reflection into mel Logical Reflection. The logical reflective features of MEL [4], together with its logical framework capabilities, make it possible to *internalize* the representation $\Phi : Spec\mathcal{L} \longrightarrow SpecMEL$ of a formalism $\mathcal{L}$ in MEL, as an equationally-defined function $\overline{\Phi} : Module_{\mathcal{L}} \longrightarrow Module$, where $Module_{\mathcal{L}}$ is an equationally defined data type representing specifications in $\mathcal{L}$, and *Module* is the data type whose terms, of the form $\overline{(\Sigma, E)}$, metarepresent MEL specifications of the form (Σ, E). We can apply this general method to the case of our algebraic semantics

$$reflect_{\mathrm{MOF}} : MOF \longrightarrow SpecMEL.$$

Then, the reflective internalization of the MOF algebraic semantics $\overline{reflect}_{\mathrm{MOF}}$ becomes an equationally-defined function

$$\overline{reflect}_{\mathrm{MOF}} : ModelType\{\mathrm{MOF}\} \longrightarrow Module.$$

where *Module* is the sort whose terms represent MEL theories in the universal MEL theory (see [4]).

The function $reflect_{\mathrm{MOF}}$ is completely defined in [5] and is implemented as $\overline{reflect}_{\mathrm{MOF}}$ in the prototype that is available at [6]. By using the theory $reflect_{\mathrm{MOF}}(\overline{\mathrm{RDBMS}})$, the table PERSON in the relational schema that appears in Fig. 2 is defined as the term

```
<< < 'column.0 : Column | nnv : true, owner : 'table.0, type : VARCHAR, name : "name" >
< 'column.1 : Column | owner : 'table.0, type : NUMBER, name : "age" >
< 'column.2 : Column | key : OrderedSet{ 'key.0 },
   nnv : true, owner : 'table.0, type : VARCHAR, name : "person_PK" >
< 'key.0 : Key | column : OrderedSet{ 'column.2 }, owner : 'tables.0, name : "Person_PK" >
< 'table.0 : Table | name : "Person", key : OrderedSet{'key.0},
   column : OrderedSet{ 'column.0 :: 'column.1 :: 'column.2 } > >>.
```

If we represent this term as the constant `model`, we can automatically check whether this model conforms to its metamodel by evaluating the following membership in Maude:

```
red model :: ModelType{rdbms} .
result Bool: true
```

5   Related work

The meaning of the *metamodel* notion has been widely discussed in the literature, see for example [7,8,9,10]. There is a consensus that a metamodel can play several roles: as *data*, as *type* or as *theory*. In this paper, we have formally expressed each of these roles by means of the notions of metamodel definition $\overline{\mathcal{M}}$, model type $\mathcal{M}$, and metamodel realization $reflect_{\mathrm{MOF}}(\overline{\mathcal{M}})$, respectively.

The current MOF standard does not provide any guidelines to implement a reflective mechanism that obtains the semantics of a metamodel. An informal attempt to realize MOF metamodel definitions as Java programs is provided in the Java Metadata Interface (JMI) specification [11], which is defined for a previous version of the MOF standard. A mapping of this kind has been successfully implemented in modeling environments such as the Eclipse Modeling Framework. By contrast, our $reflect_{\mathrm{MOF}}$ function gives us an executable formal specification of the algebraic semantics of any metamodel $\overline{\mathcal{M}}$ in MOF.

Poernomo gives a formal metamodeling framework based on Constructive Type Theory [12], where models, which are define as terms (token models), can also be represented as types (type models) by means of a reflection mechanism. In this framework, the conformance relation is implicitly provided by construction: only valid models can be defined as terms, and their definition constitutes a formal proof of the fact that the subject belongs to the corresponding type, by means of the Curry-Howard isomorphism.

[13] describes a metamodeling framework, based on Maude, which also represents graphs as terms by taking advantage of the underlying term matching algorithm modulo associativity and commutativity. In this work, the authors address the model subtyping relation that can be defined between two model types and type inference to deal with model management scenarios. Their work is based on the data version of metamodels, i.e., over metamodel definitions. A difference compared to our work is the reflective semantics for MOF metamodels that we have defined in our framework.

6   Conclusions and Future Work

In this work we have proposed an algebraic semantics for the MOF metamodeling framework, formalizing notions not yet clear in the MOF standard. In our approach, we give an explicit formal representation for each of the different notions that may be involved in a metamodeling framework: model type $\mathcal{M}$, metamodel realization $reflect_{\mathrm{MOF}}(\widetilde{\mathcal{M}})$, and metamodel conformance $\widetilde{M} : \mathcal{M}$. Our work provides an algebraic executable formalization of the MOF standard that can be reused for free, in standard-compliant frameworks. At present, the prototype, available at [6], implements the MOF framework in Maude and uses the EMF as the metamodeling front-end.

We plan to use this framework as the kernel of a model management tool suite that provides support for QVT and graph-based model transformations within the EMF. For this we have relied on the experience gained in previous prototypes that gave algebraic executable specifications for OCL [14], QVT [15] and model management operators [16]. Our framework supports the application of formal analysis techniques, such as inductive theorem proving and model checking, to model-based and graph-based systems by means of the underlying Maude framework and its formal tools [4]. In addition, grammar-based software artifacts can also be related to models by specifying context-free grammars as MEL signatures. This last feature makes our framework also suitable for forward and reverse Model-Driven Engineering.

We are currently working on a graph transformation tool that provides support for OCL and QVT. This tool is being developed entirely in Maude and uses rewriting logic to support graph transformations. In future work, we plan to apply the algebraic MOF framework together with the aforementioned QVT model transformation tool and Maude-based formal verification techniques to model management scenarios, where formal verification techniques play an important role. In particular, we are considering the formal analysis of real-time embedded systems in the avionics specific domain that are developed by following a model-driven approach, by using model-based languages like the Architecture Analysis and Design Language (AADL) [17].

Acknowledgments. This work has been partially supported by the project META TIN2006-15175-C05-01, by the ONR Grant N00014-02-1-0715, by NSF Grant IIS-07-20482, and by the project SENSORIA, IST-2005-016004.

References

1. Object Management Group: Meta Object Facility (MOF) 2.0 Core Specification (ptc/06-01-01) (2006), http://www.omg.org/cgi-bin/doc?formal/2006-01-01
2. Eclipse Organization: The Eclipse Modeling Framework (2007), http://www.eclipse.org/emf/
3. Meseguer, J.: Membership algebra as a logical framework for equational specification. In: Parisi-Presicce, F. (ed.) WADT 1997. LNCS, vol. 1376, pp. 18–61. Springer, Heidelberg (1998)
4. Clavel, M., Durán, F., Eker, S., Meseguer, J., Lincoln, P., Martí-Oliet, N., Talcott, C.: All About Maude. In: Clavel, M., Durán, F., Eker, S., Lincoln, P., Martí-Oliet, N., Meseguer, J., Talcott, C. (eds.) All About Maude - A High-Performance Logical Framework. LNCS, vol. 4350, Springer, Heidelberg (2007)
5. Boronat, A., Meseguer, J.: Algebraic semantics of EMOF/OCL metamodels. Technical Report UIUCDCS-R-2007-2904, CS Dept., University of Illinois at Urbana-Champaign (2007), http://www.cs.le.ac.uk/people/ab373/papers/ UIUC-TR-MOF-OCL-Boronat-Meseguer.pdf
6. The ISSI Research Group (The MOMENT Project), http://moment.dsic.upv.es
7. Ludewig, J.: Models in software engineering - an introduction. Inform., Forsch. Entwickl. 18(3-4), 105–112 (2004)
8. Seidewitz, E.: What models mean. Software, IEEE 20(5), 26–32 (2003)
9. Kuhne, T.: Matters of (meta-) modeling. Software and Systems Modeling (SoSyM) 5(17), 369–385 (2006)
10. Rensink, A.: Subjects, models, languages, transformations. In: Bézivin, J., Heckel, R. (eds.) Language Engineering for Model-Driven Software Development. Internationales Begegnungs- und Forschungszentrum für Informatik (IBFI). Dagstuhl Seminar Proceedings, vol. 04101, Schloss Dagstuhl, Germany (2004)
11. Java Community Process: The Java Metadata Interface (JMI) Specification (JSR 40) (2002), http://www.jcp.org/en/jsr/detail?id=40
12. Poernomo, I.: The meta-object facility typed. In: Haddad, H. (ed.) SAC, pp. 1845–1849. ACM, New York (2006)
13. Romero, J.R., Rivera, J.E., Durán, F., Vallecillo, A.: Formal and Tool Support for Model Driven Engineering with Maude. Journal of Object Technology 6(9), 187–207 (2007), http://www.jot.fm/issues/issue_2007_10/paper10/
14. Boronat, A., Oriente, J., Gómez, A., Ramos, I., Carsí, J.A.: An Algebraic Specification of Generic OCL Queries Within the Eclipse Modeling Framework. In: Rensink, A., Warmer, J. (eds.) ECMDA-FA 2006. LNCS, vol. 4066, pp. 316–330. Springer, Heidelberg (2006)
15. Boronat, A., Carsí, J.A., Ramos, I.: Algebraic specification of a model transformation engine. In: Baresi, L., Heckel, R. (eds.) FASE 2006 and ETAPS 2006. LNCS, vol. 3922, pp. 262–277. Springer, Heidelberg (2006)
16. Boronat, A., Carsí, J.A., Ramos, I.: Automatic Support for Traceability in a Generic Model Management Framework. In: Hartman, A., Kreische, D. (eds.) ECMDA-FA 2005. LNCS, vol. 3748, pp. 316–330. Springer, Heidelberg (2005)
17. SAE: AADL (2007) http://www.aadl.info/

A Formal Framework for Developing Adaptable Service-Based Applications

Leen Lambers[1], Leonardo Mariani[2], Hartmut Ehrig[1], and Mauro Pezzè[2]

[1] Department of Software Engineering and Theoretical Informatics
Technical University Berlin
Franklinstrasse, 28/29 - 10587 Berlin
{leen,ehrig}@cs.tu-berlin.de
[2] Department of Informatics, Systems and Communication
University of Milano Bicocca
via Bicocca degli Arcimboldi, 8 - 20126 Milano
{mariani,pezze}@disco.unimib.it

Abstract. Web services are open, interoperable, easy to integrate and reuse, and are extensively used in many application domains. Research and best practices have produced excellent support for developing large-scale web-based applications implementing complex business processes.

Flexibility and interoperability of web services make them well suited also for *highly-customizable reactive service-based applications*, that is interactive applications which serve few users, and can be rapidly adapted to new requirements and environmental conditions. This is the case, for example of personal data managers tailored to the needs of few specific users who want to adapt them to different conditions and requests. Classic development approaches that require experts of web service technologies do not well support this class of applications which call for rapid individual customization and adaptation by non-expert users.

In this paper, we present the formal framework of a model-based approach that provides expert users with the ability of rapidly building, adapting and reconfiguring reactive service-based applications according to new requirements and needs. Moreover this formal approach will presumably allow adaptations and reconfigurations by non-expert users as well. The underlying technique integrates two user-friendly, visual and executable formalisms: live sequence charts, to describe control flow, and graph transformation systems, to describe data flow and processing. Main results of the paper are the specification and semantics of the integration and early analysis techniques revealing inconsistencies.

1 Introduction

Internet-based systems often expose functionality through publicly available web services. The many available services provide to end-users the interesting opportunity to satisfy their emerging needs by implementing and executing client applications that integrate these services. For instance, users can easily obtain applications managing personal mobility by integrating web services that provide maps, traffic information and weather forecasts [1].

J. Fiadeiro and P. Inverardi (Eds.): FASE 2008, LNCS 4961, pp. 392–406, 2008.
© Springer-Verlag Berlin Heidelberg 2008

Unfortunately, end-users often do not have enough skill to develop such client applications and software experts are usually not interested in developing systems that satisfy needs of few or even single users. Thus, notwithstanding the many available web services and the existence of well-suited engineering processes [2,3], personal service-based applications seldom exist. In practice, users spend large amount of time by manually repeating interactions with web services.

In this paper, we present the formal foundations of a requirement-driven iterative methodology, early described in [4], for semi-automatically developing, adapting and reconfiguring *highly customizable reactive service-based applications*. The methodology enables expert users to quickly specify and develop service-based applications, and common users to adapt and reconfigure applications to meet emerging and evolving requirements that cannot be effectively managed with standard engineering processes [2,3]. Our technique merges interactions which should be adopted by the applications into an integrated model that describes the control flow by means of LSCs [5], and the data flow and data processing by means of GTs [6,7]. The integrated model represents the behavior of the application and can be automatically executed and analyzed. The sample interactions can be specified by expert users through a visual and intuitive interface analogous to the Play-In approach [5]. Moreover this interface presents analysis results and automatically generates solutions to inconsistencies in the integrated model.

This paper formally describes the integration of LSCs with GTs and early proposes integrated analysis techniques of the integrated model to identify inconsistencies and errors. We validated the technique by specifying a Personal Mobility Manager (PMM), which is a reactive service-based application designed to satisfy requirements related to individual user mobility [1]. The paper is structured as follows. Section 2 provides background information about LSCs and GTs. Sections 3 and 4 present our formal integrated models and automated analysis techniques, respectively. Finally Section 5 discusses related work and summarizes the main contributions of this paper.

2   LSC and GT

In this Section, we introduce the two modeling languages, LSCs and GTs, that we integrated to specify and generate adaptable service-based applications.

Live Sequence Charts. LSCs have been introduced in [5] as an extension of message sequence charts to express liveness, i.e., the existence of possible, necessary and mandatory behaviors, both globally to a collection of charts and locally to single charts. LSCs can be universal and existential. A universal chart consists of a prechart and a main chart, if an execution satisfies a pre-chart it must also satisfy the main chart. Existential charts are charts that need to be satisfied by all runs.

Example 1. An example of a universal LSC is given in Figure 1 (a). This LSC specifies the control flow of messages that are exchanged in the PMM when users identify a route connecting two places by taking traffic intensity into consideration. LSCs can contain guards that indicate conditions under which execution is suspended, e.g., the LSC in Figure 1 (a) requires *Means.name = car* to be fullfilled.

LSCs can have local variables. For instance, the LSC in Figure 1 (a) includes local variables created by instantiation to transmit values to web services (e.g., variable
Dep in Figure 1 (a)) or to store return values sent (e.g., variable *Route* in Figure 1 (a)).
To cope with the complex structure of the state of object-oriented programs, we associate each LSC with a local graph that represents local variables. The existence of local
graphs support the use of GT rules to create/modify/read local variables.

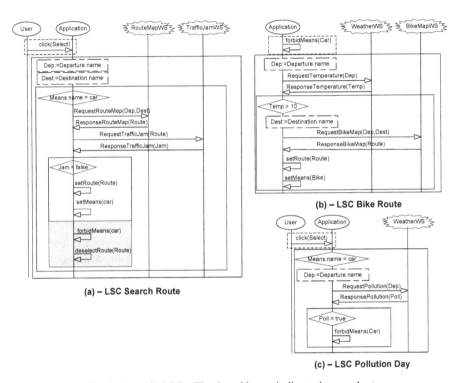

(a) – LSC Search Route

(b) – LSC Bike Route

(c) – LSC Pollution Day

Fig. 1. Example LSCs. The dotted boxes indicate the pre-charts.

Graph Transformations. In our integrated model, possible state changes and computations are specified with a set of graph transformation rules. A rule consists of a left and
right hand side (lhs and rhs resp.), both typed over a class diagram of the application.
The lhs indicates the objects, connections and attribute values that must be present before applying a rule. The rhs indicates the result of the application of the rule. Objects
and connections that are present in both the left and right hand sides are preserved by
the application of the rule. Objects and connections that are present in the lhs and not
in the rhs are deleted by the application of the rule. Objects and connections that occur
only in the rhs are added. If attribute values differ between lhs and rhs, the application
of the GT rule modifies their values. Rules can include a negative application condition
(NAC) that describes which objects, connections or attribute values are forbidden before applying the rule [8]. A detailed and formal description of typed, attributed graphs
and graph transformation can be found in [6,7].

Example 2. Figure 2 shows a few examples of graph transformation rules. The rule *setRoute(Route)* creates a *Route* object and preserves the existence of the Route *Variable*; rule *setMeans(car)* modifies the value of attribute *means* and rule *forbidMeans (car)* sets the forbidden attribute of the user to car. The NAC of rule *setMeans(car)* specifies that it cannot be applied if the user's attribute *forbidden* is set to car.

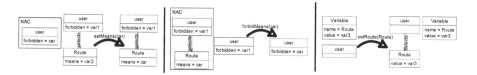

Fig. 2. Example of graph transformation rules

3   First Result: Integrating LSC and GT

We specify highly customizable reactive service-based applications by integrating LSCs and GTs: a disjoined set of graphs represents the current state of the system (a single graph can represent the state of either the application under development or a web service); LSCs describe the flow of messages exchanged between the user, the application, and web services (user inputs as the *click(Select)* message shown in the LSC in Fig. 1 (a) are modeled with messages from the user to the application); and GT rules indicate the changes on the system state induced by sent and received messages. The idea is that every time a LSC is traversed, each message in the LSC triggers the application of the GT rule associated with the message. For example, the reception of the message *setRoute(Route)* specified in the LSC shown in Fig. 1 (a) triggers the execution of the corresponding GT rule shown in Fig. 2.

Definition 1 (system participants, system state, initial system state). *We represent the participants to a highly customizable reactive service-based application as a tuple $P = (A, WS_1, \ldots, WS_n)$, where A is the application under development and $WS_1, \ldots, WS_n$ are the web services accessed by A. The application and web services have a current state that evolves with system execution. We represent this state as a typed attributed graph and we define a mapping function $gstate$ to indicate the current state of a participant, e.g., $gstate(A)$ is the current state of the application. The* system state *is indicated with the tuple $gstate(P) = (gstate(A), gstate(WS_1), \ldots, gstate(WS_n))$. States are typed over* type graphs. *We indicate the type graph associated to a participant with a mapping function TG, e.g., $TG(A)$ is the type graph of the application. It is required that the state of a participant matches its type graph, e.g., $gstate(A)$ is typed over $TG(A)$. The initial state of each participant is indicated with a mapping function $gstate_0$, e.g., $gstate_0(A)$ is the initial state of the application. The* initial system state *is indicated with the tuple $gstate(P) = (gstate(A), gstate(WS_1), \ldots, gstate(WS_n))$.*

Informally speaking, a typed attributed graph can be compared to a UML Object diagram and its type graph can be compared to a UML Class diagram [9].

Example 3. For the PMM $P=(Application, TrafficJamWS, RouteMapWS, WeatherWS)$. Fig. 3 shows an example state $gstate(P)$ for the PMM. The initial state $gstate_0(P)$ is obtained by leaving out the dotted nodes and edges. The web service areas indicate the visible behavior of web services (and eventually their conceptual state); the application area indicates the state of the application.

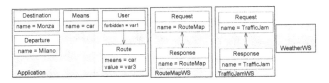

Fig. 3. An example state for the PMM system

Note that the state graph of a web service WS_i does not represent the current concrete state of the web service but the conceptual state of the web service as expected by the application A. If operations provided by a web service are specified with GT rules, our framework can automatically trace the conceptual state of web services and automatically diagnose if the application A inconsistently uses web services. If this information is not available, our framework can automatically analyze the consistency of the behavior of A, but cannot check if A consistently uses web services. GT-based specifications can be obtained from UML design documents with limited additional effort [10]. Service providers that want to ease integration of their web services can consider providing this additional description.

Operational Semantics for GT Specification. Now we define the GT based system specification and its associated semantics. Since GT rules specify how the system state is modified by each operation, they can be intuitively interpreted as a sort of *contract* that specifies how LSCs can legally invoke these operations. GT rules are usually specified by web service providers, while operations performed by the application are derived from user specifications (play-in).

When system messages are sent and received, GT rules are used to update the system state (at the end of this section we discuss how the matching process is guaranteed of being deterministic). The rule that is applied when a message is sent specifies the changes that need to be applied on the state of the sender, e.g., an attribute value can be increased to count the number of sent messages. This rule is seldom used and often consists of the empty rule. The rule that is applied when a message is received depends on the nature of the message. If the message goes from the application to a web service, the rule corresponds to the one that specifies the requested operation. If the message goes from the web service to the application, the rule consists of transferring the return value generated by a web service to the application. If the message goes from the application or the user to the application, it consists of a computation that is internal to the application. In the following paragraphs we describe how to formalize these ideas. Our formalization extends the one of Harels' play-in/play-out approach [11].

Definition 2 (system message, system alphabet). *Formally, a system message M_s is described by a tuple $M_s = \langle Src, Dst, (r_1, r_2), sync \rangle$, where Src and Dst is any between $\{U, A, WS_1, \ldots, WS_n\}$ (U indicates the user of the system), (r_1, r_2) is a pair of rules such that r_1 (resp. r_2) is typed over $TG(Src)$ (resp. $TG(Dst)$) and $sync$ is a Boolean variable describing if the message is synchronous ($sync = true$) or asynchronous ($sync = false$). The set of all possible system messages, namely the* system alphabet, *is indicated with Σ.*

Given the set of messages that can be used to specify the behavior of a highly-customizable reactive service-based system, we can derive the list of message sequences that can be legally executed. This set is clearly infinite and our technique does not compute it in practice; however, its formal definition is useful to automatically identify inconsistent uses of existing operations.

Definition 3 (GT system specification and semantics). *A GT system specification is a tuple (P, Σ) where P is a set of participants and Σ a system alphabet for P. Given a GT system specification $GTSPEC = (P, \Sigma)$, $Sem(GTSPEC)$ consists of a set of transition systems that describe the sequence of transformation rules that can be executed by each participant in P. In particular, $Sem(GTSPEC) = (Sem(A), Sem(WS_1), \ldots, Sem(WS_n))$ such that $Sem(X) = (\mathcal{G}_X, R(X), \Rightarrow, gstate_0(X))$ is a state transition system with X any of $A, WS_1, \ldots, WS_n$, $\mathcal{G}_X$ possible state values for X, $R(X)$ the GT rules occuring in the system alphabet that are typed over $TG(X)$, $gstate_0(X)$ the initial state of X and $\Rightarrow \subseteq \mathcal{G}_X \times R(X) \times \mathcal{G}_X$ with $(G, r, G') \in \Rightarrow$ if and only if the rule $r \in R(X)$ can be applied to G such that $G \stackrel{r}{\Rightarrow} G'$.*

Example 4. The rules depicted in Fig. 2 belong to $R(Application)$ because they only change the state of the application. The system reaches the state shown in Fig. 3 from the initial state by applying as last rules *setRoute(Route)* and *setMeans(car)* from Fig. 2. This state is reached after running completely through the LSC in Fig. 1 (a) following the if-branch.

Operational Semantics of the Integrated Model. Hereafter we present the semantics associated with the LSC-based specification, which is automatically obtained from scenarios provided (played-in) by users. This semantics indicates the behavior that users expect from the application under development. Differences between GT- and LSC-based semantics are used to automatically discover important inconsistencies, e.g., the existence of LSCs that activate illegal sequences of graph transformations. Moreover, we formally define the semantics of the integrated model, which specifies the behaviors that are instilled in the application under development.

Scenarios played-in by users describe a control flow of messages exchanged between participants of a highly customizable reactive service-based application. These scenarios are formally specified as LSCs. Each message included in LSCs is associated with a sender, a receiver, a system message and a location that defines at which time the message should be sent and received [11].

Definition 4 (LSC message). *A LSC message M_l included in a LSC L is a triple $M_l = (I_{src}, I_{dst}, M_s)$, where I_{src} and I_{dst} represent the source and destination lifelines [11] with I_{src} and I_{dst} participants of the system P, and M_s a system message.*

Example 5. The LSC message *setMeans(car)* shown in Fig. 1 (a) has the Application lifeline as both source and destination; its system message has an empty source rule and a destination rule that corresponds to rule *setMeans(car)* shown in Fig. 2.

LSCs describe the behavior that users expect from the application under development. We formally define the behaviors generated by a *LSCSPEC* as in [11].

Definition 5 (LSC specification and semantics). *The complete set of LSCs that are specified by users form a* LSC *system specification* $LSCSPEC = (P, \Sigma, \mathcal{S_U})$ *with* $\mathcal{S_U}$ *a set of universal LSCs. The operational semantics for LSCSPEC is defined as a state transition system* $Sem(LSCSPEC) = \langle \mathcal{V}, V_0, \Delta \rangle$ *where* $\mathcal{V}$ *is the set of possible states of* $Sem(LSCSPEC)$, V_0 *is the initial configuration and* $\Delta \subseteq \mathcal{V} \times (\mathcal{E} \cup \bigcup_{L \in LSCSPEC} E_L) \times \mathcal{V}$ *the set of allowed transitions with* E_L *the set of events for each LSC L. A state* $V \in \mathcal{V}$ *is defined as* $V = \langle \mathcal{RL}, Violating \rangle$ *where* $\mathcal{RL}$ *is the set of currently running LSCs and* $Violating$ *indicates by True or False whether the state is a violating one. The initial configuration is* $V_0 = \langle \phi, False \rangle$.

If we remove behaviors that are specified in LSCs and do not satisfy the constraints imposed by GT rules, we obtain the set of behaviors that are instilled into a highly-customizable reactive service-based system. In the following therefore we define how both specification techniques interplay on the syntactical and semantical levels. We therefore define an integrated system specification and its semantics by runs allowed by the specification. Informally, a run includes a sequence of observable events occurring when running the system.

Definition 6 (integrated system specification). *A LSC* L *is compatible with a GT system specification* $GTSPEC = (P, \Sigma)$ *iff for each message* $M_l = (I_{src}, I_{dst}, M_s)$ *in* L *such that* $M_s = (Src, Dst, (r_1, r_2), sync)$ *it holds that* $Src = I_{src}$ *and* $Dst = I_{dst}$. *An* integrated system specification $LGTSPEC = (GTSPEC, LSCSPEC)$ *consists of a GT system specification* $GTSPEC = (P, \Sigma)$ *and a LSC specification* $LSCSPEC = (P, \Sigma, \mathcal{L})$ *such that every LSC* $L \in \mathcal{L}$ *is compatible with GTSPEC.*

The play-in GUI in which the expert users instill sample interactions allows creation of compatible specifications only.

Definition 7 (run consistent with LSC specification). *Given a LSC system specification* $(S, \Sigma, \mathcal{L})$, *a run* r *represents a system execution and is defined as a sequence of visible events* $e_1 \ldots e_m$, *with* $e_j \in M_L \times \{Send, Recv\}$, $L \in \mathcal{L}$ *and* M_L *a LSC message. A run* r *is consistent with LSCSPEC if, starting from* V_0, *the rules of* Δ *can be applied iteratively to the events in* r, *and to the hidden events generated between them, without reaching a violating transition.*

Example 6. An example run for the LSC shown in Fig. 1 (a) is *(Click(Select),Send) (Click(Select),Rcv)... (setMeans(car),Send)(setMeans(car),Rcv).* This would be the begining and end of a consistent run with *LSCSPEC* for the case that the user has chosen to take his car and there is no traffic jam.

A run can be mapped to the corresponding set of system-level events. Thus, we can preserve the sequence of events removing information about lifelines, which are useful at the specification level, but not necessary at this point. Given a GT system specification *GTSPEC*, a *system run* is consistent with *GTSPEC* if the sequence of operations executed by each system participant is accepted by its GT-spec. Note that in the following definition we use the notation *part* (resp. *gt*) to indicate a system participant (resp. rule) associated with the event.

Definition 8 (system run consistent with GT specification). *In particular, given a run* $r = e_1 \ldots e_m$, *with* $e_j = ((I^j_{Src}, I^j_{Dst}, M^j_s), x^j)$, *its associated* system run *is* $r_S = e_{1,S} \ldots e_{m,S}$ *with* $e_{j,S} = (M^j_s, x^j) \in \Sigma \times \{Send, Recv\}$. *Given GTSPEC* = (P, Σ), *a system* run $r_S = e_{1,S}, e_{2,S}, \ldots, e_{m,S}$ *is consistent with GTSPEC if for each participant* X *in* P, *there exists both a sequence of GT rules* $s_X = s_0 s_1 \ldots s_n \in Sem(X)$ *with* $s_i \in R(X)$ *and an isomorphic mapping* map_X *assigning to each event* $e_{i,S}$ *in* r_S *such that* $part(e_{i,S}) = X$ *a unique rule* s_j *in the transition sequence* s_X, *i.e.,* $map_X : \{e_{i,S} | i \in \{1, \ldots, m\}, part(e_{i,S}) = X\} \to \{1, \ldots, n\}$. *Moreover, the mapping* map_X *must satisfy the following properties: compatibility with gt, i.e., if* $map_X(e_{i,S}) = j \Rightarrow gt(e_{i,S}) = s_j$, *and preserve ordering of events, i.e., if* $i \leq j$ *and* $part(e_{i,S}) = part(e_{j,S}) = X \Rightarrow map_X(e_{i,S}) \leq map_X(e_{j,S})$.

Example 7. An example consistent run, corresponding to the case of a user taking a car when a traffic jam exists, for the LSC shown in Fig. 1 (a) is *(Click(Select),Send) (Click(Select),Rcv)... (deselectRoute(Route),Send)(deselectRoute(Route),Recv)*. The corresponding system run would be inconsistent with *GTSPEC* since rule *deselectRoute(Route)* cannot be applied. The reason is that *Route* has never been selected, thus it is impossible to deselect it. This is formally expressed by the sequential dependencie of rule *deselectRoute(Route)* from *selectRoute(Route)*. These kinds of inconsistencies are automatically detected by analysis techniques presented in the next section.

Definition 9 (semantics of integrated specification). *Given an integrated system specification LGT* = *(GTSPEC, LSCSPEC), a run* r *is consistent with LGT if its associated system run* r_S *is consistent with GTSPEC and* r *is consistent with LSCSPEC. Given a system specification LGT* = *(GTSPEC, LSCSPEC), then Sem(LGT) consists of all LGT consistent runs.*

Play-Out. We now describe how an integrated specification can be executed. The process of executing traces is called *play-out*. A trace executed by an integrated specification *LGT* is not necessarily a *LGT* consistent run. In particular, given a system event e, the event is played-out executing the following steps (we call this sequence of steps $gtstep(e)$, in contrast with the original definition in [11] which was called $step(e)$).

gtstep(e)

1. Apply $\Delta(e)^1$.
2. Change the system state according to the system event e:
   (a) if $(e = \langle M_s, Sent \rangle$ and $M_s = \langle Src, Dst, (r_1, r_2), false \rangle$ apply the rule r_1 to $gstate(Src)$

---

[1] $\Delta(e)$ indicates that the event is initially processed as in the original Harel et al.'s approach.

(b) else if $(e = \langle M_s, Recv \rangle$ and $M_s = \langle Src, Dst, (r_1, r_2), false \rangle)$ apply the rule r_2 to Dst

(c) else if $M_s = \langle Src, Dst, (r_1, r_2), true \rangle$ apply r_1 to $gstate(Src)$ and r_2 to $gstate(Dst)$ in parallel

When playing out a certain system event it is possible that a transition system Sem $(LSCSPEC)$ reaches a Violating state as defined in [11] or that one of the transition systems in $Sem(GTSPEC)$ cannot be propagated. This happens when we execute an inconsistent LGT run/trace. Finding out and/or foreseeing inconsistent runs is the subject of section 4, which presents analysis techniques for this problem.

Matching of rules. The process of selecting the instances where the rule must be applied is known as matching. Formally this match is expressed by a suitable morphism of the lhs of a rule into the state graph G. In general, we can have three main possibilities: (1) no matching, (2) single matching and (3) multiple matchings. No matching corresponds to the impossibility of finding any matching (and thus the rule cannot be applied to the current state). Single matching represents the existence of a unique match (and thus the rule can be applied in a unique way). Multiple matching corresponds to many possible matchings between the rule and the current state (and thus the rule can be applied in several ways). For instance, if the current state of an application includes multiple active users, the rule *setRoute(Route)* shown in Figure 2 can be applied to any of the users.

In our approach we assume deterministic matching. Thus the system specification should forbid multiple matching. To guarantee that this property is fulfilled, we restrict the possible structure of the disjoint graphs in S to type graphs with cardinalities that satisfy the following properties: (1) only one copy of any type of object can be instantiated, i.e. the cardinality of each type is minimal zero and maximal 1; (2) if multiple instances of a certain type are allowed, we require that all rules that affect this object type either use an identifier to select the exact instance or select all instances; (3) cardinality of each edge is between 0 and 1.

4   Integrated Analysis

System specifications instilled by expert users in the Play-In GUI or specification reconfigurations demanded by users may be inconsistent. For instance, in the *GTSPEC* an object trip must always be initialized before it can be populated with routes, and simultaneously, in the *LSCSPEC*, a scenario is present where routes are added to a trip without initializing it. Such kind of inconsistencies can be easily introduced into an integrated specification because during system design or reconfiguration the expert user (or user even less) is usually concentrated on a single LSC or GT, without considering all possible interplays with other GTs, LSCs and combinations of them.

Due to Play-In of the system behavior single operations are organized within LSCs and therefore we we can intuitively assume that the required behavior from the system is given by all consistent runs in $Sem(LSCSPEC)$. However, these single operations are represented by *GTSPEC* and further constraint the behavior of the system, since it is not always possible to execute all single operations in any order. The gap between the behavior intended by expert and end-users and the behavior exhibited by the system under development is given by the set *Suppressed Runs* of runs consistent with all LSCs but not consistent with the integrated system specification due to the effect of single operations. Such a suppressed run is presented in Example 7. Our analysis points out runs that are in *SR* in order to make sure that in the end expert users (or users) are aware of runs that are automatically suppressed. If this suppression is not desired it can be repaired and the reconfigured behavior can be instilled into the specification.

Definition 10 (suppressed runs)
$SR = \{r | r \text{ consistent with } LSCSPEC\} \setminus \{r | r_S \text{ consistent with } GTSPEC\}$

In the following, we present the analysis techniques that identify suppressed runs due to the interplay of GT operations with single LSCs and multiple LSCs. Problems due to *LSCSPEC* and *GTSPEC* only are addressed with analysis techniques specific for the single techniques [11,7].

Second Result: Consistency Analysis of Single LSCs. Analysis of single LSCs consists of the identification of suppressed runs due to the interplay of GT operations with single LSCs. The analysis techniques for revealing suppressed runs are based on both the identification of possible runs generated by LSCs and conflicts and dependencies between GT rules. Therefore at first we present these supporting techniques and thereafter the final analysis techniques.

Generation of Runs Associated to LSC. Given an LSC l, we can derive a Control-Flow Graph (CFG), denoted with $cfg(l)$, that represents a (super-)set of the runs generated by l. Each edge in the CFG is labeled with the name of a message, thus a sample run can be obtained by following the path from the starting node to the ending node. The translation of an LSC to a CFG is straightforward and consists of removing conditions from the LSC and suitably mapping constructs used in LSC to constructs of CFG. Features that are straightforwardly mapped from LSC to CFG are conditions, IfThenElse constructs, subcharts and loops. It is subject of future work to consider in the analysis also hot and cold temperatures in the LSCs as introduced in [5]. Thus for now we don't distinguish between provisional (cold) and mandatory (hot) behavior. Since the set of runs specified by a CFG can be infinite because of the loops, we extract a finite set of runs to analyze by only considering runs that traverse a node in a CFG a tunable finite number of times. Note that runs described by a CFG may not always be runs generated by the corresponding LSC because CFGs abstract from conditions specified in LSCs. This may generate false alarms that can be removed though by checking in the original LSC if the problematic run really occurs.

Definition 11 (LSC and GT unfolding). *Given an LSC l, we define $U_k(cfg(l))$ as the LSC unfolding consisting of all possible runs generated by l that traverse a same node in $cfg(l)$ at most k times. Given $U_k(cfg(l)) = \{ex_1, \ldots, ex_n\}$, where $ex_i = \langle M_{S,1}, \ldots, M_{S,n_i} \rangle$ is a sequence of system messages representing a path in the CFG, each ex_i can be mapped to the corresponding sequence of GT rules $seq_t(ex_i)$ by replacing each message $M_{S,j} = \langle Src_j, Dst_j, (r_{1,j}, r_{2,j}), sync_j \rangle$ in the original sequence with: $r_{1,j}, r_{2,j}$, if $sync = false$ or $r_{1,j} + r_{2,j}$, if $sync = true^2$. Given an LSC l,*

---

² The operator $+$ indicates parallel execution of two rules.

we denote the set of all sequences of GT rules obtained from l by the GT *unfolding*
$seq_t^k(l) = \{seq_t(ex)|ex \in U_k(l)\}.$

Conflicts and Dependencies Between Rules. GT rules cannot be always applied in any order. In some cases, the application of a rule can be necessary to apply other rules, while in other cases the execution of a rule can disable the execution of other rules. For instance, if you remove a planned route, you are not allowed to modify that route anymore. A specification $GTSPEC$ can be analyzed to identify two kinds of relations between rules: conflicts and dependencies. We say that rule g_1 may disable rule g_2 iff g_1 may delete/add state entities that are required/forbidden by g_2 (*conflict*). We say that rule g_1 may cause rule g_2 iff g_1 may delete/add state elements that are forbidden/required by g_2 (*sequential dependency*) [12].

Identification of Suppressed Runs. In order to identify all suppressed runs in a single LSC l we should check which runs belonging to the LSC unfolding $U_k(cfg(l))$ correspond to sequences of GT rules in the GT unfolding $seq_t^k(l)$ which are inconsistent, i.e., that cannot be applied to the system state. In [13] criteria are formulated which ensure the applicability of GT rule sequences. If these criteria are fulfilled, the rule sequence is applicable. We call these sequences *non-suspicious.* Thus we only have to analyze rule sequences which do not fulfill the above-mentioned criteria and we call them *suspicious sequences.* The set of suppressed runs in an LSC is then a subset of the set of runs corresponding to suspicious sequences and thus we narrowed down the search analysis.

Definition 12. *[(non-)suspicious sequences]*
A sequence $ex_t = \langle r_1, \ldots, r_i, \ldots, r_j, \ldots, r_n \rangle \in seq_t^k(l)$ is defined to be non-suspicious if it satisfies four criteria: (1) (initialization) the first rule is applicable on the initial system state; (2) $\not\exists r_i$ that can eliminate nodes; (3) (no impeding predecessors) ex_t does not contain a rule r_i that may disable rule r_j and $i < j$; (4) (enabling predecessor) if a rule r_i is not applicable on the initial system state $\exists r_j$ which causes r_i and $j < i$. A sequence is defined to be suspicious if at least one of these criteria is not satisfied.

The third rule guarantees the absence of conflicting operations in the sequence. The fourth rule guarantees that prerequisites for executing an operation are satisfied. The second rule guarantees that no unwanted dangling edges are created by the application of a rule; informally speaking this is similar to guaranteeing that no undesired null references are generated in the state of an object-oriented system.

If a rule sequence is suspicious it has to be further investigated in order to find out if the corresponding run is really a suppressed one. This can be done by trying to construct a *concurrent rule* for the sequence. The concurrent rule of a rule sequence $\langle r_1, \ldots, r_n \rangle$ for rules with NACs is constructed as described in [14] (unique matching guarantees uniqueness of the concurrent rule). If the construction is valid, the run is consistent; if it is not the run will be a suppressed one. These identified suppressed runs can now be presented to the expert user (or user) who can decide (with means of an automatic correction mechanism as explained in the next paragraph) if it should be suppressed or it should be part of the intended behavior and should be repaired.

Note that the search for suppressed runs can be further optimized by using shift equivalence as described in [7] and explained also in [13]. Shift equivalence determines equivalent classes of GT rule sequences. Two sequences are in a same class if their application produces the same result and one can be obtained from the other by iteratively switching rules. This means that it is sufficient to analyze one sequence for each class, and avoid analysis of sequences that can be obtained by switching rules.

We can identify now two classes of problematic LSCs: erroneous LSCs and LSCs containing warnings. An LSC is said to be *erroneous* if it never produces any feasible behavior. For instance, an LSC that removes the user *admin* from a system and then performs an action that requires the rights of an *admin* to be completed cannot ever be successfully completed. An LSC includes *warnings* if it includes suppressed runs that should be investigated further, but others that are consistent. For instance, consider an LSC including a message that removes a route with a given identifier from a planned trip and a message that modifies the same route. If the second message can be exchanged after the first, this can be the reason for a suppressed run or warning.

Definition 13 (erroneous LSC, LSC with warnings). *An LSC l is erroneous if it only contains suppressed runs. This means that each suspicious sequence in the GT unfolding $seq_t^k(l)$ corresponds to a suppressed run in the LSC unfolding $U_k(cfg(l))$. A LSC l contains a* warning(s) *if a suspicious sequence(s) in $seq_t^k(l)$ corresponds to a suppressed run in $U_k(cfg(l))$, but at least one consistent run in $U_k(cfg(l))$ exists.*

Example 8. Our analysis technique signaled an inconsistency in the LSC in Fig. 1 (a) in the else branch to the condition *Jam=false*. There are two messages in this branch, one to forbid the use of the car and one to remove the selected route. However the route is selected only in the if branch, thus there is no route to remove. This run is suspicious because condition (2) of Def. 12 does not hold for the message *deselectRoute(Route)*. Since a concurrent rule cannot be determined, this run is inconsistent, thus a warning is generated.

Third Result: Consistency Analysis of Multiple LSCs. Multiple LSCs can be analyzed by composing LSCs, i.e., considering the LSCs that can be activated by another LSC, and then analyzing the composition with techniques for analyzing single LSCs. Unfortunately, this approach may suffer from scalability problems.

In our case, we can largely benefit from working with reactive systems, i.e., systems in which executions are triggered by user interactions. This is important information because any execution can only be triggered by user inputs. In our integrated model, user inputs coincide with messages going from the user to the application. Therefore, we can limit the analysis of multiple LSCs to composed executions that can be obtained by starting from an LSC with a pre-chart that exclusively includes user inputs and considers the LSCs that it can recursively activate, instead of considering the composition of all LSCs. The analysis of single LSCs can be directly applied to the analysis of multiple LSCs by extending the unfolding process to the activation of other LSCs. According to the experience reported at the end of this section, this optimization makes the analysis feasible without loss of information.

Example 9. In case of pollution, the LSC shown in Fig. 1 (c) activates the LSC in Fig. 1 (b), thus bike is selected if the temperature is high enough. If there is also no traffic jam, the LSC in Fig. 1 (a) selects car as transportation mean. However, bike has been already selected and the run includes an inconsistency. The inconsistency is due to the application of two rules with conflicts, $forbidMeans(Car)$ and $setMeans(Car)$. In fact, a concurrent rule expressing the application of both runs cannot be built.

Correction Mechanisms. When either a warning or error is identified, our technique can automatically suggest possible corrective actions which can be presented in a suitable way also to end users. Candidate solutions are generated depending from the reason of the inconsistency. For example, if a sequence of GT rules $ex_t = \langle r_1, \ldots, r_n \rangle \in seq_t^k(lsc)$ includes rules r_i and r_j leading to the non-satisfaction of criterion 3 in Def.12 our technique automatically generates a new sequence ex_t' obtained by applying any of the following strategies: (1) switch r_i and r_j, (2) delete r_i or r_j and (3) add a message r, which overrides the effect of r_i, between r_i and r_j. If necessary, expert users can play-in tailored solutions to address conflicts between system messages. If now the new sequence ex_t' corresponds to a consistent run, our technique proposes the solution to the user. If the user accepts the solution, our system applies the corrective action applied on the sequence to the faulty LSC. Afterwards, we compute the unfolding of both the modified and the updated LSC and we present the set of behaviors that have been removed and added as a consequence of the modification to the user. Finally, to detect possible side effects of the change, the new version of the integrated model is analyzed to find eventual problems due to the interplay of multiple LSCs. If no problems are detected, the change is definitive.

Example 10. Our technique can automatically correct the problem presented in Example 8 by deleting the message *deselectRoute(Route)*. A correction mechanism for the Example described in Example 9 could be to delete the rule $forbidMeans(Car)$ from LSC (c) in Fig. 1. Moreover the following tailored solution proposed by the expert user for the conflict described in Example 9 could be accepted by the end user as a possible reconfiguration. The rule $forbidMeans(car)$ is weakened to a rule $warning(pollution)$ which warns the user about pollution day instead of forbidding him to use his car.

Early Validation. We used an integrated model to describe the PMM system [1] and we analyzed the model for consistency. Validation highlighted effectiveness of both switch equivalence and selection of suspicious sequences. In fact, single LSCs generated 8 sequences to be analyzed, which have been reduced to 1 by selection of suspicious sequences. This suspicious sequence is generated by the LSC in Figure 1 (a) and resulted to be inconsistent as described in Example 8 and corrected as described in Example 10. Thus, we verified again consistency of single LSCs and we analyzed multiple LCSs. Since we do not have complete tool support yet, we limited the analysis of multiple LSCs to pairs of LSCs. When analyzing multiple LSCs, the three LSCs in Figure 1 generated 194 sequences to be analyzed. Switch equivalence reduced the sequences from 194 to 5. Selection of suspicious sequences further reduced to 2 the sequences to be analyzed. These sequences resulted to be inconsistent. They are generated by the interplay of LSC (a) and LSC (b) as explained in Example 9. The use of both selection of suspicious sequences and switch equivalence demonstrated the scalability of the analysis technique.

5 Related Work and Conclusions

Other work suitably integrated multiple formalisms to describe aspects related to both data and interactions, even if not specifically designed to describe interactions in service-based applications. Harel et al. integrated LSCs with statecharts [15] in order to synthesize the behavior of a set of LSCs. Whittle et al. integrated sequence charts and OCL to synthesize into statecharts the behavior of component-based systems [16]. Statecharts describe state changes of objects, but, in contrast with graph transformations, they cannot specify how the object structure, i.e., the object graph, of an application changes. Therefore it is not possible to exploit the available analysis techniques for graph transformation to reveal inconsistencies. Finally, several work integrated UML-based dynamic models, e.g., activity and sequence diagrams with GTs in different application domains. FuJaBa integrates story diagrams (a kind of activity diagrams) with graph transformations to obtain a result close to the one presented in this paper [17]. Mehner et al. integrated activity diagrams and GTs to describe aspect-oriented software [18]. The former technique does not support an analysis similar to the one described in our approach. The latter supports consistency checks, but does not formally describe the operational semantics of the integrated specification, thus it does not support automated code generation. Moreover, activity and story diagrams do not allow to specify several features inherent to LSCs, such as cold/hot features and prechart/mainchart structure.

In this paper, we presented a formal framework for a model-based approach for the development of highly-customizable reactive service-based applications. The technique is based on the integration of the visual languages LSCs and GTs. Main results of this paper are the specification and semantics of the integrated model together with early analysis techniques revealing inconsistencies. Based on this formal framework it is possible to iteratively develop distributed service-based applications by incrementally modifying the specification, collecting feedbacks from the analysis of the specification and adapting the desired behavior as soon as individual user requirements change. The technique has been experienced with a service-based system for the management of personal mobility information. The formal framework as presented in the paper has been worked out for this service-based application. The empirical experience provided confidence over the capability to manage realistic applications.

In the future, we aim to push forward the complete development of prototype tools enabling a comfortable play-in of the system behavior or system reconfigurations together with a suitable play-out (visualization + code generation) of the system behavior together with analysis results and corresponding correction mechanisms.

References

1. Lorenzoli, D., Mussino, S., Pezzè, M., Schilling, D., Sichel, A., Tosi, D.: A soa-based self-adaptive personal mobility manager. In: IEEE Conference on Service Computing (2006)
2. Nguyen, T.N.: Model-based version and configuration management for a web engineering lifecycle. In: 15th international conference on World Wide Web (2006)
3. Brambilla, M., Ceri, S., Fraternali, P., Manolescu, I.: Process modeling in web applications. ACM Transactions on Software Engineering and Methodology 15(4), 360–409 (2006)

4. Lambers, L., Ehrig, H., Mariani, L., Pezzè, M.: Iterative model-driven development of adaptable service-based applications. In: Proceedings of the International Conference on Automated Software Engineering (2007)

5. Damm, W., Harel, D.: Lscs: Breathing life into message sequence charts. Formal Methods in System Design 19(1), 45–80 (2001)

6. Ehrig, H., Ehrig, K., Prange, U., Taentzer, G.: Fundamentals of Algebraic Graph Transformation. EATCS Monographs in Theoretical Computer Science. Springer, Heidelberg (2006)

7. Ehrig, H., Engels, G., Kreowski, H.-J., Rozenberg, G. (eds.): Handbook of Graph Grammars and Computing by Graph Transformation, vol. 1. World Scientific, Singapore (1999)

8. Annegret Habel, R.H., Taentzer, G.: Graph grammars with negative application conditions. Fundamenta Informaticae 26, 287–313 (1996)

9. Kuske, S., Gogolla, M., Kollmann, R., Kreowski, H.-J.: An integrated semantics for uml class, object and state diagrams based on graph transformation. In: Third International Conference on Integrated Formal Methods. LNCS, Springer, Heidelberg (2002)

10. Baresi, L., Heckel, R.: Tutorial introduction to graph transformation: a software engineering perspective. In: Corradini, A., Ehrig, H., Kreowski, H.-J., Rozenberg, G. (eds.) ICGT 2002. LNCS, vol. 2505, Springer, Heidelberg (2002)

11. Harel, D., Marelly, R.: Come, Let's Play - Scenario-Based Programming Using LSCs and the Play-Engine. Springer, Heidelberg (2003)

12. Hausmann, J., Heckel, R., Taentzer, G.: Detecting conflicting functional requirements in a use case driven approach: a static analysis technique based on graph transformation. In: International Conference on Software Engineering (2002)

13. Lambers, L., Ehirg, H., Taentzer, G.: How to ensure or eliminate the applicability of a sequence of rules. In: Proceedings of the Seventh International Workshop on Graph Transformation and Visual Modeling Techniques, EASST (submitted, 2008)

14. Lambers, L., Ehrig, H., Orejas, F., Prange, U.: Parallelism and concurrency in adhesive high-level replacement systems with negative application conditions, ENTCS (to appear, 2008)

15. Harel, D., Kugler, H., Pnueli, A.: Synthesis revisited: Generating statechart models from scenario-based requirements. In: Formal Methods in Software and Systems Modeling, pp. 309–324 (2005)

16. Whittle, J., Schumann, J.: Generating statechart designs from scenarios (2000)

17. Fujaba Developer Team: Fujaba home page (2005), http://www.fujaba.de

18. Mehner, K., Monga, M., Taentzer, G.: Interaction analysis in aspect-oriented models. In: proceedings of the IEEE International Requirements Engineering Conference (2006)

Language-Based Optimisation of Sensor-Driven Distributed Computing Applications

Jonathan J. Davies, Alastair R. Beresford, and Alan Mycroft

Computer Laboratory, University of Cambridge,
15 JJ Thomson Avenue, Cambridge, CB3 0FD, UK
Firstname.Lastname@cl.cam.ac.uk

Abstract. In many distributed computing paradigms, especially sensor networks and ubiquitous computing but also grid computing and web services, programmers commonly tie their application to a particular set of processors. This can lead to poor utilisation of resources causing increased compute time, wasted network bandwidth or poor battery life, particularly if later changes to the architecture or application render early decisions inappropriate. This paper describes a system which separates application code from the description of the resources available to execute it. Our framework and prototype compiler determines the best location to execute different parts of the distributed application. In addition, our language encourages the programmer to structure data, and the operations performed on it, as monoids and monoid homomorphisms. This approach enables the compiler to apply particular program transformations in a semantically-safe way, and therefore further increase the flexibility of the assignment of application tasks to available resources.

1   Introduction

Sensor networks [1] are composed of many low-power computer nodes; each node contains one or more sensors, a small processor and one or more methods of communication. Nodes collaborate to collect, process and distribute data from their own sensors as well as data from other nodes. The ultimate goal of a sensor network is to deliver a pertinent *summary* of the raw sensor data to a sink node or gateway. For example, raw temperature readings from sensors might be summarised into minimum, mean and maximum values. Raw data is not delivered to the gateway since either the available network bandwidth makes it infeasible or the power budget of the sensor nodes makes it undesirable.

When building sensor networks today, a programmer will typically take a sensor platform such as the Mica Mote and write code for the platform directly in a low-level language such as nesC [2]. This approach to systems building results in *early physical binding* since the programmer must decide at design time the places at which data is processed and summarised. This can lead to poor utilisation of resources, such as increased compute time, wasted network bandwidth or poor battery life, particularly if later changes to the architecture or application render early decisions inappropriate. This paper describes a system which separates application code from the description of the resources available to execute it.

J. Fiadeiro and P. Inverardi (Eds.): FASE 2008, LNCS 4961, pp. 407–422, 2008.
© Springer-Verlag Berlin Heidelberg 2008

This allows *late physical binding* of the application since the components of the application can be optimised for execution on available resources after the components have been written or modified.

This work is not only relevant to sensor networks. Ubiquitous computing envisions an era when computers "weave themselves into the fabric of everyday life until they are indistinguishable from it" [3]. Such a system requires sensors to gather information about the real world in order to interact seamlessly with its inhabitants. In addition, our work is applicable to on-going research in Grid Computing [4] which utilises data and processing capabilities in many different physical locations and across organisational boundaries. Grid Computing enables scientists to write programs which are distributed over multiple computers and access repositories of data which are sufficiently large that moving programs onto processors near the data source is much easier than moving the data itself. We believe there is a strong analogy between the requirement to fix sensors at a particular physical location in a sensor network and the position of a petabyte data store in the Grid: both are infeasible to move.

When introducing web services as components of the Semantic Web, Berners-Lee et al. describe a scenario where a patient wishes to book an appointment with a doctor [5], necessitating the sharing of calendar data. Determining what data should be transferred where is not obvious: for example, should appropriate diary times be transferred to the doctor's computer for comparison, or to the patient's? Here a qualitative measure of 'confidentiality' might replace latency or bandwidth as a metric for optimal placement.

Our approach allows application programmers in these fields to define the tasks which constitute a program separately from the topology of the network of processors and data sources. The tasks are described in such a way (Sect. 2) that permits late binding to processors by our compiler. Our language encourages programmers to identify particular kinds of program task to allow the program to be analysed and to determine whether particular program transformations can be performed safely. These transformations (Sect. 2.2) enable the program to be better-suited to execution in a particular network of processors. We observe that sensor data often forms a *monoid* and exploit this in both the language design and the optimisation framework. We then describe the syntax of the language (Sect. 3) and the implementation of the compiler (Sect. 3.3).

2   Computational Model

Applications in sensor networks usually involve executing a set of tasks to collate, process and distribute sensor-related information, where a task is a set of instructions which must be executed sequentially on a single processor. Our aim is to make tasks and the datatypes they operate over (i) simple to specify and (ii) structured so that program optimisations are possible.

Formally, we model the tasks representing an algorithm as a directed graph $G^t = (E^t, V^t)$ called the *task graph*. The set of vertices, V^t, are the tasks and the edges, E^t, indicate the direction of data flow between tasks. An edge (v_1, v_2)

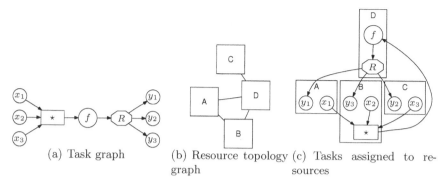

(a) Task graph   (b) Resource topology (c) Tasks assigned to re-
                      graph   sources

Fig. 1. Example graphs

indicates that task v_2 receives the output of task v_1, and that v_2 cannot com-
mence execution until the execution of v_1 is complete. An example is shown
in Fig. 1(a). We define algorithms in terms of six kinds of task. These differ in
terms of the type and number of inputs and outputs, and are sufficient to express
any algorithm. We present them intuitively first, then explain the underpinning
theory.

Source tasks are points where data is produced, drawn as circles. A source
task has no inputs and one output. Although they only have one output
edge, multiple values can be emitted in a sequential fashion. In other words,
a source task produces a stream of values. For example, in a sensor network,
a thermometer which outputs the temperature once per minute is modelled
as a source task.

Sink tasks are points where data is consumed, drawn as circles. A sink task
has one input and no outputs.

Processing tasks are functions which transform data of one type to another
type, and are drawn as circles.

Merge tasks are functions which combine two items of data of a particular type
into a single value of that type, and are drawn as rectangles. A merge task
has two inputs, a single output and is commutative and associative. More
than two items of data can be combined into a single value by chaining
several merge tasks together in any order. For convenience, we draw a chain
of merge tasks combining n items of data as a single n-ary task.

Merge tasks are particularly important in applications where a large number of input values from different sources need to be processed, such as sensor
networks or grid computing. Because of the wealth of input data, it is usually
necessary to be able to aggregate data into a significantly smaller amount of
information to make their processing and interpretation more manageable.

Because merge nodes combine data which may have different data rates
and sensor applications must be resilient to the failure of a subset of sensors,
each merge chain can be given a specified timeout after which it produces a
result based on the available inputs.

Split tasks are functions which decompose a single item of data of a particular
type into two values of that same type, and are drawn as rectangles. These
values must be constructed such that, when fed into a merge task, the original
item of data is yielded. Thus, split tasks can be thought of as the inverse of
merge tasks. As with merge tasks, an item of data can be split into more
than two parts by chaining several split tasks, and we draw such a chain as
a single n-ary task.

Split tasks allow large items of data to be *partitioned* into smaller items
so that computation can be performed in parallel. This permits a *divide-
and-conquer* approach to data processing.

Replication tasks are functions which copy a value into a pair of identical
values, and are drawn as octagons. A replication task thus has a single input
and two outputs. As before, a chain of replication tasks can be constructed
in order to generate more than two replicas of a value, and is drawn as a
single n-ary replication task.

Datatypes are defined in terms of underlying sets from which values are drawn
(e.g. the natural numbers) along with operations, or tasks, that may be performed on them.

Some datatypes which hold values of type T also have a binary operation $\star$:
$T \times T \to T$ which is associative and commutative, and have an identity element
$i \in T$ such that $\forall a \in T . i \star a = a$. The identity element denotes the datatype's
'empty' value. These datatypes are of particular interest because their operation
$\star$ is equivalent to the definition of merge tasks above. Thus, using $\star$, several items
of data of the same type can be combined into a single item of that type.

Such a datatype is modelled mathematically as a *commutative monoid* $(T, \star, i)$.
Some examples of simple commutative monoids are set union $(\mathcal{P}(S), \cup, \emptyset)$, addition $(\mathbb{R}, +, 0)$ and maximisation $(\mathbb{R}, \max, -\infty)$. We refer to these datatypes as
being *mergeable*. Associativity and commutativity reflect the idea of summaris-
ing data from a *set* of physically distributed sensors.

Since a split task for a particular datatype is an inverse of its merge task, it
follows that mergeable datatypes necessarily support split operations. By analogy with the monoid $(\mathbb{N}, \times, 1)$, where merging is multiplication, splitting is factorisation into a pair of factors. Note that while splitting merely needs to be
a right-inverse for merge, and therefore many split operations may exist for a
given merge operation $\star$, we will nonetheless use the notation $\star^{-1}$.

In an application which processes data, it is not always enough to manipulate
data within a single type, so functions $f : T_1 \to T_2$, where $T_1 \neq T_2$, are necessary in order to transform data into a new type. We refer to such functions
as *processing* functions. An example of a processing function is list2hist which
converts a multiset of temperature readings (encoded as a list) into a histogram.

A processing function f is a *monoid homomorphism* if it transforms data from
one monoid $(S, \star, i_1)$ into data from another monoid $(T, \otimes, i_2)$ whilst satisfying
two properties:

$$f(i_1) = i_2, \tag{1}$$
$$f(a \star b) = f(a) \otimes f(b). \tag{2}$$

An example of a monoid homomorphism is a function $f(x) = e^x$ from monoid $(\mathbb{N}, +, 0)$ to monoid $(\mathbb{R}, \times, 1)$. It is trivial to check that $f(0) = 1$ and $f(a + b) = f(a)f(b)$. A more realistic example is list2hist above.

Monoids (identifying merge tasks) and homomorphisms (enabling certain transformations—see below) are marked syntactically. Programmers are expected to identify which datatypes and functions are appropriate to treat in these ways. We believe that programmers will be able to easily identify these in everyday applications. In the worst case, when these are overlooked, this merely results in a smaller range of placement optimisations being available to the compiler.

In practice, the constraints of computation mean that real implementations of datatypes are not necessarily perfect monoids. For example, addition and multiplication are only approximately associative in floating point arithmetic, thus we cannot faithfully implement the monoid $(\mathbb{R}, +, 0)$. Similarly, certain thresholding operations, e.g. $f(a) = \lfloor a \rfloor$, do not satisfy property (2) to be homomorphisms; timeouts further complicate the issue. Nevertheless, we expect programmers to identify these as monoids to reap the benefits that brings; a formal treatment would involve adding a metric space structure to monoids and adding a continuity requirement for homomorphisms and then to argue that the approximate behaviour is 'close enough' for a given application.

2.1   Example

In sensor networks, it is common to want to find the arithmetic mean of a large number of sensor readings. The centralised approach would gather and sum all the readings at the sink node and divide by the number of readings received. Partitioning the problem into smaller subsets of readings means that we can reach an answer using less energy or more quickly as several additions can be executed in parallel. However, the arithmetic means of arbitrary, distinct subsets of readings cannot be readily combined into the overall mean, because the number of readings contributing to each subset's mean is lost. A solution to this problem is to keep a running total of the number of readings in each partition. Adopting this approach, we can express the arithmetic mean of a set of numeric values by employing two processing functions—one a homomorphism, the other not.

A set of real numbers is represented by the monoid $(\mathcal{P}(\mathbb{R}), \cup, \emptyset)$. We use an intermediate monoid $(\mathbb{R} \times \mathbb{N}, \oplus, (0, 0))$, where $(a_1, n_1) \oplus (a_2, n_2) \equiv (a_1 + a_2, n_1 + n_2)$, to store the numerator and denominator in the calculation of the arithmetic mean. The homomorphism to convert the set of numbers into this form is

$$h(\emptyset) = (0, 0)$$
$$h(\{x\} \cup xs) = (x, 1) \oplus (h(xs)).$$

Values from this monoid can then be transformed into the desired result using a non-homomorphic function, $g(x, n) = x/n$. An example task graph for this application is depicted in Fig. 2(a). The sum and count of two sets of values are computed by h before being combined by the $\oplus$ merge task. Finally the mean is computed by g.

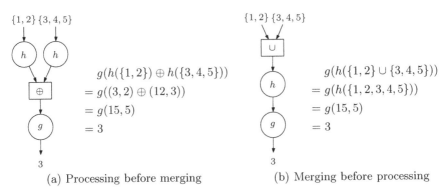

(a) Processing before merging   (b) Merging before processing

Fig. 2. Example task graphs for computing the arithmetic mean of two sets of values in a distributed fashion

2.2   Program Transformation

An advantage of identifying datatypes which are monoids and processing functions which are monoid homomorphisms is that static analysis can be used to transform the program whilst maintaining semantic integrity.

For some programs, it is possible to express the graph of tasks in a variety of semantically-equivalent ways. For example, the task graph shown in Fig. 2(a) can be equivalently expressed as shown in Fig. 2(b). The former is a conversion to numerator-denominator pairs (*processing*) for both of the sets, followed by the summing function $\oplus$ (*merge*), and finally g. The latter is a union operation (*merge*) on the two sets, followed by the conversion by h to the numerator-denominator pair (*processing*), and finally g. The general form of this transformation is depicted graphically in Fig. 3. We refer to this transformation as Merge–Processing.

In general, we note that property (2) above implies that merging before processing will yield the same result as processing before merging *if and only if the processing function is a monoid homomorphism*. This means that it is useful for a programmer to be able to express to a compiler when a processing function is a homomorphism, so the compiler knows when the transformation can be applied and is guaranteed not to affect the semantics of the program.

In the cases where a processing function is not a homomorphism, information is lost when it is executed, and this means that performing merging before processing will not yield the same result as processing before merging. As noted earlier, functions merely approximating homomorphisms will in not in general give bit-identical values, but sufficient for purpose if carefully marked as homomorphisms.

Using the Merge–Processing program transformation has several implications. Firstly, there are more tasks on the right side of the transformation than on the left. Depending on the computational complexity of f, $\star$ and $\otimes$, the overall amount of work involved may be different. Moreover, the volume of data flow

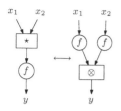   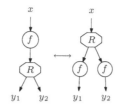   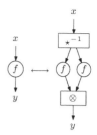

Fig. 3. Merge–Processing   **Fig. 4.** Processing–Replication   **Fig. 5.** Farm

may be affected by the transformation, depending on the relative sizes of the pre- and post-processing datatypes.

To exemplify these differences, consider an application which processes video data and extracts the number of people seen. If there are multiple video cameras, one distributed version of this application could involve appending all of the videos (*merging*) and then running the person-recognition algorithm on it (*processing*). Applying the transformation yields an alternative expression of the application in which the person-recognition algorithm (*processing*) is run on each individual video, and then the number of people are summed to a single value (*merging*). Since video data has a significantly higher data rate than the integer count, there is less network traffic required in the latter version of the algorithm.

2.3 Other Transformations

A second transformation, Processing–Replication, is similar to the transformation described above, but involves swapping the order of processing and replication tasks rather than processing and merge tasks. Rather than performing some processing and then replicating the result, we can replicate the input and process each replica individually. This transformation is depicted in Fig. 4. On the right, the amount of work is doubled and the volume of data flow may be affected.

The symmetry between split tasks and merge tasks gives rise to a transformation called Farm, depicted in Fig. 5. A processing task can be replaced by an array of processing tasks which each tackle a part of the input data. Although the transformation shows only two processing tasks, repeated application of the transformation can give rise to a larger number of processing tasks. This transformation facilitates the parallelisation of data processing, so is applicable to grid computing where a large problem is commonly divided into a number of smaller problems processed in parallel. This paradigm is familiar from popular distributed computing applications such as SETI@Home.

A further transformation, Split–Merge (Fig. 6), follows from the definition of a split task for a particular type as an inverse of the merge task for that type. Transformation Split–Merge is valid because $\forall x.\ \star\ (\star^{-1}(x)) = x$. The final transformation, Replication–Split, involves the exchange of replication and split tasks, shown in Fig. 7. This transformation also preserves the semantics of the program.

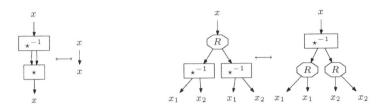

Fig. 6. Split–Merge   **Fig. 7.** Replication–Split

2.4   Task Assignment

As well as describing the program's algorithm as a task graph $G^t = (E^t, V^t)$, the network of processors in which it is to be executed must also be known. Program tasks can then be assigned to a processor for execution.

The network is modelled as a graph $G^n = (E^n, V^n)$, where now vertices V^n model processors and edges E^n model communication links between processors. An example is shown in Fig. 1(b). The processing nodes, which have local memory, are not assumed to be homogeneous in their processing power or communications capabilities.

An assignment function $A : V^t \to V^n$ maps tasks to processing nodes. Source and sink vertices in the task graph must be mapped to the particular nodes in the network where data is produced and consumed, respectively. Other tasks can be mapped to reachable network nodes. An example of an assignment function is shown pictorially in Fig. 1(c), where $\star$ is mapped to processor B and f and R are mapped to processor D.

The decision about which nodes to use impacts on the duration of execution of the algorithm; the privacy of the originators of the data; the amount of network bandwidth consumed; and a variety of other factors. The efficacy of the assignment is described quantitatively by a *cost function* specific to each application. A cost function $C : G^t \times G^n \times (V^t \to V^n) \to \mathbb{R}$ is a function of an assignment function yielding a real number indicating the cost of the assignment. Applications will use a cost function which embodies the trade-offs they desire between relevant metrics. Finding an optimal assignment with respect to a cost function is a well-studied research area [6] and is known to be NP-complete in general; we describe our strategy in Sect. 3.3.

So that a cost function can compute the values of relevant metrics, the graphs G^t and G^n must be weighted. Nodes of the resource graph (processors) are weighted with values describing their computational characteristics, such as processor speed. Edges of the resource graph (communication links) are weighted with values characterising the links, such as maximum throughput or latency. Nodes of the task graph (tasks) are weighted with values describing their requirements, such as the number of instructions constituting them. Edges of the task graph (data flow) are weighted with values characterising the data, such as the size of the data or its level of confidentiality.

3   Language

There are various ways in which the computational model described above could be encoded in a programming language. One approach is task-oriented, in which each processing and merge task is a first-class citizen. Instead, we chose a datatype-oriented approach in which merge tasks and processing tasks are encapsulated in the definitions of the datatypes they operate on. This approach ties in well with the modelling of some datatypes as commutative monoids, with their associated binary operation. For datatypes which can be modelled in this way, it is natural to encapsulate the underlying set, binary operation and identity element in a single logical unit. Processing tasks which can process data of a particular datatype are also encapsulated within that same logical unit. The datatype-oriented approach fits in well with object-orientation (our prototype implementation uses Java).

Along with the datatype definitions, the framework must be supplied with the task graph, the resource graph and a task assignment function. In the current implementation, these are defined in a *co-ordinator* file, although logically they need not be grouped together into a single module. The description of the cost function by which to evaluate an assignment function is described in a separate file. The resource graph is not required at design time; rather, it must be provided just before compilation. Presently, the program must be recompiled whenever the topology changes.

Our compiler uses the task graph and resource graph in the co-ordinator definition in order to derive a total task assignment function mapping each task to the processor found to be most appropriate to execute it. The compiler can then distribute the merge tasks and processing tasks contained in the datatype declarations to the chosen processors.

3.1   Datatype Declarations

Each datatype is defined in its own file and has a syntax built on top of a Java class in our current implementation; this could easily be adapted for use with other languages. Metrics that are used by the cost function to evaluate a mapping are also specified in this file. A datatype is declared using the `datatype` keyword. To facilitate physical redistribution, static methods and static fields (except public static final fields) are not permitted in datatype declarations.

As described above, some datatypes are *mergeable*. Declarations of such datatypes use the `mergeable` modifier to indicate this. Figure 8 shows the datatype declaration for the monoid $(\mathbb{R} \times \mathbb{N}, \oplus, (0,0))$ used in the arithmetic mean example in Sect. 2.1, which is a typical mergeable datatype. The use of the `mergeable` modifier entails three requirements: (1) The datatype is a monoid so must have an identity element. This is implemented by requiring that mergeable datatypes support a constructor which takes no arguments. (2) It must also have a constructor to create a *singleton* instance of the datatype. In other words, a means of wrapping a single element from the underlying set of values must be provided, to allow new items of data to be instantiated. (3) The binary merge

```
mergeable datatype PartialAv {
    private double numer;
    private int denom;

    public PartialAv() [cpu=0, out size=1] {          Identity element, (0,0).
        this(0, 0);
    }

    public PartialAv(double numer, int denom) {       Singleton constructor
        this.numer = numer;                           for choosing a value
        this.denom = denom;                           from ℝ × ℕ.
    }

    public PartialAv merge(PartialAv a)               Merge function, ⊕.
        [cpu=1, out size=sum]                         Cost annotation.
    {
        return new PartialAv(this.numer + a.numer,
            this.denom + a.denom);
    }
                                                       Processing function, g,
    processto Average [cpu=1, out size=1] {            returning an instance of
        return new Average(this.numer / this.denom);  the Average datatype,
    }                                                  not defined here.
}
```

Fig. 8. Datatype declaration representing the monoid $(\mathbb{R} \times \mathbb{N}, \oplus, (0,0))$

operation must be specified. This is implemented by requiring that mergeable datatypes of type α support a publicly visible method merge which takes an argument of type α and returns a value of type α. The merge function is specified such that the expression $a = a_1 \star a_2$ can be expressed in the fashion a = a1.merge(a2).

Some datatypes define an operation to split them into a pair of smaller elements. Whilst it is necessarily true that all mergeable datatypes are also splittable in theory, it may be that the algorithm for implementing splitting is significantly harder to implement than merging. For example, in the monoid $(\mathbb{N}, \times, 1)$, merging is multiplication (easy) but splitting is factorisation (hard). It is also conceivable that the converse is true for some datatypes: it may be much easier to express a split operation than a merge operation. Therefore, it is not mandatory that mergeable datatypes support a split operation. The splittable modifier is used on datatypes which implement a split operation as a publicly visible method which returns a pair of items (currently implemented as an array). Programmers of datatypes that are both mergeable and splittable need to ensure that the split operation is the inverse of the merge operation; in general it is undecidable for a compiler to check this statically, but it can be easily unit tested.

In the computational model, a processing task transforms data of one type into another type. Each datatype thus has zero or more other datatypes into which it can be processed. For each such possibility, the datatype declaration contains the code describing the processing task. These are defined in processto functions, which must each return an object of the target type. In our Java-based implementation, this is implemented in the 'source' datatype's declaration rather than as a constructor in the 'destination' datatype's declaration so that private members of the source datatype can be accessed. Note that the presence of a processing function in a datatype's declaration does not imply that it will necessarily be part of a task graph; it merely indicates that such a function exists. Processing functions which are monoid homomorphisms are marked with the homomorphism keyword, to notify the compiler that transformations appropriate to homomorphisms can be safely applied in applications using this function.

Annotations describing the values of various metrics that are employed by the cost function are required for processto functions, merge functions, split functions and constructors which are used as source tasks. The metrics are specified as a comma-separated list of (*key*, *value*) pairs, enclosed in square brackets, where the key is a string known to the cost function and the value is a simple arithmetic expression. Keys may include the out modifier to indicate that they are metrics characterising data on egress edges from the corresponding node in a task graph. Other values characterise the node itself. For processing functions, egress edge values may use the special value in to refer to the value of the input for the corresponding key. For merge functions, egress edge values may use the special values sum, max, min, avg to refer to the sum, minimum, maximum or average of the input values for the corresponding key.

For example, a merge task may be annotated with cpu=50, out size=sum, out privacy=max to indicate its CPU load; that the size of the output is the sum of the sizes of its inputs; and that the degree of sensitivity with respect to privacy is the largest such from among its inputs.

It is necessary for these annotations to be attached to the definitions of the functions, rather than the task graph, because the compiler is free to apply transformations to the task graph, and needs to know the values of the metrics on nodes and edges which it creates in the graph.

3.2   Co-ordinator Definition

The cornerstone to the programmer's description of an application is the definition of the *co-ordinator*. This file contains the ingredients which describe the application with sufficient flexibility to allow the compiler to determine a strategy for executing it. Although we implement datatype declarations using a Java-like syntax, the co-ordinator language is largely independent of that used in the rest of the application. An example co-ordinator for the temperature-averaging application for three sensors is shown in Fig. 9.

A co-ordinator is defined using the coordinator keyword. It contains three kinds of definition:

Initial task graph. The taskgraph block is used to specify an initial task graph, giving to each task an identifier which has scope throughout the co-ordinator definition. The links between tasks, indicating the direction of data flow, are also specified.

Source tasks can optionally be given a list of arguments which are to be passed to the constructor of its datatype, if any are required. In a sensor network, the source tasks generate the application's input data, so the

```
coordinator CoordAv {
    taskgraph {
        source<TempSet> c0 ["/dev/ttyS0"], c1 ["/dev/ttyS0"], c2 ["/dev/ttyS0"];
        merge<TempSet> m0 [1 => inf, 2 => inf, 3 => inf];
        process<TempSet, PartialAv> p0;
        process<PartialAv, Average> p1;
        sink<Average> s0;

        c0 -> m0; c1 -> m0; c2 -> m0;
        m0 -> p0;
        p0 -> p1;
        p1 -> s0;
    }

    resourcegraph {
        sensor0: 192.168.0.100 [speed => 2];
        sensor1: 192.168.0.101 [speed => 2];
        sensor2: 192.168.0.102 [speed => 2];
        host3:   192.168.0.103 [speed => 10];

        sensor0 -- host3   [bandwidth => 5, latency => 1];
        sensor1 -- sensor0 [bandwidth => 1, latency => 1];
        sensor2 -- host3   [bandwidth => 5, latency => 1];
    }

    mapping {
        c0 -> sensor0;
        c1 -> sensor1;
        c2 -> sensor2;
        s0 -> host3;
    }
}
```

Fig. 9. Example co-ordinator definition for the temperature-averaging application

arguments can be used to create an instance of the source datatype appropriate to each source task.

Merge tasks specified in the task graph can be annotated with an array of timeouts. For an n-ary merge task, timeouts are specified for each number of potential inputs received from 1 to n. The timeout for m inputs indicates the longest duration of time the task should wait after having received $m - 1$ input values for the next. The special value inf denotes an infinite duration, implying that it is not acceptable for the merge task to produce an output without having received further input values. The value 0 denotes that no further inputs are necessary. If no timeouts are specified, it is assumed that the timeout for all numbers of inputs up to and including n are infinite. (Infinite timeouts are generally undesirable in sensor networks as the failure of one sensor should not prevent the system from producing output.)

Resource graph. The resourcegraph block defines the processors in the network (four are used in Fig. 9) and the connections between them. An identifier and the hostname is specified for each, along with the values of metrics that are employed by the cost function. For each communication link, values of metrics that are employed by the cost function are specified.

Base mapping. The mapping block specifies an assignment function from tasks to processors. The assignment function derived by a compiler is only permitted to be a superset of the mapping specified here. This is particularly relevant in sensor networks, where a source task must execute on a particular processor because it has the sensor to be sampled, and where a sink task must execute on a particular processor because it needs to know the result of the processing. However, this feature can also be used by the programmer to lock other code to a particular processor if desired.

3.3 Current Implementation

In our current implementation we use Polyglot [7] to translate the co-ordinator definition to instantiate appropriate instances of datatype declarations and generate standard Java source code. The Java source code is then compiled using a conventional Java compiler, producing a JAR file for each processor.

During compilation, the compiler analyses the task graph and the resource graph to determine the best locations to execute the tasks. As part of this process, the annotations associated with processors and communication links in the co-ordinator file are combined with the cost function to determine the relative suitability of any particular mapping of tasks to processors. As noted earlier this is a well-studied area, and we have not developed a state-of-the-art assignment algorithm, but have used a simple technique [8] to explore both task assignment and program transformation simultaneously. In our solution, we initially assign all unmapped tasks to reachable nodes with the largest aggregate connectivity. We then use a method of steepest descent to iteratively search for improvements in two phases: firstly, we determine all possible immediate program transformations; secondly, for every program transformation we consider moving each task in turn to alternative processors in the resource graph. Finally we select the program transformation and task movement combination with the lowest cost as the starting point for our next search iteration. We terminate our search when no further improvements can be found.

The current implementation automatically generates Java RMI code to enable inter-task communication. For sensor networks, RMI is not ideal, since this approach requires a central RMI registry to be present, but this could easily be replaced by an alternative communications paradigm.

4   Related Work

In Web Services, the Business Process Execution Language (BPEL) [9] is used to describe high-level 'business protocols': stateful workflows between web services. This standard aims to separate the deployment information (where the services are executed) from the description of the protocol. Thus, an application specified in BPEL supports late binding to physical resources, as any resource supporting a particular interface could be employed to execute a task.

The Grid Computing paradigm tends to identify networks of computers as either *compute grids* or *data grids*. Compute grids involve participating computers running an execution environment into which jobs are sent by a co-ordinator, to allow an application to benefit from parallelisation. Data grids are common in the scientific community where a large corpus of data is made available to collaborators across the globe. In data grids, the question of where data integration and processing is done is paramount. So as not to incur large volumes of network traffic, processing is moved close to the data. The OGSA-DAI framework [10] achieves this using a scripting language whose programs are sent over the grid and executed close to the data. The idea of moving processing close to a data source is a particular case of the general principle of optimising the arrangement of tasks envisioned in this paper; a fixed sensor node can be thought of in the same way as a large, immovable corpus of data.

Ennals et al. describe an approach to programming network processors using a domain-specific language PacLang which permits the description of applications in an architecturally-neutral fashion [11]. An Architecture Mapping Script describes which core should execute which application task, in a similar fashion to a co-ordinator file. Furthermore, a set of transformations can be applied to enable programs to be partitioned into different arrangements of tasks, to allow the program to be better-suited to execution on a particular architecture. This work exploited linear types as the basis for the transformations; we have adopted the approach of modelling datatypes as monoids to similar effect, although these approaches are not mutually exclusive.

Program transformations are also exploited to aid task assignment in distributed query processing. It is the job of a query optimiser [12] to choose the best strategy for executing a distributed database query; this may involve rewriting the query.

Kremer et al. have implemented a compiler framework to allow an application which would otherwise run solely on a mobile device to be off-loaded onto a server [13]. Similar work has been undertaken by Li et al. at the function-call level [14] and by Ou et al. at the Java bytecode level [15]. These are specific instances of the kind of application considered in this paper, but they do not consider whether applications can be transformed to permit parallelised execution.

In sensor networks, J-Orchestra [16] is a system which automatically partitions applications into tasks, and allows developers to manually assign tasks amongst machines. The Titan framework [17] has been designed to permit dynamic reconfiguration of which processors execute which tasks for body-area sensor networks.

Some of the theoretical underpinnings of our work were greatly inspired by Afshar's use of monoids and monoid homomorphisms in parallel data-processing applications [18].

5   Conclusion

We have created a language which can be used to write applications for distributed systems. The separation of the task definitions from a notion of where in the system they are to be executed allows a compiler to derive a mapping of tasks to processors. This mapping can be improved by performing various program transformations that change the task graph. Programmers are encouraged to express datatypes as monoids and functions as homomorphisms to enable safe use of a wider range of task placement transformations.

We have approached this work from the direction of sensor networks, but we believe that our ideas are more globally applicable. It is already evident that some concepts are readily applicable to Ubiquitous Computing, Grid Computing and Web Services. We hope that this work is a stepping-stone towards a full calculus with primitives that encompass all of these paradigms.

We have assumed a static network topology. In practice, many sensor networks contain mobile nodes, meaning that an initially optimal assignment of tasks may quickly become sub-optimal. Similarly, in practice, nodes and communication links will fail. A simple adaptation of our work would be to collect nodes into logical groups from which nodes can leave and join, but where the characteristics of each group remain largely constant. In addition, we have assumed a single, omniscient co-ordinator, which is impractical, and therefore we plan to investigate a distributed approach to co-ordination.

The examples used in this paper have been kept simple to ease comprehension. We believe that it is more generally applicable to larger applications; the application which inspired this work was the automatic generation of road maps based on sensor data collected from road vehicles [19]. This application was originally implemented in a non-distributed fashion in Java; we realised that in order to make it distributed a lot of boiler-plate code would be required which could be generated automatically. Furthermore, we realised that it was inappropriate to make task placement decisions at design-time. We are in the process of re-implementing this application using our framework.

Acknowledgments. The authors gratefully acknowledge the support and vision of Andy Hopper and comments and suggestions from Andrew Rice and the anonymous reviewers. We are also grateful for the financial support provided by EPSRC.

References

1. Akyildiz, I.F., Su, W., Sankarasubramaniam, Y., Cayirci, E.: Wireless sensor networks: a survey. Computer Networks 38, 393–422 (2002)
2. Gay, D., Levis, P., von Behren, R., Welsh, M., Brewer, E., Culler, D.: The nesC language: A holistic approach to networked embedded systems. In: Proceedings of Programming Language Design and Implementation (PLDI), pp. 1–11 (2003)
3. Weiser, M.: The computer for the 21st century. Scientific American 365(3), 94–104 (1991)
4. Foster, I., Kesselman, C., Nick, J.M., Tuecke, S.: Grid services for distributed system integration. IEEE Computer 35(6), 37–46 (2002)
5. Berners-Lee, T., Hendler, J., Lassila, O.: The semantic web. Scientific American 284(5), 28–37 (2001)
6. Kwok, Y.K., Ahmad, I.: Static scheduling algorithms for allocating directed task graphs to multiprocessors. ACM Computing Surveys 31(4), 406–471 (1999)

7. Nystrom, N., Clarkson, M.R., Myers, A.C.: Polyglot: An extensible compiler framework for Java. In: Hedin, G. (ed.) CC 2003. LNCS, vol. 2622, pp. 138–152. Springer, Heidelberg (2003)
8. Davies, J.J., Beresford, A.R.: Scalable, inter-vehicular applications. In: Meersman, R., Tari, Z., Herrero, P. (eds.) OTM-WS 2007, Part II. LNCS, vol. 4806, pp. 876–885. Springer, Heidelberg (2007)
9. Business Process Execution Language for Web Services: Version 1.1 (2003), http://www-106.ibm.com/developerworks/webservices/library/ws-bpel/
10. Antonioletti, M., Atkinson, M., Baxter, R., Borley, A., Chue Hong, N.P., Collins, B., Hardman, N., Hume, A.C., Knox, A., Jackson, M., Krause, A., Laws, S., Magowan, J., Paton, N.W., Pearson, D., Sugden, T., Watson, P., Westhead, M.: The design and implementation of grid database services in OGSA-DAI. Concurrency and Computation: Practice and Experience 17, 357–376 (2005)
11. Ennals, R., Sharp, R., Mycroft, A.: Task partitioning for multi-core network processors. In: Bodik, R. (ed.) CC 2005. LNCS, vol. 3443, pp. 76–90. Springer, Heidelberg (2005)
12. Ioannidis, Y.E.: Query optimization. ACM Computing Surveys 28(1), 121–123 (1996)
13. Kremer, U., Hicks, J., Rehg, J.H.: A compilation framework for power and energy management on mobile computers. Technical Report DCS-TR-446, Rutgers University (2001)
14. Li, Z., Wang, C., Xu, R.: Computation offloading to save energy on handheld devices: A partition scheme. In: CASES 2001, pp. 238–246. ACM Press, New York (2001)
15. Ou, S., Yang, K., Liotta, A.: An adaptive multi-constraint partitioning algorithm for offloading in pervasive systems. In: PerCom 2006, pp. 116–125 (2006)
16. Liogkas, N., MacIntyre, B., Mynatt, E.D., Smaragdakis, Y., Tilevich, E., Voida, S.: Automatic partitioning for prototyping ubiquitous computing applications. IEEE Pervasive Computing 3(3), 40–47 (2004)
17. Lombriser, C., Roggen, D., Stäger, M., Tröster, G.: Titan: A tiny task network for dynamically reconfigurable heterogeneous sensor networks. In: Kommunikation in Verteilten Systemen (KiVS), Informatik aktuell, pp. 127–138. Springer, Heidelberg (2007)
18. Afshar, M.: An Open Parallel Architecture for Data-intensive Applications. PhD thesis. Technical Report UCAM-CL-TR-459, University of Cambridge (1999)
19. Davies, J.J., Beresford, A.R., Hopper, A.: Scalable, distributed, real-time map generation. IEEE Pervasive Computing 5(4), 47–54 (2006)

Clint: A Composition Language Interpreter (Tool Paper)

Javier Cámara, Gwen Salaün, and Carlos Canal

Department of Computer Science, Universidad de Málaga, Spain
{jcamara,salaun,canal}@lcc.uma.es

1 Introduction

Composition of components or services is a crucial issue when building new applications by reusing existing pieces of software. This task turns out to be tedious when behavioural descriptions, acknowledged as one of the essential parts of component interfaces, are taken into account. Furthermore, mismatches may exist between component interfaces, and adaptation [2] is necessary to help the designer to solve them.

In this tool paper, we present Clint, a composition language interpreter. Clint accepts as inputs (i) behavioural interfaces described using Labelled Transition Systems (LTSs), and (ii) a composition specification. The latter is described using vectors that make explicit component interactions, and an LTS labelled with vectors to define an order on the application of some interactions [5] (important to solve some specific mismatch cases). Clint implements step-by-step simulation for the aforementioned inputs, as well as techniques to validate the composition specification, avoiding undesirable situations such as unexplored parts of the composition or deadlock states.

In the remainder of this paper, Section 2 introduces behavioural interfaces and composition specifications. In Section 3, the main functionalities of Clint are presented. Section 4 draws up some concluding remarks.

2 Behavioural Interfaces, Composition and Adaptation

Behavioural interfaces of components are described using par-LTSs (A, S, I, F, T) [4], referred to as LTSs in the rest of the paper for short, where A is a set of labels called alphabet representing message emissions and receptions (respectively written using ! and ?), S is a set of states (either basic or concurrent), $I \in S$ is the initial state, $F \subseteq S$ are final states, and $T \subseteq S \times A \times S$ are transitions. Par-LTSs extend basic LTSs by taking into account concurrent behaviours. This is achieved by introducing *concurrent states*. These states are identified by two or more labels, one for each concurrent branch.

A *composition specification* describes composition constraints and adaptation requirements. *Vectors* relate messages used in different components to implement interactions. A vector for a set of components C_i with $i \in \{1, .., n\}$, is a tuple

J. Fiadeiro and P. Inverardi (Eds.): FASE 2008, LNCS 4961, pp. 423–427, 2008.
© Springer-Verlag Berlin Heidelberg 2008

$\langle l_1, \ldots, l_n \rangle$ with $l_i \in A_i \cup \{\varepsilon\}$, where each A_i is the alphabet of component C_i and ε means that some component does not participate in the interaction, e.g., $\langle c_1 : comm!, c_2 : \varepsilon, c_3 : comm? \rangle$ for components $\{c_1, c_2, c_3\}$. Constraints on the application ordering of vectors can be given with an LTS whose alphabet is a set of vectors. A composition specification, for a set of components C_i with $i \in \{1, \ldots, n\}$, is a couple (V, L) where V is a set of vectors for components C_i, and L is an LTS whose alphabet is V.

Clint relies on adaptation techniques and algorithms presented in [4] to generate execution traces from behavioural interfaces and a composition specification. However, the composition and adaptation engine is implemented as an external module. Therefore, it makes Clint generic at this level, and allows to take into account other adaptation techniques as those proposed in [3,5,8,9].

3   Overview of Clint

Clint implements both a composition and adaptation engine, and a graphical user interface to load, visualise and modify the different inputs. The graphical interface is also used to animate and validate the composition of an arbitrary number of components. The tool has been implemented in Python, using the wxWidgets toolkit technology for the development of the user interface. The prototype accepts component interfaces described using an XML-based format or a textual format. The composition specification is written using another XML-based notation specific to the tool.

Once the inputs are loaded, Clint uses the Object Graphics Library (OGL) to visualise component interfaces and the composition specification. These inputs can be edited and modified making use of the graphical interface. As regards animation and validation techniques, first, interactive simulation of the composition can be performed in two different modes:

- Safe mode (default). The interface offers the user only *safe* vectors for selection (*i.e.*, there exists at least one correct termination state of the system after its application).
- Unsafe mode. The interface offers all applicable vectors to the user. This allows the possibility of applying vectors leading to incorrect compositions, but it may be interesting in order to observe and understand potential flaws of the composition process.

Additionally, the tool is able to perform validation on the composition specification *wrt.* component LTSs. The basic idea is to generate automatically many random execution traces using the composition engine (unsafe mode). From such a set of traces, states and transitions are labelled with the number of times they are traversed. These traces are also used to identify unreachable states or transitions which are never traversed in the composition specification. Clint colours the composition specification, highlighting such unreachable states and transitions in the graphical representation. Moreover, Clint can extract traces leading to deadlock situations. Indeed, when a non-final state in the composition specification is reached where no further vectors can be applied, the tool identifies the sequence of vectors which has lead to the current situation as a deadlock trace.

Figure 1 gives an overview of Clint. The *simulation toolbar* on the top left side of the interface, is used to control the evolution and mode of the simulation. Just below, the *applicable vectors* panel displays the set of currently applicable vectors. In this panel, the user can successively select vectors to be applied in every step of the composition, visualising at the same time the effects of the application of a specific vector on the graphical representation of component interfaces and the composition specification on the right. We can also observe the *simulation state* panel, which displays the current states of the components and the composition specification. Finally, the *simulation trace* panel displays the trace of the current simulation, including vectors applied, as well as the actions performed by components and the composition engine.

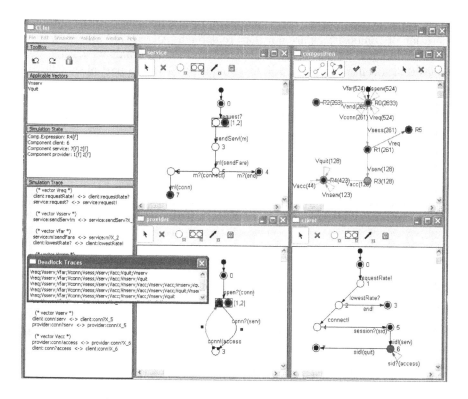

Fig. 1. Validation of a rate finder service using Clint

Clint has been validated on more than 200 examples, either small ones to experiment boundary cases, or real-world examples such as travel agency, push-out advertisements, multi-device service, rate finder service, on-line computer material store, video-on-demand, music player, disk manager, library management systems, a SQL server and several other client/server systems. For a comprehensive description of several real-world examples, such as a rate finder service or a push-out advertisement service, see the Clint webpage [1].

4   Concluding Remarks

In this paper, we have presented Clint, a graphical and user-friendly tool to specify and validate compositions of component behavioural descriptions. Our tool is being applied to the WF/.NET 3.0 platform in order to support the reuse and composition of such components [7]. Compared to other tools such as LTSA [6], Clint focuses on the specification and validation of the composition, whereas LTSA focuses on the component description, and relies on basic synchronization techniques. As regards future work, our main perspective aims at extending Clint to support the incremental construction of the composition specification. Indeed, the writing of this specification by a designer is a difficult and error-prone task. On the other hand, approaches dedicated to the automatic generation of compositions are not mature enough. An assisted approach seems to be a good trade-off between complete automation and manual writing of the composition specification. Clint will be extended to accept a partial specification of the composition, point out composition issues, and propose possible solutions or further message correspondences to complete this specification. We also plan to extend validation techniques by connecting Clint to model-checking tools, such as SPIN or CADP.

Acknowledgements. This work has been partially supported by the project TIN2004-07943-C04-01 funded by the Spanish Ministry of Education and Science (MEC), and project P06-TIC-02250 funded by the Andalusian local Government. We thank C. Joubert and E. Pimentel for their fruitful comments.

References

1. Clint - version 01 / September 2007 (Available from J. Cámara's Webpage)
2. Becker, S., Brogi, A., Gorton, I., Overhage, S., Romanovsky, A., Tivoli, M.: Architecting Systems with Trustworthy Components. In: Reussner, R., Stafford, J.A., Szyperski, C.A. (eds.) Architecting Systems with Trustworthy Components. LNCS, vol. 3938, Springer, Heidelberg (2006)
3. Bracciali, A., Brogi, A., Canal, C.: A Formal Approach to Component Adaptation. Journal of Systems and Software 74(1), 45–54 (2005)
4. Cámara, J., Salaün, G., Canal, C.: Run-time Composition and Adaptation of Mismatching Behavioural Transactions. In: Proc. of SEFM 2007, IEEE Computer Society Press, Los Alamitos (2007)
5. Canal, C., Poizat, P., Salaün, G.: Synchronizing Behavioural Mismatch in Software Composition. In: Gorrieri, R., Wehrheim, H. (eds.) FMOODS 2006. LNCS, vol. 4037, Springer, Heidelberg (2006)
6. Magee, J., Kramer, J.: Concurrency: State Models & Java Programs. Wiley, Chichester (1999)

7. Cubo, J., Salaün, G., Canal, C., Pimentel, E., Poizat, P.: A Model-Based Approach to the Verification and Adaptation of WF/.NET Components. In: Proc. of FACS 2007. ENTCS, Elsevier, Amsterdam (to appear, 2007)
8. Mateescu, R., Poizat, P., Salaün, G.: Behavioral Adaptation of Component Compositions based on Process Algebra Encodings. In: Proc. of ASE 2007, IEEE Computer Society Press, Los Alamitos (2007)
9. Motahari Nezhad, H.R., Benatallah, B., Martens, A., Curbera, F., Casati, F.: Semi-Automated Adaptation of Service Interactions. In: Proc. of WWW 2007, ACM Press, New York (2007)

Author Index

Lecture Notes in Computer Science

Sublibrary 1: Theoretical Computer Science and General Issues

For information about Vols. 1– 4638
please contact your bookseller or Springer